Insurance Administration

LOMA (Life Office Management Association, Inc.) is an international association founded in 1924. LOMA's mission is to help member companies in the insurance and financial services industry improve their management and operations through quality employee development, research, information sharing, and related products and services. Among LOMA's activities is the sponsorship of the FLMI Insurance Education Program—an educational program intended primarily for home office and branch office employees.

The **FLMI Insurance Education Program** consists of two levels—Level I, "Fundamentals of Life and Health Insurance," and Level II, "Functional Aspects of Life and Health Insurance." Level I is designed to help students achieve a working knowledge of the life and health insurance business. Level II is designed to further the student's career development by providing a more detailed understanding of life and health insurance and related business and management subjects. Upon the completion of both levels, the student is designated a Fellow of the Life Management Institute (FLMI) and is awarded a diploma.

Insurance Administration

Jane Lightcap Brown, FLMI, ACS, ALHC

FLMI Insurance Education Program
Life Management Institute LOMA
Atlanta, Georgia

LOMA®

Author:	Jane Lightcap Brown, FLMI, ALHC, ACS
Project Managers:	Katherine C. Milligan, FLMI, ALHC Ernest L. Martin, Ph.D., FLMI Lana S. Kendig, FLMI, ALHC, CLU
Editors:	Joyce Abrams Fleming, J.D., FLMI, ACS, AIAA, ALHC, HIA, MHP Martha Parker, FLMI, ACS, ALHC, AIAA
Copyeditor:	Robert D. Land, FLMI, ACS
Printing Coordinator:	Elizabeth A. Pedley
Cover Design:	Zoila Harmouche and Sally Miller Farnham
Administrative Support:	Debra Bailey Helwig, Cara Taylor, and Marion Markus
Typography:	Puffin Typography: BJ Nemeth and Heather King
Printing:	RR Donnelly & Sons Company
Cover Photography:	Images © 1996 PhotoDisc, Inc.

ISBN 0-939921-94-4

Library of Congress Catalog Card Number 97-70687

Printed in the United States of America

Contents

Preface

The only thing I was fit for was to be a writer,
and this notion rested solely on my suspicion
that I would never be fit for real work,
and that writing didn't require any.

Russell Baker, *Growing Up*

When people ask me what I do for a living and I tell them I write textbooks for the life and health insurance and financial services industry, they usually assume that I work alone. They apparently envision me sitting for months or years at a computer, poring through thick stacks of reference materials and deciding, paragraph by paragraph, what to include and how to include it.

"How do you know what to put in a textbook?" they sometimes ask. "Isn't that a tremendous responsibility?"

Their questions point toward the truth of textbook-writing at LOMA. Deciding how to handle the responsibility of developing a textbook that will have a positive influence on the industry education and professional development of thousands of students requires more than one person's abilities. Planning, researching, writing, editing, and producing a textbook demand the combined efforts of many people. Although the author is responsible for numerous aspects of the textbook, the final product represents the collaboration of experts in the insurance industry and staff members at LOMA.

This textbook, *Insurance Administration,* is the product of exactly this kind of collaboration. Intended to provide a solid introduction to multiple facets of administering life and health insurance coverages and annuities, *Insurance Administration* has been designed especially for students in LOMA's FLMI Program. The textbook is also useful for anyone interested in knowing more about the complex interactions required to ensure that life and health insurance and annuities are accurately and professionally administered and that an insurer's many customers are accorded the highest quality attention and service.

Textbook Development Panel

I myself am more and more inclined to agree with
Omar and Satchel Paige as I grow older:
Don't try to rewrite what the moving finger has
writ, and don't ever look over your shoulder.

Ogden Nash, *There's Always Another Windmill*

Actually, writers at LOMA *do* look over their shoulders, and look back often, in hope that their reviewers can provide the answers necessary to develop each chapter. *Insurance Administration* required more than the usual number of reviewers because its subject matter covers such a broad spectrum—from underwriting and reinsurance to claims and policyowner service, including both life and health coverages on individuals and groups, and with a final chapter on annuity administration. To gather a panel of experts on all these topics was essential in order for the textbook to reflect the best practices of the life and health insurance industry and to ensure that the textbook would be as nearly current, accurate, and complete as possible.

On behalf of LOMA and its membership, I would like to thank the reviewers who read and commented on each chapter as it was drafted, who shared research documents and directed me to other resources, who patiently answered numerous questions, and who gave generously of their time and expertise.

Whole-Text Reviewers

Thomas L. Clagg
Vice President & Associate General Counsel
Lincoln National Life Insurance Company

Barbara J. Gardner, FLMI, ACS
Vice President
Metropolitan Life Insurance Company

E. Ruth Gardner, AALU
Senior Underwriter, Individual Life
The Mutual Life Assurance Company of Canada

Sandra K. Holmes, FLMI
Vice President, Individual Insurance
Amerus Life Insurance Company

Beryl Piggott, FLMI
Supervisor of Operations Support
North American Life Assurance Company

L. Jack Powell, FLMI, ALHC, ACS
Vice President, Agency Worksite Marketing
Central States Health & Life Company of Omaha

Robert T. Riggio
Assistant Vice President
Metropolitan Life Insurance Company

Paula J. Ringler, FLMI, ACS
Vice President, Individual Customer Service
American United Life Insurance Company

Lawrence B. Ruark, FLMI, CLU, ACS, AIAA
Senior Compliance Analyst
Sun Life Assurance Company of Canada

Susan Silverman, FLMI, ACS
President
The Silverman Group

Underwriting and Policy Issue

William J. Clyne, FLMI, FALU
Corporate Vice President (retired)
New York Life Insurance Company

Mike Egan, RHU, FLMI
Director, Life & Health Underwriting
USAA Life Insurance Company

Joan Fitzgerald
Territorial Underwriting Manager
The Guardian Life Insurance Company

John H. Jones, Jr., FLMI, AALU, CLU, ChFC
Chief Underwriter
Standard Life & Accident Insurance Company

Thomas O. Jones, FLMI, ACS
Corporate Vice President
New York Life Insurance Company

Janet A. Nosko, FLMI, FALU
Executive Underwriting
North American Life Assurance Company

Connie Nunnally, FLMI
Senior Underwriter
Canada Life Assurance Company

Jerry J. Ross, FLMI
Manager, Customer Service & Central Benefit Payment Office
Manulife Financial

Larry Segel, M.D., CBIM, FLMI, ALHC, ACS
Assistant Vice President, Medical Research and Development
Manulife Financial

Carol J. Waage, FLMI, ACS
Technical Support Officer
Fortis Benefits Insurance Company

Sheryl J. White, FLMI
Second Vice President, Learning & Development
Fortis Benefits Insurance Company

Reinsurance Administration

Richard P. Allen, FLMI
Director, Sales & Service, Individual Reinsurance
CNA Insurance Companies

Raymond Berberi
Vice President, Administration
Swiss Re Life Canada

John C. Broshar, FLMI, ALHC
Vice President, Claims (retired)
Munich American Reassurance Company

Robert J. Flannery, FSA, FLMI, CLU, ChFC, MAAA
Assistant Vice President & Actuary, Annuities/Life Products
USAA Life Insurance Company

William J. Hazlewood, FLMI/M, CLU, ChFC
Vice President, Marketing
Mercantile & General Reinsurance Company

Ross A. Morton, FLMI
Executive Vice President
RGA Life Reinsurance Company of Canada

Richard J. Shields, ALHC
Vice President, Reinsurance
Reinsurance Group of America, Inc.

Carol Squire
Reinsurance Specialist
USAA Life Insurance Company

Lawrence Vranka
Vice President, Consulting & Claims Services
Metropolitan Life Insurance Company

Claim Administration

John Abbott, ALHC, FLMI
Associate Director, Benefit Resources
Northwestern Mutual Life Insurance Company

Diane Bezdikian, FLMI, HIA
Director, Group Claims
Canada Life Assurance Company

Lucille Chatham
Second Vice President, Claims
Conseco Companies

Susan Fe Duke
Claims Consultant
Mercantile & General Reinsurance

William G. Kasalko, ALHC
Executive Director, Policyholder Services
General American Life Insurance Company

Sharon W. Lee, FLMI, ALHC, ACS
Manager, Full Service Teams
North Carolina Mutual Life Insurance Company

Terry Lowe, FLMI, CLU, ChFC, ALHC
Superintendent, Life & Health Claims
State Farm Insurance Companies

Calvin Robinson, FLMI/M, ALHC
Vice President & Associate General Counsel
Woodmen of the World Life Insurance Society

Mary Scheer
Second Vice President, Claims
Central States Life & Health Insurance Company

Kerry Turner, FLMI, ALHC, HIA
Manager, Case Management Services
Blue Cross Life Insurance Companies

Policyowner Service

Christian Belanger
Product Manager
Blue Cross Life Insurance Company

Susan Calame, FLMI/M, ACS
Manager, Customer Services
Westfield Life Insurance Company

Kim I. Gibson, FLMI, ACS
Manager, Client Services
United Heritage Mutual Life Insurance Company

Sue A. Jacobson, FLMI, ACS
Supervisor, Services
CUNA Mutual Life Insurance Company

J. Paul Lynch
Director, Life Policy Administration
Maritime Life Assurance Company

Erik Mathiesen, FLMI
Assistant Vice President, Customer Service
Manulife Financial

King Mawhinney, FLMI, CLU, HIA, ChFC, ACS
Vice President, Health Insurance
USAA Life Insurance Company

R. J. "Sam" Schwarztrauber, ALHC
Consultant & Team Leader (retired)
General American Life Insurance Company

Annuity Administration

Mary Jo Ardington, CLU, ChFC
Associate Counsel
Lincoln National Life Insurance Company

Jane A. Benedict
Compliance Analyst
Sun Life of Canada (U.S.) Annuity Service Center

Lynda Bonney, CA
Vice President, Pensions
Crown Life Insurance Company

Peter J. Farley
Vice President, Annuity Premium Services
TIAA-CREF

Lauren Littlefield, FLMI
Director, Annuity Retirement College
Aetna Life & Annuity

Sheila E. Sandy, ALHC, ACS
Manager, Annuity Services
Amerus Life

Lisé White, FLMI, ACS, AIAA
Assistant Vice President & Director, Annuity Administration
Security Benefit Life Insurance Company

Technical Advisors

It was a dark and stormy night.
Suddenly a scream pierced the air . . .
Good writing takes enormous concentration.

Charles Monroe Schulz, *Peanuts* (1988)

Good writing also takes enormous amounts of information, not all of which is readily accessible. In addition to the industry experts who served as reviewers for chapters and sections of the textbook, I am also indebted to many other persons who lent their time and knowledge. These persons helped in numerous ways: checking segments of the textbook, suggesting examples and figures, providing samples of their companies' forms and documents, lending books and articles, and directing me to information sources and other industry experts. These contributions helped shape and enhance *Insurance Administration.*

John Adanski
Manager, Disability New Business
Guardian Life Insurance Company

DonnaMarie Arrigo
Manager, Agency Operations Support
Guardian Life Insurance Company

David D. Baals
Chief Underwriter
Lincoln National Life Insurance Company

Robert A. Baker
Assistant Vice President, Group Operations
CNA Insurance Companies

Frank Boeckmann
Actuary
Blue Cross/Blue Shield of Illinois

James C. Carnicom
Special Risk Underwriter
CNA Insurance Companies

Brian T. Casey
Attorney at Law
Morris, Manning & Martin

Elizabeth Chacko, ACS
New Business Health & Annuities
North American Life Assurance Company

James H. Cooper
Underwriting Officer
ING America Life

Christine Dalpan, FLMI
Human Resources Director
Unity Mutual Life Insurance Co.

Mary Daly, FLMI, AALU
Director of Human Resources & General Services
Mutual Group (U.S.)

Joseph De Kasar, FLMI, AALU
Second Vice President, Underwriting
Guardian Life Insurance Company

Tony Degagne
Manager, U.S. Underwriting
North American Life Insurance Company

Thomas E. Deighan, CLU, ChFC, FLMI
Vice President, Life/Health Underwriting
State Farm Life Insurance Company

Dave Doss
Vice President, Underwriting
American Mutual Life Insurance Company

L. David Downey, CLU, FLMI, ACS
Director, Individual Life & Health Administration
Nationwide Life Insurance Company

Larry Fite
Underwriting Director, Individual Insurance
General American Life Insurance Company

Kathy Giddings
Manager, Underwriting
Central States Health & Life Company

Philip E. Glassley, FLMI
Vice President, Individual Underwriting
American United Life Insurance Company

Mary Gordon
Group Medical Underwriter
Mutual Life Assurance Company of Canada

Linda Guest, FLMI, ACS
Office Manager
Murdock-Taylor/The Guardian

Richard A. Hansen, CLU, ChFC
Senior Vice President, Corporate Office of Business Conduct
New York Life Insurance Company

Nancy Heerts, FLMI
Senior Underwriter
Canada Life Assurance Company

Yung Ho, FLMI/M
Application Project Director
New York Life Insurance Company of Canada

Jerry Hogya, FLMI
Manager, Financial Systems Support & Development
Mutual of Omaha

Vance F. Howard, FLMI
President & CEO
North American Company for Life & Health Insurance

Thomas Jackson
Senior Underwriting Consultant
American United Life

Kenneth C. Johnson
Manager, Group Department
Standard Life & Accident

Robert G. Kanceruk, FLMI
Group Underwriting Associate
North American Life Assurance

Richard Lacroix
Vice President, Life & Health National Accounts
Massachusetts Mutual Life Insurance Company

Jerry Lotter, FLMI
Director, Individual Health Reinsurance Underwriting
Lincoln National Life Insurance Companies

Michael A. McCarney, FLMI, CLU
Assistant Vice President, Group Benefits & Group Reinsurance
CNA Insurance Companies

Jill Meyer, FLMI
Manager, Operations
Rocky Mountain Life Insurance Company

Linda Miller, CLU, ChFC, ACS, AIAA
Office Manager
Murdock-Taylor/The Guardian

Arlette Mooney
Director, Underwriting
Metropolitan Life Insurance Company

Nancy Nichols, FLMI, ALHC
Field Administration Manager
Fortis Information Systems

Jane Olivier
Group Benefits
Safeco Insurance Company

Thomas L. Ponsot, FLMI
Assistant Vice President & Chief Underwriter
Lincoln National Life Insurance Company

Raymond L. Prosser
Vice President & Associate General Counsel
Lincoln National Reinsurance

Christine M. Ramsay
Group Medical Underwriter
Mutual Life Assurance Company of Canada

Jerry R. Robinson, FLMI
President & CEO
Rocky Mountain Life Insurance Company

Emilio Rubi
Technical Underwriting Director, Long Term Care
AMEX Life Assurance Company

James V. Schibley
Vice President & Associate General Counsel
Lincoln National Life Insurance Company

Susan Souder
Marketing Communications Consultant
Lincoln National Reinsurance

David Stephens
Senior Underwriting Consultant
General American Life

Sonya Thomason
Junior Underwriter, Life & Health
ING/Atlanta

William G. Wanless, FLMI, ALHC
Senior Consultant, Litigation, Employee Benefits Division
London Life Insurance Company

Gary Weinstein
Supervisor, Group Life & Health Underwriting
Mutual Life Assurance Company of Canada

Zandy Wennerstrom
Personnel Assistant
Life Partners Group

LOMA Staff

One writer excels at a plan or a title page,
another works away the body of the book,
and a third is a dab at an index.

Oliver Goldsmith, *The Bee*

As I mentioned in beginning, *Insurance Administration* is the product of many hands, some of which belong to LOMA staff members who have coordinated their efforts to ensure that *Insurance Administration* functions effectively as a learning resource.

LOMA staff who were involved in developing and producing *Insurance Administration* include William H. Rabel, Ph.D., FLMI, CLU, Senior Vice President, Education Division, whose encouragement and support were invaluable. Katherine C. Milligan, FLMI, ALHC, Assistant Vice President, Education Division; Ernest L. Martin, Ph.D., FLMI, Assistant Vice President, Education Division; and Lana S. Kendig, FLMI, ALHC, CLU, Assistant Vice President, Education Division, served as project managers and helped immensely in shaping the textbook. Joyce Abrams Fleming, J.D., FLMI, ACS, AIAA, ALHC, HIA, MHP, Director, Curriculum, edited the chapters and assisted in production. Martha Parker, FLMI, ACS, ALHC, AIAA, Senior Associate, Examinations, served as examination editor. Robert D. Land, FLMI, ACS, copyedited the textbook and drafted the index. Lisa Kozlowski, FLMI, ALHC, ACS, drafted the glossary. David F. Johnson developed the Fast Facts.

Olivia Blakemore, Technical Assistant, Information Center, helped in locating research materials and other information. Zoila Harmouche, Graphics Manager, and Sally Miller Farnham, Editorial/Desktop Publishing Coordinator, prepared the cover and interior designs. Elizabeth A. Pedley, Business Coordinator, Curriculum, made arrangements for printing the textbook. Administrative support was provided by Cara Taylor, Marion Markus, and Debra Helwig. Sally Miller Farnham and Jamie Thaman proofread the typeset text.

Textbook Features

Numerous study aids in *Insurance Administration* assist students to master and apply the textbook information.

- **Learning Objectives:** The first page of each chapter contains a list of learning objectives to help students focus their studies and gain an overview of the chapter's contents.

- **Chapter Outlines:** The first page of each chapter also provides students with an outline of the central sections of the chapter and will show how the subjects in the chapter relate to each other.

- **Key Terms and Concepts:** At the end of each chapter is a list of the key terms and concepts discussed in the chapter. All key terms and concepts are also gathered into a glossary at the end of the textbook.

- **Insights:** Adaptations of articles from industry publications, brief articles written by industry specialists especially for *Insurance Administration,* and other materials appear throughout the textbook to amplify the descriptions of selected topics and to help students envision the human side of the life and health insurance industry.

- **Fast Facts:** Interesting statistics and other items of information relating to the main topics are used throughout the textbook to add depth and interest to the material.

Prep Pak and Instructor's Kit

LOMA's Prep Pak to accompany *Insurance Administration* is required as part of the preparation for the FLMI examination on the textbook.

The Prep Pak provides valuable guidance for students in mastering the textbook material. Included in the Prep Pak are review exercises for each chapter, practice examination questions, a full-length sample examination in both paper form and as interactive software, and appendices with answers to every question in the Prep Pak, and interactive software. LOMA recommends that this study aid be used in preparing for the FLMI examination on *Insurance Administration.* **Studies of FLMI students have shown clearly that those who use Prep Paks perform consistently and significantly better on examinations than do students who do not use these study aids.**

In addition, the Instructor's Kit for *Insurance Administration* includes a list of teaching objectives and materials needed for each lesson, a teaching outline of the material, and a number of learning activities in the form of transparencies, activity sheets, and action-learning activities.

As Robert Frost wrote in *Collected Poems,* "No tears in the writer, no tears in the reader." I hope that reading and learning from this textbook will prove as informative, interesting, and challenging as the researching, writing, and production were for me.

Jane Lightcap Brown, FLMI, ALHC, ACS
Senior Associate

CHAPTER ONE

Overview of Insurance Administration

Learning Objectives

After studying this chapter, you should be able to

- List the responsibilities of insurers to their customers
- Explain the focus of underwriting, reinsurance, claims, and policyowner service
- Describe the insurance functions of marketing, actuarial, accounting, legal, human resources, and information systems
- List and describe ways that computer-based technology is used in the functions of insurance administration

Chapter Outline

The Administration of Insurance

Responsibilities of Insurers to Customers

Insurance Administration Functions

Underwriting
Reinsurance
Claims
Policyowner Service

Other Insurance Functions

Marketing
Actuarial
Accounting
Legal
Human Resources
Information Systems

Computer-Based Technology in Insurance Administration

Personal Computers
Expert Systems
Electronic Data Interchange
Integrated Image Processing

Like every dynamic industry, the life and health insurance industry has numerous functions and interrelationships. You're beginning a study of the functions involved in ***insurance administration,*** which we are defining as the activities associated with assessing risk and issuing policies, obtaining reinsurance, handling claims, providing policyowner service, and administering annuities. In this textbook, you'll learn about the activities of insurance administration and the important role of these activities within life and health insurance companies.

This course in the activities of insurance administration assumes that you have a basic understanding of individual and group life and health insurance products and annuities.* Throughout this textbook, we'll examine the insurance administration activities performed for these types of products. As you study the material in this textbook, you'll learn more about the ways that employees working in the functions of insurance administration cooperate to fulfill an insurer's responsibilities to its customers. If you work in or with an insurance organization, you'll also gain a greater appreciation of the ways you may enhance the productivity, efficiency, and effectiveness not only of your own area but of other areas in your company.

The Administration of Insurance

The activities of insurance administration connect an insurer and its customers from the time of application for a policy through the time of claim settlement. After a customer applies for insurance coverage or for modifications to existing coverage, the functions involved in insurance administration act to provide every customer with proper policy service.

The four functions that administer insurance contracts include underwriting (which is typically considered a part of *new business*), reinsurance, claims, and policyowner service. We'll begin with a discussion of the responsibilities of insurers to their customers. We'll demonstrate the importance of insurance administration in enabling an insurer to fulfill its responsibilities. Then we'll give you an overview

* Health insurance generally includes both medical expense and disability income coverage. In this textbook, we'll use the term *health insurance* to refer to both medical expense coverage and disability income coverage. We'll use the term *disability income* to refer only to disability income coverage.

of the four insurance administration functions and of the areas of an insurance company with which those functions coordinate. Finally, we'll discuss the computer-based technology used in insurance administration functions.

Responsibilities of Insurers to Customers

Many of the customers of an insurance company do not receive insurance coverage from the insurer. These customers include marketers (such as agents and brokers), account holders (such as doctors and nurses, hospitals, and clinics), reinsurance companies, beneficiaries, shareholders of stock companies, and others who come into contact with the insurer from a business perspective. On the other hand, the ***premium-paying customers*** of an insurance company include its insureds, policyowners and policyholders, and annuitants and annuity owners. In this textbook, we'll use the term *customers* to refer to premium-paying customers only, although you can see that an insurer has many other types of customers. Furthermore, for the sake of simplicity, we will assume that an applicant and a proposed insured are the same person unless otherwise specified. We will, therefore, use the terms *applicant* and *proposed insured* interchangeably.

Fast Fact

As of 1995, the Japanese owned the most life insurance per person in the world, with an average (expressed in U.S. dollars) of approximately $165,250 per person in coverage, followed by the Dutch ($50,200), the Americans ($48,000), and the Canadians ($39,572).

Source: American Council of Life Insurance. Cited in *Canadian Life and Health Insurance Facts,* 1996: 28.

For practical, ethical, and legal reasons, an insurer has responsibilities to its customers. From a practical perspective, the insurer intends to operate its business in a profitable manner. From an ethical perspective, the insurer approaches its business in an honest way that protects the interests of all concerned. And from a legal perspective, the insurer must provide the benefits specified in the contracts between the insurer and its customers and must otherwise adhere to the requirements imposed by law. To be successful, an insurer needs to carefully manage and administer its responsibilities, many of which relate directly to the functions involved in insurance administration.

In accepting risks, an insurance company has a responsibility to *follow consistent risk selection practices.* The insurer must examine carefully every application for insurance and accept or decline each insurance application according to established guidelines. These guidelines, based on the insurer's and the industry's experience and actuarial projections, must be the same for every comparable case. The underwriting performed as a part of insurance administration helps to ensure fair, consistent risk selection.

Insurers also have a responsibility to *provide prompt and equitable claim handling.* Providing equitable claim settlement includes assessing every claim in accordance with the terms of the contract. Insurers also have a responsibility to deny any claim that is not covered by an insurance policy or is not valid.

Another responsibility of insurers to their customers is to *provide excellent customer service* in all aspects of the business. When a premium-paying customer applies for new coverage, adds a rider to existing coverage, requests a change of beneficiary, submits a claim, or interacts with the insurer in any other way, the customer expects and deserves prompt, correct, empathetic, and tactful responses from the insurer. Similarly, when an employee within the insurance company or a marketer asks for information or conducts other business with the insurer's employees, the transaction should be conducted in an equally prompt, correct, empathetic, and tactful manner.

Preserving customers' privacy and ensuring confidentiality are also essential responsibilities of insurance companies. Further, insurers must take care to use only lawful, reasonable, and ethical means of obtaining information. Insurers should use only accurate information, restrict access to personal information to only those persons who have a business-specific need for it, and establish written guidelines for information handling so that employees will know exactly how to treat confidential information. Successful implementation of the activities involved in insurance administration protects customers' privacy and confidentiality.

In creating and fulfilling the provisions of insurance contracts held by premium-paying customers, insurers have a primary responsibility to *maintain adequate financial resources* to pay the agreed-upon benefits if losses occur. Insurers must, therefore, conduct business so that they remain financially stable and profitable. To strengthen their financial positions, insurers focus on using resources wisely, reducing waste, managing expenses, and becoming more efficient in fulfilling the tasks required to service their clients effectively. Efficiently and effectively administered coverage helps protect an insurer's financial position and enables the organization to provide top-quality insurance protection.

An insurer's responsibility to *establish and maintain ethical business practices* encompasses a wide variety of activities and behaviors. Every area of an insurance company, including those areas involved in the activities of insurance administration, is responsible for ethical behaviors. Nearly every insurer develops a code of ethics by which to guide its business practices. For an example of such a code of ethics, read Insight 1-1, which shows the code of ethics of one insurance company.

Insurance Administration Functions

Now we'll look briefly at the insurance administration functions of underwriting, reinsurance, claims, and policyowner service. We'll examine each of these functions in detail in later chapters.

Insight 1-1 Code of Ethics of North American Life Assurance Company

Our Obligations to the Company
The company and all its employees must comply, without exception, to the laws and regulations of each jurisdiction in which the company does business. This basic requirement means each of us should be familiar with those laws and regulations that affect our work with the company. Our business conduct should exceed the minimum required by law and at all times be able to withstand close public scrutiny.

Generally speaking, most actions that are illegal are obvious: fraud, falsifying records, negligent advice, rebates, bribery, infringement of copyrights, unauthorized use of the company's or clients' funds or property, and defamatory statements about others.

The company expects the highest ethical conduct from its employees. Our continuing obligation is to conduct all our business activities in a manner deserving of the trust our policyholders have placed in us. We must therefore respect the privacy of our customers and deal honestly, fairly, and courteously with our applicants, policyholders, and others with whom the company has a business relationship, including our competitors.

Our Obligations to Our Customers
The company is committed to providing quality service to its customers. We know that business success depends on satisfied customers.

Our customers expect and deserve prompt, accurate, and courteous communication from us at all times. They trust us to provide competitive products to protect their financial security and to treat their personal information in the utmost confidence. We must consistently act in a manner that justifies our customers' trust. This means providing quality products and services, making prudent investments, effectively managing company resources, and acting with respect and honesty at all times.

Our communications with our customers must be clear and accurate. We have an obligation to ensure any statement we make is understood by our customers and to clear up misunderstandings promptly. We must be truthful in our representation of the company and its products.

Our Obligations to Our Fellow Employees
The company is committed to the principles of equality and fairness in employment. A positive working environment, protective of the rights of all employees, is fostered by mutual respect, trust, and fair play. We should acknowledge and appreciate the diversity of backgrounds and opinions each of us brings to the workplace and treat our fellow employees in the way we would like to be treated.

Our Obligations to Our Suppliers
All suppliers of goods and services to the company must have a chance to compete fairly for our business. They must know that the company will always select the qualified supplier who will provide the highest quality at the lowest price within our specifications.

Adapted by permission of North American Life Assurance Company.

Underwriting

Underwriting is one of the activities that make up the insurance function known as *new business.* The flow of business into an insurance company begins with marketing activities that produce applications for insurance. The general term used to describe all the activities required to market insurance, submit applications for insurance, evaluate the risks associated with those applications, and issue and deliver insurance policies is ***new business.***

The term *new business* can have a variety of meanings. Marketers, such as agents and brokers, may think of new business as potential clients, as all the activities they engage in to sell insurance, or as applications submitted. Insurance company employees may think of new business as applications received or as the area of the insurer that receives applications, selects the risks, and issues policies. To complicate the meaning further, some "new business" submitted to insurers requires no underwriting (for instance, guaranteed-issue products and annuities). In this textbook, we use the term *new business* to refer to insurance applications submitted and to the activities of receiving applications, selecting risks for products that require underwriting, and issuing policies.

One of the primary activities of new business is underwriting. The purposes of ***underwriting*** are (1) to assess and classify the degree of risk represented by a proposed insured or a group of insureds with respect to a specific insurance product and (2) to make a decision to accept or decline the risk. Sound underwriting decisions are extremely important in ensuring that an insurer will remain financially strong and will be able to fulfill its responsibility to pay legitimate claims. If an insurer accepts too many questionable risks without making appropriate premium adjustments, the insurer will pay more in claims than it can afford. If an insurer fails to accept enough appropriate risks at appropriate rates, the insurer will not prosper.

After an application for coverage is approved, the underwriter transfers documents and electronically stored information to the policy issue staff. ***Policy issue*** involves preparing the insurance contract, including modifying the applied-for coverage according to instructions from the underwriter, and facilitating the delivery of the policy to the customer. Although underwriting and policy issue are distinct, they are closely related and are often combined within a single operating unit within an insurance company.

Reinsurance

Insurance coverage for insurers is called ***reinsurance,*** which is broadly defined as a form of insurance that enables an insurer to be indemnified, or paid, for covered losses claimed under insurance policies it has issued. Briefly, reinsurance is insurance for an insurer. In a reinsurance arrangement, one insurer transfers a portion of risk to a second insurer, which accepts responsibility for paying part of the claims of the first insurer in exchange for part of the premium. The persons who work in reinsurance are responsible for selecting coverage from another insurance company that will share the risk of certain coverages.

In our discussion of reinsurance, we'll not only examine the ways in which insurers obtain reinsurance to share the risk on a case, but will also give you a thorough introduction to the subject of reinsurance. We'll explain various types of reinsurance coverage, the relationship between an insurer and a reinsurer, the features of reinsurance treaties, and the administration of reinsurance.

Claims

An insurer has a legal and an ethical obligation to pay every legitimate claim and to deny the liability for all other claims. As a part of the activities of insurance administration, the ***claim*** function assesses each claim made under insurance coverage and decides whether each is justified. Legitimate claims are paid according to the terms of the policy. The insurer's liability for other claims is denied.

Fast Fact

At the beginning of 1996, approximately 44 percent of the insurance companies in the United States maintained bilingual employees to help provide services to ethnic policyowners.

Source: James O. Mitchel, "Winning with Diversity: How Are We Doing?" *LIMRA's MarketFacts,* January/February 1996: 24.

Policyowner Service

Maintaining a positive relationship with all its customers is essential for an insurance company. ***Customer service*** refers to the activities, consistent with contractual provisions, that help keep customers satisfied with an insurer. ***Policyowner service*** is a type of customer service that includes all the service activities performed for marketers and for persons or parties who own or hold insurance policies and annuities. Successful insurers provide top-quality customer service and policyowner service to all their customers.

Other Insurance Functions

Staff in the insurance administration functions typically coordinate many aspects of their work with other functions of an insurance company. The other functions that most often interact with those of insurance administration are marketing, actuarial, accounting, legal, human resources, and information systems. We'll introduce these functions now, and throughout this book we'll discuss their interactions with the insurance administration functions.

Marketing

Marketing is the way an insurer identifies its customers, defines and develops the products that its customers want, conducts sales activities, and distributes products to customers. In addition to these primary activities, marketing seeks to enhance the insurer's competitive position by (1) gathering information about the insurer's business environment, including data on its competitors, and (2) assessing the insurer's sales performance in the marketplace.

Insurers distribute their products in various ways, including by agents, by brokers, and by direct response methods. In this book, we'll refer to any person or entity that sells insurance as a ***marketer.***

Actuarial

An insurer's ***actuarial*** staff members apply mathematical principles to insurance to predict the rates of illness, injury, disability, and death among insureds. Actuarial staff members also calculate legal reserve liabilities and the premium rates for insurance products, and conduct research on trends in mortality and morbidity rates, policy lapses, policy loans, company expenses, and interest rates. An insurer uses actuarial information to develop assumptions used in pricing products and in selecting risks.

Accounting

The process of collecting, analyzing, and reporting financial data is known as ***accounting.*** The accounting staff in an insurance company develop information that is used throughout the insurance company to make decisions and to satisfy financial reporting requirements.

Legal

The ***legal*** function of an insurer helps an insurer follow the laws and regulations affecting the insurer's relationships with customers, prospective customers, employees, marketers, other insurers, vendors, and government agencies. An insurer's legal function protects the insurer's legal rights and reviews company activities to be certain the insurer fulfills its legal responsibilities.

Many insurers have established compliance functions, which may be part of the legal function or may operate independently of it. ***Compliance*** is the function responsible for ensuring that an insurer and its marketers follow all applicable state, provincial, and federal insurance requirements and regulations, as well as the requirements of organizations that regulate insurance.

Human Resources

Human resources monitors the availability of qualified workers; recruits and screens applicants; helps select qualified employees; plans and presents appropriate orientation, training, and development for each employee; and administers employee benefit programs. Human resources also guides an insurer's management in conducting performance appraisals of employees and in determining compensation levels for various jobs. Finally, human resources assists with employee separations resulting from resignation, layoff, retirement, or discharge.

Information Systems

The function called ***information systems*** facilitates data processing and enables the resulting information to be made available to employees who need it. Most insurance companies have installed computers and other electronic devices to enhance the speed, accuracy, and efficiency of work activities. An automated office system enables an insurer to perform tasks that otherwise would be done manually or would be performed by outside vendors.

Computer-Based Technology in Insurance Administration

Most insurers use computer-based technology to support the functions of insurance administration. This technology includes personal computers, expert systems, electronic data interchange (EDI), and integrated image processing.

Personal Computers

A ***personal computer*** is a type of computer designed for use by an individual. Personal computers can enhance accuracy in the functions of insurance administration by guiding users to enter correct, complete information. Users who have access to sophisticated computer systems can also locate information about medical conditions, rating requirements, coverage requirements, guidelines for underwriting, and many other aspects of underwriting, as well as information relating to the reinsurance and claims functions. Networking, or linking, personal computers among functional areas allows many users of personal computers to access the same information and computer resources at the same time. Networking computers also enables marketers to communicate directly with insurers and can speed the handling of all aspects of insurance administration.

Expert Systems

An ***expert system*** is a computer application that manipulates information based on established facts and an insurer's experience data to suggest solutions to problems. Research information and commentary from the insurer's staff and from outside experts can become part of the expert system and can be used for all insurance administration functions, as well as for actuarial studies, auditing, performance appraisal, strategic planning, and many other purposes. An insurer can, therefore, benefit from an expert system's consistency, quick turnaround time, and speed for many kinds of underwriting decisions, while also making use of the underwriter's experience and sense of judgment.

To give you only a few examples, an expert system can identify whether a proposed insured's age and amount of insurance requested fall within the applied-for policy's requirements. An expert system can also itemize regulations in certain states and provinces and otherwise assist the underwriter in identifying and resolving potential underwriting problems and opportunities. When claims are submitted on coverage that has been underwritten, the expert system can match the claims against the original underwriting information to judge the accuracy of underwriting decisions. Insight 1-2 presents additional information about the development of expert systems used in underwriting, the first area of insurance administration that we'll discuss.

Insight 1-2 The Development of Expert Systems in Underwriting

The use of expert systems in underwriting has developed through generations of systems that have progressively increased in complexity. These include the following:

First Generation: Screening Systems
Screening systems were developed by larger companies in the 1970s to decrease general expenses. These systems allowed for the entry of information from the application and screened out or accepted clean nonmedical cases that previously were handled by manual jet screening units. The remainder of the cases were referred to underwriters.

Second Generation: Information Display Systems
These systems appeared in the mid-1980s and were designed to save underwriters time and thereby improve productivity. Information display systems provided underwriting manuals in an automated format and allowed users to rapidly search underwriting materials.

Third Generation: Initial Underwriting Systems
These systems were developed to improve service to the field by approving some cases automatically and eliminating cases not needing review by an underwriter. Advances in technology have made these systems feasible only in the past few years. Initial underwriting systems extend the capability of the first-generation systems and go beyond screening to identify underwriting problems, automatically underwrite some cases, and order further information on other cases.

Fourth Generation: Expert Decision Assistance Tools
These decision assistance systems help underwriters both analyze complex impairments and manage their administrative workload. Using fourth-generation systems can reduce claim expenses by enhancing consistency in the underwriting process.

Fifth Generation: Total Underwriting Systems
A new generation of underwriting systems integrates all the components discussed above into a single information system that handles the entire underwriting process. These systems can provide advantages in general expense reduction, improved service to the field, and claim expense reduction. The system's multiple components include application data entry, screening, initial underwriting, process requirements, workflow management, information display, impairment underwriting, and management information.

Adapted by permission of Lincoln National Life Reinsurance Company, from *Medical Resource,* March/April 1990: 5.

Electronic Data Interchange

Another use of technology in insurance administration is ***electronic data interchange (EDI)***, a computer-to-computer information exchange. By establishing a uniform, standardized format for information, companies in any industry and in any country can exchange computer-readable data efficiently and cost-effectively. EDI provides companies with a fast, automated, paperless, postage-free information flow. EDI is neither company-specific nor company-owned, but is a public standard for electronic movement of data.

For instance, staff in underwriting and claims may use EDI to exchange information quickly with marketers, paramedical companies, medical laboratories, inspection agencies, regulatory bodies, banks, and any other entities with which the insurer does business. The types of information exchanged include laboratory test results, medical test billing and payment information, life insurance and annuity applications and the reports on their status, and premium billing and payments. Insight 1-3 explains how EDI is being used to transmit health care data on the Internet.

Integrated Image Processing

Integrated image processing is a computer-based approach to capture, index, store, retrieve, and distribute documents in electronic form. Integrated image processing scans documents with a machine that functions much like a photocopier and that produces digitized copies of the documents for electronic storage. Employees use personal computers to request certain documents, which can be displayed on high-resolution monitors and printed if necessary. Integrated image processing saves time and enables employees to request information easily, thereby enhancing their ability to make fast, accurate decisions.

Key Terms and Concepts

insurance administration
premium-paying customers
new business
underwriting
policy issue
reinsurance
claims
customer service
policyowner service
marketing
marketer
actuarial
accounting
legal
compliance
human resources
information systems
personal computer
expert system
electronic data interchange (EDI)
integrated image processing

Insight 1-3 The Newest Expressway on the Information Superhighway

Just about everything is being transmitted over the Internet these days, so why not use it for electronic data interchange (EDI)? Although the Internet hasn't been adopted wholeheartedly in the health care industry yet, it is being touted as a fast, economical means of network communication.

According to Kepa Zebuldia, vice president of development for Oklahoma-based Synaptek, a claims clearinghouse that now is part of Envoy/NEIC, the Internet fulfills many of EDI's requirements: high availability and accessibility, reliability, cost-effectiveness, connectivity, confidentiality, and security.

The last two concerns, however, are making the industry leery about using the Internet to transmit sensitive health care information. "Although security is a major issue, it becomes a routine concern because just knowing that there is the potential for hackers in a worldwide network forces users to take precautions," Zebuldia says.

"Those using the Internet for personal information will have sophisticated security management. As far as confidentiality is concerned, encryption [use of an algorithm to scramble and unscramble data] is available," she says.

While only a few companies using EDI have developed pilot programs using the Internet, many more companies anticipate a movement in that direction. Healthcare Interchange Inc. (HII), a St. Louis–based insurance claims clearinghouse, is no newcomer to EDI. But now it has gone one step further by using the Internet as a universal connection line. Providers such as the St. Louis University and Washington University Schools of Medicine have opted to transfer claims to HII via the Internet. HII, in turn, edits and tracks the claims electronically, then sends them to major regional carriers and national payers.

But these activities are not performed via the Internet. In essence, the Internet serves as a remote terminal to HII's office. To expedite the collection process, HII uses a new application that fully integrates the billed claim information with the claim payments to provide all the necessary information to the participating collection agency.

David Granansky, HII account manager, is aware of the problems on security and confidentiality associated with the Internet. "The Internet eliminates our need to have a bank of phones and modems tied up during interchange and support for the end user's connection," Granansky says. "Everyone wants to find uses on the Internet, so as an EDI clearinghouse, we want to make sure it is available."

MedSoft Online's Medical Web Online Internet Communications Network hit the market recently. The new network enables physicians in any location to order medical procedures, receive and store those results electronically, check patient insurance eligibility, make referrals, request authorization, and track utilization and encounters.

The software allows a physician to order any procedure by CPT (current procedural terminology) code from up to nine locations, including pharmacies, hospitals, and laboratories. The procedures are assigned to the doctor and can be coordinated with billing, if desired.

In addition, by gathering information from a doctor's practice management system, Medical Web Online can keep track of utilization by procedure code, outlining how often the procedures occur and how much they cost, for the benefit of the payer.

For the managed care plan, Medical Web Online provides encounter, capitation-management and utilization data, and referral and preauthorization services so that the plan can track its providers' activities.

CHAPTER TWO

Scope and Organization of Underwriting

Learning Objectives

After studying this chapter, you should be able to

- Explain the effect of antiselection on risk assessment
- Discuss the characteristics of a risk class, and distinguish among the preferred, standard, substandard, and declined risk classes
- Define the impact of an insurer's underwriting philosophy, underwriting guidelines, and experience in guiding the insurer's underwriting decisions
- List and define four basic activities of the underwriting process
- Explain the procedural differences in policy issue for individual and group coverages
- Explain the job accountabilities of an underwriter, a chief underwriter, and medical and clerical staff
- Summarize two approaches to case assignment in underwriting
- Define independent, team, jet unit, and committee underwriting
- Explain the reasons that underwriters are given various levels of decision authority

Chapter Outline

To begin our discussion of insurance administration, we'll examine the scope and organization of underwriting. After you gain an overview of the purposes and procedures of this essential insurance administration function, you'll be ready to examine underwriting in more detail and to learn how underwriters examine risks and make decisions about them.

We'll begin by discussing risk assessment, a concept that forms the foundation of underwriting, and we will explain the importance of an insurer's underwriting philosophy and underwriting guidelines. Next, we will present an overview of the underwriting process and will explain the procedures involved in policy issue. We'll conclude by explaining how underwriting is organized and how decision options and authority levels are assigned.

Risk Assessment

An insurer designs its premium structure so that each insured person or group is charged premiums according to the amount of risk that each represents in relation to others insured by the product. A person who represents a greater amount of risk is charged a proportionately greater premium for coverage.

Underwriting is responsible for ***risk assessment,*** which involves ascertaining the degree of risk represented by each proposed insured person or group according to a range of criteria established when the insurance product was designed and priced. Underwriters assess individual applicants and groups for coverage and evaluate the level of risk according to an individual applicant's impairments or a group's characteristics. For purposes of insurance, an ***impairment*** is any aspect of a person's health, family history, occupation, activities, or lifestyle that could increase that person's expected mortality or morbidity risk. Underwriting for life insurance is particularly concerned with ***mortality,*** which is the relative incidence of death occurring among a given group of people. Underwriting for health insurance is particularly concerned with ***morbidity,*** which is the relative incidence of sickness and injury occurring among a given group of people.

In assessing the degree of risk represented by a proposed insured, an underwriter considers the factor of antiselection, which produces a higher degree of risk. ***Antiselection*** is the tendency of people who suspect or know they are more likely than average to experience loss to apply for or renew insurance to a greater extent than are people who lack such knowledge of probable loss. For example, a person who believes he has a serious illness may be more likely to purchase insurance than a person who believes he is in good health.

After evaluating the degree of risk, the underwriter decides whether to (1) issue insurance as applied for, (2) issue insurance with certain modifications in coverage or premium rate, or (3) decline to issue insurance. The role of underwriting is to accept the greatest number of qualified proposed insureds while keeping the insurer financially sound. Insight 2-1 presents one insurance executive's view of this balance.

During risk assessment for individual life insurance, applicants are assigned to risk classes. A ***risk class*** is a group of insureds who represent a similar level of risk to an insurance company. Although each insurer defines the parameters of its own risk classes, most insurers identify classes as preferred, standard, substandard, and declined.

- The ***preferred class*** is defined in various ways, but is generally used to designate proposed insureds whose anticipated mortality is significantly lower than average and who represent the least degree of risk. Some insurers establish "preferred smoker" and "preferred nonsmoker" subclasses. Increasing numbers of insurers underwrite according to use or nonuse of any tobacco product during a specified period.

- The ***standard class*** includes persons whose anticipated mortality is regarded as higher than the mortality predicted for persons in the preferred class, but lower than the mortality predicted for persons in the substandard class. Traditionally, the standard class has been divided into standard nonsmoker and standard smoker.

- The ***substandard class,*** also called *special risk,* usually includes persons whose anticipated mortality is significantly worse than average. Many insurers establish this class for proposed insureds who are recovering from serious illnesses or accidents, or whose occupations or avocations produce a greater risk of illnesses or accidents.

- The ***declined class*** is used only for proposed insureds whose impairments and anticipated extra mortality are so great that the underwriter cannot justify issuing coverage for them.

During risk assessment for individual health and disability income insurance, applicants are generally evaluated according to their age, impairments, and type of coverage requested, but are not typically assigned to risk classes as are persons who apply for life insurance coverage. Risk assessment for group life and health insurance gener-

Insight 2-1 Underwriting as a Balancing Act

"Insurance is one of the few businesses that must simultaneously drum up clients and turn down would-be buyers," says Robert A. Spittel, FLMI, former vice president of underwriting at Prudential of America Life Insurance Company (Canada).

According to Spittel, "Assessing risks is not easy. If you believe you are only in the business to say 'No,' you won't be around very long, while saying 'Yes' too readily will also bring trouble. Underwriting is as much an attitude as a set of rules. It's a willingness to look a little deeper, not being afraid to admit 'I don't understand,' a desire to work with field people, a determination to look for ways to help marketers complete a sale."

ally does not involve risk classes; instead, risk assessment is based on such factors as the type of industry, the types of employees or others to be insured, the type of coverage, and the amount of coverage. We'll discuss risk assessment for group insurance coverage in Chapters 9 and 10.

Underwriting Philosophy and Underwriting Guidelines

An insurer's ***underwriting philosophy*** (also referred to as the insurer's *underwriting objectives*) guides its risk selection and classification procedures. The underwriting philosophy generally reflects the insurer's strategic business goals and includes its pricing assumptions for products. An insurer's underwriting philosophy strongly shapes its underwriting guidelines.

Underwriting guidelines are general standards that specify the parameters within which an applicant may be assigned to one of the risk classes established for each insurance product. These guidelines for individual coverages typically encompass a number of characteristics including, but not limited to, height and weight, blood pressure, cholesterol levels, presence of specific impairments (such as coronary artery disease, diabetes, and cancer), and indications of specific behaviors (such as substance abuse, driving while intoxicated, tobacco use, and participation in certain avocations). For group coverages, as mentioned earlier, the underwriting guidelines typically cover such factors as the type of industry, the employee classes and the age demographics of the group, and the type and amount of coverage requested.

In establishing its underwriting philosophy and underwriting guidelines, an insurer considers its experience. The ***experience*** of an insurer may be expressed as the inferences drawn from the cumulative events of a certain type (for example, claims) that, taken together, express historical trends with respect to an insurance product. An insurer's experience is a useful guide for the insurer's future actions and decisions, especially for establishing underwriting requirements, risk classes, and premiums for new coverages.

As an insurer's experience changes over time, the insurer may modify its underwriting philosophy and underwriting guidelines. However they evolve, an insurer's underwriting philosophy and underwriting guidelines focus on approving and issuing coverage that is (1) equitable to the insureds, (2) equitable to the insurer, and (3) deliverable by the marketer.

Equitable to the Insureds

Risk classification maintains equity among insureds and groups by ensuring that each insured pays a premium rate that reflects the degree of risk that the insured represents. For example, a person who represents the type of risk defined as standard when an insurance product was developed is assigned to a standard risk class and is charged a standard premium rate for a person of that age. Another person who represents a significantly greater-than-average risk is usually assigned to a substandard risk class and is charged a higher premium rate. A third person who represents an unacceptable level of risk is not issued coverage. Similarly, two groups of employees proposed for long-term disability income coverage may be accepted for coverage, but may be charged different premium rates because their work represents different levels of risk. By requiring a higher premium rate or by declining to cover a proposed insured or proposed group that represents a high risk of loss, an insurer protects the coverage of all its insureds.

In order to maintain equity among insureds, risk assessment and risk classification must be as objective as possible—that is, the risks must be evaluated fairly, without bias or prejudice. Being objective in underwriting is sometimes difficult, however, because an underwriter makes decisions under considerable pressure from marketers, actuaries, and insurance company management. Marketers want underwriters to issue coverage quickly and to assign proposed insureds to preferred or standard classes. Actuaries want underwriters to use risk classification methods that keep morbidity and mortality rates very close to those on which the pricing assumptions for the insurance product are based. The insurer's management wants underwriters to accomplish both these objectives—fast issue and favorable morbidity and mortality results—while keeping underwriting costs as low as possible.

Equitable to the Insurer

An insurer's underwriting guidelines help to assure that the underwritten coverage will be equitable to the insurer. Without assigning each person or group equitably to a risk class, an insurer may find that it has approved a block of policies which, on the whole, represent an unacceptably high level of risk. A ***block of policies*** (also known as a *block of business*) is a group of policies issued to insureds who are all the same age and the same gender, and in the same risk classification. An insurance company that has issued a high-risk block of policies may receive an excessive number of claims and may be less able to pay all legitimate claims. Moreover, without sound risk classification, an insurer may price a product too high to compete favorably in the marketplace. Finally, an approach of "one price fits all" can result in product pricing that is not competitive.

Deliverable by the Marketer

An applicant for individual insurance makes the final decision whether to accept an insurance policy at the time the policy is delivered. If a buyer chooses not to accept a policy when a marketer attempts to deliver it, the policy is said to be ***undeliverable*** or *not taken.* One of many reasons that a policy may be undeliverable is that an underwriting decision to classify a proposed insured as representing a high risk can result in a premium rate that is higher than the buyer anticipated, or in coverage that is different from that which the buyer expected.

When a marketer presents information about an insurance product to a proposed insured, the marketer usually quotes a premium that is based on the insurer's standard premium rates. If the underwriter's assessment has resulted in assigning the proposed insured to a substandard class, the application is said to be *rated.* ***Rating*** an application means approving a higher-than-average risk by charging a higher-than-usual premium rate for the coverage applied for, by reducing the amount of coverage to be provided, or by doing both. When an application is rated, the marketer may have difficulty delivering the policy to a client. For group coverage, the same principle applies: a proposed group may refuse to purchase a policy that requires a premium greater than the amount the group expects to pay for a specified amount of coverage, or that offers less coverage than the group wishes to obtain at a specified price.

One of the greatest challenges facing the underwriter is explaining tactfully and persuasively to a marketer the reasons for rating or declining an application for insurance so that the marketer will be satisfied that the underwriting decision was equitable. A successful underwriter not only makes defensible decisions, but also earns the confidence and respect of marketers in doing so. Underwriters help form a productive relationship with marketers by

- Completing work on each case in a timely manner
- Keeping the marketer informed of progress in cases that are delayed because of requirements for additional information
- Communicating fully to the marketer the reasons for an adverse decision
- Making use of opportunities to educate the marketers and their staffs about the insurer's underwriting philosophy and guidelines

Overview of the Underwriting Process

As you now know, underwriting is the process of (1) assessing and classifying the degree of risk represented by a proposed insured or a group of proposed insureds and (2) making a decision to accept or decline the risk. Whether underwriting an individual or a group, underwriters follow a general rule: approve the coverage as applied for if the proposed insured represents an acceptable risk, and decline the risk or establish other conditions if the proposed insured represents an excessive risk.

In certain situations, such as those concerned with small amounts of life or health coverage for large numbers of proposed insureds, underwriting can be so routine that much of it can be handled automatically, often by specialized computer systems. Underwriting is as much an art as a science, however, and thus may require human interaction, especially for complex or unusual cases.

The underwriting process consists of four activities: (1) performing field underwriting, (2) reviewing the application for insurance, (3) gathering additional information to make a sound decision, and (4) making an underwriting decision on the case.

Performing Field Underwriting

Underwriting a proposed insured often begins well before an application for insurance reaches the insurer. ***Field underwriting*** is the process of gathering initial information about a proposed insured and screening persons for whom a specific type of coverage may be appropriate. Consider the following two typical situations:

An insurance marketer learns of a prospective purchaser of group insurance, contacts the group's management, and arranges a meeting. At the meeting, the marketer and the prospect determine a need for insurance and choose an appropriate group plan. After contacting a group representative to obtain a proposal for the desired coverage, the marketer completes an application for coverage on the group and submits the application to the insurer. By assessing the group's qualifications for coverage, the marketer has performed field underwriting.

A 60-year-old woman receives a direct mail solicitation for an insurance policy. She reads the promotional materials that say, "If you are between the ages of 25 and 65, you may be eligible for. . . ." The woman calls the toll-free telephone number listed in the mailing and asks the insurer's representative some questions. Satisfied that she wants the coverage, she answers the application questions asked by the insurer's representative and applies for a policy by telephone. In this situation, the insurer has performed field underwriting by using informational materials that enabled the woman to pre-screen herself.

Field underwriting refers to information-gathering activities during which a marketer determines an applicant's suitability for insurance coverage. If field underwriting indicates that a person or group represents an inappropriate risk, the marketer may discourage the prospect from applying for the coverage, thus saving the insurer the expense of evaluating that risk.

Marketers also contribute to effective underwriting by reporting complete information. If a proposed insured for individual coverage admits to having health problems, the marketer can facilitate underwriting by gathering such information as the precise name of each medical problem; dates and types of treatment, medication, and surgery; and the names and addresses of the proposed insured's physicians and other health care providers, and dates of visits to them. Most insurance applications include an ***agent's statement,*** reserved for the marketer's comments about the applicant or the proposed insured. Some marketers provide such information in a letter addressed to the insurer. We'll discuss the agent's statement in connection with health insurance applications in Chapter 8.

Fast Fact

Of the 120 U.S. companies writing long term care insurance in 1996, 85 percent reported using a telephone interview as part of the screening process. A face-to-face interview was used 62 percent of the time in screening an application.

Source: Barry D. Eagle, "Lifestyle, Mental Factors Key to LTC Underwriting," *Best's Review (Life/Health),* August 1996: 70–72.

Reviewing the Application for Insurance

After field underwriting is complete and the marketer sends the case to the insurer, the underwriting staff assigns the case a number or code for identification and tracking purposes. The application goes through a manual or an automated checking process to verify that the application form is the proper one for the state from which it was submitted, the age of the proposed insured is appropriate for the amount and type of coverage applied for, and the marketer is licensed to sell the type of coverage requested.

Next, the staff search the insurer's records for information, such as previous health insurance claims or life insurance applications submitted by the proposed insured. Most insurers perform the search by using computers. After the information, if any, is attached to the application, the case is assigned to an underwriter or to a special team of underwriters.

In reviewing an insurance application, the underwriter assesses the information it contains according to the underwriting guidelines established by the insurer for the applied-for coverage. The underwriter also looks at other documents submitted with the application. These documents may include the results of medical examinations, the results of laboratory and diagnostic tests, and questionnaires completed by the marketer or applicant.

Gathering Additional Information

To assess some cases, the underwriter needs additional information. The amount of additional information can be as small as the response to a single question that was left blank on an application, or as extensive as the results of a complete medical examination. As the amount of requested information increases, so do the cost and the time required to obtain and assess the information.

For each insurance product, most insurers develop a ***table of underwriting requirements*** to specify the kinds of information the underwriter considers in assessing the insurability of a proposed insured. Generally, applications that represent a greater degree of risk—for example, large amounts of coverage or insurance for persons at advanced ages—require greater amounts of information for underwriting.

Figure 2-1 shows a sample table of individual underwriting requirements for various ages and amounts of life insurance coverage. As the amount of insurance applied for increases within each age grouping, the amount of underwriting information also increases. For example, a person between the ages of 31–40 may apply for up to $99,999 of life insurance on a ***nonmedical basis***—that is, without being required to undergo a medical examination. To apply for up to $300,000 of life insurance, that person would need a blood profile, and to apply for up to $1,000,000 of coverage, that person would need both a blood profile and a paramedical examination. An underwriter might request even more information if the applicant had certain impairments.

Note also that as the age of persons applying for a given amount of insurance increases, the evidence of insurability required for underwriting also increases, and that the amount of insurance that may be applied for without medical proof of insurability decreases. On this chart, all ages above 51 require at least a paramedical examination as evidence of insurability, even for a moderate amount of coverage. Certain underwriting sources mentioned in the chart—for instance,

Figure 2-1. Table of individual life insurance underwriting requirements by age and amount.

Age at Last Birthday	Total of All Coverage	Underwriting Requirements
0–15	Up to $ 500,000	Nonmedical
	$ 500,001 to $1,500,000	Paramedical, Attending Physician's Statement (APS)
	$1,500,001 to $3,000,000	Medical, APS
	$3,000,001 and up	Medical, APS, electrocardiogram (ECG)
16–30	Up to $ 99,999	Nonmedical
	$ 100,000 to $ 400,000	Nonmedical, blood profile
	$ 400,001 to $1,500,000	Paramedical, blood profile
	$1,500,001 to $3,000,000	Paramedical, blood profile, ECG
	$3,000,001 and up	Medical, blood profile, ECG, inspection report
31–40	Up to $ 99,999	Nonmedical
	$ 100,000 to $ 300,000	Nonmedical, blood profile
	$ 300,001 to $1,000,000	Paramedical, blood profile
	$1,000,001 to $2,000,000	Paramedical, blood profile, ECG
	$2,000,001 and up	Medical, blood profile, ECG
41–45	Up to $ 99,999	Nonmedical
	$ 100,000 to $ 500,000	Paramedical, blood profile
	$ 500,001 to $1,500,000	Paramedical, blood profile, ECG
	$1,500,001 to $3,000,000	Medical, blood profile, ECG
	$3,000,001 and up	Medical, blood profile, ECG, X-ray, inspection report
46–50	Up to $ 50,000	Nonmedical
	$ 50,001 to $ 99,999	Paramedical
	$ 100,000 to $ 200,000	Paramedical, blood profile
	$ 200,001 to $1,000,000	Paramedical, blood profile, ECG
	$1,000,001 to $3,000,000	Medical, blood profile, ECG
	$3,000,001 and up	Medical, blood profile, ECG, X-ray, inspection report
51–60	Up to $ 99,999	Paramedical
	$ 100,000 to $ 750,000	Paramedical, blood profile, ECG
	$ 750,001 to $2,000,000	Medical, blood profile, ECG
	$2,000,001 and up	Medical, blood profile, ECG, X-ray, inspection report
61–70	Up to $ 49,999	Paramedical
	$ 50,000 to $ 99,999	Paramedical, ECG
	$ 100,000 to $1,000,000	Medical, blood profile, ECG
	$1,000,001 and up	Medical, blood profile, ECG, X-ray, inspection report
71 and up	Up to $ 49,999	Paramedical, ECG, APS
	$ 50,000 to $ 99,999	Medical, ECG, APS
	$ 100,000 to $ 500,000	Medical, blood profile, ECG, APS
	$ 500,001 and up	Medical, blood profile, ECG, APS, X-ray, inspection report

APS, medical examination, and inspection report—will be defined and discussed later.

A typical table of underwriting requirements for group life and health insurance coverage contains similar specifications. Unless a group is very small, the requirements are usually figured according to the demographics of the whole group. For example, a group's characteristics may permit an insurer to underwrite monthly short-term disability income coverage up to $2,000 as guaranteed issue requiring no other underwriting information. A group member who is eligible for a monthly benefit greater than $2,000, however, is usually required to supply evidence of insurability.

Sometimes an underwriter speaks directly with the staff of an attending physician in order to gather information—for instance, to learn more about a specific disorder, to verify dates and details of treatment, and to clarify the reasons for certain diagnoses and medications. Personal contact permits an underwriter to obtain precise information and increases the underwriter's knowledge about medical matters. Further, such contact makes the underwriter more accurate and productive in assessing cases.

Making an Underwriting Decision

After considering all the relevant data, the underwriter makes a decision on the case. Depending on the type and amount of coverage and the underwriter's experience, the underwriter's decision may be subject to review by a more experienced underwriter, an underwriting manager, or, in some cases, the insurer's medical director.

If the underwriter decides to issue coverage as applied for, the underwriter releases the file to the policy issue function, which produces a policy and delivers it to the marketer or to the proposed insured. The underwriter or a member of the underwriting staff communicates the underwriting decision to the marketer. If the decision is either to issue coverage with modifications or to decline coverage, the underwriter usually tells the marketer the reason for the decision, without violating the insurer's and the jurisdiction's rules about confidentiality.

Policy Issue

After underwriting is complete and coverage has been approved, an insurance company issues a policy for delivery (usually via a marketer) to the insured person or group. Using automated systems, most insurers can produce policy documents promptly and accurately. An insurer's information system typically creates a client record and verifies that the initial premium payment has been received and that all policy requirements have been met.

For most coverages, policy pages are standardized and do not have to be customized for each proposed insured. Policies for coverage that has specialized features can also be produced by an information system, which customizes certain pages with information on the type of plan and benefits, amount of coverage, premium amount, and other information that is particular to the insured person or group.

Fast Fact

The average size of ordinary life insurance policies has grown steadily larger for most of the century. In 1920, the average policy was for $1,990; in 1980, $11,920; in 1995, $49,980.

Source: American Council of Life Insurance, "Average Size Life Insurance Policy in Force in the United States," in *1996 Life Insurance Fact Book*, 1996: 21.

Individual and Group Policy Issue Procedures

The procedures for policy issue differ slightly for individual and group coverage. Individual coverage and annuities require only that a document be produced and delivered, usually by the marketer, to the insured person or annuity owner. Group coverage, by contrast, requires an installation process.

Installing a group contract includes enrolling each employee or other covered person. The insurer's information system produces not only a contract for the group policyholder, but also a certificate and an enrollment card for each covered person. During installation, the marketer or group representative presents information about the insurance plan to the covered persons and distributes a certificate to each person. Each covered person completes an enrollment card. We'll discuss the group enrollment process in more detail later in Chapter 10.

Organization of Underwriting

All of a company's functions are organized to fulfill their purposes within the company. In organizing any company function, the company's leadership gives each person and group appropriate authority to fulfill certain tasks. The leadership also combines the work activities efficiently, establishes effective reporting relationships, and arranges suitable communication links and technological support.

Overseeing the underwriting activities is the chief underwriter, who is usually a specialist in risk selection and a strong generalist in customer service and claims. The chief underwriter is responsible for monitoring the cost and quality of underwriting, including making decisions on vendors and services the insurer uses for medical information, inspection reports, and similar resources. In addition to handling personnel matters and underwriter training, the chief underwriter serves as a liaison with the insurer's reinsurance and claims functions. In most insurance companies, the chief underwriter suggests age and amount requirements to the actuaries, who use the information in establishing prices and other information for products.

In some insurance companies, the chief underwriter works with the insurer's legal staff on contract wording.

Under the leadership of the chief underwriter, the underwriters are accountable for assessing risks according to relevant information and making appropriate decisions. To work effectively, each underwriter must develop detailed, wide-ranging knowledge that takes years to master. An underwriter gradually gains an understanding of the insurer's products and marketing distribution system, underwriting philosophy and guidelines, and customer service. In assessing risks, the underwriter becomes familiar with business-related information, special risk evaluation, and medical information. Figure 2-2 lists more specifically the types of information that underwriters are generally required to know in order to fulfill their accountabilities.

Most insurers also employ physicians as medical experts for underwriting. Large insurers usually appoint a medical director to lead a medical underwriting staff composed of physicians and other medical

Figure 2-2. Information underwriters need to know.

Business-Related Information

- The insurer's products and pricing assumptions
- The insurer's marketing distribution systems and the ways the underwriter may communicate with marketers
- The insurer's underwriting philosophy, guidelines, and requirements
- Sources of underwriting information
- The insurer's computer-based system
- Customer service principles applied to internal and external customers, including written and telephone communication skills

Special Risk Evaluation

- Underwriting for occupation, avocation and hazardous activities, civilian and military aviation, alcoholism, drug abuse, criminal activity, foreign residence, recent immigration, and other topics

Medical Information

- The circulatory system, blood pressure, coronary artery disease, congenital heart disease, heart arrhythmia and murmurs, cerebral vascular disease, and peripheral vascular disease
- Neurology
- Endocrine and metabolic disorders
- Respiratory disorders
- Urinary and reproductive system disorders
- Musculoskeletal disorders
- Digestive system disorders
- Eye, ear, nose, and throat disorders
- Blood disorders
- Psychiatric disorders

personnel. The responsibilities of the medical staff include developing and updating the insurer's medical underwriting guidelines, as well as consulting with underwriters on cases with unusual or difficult medical histories.

Some insurers establish separate underwriting units to handle various types of applications—for life, disability, health, and other types of coverage. Generally, insurers organize the work of underwriting according to a case assignment system, a work division system, or a combination of the two systems. Figure 2-3 outlines these systems for organizing underwriting.

Figure 2-3. Systems for organizing underwriting.

Case Assignment System	Work Division System
■ Face amount requested	■ Independent underwriting
■ Type of application or policy change	■ Team underwriting
■ Geographic origin or marketer	■ Jet unit underwriting
	■ Committee underwriting

Case Assignment System

A ***case assignment system*** establishes a basis for giving a case to an appropriate person or group for underwriting. The case assignment system enables an underwriter to specialize in certain types of cases. The basis used to assign case files to underwriting varies depending on the size of the insurer, the number of applications usually received, and the difficulty of the cases to be underwritten. Most common case assignment systems distribute case files according to (1) the face amount requested, (2) the type of application or policy change, (3) the geographic origin of the application or the location of the marketer submitting the application, or (4) the last name of the applicant.

A drawback of the case assignment system is that underwriters may become well informed only about their own areas of specialization. As a result, employees' vacations and absences may cause an underwriter to work temporarily—and probably less productively—with "unfamiliar" cases. This problem can be reduced, however, by periodic rotation of assignments and cross-training so that several underwriters become familiar with the characteristics of other types of cases.

Face amount requested. Some insurers assign life insurance cases to underwriters according to the face amount of the coverage requested. Disability cases may be assigned according to the monthly benefit amount applied for, and health insurance cases may be assigned according to the policy limit. In this type of case assignment system, each underwriter is assigned only cases for amounts that the underwriter is authorized to approve.

Type of application or policy change. If cases are based on the type of application or on a type of change requested—usually an increase in the coverage amount or the addition of a rider—certain underwriters may be assigned only nonmedical applications, only applications requiring a medical examination report, only combination business (that is, applications for life and health coverage on the same person), only requests for accidental death benefit (ADB) coverage, and so on. In some insurance companies, underwriters specialize in life, medical expense, or disability coverage.

Geographic origin or location of marketer. If the geographic origin of the application is the basis of an insurer's case assignment system, underwriting is divided into regional or company underwriting sections, with each section handling all business submitted by marketers within a specific geographic area. Alternatively, some insurers assign specific marketers to certain underwriters, regardless of the geographic location. Either of these case assignment methods enables an underwriter to become familiar with the quality of agents' and group representatives' business and to develop effective working relationships with the marketers.

Case assignment on the basis of geographic origin also enables underwriters to become more knowledgeable about legislative and regulatory differences among various jurisdictions, as well as to learn more about specific impairments or occupations that may be peculiar to a certain geographic region. For example, black lung disease is more likely to occur in areas where coal is mined than in other areas.

Work Division System

A ***work division system*** divides cases according to the person or group that underwrites them. Types of work division include independent underwriting, team underwriting, jet unit underwriting, and committee underwriting.

Independent underwriting. In many insurance companies, applications are assigned to underwriters who work alone to assess each risk. Some insurers assign to independent underwriters only large-amount cases or those requiring extensive research.

Team underwriting. A risk selection approach in which underwriters are divided into small groups is known as ***team underwriting.*** The team usually includes one or more senior underwriters who handle large-amount or complex cases, and one or more lower-level underwriters who handle simpler cases. A clerical unit assists the team by performing preliminary applications processing and ordering additional information.

Team underwriting usually enables team members to exercise considerable autonomy in making underwriting decisions. Members of the team are responsible for setting work assignments and establishing priorities for them. Team members make recommendations to the chief underwriter on such issues as team training and development, schedules of work and vacations, solutions to production problems, and conflict resolution. Compared to other underwriting methods, team underwriting can be more cost-effective and can provide the field force with faster service.

Jet unit underwriting. Designed to underwrite simple cases quickly, a ***jet unit*** is a risk selection approach that establishes a group of two to four employees to screen applications which meet specific criteria and to approve certain types of applications for immediate policy issue. For example, life insurance applications that are eligible for consideration by a jet unit have specific characteristics, such as the following:

- Proposed insured's age, height, and weight are within specified ranges.
- Proposed insured has no significant health problems and has an acceptable occupation.
- Application is being made for an amount of insurance below a specified limit, usually $50,000 to $100,000, depending on the applicant's age and the insurer's requirements.
- Applicant has not made an unusual beneficiary designation.
- Applicant has answered all questions on the application.
- Insurer's records contain no adverse underwriting information on the proposed insured.

A jet unit is not usually authorized to rate or decline an application except for certain specified impairments. All applications that are not issued immediate coverage are sent from the jet unit to other underwriting staff, who gather underwriting information and decide on the cases. Some jet units are equipped with electronic systems that further speed underwriting by scanning and checking applications.

Committee underwriting. Cases involving large coverage amounts or special problems, such as combinations of impairments or unusual occupations, may require committee evaluation. ***Committee underwriting*** is a risk selection approach in which a committee of highly qualified persons from inside and outside the underwriting function are called together for case assessment.

Usually the committee is composed of the chief underwriter, the medical director, and representatives from the legal, actuarial, and agency functions. Pooling their technical expertise, the committee members can reach an appropriate decision on cases that otherwise might have to be passed from person to person in a less efficient manner.

Combination System

Some insurers combine a case assignment system with a work division system. For example, a jet unit may handle only applications for health coverage under one type of policy, or an underwriting team may handle only term life insurance applications from a specific geographic area or from a certain marketer.

Decision Options and Authority Levels

Underwriters have varying levels of authority to make decisions. In this section, we'll discuss decision options and levels of decision-making authority in underwriting.

Decision Options

After examining the information in a case file, an underwriter typically has the following decision options:

1. Accept the risk and issue the coverage as requested.

2. Accept the risk, but modify the coverage requested by adding a substandard rating or limiting the coverage by attaching an exclusion rider to the policy contract. An ***exclusion rider*** is a rider that limits a policy's benefits by excluding from coverage certain specified types of risk, such as death benefits for a death resulting from an aviation accident or disability income benefits for a specified, usually pre-existing, impairment.

3. Decline the risk.

Rather than make a decision immediately, the underwriter may decide to gather more information. If the underwriter requests or waits for information before making a decision, the case will be held in a pending or suspense file. Eventually, the case will be accepted or declined. If the case is accepted, the insurer will issue a policy to the proposed insured. If the case is declined, the underwriting decision will be communicated to the marketer and to the applicant.

Authority Levels

Underwriting is not a rigid or scientific discipline with absolute rules governing every decision. Therefore, an underwriter needs the ability to make well-reasoned judgments and the authority to act on those judgments.

In general, an underwriter's authority to rate or decline an application increases with the underwriter's level of experience. Underwriters gradually receive more case approval authority as their demonstrated ability and quality of judgment improve. New underwriters are typically allowed to examine and approve only small-amount cases, and their work is reviewed by other, more experienced underwriters. By contrast, experienced underwriters and chief underwriters usually have authority to approve large-amount cases and to make decisions on more difficult, detailed cases without review by a more experienced underwriter.

An underwriter's level of authority is specified by (1) the face amount that the underwriter can approve and (2) the degree to which the underwriter may rate or decline a policy without approval or review by a more experienced underwriter.

Authority to approve specified coverage limits. Most insurers develop charts or schedules of underwriting authority to specify the highest amount of coverage that can be approved by each level of underwriter. Figure 2-4 lists sample levels of case approval authority. The dollar amounts stated in the figure are used for illustration only. Specific amounts and number of levels of case approval authority vary from one insurer to another.

Authority to rate or decline cases. Some insurers require underwriting decisions to be reviewed and approved by a higher underwriting authority when an underwriter makes a decision to rate or decline a case, even if that underwriter has authority to approve the same type of case without a rating. In other words, the underwriter's authority to approve a case as applied for does not also permit the underwriter to rate or decline the case without consulting a higher-level underwriter. Generally, an underwriter's authority to approve a rated case

Figure 2-4. Levels of case approval authority for underwriters.

Underwriter Level	Standard	Substandard & Exclusions	Declined
Junior Underwriter	$100,000 to $400,000, Clear Case	—	—
Junior Underwriter with 1 Year's Experience	$400,000	$100,000	—
Intermediate Underwriter	$500,000	$200,000	—
Intermediate Underwriter with 1 Year's Experience	$750,000	$500,000	—
Senior Underwriter	$1,000,000	$500,000	$200,000
Senior Underwriter with 1 Year's Experience	$1,500,000	$1,000,000	$500,000
Chief Underwriter	ALL AMOUNTS	ALL AMOUNTS	ALL AMOUNTS

decreases as the level of risk—represented by the substandard or special risk rating—increases.

In some insurance companies, all rated and declined cases are reviewed by an underwriter one level higher than the original underwriter. Other insurers provide that only the chief underwriter performs this kind of review. The review is performed not only to ensure that the original underwriting decision is appropriate, but also to ensure the consistency of underwriting actions, to serve as a measure of an underwriter's job performance, and to enhance marketers' confidence in the insurer's underwriting practices.

Key Terms and Concepts

risk assessment
impairment
mortality
morbidity
antiselection
risk class
preferred class
standard class
substandard class (*special risk*)
declined class
underwriting philosophy (*underwriting objectives*)
underwriting guidelines
experience
block of policies (*block of business*)
undeliverable (*not taken*)
rating
field underwriting
agent's statement
table of underwriting requirements
nonmedical basis
case assignment system
work division system
team underwriting
jet unit
committee underwriting
exclusion rider

CHAPTER THREE

Legal Issues Affecting Underwriting

Learning Objectives

After studying this chapter, you should be able to

- Summarize the ways an underwriter acts responsibly when (1) handling applications, (2) acting promptly upon applications, and (3) documenting underwriting
- Identify two legally acceptable bases for discriminating among risks, and describe six types of risk factors that are specifically mentioned in antidiscrimination legislation
- Explain the general requirements of replacement regulations
- Summarize the provisions of the Fair Credit Reporting Act (FCRA) concerning protection of consumers' privacy and confidentiality
- Explain three types of notice that an insurer must provide to applicants concerning consumer reporting agency reports
- Distinguish between a conditional premium receipt and a binding premium receipt
- Identify the provisions of the NAIC Group Life Insurance Definition and Group Life Insurance Standard Provisions Model Act and the CLHIA Group Insurance Guidelines

Chapter Outline

Legal Implications of Underwriting
Handling Applications
Acting Promptly upon Applications
Documenting Underwriting

Antidiscrimination Statutes
Gender
Physical and Mental Impairments
Blindness, Partial Blindness, and Deafness
Genetic Characteristics
Marital Status
Sexual Orientation
Canadian Antidiscrimination Statutes

Replacement Regulations

Privacy and Confidentiality Laws
Federal Privacy Guidelines and Laws
The NAIC Model Privacy Act
State and Provincial Privacy Protection

Premium Receipts
Conditional Premium Receipt
Binding Premium Receipt

Statutory Requirements for Group Insurance
Requirements in the United States
Requirements in Canada

Insurance business, like any other business, is subject to laws and regulations. If an underwriter were unaware of the legal issues affecting underwriting, the result could be large financial losses and legal penalties, as well as harm to an insurer's reputation and to its ability to continue doing business in one or more jurisdictions. Moreover, some of an underwriter's day-to-day actions in handling applications and assessing risks can affect an insurer's legal position if the insurer is brought to court.

We will look first at the responsibilities of the underwriter to handle cases so that if the file should later be subjected to court scrutiny, all underwriting decisions and actions would be judged appropriate and would be clearly documented. Then we will consider specific areas of law and regulation affecting underwriting: antidiscrimination statutes, replacement regulations, privacy laws, and legal interpretations regarding various types of premium receipts.

Legal Implications of Underwriting

To guard against legal complications for the insurance company, when evaluating a case, an underwriter should (1) handle the application carefully, (2) act promptly upon the application, and (3) accurately and fully document every step in underwriting the case.

Handling Applications

In handling completed insurance applications, underwriters avoid making alterations, check carefully for incomplete or erroneous information, and determine the need for further investigation.

Alteration of applications. Underwriters avoid altering or permitting alterations to be made on a completed application unless the applicant affirms the change in writing. Insurance applications cannot be changed except by appropriate legal procedures. Many jurisdictions provide that an application presented in court must be the original application signed by the applicant, and that no modification of the document is valid without the applicant's signed (or, sometimes, initialed) consent. Generally, an insurer cannot use a life or health insurance application as evidence in court unless a valid copy of that application was attached to the insurance contract when the policy was issued. Furthermore, without the applicant's signature or initials, the entire application is usually invalid and, therefore, inadmissible as evidence in a court of law.

Incomplete or erroneous information on applications. The underwriter remains alert for applications that contain incomplete or inconsistent information. Most missing or erroneous information is the result of human error, but sometimes it indicates the presence of misrepresentation. ***Misrepresentation*** is the presence of false or misleading statements on an application for insurance. The false information may be provided by an unscrupulous applicant or marketer who realizes that truthful information about the applicant would result in a higher premium or in denial of the application. If an application contains erroneous information—such as a false age or false dates of an applicant's active employment—or if an application omits critical information—such as failing to mention a known impairment or additional sources of income—the insurer is allowed by law to (1) deny the coverage or (2) require the applicant to revise the false or misleading statements prior to underwriting.

If an insurer does not discover the misrepresentation until after the policy is issued, the law allows the insurer to take the action of ***rescission,*** which is a legal action by which the insurer seeks to void a policy or have it declared void. The basis for such a rescission is ***material misrepresentation,*** which is a misstatement that is relevant to the insurer's acceptance of a risk. The test as to whether misrepresentation is material is whether, if the truth had been known about the misstatement, the insurer would still have issued the policy or have issued it on a different basis.

Generally, an underwriter does not accept an application containing ditto marks, dashes, or question marks. The insurer would probably be held by a court to have waived its right to obtain or use material information if an underwriter, in approving coverage, had overlooked unanswered information or had not resolved conflicting information. The insurer then is generally prevented from asserting the defense of material misrepresentation on the basis of the waived information.

Investigation of applications. An underwriter also considers the need to investigate the information recorded in an application so that the insurer cannot be held to have waived its right to certain information. Obtaining all information necessary to make every decision is sometimes difficult and not cost-effective. In some instances, an underwriter can justify not requesting medical reports. However, the underwriter also needs to understand the possible outcomes of not requesting sufficient supporting information and of not checking application information properly.

Acting Promptly upon Applications

The amount of time an underwriter takes to handle an application is important for several reasons. A practical reason is that the longer an insurer takes to handle an application, the more difficult it may be for the marketer to deliver the policy. A legal reason is that the courts of many jurisdictions have held that insurers must act within a relatively short period of time when they receive an application. If the proposed insured dies or suffers an illness or a disability before the risk is assessed, an insurer may be held liable for lack of prompt action on an application. If the insurer is held liable under these circumstances, it will have to pay benefits under the policy regardless of the proposed insured's insurability. The legal requirement that an insurer act promptly on a policy application is especially strict in cases in which an applicant submits a premium with the application. If the insurer does not respond to such an application in a timely way, it may be held to have agreed to accept the application.

Documenting Underwriting

Whether an underwriter obtains information in a case file by telephone, letter, fax, or some other means, the information forms a history of the way the insurer has handled the case. A well-documented case file provides convincing evidence to justify a risk classification decision. In investigating a proposed insured, an underwriter often makes telephone calls and receives letters, memos, faxes, computer transmissions, and other communications. All such communication and other information related to risk classification must be fully documented in the applicant's file so that all facts will be available in the event of a legal challenge.

Most companies require that an underwriting worksheet for each case be used to summarize each type of information requested and received, as well as the final decision on the case. An ***underwriting worksheet*** is a document that contains records of telephone calls, letters and other communications, documentation of requests for reinsurance, lists of reports and other information requested, and other notations that will explain clearly the manner in which the case has been handled from the time it was submitted to the insurer. If the underwriter handling the case is out of the office, another underwriter will usually be able to answer telephone inquiries on the case and to take other necessary actions by reading through the underwriting worksheet. When the insurer's internal auditors examine a case, the worksheet explains unusual or exceptional handling and the final decision.

Telephone conversations. Because a telephone conversation about a case can place a legal obligation upon the insurance company, the underwriter documents every telephone discussion in a clear and accurate written record. Documentation of telephone conversations should include several types of information:

- The full name of the person or company spoken to
- The exact date and time of the telephone conversation
- Client information, specifying the client's name and other identifying information, such as file or policy number
- A summary of the conversation, which should cover not only what issues were discussed and what questions were asked, but the responses and the actions the underwriter decided to take
- The underwriter's signature, not just his initials; including the underwriter's full name (or, if preferred, first initial and surname) enables an insurer to identify the underwriter accurately

The applicant's file. Every action an underwriter takes regarding classification of the risk represented by a proposed insured is recorded in the application file. The underwriting comments in the file provide a diary of each underwriting decision, from the first review of the application to approval or rejection of the application. The underwriter notes all results of the initial review of the application and/or supplements, rate calculations, new information obtained from telephone calls and correspondence, and other relevant information.

Each of the underwriting comments includes the date and time, the specific action taken or requested, and the underwriter's signature, not just her initials. Other information or documentation pertaining to the underwriting decision should also be in writing and should become a permanent part of the case file.

Underwriters also make sure that all comments included in an applicant's file are appropriate and free of any content that could be interpreted as indicating personal bias against an applicant or a proposed insured. Because the entire file can be subpoenaed and placed into evidence in a court of law, the presence of such comments can prove embarrassing and damaging to the insurer. Such comments could be used to support an assertion that the insurer did not deal in good faith with an applicant. Insight 3-1 lets you check your understanding of the types of comments that underwriters should and should not include in applicants' files.

The documentation in a case file could be crucial if the underwriter is ever called to testify in court about a specific underwriting decision, because the underwriter needs a solid, objective basis on which to explain the underwriting decision.

Insight 3-1 Check Yourself: What Would You Write?

Assume you're an underwriting supervisor checking some of the life and health insurance case comments handled by junior underwriters. Decide which of the following notations are acceptable to include in a case file. If you decide a notation is unacceptable, explain how the junior underwriter could correct or improve it.

Note 1. Mr. Jones from an agency in Tucson, AZ, telephoned to ask why the case on Hiram P. France has not been given a preferred rating. I told him the applicant's avocation of deep-water scuba diving and his smoker status prevented our assigning the case a preferred rating. [Signed] BP

Note 2. June 23, 1996, 10:17 A.M. —Ethel Januck called again about receiving a letter from underwriting re: her application for health insurance. She acted rude and impatient this time, as usual. I told her I'd check on it and get back to her. [Signed] M. Grimsby

Note 3. 4:15 P.M. 9/17/96—Parkerson Insurance Agency, Wichita, KS. Wayne Parkerson (316-371-XXXX) called to check on status of Marian and Walter Upson's life policy #AB1064-ZW and to see if more tests were required. I said I'd call back before noon on 9/19/96 with details. [Signed] A. Perryman

Note 1 Explanation. Unacceptable. The first name of the caller and the name of the agency, as well as the date and the time of the call and the policy number, should be included. The full name of the underwriter, or at least the first initial and surname, should be added to the note.

Note 2 Explanation. Unacceptable. The note omits the policy number. Moreover, including the comment about Ms. Janucks' being "rude and impatient" is needlessly critical and does not demonstrate a desirable attitude of good customer service.

Note 3 Explanation. Acceptable. The notation contains all necessary information, including the telephone number, and is objective and clear.

Furthermore, months or years may have passed between the time the underwriting decision was made and the time of a hearing or trial. In such a situation, the underwriter may not remember all the details associated with a case; therefore, accurate documentation will be crucial. Even in a situation in which the underwriter does have a clear memory of the details, careful documentation will reinforce his oral testimony. Insight 3-2 outlines advice for underwriters who are called to testify in courts of law and emphasizes the importance of maintaining documented records.

Antidiscrimination Statutes

In underwriting, the essential concept of equity is based on the two premises that (1) similar risks should be identified and classified together and (2) each risk selected for coverage should be charged an equitable premium for the level of risk the insurer assumes. The responsibility of an underwriter is to distinguish—that is, to discriminate fairly—among risks that are acceptable and risks that are unacceptable.

Discrimination among risks is usually legal when it is based upon (1) recognized actuarial principles or (2) actual or reasonably anticipated experience. Legislation in various jurisdictions restricts or prohibits unfair discrimination based on certain risk classification factors.

Insight 3-2 Advice for Underwriters Called to Testify in Courts of Law

■ In preparing to give testimony, review all available information about the case. Take information from your documented files.

■ In the courtroom, remain as objective as possible, and resist becoming a partisan or advocate for the insurance company or any other person or entity.

■ Do not overstate your knowledge, and don't offer opinions that go beyond your honest convictions concerning the issues of a case.

■ Don't anticipate the end of a question. Always wait until the attorney has completed the question.

■ If you don't understand a question, ask to have it repeated and restated. If you don't know an answer, say so.

■ Tell the truth. Admit every material fact, even if it is not to the advantage of the party for whom you are testifying.

■ If you wish to qualify your answer, use such words and phrases as "approximately," "about," and "in my best judgment."

■ Avoid laughing or talking about the case outside the courtroom where the jurors might observe such conduct. Do not engage in casual conversation with parties to the case, their counsel or witnesses. If a juror speaks to you, be polite, excuse yourself, and report the incident to the attorney.

From Sal Fiscina, M.D., J.D., "The Underwriter as an Expert Witness: Practical Considerations for Effective Testimony," *On the Risk,* 1988: 32–36. Adapted by permission.

In this section, we'll look briefly at some of the risk factors specifically mentioned in U.S. antidiscrimination legislation. These risk factors include gender; physical and mental impairments; blindness, partial blindness, and deafness; genetic characteristics; marital status; and sexual orientation. We'll discuss Canadian antidiscrimination statutes in a separate subsection of this chapter.

Gender

In 1976, the National Association of Insurance Commissioners (NAIC) adopted its Model Regulation to Eliminate Unfair Sex Discrimination. Most states and provinces have patterned legislation on this model and now prohibit the restriction or denial of coverage solely on the basis of gender, although gender-based actuarial tables may be used in most states and provinces. The NAIC has designed a regulation, which most states have adopted, permitting insurers to use gender-blended or unisex mortality or morbidity tables that merge risk-related information from both males and females to produce figures that can be applied to both genders equally.

Physical and Mental Impairments

U.S. laws patterned on the NAIC's Model Regulation on Unfair Discrimination in Life and Health Insurance on the Basis of Physical or Mental Impairment prohibit (1) limitation or refusal of insurance coverage or (2) premium rate differentials based solely on physical or mental impairments, unless such action is based either on recognized actuarial principles or on actual or reasonably anticipated experience.

Blindness, Partial Blindness, and Deafness

Although blindness, partial blindness, and deafness may also be covered in laws that prohibit discrimination based on physical impairments, many states have statutes that specifically prohibit discrimination on the basis of these conditions. Under the NAIC Model Regulation to Prohibit Unfair Discrimination on the Basis of Blindness or Partial Blindness, insurers are prohibited from using blindness or partial blindness as a sole basis for (1) refusing to insure, or refusing to continue to insure, an individual; (2) limiting the amount, extent, or kind of coverage available to an individual; or (3) charging an individual a different rate from the standard rate for the same coverage. In addition, a number of states have passed laws making it illegal for underwriters to discriminate against persons solely on the basis of deafness or other hearing impairments. Discrimination may, however, be based on sound actuarial principles or on actual or reasonably anticipated experience.

Genetic Characteristics

One of the most controversial issues for insurers is whether to include the results of genetic testing in underwriting decisions. Genetic testing assesses the chromosomes and genes in human cells. It enables researchers to identify normal and abnormal chromosome and gene characteristics, and thus to identify certain physical and mental conditions, including actual and potential diseases and impairments, that are wholly or partially genetically linked.

At least one jurisdiction has held that underwriters may not discriminate against proposed insureds solely on the basis of the genetic makeup that those proposed insureds exhibit. Insurers do not usually discriminate for the presence of an abnormal gene alone, but do discriminate on the basis of a disease caused by an abnormal gene. Although healthy persons possessing one of the genes *may* possibly develop the associated disease at a later time, or may pass on the genes to their children, discrimination based only on the possession of a genetic trait is considered unfair unless that gene will invariably produce disease (for example, the gene for Huntington's disease). If an applicant for insurance does have a disease caused by a genetic trait, that disease ordinarily may legally be taken into account during underwriting. For instance, an underwriter may not rate or deny coverage to a proposed insured solely on the basis that the applicant possesses a gene associated with diabetes, but may rate or deny coverage if the proposed insured also exhibits evidence of diabetes.

Fast Fact

Scientists estimate that humans have between 50,000 and 100,000 genes. Although efforts to map human genes continue, as of the summer of 1996, scientists had identified only 6,126 individual genes.

Source: Suzanne E. Stipe, "Genetic Testing Battle Pits Insurers Against Consumers," *Best's Review (Life/Health)*, August 1996: 39–43.

Marital Status

Discrimination solely on the basis of an applicant's marital status is prohibited by law in many jurisdictions. One exception to this general rule is in family coverage policies, which cover all members of a family under one contract. Legislation generally allows an insurance company to decline an application for family coverage on cohabiting single persons. Some insurers make exceptions, however, for cohabiting single persons who have children and clear insurable interest.

Sexual Orientation

Many jurisdictions have enacted regulations prohibiting underwriters from engaging in discrimination based solely on an applicant's sexual orientation. Such regulations mean that, if an applicant for insurance is known to be homosexual, the insurer cannot deny coverage or charge a higher premium solely on the basis of the applicant's homosexuality.

NAIC model guidelines, adopted by many states, prohibit underwriters from using sexual orientation to influence underwriting decisions, and from basing underwriting requirements on a person's actual or perceived sexual orientation, including making inferences based on a person's stated occupation, area of residence, or choice of beneficiary. In some states, the fact that a person has taken one or more tests for human immunodeficiency virus (HIV) cannot be used as a basis for declining coverage.

Canadian Antidiscrimination Statutes

Underwriters in Canada generally may not discriminate among life and health insurance applicants on the basis of gender, unless such discrimination is reasonably based on actuarial data. Provincial regulation is not as uniform regarding other types of discrimination. Because of the disparity in regulations, an underwriter handling business subject to Canadian laws usually needs to be knowledgeable about relevant legislation in all Canadian jurisdictions in which the underwriter's company does business.

Some provinces specifically prohibit discrimination on the basis of physical and mental impairments and other handicaps, marital status, and sexual orientation. Canadian underwriting practices are generally the same as U.S. practices concerning underwriting for genetic characteristics.

Replacement Regulations

Surrendering an insurance policy or part of the coverage of an insurance policy in order to buy another policy is known as ***replacement.*** Policy replacements are subject to regulation. While replacement of existing life insurance policies is not illegal, it may not be in a policyowner's best interest. Insurance companies typically establish programs for agency training and home office education to help ensure that when replacement occurs, it is carried out ethically and legally, with full disclosure to policyowners.

When a marketer encourages a policyowner to cancel an insurance policy and to buy a new policy from another insurer, the marketer must clearly inform the policyowner of the difference between the two policies and the financial consequences of the replacement. To help prevent unethical replacement, most states have adopted some version of the NAIC's Replacement of Life Insurance and Annuities Model Regulation, which says that replacement of policies is generally permissible if the replacing insurer provides full and fair disclosure. Certain types of policies are usually not governed by state replacement regulations; these include group policies, conversion policies, policies that replace temporary life insurance and that are issued under a premium receipt, and new policies issued by the existing insurer.

If the application for insurance indicates that the policy requested will replace existing coverage, the replacing insurer—and, thus, the underwriter in many instances—has a number of significant duties to perform. Depending on the jurisdiction involved, these duties can include

- Requiring that the marketer prepare, either with or as a part of each application, a list identifying to the best of her knowledge all existing life insurance policies proposed to be replaced.

- Obtaining a copy of the "Notice to Applicants Regarding Replacement of Life Insurance" provided to the applicant. The replacing insurer keeps these forms on file for at least three years or until the conclusion of the next regular examination of the insurer by the insurance department of its state of domicile, whichever is later.

- Immediately notifying an insurer whose policy is being replaced and furnishing that insurer with a copy of a policy summary.

Privacy and Confidentiality Laws

In the course of business operations, insurance companies need to acquire and store large quantities of personal information about their customers. ***Personal information*** includes any information that can be connected to a specific person and includes information about a person's habits, character, occupation or avocations, financial situation, credit history, health, and any other topic. Comments on the history of privacy and confidentiality in the insurance industry are found in Insight 3-3.

Insight 3-3 My Thoughts On . . . The History of Privacy and Confidentiality

Privacy is the right of an individual to limit access by others to some aspect of the person. When applied to information, privacy involves limiting the access of information so that it is beyond the range of others who lack specific authorization.

Confidentiality is a form of informational privacy that is characterized by a special relationship, such as a physician to a patient or an attorney to a client. Personal information obtained in the course of this relationship should not be revealed to others, unless the individual is made aware and consents to its disclosure.

Let me first state that confidentiality guidelines are not a modern concept to the healing professions, but antiquarian. One of the first attempts to document this responsibility for the medical profession can be found in the Oath of Hippocrates (460 to 377 B.C.) in the passage: "Whatever, in connection with my professional practice, or not in connection with it, I see or hear, in the life of men, which ought not to be spoken of abroad, I will not divulge, as reckoning that all such should be kept secret."

Historically, confidentiality and privacy in the insurance industry can be broken into seven eras from the 1800s to the present.

- The *Empirical Era* (1800s to 1905) was noted for intuitive underwriting, with a lack of objective statistical information to back decisions. Because of the lack of studies, there was inconsistency in decision making. Although insurers did appoint medical examiners, there was a minimal amount of impaired risk underwriting. Special emphasis was placed on the measurement of build and on the examination of urine.
- The *Biostatistical Era* (1905 to 1930) heralded the development of large-scale mortality studies. Now substandard risks could cautiously be insured. Testing also began to become prominent, such as the examination of blood sugars, electrocardiograms, and chest X-rays. Measuring blood pressure also came into prominence.
- The *Clinical Era* (1930 to 1950) was noted for its rapid advances in clinical medicine and increased statistical studies. This greater understanding of impairments was translated into an even larger use for the industry of testing procedures and the insuring of many more substandard lives.
- The *Tranquillity Era* (1950 to 1965) was noted for consistent and conservative underwriting and pricing practices that produced many years of excellent profitability for the insurance industry.

Throughout these first four eras, privacy and confidentiality issues changed very little. They were approached in a manner similar to the way one would behave in a patient/doctor relationship. That is, insurers were generally committed to non-disclosure or no re-disclosure of circumscribed information to any parties other than the information originator and the initial recipient, unless legitimate exceptions existed by legal or regulatory process. Moreover, disclosure was made to third parties only with explicit consent and authorization of the insured or proposed insured, and only persons with a business need-to-know could have access to any underwriting or claim information. During the next three eras, certain changes occurred to these approaches.

- The *Shopping Era* (1965 to 1985) was noted for intense competition that culminated in very aggressive underwriting, wide-scale shopping with expansion of the reinsurers, a decrease in marketer loyalty, and diminished underwriting profitability. During this era, much of the baseline privacy legislation in the United States was passed.
- The *AIDS Era* (1985 to 1990) was ushered in by the AIDS epidemic, which was feared to threaten the very viability of the insurance industry. Antiselection was aggressively defended with HIV testing supported by expansion in the insurance lab industry. Underwriting was once again recognized as a premier control function whose expertise was essential for the life of the industry. A large number of laws were passed to regulate privacy, confidentiality, and compliance.
- The *Technology Era* (1990 to the present) has been highlighted by the leap into advanced electronic technology including common use of computerized underwriting systems, electronic data interchange (EDI), image work stations, and the proliferation of fax and cell technology. AIDS hysteria has died, and the major medical issues facing the insurance industry now will be the proper use of genetic information.

Lawrence Segel, M.D., FLMI,
ALHC, ACS, CBIM, AIAA
Assistant Vice President, Medical
Research and Development
Manulife Financial

Adapted by written permission from *Marketing Options,* June 1996.

To protect the privacy of customers and the confidentiality of personal information, most jurisdictions have established extensive laws affecting the use and disclosure of that information. Insurance underwriting is subject to these laws. In this section, we will look at federal privacy laws in both the United States and Canada.

Although privacy laws enacted at the state and provincial level vary from one jurisdiction to another, most such laws are patterned on model laws and guidelines proposed by the NAIC in the United States and by the Canadian Life and Health Insurance Association (CLHIA) in Canada. We will look at the various features of model laws and guidelines to understand how state and provincial laws that are patterned on these models affect underwriting.

Federal Privacy Guidelines and Laws

In an attempt to ensure that personal information will not be inaccurate or misused, countries around the world have attempted to establish protections for that information. Internationally, the Organization for Economic Cooperation and Development (OECD) in 1980 developed guidelines on the flow and protection of personal information and privacy between one country and another. The guidelines established minimum standards for protecting the confidentiality of personal information without impeding the flow of such information from one country to another. These guidelines were endorsed by the European members of OECD and by the United States and Canada, and were also incorporated into the CLHIA's "Right-to-Privacy Guidelines." These guidelines are presented in Insight 3-4.

The U.S. Congress has passed laws regulating the collection, retention, and use of personal information. In the United States, two acts passed by Congress, the Fair Credit Reporting Act (FCRA) and the Privacy Act of 1974, help ensure the privacy and confidentiality of personal information, including insurance records.

The Fair Credit Reporting Act. The ***Fair Credit Reporting Act (FCRA),*** enacted in 1970, helps ensure that credit reporting agencies act fairly, impartially, and with respect for the consumer's right to privacy when preparing reports on individuals. Under the FCRA, only individuals are considered to be consumers; corporations and other types of businesses are not protected by this act.

Three terms used in the FCRA have specific definitions that are relevant to underwriting—*consumer reporting agency, consumer report,* and *investigative consumer report.*

When assessing the risk represented by a proposed insured and when evaluating certain claims, insurers often obtain reports from consumer reporting agencies. A ***consumer reporting agency*** is a person or an organization that regularly prepares consumer reports

Insight 3-4 CLHIA "Right-to-Privacy Guidelines"

Foreword

In providing life and health insurance to Canadians, insurance companies require significant amounts of detailed information about individuals. This information, much of which can be regarded as "personal," is required both for risk evaluation and for claim adjudication under both individual and group contracts. Indeed, it could be said that personal information is the principal raw material for life and health insurance.

In recognition of this fact, and of the potentially sensitive nature of such information, insurance companies must adhere closely to strict rules governing the protection of the confidential information they hold.

These Guidelines set a minimum standard. Insurance companies may adopt these Guidelines or may develop their own guidelines, which are at least as protective as these minimum standards.

1. Scope and Purpose of Guidelines

These Guidelines apply to the collection, verification, possession, protection, use, and disclosure of personal information acquired by a life and health insurance company in the course of its Canadian operations.

2. Definitions

"Company" means a life and health insurance company and includes its life and health insurance subsidiaries and benefit-plan-administration subsidiaries.

"Personal information" means any information relating to an identified or identifiable individual, including, but not limited to, health and financial information.

3. Collection Limitation

Only lawful means will be used to collect personal information. To the extent appropriate:

(a) such personal information will be obtained directly from the individual, and

(b) prior to collecting such information from any other source, the individual concerned will be notified or his/her written authorization obtained.

Parts (a) and (b) of this section do not apply to information supplied to the company by a group plan sponsor for the purpose of risk evaluation, administering a group plan, or claim adjudication.

4. Data Quality

Every reasonable effort will be made to ensure that the personal information obtained by the company is:

(a) pertinent to the effective conduct of the company's business;

(b) as accurate and complete as possible, consistent with the purpose(s) for which it was obtained.

5. Purpose Identification

The purpose(s) for which personal information is collected from an individual will be specified on or before the collection of information, and any change of purpose will be communicated to the individual.

6. Use and Disclosure

Personal information will not be disclosed or used for purposes other than those specified to the individual in accordance with Section #5, except:

(a) with the consent of the individual concerned; or

(b) where required by law; or

(c) where reasonably necessary, to determine eligibility for an insurance benefit or to protect the interests of the company against criminal activity, fraud, and material misrepresentation in connection with an insurance contract; or

(d) in the discharge of public duty.

7. Individual Access to Information

Each company will adopt a general policy of openness about the company's practices and policies with respect to the use and protection of personal information. In particular:

(a) Upon appropriate identification and written request satisfactory to the company, an individual will be advised of personal information about him/her retained in the company's records. A company may charge a reasonable administration fee to supply the information. Some medical information may be made available only through the individual's designated physician.

(b) Where information cannot be disclosed to the individual, he/she will be given the reasons for not disclosing information.

(c) An individual may clarify or correct erroneous personal information retained by the company. Incorrect or incomplete information will be amended, and differences as to the correctness of the information will be noted.

8. Compliance and Complaint Resolution

In order to ensure compliance with the protection of privacy guidelines, each company will:

(a) designate an officer to receive complaints;

(b) establish procedures for receiving and resolving complaints.

(continued)

Insight 3-4 CLHIA "Right-to-Privacy Guidelines," continued

Individuals dissatisfied with the complaint resolution of a company can contact the office of the insurance regulators in their province.

9. Security Safeguards
Personal information will be considered confidential, and comprehensive safeguards will be established by the company to protect that confidentiality.

A company will take the necessary measures to ensure that all employees of the company are required to conform to the company's applicable privacy guidelines.

All agents, brokers, plan sponsors, and other persons or organizations acting for or on the behalf of the company will be required to comply with the guidelines.

and furnishes them, either for profit or on a cooperative, non-profit basis, to other persons or organizations.

A ***consumer report*** is a communication from a consumer reporting agency and contains information relating to a person's creditworthiness, credit standing, or credit capacity, as well as information about the person's general reputation or personal characteristics.

An ***investigative consumer report*** is a type of consumer report that includes information gathered during interviews with persons such as friends, neighbors, business associates, and others who are associated with or who have knowledge of the consumer. An inspection report, which we will discuss in Chapter 5, is a type of investigative consumer report.

To use the reports generated by consumer reporting agencies, insurers are required to give certain types of notice to applicants. The three types of notice required by the FCRA are (1) pre-notice, (2) supplementary notice, and (3) post-notice.

- An insurer uses a ***pre-notice*** to disclose clearly and adequately to an applicant that an investigative consumer report may be made. The insurer must use the term "investigative consumer report" in its disclosure. Such disclosure must (1) be in writing, (2) be mailed or otherwise delivered to the proposed insured no later than three days after the date on which the report was first requested, and (3) include a statement informing the proposed insured of her right to obtain a disclosure of the nature and scope of the investigation requested. Figure 3-1 provides an example of the authorization portion of a pre-notice form.

- A ***supplementary notice*** is required within five days when a consumer makes a request for information respecting the nature and scope of the investigation specified in the pre-notice.

Figure 3-1. Authorization portion of a pre-notice form.

AUTHORIZATION

In order to see if (and on what basis) I qualify for insurance or for the benefits which that insurance may provide, I authorize the following:

MEDICAL INFORMATION. Physicians or practitioners; hospitals; medical or medically related facilities; laboratories; insurance companies; or the Medical Information Bureau (MIB) may give to the insurer (or any consumer reporting agency acting in its behalf) and to any of its reinsurers data and copies of records that they may have about my physical and mental health.

OTHER UNDERWRITING INFORMATION. MIB and other insurance companies may give to the insurer and to any of its reinsurers data about: my driving record; any criminal activity or association; hazardous sport or aviation activity; use of alcohol or drugs; and other applications for insurance.

EXAMINATIONS AND TESTS. The insurer may obtain physical examinations or medical tests deemed necessary to underwrite my application. These tests (where permitted by law) may include, but are not limited to, electrocardiograms, chest X-rays, and tests of blood and urine to determine, among other things, exposure to causative agents of disease (for example, exposure to the AIDS virus) and the presence of drugs. However, a separate notification/authorization form will be provided with respect to testing for the AIDS virus.

INVESTIGATIVE CONSUMER REPORT. The insurer may obtain an investigative consumer report and may tell the consumer reporting agency the amount and type of my coverage. The report may add to or confirm the types of data mentioned above. It may also contain data about: my identity; age; residence; marital status; past and present jobs (including work duties); economic conditions; driving record; personal and business reputation in the community; and mode of living; but will not include any information relating directly or indirectly to sexual orientation.

IDENTIFICATION. To obtain the data described above, the insurer may give my name, address, and date and place of birth to the above persons or organizations.

RELEASE OF INFORMATION TO OTHERS. When necessary, the insurer may give data about me that affects my insurability to: its subsidiaries; its affiliates; its parent company; its marketers and their staffs; its reinsurers; and the insurer and its reinsurers may give such data to MIB. However, this will not be done in connection with information relating to the AIDS virus.

I also authorize the release of these same types of data about any of my children who are to be insured.

This authorization shall be valid for 30 days from the date shown below. A photocopy of it shall be as valid as the original.

I know that a copy of this form is in the Insurer's statement on "Information Practices Related to Underwriting Your Application."

Date ____________________ 19 ______ ____
Signature of Proposed Insured (Annuitant)

Witness ____________________________ ____
Marketer
Signature of Spouse, if proposed for coverage; or Signature of Parent or Guardian, if Proposed Insured (Annuitant) is under 14 years.

- A ***post-notice*** must be sent to an applicant if an insurer makes an adverse decision that is based wholly or partially on information contained in a report from a consumer reporting agency. The adverse decision is typically a denial of insurance, or issuance of a policy with a substandard or special risk classification and a consequent increase in premium, or a reduction in the amount of coverage or the type of benefits applied for. The post-notice form must (1) inform the proposed insured of the adverse decision and (2) supply the name and address of the consumer reporting agency that made the report so that the applicant may obtain a copy of the report and correct any erroneous information it may contain. The post-notice does not include details contained in the report from the consumer reporting agency.

Underwriters are usually knowledgeable about the limitations on the types of information that they may ask to be included in a consumer report. The FCRA states that a consumer report regarding an applicant who has applied for less than $50,000 of insurance cannot contain certain types of adverse information, such as comments about bankruptcies, suits and judgments, and arrest and conviction records. These types of information, however, may be included in a consumer report if the policy applied for has a face amount of $50,000 or more.

Using information gathered during preparation of a consumer report, a consumer reporting agency may include adverse information in any subsequent consumer report only if (1) such information is a matter of public record, (2) such information is verified during the process of making the report, or (3) the reporting agency received the adverse information within the three-month period preceding the date that the subsequent report is furnished.

Fast Fact

As of 1996, laws in 11 states specifically prevented insurers from rejecting applications or raising premium rates based on genetic testing results. In two other states, similar bills were awaiting the governors' signatures.

Source: "Regulatory Genetics Bills Attracting Broad Support," *Best's Review (Life/Health)*, August 1996: 39–43.

The Privacy Act of 1974. Another Congressional act that has encouraged insurers to treat personal information carefully is the ***Privacy Act of 1974,*** which protects the employees of federal agencies by establishing requirements for the collection, retention, use, and distribution of personal data. This act provides that federal employees may obtain copies of confidential records that pertain to them and may have information added to their records. Moreover, the act established the Privacy Protection Study Commission, whose purpose was to study the use of personal information by both government and private industry and to recommend privacy legislation.

The NAIC Model Privacy Act

Using information contained in the report of the Privacy Protection Study Commission, the NAIC drafted the Insurance Information and Privacy Protection Act, better known as the NAIC Model Privacy Act.

Some states have enacted privacy laws based on the NAIC model. A state law patterned on the model act protects only persons who are residents of that state and who are applying for personal insurance. Persons who are applying for insurance for business purposes and corporations applying for insurance are not protected under such laws.

Laws patterned on the NAIC Model Privacy Act establish standards for the collection, use, and disclosure of information gathered in connection with insurance transactions by insurance institutions, marketers, and insurance-support organizations. The NAIC Model Privacy Act has the following stated purposes:

1. To minimize intrusions on individuals' privacy
2. To establish a mechanism that allows persons to determine what information about them relevant to insurance transactions is currently being collected or has already been collected
3. To enable such persons to have access to information collected in order to verify or dispute its accuracy
4. To limit the disclosure of collected information
5. To enable applicants and policyowners to obtain a justification for adverse underwriting decisions

To achieve these purposes, the NAIC Model Privacy Act stipulates a number of procedures that insurers must follow when a person applies for coverage, whether the coverage applied for is a new policy or a renewal or an expansion of existing coverage. The act also stipulates the manner in which compliance with these procedures will be enforced.

State and Provincial Privacy Protection

In addition to understanding state statutes modeled after the NAIC Model Privacy Act, underwriters stay informed about other state legislation affecting the collection and use of personal information. Many jurisdictions have enacted statutes that protect medical records and tax returns.

Even in jurisdictions that have not enacted privacy legislation, many insurers voluntarily observe the following practices for protecting the privacy of their customers:

1. Safeguarding the confidentiality of records
2. Conducting periodic evaluations of recordkeeping practices

3. Allowing applicants access to information obtained during a background check

4. Reviewing the operating practices of investigative firms

Underwriters and others should know to whom medical information may be released. Various state and provincial laws either *mandate* or *allow* insurers to release medical information to the following persons or entities:

- The proposed insured
- The proposed insured's physician
- Another health care provider designated by the proposed insured
- The Medical Information Bureau (which we will discuss in the next chapter)
- A reinsurer
- An employee of the insurer
- A legal guardian of the proposed insured
- A person authorized by the proposed insured to receive such information
- A law enforcement official
- A state department of health
- The insurer's legal counsel

The state laws vary considerably, but the overriding principle is that only persons with a legitimate business need-to-know or some other legitimate need-to-know—such as the proposed insured himself or his physician or guardian—should receive the information. Not all states and provinces mandate or allow all of the above persons to receive medical information. The underwriter, therefore, learns what is allowed or mandated in each state or province.

Of particular importance to most insurers is the public concern over confidentiality of medical records containing information on such diseases as acquired immune deficiency syndrome (AIDS). The American Council of Life Insurance (ACLI) and the Health Insurance Association of America (HIAA), in their *Position Paper on AIDS and*

Insurance, state that insurers will continue to treat information about AIDS with the same level of confidentiality as they have treated all medical information. The MIB protects patient confidentiality by placing HIV test results in a code that designates only general blood abnormalities and does not specify the presence of the HIV virus or AIDS. In recent years, most states have passed laws requiring insurers to keep AIDS-related information confidential.

Fast Fact

From 1985 to 1995, life and health insurance companies in the United States spent $36 million to support education, research, and service delivery activities related to AIDS.

Source: George A. Norris, "Industry AIDS Toll Mounts, but Slowly," in *Life Association News,* July 1996: 41.

At present, there is no general legislation in Canada regarding the availability to insurers of medical information in the possession of doctors, hospitals, and other institutions, although specific legislation concerning mental health information has been passed. Concern in Canada over unauthorized distribution of personal medical information from medical care providers to insurers and certain private investigators has led to the formation of a Royal Commission on the Confidentiality of Health Records. This commission has developed a set of recommendations regarding authorization for the release of personal medical information.

To safeguard the privacy and confidentiality of personal information about their customers, many insurance companies have established procedures for handling such information. Insight 3-5 presents a series of questions designed to help companies determine how effectively they protect personal information.

Insight 3-5 Protecting Confidentiality of Personal Information

Do all employees with access to confidential information

- Have written guidelines in their area that address the protection of confidentiality and that let everyone know what they should and should not do when handling personal information?
- Know that personal information received from another insurer, or from another source, without appropriate authorization from the person in question should be returned to the sender and not copied or used?
- Understand that they also need authorization to disclose personal information to a third party?
- Appreciate that those who acquire personal information should have a legitimate business or professional reason for needing the information?
- Know that those to whom they send personal information should have a reasonable business or professional reason for needing that information?
- Know that taking work home—i.e., removing files that contain personal information from the workplace—is an unsafe business practice?
- Understand that they should not readily share personal kinds of data over the telephone with someone when they don't know the caller's true identity for certain?
- Have a policy against leaving underwriting jackets or other records lying on their desks overnight?
- Have practices and procedures in place that effectively limit access to the company's general files area and so prevent unauthorized people from accessing such files, or authorized people from doing so without business need?
- Remove certain kinds of personal medical information, such as positive AIDS-test results, from jackets and keep this especially sensitive information in a locked file?
- Sign a yearly pledge that they understand and will abide by corporate and/or department confidentiality policies and practices?

Adapted by permission of Lincoln National Life Reinsurance Company, from *Medical Resource,* November/December 1993: 13–14.

Premium Receipts

Underwriting some types of coverages, especially for large amounts or for proposed insureds with impairments, may consume a considerable period of time. Meanwhile, if the applicant has submitted the initial premium to the insurance company, many companies agree to provide temporary life insurance coverage on the proposed insured if certain conditions are met. A ***premium receipt*** is a written acknowledgment that an insurer has received the initial premium submitted with an application for insurance. Underwriters are typically familiar with the legal effects of these receipts.

Two types of premium receipts are the conditional premium receipt and the binding premium receipt.

Conditional Premium Receipt

Insurers may issue a ***conditional premium receipt*** to make the applied-for insurance coverage effective on the date of the application without necessitating the delivery of the policy. In other words, when an insurer issues a conditional premium receipt, the company makes the applied-for coverage effective *at the time of application,* provided that the underwriter subsequently finds the applicant insurable as a standard risk. Figure 3-2 shows a sample conditional premium receipt.

A conditional premium receipt provides two specific benefits—one for the applicant and beneficiary, and one for the insurance company. First, this type of receipt protects an applicant against loss of insurability and protects a beneficiary against loss resulting from the death of the proposed insured while underwriting is in progress. Second, this type of receipt helps to protect an insurer against the expense of underwriting a policy and then having it refused by an applicant, because applicants are less likely to refuse delivery of a policy for which they have already paid the initial premium, and they are more likely to remit the initial premium with the application if they receive temporary insurance coverage in return.

For the coverage to be considered effective as of the date of application, the applicant must be judged insurable according to the underwriting rules established for the specific plan applied for and for the amount of insurance applied for at the premium rate stated on the application. If, however, an applicant is judged insurable, but for a plan other than the plan applied for, or for a different amount of insurance than the amount applied for, or at another premium rate than the rate stated, then the applicant must accept the insurance as revised before coverage becomes effective.

According to the terms of a conditional premium receipt, an applicant who is found to be insurable at the time of application is covered

Figure 3-2. Conditional premium receipt.

CONDITIONAL RECEIPT

To the Marketer: Complete this receipt and give it to the applicant **only** if collecting at least the minimum payment with the application.

Received from ______________________________ the sum of $____________ in connection with an application bearing the same number as this receipt.

Date ___________

Marketer's Signature X ______________________ Marketer's Phone ______________

No insurance is provided under the terms of this receipt unless <u>all</u> of the following conditions have been met:

1. Part I of the application and Part II, if required by the company, must be completed, signed, and dated;

2. All statements and answers in Part I of the application and Part II, if required, must be true and complete;

3. All medical examinations, tests, X-rays, and electrocardiograms, if required by the company prior to issuing the policy, must be completed;

4. On the date shown on this receipt, each person to be covered must be insurable for the plan, class, and amount of life insurance and any additional benefits applied for, according to the company's underwriting rules and practices; and

5. One monthly premium or a completed allotment authorization for the plan and amount of insurance applied for must be paid/submitted on or before the date shown on this receipt.

If all five conditions have been met, then insurance will be in effect from the date shown on Part I of the application or Part II, if required.

A. The total amount of insurance applied for on the life of any person to be covered under the application bearing the same number as this receipt, as well as any other application pending with the company, including accidental death benefits, will be limited to $250,000 or the amount applied for, whichever is less prior to delivery of the policy. Any premium paid for coverage in excess of this maximum shall create no additional liability on the part of the company.

B. Insurance provided under the terms of this receipt is also subject to all terms and conditions of the policy applied for, including any suicide exclusion provision.

C. Insurance provided under the terms of this receipt will be void if this receipt is modified or altered, or if payment by check or by draft is not honored on first presentation for payment.

If the company declines to issue the policy applied for and the applicant does not accept an alternative policy offered, if any, this payment will be refunded without interest.

under the policy, even if he should become uninsurable or die before the application is actually approved by the insurer. In considering the application of a person who is known to have died during the time since the policy was applied for, underwriters do not allow knowledge of the applicant's illness or death to influence the underwriting decision.

Binding Premium Receipt

In recent years, conditional premium receipts have become a problem for insurers because many courts have interpreted such receipts to provide unconditional, immediate coverage regardless of the intention of the company or the wording of the receipt. This interpretation, called the ***interim insurance law,*** generally holds that, if the marketer has accepted payment, the applicant is covered until the insurer notifies the applicant that coverage has been terminated and returns the premium.

Because of the interim insurance law, conditional premium receipts often do not protect the insurer from temporarily assuming undesirable risks. Even if the applicant is found to be uninsurable and would not have been granted coverage under a policy, the insurer may be liable for the full policy benefit amount if an applicant who paid the initial premium and received a conditional premium receipt dies before being notified of the rejection or before the initial premium has been refunded.

Many insurance companies have responded to the interim insurance law by issuing a binding premium receipt, also called a *temporary insurance agreement (TIA)*. A ***binding premium receipt*** provides insurance coverage of a specified amount for a specified time, usually for the time required to underwrite the case. The binding premium receipt usually specifies that coverage will begin on the date the application was signed and the premium was paid. Moreover, the receipt specifies that coverage under the binding premium receipt will end on the earliest of (1) the date the insurer returns the premium; (2) a specified number of days after the insurer mails a notice of termination to the premium notice address on the application; or (3) the date coverage begins under the issued policy. Coverage under the binding receipt does not depend on the proposed insured's insurability. However, a binding receipt typically lists conditions under which the receipt provides no coverage, such as (1) material misrepresentation in the answers to the questions in the receipt or (2) death of the proposed insured from suicide or a self-inflicted injury. Figure 3-3 presents a sample binding premium receipt.

A valid binding premium receipt is a contract between an insurer and an applicant, but is not a part of the insurance policy. A binding premium receipt temporarily binds the insurer to the risk regardless of whether the insurer ultimately issues a policy to the applicant. In some jurisdictions, a binding premium receipt that contains no provision concerning revocation of the application continues in force during the specified period of 60 or 90 days even if the applicant withdraws the application. In such a situation, a proposed insured is covered for the amount specified by the binding premium receipt, even if the applicant is not continuing to seek a policy from the insurance company.

Statutory Requirements for Group Insurance

In the United States and Canada, group insurance is regulated by many of the same laws that regulate individual insurance. In addition, group insurance in the United States is regulated by legislation modeled on several NAIC model acts and is guided in Canada by CLHIA guidelines.

Figure 3-3. Binding premium receipt.

BINDING LIMITED LIFE INSURANCE COVERAGE

For premium(s) received in connection with the Application, XYZ Insurance provides a limited amount of life insurance coverage for a short time while it decides whether to issue and deliver the policy applied for. This coverage is subject to the terms and conditions set out below.

Application # ____________________ Proposed Insured ____________________

Amount of Limited life insurance coverage $____________ (Not to exceed the *lesser* of $300,000 or the amount of life insurance applied for)

	Yes	No
1. Has the proposed insured		
a. any reason to believe present health is not good?	☐	☐
b. ever had, or now have, any type of heart disease or high blood pressure?	☐	☐
c. ever had, or now have, any type of cancer, leukemia, or malignant tumor?	☐	☐
d. attained age 70?	☐	☐
2. Does all existing life insurance plus amount applied for in pending application(s) with all insurers exceed four million dollars? Include group and AD with XYZ Insurance and other insurers.	☐	☐

If any of the above questions is answered YES or LEFT BLANK, no marketer is authorized to accept a premium, and there will be NO COVERAGE.

(continued)

Figure 3-3. Binding premium receipt (continued).

TERMS AND CONDITIONS

AMOUNT OF COVERAGE—UP TO $300,000

If the Proposed Insured dies while this coverage is in effect, XYZ Insurance will pay the amount of limited life insurance coverage to the beneficiary in the application. But, the total amount payable under this coverage, plus any other binding limited life insurance coverage with XYZ Insurance, shall not exceed $300,000. There is no premium waiver coverage.

DATE COVERAGE BEGINS

Coverage under this Agreement starts when Part I of the application is completed and a premium has been accepted.

DATE COVERAGE ENDS

This coverage will end automatically on the *earliest* of the date:

- XYZ Insurance returns the premium;
- Five days after XYZ Insurance mails a notice of termination to the premium notice address on the application; or
- Coverage starts under any XYZ policy resulting from the application.

XYZ Insurance may send the notice or return premium(s) at any time.

NO COVERAGE

There is no insurance coverage if:

- There is a material misrepresentation in the answers to the questions above; or
- The proposed insured dies by suicide, or self-inflicted injury; or
- The premium check is not honored.

Premium(s) will be returned if no policy is delivered and no benefit is paid under this coverage. If a policy is delivered, premium(s) will be applied to the first policy premium. Premium is either cash, check, pre-authorized check, or employee salary authorization.

All the representations above are true and complete to the best of my knowledge and belief. They are relied on for this coverage. No marketer can waive or modify this coverage in any way.

Signature of Proposed Insured________________________ Date____________, 19____
(If below age 15, signature of parent or guardian required)

Spouse (If applicable)____

Applicant-Owner (If not signing above)_______________________________________

Witness_____________________________________ If a firm or corporation, print company name and have company officer sign.

Requirements in the United States

In the United States, state laws specify (1) the nature of groups that are eligible for group insurance, (2) certain provisions that must be included in group contracts, (3) limitations on benefits that can be provided under group coverage, and (4) the types and level of taxes that may be levied on out-of-state insurers licensed to do business within a state. In addition, most states establish the regulatory jurisdiction of each state over the underwriting practices of group insurers.

In assessing the risk represented by a group of persons who work in various states or provinces, the underwriter considers the laws that are applicable to each of those areas. Such an analysis of the group's risk can become complicated, particularly if some of the group members are affected by laws establishing requirements that are markedly different from the laws affecting other group members. Underwriters handling such cases, therefore, receive thorough training in state mandates, as well as timely updates as the laws are changed.

The Employee Retirement Income Security Act of 1974 (ERISA) does not establish requirements that directly affect underwriting, but does require groups to file certain documents that underwriters can use in assessing the risk for group coverage. ERISA is a federal law that establishes (1) the rights of participants in pension plans, (2) standards for investing pension plan assets, and (3) requirements for disclosing plan provisions and funding. Later in this text, we will discuss the documents that are filed under ERISA and that underwriters use as an information source.

Certain elements of group insurance coverage are also regulated by U.S. federal statutes, the most important of which include the Internal Revenue Code, Social Security Act, Civil Rights Act, Health Maintenance Organization Act, Family and Medical Leave Act (FMLA), Age Discrimination in Employment Act (ADEA), and Americans with Disabilities Act (ADA). ADEA and ADA are particularly important for group underwriters to understand because both acts influence an underwriter's assessment of plan schedules.

Two NAIC model acts contain standard contract provisions for group health and life insurance policies. These acts are the (1) Group Life Insurance Definition and Group Life Insurance Standard Provisions Model Act and (2) Group Health Insurance Definition and Group Health Insurance Standard Provisions Model Act. The standard provisions contained in these model acts relate to

- Incontestability
- Grace period
- Evidence of insurability

- Application made a part of the policy contract
- Misstatement of age
- Required issue of a certificate to every insured person

In addition, the model act for group life coverage states that a group life insurance contract must make provision for conversion rights (including payment of proceeds during a conversion period), naming a beneficiary, and continued coverage during disability. The model act for group health coverage states that a group health insurance contract must provide for the insurer to receive notice of a claim within a reasonable period after the claim was incurred.

Requirements in Canada

In Canada, each province has enacted legislation governing group life and group health coverage. In all provinces except Quebec, the legislation is called the Uniform Life Insurance Act, which regulates both individual and group life insurance, and the Uniform Accident and Sickness Act, which regulates individual and group health insurance. In Quebec, the legislation is called the Quebec Insurance Act, which regulates coverage for individuals and groups.

The provincial laws that affect underwriting include those that regulate the designation and rights of insured persons and beneficiaries, contract administration and premium payment, contract and certificate contents, and requirements concerning termination of coverage and transfer to a new carrier.

Group insurance guidelines provided by the CLHIA give insurers a set of generally accepted operating principles relating to group insurance. Approved by the CLHIA in 1994, the Group Insurance Guidelines replace the former Guidelines of the Superintendent of Insurance and are intended to provide a minimum standard for group insurance practices.

Topics covered by the Guidelines include

- Specifications for the principal benefits and conditions for a group plan description
- Minimum underwriting and claim administration standards to ensure the equitable treatment of insureds and claimants
- Processes to follow when a policyholder transfers coverage from one insurer to another, including coverage of disabled persons at the effective date of the replacing contract

- Requirement that a disability under a waiver-of-premium provision be reported to an insurer no later than 180 days after commencement of the disability or whatever longer period the group policy provides

- Requirement that the disability income benefit payable to an insured under a group contract shall not be reduced because of a government-sponsored cost-of-living adjustment (COLA) program occurring after the date on which the benefit becomes payable

- Provision for arbitration to settle disputes in both life and disability claims

Key Terms and Concepts

misrepresentation
rescission
material misrepresentation
underwriting worksheet
replacement
personal information
Fair Credit Reporting Act (FCRA)
consumer reporting agency
consumer report
investigative consumer report
pre-notice
supplementary notice
post-notice
Privacy Act of 1974
premium receipt
conditional premium receipt
interim insurance law
binding premium receipt (*temporary insurance agreement* [*TIA*])

CHAPTER FOUR

Underwriting Individual Life Insurance—Medical Factors

Learning Objectives

After studying this chapter, you should be able to

- Describe the typical information presented in a field underwriting manual
- List the types of insurability information contained in Part I and Part II of an application for insurance
- Describe the functions and contents of a nonmedical supplement, a medical report, and a paramedical report
- Explain the types of information an underwriter may obtain from attending and examining physicians, specialized medical questionnaires, laboratory tests, and the Medical Information Bureau (MIB)
- State the importance of the factors of age and build in classifying proposed risks
- Explain the function of the numerical rating system
- Describe the approach used in the table rating method and the flat extra premium method of medical risk assessment
- Name the kinds of medical information contained in an insurer's underwriting manual

Chapter Outline

Well before an underwriter begins to assess an application for individual life insurance, a marketer has begun risk selection. The marketer selects target markets, identifies prospects, and works with clients to determine their financial needs and to seek ways to meet those needs. Unless the insurance product is sold by direct mail or other direct contact, the marketer sees the applicant in person and has opportunities to make and report observations about the applicant that home office underwriters cannot make because they have no direct contact with the applicant. When marketers understand and properly fulfill their underwriting responsibilities, the quality of business an insurer receives is greatly improved, and the response time of underwriting is faster.

Medical underwriting is not generally needed for group life and health insurance coverage, except when small groups of just a few persons are being evaluated. In a typical group, the risk is spread among all the members of the group. The statistically low risk of the younger and healthier group members helps to offset the statistically higher risk of other members of the group. This balance helps to ensure that the overall claim experience of the group will be neither too high nor too low, and that all group members will have access to coverage. Except for noncontributory policies for which the group policyholder pays the entire premium, the members of the group typically pay an equal amount for the coverage because all are participating in the risk.

For many types of individual insurance, however, medical underwriting is a necessity. Each insured is supposed to pay an appropriate premium for the degree of risk involved in issuing the coverage. Determining the risk includes knowing the medical condition of the proposed insured. Read Insight 4-1 to see how the many factors involved in medical underwriting can produce an equitable assessment of each risk proposed for insurance.

In this chapter, we will begin our study of individual life insurance underwriting. We will explain the marketer's field underwriting manual and will discuss features of the insurance application. We'll explain how the underwriter evaluates the application, along with various kinds of medical information about an applicant's insurability. We'll also examine the approaches an underwriter uses to assess medical risk factors. Our study will continue in the next two chapters as we examine the personal, lifestyle, and financial factors that underwriters consider in evaluating the risks represented by applicants.

Insight 4-1 The Value of Medical Underwriting

An understanding of medical underwriting begins with a glance at the insurance skyline. On one horizon, you have various forms of governmental or social insurance. On the opposite skyline, you have private or commercial companies that sell various types of insurance. I emphasize the word "sell" because the need to sell is one of the major distinguishing characteristics between commercial carriers in a voluntary system of insurance and governmental types of insurance where participation is mandated.

Insurers are paid to take risks, not to reject risks. Insurance operates by spreading risk. That is, the majority who are insured and do not experience loss help pay for the misfortune of the few who sustain loss. Underwriting is the process by which home office underwriters apply their company's risk-classification system to persons who apply for coverage. Basically, the underwriter seeks to answer three questions:

- Should the applicant be insured?
- If so, for how much insurance?
- And at what rate?

Risk-classification practices are continually evolving with changing disease patterns, advances in diagnostic and therapeutic medicine, additional information on experience, and other factors. Every insurer has its own underwriting philosophy and develops its underwriting practices to reflect corporate characteristics, needs, and objectives. Basically, the corporate actuary builds a certain mortality or morbidity assumption into the price of each insurance product. Then the underwriter establishes underwriting practices that support those mortality or morbidity assumptions. Premium rates that are based on very favorable (low) mortality and morbidity assumptions require adopting conservative underwriting practices. Less strict mortality or morbidity assumptions give the underwriter a greater degree of freedom in assessing risks.

Underwriting practices are highly dependent on the age of the applicant and the amount of insurance being applied for. Younger ages and smaller amounts of insurance generally permit simplified requirements for the insurance to be approved. Fewer requirements translate into more rapid processing—and time is money.

Except for coverage types and amounts that require only basic medical information, an underwriter needs to know as much about a proposed insured's state of health as that person knows in order to assess the risk. If applicants are permitted, either by faulty design of underwriting practices or by fraud, to conceal any medical information that is of documented and material importance to that person's risk, the insurance company will take on a greater amount of risk than the premiums will pay for. Fairness is critically important to insurers and to the millions of insureds who rely on the integrity of their insurance policies.

From Donald C. Chambers, M.D., "What the General Public Should Know about the Value of Medical Underwriting," *On the Risk*, April/June 1993: 42–49. Adapted by permission.

Field Underwriting Manual

A ***field underwriting manual*** is a document developed by an insurance company for marketers to use when making initial assessments of proposed insureds. A field underwriting manual presents (1) information on the insurer's underwriting philosophy; (2) specific guidance on completing applications and on submitting changes and reinstatements; (3) brief, simple definitions of common medical terms; (4) information on specific medical impairments; and (5) other company-specific considerations, such as risk factors and age and amount limitations for specific insurance products.

The field underwriting manual includes a description of the evidence of insurability usually required for common impairments, as well as an approximate expected rating if one is applicable. The manual also gives the marketer basic information regarding various medical conditions and suggests specific questions to ask when an applicant admits having one of the conditions.

A field underwriting manual shows clearly that underwriting is not a mysterious activity, but is based on sound principles and on facts relevant to each applicant. Reviewing the field underwriting manual can help a marketer appreciate the need for submitting a detailed and accurate medical history for every applicant. Given this history, an underwriter can assess the risk objectively and fully, and, if the case meets the insurer's underwriting criteria, can then issue sound, sensibly priced coverage.

The Application for Individual Life Insurance

When a marketer submits an application to a home or branch office, that application contains information about two persons with whom the insurance company may do business. One person is the marketer, and the other person is the applicant (or the proposed insured, if different from the applicant). In examining an application, the underwriter first checks the name and license of the marketer. Knowledge about that marketer and the marketer's way of doing business can provide the underwriter with information concerning the probable quality of the submitted business and the probable accuracy of the information contained in the application.

The insurance application is one of the most important of the underwriter's risk assessment tools and serves as the basis of the contract between the insurer and the policyowner or policyholder. The application for individual life insurance is usually completed by a marketer on behalf of the insurance applicant. After preliminary processing in the marketer's office, the application and supporting documents are then sent in paper form or by computer to an insurance company's home or regional office.

The life insurance application form has traditionally consisted of two sections, Part I and Part II. Although nearly all insurers ask basically the same types of questions as those included in Part I and Part II, some insurers no longer divide the insurance application into these sections. Instead, these insurers develop various application forms that combine the questions typically included in Part I with other questions that are appropriate for the type and amount of coverage being requested. Each of the various application forms is called simply "an application." In this textbook, we'll discuss Part I and Part II of the insurance application as separate sections, but keep in mind that some insurers do not formally separate Part I and Part II.

Part I of the Application

Part I of the life insurance application identifies the proposed insured (and the policyowner, if different from the proposed insured), specifies the amount and type of coverage requested, and provides basic insurability information. The type of insurability information usually includes the following:

- Identification of the proposed insured by name, social security number (United States) or social insurance number (Canada), date of birth, country of birth, age, gender, address and telephone number, length of time at residence, occupation and current employer, and the length of time with the current employer
- Identification of the applicant, if the policy is applied for by someone other than the proposed insured
- The face amount, plan of insurance, and premium payment mode requested, and dividend options if appropriate
- Special features or riders desired
- Name of the beneficiary and relationship to the proposed insured
- Signatures of the applicant, the proposed insured, and the marketer

Part I also includes a series of questions concerning the proposed insured's avocations and aviation activities, as well as questions about the proposed insured's insurance history—that is, the total amount of insurance already in force on the life of the proposed insured with any insurance company, whether all or part of current insurance will be replaced by the coverage applied for, and whether the proposed insured has ever been rated or declined for insurance coverage. Part I includes questions concerning foreign residence and driving and criminal convictions.

When an underwriter first evaluates the information in Part I, she examines the relationship between the coverage requested and the proposed insured's age, occupation, and other characteristics that are important in evaluating the risk. If an applicant requests an unusually high amount of coverage in relation to his circumstances, the underwriter determines whether the situation indicates antiselection.

Some insurers also include in Part I a section called the agent's statement, which we introduced in Chapter 2. The agent's statement is important when, after reviewing a completed case file, the underwriter has doubts about whether to accept a risk. The agent's statement can include information about the following items:

- How long the marketer has known the proposed insured and how well the marketer knows the proposed insured
- The marketer's impression of the proposed insured's financial worth and annual income
- The marketer's opinion about whether the proposed insured might qualify for coverage at standard rates
- Whether the marketer actually saw the proposed insured when the application was completed, and, if so, whether the proposed insured appeared to be in good health and free from any defect, deformity, or abnormality
- Purpose of the insurance

The agent's statement usually includes information concerning whether the marketer is a full-time representative of another insurance company and whether the marketer has submitted an application on the proposed insured to any other insurer within the past six months. The statement may also ask the marketer to indicate whether the application is being made for a corporation and whether the application is one of several that should be handled concurrently—if, for instance, the proposed insured and another family member are applying for insurance at the same time, or if the proposed insured is applying for health coverage or an annuity at the same time she applies for life insurance. In addition, the agent's statement sometimes has space for the marketer (1) to indicate the types of medical proofs being submitted if the coverage requires a medical examination and (2) to list the name and address of the paramedic or physician who will complete the medical examination, if any, and the date scheduled for the examination.

Insurers normally specify to marketers the basic information on medical conditions the marketer should obtain from a proposed insured and should submit with the application. By developing complete information, marketers facilitate underwriting by eliminating some of the need for an underwriter to request additional information from the marketer or to order medical information.

Insurance that is issued on a nonmedical basis is offered without requiring a proposed insured to undergo a medical examination. ***Nonmedical limits*** are the total amounts of insurance that will be issued to an applicant at one time without requiring a medical examination. An insurance company usually specifies to marketers the nonmedical limits that the insurer will accept for coverage. For example, an insurer may specify the following nonmedical limits for a specific insurance product:

Age	Limit of Nonmedical Coverage
0–30	$500,000
31–40	250,000
41–45	100,000
46–50	50,000

Nonmedical limits usually apply to the total of (1) insurance being applied for and (2) insurance already in force with the insurer. For example, suppose that a proposed insured, age 44, already has $50,000 of insurance in force with an insurer and is applying for an additional $25,000 of coverage, for a total of $75,000 of insurance. If the nonmedical limit for a 44-year-old applicant for that type of coverage is $100,000, the proposed insured may be considered on a nonmedical basis according to that insurer's nonmedical limits. If, on the other hand, the proposed insured already has $50,000 of insurance in force and is applying for an additional $75,000 of coverage, the total of $125,000 exceeds the insurer's nonmedical limits for that coverage, so the proposed insured's application would not be considered on a nonmedical basis. Limits of nonmedical coverage for a specific product generally decrease as a proposed insured's age increases.

Part II of the Application

Part II of the life insurance application consists of medical information regarding the proposed insured. Part II may take one of three forms: (1) a nonmedical supplement, (2) a medical report, or (3) a paramedical report. Insurers provide information for marketers so that the marketers will know which type of Part II report (or which type of application form) to submit for each applicant. Field underwriting by the marketer is particularly important for nonmedical risks. The more thoroughly the marketer screens the risk, the better the overall quality of the insurer's business will be.

The type of Part II application required depends primarily on the proposed insured's age and the amount of coverage requested. (Remember that some insurers don't divide the application into Part I and Part II. Those insurers develop application forms that contain questions appropriate to the coverage requested.) Generally, the higher the potential risk to the insurer according to the insurer's underwriting guidelines, the more extensive the medical information required. Although an insurer needs information about a proposed insured's health history to evaluate the degree of risk represented, the insurer also needs to balance the need for such information with the cost of obtaining it.

Nonmedical supplement. The type of Part II application known as a ***nonmedical supplement*** contains health history questions that a marketer asks of a proposed insured. The nonmedical supplement serves as a substitute for a physical examination. Because it is part of the application, the nonmedical supplement becomes part of the insurance contract.

Answers to questions on a nonmedical supplement generally provide the name and address of the proposed insured's personal physician and the date, reason for, and results of consultations within the past 5 to 10 years. The nonmedical supplement also contains questions concerning whether the proposed insured has ever had or been treated for specified medical conditions or for any other injury, disease, or disorder. The supplement may also ask about drug, tobacco, and alcohol use; family history of medical impairments; the age of the proposed insured's parents and siblings; and, if a parent or sibling is deceased, the cause of death. According to the results of information provided on the nonmedical supplement, the underwriter can request additional information about the proposed insured.

Fast Fact

In one study of 34,000 men over a 40-year period, 20 percent of male non-smokers died between the ages of 35 and 69 years of age—but 50 percent of the male smokers in the study group died during the same period.

Source: John Ormondroyd, "Cigarettes and Whiskey and Wild, Wild Women," *On the Risk*, July–September 1995: 77–80.

Medical report. The second type of Part II application is a ***medical report,*** which is the most extensive of the three types and is designed to be completed by both the proposed insured and a physician. In one section of a medical report, an examining physician records the proposed insured's answers to questions that are the same as or similar to those asked on the nonmedical supplement and the paramedical report. The proposed insured signs the medical report form to verify that the information given was correctly recorded by the physician. Because this section of the medical report is part of the application, it becomes a part of the insurance contract. Figure 4-1 shows an example of this section of a medical report.

In another section of the medical report, the physician records the results of the medical examination given the proposed insured. It usually includes the proposed insured's height, weight, blood pressure, pulse rate, heart sounds, and other information. This section of the medical report is not signed by the proposed insured and does not become part of the insurance contract. Figure 4-2 presents an example of the section of a medical report showing the results of a physical examination.

Paramedical report. The third type of Part II application is a ***paramedical report,*** which contains (1) the proposed insured's answers to the same medical history questions that are included in the nonmedical supplement and the medical report and (2) the results of a physical examination of the proposed insured conducted by a paramedical examiner. As is the case for the medical report, the section of the paramedical report that contains the proposed insured's answers to questions is signed by the proposed insured and becomes a part of the insurance contract. The other portion of the paramedical report

Figure 4-1. Section of a medical report form containing questions for a proposed insured's response.

Question	YES	NO	Details of "Yes" answers. (Identify question; and include diagnoses, dates, duration and names and addresses of all attending physicians and medical facilities.)
2. To the best of your knowledge and belief do you have, or have you ever had or been treated for: (Check applicable items and give details.)			
a. Disorder of eyes, ears, nose or throat?	☐	☐	
b. Convulsions, paralysis, mental or nervous disorder?	☐	☐	
c. Pneumonia pleurisy, asthma, emphysema, tuberculosis, or other disorder of the respiratory system?	☐	☐	
d. Chest pain, high blood pressure, murmur, heart attack or other disorder of the heart or blood vessels?	☐	☐	
e. Intestinal bleeding, hepatitis, ulcer, hernia, colitis, diverticulitis, or other disorder of the stomach, liver, gallbladder, pancreas, rectal or other intestinal disorders?	☐	☐	
f. Sugar, albumin, blood or pus in urine; venereal disease; stone or other disorder of kidney or bladder?	☐	☐	
g. Diabetes; thyroid or other endocrine disorders?	☐	☐	
h. Arthritis, gout, or disorder of the back or spine, muscles or bones?	☐	☐	
i. Tumor, cancer or disorder of skin?	☐	☐	
j. Any other mental or physical disorder not listed above?	☐	☐	
k. Any disease of the prostate or testes if male; of the uterus, ovaries or breasts if female?	☐	☐	
3. Have you ever received treatment or consulted a physician for allergies, anemia, disorder of the blood, lymph glands, Herpes Simplex, or an acquired disorder of the immunity system?	☐	☐	
4. a. Have you had any change in weight in the past year?	☐	☐	
b. Are you now under regular observation or taking treatment?	☐	☐	
5. Have you within the past 5 years:			
a. Had a checkup, consultation, illness, injury or operation?	☐	☐	
b. Been a patient in a hospital, clinic or other medical facilities?	☐	☐	
c. Had an electrocardiogram, X-ray or other diagnostic test?	☐	☐	
d. Been advised to have any diagnostic test, hospitalization, or surgery which was not completed?	☐	☐	
6. Have you had an application for life or health insurance declined, postponed, canceled, rated or restricted?	☐	☐	
7. Have you ever been treated for alcoholism or been advised by a physician to discontinue the use of alcohol for health reasons?	☐	☐	
8. Have you ever used any intravenous drugs, narcotics, barbiturates, excitant drugs, hallucinogens, tranquilizers unless on the advice of a physician?	☐	☐	
9. Have you smoked one or more cigarettes in the last 12 months? If yes, number of packs per day ______	☐	☐	
10. Did the natural parent or sibling of the Proposed Insured die prior to age 60 of cardiovascular disease?	☐	☐	

Figure 4-2. Section of a medical report form showing the results of a physical examination.

Details of "Yes" answers. (Identify Item.)

1. HEIGHT (IN SHOES)	WEIGHT (CLOTHED)	CHEST (FULL INSPIRATION)	CHEST (FORCED EXPIRATION)	ABDOMEN, AT UMBILICUS RELAXED
FT. IN.	LBS.	IN.	IN.	IN.

Did you weigh? ☐ Yes ☐ No Did you measure? ☐ Yes ☐ No

Weight change in past year? _________ lbs. ☐ Gain ☐ Loss – Cause?

Is appearance unhealthy or older than stated age? ☐ Yes ☐ No

2. Blood Pressure (Record all readings)

	AT REST	AFTER EXERCISE	3 MINUTES LATER
Systolic			
Diastolic			

3. Pulse:

	AT REST	AFTER EXERCISE	3 MINUTES LATER
Rate			
Irregularities Per Min.			

4. Heart: (a) Is there any cyanosis, dyspnea, edema, arteriosclerosis, peripheral vascular or other cardiovascular disorder? ☐ Yes ☐ No

b. Is heart enlarged? ☐ Yes ☐ No (If yes, describe)

c. Is murmur present? ☐ Yes ☐ No (If yes, complete 4d)

d. Murmur is: ☐ Systolic ☐ Apical ☐ Soft (Gr. 1 - 2)

☐ Constant ☐ Transmitted ☐ Presystolic ☐ Basal ☐ Mod. (Gr. 3 - 4)

☐ Inconstant ☐ Localized ☐ Diastolic ☐ Other ☐ Loud (Gr. 5 - 6)

After exercise: ☐ Unchanged ☐ Increased

☐ Decreased ☐ Absent

Show Location Of:

Apex by X

Area of murmur by (dotted circle)

Point of greatest intensity by O

Transmission by →

Your impression?

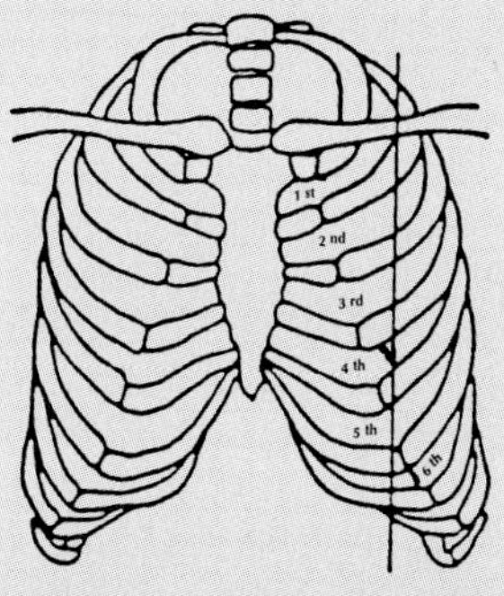

5. Is there on examination any abnormality of the following: (Check applicable items and give details.)

	YES	NO
a. Eyes, ears, nose, mouth, pharynx? . . . . . (If vision or hearing markedly impaired, indicate degree and correction.)	☐	☐
b. Skin (incl. scars); lymph nodes, blood vessels (incl. varicose veins)?	☐	☐
c. Nervous system (include reflexes, gait, paralysis?	☐	☐
d. Respiratory system?	☐	☐
e. Abdomen (including scars)?	☐	☐
f. Genitourinary system (include prostate)?	☐	☐
g. Endocrine system (include thyroid and breasts)?	☐	☐
h. Musculoskeletal system (include spine, joints, amputations, deformities)?	☐	☐
6. a. Are there any hernias?	☐	☐
b. Any hemorrhoids?	☐	☐
7. Have you any pertinent information not brought out above?	☐	☐

containing physical examination results is not signed by the proposed insured and does not become a part of the insurance contract.

A paramedical examination is generally used when the face amount of coverage is not high enough to warrant the cost of a full medical examination, but is too high for the insurer to rely on a nonmedical supplement alone.

A paramedical report is similar to, but less extensive than, a medical report. The paramedical examiner does not usually listen to the heart and lungs, for example, as does a physician when conducting an examination for a medical report. If the information on a paramedical report indicates a medical impairment, an underwriter can request a full medical examination of the proposed insured. More and more insurers use paramedical instead of medical examinations because paramedical exams are less expensive and faster and, in many cases, provide all the information needed for accurate underwriting. Insight 4-2 discusses electronic applications that can speed paramedical examinations.

Insight 4-2 The Electronic Paramedical: The New Revolution in Underwriting

In the underwriting process for life and health insurance, the paperless paramedical examination provides underwriters with more accurate and complete medical information on applicants and helps insurers issue policies faster. Using this technology, insurance companies gain the advantage of improved underwriting decision making, decreased underwriting expenses, and greater marketer and client satisfaction.

Electronic paramedicals enable medical examiners to record all medical underwriting information onto a computer that is programmed with various insurers' medical forms. Using an electronic pen, the medical examiner completes Part II of the application, signs the form and obtains the applicant's signature on it, and submits the form to the insurer. The signatures and heart chart are stored as graphics files and can, therefore, be viewed on the underwriters' computers at the insurer's office.

Electronic forms prompt the paramedical examiner to answer all the questions. If a question is not answered, the system does not allow the examiner to move on to the next one. Therefore, the insurer receives complete information on which to base an underwriting decision, and marketers avoid the need to call proposed insureds to gather information required on the application. The process also saves time and money. Faster than conventional paper forms, the electronic forms arrive almost immediately at the insurance company. The insurer's office staff no longer has to type information from paper applications into a computer system, and underwriters can retrieve information quickly without having to wait for paper files to be located and transported. Several underwriters may view the same information simultaneously and may collaborate to evaluate the risk on difficult cases. Because there are no papers involved, there are no papers to misplace. And no one wastes time deciphering handwriting or telephoning the paramedical service for missing or incomplete information.

When underwriters speed up their application review process, the insurer can issue policies faster, with the result that customers receive coverage faster. The electronic process thus helps prevent impatient applicants from taking their business elsewhere. Electronic paramedicals can provide underwriters and marketers with the competitive edge they need in a challenging marketplace.

From Paul Kolacki, "The Electronic Paramedical: The New Revolution in Underwriting," *On the Risk,* April/June 1996: 41–42. Adapted by permission.

Sources of Medical Information

The medical information necessary to evaluate a risk comes from a variety of sources. These sources include the Medical Information Bureau (MIB), the attending or examining physician, and laboratory tests.

The underwriter's goal in ordering information about an applicant's medical condition is to have enough data to assess the risk fairly without accumulating excessive or unnecessary information, incurring excessive costs, or taking too much time. Before requesting information, underwriters consider the following factors:

- The cost of obtaining the information
- The value of the information in assessing an applicant's mortality or morbidity risk
- Any inconvenience that providing the additional information may cause the marketer or the proposed insured
- The length of time required to gather the information

Fast Fact

A common chemical analysis of blood, saliva, or urine to test for the presence of nicotine is called a cotinine test. According to one study, over 20 percent of British life insurance companies surveyed said that they use a cotinine test to screen tobacco users from non-users.

Source: Tony O'Leary, "Back Behind the Smokescreen: A UK Cotinine Update," *On the Risk,* April–June 1996: 59.

Medical Information Bureau

An underwriter may request information about a proposed insured from the ***Medical Information Bureau (MIB),*** a nonprofit organization established to provide coded information to insurers concerning impairments that applicants have admitted to or that other insurance companies have detected in connection with previous applications for insurance. Such information is provided only to initiate further investigation, because the MIB strictly prohibits its member companies from using MIB information as the sole basis of an unfavorable underwriting decision, except under clearly defined and limited conditions.

The MIB system exists because of the concern of life and health insurers that some applicants may, either inadvertently or deliberately, not inform insurers about impairments that may affect insurability. If underwriters had no means of detecting and investigating these unadmitted impairments, some persons might obtain insurance coverage at insufficient premium rates or while they have uninsurable medical conditions. The MIB operates to protect life and health insurance companies and, ultimately, to protect other purchasers of life and health insurance from persons who knowingly or unknowingly do not admit information about their insurability.

In interacting with the MIB, underwriters engage in two primary activities: reporting and requesting impairment information. Provisions of the MIB establish requirements for these two activities, as well as requirements for underwriting on the basis of MIB information and procedures for confidentiality and consumer protection.

Reporting information. The MIB furnishes its members with a confidential list of factors that are considered important to risk selection. Each case file is screened for these factors. When one of the MIB factors is found in a case file, regardless of whether the risk involved has been judged to be standard, substandard, or uninsurable, the presence of that factor is reported to the MIB in the form of a three-digit code along with information identifying the proposed insured. Member companies do not send the MIB information about (1) specific amounts of insurance applied for or issued, (2) underwriting and claims decisions, or (3) other information received in connection with life, health, and disability insurance claims.

Requesting information. An underwriter may ask the MIB to search its computer files for coded information about a proposed insured. If this search shows that another insurer previously reported coded information resulting from an underwriting evaluation of an application submitted to that insurer, the inquiring insurer is sent those codes. If the information in the codes is not revealed in the application documents submitted to the inquiring insurer, that insurer is alerted to make its own investigation if it deems such an investigation necessary.

Underwriting on the basis of MIB information. If an underwriter's investigation does not verify the MIB's coded information, the underwriter can request details through the MIB, which asks the reporting insurer for further information. The reporting insurer is not obligated to furnish such details. Coded information received from the MIB may be used in considering a proposed insured's insurability when, and only when, the underwriting member company can certify the following information:

- No further investigation is needed to ensure that the application being considered and the MIB-coded medical information refer to the same person.

- The underwriting insurer has obtained from the reporting member company either (a) the documents or summaries of the documents that are the basis of the reporting member's report to the MIB or (b) advice from the reporting member that the MIB-coded information is verified by information from either a medical source or the proposed insured.

When MIB-coded information is used to consider a proposed insured's insurability, MIB rules require that the insurer furnish the proposed insured with a notice complying with the Fair Credit Reporting Act (FCRA) and other applicable laws.

Confidentiality and consumer protection procedures. Current MIB rules require that all MIB information be kept strictly confidential. Access to MIB information must be restricted to authorized medical, underwriting, and claim personnel of each member company. Further, member companies maintain internal security procedures to prevent the exposure or release of MIB information to

- A company that is not a member of the MIB
- A non-member corporate affiliate of a member company
- A consumer reporting agency
- Any other individual or organization

In order to ensure the accuracy of MIB information, member companies are required (1) to maintain internal procedures to cancel, correct, or supplement information submitted to the MIB and (2) to notify the MIB if the company has reason to believe that a report received from the MIB contains inaccurate or incomplete information. MIB rules also require that no member shall request information pertaining to any person unless that person has given written consent using a form prescribed by the MIB and expressly naming the MIB as an authorized source.

Requests to Physicians

A physician who has provided medical care for a proposed insured is usually called an *attending physician.* A physician who performs an examination of a proposed insured at the request of the insurance company is usually called an *examining physician.* When an underwriter reviews an application on which the health history requires clarification, the underwriter can request a statement from the attending physician or can ask the examining physician for more information. The underwriter can also request information about the proposed insured in a specialized medical questionnaire or a physician interview.

The attending physician's statement (APS). The ***attending physician's statement (APS)*** is a report by a physician who has treated, or who is currently treating, the proposed insured. An APS is the most frequently ordered additional source of medical information.

Although requesting an APS can increase the time required to assess a risk, an APS is usually worth waiting for on a difficult case because it can provide invaluable information on an applicant's insurability. In most cases, an underwriter tries to minimize the number of APSs requested for an applicant in order to save time and expense. If a proposed insured names several attending physicians, the underwriter tries to determine which physician or physicians can provide the most complete picture of the proposed insured's health history.

An underwriter usually requests an APS to obtain specific information that has not been developed—or not developed in sufficient detail—on the nonmedical application, in the report of the examining physician or paramedical technician, or in the nonmedical supplement. Underwriters most frequently order APSs when (1) a visit to a doctor has been reported as a routine checkup, (2) a specific illness or medical history has been mentioned, (3) the amount of insurance is very large, (4) information from the MIB is unfavorable, or (5) the proposed insured is at an advanced age.

Underwriters classify checkups as either routine checkups or history checkups. A ***routine checkup*** is one that was not motivated by a symptom or health problem. Usually, a person who undergoes an annual checkup, an employment exam, or a flight physical is having a routine checkup. A ***history checkup*** is one that was very likely prompted by a symptom or health problem. A history checkup is usually listed on the application as routine, although the underwriting file reveals a prior history that could have prompted a visit to the doctor. Most checkups—especially those that require the applicant to be hospitalized or that include X-rays, EKGs, or other special studies—are considered history checkups. Note, however, that X-rays and EKGs may be considered part of a routine checkup for a person of advanced age.

Many insurers have devised guidelines to help underwriters determine whether to order an APS when the insurance application indicates that the applicant has had a recent checkup. These guidelines are usually based on the age of the proposed insured and the amount of insurance applied for.

The fact that an application indicates a checkup does not always indicate the need for an APS, even when a proposed insured has recently visited a doctor. An underwriter can decide not to request an APS, even though a checkup was prompted by a health problem, if the condition that prompted the medical treatment was relatively minor, such as a fracture, appendectomy, tonsillectomy, hernia, or hemorrhoids. Moreover, when the amount of insurance does not exceed a level specified for a certain age and when the proposed insured appears to be in good health, the underwriter generally does not order an APS merely because the proposed insured has had a checkup.

When a description of a checkup is clear and specific, an underwriter will be more likely to accept the stated reason for that checkup. However, a vague description of a checkup recorded on an insurance application will more likely cause the underwriter to order an APS. For example, the notation "Checkup, 1995" is more likely to raise questions than the notation "Checkup, 1995, not prompted by symptoms, no adverse findings." The underwriter might also read more significance into a checkup that was performed at a young age and that included special laboratory tests. An applicant's occupation and income level could also provide information about whether a visit to a doctor was for a routine checkup. Persons with high incomes or those whose employers routinely pay for checkups are more likely to have frequent checkups than are persons with low incomes or without employer assistance in paying for checkups.

Sometimes an underwriter needs detailed information concerning an impairment. In such a situation, the underwriter asks an attending physician for a history statement. A ***history statement*** is an APS concerning a specific health condition that has been admitted by a proposed insured. Some conditions—such as nervous disorders, cancer, heart conditions, and diabetes—call for a history statement in almost every instance.

An underwriter typically orders a history statement when

- A proposed insured has visited well-known medical facilities
- A proposed insured has traveled significantly far from home or work to obtain medical treatment
- A proposed insured has recently consulted more than one physician
- Information in a case file contradicts a proposed insured's answers on the application
- The proposed insured has been admitted to a hospital
- There is evidence of overinsurance

Overinsurance refers to an amount of applied-for insurance that is excessive in relation to the potential loss for which coverage is being purchased. An underwriter determines the reason for apparently excessive applied-for coverage because overinsurance sometimes suggests a problem such as an unadmitted health history or an intent to commit suicide.

Specialized medical questionnaire. The underwriter might request more detailed information about certain conditions such as coronary artery disease, chest pain, or diabetes by asking an attending or examining physician to complete a ***specialized medical questionnaire,*** a questionnaire that requests detailed information on a specific illness or condition. Many insurers develop questionnaires on such potentially serious impairments as epilepsy, respiratory impairments, mental or nervous disorders, gastrointestinal problems, chest pain, neck or back pain, high blood pressure, bone or joint pain, immunodeficiency, and cancer. Figure 4-3 is an example of a specialized medical questionnaire requesting detailed information concerning diabetes.

Physician interviews. In reaching a sound decision, an underwriter sometimes speaks directly with an attending or examining physician to gather additional information on a proposed insured's specific disorder, to verify dates and details of treatment, and to clarify the reasons for certain diagnoses and medications. Three specific situations in which an underwriter may need to interview a physician concerning a medical report involve (1) omitted or incomplete information, (2) an apparently unadmitted health history, or (3) a need to verify an initial examination finding by a partial reexamination, called a *recheck*.

Sometimes an underwriter finds that information obtained from a source such as an APS or an MIB report discloses a medical impairment or a condition that was not reported on the application for insurance. Because the third-party information may be incorrect, the underwriter is careful not to reach a conclusion before interviewing the physician.

At times, an underwriter may find information in the case file that causes doubt about certain medical findings. In such a situation, the underwriter decides whether to act on the available information or to interview a physician and request a recheck of the original findings. Typically the underwriter makes this decision by considering a number of elements, including the proposed insured's age and gender, the amount and plan of insurance requested, the proposed insured's health history, the results of other tests, and impairments and conditions noted in the case file.

An underwriter does not routinely order a recheck. The underwriter would request a recheck if (1) evidence indicates that previous test results are unreliable, (2) the recheck will make a more favorable rating possible, or (3) the recheck is needed to add an extra degree of accuracy to the risk assessment.

Laboratory Tests

Laboratory tests are usually ordered by the marketer in accordance with the insurer's published underwriting requirements (recall the chart of such requirements in Figure 2-1). The tests are performed when the medical or paramedical examination is conducted, and detailed reports of the findings are produced by commercial laboratories. An underwriter may also order laboratory tests to provide information needed to make a sound decision. A urinalysis is routinely ordered on all medical examinations, and a blood profile is routine for many examinations. In addition, a chest X-ray and an EKG are required at

Figure 4-3. Specialized medical questionnaire concerning diabetes.

Name of Proposed Insured	USAA #

1. Period of time under your observation as a patient: From ____________ 19___ to ____________ 19___

2. If known, please give date diabetes diagnosed ____________

3. Does the patient report regularly for examination and advice? Yes ___ No ___ How often? ____________

____________ Date of last visit ____________

4. What are the diet and insulin or oral agent prescriptions?

DIET		INSULIN and/or	ORAL AGENT
Carbohydrates	Gms.	Type?	Kind?
Protein	Gms.	Total Units Per Day?	Tablets Per Day?
Fat	Gms.	None?	None?

If the diet is not calculated in grams of carbohydrates, protein, and fat, or not measured or estimated from appropriate food exchange lists, what diet program is followed? (Please give details under 8 below):

Does the patient disregard your advice concerning the diet, and insulin or oral agent prescriptions, or make changes without prior discussion with you? ____________

Has it been necessary to increase the amount of insulin or oral agent without an increase in the diet? ____________

5. What levels of blood and urine sugar have been recorded in the past two years?

BLOOD SUGARS					URINE SUGARS				
Date					Date				
Fasting					Fasting				
Non-fast					Non-fast				

6. Is there evidence or history of: Repeated infections? ________ Elevated blood pressure? ________ Kidney Disease? ________ Impaired circulation? ________ Heart disease? ________ Gain or loss in weight? ________ Diabetic coma? ________ Retinitis? ________ Arteriosclerosis? ________ Shock or frequent insulin or hypoglycemis reactions?________

Other illness? ____________

7. Have any electrocardiograms been made on this patient? ________ If available, we should appreciate your mailing them to us for our review. They will be returned promptly. If not available, please include findings under 8 below.

8. Please use this space to amplify answers to the above and for any comments you care to make regarding your patient's ability to handle the disease.

____

____

____

____

Date	Signature of Physician M.D.

various age and amount levels. Figure 4-4 provides a brief description of these four tests.

Deciding whether to order tests for underwriting purposes is sometimes difficult, particularly when an underwriter discovers an abnormality during underwriting. Insight 4-3 discusses some of the considerations involved in making a decision to order more tests.

Insurers keep the results of laboratory tests confidential to all parties except for those with a legitimate need to know the results. In testing the blood of a proposed insured for the presence of HIV antibodies, insurers obtain permission from the proposed insured for such testing and provide advance notice to the proposed insured concerning (1) the purpose of the test, (2) the meaning of normal and positive test results, and (3) the fact that test results will be sent to the MIB and may be disclosed to any MIB member company to which the proposed insured applies for life or health insurance coverage. These insurers usually inform the proposed insured that positive HIV

Figure 4-4. Four tests commonly ordered for underwriting.

Electrocardiogram. An electrocardiogram (EKG) is a graphic record of the electrical forces produced by the heart and is a diagnostic tool for detecting a disease or an abnormality of the heart. A resting EKG is one taken when a proposed insured is at rest and the heart is beating at its normal rate. An exercise EKG (or stress EKG) is the same test taken during and after a proposed insured has engaged in a strictly defined amount of exercise. The duration of the exercise depends on the person's age and build. In cases that call for EKGs, general industry practice is to obtain a resting EKG. Although an exercise EKG provides a more detailed analysis of a proposed insured's cardiac condition, underwriters usually request it only at higher age and amount combinations because the test is expensive and time-consuming, and it represents some degree of physical risk.

Urinalysis. Analysis of a urine specimen is frequently required because it can detect albumin, sugar, blood, hypertension medication, and certain drugs. Because urinalysis can also detect nicotine in urine, insurers use this test to verify whether a declared nonsmoker is qualified for nonsmoker rates. When urinalysis is performed in the insurer's home office or in a laboratory chosen by the insurer, the requirement is usually referred to as a *home office specimen (HOS)*.

Blood chemistry profile. A blood chemistry profile is a series of laboratory tests that study and report on the blood cells in a sample of blood. Most insurers require glucose, cholesterol, and liver function tests for certain ages and coverage amounts, but may order additional blood analysis if it seems warranted. In addition, a test for human immunodeficiency virus (HIV) is included in nearly all insurers' requirements.

Chest X-ray. For applications at higher age and amount combinations, most insurers require that the proposed insured submit a chest X-ray taken from a distance of six feet. If a proposed insured has had such an X-ray taken recently, the underwriter usually accepts an APS concerning that X-ray. Occasionally, however, in the upper age limits and for higher amounts, the underwriter requires the film to be sent to the insurer for review.

Insight 4-3 Testing for Cause: Challenges for the Underwriter

The considerations when testing for cause—ordering an additional test based on an abnormality discovered during underwriting—are different than those for screening tests. Tests for cause are generally not useful unless the impairment is important from a morbidity or mortality point of view and unless there is a significant likelihood that the test result will change the risk assessment. Communicating the reason for an additional test to the marketer will increase the probability that the test will serve its intended purpose of improving risk classification and providing the proposed insured with a lower-cost product.

Unlike screening tests, which are obtained on large numbers of applicants based on age, amount of insurance, and the prevalence of a given impairment, tests ordered for cause are based on abnormality of the health history or a prior screening test. Such requests complicate the underwriting process and increase the likelihood that the applicant will take the business elsewhere.

If the underwriter is considering asking for an additional test, she might consider how the results would change the underwriting action. Unless the test will add significant new information to the case, the expense of ordering the test and the inconvenience to the proposed insured are not justified. Ideally, the underwriter imagines herself in the position of the applicant and asks, "If I were the proposed insured, would this abnormality concern me?" If not, it probably isn't worth pursuing further. But if the symptoms or findings would be important to a proposed insured, chances are that he would agree and be willing to have the additional test.

Generally, ordering an additional test should be presented as an opportunity to provide a service for the proposed insured. A positive test would suggest that a serious disorder may be present; a negative result will enable the insurer to provide the applicant with a lower-priced product.

Adapted by permission of Lincoln National Life Reinsurance Company, from *Medical Resource*, July/August 1990: 6–7.

antibody or antigen test results or other significant blood abnormalities will adversely affect the application for insurance and that the application may be declined, an increased premium may be charged, or changes may be made in the applied-for policy.

Assessing Age and Build

Underwriters use the factors of age and build to classify proposed risks for individual life insurance.

The Age Factor

Placing each applicant for life insurance into the correct risk classification involves assessing information on every factor that might affect that person's longevity. The most important single factor affecting the length of time a person may live is that person's current age.

Because of its importance in assessing risk, age can render a person uninsurable regardless of other factors affecting insurability. Nearly all insurers establish upper age limits beyond which the insurers will not issue insurance. Thc upper age limits usually vary according to the insurance product applied for and are generally lower for term insurance (an average upper-limit age is about 75) and higher for whole life insurance (an average upper-limit age is about 80).

In submitting an application for life insurance, a person is not required to provide proof of age for several reasons:

- Relatively few applicants misstate their ages at the time of application.
- If proof of age is needed at the time of a claim, it is usually available.
- Most insurance policies contain a misstatement-of-age clause that can be applied to resolve problem cases by adjusting the amount of benefits.

The Build Factor

A person's build includes the relationships among his height, weight, and distribution of the weight. Build includes such elements as (1) whether a person has small, medium, or large bone mass; (2) the amount and distribution of excess weight, if any; and (3) the relative amounts of fat, muscle, and bone, as well as the degree to which the person appears athletic or unathletic.

To evaluate build, an underwriter typically uses a ***build chart,*** which is based on established studies and which indicates average weights for various heights for each gender, along with the mortality debits associated with increases in weight. Figure 4-5 illustrates part of a typical build chart. A proposed insured whose weight is greater than average is given plus values according to the range within which the weight falls. For example, a person who is 5 feet 7 inches tall and weighs 247 pounds is given +50 because the weight listed for that height is more than 245 pounds (+50), but less than 255 pounds (+75). The numbers such as "+25" indicate the unfavorable effect on mortality associated with increased weight and will be discussed later in this chapter. Note that a different build chart would be appropriate for persons in certain ethnic groups that typically have smaller or larger statures.

Fast Fact

In 1994, one in three people in the United States was at least 20 percent heavier than the ideal weight.

Source: National Center for Health Statistics. Cited in "Build/Obesity," *Underwriter Alert,* October/November 1994: 1.

In addition to comparing an applicant's height and weight to the averages on a build chart, an underwriter considers the distribution of the person's weight by examining measurements of the expanded chest and the abdomen. Generally, an obese person exhibits a large abdominal measurement relative to the chest measurement, whereas a non-obese person exhibits a small abdominal measurement relative to the chest measurement.

Figure 4-5. Build chart.

Adult Build Chart
Age 16 and over (feet and inches/pounds)

Ht.	Avg. Male Wt.	Avg. Female Wt.	+25	+50	+75	+100	+125	+150	+200	+250	+300
4′8″	121 lbs	105 lbs	180 lbs	190 lbs	200 lbs	215 lbs	220 lbs	230 lbs	240 lbs	245 lbs	255 lbs
4′9″	124	108	185	195	205	215	225	235	245	255	260
4′10″	127	112	190	200	210	220	230	240	250	255	265
4′11″	130	116	195	205	215	225	235	245	255	260	270
5′0″	133	118	195	205	220	230	240	250	255	265	275
5′1″	136	122	205	210	225	235	245	250	260	270	280
5′2″	139	125	205	215	230	235	245	255	265	275	285
5′3″	143	129	210	220	230	245	255	265	275	280	290
5′4″	147	132	220	225	240	250	260	270	280	290	300
5′5″	151	135	225	235	245	255	265	275	285	295	305
5′6″	155	138	230	240	250	260	270	285	295	305	315
5′7″	159	143	235	245	255	270	280	290	300	310	320
5′8″	163	146	240	250	265	275	285	300	310	320	330
5′9″	167	151	250	260	270	285	295	305	320	330	340
5′10″	172	154	255	265	280	290	305	315	325	335	345
5′11″	176	158	260	275	285	300	310	325	335	345	355
6′0″	181	162	270	280	295	305	320	330	340	355	365
6′1″	185	166	275	290	300	315	325	340	350	360	370
6′2″	190	169	285	300	310	325	335	345	360	370	380
6′3″	195	173	290	305	320	330	345	355	365	380	390

An underwriter also considers recent gains or losses in an applicant's weight. Substantial or rapid gains or losses in weight may indicate medical impairments.

In considering an application for juvenile insurance, the underwriter usually declines a proposed insured whose weight is five pounds or less or who is in a hospital for any reason. Most insurers reconsider such a proposed insured at three months of age, provided the child has reached at least the minimum weight for his height. An APS is usually required for reconsideration. If a child is below the minimum weight established for his height, or if a child has lost weight or has failed to gain enough weight within the past year, the underwriter obtains an APS.

Assessing Medical Factors

Medical factors are very important in underwriting decisions. To be consistent in evaluating the risk represented by medical factors, insurers depend on statistical information developed during large-scale studies of medical impairments. These studies have generally compared the relative mortality experience of impaired persons to that of unimpaired persons, and have revealed mortality patterns by age, gender, elapsed time, and other factors. The medical impairment studies have guided actuaries in establishing rate classes for insurance.

An underwriter assesses the medical risk presented by a proposed insured by using the numerical rating system, the table rating method, the flat extra premium method, or some combination of these approaches. While making such assessments, the underwriter uses information in an underwriting manual.

The Numerical Rating System

Information from impairment studies and from insurers' experience has been used to develop the numerical rating system. Insurers have used information from impairment studies to measure the excess mortality of impaired lives and to relate that mortality experience to the mortality and life expectancy of their insureds. Insurers are thus prepared to classify substandard risks into categories, each of which is rated or charged an amount of premium appropriate to the degree of risk that the category represents. Using this approach, insurers can decide to extend coverage to persons who earlier would have been declined because of their impairments.

The ***numerical rating system*** is a method of assigning numbers to individual proposed insureds according to the degree of risk they present to the insurer. These numbers are then used to determine the appropriate risk class in which to place each proposed insured. The numerical rating system assigns a positive or negative number to characteristics that have been determined statistically to have a positive or negative impact on the mortality or morbidity risk presented by individuals. The total numerical rating an applicant receives determines his risk classification. The higher the total, the higher the degree of risk presented by the applicant.

The numerical value of the average, or standard, mortality risk is set at 100, indicating 100 percent of standard mortality. An applicant's medical, personal, lifestyle, and financial characteristics that have a favorable effect on mortality are assigned "minus" values (such as –25) and are called ***credits.*** The net effect of credits is to lower the number indicating an applicant's predicted percent of standard mortality. If an applicant maintains a desirable weight, does not smoke, has no family history of certain diseases, or has a good driving record, she may be assigned credits.

In contrast, an applicant's medical, personal, lifestyle, and financial characteristics that have an unfavorable effect on mortality are assigned "plus" values (such as +25) and are called ***debits.*** The net effect of debits is to increase the number indicating an applicant's predicted percent of standard mortality. If an applicant is employed in a hazardous occupation or has suffered complications from recent surgery, she may be assigned debits.

Combining debits and credits with the basic standard value of 100 produces the numerical value of the risk presented by an individual applicant. For example, suppose Alfredo de Santo's medical records indicate that he has a slightly enlarged heart. The insurer from which Mr. de Santo is requesting coverage typically assigns a debit of +50 to such an impairment, indicating that a person with this type of impairment represents 150 percent of the mortality rate for standard risks. If Mr. de Santo's other characteristics indicate no other impairments, and if he has no characteristics that decrease his predicted mortality, then the figure representing his predicted percent of standard mortality is 150 (100 points representing standard mortality plus 50 points representing the additional risk). Figure 4-6 presents a typical life underwriting worksheet showing debits and credits assigned.

In developing premium charges for substandard risks, insurers assume that the mortality pattern of a given impairment or characteristic will remain constant, increase with age, or decrease with age. Insurers charge for substandard risks by imposing a table rating, charging a flat extra premium, or combining these two methods.

The Table Rating Method

Insurers adjust premium rates to compensate for extra mortality by using the ***table rating method,*** by which substandard risks are divided into broad groups according to their numerical ratings. The extra mortality for each group is expressed as a percentage of standard mortality as has been shown by the insurer's actual mortality experience and is presented in an ***extra-percentage table.*** Each table is labeled by either a number or a letter of the alphabet. Figure 4-7 shows a representative extra-percentage table. The table rating method is appropriate when a risk shows a pattern of extra mortality that increases with age, as is found in hypertensive and overweight persons. Table ratings are used for the majority of extra risks and are generally the same from one insurer to another.

According to Figure 4-7, the total mortality for each class is figured as 100 (representing standard mortality) plus the total of debits (representing extra mortality). Note that the number assigned to each table represents an additional increment of extra mortality. If the additional

Figure 4-6. Typical life underwriting worksheet.

Life Underwriting Worksheet

Life App $ 250,000
ELR ✓ $

☑ WP ☑ AD ☐ GB ☐ VB ☐ PUA

Personal	+/−
☑ Male ☐ Female ☑ Non-Smoker ☐ Smoker	
Age: 47	
Height 5′11″ Weight 255	+75
Family History both parents alive 75 71	−10
MB ☐ Yes ☐ No	
General	
Diabetic onset age 40 control by diet only good control by both blood results + APS.	+50
Normal ECG.	−25
	+90
☐ ELR / CTB ☐ Male ☐ Female ☐ Non-Smoker ☐ Smoker	
Age:	
Height Weight	
Family History	
MB ☐ Yes ☐ No	
General	

Request	Requirements	Receive	Clear	Waive
✓	Para	✓	✓	
	Med			
✓	Ekg	✓	✓	
	X-Ray			
	Spec ☐ 1 ☐ 2			
✓	Blood Profile	✓	✓	
	Insp. ☐ MVR 47 ☐			
✓	Aps/Dr Smith	✓		
	Aps/Dr			
	EP 18 ☐ 1 ☐ 2			
	23 ☐ 25 ☐ 28 ☐ F37 ☐			
	Smoking Q F170			
	Fin. Ques. 17			
	Reinsurance 45			
	Branch Reply 02			
	Replacement 29			

Financial Calculation	Life	A.D.
In Force (all Co's)		
New (all Co's)		
Total		

Income: | Required Income

Factor: | $

Figure 4-7. Representative extra-percentage table.

Table or Substandard Class	Total Mortality = Standard Mortality + Extra Mortality
1 or A	125 (100 + 25)
2 or B	150 (100 + 50)
3 or C	175 (100 + 75)
4 or D	200 (100 + 100)
5 or E	225 (100 + 125)
6 or F	250 (100 + 150)
8 or G	300 (100 + 200)
10 or H	350 (100 + 250)
12 or J	400 (100 + 300)
16 or K	500 (100 + 400)

increment is 25, multiplying the table number by 25 results in the additional debits to be assigned for increased mortality. As examples, a case that is rated as Table 1 or A represents 125 percent of standard mortality (100 for standard mortality + 25 [1 × 25] for Table 1 or A rating), whereas a case that is rated Table 5 or E represents 225 percent of standard mortality (100 for standard mortality + 125 [5 × 25] for Table 5 or E rating). At the higher ratings, each number still represents 25 percent increased mortality; for instance, a Table 12 rating represents 400 percent of standard mortality (100 + 12[25]).

In some situations, the total of the debits appears to overstate the risk represented by a proposed insured. In such situations, the underwriter may decide to add only a percentage of some of the debits (for example, 50 percent of a debit) to represent accurately the total risk represented by the proposed insured.

The Flat Extra Premium Method

The ***flat extra premium method*** is used mainly in cases involving extra mortality that is considered to be either constant or decreasing with age. This method provides that for every $1,000 of insurance, a specified extra dollar amount will be added to the standard premium.

The amount of extra premium varies in amount according to the amount of risk represented by the impairment or characteristic, but does not vary from year to year during the time the extra premium is charged. For example, an insurer may charge $2 per thousand for a mild impairment, but $7 or $15 per thousand for a more serious impairment. Whatever the amount charged, it will remain the same ($2 or $7 or $15) throughout the period that the flat extra premium is charged.

An insurer may charge a ***temporary flat extra premium*** for an impairment for which the extra mortality risk is expected to decrease and eventually disappear over a limited time period. A temporary flat extra premium is charged for such impairments as cancers in remission and heart conditions from which the insured is recovering. An insured does not have to ask to have a temporary flat extra premium removed. Most insurers program their information systems to remove this type of premium at the appropriate time.

When insurers do impose a flat extra premium for a medical impairment, the extra premium is almost always temporary. A ***permanent flat extra premium*** is charged, however, for cases in which a nonmedical risk is expected to remain constant throughout the life of the policy. This type of rating is most commonly used for hazardous occupations or dangerous avocations.

Combining Methods

Insurers often use a combination of a flat extra premium and a numerical or table rating when the risk of death is expected to increase during a certain period and to decrease after that period. For example, experience has shown that a person who has already had a heart attack is more prone to heart attacks than is a person who has never had one. This increased risk is greatest during the first 10 years following the initial attack. After 10 years, the risk is much lower, although it still exists. Thus, a proposed insured who suffered a heart attack two years before applying for life insurance might be accepted with a percentage table rating of 200 percent (Table D in Figure 4-7), plus $10 flat extra premium per $1,000 of coverage for each of the next eight years. After eight years, the $10 flat extra premium would automatically be removed, but the table rating would continue.

Underwriting Manual

The debits and credits and the flat extra ratings that insurers assign to insurance risks vary from one insurer to another because of differences in assumptions about expected mortality. The information an insurer uses to assign relative values to life insurance risks is contained in an ***underwriting manual,*** which may be in paper form or on the insurer's information system. An underwriting manual typically provides descriptive information on impairments and serves as a guide to underwriting action. An underwriting manual is not to be confused with a field underwriting manual, which we have described as a document used by marketers to make initial assessments of proposed insureds.

The underwriting manual typically includes (1) a description of various impairments; (2) a list of debits or credits, or both, for specific impairments and characteristics; (3) a statement of the amount of flat extra premium to be charged for certain impairments and characteristics; and (4) extra-percentage tables to be used for table ratings.

Each underwriting manual also includes an index listing synonyms and derivative terms for characteristics, with page references. Most manuals also include a laboratory section that lists basic laboratory test data and a "normal" range of values for the most commonly used laboratory tests. To help underwriters interpret medical information, many manuals contain a glossary of symptoms and medical terms, as well as a list of medical and insurance abbreviations and definitions.

The suggested ratings in an underwriting manual vary according to the status of each condition. For example, in the medical section under respiratory disorders, an underwriting manual may list *asthma,* noting that an applicant who has not suffered an attack within the past five years may be given zero credits, a number that has no effect on the applicant's final total. In contrast, an applicant who currently suffers from asthma may be given a rating between +25 and +250, or may be declined, depending on the severity of the condition. Some characteristics about which insurers have gathered extensive, experience-based information are easier to assess than others that occur less frequently and on which insurers can gather only sparse data. An underwriting manual provides detailed information to enable an underwriter to make objective judgments concerning these less frequently encountered characteristics. Most insurers emphasize that the suggested actions and ratings listed in their underwriting manuals are intended to be flexible and may be modified by an underwriter according to individual circumstances.

Key Terms and Concepts

field underwriting manual
Part I
nonmedical limits
Part II
nonmedical supplement
medical report
paramedical report
Medical Information Board (MIB)
attending physician's statement (APS)
routine checkup
history checkup
history statement
overinsurance
specialized medical questionnaire
build chart
numerical rating system
credits
debits
table rating method
extra-percentage table
flat extra premium method
temporary flat extra premium
permanent flat extra premium
underwriting manual

CHAPTER FIVE

Underwriting Individual Life Insurance—Personal and Lifestyle Factors

Learning Objectives

After studying this chapter, you should be able to

- Describe the contents and underwriting uses of an inspection report and a personal interview report
- Define two general types of specialized questionnaires used to gather underwriting information
- Explain the importance of insurable interest in the formation of a legally binding insurance contract
- Discuss the importance of phrasing the beneficiary designation correctly
- Identify the components of insurable interest for third-party applicants and for business relationships
- Define and explain the importance to underwriting of moral hazard
- List five factors that contribute to poor persistency
- Explain the personal and lifestyle factors used in underwriting
- Discuss underwriting for immigrants and foreign citizens

Chapter Outline

Sources of Personal and Lifestyle Information

Motor Vehicle Record

Inspection Report

Personal Interview Report

Specialized Personal Questionnaires

Underwriting Manual

Assessing Personal Factors

Insurable Interest

Moral Hazard

Persistency

Age

Gender

Assessing Lifestyle Factors

Occupation

Driving History

Avocations and Professional Sports

Tobacco Use

Alcohol Use

Substance Abuse

Criminal History

Civilian and Military Aviation

Military Status

International Residence and Travel

We have seen the importance of medical factors in assessing insurance risks. The risk represented by a proposed insured, however, is composed of more elements than just health factors. The activities a proposed insured pursues can significantly affect the quality and probable length of the person's life. In this chapter, we will look at the personal factors and lifestyle elements that impact risk evaluation for individual life insurance.

We'll begin by discussing the sources of personal and lifestyle information about a proposed insured. Next we'll examine the personal factors, including insurable interest, moral hazard, persistency, age, and gender, that are considered in underwriting. We'll also discuss lifestyle elements, including occupation, driving history, avocations and professional sports, tobacco and alcohol use, substance abuse, criminal history, civilian and military aviation, military status, and international travel and residence.

Sources of Personal and Lifestyle Information

To assess the risks posed by personal and lifestyle characteristics of proposed insureds, underwriters have access to many sources of information, including the motor vehicle record (MVR), the inspection report, the personal interview report, specialized personal and lifestyle questionnaires, and the underwriting manual. We will define each of these sources and will explain a little more about their underwriting uses. In later sections of this chapter, we'll show how these information sources are used in underwriting.

Motor Vehicle Record

A ***motor vehicle record (MVR)*** typically contains information about a person's driving history, including information about traffic violations and arrests and convictions for driving-related incidents. The MVR is usually available from consumer reporting agencies and, in most jurisdictions, from public records. The underwriter uses information in the MVR to assess the degree of risk represented by a proposed insured's driving habits.

Inspection Report

An ***inspection report,*** which is a type of investigative consumer report, is developed by a consumer reporting agency concerning a proposed insured's personal life, activities, occupation, and economic standing. The information in an inspection report can be important to an underwriter in verifying information from the applicant and the marketer.

To compile an inspection report, an inspector uses a variety of public records and sometimes interviews the proposed insured and some of the proposed insured's friends, neighbors, and business associates. The proposed insured usually signs a release form that is part of the application and that authorizes various persons to release information for the inspection report. Some insurers provide only the notice required by the Fair Credit Reporting Act (FCRA) informing a proposed insured that an inspection report may be requested.

Inspection reports vary according to (1) the depth of information included, (2) the number of sources consulted, and (3) the length of time covered by the report. The use of inspection reports varies from one insurer to another, but very few insurers require inspection reports on all proposed insureds. The primary factor limiting the use of inspection reports is their cost. Insurance companies carefully weigh the value of an inspection report against its cost, and they generally establish a coverage amount above which inspection reports are routinely ordered. Insurers also reserve the right to order, at the underwriter's discretion, inspection reports on applications for lower amounts. Inspection reports are seldom ordered on small-amount policies because the cost of such a report is too high to be cost-effective.

Details of the inspection report generally include the proposed insured's gender; date of birth; height and weight; health history including significant impairments; and, less commonly, medications, including type of drug and dosage. Such a report typically includes the name and address of the proposed insured's attending physician, as well as the date and cause of death if either of the proposed insured's deceased parents are deceased. Concerning the proposed insured's occupation, the inspection report tells the type of business and length of time involved in it, and the typical duties performed by the proposed insured. The inspection report also notes the type and frequency of alcohol use, tobacco use, and drug use (other than prescribed medications). Other information may cover avocations, driving history (which may be detailed in an MVR), police record (including arrests and convictions), and total insurance coverage.

The underwriter may request that the inspection report cover the finances of the proposed insured. Such a financial report usually describes the assets and liabilities of the proposed insured, including cash, stocks and bonds; earned and unearned income; real estate; automobiles; personal possessions; business equity; and any other resources.

Personal Interview Report

Consumer reporting agencies or the insurer's underwriters can develop a ***personal interview report,*** which contains the same type of information as an inspection report, but uses *only* the proposed insured as a source. One advantage of a personal interview report is that it allows underwriters to discuss health information in the medical report furnished by the insurer's examining physician. Personal interview reports also serve to verify the thoroughness of the marketer during the application process.

Some personal interview reports are broad in scope, whereas others are limited to single, specific areas of concern, such as the proposed insured's financial status, occupation, or avocation.

Specialized Personal Questionnaires

Insurers have developed many different kinds of specialized questionnaires designed to allow underwriters and other investigators to gather information needed for complete and accurate underwriting of the risk. These questionnaires generally fall into two types: those concerning medical impairments—such as diabetes, heart attack, and chest pain—and those concerning personal factors, such as aviation, avocation, residence, and occupation.

In Chapter 4, we discussed specialized medical questionnaires and presented an example of a medical supplement questionnaire for diabetes. In this chapter, we will discuss specialized personal questionnaires and include examples of several specialized personal questionnaires, including those for avocations, alcohol usage, and drug usage.

Specialized personal questionnaires typically ask for information that tells the underwriter the extent of the proposed insured's participation in a specified activity that is known to be related to additional mortality or morbidity. In addition, these questionnaires ask for proof that the proposed insured is qualified or certified to take part in the specified activity.

Developing and refining personal questionnaires usually requires the insurer to have a great deal of statistical information concerning the relationship of specific activities to deaths and injuries. The quality of specialized personal questionnaires is verified in two ways. First, questionnaire forms that are to be signed by proposed insureds and made part of the insurance contract must be approved by insurance regulatory authorities. Second, insurance companies doing business with reinsurers usually submit their questionnaires to the reinsuring companies to be certain the reinsurers agree that the correct information is being gathered about proposed insureds. Because a reinsurer is liable in whole or in part for the amount of the coverage being purchased, the reinsurer has a strong interest in seeing that the ceding insurer's questionnaires ask the questions necessary to assess each risk correctly.

Many insurers rely on standard questionnaires that have been used in the industry for years and proved accurate in gathering information needed for underwriting. In consultation with actuaries, some insurers use their experience data to modify existing questionnaires to fit their specific markets. For example, an insurer that historically has underwritten the lives of coal miners may have gathered detailed data on the kinds of mining jobs that are more or less likely to be involved in accidents or deaths. That insurer may modify its occupation questionnaire to include certain questions relating to a coal miner's job duties so that the rate class and the premium charged are accurate in reflecting the insurer's experience.

Underwriting Manual

An underwriting manual typically contains information to guide the underwriter in assessing personal and lifestyle information about a proposed insured. The personal and lifestyle topics generally covered in an underwriting manual include

- Alcohol and drug use
- Motor vehicles and aviation
- Avocation
- Financial issues
- Foreign residence

We'll discuss each of these topics in more detail later in this chapter.

Assessing Personal Factors

In underwriting individual life insurance applications, an underwriter looks carefully at several personal factors that can have an impact on an applicant's risk classification. These personal factors include the presence of insurable interest and the appropriateness of beneficiaries; the possibility of moral hazard; probable persistency; age; and gender.

Insurable Interest

At inception, contracts of insurance are considered to be binding only if the insured, the owner (if different from the insured), or the beneficiary would suffer a genuine, foreseeable loss if the event insured against were to occur. The condition in which a person or an entity would suffer a genuine loss if the event insured against were to occur is called ***insurable interest.*** Underwriting determines whether insurable interest, where required, is present; if it is not present where required, an insurer does not issue insurance because lack of insurable interest may void any contract of insurance.

Before approving an application for insurance, an underwriter determines that insurable interest exists between the proposed insured and the applicant (if different from the proposed insured), and between the proposed insured and the proposed beneficiary. To establish insurable interest, evidence must be shown that the proposed insured, the applicant, and/or the designated beneficiary will suffer an economic loss in the event of the insured's death. Unless insurable interest is established, an insurer will not issue coverage.

Insurable interest often exists where the insured and the beneficiary share a close relationship by blood, marriage, or dependency. An underwriter generally assumes that the proposed insured's spouse, parent, child, grandparent, grandchild, brother, and sister have an insurable interest in the life of the proposed insured. The underwriter assumes, however, that no insurable interest exists between the proposed insured and an aunt, uncle, niece, nephew, cousin, or relative by marriage, unless a dependent relationship exists between them. For example, a child who is dependent on a cousin, aunt, or nephew for support has an insurable interest in that person's life.

Because the death of a child usually results in only funeral expenses, but no dependency expenses to a family, most insurers anticipate that insurance on the life of a child is being purchased for the future benefit of the child, such as to provide the child with an early start on a life insurance program when premiums are low. Most insurers limit the amount of coverage on a child and require written parental consent when a third party—including any relative further removed than a grandparent—applies for insurance on a child, or else applies to be the owner of the policy. Further, the amount of insurance on the life of the child must have a logical relationship to the amount of life insurance on the parents' lives.

Marriage usually establishes an insurable interest of either spouse in the life of the other, although an insurer may limit the dollar amount of coverage on the life of a spouse who does not have an income. Moreover, most insurers do not permit a nonworking spouse to have more insurance than the working spouse. When one spouse is paying the premium for the other spouse's insurance, most insurers require that the other spouse not be insured for an amount greater than the amount of insurance on the premium-paying spouse.

Exceptions to this general rule occur when the death of one spouse would result in a greater economic loss to the family than would the death of the other spouse. For example, one spouse might leave a substantial estate at death on which inheritance taxes would have to be paid, or the spouse could be the recipient of trust income on which the family is dependent and which would terminate on the spouse's death.

Beneficiary designation. Several underwriting considerations are involved regarding the beneficiary named in the application. These considerations include the presence of insurable interest and the phrasing of the beneficiary designation.

In a legal sense, a person can apply for as much insurance coverage on her own life as an insurer is willing to issue and can name anyone she wishes as the beneficiary. Therefore, the underwriter rarely checks the beneficiary designation on an application submitted by a proposed insured. On the other hand, if a third party submits an application for insurance on the life of another person, the underwriter determines whether the named beneficiary has an insurable interest in the life of the insured, according to the laws of the prevailing jurisdiction. If the underwriter determines that insurable interest is questionable or not present, further investigation is necessary to determine the existence of insurable interest.

Phrasing the beneficiary designation correctly is essential so that the proceeds may be paid in a timely fashion and in the manner the policyowner intended. Many insurers establish certain requirements for phrasing the beneficiary designation at the time the application is completed. For example, where beneficiaries are designated by name, insurers require that the beneficiaries be specified by both given name and surname, as well as by their relationship to the insured. For example, instead of identifying "my brother Osamu" or "my cousins" as beneficiaries, an applicant specifies "my brother Osamu Akiko" or "my cousins Yuka Yamasaki and Toshio Hirose." Some insurers' applications also ask for beneficiaries' Social Security or social insurance numbers.

When naming minor children as beneficiaries, an applicant is required to include each child's birth date. Moreover, many insurers prohibit the designation of beneficiaries by class. For instance, a designation such as "children of the insured" or "grandchildren of the insured" would not be permitted. A class designation may make it difficult for the insurance company to determine that it has identified all persons who are eligible for inclusion in the class. Suppose, for instance, a widow specifies her children as beneficiaries to a whole life policy on her life. Several years later, she marries a man who has two children. Unless the beneficiary designation specifies exactly which children are to be included as beneficiaries, the result may be a time-consuming judicial process to determine the insured's intent.

If an applicant names two or more persons as beneficiaries, the applicant is required to specify the share of the proceeds that each beneficiary is to receive. Most insurers prefer that these shares be expressed as fractions or percentages rather than as dollar amounts in order to prevent misunderstanding on the part of the beneficiaries if the proceeds payable on the insured's death are different from the face amount of the policy. Such differences might occur if the policy amount were reduced by an outstanding policy loan or by a collateral assignment of the policy, or if the amount were increased by an accidental death benefit or paid-up additions. For example, on a $100,000 policy, the share of the proceeds to be received by each beneficiary would be expressed as "husband Franklin Rhodes 3/5, daughter Diana Rhodes 1/5, daughter Kathleen Rhodes 1/5" rather than as "husband Franklin Rhodes $60,000, daughter Diana Rhodes $20,000, daughter Kathleen Rhodes $20,000."

Third-party applicants. A person who applies for coverage on the life of another person is called a ***third-party applicant.*** In general, a third-party applicant must show evidence of insurable interest in the life of the person to be insured. Some jurisdictions make exceptions for a spouse who wishes to purchase insurance on the life of the other spouse, for a parent who wishes to purchase insurance on the life of a minor child, and for a grandparent purchasing coverage on the life of a grandchild.

Often, the third-party applicant is also the beneficiary of the policy. Sometimes, however, a third-party applicant names another person as the beneficiary. Because this situation creates the possibility of speculation or antiselection, some insurers and some states require that a third-party beneficiary have an insurable interest in the life of the insured at the time the insurance is issued.

Business relationships. Businesses often purchase insurance coverage on certain persons for business purposes. Such coverage is a type of third-party insurance and requires the presence of insurable interest. An insurable interest is considered to be present in coverage requested for business purposes if the premature death of one person in a business relationship would cause serious financial loss to the surviving person or persons or to a business. In such a situation, the person or organization that would suffer a financial loss has an insurable interest in the life of the person whose premature death would cause a loss.

We'll discuss underwriting for business insurance in Chapter 7.

Moral Hazard

Moral hazard is a characteristic that may exist when the reputation, financial position, or mental state of an applicant or a proposed insured indicates that the person might cause a loss intentionally or might fail to limit a loss after it occurred. For life insurance, moral hazard may exist when a proposed insured who is suffering from severe depression and exhibiting suicidal tendencies applies for a large amount of life coverage. For health insurance, moral hazard may exist if a proposed insured has a history of submitting fraudulent or highly questionable claims for medical expense reimbursement.

Information gathered during underwriting may indicate that an applicant has a record of unethical business operations or a conviction for tax evasion, business fraud, drug abuse, or similar offenses. The underwriter carefully investigates an application from a person with such a record. Sources such as the MIB, APS, inspection report, MVR, specialized questionnaires, marketer's statement, and a personal interview may cause an underwriter to question whether pertinent information was deliberately withheld or misrepresented. If the underwriter finds that an applicant or a proposed insured has been involved in dishonest practices or otherwise exhibits behavior that might lead to intentional or prolonged losses, the underwriter either rates the coverage or denies it.

Not every instance of omitted or inconsistent information constitutes moral hazard. For example, an applicant who neglects to include on an application the fact that several nonmalignant skin growths were surgically removed many years ago may not be trying to deceive the insurer. The applicant may have forgotten about the procedure or may have assumed that, because the growths were not malignant, the insurer wouldn't be interested in the fact that the growths once existed.

Persistency

Another factor an underwriter considers is ***persistency,*** which refers to how well a policy or group of policies remains, or persists, in force. A policy or group of policies that remains continuously in force for a long time is considered to have good persistency. A ***policy lapse*** is a termination of insurance coverage that occurs as a result of nonpayment of premium (and, for life insurance, before the policy has accumulated cash values). When a policyowner fails to make a premium payment, the insurer is allowed by law to terminate the coverage. Frequent lapses—in a class of policyowners, for a certain marketer's class of business, or in the coverage for an individual policyholder—are said to indicate poor persistency.

An insurer's persistency experience is a major factor in achieving the insurer's desired financial results. The expenses the insurer incurs in the first year of a policy usually exceed the policy's first-year premium. These expenses include the insurer's costs for underwriting the coverage and issuing the policy, as well as the marketer's first-year commission. In establishing an insurer's premiums, actuaries anticipate that the insurer will make up those first-year expenses in subsequent years as premiums are paid. However, an insurance company that experiences poor persistency loses money, because the insurer does not make up the first-year expenses.

Underwriters generally consider any of the following to be a sign of possible poor persistency:

- An applicant with a low income
- An applicant in a less-skilled occupation
- An applicant who has previously allowed a policy to lapse
- A request for monthly premium payments that are not to be paid by an automatic payment method
- An application for a term rather than a whole life policy

An underwriter who decides that an application indicates a high probability of poor persistency usually declines to issue a policy.

Age

The age of the proposed insured influences the underwriter's underwriting decision. One reason is that, in most cases, physical impairments become more severe and more complex with advancing age. Another reason is that the age of the proposed insured, coupled with the amount of coverage already in force and the amount applied for, helps the underwriter to resolve questions of possible antiselection.

For example, a 60-year-old man purchasing life insurance for the first time is statistically a greater risk for possible antiselection than a 60-year-old man who has purchased insurance throughout his adult life. The fact that the first man has decided to purchase coverage only at an older age, perhaps as a result of sudden concern for his declining health, indicates the possibility of antiselection. An underwriter would be similarly concerned about the possibility of antiselection if a 28-year-old woman, earning a moderate amount of money annually, wanted to purchase an amount of life insurance far in excess of the usual amount purchased by someone in her circumstances.

However, an underwriter considers all aspects of each case and seeks an explanation that will permit approval of the requested coverage. If the 60-year-old man mentioned above has had life insurance provided by an employer and then, because of a change of jobs, must provide his own life insurance, an underwriter would be less likely to suspect antiselection. Similarly, if the 28-year-old woman mentioned above has married a man with three small children and wants to provide for their education in the event of her death, an underwriter would consider that circumstance in evaluating the risk and would be less likely to think of antiselection as a factor affecting the application.

Considerations for young, middle-aged, and old applicants. Young applicants, generally ages 15 through 39, typically present few underwriting problems. In considering applications from young persons, an underwriter normally has all the selection tools needed to identify unacceptable levels of extra mortality, which usually concern factors relating to accidental death, such as driving history and alcohol or substance abuse. When no unusual or questionable situation is present, an underwriter reaches a decision by considering the applicant's age, plan of insurance, amount of insurance in force, insurable interest, and earned income in relation to the amount of insurance requested.

Middle-aged applicants, generally ages 40 through 65, are of more concern from a health perspective. Many people begin having physical problems after age 40. The underwriter, therefore, examines more closely the possibility of antiselection in applications from such persons, even for lower amounts of coverage. If the proposed insured has no other insurance in force, the underwriter may question why the applicant has waited until now to purchase life insurance protection. If an applicant is purchasing insurance to help pay estate taxes, the question of "Why now?" may be satisfactorily answered. On the other hand, the applicant or the proposed insured may recently have become aware of health problems.

For old applicants, generally ages 66 and older, an underwriter considers several additional aspects of insurability. In general, the older the proposed insured, the greater the chance that the person will have developed a physical impairment or limitation. A 68-year-old woman who does not admit to having seen any doctors during the previous five years or who lists only minor or very few injuries or illnesses is not typical. For such an applicant, the underwriter tends to conduct a very thorough review.

The underwriter may find valid reasons for approving the coverage. Some beneficiaries are not adequately supported by savings, government benefits, and other means. Also, some older people who previously lacked the financial means to purchase life insurance may finally apply for it to pay their last expenses or to pay estate taxes.

An additional consideration for underwriting elderly applicants involves recent death of a spouse. Insight 5-1 discusses mortality factors associated with bereavement.

Fast Fact

Although older applicants generally represent higher mortality risks, insurers are interested in providing products to older people because seniors are the fastest growing portion of the population, and because they are interested in estate planning. By the year 2040, more than 1 in every 5 Americans will be over 65 years of age.

Source: Tom McWilliams, "Older Age Underwriting," *On the Risk,* January–March 1996: 91–97.

Insight 5-1 Mortality of Bereavement

Bereavement is a situation that most of us have either read about or experienced within our own families. A close married couple lives together quite functionally until one of the partners dies. The other spouse, often seemingly healthy, dies very shortly afterwards. Underwriting the surviving spouse without knowing any of the social factors that might be involved could result in significant, different-than-expected mortality.

The insurance industry is aware that the health of a spouse is often related to the health of the other partner. Studies have found that suddenly widowed men were 52 percent more likely to die within the next year than their married counterparts. This rate dropped to 13 percent when the female spouse had had a chronic illness preceding death. The risk of death was magnified for widowers under the age of 65 when their wives died suddenly and was even higher for widowed husbands under the age of 50.

For widows, the risk of mortality was weaker than it was for men. Suddenly widowed women were only 1 percent more likely to die in the next year, but had a higher overall death rate of 49 percent after a prolonged or chronic illness of the male spouse. However, widows aged 65 and older whose husbands died of a chronic illness had a lower rate of death than their counterparts. Three possible reasons accounted for this finding:

1. The widowed women no longer bore the burden of being caregivers to their husbands.
2. The social support for widowed women was quite strong.
3. The women were capable of adequate self-care.

The major effect of bereavement in the life-span of female surviving spouses is found mainly in the second year after the death of the male partner, but in men this effect is found almost exclusively in the first six months to a year following the loss of the female partner. Depression is markedly higher in the recently widowed and can lead to less self-care and higher suicide rates. Coronary heart diseases are higher, possibly because of the parasympathetic dominance of the nervous system in grieving. The risk of suicide in both male and female widowed persons appears to be highest in the first one to two years after a spouse's death. Deaths from tuberculosis, influenza, pneumonia, and cancer are higher in the two years following the death of a spouse than would be predicted normally.

The existing studies probably do not number enough to offer comprehensive conclusions, but one postulated factor behind some of these findings is *homogamy,* which is best explained as the tendency of those with medical or physical afflictions to marry those with similar limiting conditions. Moreover, environment is also suspected as a cause, in that spouses who share the same unfavorable environment (unhealthful living conditions, smoking, and others) will also share the likelihood of earlier untoward events occurring to each of them individually.

The studies seem to point to four consistent findings:

1. Men are at consistently higher risk than women following the loss of a spouse.
2. Younger widowed are at a higher risk than older widowed.
3. Young widowed do poorly after the death of a spouse from chronic disease.
4. Preexisting illness in the survivor has an even higher mortality than expected after the loss of a spouse.

The underwriter must be aware of these and other factors when a suddenly widowed person applies immediately for insurance or when a couple apply for joint-and-survivor coverage and one person is to be underwritten as uninsurable based on probable impending mortality. Studies have shown that caution is appropriate in such cases.

From Robert Goldstone, M.D., "Mortality of Bereavement," *On the Risk,* January/March 1995: 32–33. Adapted by permission.

Gender

Insurers' experience, the pressure of competition, and state, provincial, and federal laws have caused insurers to disregard the gender of the proposed insured in determining the amounts and types of insurance coverage issued.

Assessing Lifestyle Factors

The term "lifestyle" is used in underwriting to refer to occupation, driving history, avocations and professional sports, tobacco and alcohol use, substance abuse, criminal history, civilian and military aviation, military status, and international travel and residence. The term "lifestyle," as used in underwriting and in this textbook, neither refers to nor implies sexual orientation.

Occupation

A proposed insured's occupation is usually not an underwriting factor unless it could be considered hazardous by the insurer's standards. In most cases, occupations that are not listed in an insurer's underwriting manual are not considered hazardous regardless of their nature, but sometimes an unlisted occupation is evaluated as to the extent of its hazard, especially if it resembles one that is listed.

Because the workplace has become increasingly safe, the percentage of policies rated for occupation has diminished dramatically. Occupation is a far more significant underwriting factor in disability income insurance than in life insurance. In Chapter 8, we'll discuss underwriting for disability income coverage.

Gathering complete underwriting information related to an applicant's present or past occupation, especially for elderly persons, requires that an underwriter obtain the following information:

- Jobs the proposed insured has held
- The working conditions on those jobs, especially hazardous conditions and the measures used to protect the proposed insured from them
- Indications of work-caused illness or sickness among the proposed insured's coworkers

An underwriter typically assesses two kinds of occupational hazards: accident hazards (such as working on high-rise construction) and health hazards (such as exposure to toxic chemicals). Accident hazards are more common among some workers, such as lumber workers and demolition experts, while health hazards are more common among other workers, such as those involved in manufacturing asbestos products. Moreover, some workers—coal miners and persons who manufacture silicon abrasives, for example—are subject to both types of hazards.

For occupations that present extra hazard, an underwriter can refer to the occupations section of the insurer's underwriting manual, which lists occupations that always require an increased premium and occupations that require an increased premium only for accidental death or waiver-of-premium coverage. Although some medical impairments can be underwritten as standard if the extra risk is likely to occur after the policy has been in force for some time, hazardous occupations are always rated because the extra mortality risk could occur at any time.

A rating for occupation may be reduced or removed when the insured's occupation changes. Generally, insurers require that an insured person who has previously been in a hazardous occupation must work for at least one year in a less-hazardous occupation and must not be likely to return to the former, more hazardous occupation.

Driving History

Because motor vehicles are involved in many accidental deaths, underwriters pay considerable attention to a proposed insured's driving history. Underwriters consider the number, type, and recency of traffic violations; the use of alcohol; and substance abuse. Proposed insureds who have numerous traffic violations pose generally greater risks for fatal motor vehicle accidents and for nonfatal accidents that produce serious injuries. A proposed insured who has been cited for accidents or other traffic violations while driving under the influence of alcohol or other substances requires special underwriting. If a proposed insured has a history of abusing a substance such as cocaine, heroin, amphetamines, or hallucinogens, and has an unfavorable driving history as well, the usual action is to decline coverage. The underwriter also considers whether the proposed insured suffers from epilepsy, certain cardiovascular disorders, neuroses and psychoses, sleep apnea, or any other impairments that may affect motor vehicle operation, and whether the proposed insured routinely takes medication that may hinder effective operation of a motor vehicle. For persons who have unfavorable driving histories, most insurers use flat extra premiums.

In order to obtain information about a proposed insured's driving record, an underwriter may request an inspection report and/or an MVR, both of which we described earlier in this chapter. An inspection report usually includes information on the proposed insured's driving history. In addition, most insurers attempt to identify poor drivers by including in the application a question asking if the proposed insured has been convicted of a moving traffic violation or has had a motor vehicle accident within the last three years.

Figure 5-1. Multiple avocations questionnaire.

FULL NAME (PRINT) ______________________ DATE OF BIRTH MO. DAY YR.

SECTION A AUTOMOBILE, MOTORCYCLE AND/OR POWERBOAT RACING

1. Type of racing? ☐ Midget ☐ Go-Kart ☐ Sports Car ☐ Modified Stock ☐ Drag Racing ☐ Motorcycle ☐ Powerboat ☐ Other (explain) ______
2. Make? ______ Model? ______ Displacement? ______
   Class? ______ Engine Make & Model? ______ HP? ______
3. (a) Number of races 12–24 months ago? ______ (b) Past 12 months? ______
   (c) Date of last race? ______ (d) Est. next 12 months? ______
4. Type of race? ☐ Midget ☐ Sports Car ☐ Stock Car ☐ Championship ☐ Drag ☐ Kart ☐ Hillclimb ☐ Cross Country ☐ Hound & Hare ☐ Moto-Cross ☐ Other (explain) ______
5. Type of course? ☐ Paved ☐ Dirt ☐ Drag Strip ☐ Oval ☐ Other (explain) ______
6. Where do you race? ☐ Local? If not, where? ______
7. Competition against? ☐ Other Cars ☐ Clock ☐ Straightaway ☐ ______
8. Average speed? ______ Top speed? ______ Average miles per race? ______
9. Is your racing? ☐ Professional ☐ Amateur ☐ Other (explain) ______

SECTION B UNDERWATER DIVING (SKIN OR SCUBA)

1. What type of equipment do you use? ______
2. Location of diving activities? ______ Diving for pleasure? ______ Pay? ______
3. Do you belong to club or association? ______ Do you ever dive alone? ______
4. Depth of Dives

	During Past 12 Months		Expected Next 12 Months	
	No. Dives	Average Time	No Dives	Average Time
a. Less than 40 feet				
b. 40 feet to 60 feet				
c. 60 feet & over				
d. Maximum depth obtained				

SECTION C PARACHUTE JUMPING AND SKY DIVING

1. Are you now a member of any parachute or sky diving club or association? ______
2. Are all of your jumps made under auspices of your club or association? ______
3. (a) Number of jumps 12–24 months ago? ______ (b) Past 12 months? ______ (c) Next 12 months? ______
4. Do you participate in delayed chute opening competition or other stunts? ______
5. Location of jump areas? ______ Date of last jump? ______

REMARKS IDENTIFY SECTION AND QUESTION

I represent that the foregoing answers and statements are correctly recorded, complete, and true to the best of my knowledge and belief.

Date ______ MO. DAY YR. X ______ SIGNATURE OF PROPOSED INSURED (OR PARENT IF PROPOSED INSURED IS UNDER AGE 18)

______
SIGNATURE OF SOLICITING AGENT

______
AGENCY NO.

Avocations and Professional Sports

An applicant's choice of leisure activities, or avocations, influences risk appraisal. To gather information about an applicant's avocations, underwriters use specialized personal questionnaires. Such a questionnaire may focus on just one activity or may gather information on several avocations. An example of a multiple avocations questionnaire is shown in Figure 5-1.

In underwriting avocations, an underwriter depends on the available rating schedules derived from the insurer's experience. The underwriter also considers the applicant's age and lifestyle elements to determine whether an extra premium should be charged for participation in an avocation that may add to an applicant's risk.

Underwriting manuals provide guidelines for assessing the risk associated with specialized vocations and avocations. As an example, Figure 5-2 depicts a section of an underwriting manual showing suggested underwriting actions for the avocation of scuba diving.

Many of the ratable avocations listed in insurers' underwriting manuals are pursued by professionals as well as by amateurs. As examples, automobile racing, boxing, wrestling, and rodeo riding can be either avocations or occupations. The underwriter usually distinguishes between persons who pursue such an activity as an occupation (professional) and those who do it as an avocation (amateur).

Deciding whether a professional or an amateur is likely to represent a greater degree of risk depends entirely on the circumstances of each case. In some sports, most professionals have more training and use safety equipment more consistently than do amateurs. In other sports, the risk to the amateur is substantially less than to the professional. Insight 5-2 discusses some of the underwriting implications for former athletes.

Tobacco Use

People who use tobacco in any form show greater morbidity and mortality at every age than people who don't. Using tobacco causes or contributes to many impairments and aggravates other health problems. Some insurance companies place smokers into a standard classification and nonsmokers into a preferred classification. As a result, insurers generally provide lower premiums for tobacco nonusers than for tobacco users. Some insurers have developed separate premium schedules for tobacco users and nonusers. Other insurers use the results of underwriting to adjust premium rates for nonusers. Under this approach, tobacco use and nonuse are considered risk factors that require mortality debits or credits, respectively.

Fast Fact

According to the experience of one insurance company, 13.8 percent of insurance applicants who claimed they did not use nicotine tested positive for nicotine use. The increase in risk associated with these nicotine users would generate $1.6 million in additional premiums every year above the rates for nonsmokers.

Source: "The Butt Stops Here," *Underwriter Alert,* October/November 1996: 5.

Figure 5-2. Underwriting manual information for scuba diving.

Scuba Diving

Underwriting Action: The following guidance applies to recreational diving and instruction. Guidance pertaining to diving that is required as part of occupational duties (other than recreational instruction) is located in the section under Occupation.

IC = Individual consideration
U Dec = Usually decline

Open Water Diving	Rating or Underwriting Action
To 75 feet:	
With open water certification or with a qualified instructor	0
Other	IC
75–100 feet:	
Experienced divers, including instructors, actively participating in diving activity (includes persons who dive at least 5 times annually and who have a minimum of 10 total dives)	0
Other	$2.50
100–130 feet:	
Experienced divers, including instructors, who demonstrate proficiency by diving a minimum of 10 dives annually and hold Advanced Open Water Certification	0
Other	$3.50–$5.00
130–150 feet:	
Experienced divers with advanced certification	
Less than 10 deep dives per year	$3.50
10 or more deep dives per year	$5.00 up
Other	IC
150 feet or deeper:	
(normally considered well beyond the capacity of recreational diving)	U Dec
Specialty Diving	
Cave diving (the minimum rating applies only to certified cave divers with demonstrated proficiency in cave diving)	$5.00–$7.50
Photography	Classify as Open Water Diving
Spear fishing	Classify as Open Water Diving
Salvage or treasure diving (rating depends on diving experience and certification, depth, conditions, nature of equipment used, and size of project)	$2.50–$7.50
Wreck diving	
No penetration into the wreckage	Classify as Open Water Diving
With penetration into the wreckage (minimum rating applies to divers with advanced certification diving in wreck sites that are frequently explored)	$2.50–$7.50

Insight 5-2 Underwriting Former Athletes

What are the implications for underwriting former athletes? Do former athletes live longer than non-athletes? What causes the eventual demise of former athletes? Do they suffer the same kinds of maladies as those who abstain from the wear-and-tear of sports? Are former athletes at greater risk for certain ailments?

In the early years of this century, it was widely believed that competitive athletics had detrimental effects on the heart and blood vessels. Studies showed that students who took part in major sports had a propensity toward enlarged hearts. Medical research now shows that healthy hearts enlarge through endurance training, and when such training ceases, the heart generally returns to its former size.

No clear evidence supports the idea that former male athletes die more frequently from cardiovascular disease than males from the general population. Evidence suggests that it's the body build type many athletes have that may result in a greater tendency toward cardiovascular disease at a younger age. But the risk of cardiovascular problems lessens if the former athletes stay active later in life. One study showed that more cardiovascular deaths were suffered by high school basketball players than other males. But since, again, the study's numbers were relatively small, the results could be interpreted as mere coincidence.

What about women athletes? Women have only begun to stake their claim in the intercollegiate sports arena, so facts and records aren't as widely available as those for men. A study by Harvard researchers of 5,398 women ages 21 to 80, from eight colleges and two universities, revealed that 49 percent were former athletes. This study included not only women who had participated in a varsity sport, but also women who had played on intramural teams for at least one year.

Strikingly, women athletes were less likely to contract several forms of cancer. Non-athletes tallied 28 cases of nonfatal cancer of the reproductive system, compared to only 9 cases among the former women athletes. In addition, the former sports participants showed 24 cases of breast cancer, compared to 45 from the other group. The authors of these studies believe the lower numbers of cancer cases in the female athletes may be a result of diminished production of estrogen.

From Scott Gerace, "Athletes vs. Themselves: Are They Defeating Their Life Expectancy?" *Contingencies,* May/June 1995: 53–56. Adapted by permission.

Insurers have developed a number of approaches to identifying tobacco users, as follows:

- Including a smoking question on the application or medical examination form
- Requesting the medical examiner, paramedical examiner, and/or attending physician to comment on an applicant's tobacco use
- Testing a sample of an applicant's urine for nicotine or traces of nicotine
- Requiring an inspection report that comments on tobacco use
- Interviewing the applicant and other family members or the applicant's spouse*

* Gary Lee, "Smoking Habit Misrepresentation Issues and Suggestions," *On the Risk,* July/September 1992: 31–32.

Insight 5-3 Underwriting and Tobacco Use Misrepresentation

The health and economic consequences of cigarette smoking are extensively documented in the medical literature. The evidence overwhelmingly leads to the conclusion that smoking is the leading single preventable cause of death in our society today.

As a result of the creation of inexpensive policy rates relative to those previously available, insurers have inadvertently created a financial incentive for proposed insureds who use tobacco to be less than truthful on their applications. Life risk premium rates for tobacco users can be twice the rate charged to nonusers. Thus, another form of antiselection is born.

Responses to Material Misrepresentation of Tobacco Use

In the past, many insurers responded to material misrepresentation of tobacco use status by adjusting the amount of policy payment to equal the sum the premiums would have purchased on a tobacco user basis. More recently, some insurers are moving instead to rescind coverage when such misrepresentation is found. Courts in the United States have ruled recently in favor of insurance companies in deciding contractual liability when the insured has materially misrepresented tobacco use status.

In Canada, even more strict response to tobacco status misrepresentation has been evident. The Canadian Life and Health Insurance Association and the Canadian Institute of Underwriters have made uniform recommendations to their respective member companies to void the contract without refund of premium, whether within or beyond the contestable period, when material misstatement of tobacco use is discovered.

Improving Underwriting Controls on Misrepresentation

Prudent underwriting considers carefully the following suggestions for improving control as underwriters distinguish between applicants who use tobacco and those who do not:

- Create and refine systems to monitor each book of business and to report findings to the actuarial function
- Modify smoking application supplements or questionnaires to include full disclosure of the ramifications of material misstatement
- Inform field representatives of the insurer's policy concerning misrepresentation of tobacco use, and ask them to participate in more effective field underwriting
- Consider lengthening the insurer's duration requirement for nonuser qualification from 12 months to 24 months or longer

From Gary Lee, "Smoking Habit Misrepresentation Issues and Suggestions," *On the Risk,* July/September 1992: 31–37.

Underwriters are especially careful to classify tobacco users and nonusers correctly to avoid charging inappropriate premium amounts. Insight 5-3 presents suggestions for ensuring the accuracy of underwriting for tobacco use.

Alcohol Use

Because alcohol use can lead to alcoholism, which is considered a disease, both alcohol abuse and alcoholism are investigated during underwriting just as one would investigate any other health history or disease. Current evidence of excessive alcohol use may indicate a more serious problem in the future, as the person increases the use of alcohol or suffers from the cumulative effects of many years of abuse.

In underwriting cases in which alcohol abuse or alcoholism is present, underwriters face three problems:

- Obtaining sufficient information about the level of alcohol use

- Underwriting despite a lack of medical data on alcohol abuse and alcoholism
- Coping with the lack of standardized terminology for describing situations of alcohol abuse and alcoholism

Obtaining information. The underwriter is concerned with not only how much a proposed insured drinks, but also with what happens when that person drinks. Therefore, the underwriter needs to learn the effects of alcohol on that person's judgment, driving ability, work, and physical well-being.

Obtaining information about a proposed insured's use of alcohol can be very difficult. Underwriters usually gather information from inspection reports, personal interviews, alcohol usage questionnaires, MVRs, APSs, and liver screening tests.

Using an alcohol usage questionnaire, an underwriter can gather valuable information about alcohol use. Such a questionnaire usually asks a proposed insured to provide information on his consumption of alcoholic beverages, as well as details about any conditions that may have resulted from or be related to alcohol use. Some insurers obtain answers to an alcohol usage questionnaire over the proposed insured's signature, with the intent of attaching the questionnaire to the policy for possible use if death occurs during the contestable period. A sample of an alcohol usage questionnaire is shown in Figure 5-3.

Lack of medical data. To make valid assessments of a proposed insured's use of alcohol, an underwriter needs relevant medical data. Unfortunately, systematic efforts to collect long-term data about alcohol use have been made only recently. Little information is available concerning the early stages of the disease of alcoholism.

Lack of standard terminology. The general public typically uses the word "alcoholism" as descriptive of any form of excessive drinking, rather than as a clinical term describing a specific type of alcohol use behavior. Furthermore, alcoholism is defined differently by various authorities, and no precise clinical distinction has yet been established between alcoholism and alcohol abuse. The underwriter, therefore, makes a determination based on the available information and medical data, and on the underwriter's experience in classifying risks.

The underwriter keeps in mind the fact that alcohol use mentioned in an inspection report may be understated. Alcohol use noted in an APS or a medical report, however, reflects what the proposed insured has admitted to a physician or paramedical examiner, or what that doctor or examiner has observed. If an underwriter has to

Figure 5-3. Alcohol usage questionnaire.

Name of proposed person insured

Date of birth (Day/Month/Year)

1 Do you presently use alcoholic beverages? Yes ☐ No ☐

If yes, please record the quantity in each category below for each time period

Beverage	Daily consumption	Weekly	Monthly	Date of last drink
Wine (in ounces)				
Beer (in 12 oz. bottles)				
Liquor (in ounces)				

2 Did you ever drink substantially more than you have indicated above? Yes ☐ No ☐

If yes, complete the following:

Beverage	Daily Consumption	Weekly	Monthly	Date started	Date of last drink
Wine					
Beer					
Liquor					

3 What is the date you last consumed any alcohol?

4 Have you ever consulted a doctor, been advised by a doctor, or received treatment because of your alcohol use? Yes ☐ No ☐

If yes, indicate dates, names and addresses of any doctors, hospitals or treatment centres below:

5 Are you now or have you ever been a member of Alcoholics Anonymous? If so, when? Yes ☐ No ☐

6 Since you stopped drinking have you suffered any relapses? Yes ☐ No ☐

If so, when? Duration?

7 Have you ever been charged with impaired driving, lost your job, or been arrested due to the influence of alcohol? Yes ☐ No ☐

If yes, give details.

8 Additional Comments

I, the proposed person insured, declare that the above statements and answers are mine and that after reviewing them, find them complete and true to the best of my knowledge and belief. I agree that this statement shall form part of my application for life insurance to ABC Life.

Signature of proposed person insured

Date (Day/Month/Year)

Signature of witness

choose between contradictory reports of alcohol use from an inspection report and from a statement made by a physician, the underwriter usually chooses the doctor's statement.

Admitted membership in an alcohol treatment program such as Alcoholics Anonymous (AA) is usually evidence of alcoholism. An underwriter who determines that a proposed insured is a member of AA checks further to verify whether alcohol use is continuing or has stopped.

Substance Abuse

Substance abuse generally refers to the excessive use of any of a variety of several substances, including the following:

- Narcotics, such as codeine, morphine, or heroin
- Hallucinogens, such as mescaline, marijuana, LSD, or PCP
- Stimulants, such as amphetamines or cocaine
- Sedatives, such as barbiturates

Persons who abuse these substances may have or may develop psychological impairments, physical dependence, or personality disorders that can constitute additional risk.

Many of the considerations involved in underwriting cases in which there is excessive use of alcohol also relate to the abuse of other substances. Essentially, the underwriter is concerned with whether a proposed insured makes inappropriate use of substances and the extent to which this type of abuse may increase the chance of death.

A distinct difference between alcohol abuse and the abuse of some other substances is that alcohol is legal and, if used in moderation, acceptable in our society, whereas the use of illegal substances is not acceptable. The fact that an applicant uses illegal substances, therefore, raises the question of moral hazard. Underwriters need to remain as well informed as possible about these and other new drugs, both legal and illegal.

Gathering information about an applicant's substance abuse is often difficult, especially because positive answers to questions concerning a person's use of illegal substances can be incriminating. In using tests to check for the presence of illegal substances, an underwriter verifies that the tests are conducted properly and that the test results are kept confidential. An underwriter is generally persistent in seeking detailed information in every case in which substance abuse is suspected because such abuse can add substantially to the degree of risk that a proposed insured represents. Some insurers use a drug usage questionnaire like the one in Figure 5-4.

Figure 5-4. Drug usage questionnaire.

Name of proposed person insured	Date of birth (Day/Month/Year)

1 Are you now using or have you ever used:

Opium derivatives: heroin, morphine, Demerol, methadone	Yes ☐	No ☐
Barbiturates: Amytal, Phenobarbital, Seconal, Nembutal	Yes ☐	No ☐
Marijuana: hashish, cannabis	Yes ☐	No ☐
Amphetamines: Benzedrine, Dexedrine, Methedrine	Yes ☐	No ☐
Cocaine, Crack	Yes ☐	No ☐
Hallucinogens: LSD, DMT, mescaline, peyote, psilocybin	Yes ☐	No ☐
IV drug use: Yes ☐ No ☐ / Other (explain):	Yes ☐	No ☐

2 If yes to above, please give details:

Type(s)	Usual quantity	Frequency of use	Duration From	Duration To	Date last used (Month/Year)

3 Have you ever sought medical treatment because of drug usage? Yes ☐ No ☐
If yes, state dates and names of doctors and the institutions consulted:

	Date (Month/Year)	
	Date (Month/Year)	

4 Have you ever been to Emergency for drug or alcohol related problems? If yes, give dates and details. Yes ☐ No ☐

5 Are you a member of Narcotics Anonymous or similar association? Yes ☐ No ☐

6 Have you ever been confined to bed or lost a job due to excessive use of any drug? Yes ☐ No ☐
If yes, give dates and details

7 Have you ever been arrested or charged in connection with drugs? Yes ☐ No ☐
If yes, give dates and details

8 Have you ever suffered from a liver disorder? Yes ☐ No ☐
Explain

9 Give amounts, type and frequency of alcohol consumption:

I, the proposed person insured, declare that the above statements and answers are mine and that after reviewing them, find them complete and true to the best of my knowledge and belief. I agree that this statement shall form part of my application for life insurance to ABC Life.

Signature of proposed person insured	Date (Day/Month/Year)
Signature of witness	

Criminal History

Proposed insureds with a history of criminal or illegal activities are investigated carefully so that the insurer will not be exposed to excessive risk by insuring such persons. Ranging from arson and assault to fraud and vandalism, criminal activity in the history of a proposed insured usually results in the case's being either rated or declined. Although the underwriter cannot predict that criminal activity will recur, such a case requires a thorough review of the facts, an extensive inspection report, and detailed interviews with persons who are likely to know the current activities and character of the proposed insured.

In assessing a case in which criminal history is present, the underwriter typically considers that the extent of an applicant's criminal activity may be difficult to assess because information is reported only for incidents for which the applicant was arrested. Moreover, the true nature of a criminal offense may be concealed by a plea bargain.

Assessment of criminal activity is normally made on the basis of the length of time the applicant was involved in crime; the applicant's history in relation to police, courts, and correctional institutions; and the nature of the offense or offenses committed. Persons who have been arrested for multiple or violent crimes, who have been involved in criminal activity over a period of time, or who have a history of criminal activity coupled with alcohol abuse, drug abuse, compulsive gambling, extreme aggression, or severe psychological problems are rarely, if ever, accepted for coverage. Insurers generally give more lenient consideration to applicants who have no history of violent crime and who have noncriminal family members, consistent work records, and associates and friends who are not involved in criminal activity.

Civilian and Military Aviation

Because the federal government has kept statistics on aviation accidents and fatalities since the early days of aviation, underwriters and actuaries have a reliable data base from which to assess the degree of risk involved in aviation activities. Although civilian and military aviation are underwritten somewhat differently, the primary sources of information for both include the application for insurance, the aviation questionnaire, the medical examination, the APS, the inspection report, and the personal history interview.

Underwriting civil aviation. Civil aviation includes air ambulance, ballooning, commercial aviation, crop dusting, fire fighting, power line and pipe inspecting, mail service, mapping, policing, racing, sightseeing, and weather or traffic control. Civil aviation also includes flying for pleasure.

Fast Fact

The risk involved in civil aviation depends not only on the experience of the pilot, but on what kind of craft is being flown. The fatality rate for those engaged in hang gliding is 40 per 100,000. For private small-plane aviators, the fatality rate is 145 per 100,000—but for people who built their own planes from kits, the fatality rate is 312 per 100,000.

Source: "Homebuilts Have the FAA Worried," *Underwriter Alert,* February/March 1996: 9.

For most civil aviation, the proposed insured's total hours of flying experience and the number of hours that the person plans to fly annually are important information. Another factor that underwriters consider is the aviation certificate or ratings that the proposed insured holds. The presumption for underwriting is that pilots and crew members with more experience also have a greater degree of skill and are less likely to be involved in aviation accidents.

An underwriter may also consider the type of medical certificate held by a proposed insured to learn about aviation activity that the proposed insured is considering or that was omitted from the aviation questionnaire. The medical certificate is the only proof required for a pilot to be medically certified to fly. Generally, agencies that certify pilots, such as the Federal Aviation Administration (FAA) in the United States, have established no method of exchanging information with other agencies (such as the MIB) and do not use reports from any agency to check pilots' physical preparedness for flight. Therefore, the underwriter is alert to the possibility that a proposed insured may have omitted some relevant impairment information in order to obtain an aviation medical certificate. The underwriter is also aware that, even if a person is denied a medical certificate, numerous appeal mechanisms enable a person with even severe medical impairments such as alcoholism or a history of coronary bypass surgery to obtain medical certification. In short, a proposed insured who holds an aviation medical certificate is not necessarily a standard risk for insurance.

The general underwriting action for civil aviation risks is to charge an extra premium for the aviation hazard. Another approach is to issue the policy with an aviation exclusion rider. Generally, aviation exclusion riders are used only in cases in which the aviation hazard (1) is too great for any coverage or (2) cannot be measured.

In assessing risk for pilots flying employer-owned aircraft, an underwriter ascertains whether the pilot has an airline transport certificate or a commercial certificate with an instrument flight rating, indicating that the pilot is qualified to fly in all weather conditions. A pilot who does not hold one of these certificates is usually charged an extra premium.

Underwriting military aviation. Many of the considerations applied to underwriting civilian aviation also apply to underwriting military aviation. The underwriter looks carefully at the age, duty area, and type of aircraft of all proposed insureds who are military aviators. Statistically, younger pilots have more accidents than older pilots. Also, military personnel flying in the reserves and the National Guard have fewer accidents than do military personnel flying in other branches of the armed forces. Proposed insureds who pilot or serve as crew members on such aircraft as attack bombers, attack fighters, and observation or reconnaissance aircraft are typically charged higher premiums than are persons who pilot or serve as crew members on such aircraft as research, utility, or transport aircraft.

Proficiency flying is done by pilots whose duties no longer include regular flying, but who fly very limited hours to maintain their flying proficiency and flight pay. Generally, proficiency flying is treated on a more favorable basis than is other military aviation.

Generally, the flat extra premiums for military aviation are higher for persons younger than 30 than for persons age 30 and over. Also, the flat extra premiums charged for pilots are usually higher than the premiums charged for aviation crew members. In most military aviation cases, persons who serve in hazardous places are not acceptable risks and are declined.

Military Status

Underwriters generally treat military status as a separate area of risk assessment. If a country is not at war or involved in a military conflict, most insurers approve military personnel for coverage at standard rates. Career military personnel in particular are generally considered good risks and are underwritten as if they were civilians.

Many insurers, however, do not issue coverage to noncareer military applicants from the lower pay grades because these persons have demonstrated statistically higher-than-average lapse rates and higher-than-average accidental death rates. Insurance companies that do issue coverage to noncareer, lower-pay-grade applicants usually limit the total amount of insurance granted to an amount below the insurers' normal retention, do not offer term insurance, and do not issue accidental death benefit coverage.

Most insurers do not include war exclusions in their policies. If an armed conflict broke out, most insurers would refuse an application from military personnel for as long as the conflict lasts. Some insurance companies, however, issue individual life insurance coverage at standard rates to all military personnel who do not exhibit extraordinary risk other than that associated with military service.

International Residence and Travel

Many insurers in the United States and Canada do not approve coverage for applicants whose permanent residence is in a foreign country because of the difficulty of gathering complete underwriting information and, if coverage is issued, of conducting an adequate, cost-effective claim investigation. Insurance companies that do considerable business in foreign countries and that have established foreign offices, however, typically charge special premium rates for coverages in those countries and do issue insurance to persons residing there either temporarily or permanently.

In considering international travel and residence as a risk selection factor, the underwriter is usually concerned with extended residence abroad. Vacation trips of three to six months' duration are usually of no concern to the underwriter unless a proposed insured plans to travel to an area with great political unrest, military activity, or known deadly disease. Most insurers remove extra premiums after an insured has returned to the United States or Canada and has remained there for one to two years.

When reviewing an application in which prolonged foreign residence is indicated, the underwriter gives the case extra attention. Considerations include the living conditions prevailing in the area, the possibility of exposure to disease, and the availability of reliable medical and sanitary facilities. The underwriter generally seeks information, often from a questionnaire focused on foreign residence, on the following topics:

- The purpose of travel and the proposed insured's duties in the new location
- The name of the city where the proposed insured will live, or the name of the closest large city and the distance from it to the city of residence
- The date of arrival and the anticipated date of permanent return to the United States or Canada
- The birthplace and citizenship of the proposed insured
- Medication the proposed insured will take while in foreign residence

Underwriters also take into account the degree of political stability in the country in which the proposed insured plans to travel or reside. In unstable areas of the world, employees of certain companies have become the targets of assassination or kidnap attempts. Applications indicating travel or residence in a politically unstable country are usually declined.

One of the most important questions in all applications in which foreign travel and residence are involved is the type of insurance requested. In general, when an applicant requests the cheapest possible term insurance and wishes to make monthly payments for it, the underwriter considers the coverage to be "trip insurance" with probably poor persistency. Therefore, the underwriter usually declines the risk.

Some cases involve proposed insureds who travel internationally for business or diplomatic reasons. An employer may purchase insurance on an important employee as a means of inducing the employee to travel internationally by providing protection for the employee's family. Career foreign service personnel may present varying risks for an insurer because they typically spend a great deal of time away from their home country and are subject to relocation from one country to another, perhaps to a politically unstable area.

A number of insurers will not provide special benefits such as waiver-of-premium and accidental death benefits for proposed insureds living abroad, unless the persons are living in Europe, Japan, Australia, and some other countries. These insurers take the position that an insured's foreign residence makes it difficult and expensive to conduct thorough investigations if benefits are claimed. Death is usually verifiable wherever a person may be, but "disability" and "accident" may be open to different cultural interpretations and, because of language differences and the distance involved, may be difficult to substantiate or disprove.

Immigrants and citizens of foreign countries. Underwriting immigrants and citizens of foreign countries is based on individual consideration of the class of risk presented, the reason for the insurance purchase, the reputation of the submitting marketer, and the quality of the marketer's previously submitted business. Generally, insurers give favorable consideration to immigrants and foreign countries' citizens who

- Intend to become permanent residents of the country in which the insurer does business
- Possess a permanent resident visa
- Do not travel at all or travel only infrequently to their country of origin

If an immigrant or citizen of a foreign country has lived in the new country for less than six months, most insurers require a medical examination and a complete blood profile for any amount of life insurance coverage.

Most insurers do not issue coverage to foreign nationals who are only visiting or temporarily living in North America because of a concern that the policy may lapse upon the person's departure. Such a person has little apparent reason to own a policy issued outside the native country.

Key Terms and Concepts

motor vehicle record (MVR)
inspection report
personal interview report
insurable interest
third-party applicant
moral hazard
persistency
policy lapse

CHAPTER SIX

Underwriting Individual Life Insurance—Financial Factors

Learning Objectives

After studying this chapter, you should be able to

- Explain the types of financial information an underwriter obtains from the application for insurance, the marketer, and the inspection report
- Identify the information an underwriter obtains from a W-2 or T4 form and from an income tax return and a specialized financial questionnaire
- Identify the information an underwriter may obtain from each of five financial statements
- Explain the relationship of insurable interest, antiselection, and speculation to financial underwriting
- Discuss the importance to sound financial underwriting of an applicant's (1) net worth and income, (2) ability to pay for insurance, and (3) insurance in force
- Use two methods to calculate the amount of coverage a proposed insured with a specified income should usually be able to purchase
- Use a factor table to calculate the maximum amount of coverage an underwriter usually approves for persons in specific age ranges
- Explain how an underwriter evaluates the amount of in-force insurance and assesses applications for large amounts of life insurance

Chapter Outline

Sources of Financial Information

The Application for Insurance
The Marketer
Inspection Report
Tax Forms
Specialized Financial Questionnaire
Financial Statements
Financial Worksheet

Assessing the Need for Insurance

Family Income Protection
Estate Settlement
Charitable Benefit

Insurable Interest, Antiselection, and Speculation

Insurable Interest
Antiselection
Speculation

Assessing Financial Factors

Net Worth and Income
Ability to Pay for Insurance
Insurance in Force
Large-Amount Cases

Besides considering medical, personal, and lifestyle factors, underwriters often look at financial information—the proposed insured's worth, income, and financial reputation. Insurers have learned from experience that if people buy more life insurance than they can afford and need, an insurer's persistency and mortality results are likely to be adversely affected. Inadequate finances do not necessarily produce extra mortality, although they may indicate the possibility of speculation and antiselection. The underwriter, therefore, approves insurance coverage on the basis of the applicant's real need for insurance, including the presence of a genuine potential financial loss in the event of the proposed insured's death.

Although financial factors are relevant in underwriting both personal and business insurance, we'll postpone discussion of business insurance to the next chapter. In this chapter, we'll focus on ***personal insurance,*** which can be defined generally as insurance purchased by individuals for the ultimate benefit of persons who have a direct financial interest in the life of the proposed insured. The proceeds from personal insurance are typically used for income replacement, family needs and expenses, and payment of estate taxes.

An underwriter assesses the financial status of an applicant for life insurance to see that the amount of insurance applied for is consistent with the anticipated amount of loss in the event of the applicant's death. A person's ***financial status*** is defined as a person's current income expressed in terms of amount, sources, and permanency, and by the person's ***net worth,*** which is the difference between the person's assets and liabilities.

In examining the financial factors pertaining to personal insurance, we'll begin by discussing the sources of financial information used for underwriting. Next, we will look at the ways underwriters evaluate an applicant's need for personal life insurance, and we will examine the significance of insurable interest, antiselection, and speculation. We'll conclude by showing how underwriters assess financial factors that help justify the underwriting decision.

Sources of Financial Information

The underwriter relies on three main sources of information to assess an applicant's financial situation: (1) the application for insurance, (2) the marketer, and (3) the inspection report. For large-amount or unusual cases, the underwriter may order additional evidence such as an income tax return, a personal balance sheet, or a specialized financial questionnaire. The underwriter also may use information from a W-2 form in the United States or a T4 form in Canada. These forms are generally filed by employers for each employee from whom income tax or other types of tax have been withheld or who has satisfied other, specified federal tax requirements. In addition, financial statements from a proposed insured's own business may be used to gather information for underwriting personal insurance. The amount and type of financial information requested are generally determined by the amount of coverage requested. The underwriter may use a financial worksheet to consolidate financial information from these sources.

The Application for Insurance

The application for insurance provides the underwriter with an initial picture of the proposed insured's financial status. The application shows the proposed insured's age, occupation, and income; the amount of insurance in force; the cost and amount of the coverage requested; and the relationship between the proposed insured and the proposed beneficiary.

In examining this information, the underwriter looks for consistency before making a judgment regarding the appropriateness of the amount of insurance requested. For example, if a proposed insured already has several small-amount life insurance policies that have been in force for years and now wishes to purchase a large additional amount of coverage, the underwriter determines whether the new coverage can be justified according to the proposed insured's current income and ability to pay for the coverage.

The Marketer

The marketer's business relationship with the insurance company also influences the underwriter's decision whether to ask for additional information concerning a proposed insured's financial status and the reason for the insurance purchase.

In a situation in which the underwriter has questions or doubts about the justification for requested insurance, the underwriter typically communicates with the marketer to clarify the available information. If doubts persist, the underwriter may then request more information from the marketer, the proposed insured, or an inspection agency. When a proposed insured requests unusually large amounts of coverage, the underwriter usually requires that the marketer submit a letter explaining (1) the purpose of the insurance and (2) the method used to determine the amount of coverage requested. If an underwriter doesn't know the marketer well and needs to check on the quality of business submitted, the underwriter typically orders an inspection report.

Inspection Report

Another of the underwriter's sources of financial information is the inspection report. In the last chapter, we discussed the contents of the inspection report and noted that financial information is included. We said that the inspection report may include the assets and liabilities of the proposed insured, including these elements:

- Cash, stocks, and bonds
- Real estate
- Automobiles and personal possessions
- Business equity
- Other sources of assets and liabilities

In addition, the inspection report can provide the underwriter with information on the proposed insured's earned and unearned income, as well as details of the credit record.

Many insurers do not use an inspection report for financial underwriting on most amounts of personal life insurance. Instead, for cases under $500,000, the underwriter generally relies on the marketer and the information in the application to justify the amount of coverage requested. For cases above $500,000, the underwriter usually interviews the proposed insured's accountant or bank to verify information in the application and other documents.

Further, for large-amount cases, the marketer usually is required to complete a financial questionnaire over the applicant's signature or provide an audited financial statement to show the income, net worth, and sources of income. If the questionnaire or the audited financial statement reveals that an applicant's finances are not consistent with the amount of coverage requested, and if the case file doesn't already include an inspection report, the underwriter may order an inspection report that includes considerable financial information. The underwriter may ask the inspection agency to interview the proposed insured's attorney, tax adviser, or accountant to check facts on the application. The underwriter may also ask the inspection agency to check especially for a lien (a claim on property in connection with a debt), bankruptcies, credit history, outstanding lawsuits, criminal records, and outstanding debts in the financial history of the proposed insured.

The bankruptcy of a proposed insured poses certain underwriting problems. The increased risk associated with bankruptcy includes persistency problems and the possibility of antiselection resulting from suicide and accidental death. If the inspection report reveals that a proposed insured is currently involved in a bankruptcy, many insurers

Fast Fact

A typical American household experiences its highest income when the adult or adults in it are between 45 and 54 years of age—but the discretionary income with which households purchase insurance generally peaks when the adults are between 55 and 59 years of age.

Source: Mary Hine and James C. Weide, "Are Product Designs, Distribution Systems Keeping Pace with Demographic Changes?" *Reinsurance Reporter,* First Quarter 1994: 5–6.

deny coverage until the proposed insured has been released from bankruptcy. Some insurers, however, may approve applications from persons involved in certain types of bankruptcies. Insight 6-1 presents additional information concerning three types of bankruptcies in the United States and possible underwriting approaches for each.

Tax Forms

An underwriter can gather valuable information from an applicant's W-2 form (in the United States) or T4 form (in Canada), as well as federal, state, or provincial income tax returns. Such forms enable the underwriter to verify financial information obtained from the application and other sources.

W-2 form or T4 form. When an underwriter needs to investigate an applicant's finances, the W-2 form in the United States provides the

Insight 6-1 Underwriting Approaches for Three Types of Bankruptcies

A current or recent bankruptcy involving a person applying for insurance has long been a concern for life underwriters. Because the number of bankruptcy filings is increasing, underwriters may consider various approaches to three types of bankruptcies. Each type of bankruptcy is named according to the chapter that explains it in the United States Federal Bankruptcy Reform Acts.

Personal Bankruptcy: Chapter 7
Chapter 7 is the most commonly used form of bankruptcy and is usually filed by persons without a regular income and with few assets. In Chapter 7, debtors are freed from many of their obligations by agreeing to give up most of their assets. Certain categories of debt—including federal, state, and local taxes; recent student loans; child support; and alimony—are not forgiven or discharged in a Chapter 7 bankruptcy.

In most cases, underwriters decline a life insurance application from a person undergoing a Chapter 7 bankruptcy. Such a person has little, if any, current income and is involved in liquidating most assets. Therefore, the person has little ability to pay for new life insurance. Underwriters also check an application from a person who has recently discharged a Chapter 7 bankruptcy to ensure that financial figures indicate adequate financial recovery.

Personal Bankruptcy: Chapter 13
In a Chapter 13 bankruptcy, a debtor agrees to repay part of what is owed from future earnings, over a three- to five-year period and is permitted to do so without being pressured by creditors during the repayment period. The repayment plan is administered by a court-appointed bankruptcy trustee. To file under Chapter 13, a person must have regular income from employment and must not have more than $350,000 in secured debt (such as a home mortgage) or more than $100,000 in unsecured debt (such as credit card debts). Some insurers consider a person who has filed a Chapter 13 bankruptcy to be insurable.

Business Bankruptcy: Chapter 11
A Chapter 11, or business reorganization, bankruptcy allows a business debtor to continue operations free from pressure by creditors, while the debtor devises a plan of reorganization to rehabilitate the business and to repay its debts, at least partially. A Chapter 11 bankruptcy can be filed by an individual or a married couple in business, or by a partnership or a corporation. Some insurers feel that a business undergoing a Chapter 11 bankruptcy is insurable.

From John W. Lawson, AALU, FLMI, "Bankruptcy: Implications for Life Underwriting," *On the Risk*, April/June 1994: 78–80. Adapted by permission.

underwriter with relevant information about the amount of money paid to the proposed insured by an employer, including the following:

- Gross pay
- Wages, tips, and other compensation, such as commissions or bonuses
- Federal and state income tax withheld
- Social Security tax withheld
- Medicare tax withheld
- Pension plan contributions

In Canada, the T4 form provides information that is similar to that provided by the W-2. The T4 also includes a statement of the applicant's reportable income and the amount of taxes deducted. The primary differences between the T4 and the W-2 are that (1) the pension plan noted on the T4 is termed either the Canada Pension Plan or the Quebec Pension Plan and (2) the T4 reports deductions not only for the pension plan, but also for unemployment insurance premiums, registered pension plan contributions, employment commissions, union dues, and charitable donations.

The T4U, a special form of T4, includes the amount of maternity benefits or unemployment insurance compensation (UIC), if any, received during a specified period. If the T4U indicates a period of unemployment, the underwriter typically investigates the matter to be sure the proposed insured has sufficient funds to pay for insurance.

Information from the T4 is typically used to verify an applicant's personal income when the coverage amount requested is over $1,000,000. For very large coverage amounts, the underwriter ordinarily supplements the T4 with information concerning the purpose for the insurance and the applicant's annual income. The underwriter may require the applicant to sign a supplementary form that attests to the following information:

- The reason for applying for insurance
- The income and approximate net worth of the proposed insured
- The income and approximate net worth of the applicant if that person is not the proposed insured
- The amount of insurance in force (excluding the current application)

The supplementary form usually includes the question "If the applicant is not the life insured, what financial loss will the applicant suffer on the death of the life insured?" and provides space for comments. If coverage is approved, the supplementary form is attached to and becomes a part of the life insurance contract.

Income tax return. Underwriters can request copies of income tax returns from the marketer or the proposed insured in order to make a full assessment of the proposed insured's financial status. Particularly when amounts are itemized, an income tax return from the United States or Canada provides a great deal of financial information about a proposed insured, including the following items:

- Earned income
- Taxable and nontaxable interest income and dividend income
- Alimony received or paid
- Business, farm, and investment income or loss
- Unemployment compensation
- Social Security benefits
- Medical or dental expenses
- Gifts to charity, job expenses, and miscellaneous deductions

An underwriter can use information from an income tax form to assess many aspects of a proposed insured's insurability. For example, when an applicant has listed unemployment compensation, the underwriter may question whether the applicant is steadily employed and can pay for insurance. If an applicant lists a considerable deduction for medical or dental expenses, the underwriter may seek further information about the applicant's health, especially if other information indicates that the applicant may have a significant health impairment.

Instead of an income tax form, some insurers prefer to use statements from a proposed insured's banker or certified public accountant, especially for large-amount cases. The statements typically cover several years and report gross income, net income, net worth, and financial losses. When available, such statements have credibility because they have been compiled by professionals, who submit with the statements a certificate that the statements are accurate.

Specialized Financial Questionnaire

The underwriter can also obtain financial information about an applicant by using a specialized financial questionnaire signed by the proposed insured. Such a questionnaire requests specific details about the financial situation of the proposed insured. In handling specialized financial questionnaires, the underwriter is especially careful to adhere to the insurance company's rules of confidentiality. An example of a specialized financial questionnaire is shown in Figure 6-1.

The underwriter carefully checks questionable items of information on the questionnaire. For example, if a proposed insured lists numerous investments in stocks and bonds or other investment instruments, the underwriter may secure brokerage statements and may request information from brokers and other knowledgeable persons to ascertain the current and projected value of the investments. Colleagues in the insurer's investment department can also provide invaluable help to the underwriter. Occasionally, the underwriter may obtain documentation that verifies the value of real estate and of personal possessions such as jewelry, art, automobiles, aircraft, and boats. The underwriter checks especially the amounts invested in the proposed insured's own company, particularly if the company's value has decreased.

If the applicant is requesting personal life insurance as a means of paying a future estate tax liability, the underwriter may also use a specialized questionnaire to ask about the value of the applicant's estate, the composition of the estate (for instance, property, investments, and other sources of assets), the estimated value and the dates of all gifts made from the estate, the applicant's estimated liability for estate tax, and the name of the person who is liable for estate tax on the applicant's death.

Financial Statements

When a proposed insured who owns a business wishes to purchase a considerable amount of personal life insurance, the underwriter may request financial statements relating to the business in order to determine the stability of the business and to rule out possible antiselection. These statements may include an income statement, a statement of cash flows, a balance sheet, a statement of changes in financial position, and an annual report.

An ***income statement,*** also called a *profit and loss statement,* is a financial document that provides information on the net results of a business's operations during a certain interval such as three months or one year. The income statement attempts to match the revenues or income for the specified period with the expenses or costs of doing business during that period.

Figure 6-1. Financial questionnaire.

Name: ______________________ Birthdate: ______________________

Amount applied for: ______________________ Beneficiary: ______________________

Purpose: Personal ________ (Complete schedule A) Business ________ (Complete schedules A&B)

Amounts In Force	Purpose	Year(s) Issued	WP or ADB Amounts
Pending			

SCHEDULE A — PERSONAL COVERAGE

Purpose: estate planning ____________ creditor ____________ income replacement ____________

other ____________ How was amount determined? ______________________

PERSONAL INCOME AND NET WORTH

ANNUAL EARNED INCOME

Salary (or Draw if self-employed) $ ________
Bonus $ ________
Commission $ ________
Other Earnings $ ________
Total Earned Income $ ________

ANNUAL UNEARNED INCOME

Dividends $ ________
Interest $ ________
Net Rentals $ ________
Other $ ________
______________ $ ________
______________ $ ________
Total Unearned Income $ ________

ASSETS

Cash $ ________
Net Cash Value Life Insurance $ ________
Real Estate $ ________
Business Equity $ ________
Stock (not in above) $ ________
Bonds $ ________
Other ______________ $ ________
______________ $ ________
______________ $ ________
Total Assets $ ________

LIABILITIES

Mortgages $ ________
Personal Loans $ ________
Liens/Judgements $ ________
Other ______________ $ ________
Total Liabilities $ ________

NEW WORTH $ ________

I declare that the above information is true and complete and shall form part of the application on my life with ABC Life Insurance Company.

Date: ______________________

Witness: ______________________ ______________________

(Proposed Insured)

Particularly for large-amount applications, many insurers request a ***statement of cash flows,*** which indicates the amounts of actual cash received or paid in the day-to-day operation of a business. A statement of cash flows can be developed on demand, particularly if a business has an automated financial records system. Most businesses, however, prepare a statement of cash flows on a quarterly basis. A statement of cash flows is valuable in helping an underwriter to assess a firm's ability to produce adequate future cash flows. This statement also helps the underwriter determine why gaps, if any, exist between a company's net income and the amount of cash received. A company that shows increasing deficiencies in cash flow from year to year may be in financial difficulty.

A ***balance sheet*** is a financial document that provides a statement of the business's financial position on a certain date. The balance sheet includes information on the business's assets, which are the resources owned by the business; the business's liabilities, which are the debts that the business must pay; and the net worth of the business, which is the equity of the owners or proprietors of the business, and represents, in general terms, the value of the business.

Another financial document, a ***statement of changes in financial position,*** also called a *sources and uses of funds statement,* provides information on the resources that the business used during a certain period and the ways in which those resources were used. The statement of changes in financial position generally indicates the amount and sources of money the business generated during the specified period, the ways in which items were purchased and paid for, the ways that debts were paid, the distribution of profits and dividends, and other information relative to the business's financial position.

An ***annual report*** is a financial document that an incorporated business issues to its stockholders and that usually includes independently audited financial statements, along with information from the business's management team concerning the organization's current and future business position and performance.

In assessing financial statements for a personal business, an underwriter usually takes the following considerations into account:

- The historic trend of profit or loss in the business, typically for a period of at least the three to five years prior to the date of application for insurance
- The relative performance of the business in its industry during the same three- to five-year period
- Financial obligations to which the business is or will be committed
- Evidence of plans to expand, restructure, or sell the business

The underwriter keeps in mind that the debt of a business can rise and fall substantially during the year. Therefore, the underwriter typically uses annual financial statements, not recent quarterly reports, in determining the amount of debt a company carries. Using a recent quarterly report could present a distorted view of the company's financial strength or weakness.

Financial Worksheet

Underwriting the financial aspects of a life insurance case may require an underwriter to examine a number of sources and to understand a great deal of detailed information. To organize this information and to clarify an applicant's financial situation, the underwriter may use a financial worksheet similar to the one shown in Figure 6-2. The worksheet is meant to produce rough estimates only.

Assessing the Need for Insurance

Fast Fact

According to one industry survey, 35 percent of U.S. householders believe they do not have enough insurance.

Source: Sally A. Bryck and Cheryl D. Retzloff, "Life Insurance: Who Wants It?" *LIMRA's MarketFacts,* November/December 1996: 23–31.

Evaluating a proposed insured's financial situation includes an assessment of that person's need for insurance. Insurers are justifiably wary of an application requesting coverage that is far in excess of the proposed insured's expected needs because such an application may indicate that the applicant is selecting against the insurer.

Generally accepted financial purposes for purchasing personal life insurance include family income protection and estate settlement. Some insurers approve coverage to benefit a charitable institution.

Family Income Protection

Family income is funds needed to replace the ordinary living expenses formerly paid by the income of a deceased person whose wages or other income supplied the needs of a family. As is true for the costs of estate settlement, the underwriter generally approves coverage for family income if the need for that income is clearly shown.

Estate Settlement

Estate settlement is the process of paying debts after a person's death. The process of estate settlement typically requires funds to pay taxes, as well as medical expenses not covered by other insurance, funeral costs, attorney's fees and other costs incurred to settle the estate, and repayment of debts owed by the insured person. Life insurance can provide the funds needed to pay these costs. The underwriter usually approves coverage intended to pay such expenses when evidence of the likely obligations is clear.

Figure 6-2. Financial worksheet.

Financial Worksheet

Name ______________________ No. of dependents __________

Age __________ Amount and plan requested ______________________

Available income __________ Insurance in force $ ______________

Needs:

Education fund __________

Emergency fund __________

Estate taxes __________

Last expenses __________

Monthly income __________

Mortgage redemption __________

Other __________

Total insurance needs $ __________

Total insurance in force $ __________

Balance insurance needed $ __________

Cost of total insurance in force and requested — Annually $ __________ Monthly $ __________

Decision ______________________

____

____

If an heir is forced to sell assets to pay estate taxes, the result is often a substantial financial loss, especially considering the price the same assets might have brought in a more favorable market. Insurance to cover estate taxes eliminates the need for a forced sale. Most insurers approve an amount sufficient to pay all anticipated estate taxes.

Charitable Benefit

Sometimes the beneficiary listed in an application for life insurance is a charitable institution. If a person has been making regular contributions to a charitable organization, the contributions will cease when that person dies. The insurance proceeds can be considered as replacing that person's lost future contributions.

If a charitable institution applies for the coverage and intends to pay the premiums on this type of policy, the underwriter attempts to discover what financial loss the charity will bear through the death of the proposed insured. Besides being a contributor, the proposed insured may have other value to the organization, for example, as a leader or fund-raiser, so that the death of the proposed insured would result in considerable loss to the charity. If the proposed insured plays no such role, however, the underwriter either finds other justification for issuing the coverage or denies the coverage.

Insurable Interest, Antiselection, and Speculation

We have already introduced the topics of insurable interest and antiselection. In assessing financial factors, the underwriter protects both the insurer and other insureds by making certain (1) every case has a valid insurable interest, especially in relationship to the amount of insurance requested, (2) antiselection is not present, and (3) speculation is not a factor, particularly for cases in which a large amount of insurance is involved.

Insurable Interest

Determining the value of a human life is difficult. An underwriter, however, typically ensures that a balance exists between the amount of insurance requested and the potential financial loss to a beneficiary if an insured person dies. As we have noted, the underwriter checks carefully to be sure that each beneficiary has an insurable interest in the continued life of the proposed insured, that the amount of coverage requested is justified in relationship to the insurable interest of the beneficiary, and that the reasons for purchasing coverage are justifiable.

In assessing insurable interest, the underwriter often projects the loss into the future, particularly if the proposed insured provides a considerable amount of financial assistance to a beneficiary, as a parent would provide for a child, or one spouse would provide for the other spouse. In such a situation, the underwriter estimates the amount of financial loss to the beneficiary for a specified number of years to arrive at a total amount that insurance would reasonably cover. In making projections, the underwriter considers not only the needs of the beneficiary, but also the proposed insured's age, occupation, and potential for increased earnings.

Some cases present the underwriter with the problem of questionable beneficiaries—those who apparently have little or no insurable interest in the life of the insured person. The underwriter may question the presence of insurable interest if the named beneficiary is not the applicant's estate or the applicant's spouse, child, parent, grandparent, grandchild, or sibling, or if the named beneficiary has no clear financial interest in the continued life of the proposed insured. An underwriter investigates closely to determine the presence of insurable interest if the beneficiary is a friend, a creditor, an aunt, an uncle, a cousin, or a former spouse without dependent children for whom the applicant is financially responsible. Note that, in most jurisdictions, a proposed insured who is also the applicant can name anyone as the beneficiary.

Antiselection

Some applicants have a strong financial need that they do not disclose in making an application for insurance. They apparently hope that the financial need will not become apparent during underwriting. In such cases, the possibility of antiselection arises, with resultant potential financial harm to the insurer and its other insureds.

Moreover, an underwriter is aware of possible antiselection for elderly applicants. Whereas insurance may not be suitable for income protection for the elderly, many elderly persons have sizable estates for which insurance can provide vital estate tax protection. An underwriter usually approves coverage for such persons after investigation to be sure that antiselection is not a factor in the case.

Speculation

The possibility of speculation arises when the amount of insurance exceeds the potential financial loss that a beneficiary might suffer if an insured person were to die. Consider the situation of a parent of several children who applies for life insurance on only one of the children. Typically, the underwriter checks carefully to be certain that the child proposed for coverage does not have a life-threatening illness or impairment. In such a situation, a seriously ill child who requires expensive medical treatments might represent a financial liability to a family rather than a potential financial loss if the child were to die.

An application for insurance on aged, dependent parents requires special examination, because such an application may present an element of speculation. Unless the coverage is intended as burial insurance or as coverage to pay for other final expenses or estate taxes, insurance on an older proposed insured who is supported by an adult child does not reflect an insurable risk if the child pays the premium and will also be the beneficiary. Upon the death of the proposed insured, the adult child not only would receive the death benefit, but would also be relieved of support expenses. The underwriter might, however, approve coverage on the life of an elderly parent who was providing a service, such as babysitting for grandchildren.

Assessing Financial Factors

Financial underwriting for life insurance is based on the assumption that the coverage an insurer issues will compensate for a loss, but will not be so great that the money will represent a profit to the beneficiary or beneficiaries. In considering each case, the underwriter looks at the applicant's financial status and the amount of insurance already in force. Even if an applicant is applying for only a small amount of insurance, the underwriter may not approve the coverage if the applicant already has a sufficient amount of coverage in force.

Most proposed insureds demonstrate a clear need for the requested amount of coverage. In a few cases, however, the amount of coverage requested does not seem appropriate, at least not initially. In these cases, the underwriter judges the applicant's appropriateness of the amount of insurance requested according to three financial factors: the applicant's (1) net worth and income, (2) ability to pay for insurance, and (3) insurance in force. After discussing these factors, we'll look at the special challenge of underwriting large-amount cases.

Net Worth and Income

From an underwriting perspective, a person's net worth—the difference between that person's assets and liabilities—represents the estimated economic value of that person's life. Income is one of the elements used to determine the amount of financial loss that would occur in the event of a person's death. Life insurance in force is not considered part of a person's net worth. Elements that the underwriter considers include current income, potential income, and taxes.

Current income. The amount of income of a proposed insured has a specific relationship to the amount of loss that person's death could cause and to the amount of coverage that an underwriter would probably approve. To use a simplified case as an example, suppose Nina Porter is a 36-year-old woman whose gross income is $45,000 per year and provides the sole financial support of three children ages 4, 8, and 12. In the event of Ms. Porter's death, the financial loss to the children would be at least $45,000 a year for at least the next 14 years—until the youngest child reaches the age of 18. Moreover, Ms. Porter's earnings could be expected to increase during that time period. The cost of paying for the children's college education and the impact of expected annual inflation may also be considered important for the case. Assuming that Ms. Porter is in good health, most underwriters would approve life insurance coverage to supply the needed amounts of financial support for her children as beneficiaries—say, $500,000 to $750,000. On the other hand, few underwriters would approve coverage for Ms. Porter in the amount of $10 million, because that amount of coverage bears no apparent relationship to her income.

The job of the underwriter includes determining the approximate level of the proposed insured's income and its importance to the named beneficiaries. The underwriter keeps in mind that a person may have income from various sources, some of which are fairly permanent, and some of which are transient. The underwriter also decides which source or sources of income can be used to determine whether the applicant can afford to buy the amount of insurance requested.

Possible sources of income include salary from a full-time job, salary from a part-time job, spouse's salary, bonuses, commissions, expense allowance, profit sharing, investment income, capital gains, dividends, and inheritance. The underwriter decides which sources of income to count in deciding the amount of loss that might be caused by the death of the proposed insured. Generally, underwriters treat each of these potential income sources in the following ways:

Income Counted	Income Not Counted
■ Salary from full-time job	
■ Salary from part-time job	
■ Spouse's salary	
■ Regular bonuses	■ Irregular bonuses
■ Commissions	■ Expense allowance
■ Profit sharing not deferred until retirement	■ Profit sharing deferred until retirement
■ Investment income not deferred until retirement	■ Investment income deferred until retirement
■ Investment income expected to continue after the applicant's death	
■ Capital gains regular for at least five years	■ Irregular capital gains
■ Dividends regular for at least five years	■ Irregular dividends
■ Inheritance currently disbursed	■ Anticipated inheritance

To assess a case in which a proposed insured has a large, unearned income that will continue after the applicant's death, the underwriter determines whether, aside from a provision to pay estate taxes, the proposed insured demonstrates a genuine need for insurance. If the beneficiary will suffer no economic loss beyond the amount needed for final expenses and estate taxes, the underwriter may justifiably question whether a real need exists for the full amount of coverage requested.

Fast Fact

Only 70 percent of the wealthiest American households have an estate plan, and, despite life insurance's estate tax advantage, only 30 percent say that they have purchased life insurance specifically to pay for estate taxes.

Source: Robert M. Baranoff, "Estate Planning: The Market and the Competition Are Growing," *LIMRA's MarketFacts*, July/August 1995: 46–48.

Potential income. The underwriter considers the potential earning power of a proposed insured who is in the process of establishing a career. The underwriter cannot fairly consider the potential income of a person whose current income is irregular or insecure—for instance, someone who has no business experience and who is starting a new company, or someone whose sole income is derived from participation in a minor league sport.

Taxes. Taxes complicate the underwriter's assessment task because usually a substantial difference exists between an applicant's gross income and net (after-tax) income. Usually, underwriters use pre-tax figures, making the necessary adjustments for taxable income in cases in which the inclusion of taxes produces a significantly different picture of an applicant's finances.

Ability to Pay for Insurance

Determining a proposed insured's ability to pay for the insurance requested requires the underwriter to make an informed estimate of the proportion of the person's net worth (and income, if applicable) that could reasonably be spent for the insurance purchase. Each insurer establishes its own guidelines for making this determination. However, underwriters generally use three general rules to determine ability to pay: the percentage of income rule, the 20 percent rule, and factor tables. These rules are used as guidelines, not as rigid decision-making tools.

Percentage of income rule. A ***percentage of income rule*** stipulates the amount of money an applicant can afford to spend on insurance according to the applicant's income. Each insurer stipulates its own version of the rule. As an example, one insurer's percentage of income rule might specify that, when purchasing life insurance, a person can afford to spend no more than 7 percent of the first $10,000 of the person's gross income, 12 percent of the next $15,000, and 20 percent of the remainder. According to this insurer's percentage of income rule, an applicant who earns $100,000 a year can afford to pay $17,500 annually for life insurance coverage ($700 + $1,800 + $15,000).

20 percent rule. Another, similar method of determining the amount of coverage a proposed insured may purchase is known as the 20 percent rule. Under the ***20 percent rule,*** a maximum of 20 percent of the applicant's gross earned income can be used to buy life insurance. For example, an applicant who earns $100,000 annually could afford to spend $20,000 ($100,000 × .20) a year on life insurance.

Factor tables. A ***factor table*** shows the maximum amount of insurance, expressed in multiples of a person's salary or total income, that an insurer will typically approve without question in each of several age ranges. An insurer's factor table is typically updated every five years or so to reflect changes in the economy and in the insurer's underwriting guidelines, which may change according to revisions in the insurer's product line and claims experience.

Because each insurer develops its own factor tables, the amount of insurance a person can buy may vary widely from one insurer to another. Figure 6-3 shows a typical factor table for life insurance; the table specifies the amount of insurance, figured as a multiple of a proposed insured's current gross income, that may be purchased at specified ages.

According to the information in Figure 6-3, a proposed insured who is 33 years old and whose gross income is $40,000 a year may be approved without question for a maximum of $680,000 of life insurance ($40,000 × 17). If the same applicant had applied for life insurance at age 26 and had the same amount of income, he could have been approved for a maximum of $720,000 of life coverage ($40,000 × 18).

An underwriter is usually not bound absolutely by the numbers in a factor table. Higher amounts of coverage can be approved for persons whose current income is low but who can be expected to have higher earnings in later years. For example, young doctors, attorneys, and financial consultants may be expected to earn more money as they gain more experience and develop larger practices. Applicants whose occupations would not ordinarily be expected to produce increased earnings over time may also qualify for higher amounts than factor table rating provides.

For example, suppose that Sarah Streator is a 24-year-old salesperson, has a current annual income of $32,000, and applies for $1,000,000 in life insurance. Ms. Streator's income tax reports indicate that for the past three years her sales commission income has steadily increased. If the insurer uses the factor table shown in Figure 6-3, the underwriter

Figure 6-3. A typical factor table for whole life insurance.

Age	Multiple of Current Annual Income
20–24	20
25–29	18
30–34	17
35–39	15
40–44	12
45–49	11
50–54	9
55–59	8
60–64	6
65 and over	5

will most likely approve a maximum of approximately $640,000 in coverage for Ms. Streator. After noting the increasing amounts of sales commission income on Ms. Streator's recent income tax reports, the underwriter realizes that Ms. Streator's demonstrated skill in sales is likely to mean her income will increase within the next 5 to 10 years, so that her ability to pay for insurance is also likely to increase. Therefore, if Ms. Streator's health is satisfactory and no other negative factors are present in the case, the underwriter is likely to approve the higher amount of coverage.

Insurance in Force

A third financial factor for underwriting is the amount of insurance that a proposed insured currently has in force. The underwriter uses information on the application to determine this amount. In order to rule out the elements of speculation and antiselection, the underwriter makes certain that the proposed insured is not overinsured. Each insurer sets its own limits for the total acceptable amount of in-force coverage.

In some insurance companies, the calculation for the amount of insurance in force includes an accidental death benefit (ADB), which doubles or triples the face amount of the policy in the event of accidental death. Some insurers establish separate limits for face amount coverage and for ADB coverages.

Life insurance coverage paid for by the proposed insured's employer is typically included as in-force coverage. Even though such insurance is usually requested and owned by the employer, the insured chooses the beneficiary. The underwriter also includes as personal insurance any in-force business insurance that covers the proposed insured's life. For example, if a corporation owned by the proposed insured's family is the beneficiary of an individual policy on the proposed insured's life, that policy is counted as personal insurance in force, even though the policy is not part of the proposed insured's compensation and even though the corporation pays the premium. By contrast, the death benefits of pensions and Social Security are usually small and generally are not considered to be insurance in force.

Large-Amount Cases

Underwriting life insurance applications for unusually large amounts of coverage presents the underwriter with a special challenge. When underwriters act on applications for amounts higher than the insurer's retention limit, they do so only because reinsurance is available. However, the cost to the insurer of large amounts of reinsurance can offset part or all of the profit from a given policy.

The mortality of large-amount risks is statistically higher than that of so-called normal risks, and the possibility of antiselection tends to be greater for large policies. In underwriting an application for a substantial amount of coverage, the underwriter needs to know considerably more about the applicant's financial background than is necessary for smaller-amount cases.

Key Terms and Concepts

personal insurance
financial status
net worth
income statement (*profit and loss statement*)
statement of cash flows
balance sheet
statement of changes in financial position (*sources and uses of funds statement*)
annual report
family income
estate settlement
percentage of income rule
20 percent rule
factor table

CHAPTER SEVEN

Underwriting Specialized Policies and Supplemental Coverages

Learning Objectives

After studying this chapter, you should be able to

- Explain how business insurance differs from most personal insurance
- Describe the types of information an underwriter gathers by using a business financial supplement
- List and explain six criteria an underwriter uses in estimating the value of a business
- Distinguish among the debt-to-equity ratio, current ratio, quick ratio, and return on equity, and explain how each is calculated and interpreted in underwriting business coverages
- Discuss the underwriting considerations for the following types of business coverages: creditor insurance, partnership insurance, sole proprietorship insurance, key-person insurance, and split-dollar plans
- Explain the typical underwriting approach for multi-life products, industrial insurance, juvenile insurance, individual guaranteed-issue products, and direct response products
- Discuss the importance of antiselection and underwriting standards in connection with policy replacements

Chapter Outline

Underwriting Business Insurance

Insurable Interest

Medical, Personal, Lifestyle, and Financial Factors

Estimating the Value of a Business

Assessing Risk

Underwriting Multi-Life Products and Industrial Insurance

Underwriting Juvenile Insurance

Handling Guaranteed-Issue Products

Direct Response Products

Underwriting Policy Replacements

Antiselection in Policy Replacements

Underwriting Standards in Policy Replacements

Possibility of Churning or Twisting

1035 Exchanges

Underwriting Supplementary Coverages

Waiver of Premium for Disability

Accidental Death Benefit

Family Benefit

Guaranteed Insurability

Now that you've learned how underwriters assess the risk for individual life insurance, we'll examine the underwriting considerations for certain specialized life insurance coverages. You'll see that many of the same factors that are assessed in underwriting individual life coverages are also used to determine the degree of risk represented by applicants for specialized coverages.

In this chapter, we'll begin by discussing the underwriting considerations for business insurance, multi-life products and industrial insurance, juvenile insurance, and guaranteed-issue and direct response products. We'll also examine the underwriting approaches for policy replacements and for certain supplementary coverages including waiver of premium for disability, accidental death benefit, family benefit, and guaranteed insurability.

Underwriting Business Insurance

You have learned that underwriters consider medical, personal, and financial factors in underwriting individual life insurance. Underwriters examine these same factors in underwriting business insurance. After we define business insurance and its requirement of insurable interest, we'll look at underwriting approaches used for specific types of business insurance, including creditor insurance, partnership insurance, sole proprietorship insurance, key-person insurance, and split-dollar plans.

Insurable Interest

Business insurance is coverage intended to serve the insurance needs of a business organization rather than those of an individual. Business insurance differs from most personal insurance in that business insurance is usually third-party insurance, so that the proposed insured is not the applicant and will not be the policyowner if a policy is issued. An exception is sole proprietorship insurance, for which the proposed insured and the policyowner are the same.

In assessing the risk for business insurance, the underwriter ascertains whether insurable interest exists. For business purposes, an insurable interest is usually considered to be present if the premature death of one party in a business relationship would cause serious loss

Fast Fact

According to a survey of underwriters, 67 percent of underwriters working in life insurance had 10 or more years of experience, and 34 percent had over 15 years of experience.

Source: Home Office Life Underwriters Association/Institute of Home Office Underwriters, "1994 Life Insurance Requirements Survey," *On the Risk,* January/March 1995: 85.

to the surviving parties or to the business. Therefore, a business has an insurable interest in the lives of certain key employees who are essential to the continued success of the company. In addition, in some situations the owners of a business have an insurable interest in each other's lives. A creditor also has an insurable interest in the life of a debtor.

Medical, Personal, Lifestyle, and Financial Factors

Using many of the same sources and procedures as when gathering information for personal insurance, the underwriter of business insurance collects and assesses medical, personal, lifestyle, and financial information.

To gather medical information, the underwriter reviews the application and may order an APS and laboratory tests. The underwriter may also use an inspection report, a personal interview report, and specialized questionnaires to gather personal and lifestyle information about the proposed insured.

Financial assessment for business insurance focuses on the finances of the business, more than on the finances of the proposed insured. The underwriter examines the financial condition of the business in order to be satisfied that there is a legitimate need for the insurance and that the business will be able to pay the premiums.

To collect financial information in connection with a business insurance application, the underwriter typically uses many of the same sources used to collect financial information for personal insurance, such as the application for insurance, the agent's statement, an inspection report, W-2 or T4 forms, business income tax returns, a specialized financial questionnaire, and business financial statements. In addition, if a lender has required the proposed insured to be covered by a specific amount of insurance, the underwriter usually asks the marketer to obtain copies of relevant personal and business loan documents.

In addition to these documents, an underwriter may use a specialized questionnaire called a ***business financial supplement.*** This document requests information concerning the type of business, the current financial condition of the business, and the purpose for which the insurance is being requested. This type of supplement is also occasionally used for underwriting personal insurance when the value of a proposed insured's business is important in assessing that person's financial worth. Figure 7-1 shows a typical business financial supplement.

For business coverage applications, the underwriter assesses these documents in much the same way as for personal coverage applications. One special consideration for business coverages is that a business's audited financial statements may need investigation because acceptable methods of valuing assets and liabilities, and of reporting profits and earnings, vary widely. The underwriter can consult with persons

Figure 7-1. Business financial supplement.

I. NAME OF COMPANY ______________________________

II. TYPE OF ORGANIZATION ☐ Corporation ☐ Partnership ☐ Sole Proprietorship

III. Please attach a copy of your Company's ***latest audited financial statements*** (Balance Sheet and Profit & Loss).
If not available, complete the following questions:

A. CURRENT COMPANY BOOK VALUE

Assets $ __________
Liabilities $ __________
Net Worth $ __________

B. CURRENT COMPANY MARKET VALUE

Market Value $ __________
Insured's % Ownership __________%
Market Value of Insured's % Ownership $ __________

C. COMPANY NET PROFIT — Past Two Years (Before taxes and bonuses)

19____ $ __________
19____ $ __________
This Year (Est.) $ __________

D. What other Stockholders, Partners, or Key Persons are also being insured in favor of the Company? (Please name)

____
____
____

IV. (Check at least one box and furnish details)

☐ KEY PERSON

A. Why is the person to be insured important to the Company? What special skills, knowledge, or abilities does he/she possess which makes insurance necessary?

____
____

B. How is it expected that the proceeds will be utilized? ______________________________

____
____
____

☐ STOCK REDEMPTION/BUY AND SELL

A. Is there a written agreement: In effect? (Attach signed Copy)
Contemplated? Give expected finalization date __________

B. How is business being valued in the Agreement? ______________________________

☐ BUSINESS LOAN

A. Name and address of the lender: ______________________________

____

B. Amount of Loan $ __________ C. Date of Loan: __________

D. The repayment terms are: ______________________________

____

E. The purpose of the loan is: ______________________________

____

F. Is lender requiring the insurance? ☐ Yes ☐ No

I understand that ABC Life Insurance Company will rely on the above statements in determining the need and justification for the insurance applied for, and I represent that all answers are true and accurate statements to the best of my knowledge and belief as of the date of application for life insurance. A photographic copy of this statement may be attached to and made part of any insurance contract issued.

Signature of Proposed Insured ______________________________ Date __________

Signature of Owner ______________________________ Date __________

Witnessed by ______________________________ Date __________

in the insurer's legal, investment, and accounting functions to help investigate and understand these financial documents.

The financial health of a business is often difficult to assess. Underwriters who specialize in business insurance are trained to look for indications that a business is in financial difficulty. These indications include such elements as negative cash flow from operations, unusual financing arrangements, and dependence on a single project to keep the business going. Figure 7-2 lists these and other characteristics of businesses in poor financial health.

Estimating the Value of a Business

Underwriting an application for business insurance requires the underwriter to make an analysis of the financial strength of the business by assessing a number of criteria, including the following:

- Tangible assets (such as buildings, equipment, and inventory)
- Intangible assets (such as goodwill, an established customer base, favorable industry reputation, market presence, franchise value, name recognition, desirable location of the business, trademarks, logos, and patents)
- Historic trend of profit or loss in the business, especially its average earning capacity over a period of at least three to five years prior to the date of application for insurance
- The relative performance of the business in its industry during the same three- to five-year period
- Current economic conditions and the future outlook of the business sector in which the business operates and of the economy as a whole
- Probable ability of the business to be self-sustaining by (1) hiring and retaining employees and (2) retaining current customers and attracting new ones
- Book value and recent sales of the company's stock, if any, and the dividend-paying capacity of the business
- Financial obligations to which the business is or will be committed
- Evidence of plans to expand, restructure, or sell the business

One of the challenges for every underwriter in estimating the value of a business is knowing enough about the business to make an

Figure 7-2. Characteristics of businesses in poor financial health.

Negative Trends

- Recurring operating losses
- Inadequate financing
- Negative cash flows from operations
- Declining sales or revenues
- Excessive debt

Other Indications

- Credit defaults, credit denial, or restructuring
- Unusual financing arrangements
- Sale of substantial assets
- Bankruptcy

Internal Matters

- Labor strife
- Dependency on a single project

External Matters

- Litigation
- Loss of patents, copyrights, franchises, key customers, etc.
- Catastrophes without adequate insurance

Adapted by permission from *Journal of Accountancy*, January 1989: 24–31.

equitable, accurate assessment of its worth. Because industries grow, change, merge, and diversify, underwriters continually update their knowledge not only of business in general, but of specific industries. Insight 7-1 discusses the elements required to evaluate a business in one industry.

In order to avoid antiselection, the underwriter of business coverage looks at all facts revealed by the financial sources to be sure a company is in good financial health. Specifically, the underwriter assesses the company's solvency, liquidity, and profitability.

Considered in isolation, the figures concerning solvency, liquidity, and profitability mean little, if anything. The underwriter typically compares these figures for a business to the norms established by the insurance industry and to the figures of other businesses in the same or similar industries.

Solvency. A company's ***solvency*** is the company's ability to pay its debts on time. A business that is unable to maintain sufficient funds to pay its debts not only may be unable to pay insurance premiums, but also may be likely to suffer financial failure. In either situation, such a company is not a sound candidate for business coverage. One way to calculate a company's solvency is to determine a ***debt-to-equity***

Insight 7-1 Financial Analysis of Agribusiness

Farming was a way of life for much of America until this century. Much has been written about the farm family's demise in recent decades. But since the first time a farmer ever took produce, livestock, or dairy products to a town market, farming has been a business. As the 21st century proceeds, agribusiness is one of America's largest industries, with ownership and wealth concentrated in significantly fewer hands than a century ago.

Agribusiness encompasses commercial feedlots as well as small dairy farms . . . grain elevators and fruit and vegetable farms . . . tree crops and hog or cattle farmers . . . co-ops, middlemen, and large food-processing companies. The financial analysis of agribusiness is as diverse and complex as the myriad types of farm operations. Reviewing the underwriting considerations for one type of agribusiness—dairy farming—is instructive.

The majority of the 175,000 dairy farms in the United States are concentrated in the midwest states. Dairy farmers experience wide fluctuations in the price of milk products. To guarantee an adequate supply of milk at reasonable prices, the federal government has long been involved in regulating the dairy industry. Nonetheless, dairy income is always volatile, so the Farm Credit System and Farmers Home Administration are deeply involved in farm financing, along with county banks and specialized branches of larger banking companies.

The underwriter may find that tax returns, supplemented by financial statements and cash flow statements prepared by the farmer without the assistance of professional financial advisers, are the only source of cash flow information available. Financial statements typically include the dairy herd, with cows listed as a current asset due to inventory value or an intermediate-term asset due to normal turnover rate (the latter is more accurate because cows are not immediately convertible to cash). The fact that cattle prices are highly localized affects asset evaluation. Financial statements also include monthly payments, settlements or advances on milk pools from which the farmer receives gross pay, and other current assets such as stocks, bonds, and life insurance cash values. Other intermediate assets include farm equipment, usually valued at cost less annual depreciation. Real estate is probably the largest long-term asset, but local appraisal values vary widely.

Dairy farm current liabilities include loans against the herd, equipment, and grain supplies. Lenders check with trade creditors to determine the financial stability and debt management habits of farmers, and may be able to provide underwriters and inspection companies with verifying information. Long-term liabilities include the first mortgage on real estate and second mortgages from private contracts or the Farmers Home Administration.

Dairy farms earn monthly gross revenues from milk sale, but feed costs take as much as half of these revenues. Another 25 percent of revenues pay for breeding, veterinary services, testing, and supplies. The rest goes to debt reduction, capital improvements, and return on owner's equity. Milk price cycles span two to five years, during which farmers raise or lower production to influence prices. Sometimes farmers go out of business when prices drop too low to cover debt. Unlike grain, which has a worldwide market, dairy products are quickly perishable. The United States market is highly regionalized, and overproduction is common, contributing to price instability.

Large amount insurance applications from dairy farmers require the full cooperation of the marketer and local inspection company staff. The underwriter can evaluate the financial risk represented by such an application only with the help of persons having local knowledge of the applicant and the prevalent market conditions.

Adapted by permission from *Underwriter Alert,* September 1994: 7–9.

ratio by dividing the company's total debt by the company's net worth. The formula for the debt-to-equity ratio is expressed below:

$$\textbf{Debt-to-Equity Ratio} = \frac{\textbf{Total Debt}}{\textbf{Net Worth}}$$

The higher a company's net worth in relation to its total debt, the more likely the company is solvent and will be able to pay its debts. The norm used by insurers for underwriting purposes is that a financially sound company has a total debt less than its net worth. In other words, the company's debt-to-equity ratio should be less than 1:1.

For example, suppose a company has a net worth of $2,350,000 and total debt amounting to $2,150,000. When we divide the company's total debt by its net worth, the result is 0.91, which is less than 1. According to the insurance industry norm, the company is considered solvent. Suppose the same company's debt were increased to $2,500,000 while its net worth remained the same. Dividing the company's total debt by its net worth would yield a debt-to-equity ratio of 1.06:1, indicating that the company's solvency is in doubt.

Liquidity. ***Liquidity*** refers to the ease with which a company can convert its assets into cash for an approximation of their true value. A company's ***current assets*** are usually the items or entities the company presently owns or to which the company has a legal claim, including inventory, investments, and other items and entities. A company's ***current liabilities*** are usually all the debt that is due and payable within the next year.

To determine a company's liquidity, many insurers calculate a ***current ratio,*** determined by dividing the company's current assets by the company's current liabilities. Thus, a business with current assets of $600,000 and current liabilities of $200,000 would have a current ratio of 3:1 ($600,000 ÷ $200,000).

If a current appraisal of asset value is available, the underwriter uses it. If such information is not available, the underwriter estimates the market value of assets. Although the desired ratio of current assets to current liabilities varies among industries, insurance companies generally consider a business to have acceptable liquidity if the business has at least $2 in current assets for every $1 in current debt, or a current ratio of 2:1. That is, the firm's current assets should be at least two times as great as the firm's current debts.

Some insurers prefer underwriters to assess a company's liquidity by examining its ability to pay its debts immediately. Immediate debt payment requires cash or its equivalent rather than monies derived from selling such assets as buildings and inventory, which may sell slowly, at a lower-than-expected price, or not at all. A company's ability to liquidate debt immediately can be calculated using a ***quick ratio,*** also called an *acid-test ratio.* The quick ratio is calculated by dividing a company's most liquid current assets (cash, liquid and short-term investments, and accounts receivable, but not including inventories) by the company's current liabilities.

Compared to the current ratio, the quick ratio is considered to provide a more realistic view of a company's debt payment abilities because the quick ratio reduces the importance of the company's non-cash assets that may be of little assistance in reducing debt immediately. The industry norm for the quick ratio varies from one industry to another, but may be as low as 1:1.

Profitability. A company's ***profitability*** measures the productivity of the company's assets and its return on investment. One way that insurers determine the profitability of a company that has issued stock is to calculate the ***return on equity,*** which is determined by dividing the company's net income by the stockholders' equity in the company. ***Net income*** is expressed very generally as the money remaining from a company's sales after deductions have been made for sales costs, operating expenses, and taxes. ***Stockholders' equity*** is the net worth of a firm determined by subtracting its total liabilities from its total assets.

Acceptable return on equity depends on the risk involved in a business. Companies operating in higher risk businesses expect a higher return, whereas companies operating in lower risk businesses are satisfied with a smaller return. In general, most insurers consider a company with a return on equity of 15 percent to be financially sound.

These approaches to assessing the financial strength of a business may be difficult to apply to nondomestic corporations whose accounting practices and business strategies differ considerably from those generally applied to domestic organizations. Determining the financial integrity of nondomestic companies requires that the underwriter develop a thorough understanding of financial statement practices in other countries. Governmental organizations and attorneys' organizations in foreign countries usually maintain and publish records of business legal problems and can provide such information that is useful for underwriting purposes.

By gathering as complete information as possible on a business, the underwriter seeks to approve coverage for appropriate risks and to deny coverage to businesses involved in commercial fraud. Insight 7-2 presents some of the warning signs of business insurance fraud.

Assessing Risk

The underwriter uses basically the same approaches to assess the risk for every type of business insurance. However, each type of business insurance coverage has slightly different requirements. We'll examine the primary underwriting considerations for several types of business coverages and riders. These types of business insurance are defined briefly in Figure 7-3 and will be discussed in more detail in this section.

Creditor insurance. ***Creditor insurance*** is designed to cover the economic loss suffered by a creditor when one of its borrowers dies before

Insight 7-2 The Warning Signs of Business Insurance Fraud

How do you avoid insuring a business involved in some kind of commercial fraud? Commercial lenders and corporate credit managers have learned to be alert to the probability of business scams. Underwriters can learn some lessons from the experience of lenders, including the following indicators of business fraud:

- True ownership of a company is often concealed by using a "front man," a very young person, because he will not have to invent a long business background. Or the front man may be an older person who retired with a clear business record and who may confer respectability on a dishonest operation.
- Double check the business backgrounds of company management if a principal claims long periods of time working in an obscure company in a foreign country, for several companies currently out of business, or as a consultant, particularly when a principal won't provide references or specific business locations from prior employment.
- Sometimes a business has been secretly sold and its former owners paid to remain with the business. The new owners may be skimming profits, selling assets, and running up credit while the former owners keep creditors satisfied. If fraud looks like normal business failure, prosecutors typically have difficulty in proving intent to defraud.
- A confusing, complex organizational structure, especially in a relatively new business, may be a sign of trouble. Principals may hide behind a maze of complicated corporate or partnership entities, some or all of which may be false.
- Be suspicious if a reference gives an instant glowing account without taking time to consult records. Trade or bank references can be faked by friends or partners of a fraudulent business person.
- Check financial statements in detail rather than looking only at the bottom line or cash flow figures. Dates on financial statements should be at regular intervals rather than on random dates. Assets that are difficult to confirm, such as marketable securities or real estate, may be suspect, as are accounts receivable shown in rounded figures or in extremely high amounts.
- If the business and its accounting or auditing firm are in different locations, find out why.
- For a new business, check the stated worth and starting capital figures to be sure they are consistent. Check assets to determine if they can be confirmed by other sources, and be sure that accounts receivable are consistent with annual sales.
- Claimed affiliations with parent companies, related businesses, subsidiaries, a difficult-to-confirm foreign company, or a well-known, legitimate company should be carefully reviewed.
- If a business looks too good to be true, it probably is.

Adapted by permission from *Underwriter Alert,* September 1996: 9.

the debt is paid. In this discussion, we are considering only business loans, not consumer loans that finance the purchase of a house or a personal vehicle. Creditor insurance provides the creditor with proceeds that are no greater than the unpaid debt, so that the principle of insurable interest is maintained. The creditor is legally entitled to only that portion of a loan that has not been repaid.

The underwriter also determines whether a borrower has means other than insurance to repay the debt. One issue to be considered in underwriting a creditor insurance application is whether money from the loan is being used to purchase something that can serve as collateral for the loan. Another issue is whether the collateral will continue to produce income to pay off the loan. If it seems likely that the borrower will be unable to repay the loan, such that the only viable means of repayment would be the life insurance benefit, then the underwriter declines the case. In such a situation, the application

Fast Fact

In 1920, there was $4 million of creditor life insurance in force in the United States. By 1995 there was more than $231 *billion* in force.

Source: American Council of Life Insurance, *1996 Life Insurance Fact Book:* 16.

Figure 7-3. Types of business insurance.

Creditor Insurance

Insurance issued to a lender to cover the life of a borrower for the amount of an outstanding loan. If the borrower dies before the loan is repaid, the policy pays the remaining debt. The face value of creditor insurance decreases to match the amount of unpaid debt.

Partnership Insurance

Insurance designed to provide funds so that the remaining partners in a business can buy the business interest of a deceased or disabled partner. A variation is *stock repurchase insurance,* which provides funds to buy stock from the estate of a deceased stockholder by other stockholders in the same company.

Sole Proprietorship Insurance

Insurance on the life of the sole proprietor of a business. The coverage is used either (1) to pay the salary of someone hired to run the business after the owner's death or (2) to compensate the owner's family for the loss of potential income because of the failure of the business after the owner's death or disability.

Key-Person Insurance

Insurance purchased by a business on the life of a person (usually an employee) whose continued participation in the business is judged necessary to the firm's success and whose death would cause financial loss to the company.

Split-Dollar Plans

Insurance that covers the life of an employee and that is paid for jointly by the employee and the employer. The employee names the beneficiary. Each year, the employer pays the portion of the premium that is equal to the increase in the policy's cash value for that year, and the employee pays the rest of the premium. If the employee dies, the employer receives an amount of the proceeds equal to the cash value of the policy, and the beneficiary of the policy receives the remaining benefits.

for creditor insurance represents an undesirable risk and possible antiselection. The underwriter may want to see the loan repayment schedule in order to obtain a better idea of the proposed insured's financial situation. Another element to consider is that a short-term creditor policy may lapse before the insurer can recover its costs or realize a profit. Generally, issuing coverage for short-term loans is not in an insurer's best interest.

If an applicant requests an amount of coverage equal to the amount of a loan, the underwriter can rarely approve the full amount. The allowable amount depends upon whether the loan is collateralized by other assets. Usually, 50 percent to 75 percent of the loan is the maximum an underwriter approves. Over the years, mortality experience from large-amount creditor coverage has consistently demonstrated the poorest experience. An application submitted a significant period after a loan was granted usually warrants deeper investigation. If the application is made at a later date, factors of antiselection may be at work—perhaps a debtor's financial situation or health has deteriorated since the loan was granted, so that the creditor wishes to ensure that the debt will be paid. The underwriter verifies, therefore, that loan payments have been made in a timely fashion and that the debtor's financial condition and health remain sound.

Partnership insurance. A business partnership is formed when two or more persons voluntarily join together as co-owners of a business. The death of a business partner can cause severe loss to a company, particularly because, under the laws of most jurisdictions, a partnership is dissolved when a change occurs in its membership. The remaining partners are bound by law to close the business and to pay an equitable share of the value of the business to the estate or the heirs of the deceased partner.

Partnership insurance provides cash that surviving partners can use to purchase the interest of a deceased partner from that partner's heirs. The partnership owns the partnership insurance policy and is the beneficiary of the coverage. To underwrite partnership insurance, the underwriter assesses the insurability of each partner covered by the policy. If one partner is uninsurable, generally the coverage can still be issued, although at a higher premium. Most insurers, however, consider that the fewer the number of partners in a business, the more conservatively the application is handled.

In gathering information to underwrite an application for partnership coverage, the underwriter typically uses a financial questionnaire that focuses on the partnership. Figure 7-4 illustrates such a partnership insurance questionnaire.

A variation of partnership insurance is stock repurchase insurance. If a person who owns a significant amount of stock in a company dies, the stock goes into that person's estate. In some situations, however, other stockholders want to buy that stock. The money to pay for the stock purchase can come from life insurance proceeds, and the coverage that provides the money is called ***stock repurchase insurance*** or *stock redemption insurance.*

In underwriting applications for stock repurchase insurance, the underwriter's main concern is that the persons who plan to buy the stock owned by the proposed insured have an insurable interest in the insured's life. The underwriter also learns (1) the present and projected value of the stock in order to determine the amount of coverage required and (2) the net worth of the business. Many insurance companies establish a rough figure of seven times the business's net worth as a maximum amount for stock repurchase coverage.

Another underwriting concern for stock repurchase insurance is the proportion of the total amount of stock owned by a proposed

Figure 7-4. Partnership insurance questionnaire.

1. Name of applicant (partner) ______
2. How many partners are there, and what are their names? ______
3. What is the nature of business transacted? ______
4. How long has the partnership been in existence? ______
5. What has been the profit/loss of the partnership over the last three years? ______
6. What has been the applicant's salary/share of profits over the last three years? ______
7. What is the current value of the partnership? How was the value established? ______
8. What is the applicant's percentage share of the partnership? ______
9. Is there a buy/sell agreement in existence? If not, is one to be executed in the near future? ______
10. Are policies to be effected on the lives of all other partners? If not, please give reasons. ______

insured. There may be no real need to insure purchase of the stock unless the proposed insured's stock holdings represent a significant portion of the company's equity. The underwriter makes sure that the lives of other major stockholders are also covered by insurance in order to rule out the possibility of antiselection.

Sole proprietorship insurance. A sole proprietorship is a business owned by one person (or, in some jurisdictions, by a husband and wife). By law, the business assets of the sole proprietor are not kept distinct from his personal assets. ***Sole proprietorship insurance*** provides coverage so that when the owner of a sole proprietorship dies, the insurance pays for the buyout of the business from the owner's heirs by the person or persons designated to become the new owner or owners.

Underwriting sole proprietorship applications requires the underwriter to make the same sort of inquiries into the proposed insured's medical, personal, lifestyle, and financial condition as would be made for personal life insurance. In addition, the underwriter examines the financial health of the business, checking to be sure the company has not incurred large debts.

Key-person insurance. An owner or employee may be so important to a company that if that person dies or leaves, the company will suffer a severe loss—of customers, investors, or management skills, for example. The term ***key person*** refers to such a person whose absence would cause a serious loss to a business. ***Key-person insurance*** is coverage that protects a business from the losses that occur when a key person dies. Figure 7-5 illustrates a typical questionnaire used to gather information necessary to assess the risk for key-person insurance.

Because a large percentage of new businesses fail within the first two to three years, underwriting key-person coverage for a new company is more conservative than for businesses with a longer history of operation. The insurer is concerned that a new business might fail before the insurer has collected enough premiums to cover the expenses of underwriting, issuing, and administering the policy.

Similarly, the size of a business is important for underwriting. Generally, as larger businesses grow, there is less likelihood that losing one person would produce a significant loss. If a business appears to have other, equally valuable employees or partners who are not being proposed for key-person coverage, the underwriter may question why only the proposed insured is being singled out.

Although the insurable interest that a business has in the life of a key person is usually obvious, certain situations may prompt the underwriter to look more closely for insurable interest. If the proposed insured is nearing retirement age and has not previously been insured by that business, the underwriter may ask why that person has become important to the company. If a company applies for a large amount of coverage on a proposed insured who holds what appears to be only a moderately important position in the company, the underwriter may investigate further to determine insurable interest.

In evaluating the amount of coverage requested on a key person, the underwriter tries to determine the value to the company in dollars of the proposed insured. This amount is usually set at 5 to 10 times the proposed insured's salary, but the underwriter may also include the dollar value of other compensation, whether in cash (such as bonuses) or in fringe benefits (such as employer-provided health insurance or use of a company car). The underwriter may also include the dollar amount of sales attributed to the key person and the cost of recruiting and training that person's replacement.

Special underwriting attention must be given to applications for insurance for key persons in multinational companies—those that operate in two or more countries. The underwriter may need to review the financial documents that are written in another language,

Fast Fact

According to a Society of Actuaries' study, key persons as a class have a much higher mortality experience than expected for their ages. The actual mortality of key persons up to age 29 in the study was 142 percent of expected mortality; for key persons ages 40 to 49, the mortality experience was 121 percent of the expected rate.

Source: "Financial Underwriting/ Disability Buy-Out," *Underwriter Alert,* June/July 1990: 3.

Figure 7-5. Key-person insurance questionnaire.

1. Name of applicant (key person) ______________________________
2. What is the key person's precise occupation? ______________________________
3. What is the nature of the business transacted by the key person's employer? ______________________________

   ____
4. How long has the employer been in business? ______________________________
5. How many employees are there? ______________________________
6. How long has the key person been employed by the employer? ______________________________
7. What has been the key person's gross salary over each of the last three years?

   This figure should include bonuses and commission. ______________________________
8. What has been the net profit/loss of the employer over each of the last three years?

   ____
9. Is the key person a shareholder in the employer's business? If so, what percentage

   of shares does the key person hold? ______________________________
10. What special abilities does the key person possess to justify classification as a key person?

    ____
11. What existing coverage is in force on the key person's life? ______________________________
12. Why has the amount of insurance applied for been chosen? ______________________________

    ____
13. Will the employer insure the lives of other employees as key persons? If so, how many lives and what amounts of coverage are proposed? Include lives already insured under key-person coverage.

    ____

that are abridged, that are unaudited, or that use accounting terms with different meanings from those in the underwriter's country.

Insight 7-3 comments further on underwriting considerations for key-person insurance.

Split-dollar plans. Under a ***split-dollar plan,*** an employer and an employee can combine their funds to buy life insurance. The insured is the employee, and the premium payment is divided between the employee and the employer. The owner of the policy may be either the employer or the employee. Each year, the employer pays the portion of

Insight 7-3 Underwriting Key-Person Insurance

For the life insurance underwriter, key-person insurance is desirable only on those employees who contribute substantially to the success of the business and whose death would result in a material financial loss to the firm. The best subjects for this form of coverage are those employees who

- Are usually found in the firm's management—although the key factor is not the person's job title, but contribution to the company
- Are found more often in smaller firms with little management depth as compared to large corporations
- Are usually highly compensated
- Enjoy the respect of the firm's customers and creditors
- Often have direct responsibility for sales or production
- Are in a decision-making position

Five ways in which a business may suffer loss at the death of a key person include

1. The loss of managerial skill and experience.
2. A loss of sales that may be due to the key employee's direct responsibility for sales or because the firm's customers have developed a "wait-and-see" attitude concerning future purchases.
3. An adverse effect on production as a result of the deceased employee's role in the production process.
4. A restriction on the line of credit that a company can acquire from suppliers or banks. The premature death of a key employee may affect the ability of a firm to acquire credit because the creditors might judge the financial stability of the business before extending more credit. If the key employee is also an owner of the firm, a lending institution may insert a clause in a loan agreement requiring immediate payment upon death. In this situation, the loss to the firm could be so severe as to prevent its survival without sufficient life insurance on the key person to pay off the loan.
5. A company without a trained backup may be faced with the expense of recruiting and training a replacement for the deceased key person.

From Wally Taylor, FALU, CLU, ChFC, FLMI, "Underwriting Key Employee Insurance," *On the Risk,* October/December 1995: 55–59.

the premium that is equal to the increase in the policy's cash value for that year, with the rest of the premium being paid by the employee. At the employee's death, the proceeds are split according to the agreement previously made between the employer and the employee; the employer receives an amount equal to the policy's cash value or the sum of the premiums paid by the employer, and the insured's beneficiary receives the remainder of the policy proceeds.

Although split-dollar plans are considered business insurance, they are underwritten in the same manner as personal insurance. The split-dollar approach is often used for partnership and key-person coverages.

Underwriting Multi-Life Products and Industrial Insurance

A life insurance contract that is written on more than one life is generally called a ***joint-and-last-survivor policy.*** If the contract provides that proceeds will be paid when the first of two or more insured persons dies, the contract is called a ***first-to-die policy.*** If, by contrast, the contract provides that payment of proceeds will occur when the second of two or more insured persons dies, the contract is called a ***second-to-die policy*** or *survivorship policy.* Some contracts provide that proceeds are paid to the named beneficiary on the death of each insured. Some insurers write policies that cover as many as 10 to 20 lives.

The underwriter makes a separate evaluation of each life to be covered under a multi-life policy. If the underwriter determines that one of the proposed insureds represents a ratable risk or is uninsurable, the policy can still be issued at an increased premium for that person. However, if one person is uninsurable, the contract usually does not contain a provision that premiums will be waived upon the death of the first insured person to die. Insight 7-4 discusses some of the challenges of underwriting survivorship products.

Industrial insurance is a form of life insurance characterized by (a) death benefits of $2,000 or less, (b) a weekly, biweekly, or monthly premium payment schedule, (c) the collection of premiums at the policyowner's home by a marketer, and (d) minimum underwriting requirements. Industrial insurance is marketed under the home service system, which relies on marketers to sell specified products and to provide premium collection and other policyowner service functions within a defined geographic territory. Most industrial policies sold are limited-payment, small-amount whole life insurance policies.

Insight 7-4 Underwriting Survivorship Products

Underwriting survivorship products is a time-consuming, difficult process. Experience has shown that because survivorship products are popular in the elderly market, underwriting has to be done in much greater depth than for products attracting a younger consumer. Requesting additional underwriting information can cause processing delays, which may be unacceptable to customers. Moreover, underwriters often experience dramatically increased workloads because they have to underwrite two lives for every application.

Because many applicants are elderly, the primary purpose of survivorship coverage is to provide for estate planning and preservation. Often, applicants request larger-than-average amounts of insurance. Since underwriting requires consideration of the second (or last) person to die, underwriters need to estimate the insurance needed when the second death occurs. Underwriters normally use the life expectancy of the younger insured in projecting the amount allowed for growth of the estate. Typically, underwriters avoid making projections that extend for more than 10 to 15 years and take a conservative approach in estimating future estate growth—usually not more than 5 to 6 percent annually.

For survivorship products, it is no longer reasonable to look at current income and use a multiple-of-income rule to determine the amount of insurance needed. Instead, a projection is made of the estate size in 10 or 15 years, including additional amounts to represent a reasonable rate of growth and the estate taxes due at the second death. To handle the task of making these estimates, underwriters need training in sophisticated tax planning approaches.

Because underwriters and actuaries coordinate their efforts in handling survivorship products, actuaries need to understand the difficulties of underwriting these risks. Similarly, underwriters need to understand how actuaries have priced these products.

Steven B. Teeple, Director of Reinsurance Underwriting, Lincoln National Reinsurance. Excerpted by permission from *Reinsurance Reporter* of the Lincoln National Life Reinsurance Co.

Underwriting standards for industrial life insurance are typically more liberal than for ordinary life insurance because of the small face amount of industrial policies. The role of the marketer in selecting proposed insureds for industrial policy coverage is generally more important for industrial life insurance than for ordinary life insurance.

Insurers usually design applications for industrial life insurance to obtain all the necessary underwriting information, so that the underwriter will not have to gather additional information. Questions on the application typically concern occupation, age, gender, height, and weight. Medical history questions on the application are less detailed and less extensive than those found on applications for ordinary life insurance. Insurers generally do not require medical examinations for industrial life insurance unless the proposed insured's medical history indicates that an examination is needed. Few insurers require an MIB check for industrial life insurance underwriting.

Most industrial insurance underwriting is performed at the clerical level or is performed by a jet unit or by computerized screening because the rate structure for this type of coverage makes little allowance for detailed assessment by an underwriter. Applications that do not meet the criteria for jet unit or computer approval are reviewed by an underwriter. Many applicants who would be rated substandard for ordinary life coverage can qualify for industrial insurance at standard rates.

Underwriting Juvenile Insurance

A ***juvenile insurance policy*** is a life insurance policy purchased by an adult to cover the life of a child. The owner of a juvenile insurance policy is usually the adult. Some jurisdictions limit the amount of coverage that can be issued on a juvenile.

The information sources an underwriter can use to assess a juvenile proposed insured are basically the same as those available for an adult. Some insurers offer a special, nonmedical juvenile application that is similar to an adult nonmedical application and that is completed by the adult applying for coverage on the child's life.

To evaluate an application for juvenile insurance, the underwriter considers many of the same factors that are needed for risk appraisal of an adult's life. These factors include the age, gender, and medical history of the child, as well as the financial status of the applicant. However, the underwriter regards several underwriting factors differently when evaluating an application for juvenile insurance. These factors include the face amount of the insurance and policy ownership.

In evaluating the appropriateness of the face amount requested, the underwriter considers whether other children in the family are similarly insured. If only one child of several is insured, or if one child is being insured for a larger amount of coverage than are the other children, the underwriter investigates the reason for such unusual treatment of one child. The underwriter's approval of the amount and plan of insurance requested on a child is based on the financial situation of the policyowner, rather than on the child's financial situation.

The underwriter also considers who will be the owner and the beneficiary of a juvenile policy. Usually, only parents, grandparents, or legal guardians are considered to have an insurable interest in the life of a child. Therefore, insurers usually require that one of these parties be either the owner or the beneficiary of the policy, or both.

When parents are not the owners of a policy covering a child, most insurers obtain the written consent of the parents and require them to attest to the correctness of responses to medical questions, as grandparents who are purchasing the policy, for example, may live at some distance and may not have knowledge of the child's current state of health. Such parental permission is kept on file with the application or is made a part of the policy in order to record the validity of the transaction. Adopted children are treated the same as natural children once the adoption is final, but usually no coverage is issued until the adoption is final.

A medical examination is seldom required for juvenile insurance, primarily for two reasons: (1) after the first year of life, the mortality rate for children is very low, and (2) most juvenile insurance applications do not involve large sums of money, and therefore do not justify expensive and complex medical examinations. If the information provided on the juvenile application indicates that the child has a health problem, or if the parent or legal guardian cannot complete the nonmedical portion of the application, then the underwriter usually requests an APS, generally from the child's physician. Most insurers approve coverage after a child has been released from a hospital after birth. However, for infants born prematurely, coverage is generally declined, but can be considered as soon as the infant's weight is normal for his age.

Some juvenile policies include a ***waiver of premium for payor benefit.*** This benefit provides that an insurer will waive payment of the policy's premiums if the adult policyowner becomes disabled or dies prior to the insured child's attainment of a specified age, usually 21. When an application requests this benefit, the insurer requires modest evidence of insurability from the payor. Typically, the payor's age, gender, occupation, height and weight, and a brief medical history are sufficient evidence of the payor's insurability. This information is typically provided as part of the regular application for juvenile coverage. A medical examination of the payor is seldom required unless the payor's medical history indicates that an examination is warranted. The waiver of premium for payor benefit is usually issued only if the payor is considered to be a preferred, standard, or slightly substandard risk.

Handling Guaranteed-Issue Products

Not all insurance requires underwriting. Certain products are sold on a guaranteed-issue basis, and no individual underwriting takes place. ***Guaranteed-issue products*** are designed so that each applicant who meets certain conditions established by the insurer is automatically issued a policy. Although most guaranteed-issue products are issued to groups, a few are issued to individuals.

The most common conditions for individual life insurance products sold on a guaranteed-issue basis include the following:

1. Uniform face amount of coverage—the proposed insured cannot select a different face amount;

2. Eligibility requirements, such as limiting coverage only to persons within a certain age range;

3. Enrollment periods or deadlines, such as a specified date by which the enrollment application must be submitted; and

4. Maximums imposed on the face amounts of guaranteed-issue policies issued to one person. These maximum amounts of coverage usually decrease as the age of the insured increases. In most jurisdictions, guaranteed-issue policies cannot be issued to persons over age 85 or 87. Some state regulations forbid selling this type of coverage to persons over age 74.

Direct Response Products

Many individual insurance products sold on a guaranteed-issue basis are sold through the direct response method. ***Direct response products*** are sold to consumers by an insurer without the assistance of a marketer, usually through direct mail, advertising in print and other media, or telephone solicitation. Many guaranteed-issue policies limit the benefit amount payable—often to a return of premiums—if the insured dies from natural causes during a specified period.

Individual life insurance products marketed using direct response methods are usually designed to serve a broad, general market segment, such as those within a certain age range or income range: for example, retired persons over age 65, or people who are between 40 and 60 years old and who are earning over $30,000 a year. Direct response life insurance marketed to people under age 40 is usually underwritten on a nonmedical basis rather than on a guaranteed-issue basis and requires limited underwriting. Direct response insurers have found that this type of coverage is often subject to a high degree of antiselection when offered to individuals who are below age 40.

If offered on a guaranteed-issue basis, most direct response products have no underwriting requirements at all. Few direct response life insurers use substandard rates, and the standard risk class generally includes persons whose anticipated mortality is assessed as high as 150 to 200 percent of standard mortality.

The applicant for guaranteed-issue direct response coverage usually does not have to undergo a medical examination, although the application typically asks several basic medical history questions, such as the following:

- Check each condition you have had or for which you have received medical treatment. (A list follows, containing impairments such as high blood pressure, heart trouble, chest pains, cancer, tumors, convulsions, and diabetes.)
- Within the last five years have you tested positive for the human immunodeficiency virus (HIV) or been told you have acquired immune deficiency syndrome (AIDS)?
- Within the last three years have you consulted a doctor, been hospitalized, or taken prescription medication?

The vast majority of persons solicited for coverage qualify for direct response products solely on the basis of their answers to the questions on the application. If the direct response insurer's underwriter determines that further information is needed, the applicant or the applicant's physician may be asked to complete a medical questionnaire. In difficult cases, medical examinations, inspection reports, or both may also be required.

Underwriting Policy Replacements

In Chapter 3, you learned that replacement involves surrendering an insurance policy or part of the coverage of an insurance policy in order to buy another policy. While replacement of existing life insurance policies is not illegal, it may not be in a policyowner's best interest. Generally, a policyowner who wishes to replace an existing policy with a new policy is allowed to do so on the basis of little or no current evidence of insurability. Such a replacement is usually made possible if the proposed insured's insurability has recently been established—typically within the past five years—by the insurer that issued the original policy.

To be eligible for a replacement, the proposed insured must be covered by a policy that was fully underwritten and that was issued within a certain recent period. A replaced policy is underwritten similarly to a routine term conversion, although a policy replacement allows a change from one insurer's policy to another insurer's policy.

Some insurers accept policy replacements on a guaranteed-issue basis, that is, without requiring evidence of insurability. Other insurers require minimal evidence of insurability, such as the answers to two simple health questions like these:

1. Is the insured now so disabled by sickness or injury that he is unable to perform all the duties of his normal job?

2. During the last five years, has the insured had high blood pressure, heart disease, diabetes, or cancer?

In insurance companies that require some underwriting for policy replacements, underwriters have the options of issuing the policy as requested, issuing the policy with a substandard rating, or declining to issue coverage.

In evaluating applications for policy replacements, the underwriter is essentially concerned with (1) the possibility that antiselection has motivated the request for the replacement, (2) the underwriting standards of the insurer that issued the policy being exchanged, and (3) the possibility of churning or twisting.

Antiselection in Policy Replacements

Particularly for proposed insureds at older ages, the underwriter checks for antiselection in policy replacements. An insured whose health has deteriorated may have an incentive to obtain a new policy at a lower premium and without evidence of insurability. Moreover, a person may wish to replace one policy for another if the new policy offers a comparatively higher interest rate on its cash value.

Underwriting Standards in Policy Replacements

The underwriter also considers the underwriting philosophy and guidelines of the insurer that originally issued the policy because, by making a policy replacement, the replacing insurer is accepting these standards as its own. If the issuing insurer's underwriting philosophy and guidelines are liberal and the replacement insurer's are conservative, the policy proposed for a replacement may not be acceptable as it was originally written. In such a situation, accepting the policy as written may lead to adverse mortality results for the accepting insurer. For this reason, insurers may exclude from their policy replacements all policies originally issued by insurers that specialize in providing coverage for substandard risks.

Possibility of Churning or Twisting

Two undesirable activities that may occur during replacement are churning and twisting. ***Churning*** is an unethical activity by which a marketer induces a policyowner to cash in a policy and buy another, even though the replacement is not in the policyowner's best interest. A marketer engages in churning in order to collect high first-year commissions. Misleading a policyowner concerning replacement or providing an incomplete comparison of the two policies to the disadvantage of the policyowner is an illegal practice known as ***twisting.*** The underwriter has a responsibility to be aware that churning or twisting may be occurring when a marketer does a high volume of replacement business.

1035 Exchanges

An income tax may be assessed when a policyowner surrenders a policy and receives its cash surrender value in a lump sum. Any portion of the cash surrender value that exceeds the cost basis for the policy is considered a gain and is taxable as ordinary income. Usually, the ***cost basis*** of an insurance policy is equal to the total net premiums paid, *plus* accumulated dividends and *minus* certain specified costs. To prevent a tax incident on replacements, many insurers use a ***1035 exchange,*** in which the cash surrender value of a replaced policy is used as the initial premium for a new policy. There is no financial gain to the policyowner on the transaction because the cash surrender value is used to pay a premium. Because there is no gain, no tax is due. The 1035 exchange is named for Section 1035a of the United States Internal Revenue Code.

Generally, a 1035 exchange is underwritten in the same manner as a new business application. Underwriters do, however, usually take two precautions. First, to prevent a gap in coverage, the original policy is not surrendered until the new policy has been approved for issue. Second, if the new policy must be issued with a substandard rating, the underwriter obtains from the applicant a letter stating that the applicant understands that a higher premium will be required if the face amount of the new policy remains the same as that of the original policy.

Underwriting Supplementary Coverages

The insurance protection provided by most life insurance policies may be expanded by supplementary benefit riders. Such riders provide additional benefits and allow existing contracts to be adapted to the needs of insureds without the expense of redrawing the contracts. If a proposed insured requests such supplementary coverage, the request is considered during underwriting. If a person who is already insured asks for supplementary coverage, the request is usually considered first by the insurer's policyowner service staff. When such a request involves only a slight increase in the insurer's risk, approval of the request can be made by policyowner service. If, however, the risk for revising the coverage may cause the insurer to bear a greater degree of risk, the policyowner service staff forwards the request to underwriting for more detailed consideration.

Four important supplementary coverages are waiver of premium for disability, accidental death benefit, family benefit, and guaranteed insurability.

Waiver of Premium for Disability

The ***waiver of premium for disability*** rider in a life insurance policy provides that, in the event an insured is totally disabled as defined in the rider, the insurance company will waive the payment of all premiums that become due during the period of disability. This rider eliminates the possibility of the insured's having to drop the basic life insurance protection when he experiences a loss of income from disability. The premiums waived by the rider are paid by the insurance company.

In underwriting the waiver of premium for disability rider, the underwriter considers such factors as age, avocation, occupation, health, and finances. Because insurance studies and Social Security reports indicate that the risk of disability increases with age, issue of the rider is normally limited to proposed insureds below age 55 or 60.

If an applicant's mortality rating is standard according to health history and physical condition, the rider is usually granted. In some situations, however, even if the policy was issued as standard, the insured's avocation or occupation may present enough of an extra hazard that the insurer may require an extra premium for the rider or may decline to issue the rider.

Underwriting for the waiver of premium for disability rider is generally unaffected by the applicant's financial circumstances. On very large amounts of insurance, however, particularly on high cash value plans, cash values may accumulate fast enough for the policy loan provision to provide the insured with a significant source of income during a disability. Loans on the cash value of the policy could provide the insured with such a large disability income that the insured might have no incentive to terminate a period of disability.

Accidental Death Benefit

The ***accidental death benefit (ADB)*** rider provides an additional death benefit above the face amount of a policy if an insured's death occurs as the result of an accident. This additional amount may be a multiple of the amount of the basic life coverage, or it may be an unrelated amount.

In underwriting ADB coverage, the underwriter usually adheres to the same principles used in underwriting basic life coverage. In certain business insurance cases, the ADB may not be justified. For example, if a business needs $100,000 to fund a buy-sell agreement, the amount is fixed and specific. The business has no reason to receive double that amount simply because the insured's death is accidental. However, individual insurance needs—as well as some business insurance needs, such as key-person coverage—are not fixed and specific, and are not as easily measured. Accidental death coverage may be an appropriate supplement to life insurance to cover an increase in the beneficiary's economic loss that results from an accidental death.

Age is the most important factor considered in underwriting the ADB rider. Most ADB riders expire when the insured reaches age 65 or 70, and insurers rarely issue ADB riders to persons over age 55 or 60. One reason for these restrictions is that accidents are more likely to happen to older persons.

Rather than trying to assess each case individually, most insurers specify that the ADB rider may be issued at standard rates to low substandard life risks, such as those rated to 200 percent mortality, but will be denied to those rated higher than 200 percent. The ADB is usually not available to applicants rated for substance abuse, particularly alcohol abuse.

Persons with certain hazardous occupations or avocations may be charged an extra premium for ADB coverage or may be denied the rider. For aviation risks, for example, most insurers exclude coverage for death resulting from an aviation accident if the insured had duties aboard the airplane.

The underwriter decides how much coverage can be included in the ADB approved for a case. The amount usually depends on the amount of life insurance in force, the amount of coverage requested, and the beneficiary designation. The underwriter also examines the appropriateness of the designated beneficiary.

Family Benefit

The ***family benefit*** rider insures the lives of an insured's spouse and children. The amount of underwriting necessary for the family benefit is limited.

To underwrite the family benefit rider, the underwriter requires insurability information for all family members, but usually the basic information on the application fills this need. A spouse and children, including those with slight impairments, are generally accepted as standard risks if the mortality rating of each family member is no higher than 200 percent. Higher mortality risks are usually declined.

Some insurers establish age requirements for family benefit riders. For example, an insurer may require that a spouse be at least 17 years old and no more than 10 to 15 years younger than the insured. The insurer may also establish an upper age limit for a spouse. To be accepted for coverage, children typically must be under 18 years of age at the time of issue. Furthermore, unless a child is handicapped and a dependent, coverage on the child ends when the child reaches age 21 or 25.

Guaranteed Insurability

A policy rider for ***guaranteed insurability (GI)*** gives a policyowner the right to buy additional insurance up to a specified amount at a specified premium rate and at specified times without providing new evidence of insurability. If the policyowner does not exercise the option under the GI rider to buy additional insurance at the time specified, that opportunity is lost; the policyowner cannot purchase the amount of insurance available under those circumstances at a subsequent option date. The purpose of the requirement to exercise options promptly is to avoid antiselection.

If the GI rider is not included in the basic policy when the policy is issued, the rider usually may be added up to 60 days after issue. The underwriter's main concern is to determine the probability of a change in insurability during the 60-day post-issue period. Some insurers allow an insured to add the GI rider more than 60 days after issue by presenting evidence of insurability.

An important underwriting factor for the GI rider is age. Usually, the maximum age for issue of the GI rider is 40 or 45. Aside from the age factor, the risk selection factors involved in underwriting the GI rider are typically the same as those considered in underwriting the basic policy. The additional coverage provided by the GI rider has the same risk class rating as the policy.

Key Terms and Concepts

business insurance
business financial supplement
solvency
debt-to-equity ratio
liquidity
current assets
current liabilities
current ratio
quick ratio (*acid-test ratio*)
profitability
return on equity
net income
stockholders' equity
creditor insurance
partnership insurance
stock repurchase insurance (*stock redemption insurance*)
sole proprietorship insurance
key person
key-person insurance
split-dollar plan
joint-and-last-survivor policy
first-to-die policy
second-to-die policy (*survivorship policy*)
industrial insurance
juvenile insurance policy
waiver of premium for payor benefit
guaranteed-issue products
direct response products
churning
twisting
cost basis
1035 exchange
waiver of premium for disability
accidental death benefit (ADB)
family benefit
guaranteed insurability (GI)

CHAPTER EIGHT

Underwriting Individual Health Insurance

Learning Objectives

After studying this chapter, you should be able to

- Describe the type of information a health insurance underwriter obtains from various documents
- List five ways an underwriter may modify medical coverage for a substandard risk
- Explain the function of impairment riders
- Discuss the importance of insurable interest, antiselection, health history, and other factors in underwriting health insurance coverages
- List and explain the four elements with which the individual disability income coverage underwriter is primarily concerned
- Distinguish between an impairment guide and a long-term care field underwriting manual
- Discuss the differences between the tools used for underwriting long-term care insurance and those used for underwriting other types of health insurance

Chapter Outline

Information Sources for Health Underwriting
Insurance Application and Agent's Statement
Medical Examination and APS
Inspection Report
Specialized Questionnaires

Underwriting Substandard Risks
Higher Premium Rate
Modifications and Exclusions

Underwriting Individual Medical Expense Insurance
Insurable Interest
Antiselection
Health History
Other Factors

Underwriting Individual Disability Income Insurance
Moral Hazard
Health
Occupation
Finances and Portion of Income Insured

Underwriting Long-Term Care Coverage
Considerations about Aging
Antiselection
Field Underwriting
Tools for LTC Underwriting

By this point in your study of insurance administration, you've looked at many aspects of underwriting individual life coverages, including the medical, personal, and financial considerations involved in assessing the risk presented by a proposed insured. Now we'll examine the underwriting issues connected with individual health coverages.

In some insurance companies, an underwriter reviews applications not only for individual life insurance, but for individual health insurance as well. As you have learned, underwriting for life coverages concerns *mortality,* which is the relative incidence of death occurring among a given group of people. Underwriting for health insurance, sometimes called accident insurance, involves *morbidity,* the relative incidence of sickness and injury occurring among a given group of people.

Although health underwriters emphasize morbidity in risk assessment, they also look at any indication of increased risk of mortality as a result of an impairment. For instance, a proposed insured is considered obese when the body weight is more than 30 percent higher than the weight established as normal for that person's height and gender. Most insurance companies would not issue health insurance at standard rates to such a person, and nearly all insurers would decline to issue disability income coverage, because obese people are statistically more likely to have higher morbidity and mortality rates than are people of average weight.

Health insurance underwriters need to learn a great deal of medical terminology and information, including the treatments for a wide variety of medical conditions. In addition, health underwriters continually expand their knowledge as medical information changes and increases. Discovery of new medical conditions and knowledge of medical advances enable health underwriters to recognize and assess new types of impairments and to understand new means of treatment.

In this chapter, we'll first look at the information sources that health underwriters use most frequently. After examining the underwriting considerations for substandard health risks, we'll discuss underwriting of several types of individual health insurance, including the following:

- Medical expense insurance, which pays benefits for treatment of sickness or injury
- Disability income (DI) insurance, which helps replace income lost as a result of sickness or injury
- Long-term care (LTC) coverage, which pays for nursing home confinement or home health care

Information Sources for Health Underwriting

In assessing risks, the health underwriter uses the same kinds of tools that the life underwriter uses. To evaluate the risk represented by a person proposed for health coverage, the health underwriter can consider the insurance application (including the agent's statement), the results of a medical examination (if one is required), an APS, an inspection report, and specialized questionnaires. Some insurers also require a blood profile and urinalysis from adults applying for medical expense coverage. These tests provide information that may not have been included on an APS, including HIV test results and details concerning cholesterol and triglyceride levels, liver function, and a nicotine and drug screen. Just as for life underwriting, the health underwriter considers the cost involved in relation to the underwriting benefit in seeking additional information about a proposed insured.

Insurance Application and Agent's Statement

The questions on an individual health insurance application typically place more emphasis on the proposed insured's occupational duties and income than do the questions on a life insurance application. Disability income applications, in particular, request extensive information on the applicant's occupation and income. Other information requested on a health insurance application is similar to that requested for life insurance coverages.

The agent's statement can be very useful to the health underwriter. A marketer usually has an opportunity to observe a proposed insured and may have personal knowledge of that person's health history and possible impairments. For instance, a marketer may notice that a proposed insured moves with difficulty from one chair to another or has trouble communicating verbally. Such observations could enable the marketer to alert the underwriter so that assessing the risk for this person is done cautiously and the person's medical history, in particular, is investigated fully. In communicating this type of information to the underwriter, the marketer plays a key role in helping ensure that an insurance company evaluates each risk appropriately. Insight 8-1 discusses responses to some marketers' views of the agent's statement.

Compared to information withheld on a life insurance application, information that a proposed insured or a marketer withholds on a health insurance application may be more important with respect to the possibility that an insured may file an early claim. The underwriter, therefore, checks all apparently omitted information or unanswered questions. If an application has been initiated by a proposed insured rather than by a marketer, the health underwriter scrutinizes the application with special care in order to guard against antiselection.

Insight 8-1 My Thoughts On . . . The Agent's Statement

Although most marketers don't seem to mind completing an agent's statement to accompany an application, some marketers doubt the usefulness of this document. "Why should I bother completing an agent's statement?" some of them say. "I wonder if anyone ever reads it. Besides, it generally isn't made a part of the policy, and it usually is not even a real part of the application!"

These comments are sometimes valid. But consider also the old truism, "You can't give an underwriter too much information." With that thought in mind, we can start to realize the value of an agent's statement during the underwriting process for any type of coverage.

For example, does the agent's statement indicate that the marketer has ordered the paramedical examination, the urine specimen, the blood profile, and other requirements? If so, the underwriter receives a positive impression of the marketer as an experienced professional.

Does the agent's statement specify when, at which provider, and at what phone number the order for requirements was placed? If so, the underwriter can make an intelligent estimate of the length of time before the requirements arrive and will know when to begin followup procedures if any are needed.

An agent may balk at reporting how long she has known the client. But consider that there are many people with very similar names and dates of birth. The fact that a marketer has known a client for a considerable period will help clarify any confusion of identity.

Similarly, an agent may not wish to report a client's income level. Yet this information is very helpful during underwriting to ensure that the person who is purchasing the insurance is able to pay the premiums and, therefore, continue to receive coverage.

In my view, marketers are "a different breed of cat." They are among the best salespeople in the world. They sell an intangible product—a piece of paper with a promise to pay "if." That "if" is very often a topic, such as death or disability, which most people would rather not discuss. So the job of the marketer is essential, and yet can be very difficult. If a policy is not issued, no promise can be kept, and no service can be performed.

Sometimes, completing the agent's statement makes the difference between the application being moved rapidly through the insurer's underwriting and policy issue procedures, or being scuttled into a sea of unanswered questions.

John H. Jones, Jr., FLMI, AALU, CLU, ChFC
Chief Underwriter
Standard Life & Accident Insurance Company

Most insurance companies instruct their marketers to obtain a detailed health history through careful questioning of each applicant. To assist marketers in advising proposed insureds and in gathering complete information, most insurers provide marketers with an ***impairment guide,*** which is a list of common impairments and the probable underwriting decision for each. By using the impairment guide, a marketer can inform a proposed insured about coverage types and amounts for which that person is most likely to be approved.

For example, if a marketer is completing a health insurance application for a proposed insured who earlier has suffered an attack of appendicitis, the impairment guide notes that if the appendicitis was not medically resolved, the probable underwriting decision will be to add an impairment rider to the policy (we'll explain impairment riders later in this chapter). If at least one month has passed since successful, uncomplicated surgery for appendicitis (and if the proposed insured has no other significant impairments), the application will probably be considered a standard risk. Figure 8-1 presents sample entries in one insurer's impairment guide.

For each impairment that a proposed insured acknowledges on the insurance application, insurers generally instruct marketers to furnish the following information for coverage that does not require a medical examination:

- Precise medical term for an impairment
- Date and duration of each attack or episode
- If a chronic or recurrent condition, the date of the first attack, frequency of episodes, and date of most recent attack
- Aftereffects and complications, if any
- Nature of treatment or medication, and date of last such treatment or medication
- Names and addresses of physicians seen, dates of visits, and sequence in which physicians were consulted
- If hospitalization occurred, dates of hospitalization, length of hospital stay, and name and location of hospital

This information is usually included in the agent's statement or in a letter attached to the application.

Medical Examination and APS

Fast Fact

As of 1995, nearly 3,000 different prescription drugs were on the market.

Source: *Underwriter Alert,* February/March 1995: 1.

Medical or paramedical examinations are less frequently required for health insurance than for life insurance. Generally, the health underwriter relies more on the information contained in the application and other documents rather than on information revealed by a medical examination. However, if the underwriter notices that an applicant for health coverage has undergone recent treatment for a serious impairment, or if the underwriter is otherwise alerted to a significant medical condition, the underwriter usually orders an APS from each of the applicant's doctors who diagnosed or treated the impairment or condition. The underwriter may require a medical examination of an applicant for disability income coverage, as we'll explain later in this chapter.

Some insurers require a blood profile and a urinalysis if these tests are not covered by an APS. These tests are usually mandatory on applications for disability income coverage.

Figure 8-1. Entries in one insurer's impairment guide.

Appendicitis Impairment	
Health	Unoperated—impairment rider Operated within one month—decline One month after successful, uncomplicated operation—probably standard
Life	Usually standard
Asthma	
Health	Mild, occasional—usually standard Moderate to severe—rate to decline
Life	Mild, occasional—usually standard Moderate to severe—rate to decline
Burns	
Health	If no impaired function—standard If possible future plastic surgery—impairment rider
Life	Usually standard
Concussion of Brain	
Health	Standard to decline after recovery depending on severity
Life	Recovered, no remaining signs—standard
Diabetes	
Health	Mild—individual consideration Others—decline
Life	Standard to decline depending on age, duration, and other medical factors
Epilepsy	
Health	Individual consideration
Life	Depends on history—rate to decline Some types standard after five years
Fractures	
Health	According to location, severity, complications, and recovery—standard, impairment rider, or both
Life	After recovery—standard

Inspection Report

Health underwriters generally order inspection reports more frequently than life underwriters order such reports. Particularly for disability coverages, a health underwriter needs to know much more about an applicant's occupation and finances than a life underwriter needs to know to assess the risk for life insurance. The results of an inspection report can verify financial information submitted on the application.

Specialized Questionnaires

Health underwriters use specialized questionnaires or supplements more often than do their life insurance counterparts. Most insurers use similar kinds of specialized questionnaires covering specific physical disorders and diseases, as we have discussed in the chapters on underwriting life insurance. Some insurers also use comprehensive general health questionnaires similar to the one shown in Figure 8-2. A ***comprehensive general health questionnaire*** seeks information on an applicant's total health condition rather than focusing on a specific disorder or disease.

Underwriting Substandard Risks

Information used for underwriting health applications is found in each insurer's health underwriting manual. Typically, the manual includes a number of impairments similar to those found in a life underwriting manual. The assigned ratings are usually classified as: (1) monthly indemnity, representing the product line of disability policies, and (2) medical expense, representing the product line of medical expense reimbursement policies. Ratings for each of these types of coverage may differ.

Like a life underwriter, a health underwriter can accept, rate, or decline an application according to the degree of risk the applicant presents to the insurance company. If a proposed insured represents a risk greater than that acceptable as a standard risk, and if the risk is not so great that the underwriter must decline the application, the underwriter can rate the application and accept the risk with a rated policy. A ***rated policy*** is a policy issued to a person considered to have a greater-than-average risk of loss. A rated policy may be issued with (1) a premium rate higher than the rate for a policy issued to a person with an average or less-than-average risk of loss, (2) modifications and exclusions, or (3) any combination of a higher premium rate, modifications, and exclusions.

Higher Premium Rate

A health underwriter evaluates the risk represented by a proposed insured by using a numerical rating system based on standard morbidity. The standard premium for health coverage is usually based on 100 percent of standard morbidity. The health underwriter indicates degrees of extra risk as debits, which are converted to rating percentages. After assigning debits to a proposed insured, the underwriter next uses a ***rating schedule,*** which is a table that enables the underwriter to convert

Figure 8-2. Comprehensive general health questionnaire.

Use this space to amplify and extend answers to questions in your application dated ____________

Question No. Additional Answers

CONCERNING THE: ____________
(Injury, illness or infirmity about which details are required)

OF: ____________
(Name of proposed covered person involved)

1. What are or were the symptoms?
2. What did the attending physician call the condition (diagnosis)?
3. When did this condition begin? How long did or do attacks last?
4. How frequent are or were the attacks (weekly, monthly, once a year, etc.)?
5. How severe are or were the attacks (very painful, totally or partially disabling, mild discomfort, required hospital care, etc.)?
6. Give dates and durations of any periods of disability (loss of work time or confinement to home).
7. When was the last attack, or the date you last had symptoms? Are there any symptoms of this condition at present?
8. Description of treatment and/or medication.
9. Names and addresses of all medical practitioners consulted for this condition.
10. Names and addresses of all hospitals, clinics, or sanitariums in which confined. Give dates of confinements.

I represent that the answers as amplified and extended above are true and complete to the best of my knowledge and are a part of my application to THE ABC LIFE INSURANCE COMPANY.

Signed at ____________ X ____________
Signature of proposed insured

Date ____________

Agent-Witness ____________ ____________
Signature of applicant, if other than proposed insured

IMPORTANT

The attached authorization should be signed by the proposed insured if there is any history of medical treatment, consultant or examination of any proposed covered person. It should also be signed by the spouse of the proposed Insured if such history refers to the spouse.

To any physician who has treated me, my spouse, or any of my children, or any hospital where I, my spouse, or any of my children has been confined.

In connection with an application to The ABC Life Insurance Company, please answer any inquiries that the company may make of you regarding the past or present condition of my health and that of any of my children. Please answer any similar inquiries with respect to my spouse if the signature of my spouse appears below. Your cooperation will be greatly appreciated by me. A photographic copy of this authorization shall be deemed as effective and valid as the original.

Date ____________

Witness ____________ X ____________ X ____________
Signature of proposed Insured — Signature of spouse of proposed Insured

the total of rating debits to a rating percentage. Each insurer develops its own rating schedule. The rating percentage from the rating schedule is added to the percentage (100) that represents the standard risk for which a standard premium is charged. To calculate the premium to be charged for the coverage, the underwriter multiplies the standard premium by the total of the standard percentage *plus* the rating percentage. A typical rating schedule is shown below.

Rating Debits	Rating Percentage
0–5	Standard (=100)
10–15	10
20–35	25
40–60	50
65–85	75
90–110	100
115–135	125
140–165	150
170–185	175
190–220	200
220 and up	Declined

For example, a proposed insured who has 30 rating debits may be assigned a rating percentage of 25. This proposed insured will be charged a premium that is 125 percent of standard premium (a percentage of 100 for standard premium plus a percentage of 25 for the rating). Thus, if the standard premium for the coverage for which this proposed insured is applying is $300.00 a year, the premium this proposed insured will be charged for the coverage is $375.00 ($300.00 × 1.25).

When a proposed insured has more than one ratable impairment and when no other instructions are given in the health underwriting manual, the health underwriter usually sums the debits. Particularly for certain impairments occurring together, however, the risk is higher than the sum of the debits—for instance, diabetes occurring with hypertension, and diabetes with overweight. Other combinations of impairments may not represent an increased risk. If the sum of debits appears to overstate the risk anticipated, the underwriter may decide that only a portion of the debits for the second or third impairment is appropriate for the total risk presented. For some proposed insureds, such as those with pre-existing conditions or continuing impairments, the underwriter may assign a rating for one impairment and an impairment rider for each subsequent impairment. A ***preexisting condition*** is a condition for which an individual received medical care during a specified period of time prior to the effective date of the proposed coverage.

Certain medical impairments may also work in combination with nonmedical factors such as occupation or avocation to increase risk significantly—for example, an applicant who has a preexisting respiratory disease and whose occupation exposes him to dust or smoke, or a cosmetologist who is sensitive to certain chemical solutions used in performing her occupational duties. The underwriter takes such combinations of medical and nonmedical factors into consideration in reaching an equitable rating.

If a proposed insured is assessed as having a rating above +50, which represents a 50 percent greater morbidity than standard, most insurers do not offer a benefit period beyond five years. At progressively higher ratings, insurers typically reduce the length of the benefit period and the amount of benefits. An insurer may charge extra premiums for only a certain length of time—for example, in a case in which an impairment is not expected to be permanent—or for the entire period for which coverage is being purchased.

Insurers typically use percentage ratings for impairments that increase the risk as the age of the proposed insured increases. For impairments for which the extra risk does not increase with age, insurers generally use ***flat rating,*** which is a rating method used for impairments that present an accident hazard but no additional health hazard. Flat rating is typically used for such conditions as a loss of a limb, such as an arm or a leg, as a result of an accident, not disease.

Modifications and Exclusions

Like life underwriters, health underwriters can also modify the coverage originally requested so that the applicant becomes insurable on some basis. The health coverage issued to an extra risk applicant can be modified using one or more of the following techniques:

1. Reduce the policy's benefit-paying period—for example, from two years to one year.

2. Reduce the benefit amount.

3. Increase the deductible amount.

4. Increase the ***waiting period,*** which is the period of time that must pass before benefits are payable to an insured. For medical expense coverage, the waiting period is a specified length of time, counted from the date of policy issue, during which the insured's medical expenses are not covered. Increasing a waiting period of 30 days to 60 days has the effect of reducing the insurer's risk on a substandard policy. For disability income coverage, the waiting period (also called the *elimination period*) is a specified length of time, beginning with the onset of a disability, during which benefits are not payable. Often, an insurer increases the waiting

period for only the impaired problem, while retaining the usual waiting period for other claims.

5. Attach an impairment rider (defined below) to the contract excluding coverage for an identified, prior health impairment. When a medical or an actuarial basis justifies the exclusion rider, an insurer has the right to use the rider for a condition not manifested but indicated as being strongly possible in the future. Suppose that a proposed insured with a family history of breast cancer has no identified breast cancer, but has developed fibrocystic disease, certain forms of which are associated with a higher risk of breast cancer. In this circumstance, the underwriter typically requires a waiver of coverage for diseases of the breasts because the proposed insured currently has a condition that can increase risk. If the proposed insured in this situation had applied for guaranteed renewable or noncancellable coverage, the application would most likely not be approved.

An ***impairment rider,*** also known as an *impairment waiver* or an *exclusion rider,* is an attachment to a policy to exclude from coverage (1) a loss arising from a specified disease or physical impairment or (2) a specific body part. An impairment rider may be used with a health policy if an applicant's health history presents the possibility of the recurrence of a disabling illness, or if the applicant has a chronic condition for which future treatment seems likely.

An impairment rider excludes from coverage a medical condition, a disease or disorder of a specified body part, or both. The impairment rider is worded in simple, straightforward terms so that a proposed insured may understand what condition is being excluded from coverage. The insurer's medical director and legal area can help an underwriter to word a rider to suit the circumstances of a specific case. A sample impairment rider that specifies the limits of coverage is shown in Figure 8-3.

To save the underwriter time in completing an impairment rider, most underwriting manuals provide the wording for a large number of conditions that might warrant the use of an impairment rider. Samples of such wording for medical conditions are shown in Figure 8-4.

Fast Fact

The first medical expense coverage for nonfatal injuries was offered in 1850 by The Accidental Death Association of London. Later that year, the Franklin Health Assurance Company of Massachusetts offered similar coverage for the first time in the United States.

Source: Health Insurance Association of America *Source Book of Health Insurance Data,* 1995: 1.

Underwriting Individual Medical Expense Insurance

The elements of insurable interest, antiselection, and health history are important in underwriting health coverages, and they are often

Figure 8-3. Impairment rider.

This Agreement is attached to and made a part of Policy No. ______________________________

issued to ____

In consideration of the issuance of said Policy, it is hereby understood and agreed that the insurance thereunder shall not cover nor shall any indemnity be payable for ______________

____

____

____

anything in said Policy to the contrary notwithstanding.

______________________	______________________
Witness	Insured

considered in different ways than they are for underwriting life insurance. We'll first discuss these elements and then examine a number of other factors. We will look at the primary elements that an underwriter assesses for individual medical expense insurance, and we will comment on disability income coverage where appropriate. In subsequent sections, we'll look at additional elements an underwriter evaluates for disability income coverage and for long-term care insurance.

Figure 8-4. Examples of wording for standardized impairment riders.

Condition Involved	Suggested Rider Wording
Cataract	Cataract or disease of, or partial or complete loss of sight of, one or both eyes, a complication thereof, treatment or operation therefor.
Conjunctivitis	Conjunctivitis or an infection or allergic disease of the conjunctivae, including complications thereof.
Phlebitis	Phlebitis, varicose veins, thrombosis, a complication thereof, treatment or operation therefor.
Raynaud's disease	Raynaud's disease or other peripheral vascular disease, a complication thereof, treatment or operation therefor.
Rheumatic fever	Rheumatic fever including a complication or residual effects thereof, treatment or operation therefor.
Varicose veins	Varicose veins, varicose ulcers, a complication thereof, treatment or operation therefor.

Insurable Interest

The health insurance underwriter does not have to establish insurable interest to the extent that the life underwriter does. For health insurance, the requirement for insurable interest is met if the applicant can demonstrate a risk of economic loss if the proposed insured requires medical care or becomes disabled. When an applicant seeks health insurance on family members, the underwriter establishes the relationship of each of those family members to the proposed insured.

Applicant relationships to a proposed insured that require an underwriter to check with the marketer include cousins, in-laws, grandparents, aunts and uncles, and common-law spouses. Most insurers require a marketer to certify that a couple living as common-law spouses have maintained the relationship for a specified period of time, usually two years or longer, before coverage can be issued.

Antiselection

Some people may seek to purchase individual health insurance to provide benefits for a health problem already known to them but not disclosed on the application. The health policies issued by most insurers guard against this type of antiselection by including a ***preexisting conditions clause,*** which states that, until coverage has been in force for a specified time—typically two years—no benefit is payable if the impairment producing the claim (1) existed prior to the issue date and (2) was not disclosed on the application.

If an applicant does not disclose a preexisting condition in the application and the insured makes a claim for medical expenses arising from that condition during the first two years that the policy is in force, the insurer will not pay benefits for that claim. On the other hand, if an applicant does disclose a preexisting condition in the application, an insurer will pay benefits for medical expenses arising from that condition at any time the policy is in force, *unless* the policy contains a waiver that specifically excludes from coverage that condition or an injury resulting from it.

Benefits for certain impairments, such as chronic depression and nervous conditions, are typically excluded by an impairment rider; some insurers, however, do not issue health insurance contracts to applicants with these or other serious impairments. An impairment rider typically does not exclude benefits for impairments that are considered temporary. For instance, if a proposed insured has sprained her knee a month before applying for coverage, but has no previous history of knee problems, most insurers would issue health insurance coverage without excluding knee problems.

Health History

When underwriting a health insurance application, the underwriter pays particularly close attention to the proposed insured's health history. Certain impairments warrant in-depth scrutiny. The health underwriter focuses especially on impairments associated with two types of concerns: (1) future medical treatment or disability, and (2) probable accidents.

A given impairment may have serious effects on the health of one proposed insured, but little or no effect on the health of another proposed insured. For one proposed insured, an impairment may increase the likelihood of future claims. For another proposed insured, the same type of impairment may be mild and have no relevant effect on that person's risk. The health underwriter is responsible for assessing the probable impact of each medical impairment and combination of impairments on the health of a proposed insured.

Future medical treatment or disability. An applicant's health is a major factor in underwriting both life and health insurance, but health underwriters pay special attention to certain health histories that life underwriters would consider insignificant. Certain impairments that are not typically considered life-threatening and thus not particularly important in life underwriting are of considerable significance in health underwriting because those impairments have been shown statistically to result in higher-than-average health claims. Such conditions as obesity, arthritis, back injuries, spinal curvature, asthma, certain kidney impairments, and mild neuroses are examples.

Probable accidents. Health underwriters also give consideration to medical conditions that may present a higher-than-average probability of accidents. Some impairments, such as epilepsy, vertigo, narcolepsy, numbness in hands and feet (neuropathy), paralysis, and impaired eyesight and hearing are often associated with accidents and are examined thoroughly in health underwriting.

In addition to looking at the probable effects of impairments, the health underwriter also examines all information relating to health conditions that have been diagnosed or treated recently. Some conditions, especially certain types of cancer, are considered more serious when they have been recently discovered or treated. If, however, such a condition has been stable for a number of years as specified in an insurer's underwriting manual, the underwriter may not consider the condition as having a significant potential effect on the future health of the proposed insured. Even a history of acute illness, such as pneumonia, may not be significant in health underwriting if the proposed insured has recovered fully.

A health underwriter may be able to accept some proposed insureds for coverage after a period of time following treatment for an impairment. Moreover, a health underwriter does not consider each impairment in isolation, but tries to obtain a clear understanding of the possible connections between various impairments and their combined effect on the proposed insured's health.

The health underwriter looks especially at the cause of each impairment. A proposed insured who has been treated for gangrene (tissue death), for instance, may have suffered the effects of an isolated incident of exposure to extreme cold; in such a case, this impairment would probably not represent a high risk to the insurer. In contrast, gangrene associated with diabetes or certain other disorders may have significant morbidity implications and is, therefore, considered with extreme caution.

Finally, the health underwriter pays special attention to factors in the life of a proposed insured that may decrease or increase the probable effect of an impairment on the person's health. For example, a proposed insured who has been diagnosed with mild to moderate asthma and who also smokes or whose lung function studies are abnormal between attacks is underwritten more cautiously than one who has asthma but does not smoke.

Other Factors

In addition to the elements above, the health underwriter considers a number of other factors, including the proposed insured's finances, existing health coverage, occupation, avocations, substance abuse, military status, driving history, foreign travel or residence, and foreign citizenship.

Finances. Most insurers that issue health coverage require that a proposed insured have a certain level of annual income to qualify for certain types of insurance. For example, one insurer requires an applicant to show an annual income of at least $7,500 to be eligible for a specific type of accident coverage, and an income of at least $15,000 to be eligible for a specific type of accident plus disability income coverage. Each insurer establishes its own eligibility requirements.

Existing health coverage. To ensure that an applicant is not overinsured, the underwriter checks the application to determine the amount and type of health insurance that the proposed insured already has in force. Verifying this information enables the underwriter to prevent duplication of coverage.

Occupation. Occupation is a major concern to the health underwriter because it plays an important role in an insurer's assumptions about morbidity. A proposed insured's occupation is of much more significance in health underwriting than in life underwriting. The health underwriter is especially concerned about occupations that produce higher-than-normal accident rates and health hazards.

Insurance companies categorize occupations according to the type and degree of peril each occupation represents. Accident perils include exposure to dangerous machinery and to the dangers of falling, fire, and the handling of heavy objects. Illness perils include exposure to dust, poisons, dampness, extreme temperatures, air pressure, and other elements. The degree to which these perils are likely to affect the health of a proposed insured determines the underwriting action to be taken.

In deciding the proper occupational classification for a proposed insured, the underwriter typically considers the job duties performed rather than the job title. The degree of risk presented by a specific occupation is determined on the basis of the most hazardous duty performed and the proportion of work time spent performing that duty.

Fast Fact

About 3 million people go scuba diving in the United States each year; 70 percent of the scuba accidents reported involve people who are 20 to 39 years of age, and 92 percent of the people who are injured in scuba accidents were in good health before their accidents.

Source: Wally Taylor, "Mortality Risks of the Recreational Scuba Diver," *On the Risk,* April–June 1996: 99–102.

Avocations. The avocation risks to which many persons are occasionally exposed are generally acceptable for health underwriting purposes. However, if a proposed insured participates more frequently than average in some avocations—for example, scuba diving, mountain climbing, and horse racing—the underwriter usually adds an impairment rider to the policy.

Substance abuse. Health or disability income insurance applicants who have a record of substance abuse, including drugs and alcohol, are investigated thoroughly. If a proposed insured has been free of substance abuse for a considerable period of time—usually a minimum of five years—and has undergone treatment for substance abuse, most insurers issue a rated policy. Abuse of alcohol or drugs within the past five years, however, typically results in an underwriting decision to decline coverage. The underwriter who finds evidence of past substance abuse obtains specific tests, including a drug screen and blood profile, to check for current use.

Military status. The military usually provides medical expense coverage for persons who are in service. Insurance companies, therefore, typically do not grant coverage to persons currently serving in the military. Some insurers, however, issue hospital indemnity coverage to such persons. If an insured person enters the military after a policy has been issued, many insurers suspend the insured's coverage for the duration of military service and resume the coverage when the insured leaves the military.

A program that provides supplementary health insurance in the United States for retired military persons and their dependents is the Civilian Health and Medical Program of the Uniformed Services, or CHAMPUS. Under this system, the federal government shares with military families the cost of health care provided by civilian hospitals and doctors. Persons insured under CHAMPUS pay premiums to government administrators, who in turn pay civilian health care providers to deliver health care.

Some insurance companies offer supplementary insurance that assists with payment for medical expenses that CHAMPUS does not cover completely. This supplementary coverage includes some hospital, medical, and surgical services. Most applications for CHAMPUS supplementary policies are underwritten on a nonmedical basis.

Driving history. If an applicant has a poor driving record, as shown by numerous arrests or accidents, most insurers severely limit benefits or decline coverage. The underwriter pays special attention to any indication that a proposed insured has a record of driving under the influence (DUI) of alcohol or other substances.

Foreign travel or residence. Foreign travel and foreign residence mainly present problems of claims administration. In handling applications involving foreign travel or residence, health underwriters generally follow the principles of life insurance underwriting, paying particular attention to the prevalence of diseases peculiar to a given area. For large-amount cases, most insurers require an inspection report that focuses on the location and frequency of the proposed insured's travel or duration of residence. Some insurers also require that a proposed insured who is a U.S. citizen and who travels in foreign countries spend at least nine months of each year in the United States, or, if the proposed insured is Canadian, in Canada.

Foreign citizenship. Most insurers in the United States require proposed insureds who have foreign citizenship to (1) reside in the United States for two years before applying for health insurance, (2) supply a copy of a visa or green card, (3) provide the name of a medical practitioner in the United States who can supply adequate medical records, and (4) show intent to remain in the United States.

Underwriting Individual Disability Income Insurance

Disability income (DI) insurance coverage presents somewhat different underwriting considerations from those presented by other types of health insurance coverages. DI coverage is intended to replace a certain portion of income that is lost during a period of disability. The DI benefit is always less than the amount an applicant receives from earned income because the DI payment is not intended to replace income completely. Full income replacement might discourage a recipient from returning to work. Rather, the purpose of DI coverage is to provide a percentage of the insured's former income during a period of disability so that the disability will not cause the insured to become destitute. The underwriter of DI coverage is primarily concerned with four elements: moral hazard, health, occupation, and finances and the portion of income insured.

Moral Hazard

For DI coverage, moral hazard is the most important underwriting element. A proposed insured who (1) intentionally includes erroneous information or withholds information on the application, (2) attempts to buy excessive amounts of DI, or (3) is otherwise unethical may present moral hazard and is investigated with extreme care.

Although the DI policy contract contains a provision defining "disability," the underwriter may have difficulty in determining (1) whether a specific illness or injury would constitute a disability and (2) what the duration of such a disability would be. In some cases, an insured person might file a claim and exaggerate the extent or duration of a disability. The insurance company is vulnerable, therefore, to antiselection by proposed insureds who later use the DI coverage for purposes for which it was not designed and priced. The potential for antiselection for DI coverage is, indeed, greater than that for life insurance and for other types of health coverage.

The underwriter determines as clearly as possible that each applicant is free of any indication of moral hazard. Being sure that the amount of DI coverage is appropriate for each proposed insured helps the underwriter reduce the possibility that the request for a DI policy may produce antiselection.

Health

Generally, more health conditions result in disability than result in death. DI coverage is usually not approved if the proposed insured has a physical condition that might make it difficult to determine whether a disability is present in the event that a claim is made. Back trouble and nervous system problems are examples of conditions that usually are not approved for DI coverage.

In assessing risk for DI insurance, underwriters typically order far more reports, including medical records, blood profile, urinalysis, and inspection reports, than do underwriters for life coverage. If a proposed insured for life coverage mentions in a questionnaire that she has a medical history of back sprains, for example, most life underwriters will not investigate further because back sprains do not usually result in death. A DI underwriter, however, typically investigates such a report because a history of back sprains is closely associated with disability.

Occupation

The DI underwriter considers occupation in more detail than the life underwriter does. The DI underwriter especially assesses the likelihood that a proposed insured may become disabled because of his occupation. To be considered an acceptable risk, an applicant for DI coverage should have a favorable employment record in a nonhazardous occupation.

Applicants whose work environment presents potential hazards of diseases or accidents, or whose employment is seasonal or otherwise irregular, are generally viewed as undesirable risks. In addition, persons who work from their homes are sometimes considered questionable risks because determining if they are continuing to work or if they have returned to work may be difficult. In certain occupations, a self-employed person who works from home and who has no considerable net worth or other means of support is also considered a poor risk for DI coverage because the person may have little incentive to return to work. An applicant who is likely to be out of work is thoroughly investigated because a person who is having difficulty finding employment may be more likely to develop or prolong a disability.

In addition, the duties or job requirements of the proposed insured play a part in the anticipated duration of a disability and, thus, in the underwriting decision. Insurance industry statistics show, for instance, that a white-collar worker who has suffered a heart attack is more likely to return to work sooner than a blue-collar worker. Similarly, a relatively minor injury such as a broken wrist could prove incapacitating to a dentist or a doctor, but would not necessarily prevent an office worker from continuing employment.

All insurance companies establish ***occupational rating classes*** into which occupations are grouped according to the relative degree of risk they present for DI coverage. Occupations that are rated as offering less relative risk include those that offer few physical dangers or psychological stresses and are stable, with little annual turnover. Occupational classes range from the most hazardous occupations, which are uninsurable, to the least hazardous occupations. When the DI underwriter assesses an applicant whose duties cross occupational lines, the classification covering the most hazardous duties is usually applied. One insurer's occupational rating classes are shown in Figure 8-5.

Finances and Portion of Income Insured

An applicant for DI coverage typically submits detailed information on finances. The underwriter examines each applicant's net worth, net

Figure 8-5. Occupational rating classes.

Class 1
Standard

This class includes persons in the least hazardous occupations; for example, attorney, auditor, bookkeeper, draftsman, insurance agent, librarian, meteorologist, pharmacist, secretary, stockbroker.

Class 2

This class generally includes (a) those in certain nonhazardous occupations in which even a minor injury can result in disability, such as most people working in allied medical professions and laboratory workers; and (b) those having office and overall supervisory responsibility in manufacturing plants or at construction sites. Examples include architect, building contractor supervising construction, medical technician, musician, supervising plant manager, surgeon.

Class 3

This class generally includes (a) blue-collar workers or persons doing light manual labor, (b) persons who drive passenger or light delivery vehicles, and (c) foremen who directly supervise manual laborers on the job and who may occasionally assist in manual activity. Examples include athletic coach, bus driver, foreman, house painter, motor freight dispatcher, plumber, taxi driver, waiter, or waitress.

Class 4
Most Hazardous

This class includes persons in the most hazardous insurable occupations; for example, boilermaker, border patrol policeman, locomotive engineer, stevedore, structural steelworker.

Uninsurable

This class includes persons who are exposed to unusual hazards and are uninsurable for any coverage; for example, certain professional and semiprofessional athletes, aerial photographer or surveyor, blaster, diver, underground miner, steeplejack, test pilot, war correspondent.

earned income (figured as gross income minus taxes), and unearned income. Each insurer establishes limits on the amount of DI insurance—usually expressed as an amount of monthly benefit—it will issue based on an applicant's earned income. This limited amount of DI coverage is expressed in an ***income replacement table.*** Figure 8-6, which is a portion of one insurer's income replacement table, shows the amount of monthly net income earned by a proposed insured with a specified annual net earned income, as well as the total monthly DI benefit that person could obtain.

For example, according to Figure 8-6, a proposed insured who has an annual net earned income of $22,000 receives approximately $1,833 monthly after taxes. According to this income replacement table, such an applicant is eligible for approximately $1,400 in monthly benefits under DI coverage.

In figuring the amount of income that a proposed insured is eligible to replace through DI coverage, the underwriter looks at both primary

Figure 8-6. Income replacement table.

Annual Net Earned Income	Monthly Net Earned Income	Total DI Benefit
$ 20,000	$1,667	$1,300
$ 22,000	$1,833	$1,400
$ 24,000	$2,000	$1,500
$ 26,000	$2,167	$1,600
$ 28,000	$2,333	$1,725
	....	
$ 40,000	$3,333	$2,400
$ 50,000	$4,167	$2,900
$ 60,000	$5,000	$3,350
$ 70,000	$5,833	$3,750
$ 80,000	$6,667	$4,100
$ 90,000	$7,500	$4,400
$100,000	$8,333	$4,700

and secondary income sources. Generally, the underwriter is concerned that if an injury prevents a proposed insured from earning income from both primary and secondary sources, then the proposed insured is eligible for insurance that covers both sources of income. If a proposed insured has income from a secondary occupation that requires skills similar to those required to perform the primary occupation, the underwriter includes the amount of secondary income in figuring the total amount of income that may be insured. If, however, the proposed insured has secondary income from an occupation that uses skills that are unrelated to the skills required to perform the primary occupation, the underwriter does not include the secondary income in evaluating the appropriate amount to insure.

For example, if a proposed insured who is a veterinarian also earns money by giving motivational speeches, an underwriter would not consider the income earned by speaking as part of the proposed insured's primary income because speaking requires a different set of skills than does the practice of veterinary medicine. If another proposed insured is employed as a high school teacher of Spanish and also teaches gardening classes to adults in the summer, however, the underwriter would include the secondary income in the total income eligible for DI coverage, because both the primary and secondary occupations require similar skills.

The underwriter considers as favorable any indication that an applicant's income is consistent or increasing over a three-year period. Conversely, if a proposed insured has suffered severe, recent decreases in income, the underwriter looks at the sources and consistency of that person's income. A severe reduction in income is usually considered to be at least 40 percent of original income. A decrease in income level is considered to be recent if the decrease has occurred within the last three years, without recovery to the original level of income.

The underwriter also looks at the stability of income of a proposed insured. Funds earned through seasonal or temporary employment are generally not considered stable and are not included under DI coverage. For example, a person who delivers new telephone directories once a year or who works at a retail store only during certain seasons is typically ineligible to have income from those sources protected under DI coverage.

If an applicant has an unusually high unearned income—for example, if his income from investments, interest, or a trust fund is 50 percent or more of his net earned income—the underwriter generally does not include the unearned income in figuring the amount of income to be covered. The reason is that a person with substantial unearned income may not depend on an earned income to the same extent as would a person without high unearned income and might, therefore, be a greater risk for a DI claim. The amount of DI coverage cannot be so great as to remove an insured's financial incentive to return to work.

Similarly, if a proposed insured has a high net worth, the underwriter checks to be sure the applicant cannot completely replace the current net earned income by liquidating assets. For instance, if a proposed insured has a net worth of $3,000,000 and an annual net income of $20,000, most underwriters would conclude that this person has no need of DI coverage. If this person were disabled so that she could not work, she has sufficient net worth to provide well for herself.

The underwriter also considers any other DI coverage protecting an applicant and uses the income replacement table to assess whether an applicant is eligible for DI benefits. For instance, an applicant who has $40,000 in annual net earned income and who has no significant unearned income or excessive net worth would be eligible for approximately $2,400 a month in DI benefits. If this applicant is already covered by some DI insurance offered by his employer, however, the underwriter usually reduces the amount of benefit that would be paid by the insurance company so that the total of DI benefits paid—by any and all insurers—does not exceed approximately $2,400 per month.

Underwriting Long-Term Care Coverage

Long-term care (LTC) insurance covers expenses that are not included under medical expense insurance and Medicare. Benefits can be provided by LTC insurance to pay for medical and other services to patients who need assistance in their own home, a nursing home, or other facility.

The benefit period for LTC insurance can be set for any length of time, starting at one year and extending to a maximum of lifetime coverage. Possible underwriting actions on most LTC products are to issue the coverage at standard rates, modify the amount of coverage available, increase the premium amount, or decline to issue the coverage.

Considerations about Aging

Underwriting LTC coverage requires a great deal of information about the ways that aging affects people. Generally, the minimum age for LTC products is 40, and the maximum age is 85. The LTC underwriter, therefore, develops a thorough knowledge of the kinds of physical and mental disorders that are part of the aging process. The LTC underwriter develops detailed knowledge of many elements of ***geriatrics,*** which is the branch of medicine dealing with the diseases and conditions of aging.

Accurate underwriting for LTC insurance also requires consideration of the applicant's physiological age in relation to his chronological age. A person's ***physiological age*** involves the relative age or youthfulness of his vital organs and their functioning. A person who has a chronological age of 75 years may be in far better health than the average person of that age, so that his physiological age may be closer to 60 or 65 than to 75. Conversely, a person who has a chronological age of 75 may be in such poor health that his physiological age may be closer to 85 or 90 than to 75.

Many older persons exhibit signs of ***cognitive impairment,*** which is a reduction in a person's ability to think, reason, or remember. Cognitive impairment involves a number of mental conditions, including the following:

- Forgetfulness
- Memory loss
- Decreased ability to think clearly
- Reduced mental keenness
- Confusion or disorientation
- Delirium or amnesia

Underwriters of LTC coverages typically understand the probable consequences of each impairment on a proposed insured's ability to live independently. One of the most common types of cognitive impairment is ***dementia,*** a general term used for mental deterioration that is characterized by loss of certain intellectual abilities such as memory, judgment, and abstract thinking, of such a degree as to interfere with social functioning. Persons who have any type of dementia typically experience decreased longevity and increased dependence, and eventually may require confinement in a long-term care facility. Another common type of cognitive impairment is ***Alzheimer's disease,*** also called *primary degenerative dementia,* which causes deterioration of a person's intellectual and cognitive functions, including memory, orientation, intellect, and judgment, and can cause deterioration of a person's speech and motor functions.

In underwriting most LTC coverages, the underwriter checks for medical conditions that, over time, will probably cause a disability in one or more of the activities of daily living so that the proposed insured requires personal, one-on-one assistance in performing those activities. The ***activities of daily living (ADLs)*** generally include eating, bathing, dressing, mobility (transferring from bed to chair or getting out of bed), and toileting. Most LTC policies provide coverage for persons who are unable to perform at least one or two of the ADLs.

Certain types of cognitive impairment may impair ADLs significantly. For example, a person suffering from dementia may be physically able to feed himself, but may not remember to eat or may forget how to feed himself. He may be able to put on his own clothes, but may wear the same items of clothing day after day. Persons with significant cognitive impairment usually require assistance with ADLs.

Some persons can manage the ADLs, but have difficulty with other, usually less essential types of activities that are called ***instrumental activities of daily living (IADLs).*** Doing one's own finances, taking care of cooking and laundry, and shopping for food and clothing are a few IADLs. Some insurance companies include IADLs in underwriting proposed insureds for LTC coverage, but others consider only ADLs.

Antiselection

A principal concern of the underwriter for LTC coverage is to help prevent antiselection by determining whether an applicant currently has acquired, or is in imminent danger of acquiring, any significant physical, mental, social, or behavioral reason to seek institutional care. A person who is disposed to seek such care is usually not accepted for LTC insurance. LTC coverage is designed and priced so as to provide for institutional care at a future time when a proposed insured develops conditions or impairments that require the care; LTC coverage is not designed and priced so as to provide such care for persons who are already suffering from incapacitating conditions or impairments at the time of application.

Field Underwriting

To assist marketers in effective field underwriting of applicants for LTC coverage, many insurers develop special field underwriting manuals that focus specifically on the requirements for this type of insurance. Generally, an ***LTC field underwriting manual*** is a guidebook that lists a number of medical conditions associated with aging and provides general underwriting criteria for those conditions. For each medical condition, the LTC field underwriting manual describes characteristics and complications, and includes questions that the marketer is expected to ask in gathering information from the proposed insured.

An LTC field underwriting manual is similar to an impairment guide in that both these publications list impairments. The publications differ in that an impairment guide provides very general information on a wide variety of impairments, whereas an LTC field underwriting manual provides more specific information on the types of conditions that persons applying for LTC may tend to exhibit. In addition, an impairment guide gives very general information about the probable underwriting decision for each impairment, whereas an LTC field underwriting manual cites more specific information about the underwriting decision for specific types of impairment.

Look again at Figure 8-1 and examine the entry for fractures in one insurer's impairment guide. Note that the impairment guide states only that, according to the location, severity, complications, and recovery from a fracture, coverage may be issued at standard rates, with an impairment rider, or both. By contrast, the listing for fractures in one insurer's LTC field underwriting manual, shown in Figure 8-7, provides more specific information for certain types of fractures (hip, spinal column, pelvis, and so on), and also lists specific fractures for which no coverage will probably be issued. Unlike the impairment guide, the LTC field underwriting manual also provides a general description of the characteristics and complications of fractures, as well as a list of questions that a marketer may ask a proposed insured in gathering information to submit with the application.

Tools for LTC Underwriting

The tools an LTC underwriter uses for assessing a proposed insured differ considerably from the tools used for underwriting other types of individual health coverages. For example, underwriters for LTC coverages do not use information from the MIB because that information is typically too general to be of use for the kind of detailed investigation necessary to underwrite LTC insurance. Few insurers use inspection reports for LTC underwriting because other sources reveal more specific and useful information.

Figure 8-7. Section of one insurer's LTC field underwriting manual.

Fractures

Characteristics and complications: Fractures are more common in women than in men, probably because of post-menopausal osteoporosis and the tendency for women to outlive men. The most common sites of fractures in our claims experience have been the hips followed by compression fractures of the spinal column and fractures of the pelvis, shoulders, and wrists. Healing of fractures in the elderly is often delayed because of reduced blood supply to the area, pre-existing arthritis, reduced nutrition, and decreased physical activity.

Questions you should ask or observe:

- Is there any evidence or indication of functional or movement limitation?
- Are narcotics used to control pain?
- Are assistive devices such as a wheelchair, walker, or crutches used?
- Is there a history of imbalance with falls and fractures?
- Is there a diagnosis of osteoporosis?

Underwriting criteria for fractures:

- Fractures of the hip, tibia, or hip replacement are acceptable six months after person regains full functional status and release from medical follow-up
- Fractures of the pelvis or vertebral body are acceptable twelve months after recovery
- Not acceptable:
    - Three or more long bone, vertebra, or pelvic fractures due to falls or osteoporosis
    - Any fracture where assistance is still required or wheelchair or walker is used
    - Curvature of the spine with secondary pulmonary problems

The underwriter for LTC products assesses each risk by using information from the application along with the results of a paramedical examination and an APS from each physician who has treated the applicant within the last three to five years. Checking for possible cognitive impairment is also an essential part of LTC underwriting. The underwriter is not concerned with projecting the amount of cognitive impairment that may develop after coverage is issued, but is concerned with any cognitive impairment that exists prior to issue of coverage. In addition to the information from the APS and the paramedical examination, the LTC underwriter checks for possible cognitive impairment by using a personal history interview, a face-to-face assessment, and a cognitive screen.

A ***personal history interview*** is a fact-finding interview that is usually conducted as a telephone conversation between the underwriter and the proposed insured or a medical caregiver of the proposed insured. To consult with medical caregivers, the underwriter verifies that each caregiver has been given permission to discuss medical information with the insurer. During the personal history interview, the parties discuss items on the application and on any other documents used in evaluating the risk. The underwriter's purpose is to check facts that have been provided and to elicit facts that may not have been included. During a telephone conversation with a proposed insured, the underwriter may ask a short list of questions designed to indicate the presence of cognitive impairment. For example, the underwriter may ask the date, the season, the current location of the proposed insured, and other questions that persons without a cognitive impairment would find simple to answer.

A ***face-to-face assessment*** involves a meeting between a proposed insured and an interviewer who represents the insurance company and who is usually employed by a vendor. Most insurance companies require a face-to-face assessment for applicants age 76 and older, although if an application reveals the possibility of significant medical conditions, or if current medical records are unavailable, an insurer may require a face-to-face assessment for a proposed insured who is younger than 76. Typical questions asked during a face-to-face assessment are shown in Figure 8-8.

As part of the face-to-face assessment, the interviewer may also use a ***cognitive screen,*** which is a test designed to determine a person's powers of recollection or short-term memory recall. One type of cognitive screen is a ***delayed word recall (DWR) test,*** which examines the ability of a proposed insured to remember a number of common words. The inability to recall between 3 and 5 words correctly from a list of 10 words is indicative of a cognitive impairment. If a proposed insured shows a significant degree of forgetfulness, the underwriter generally declines the application.

Certain health conditions and treatments place such severe limitations on a person's ability to function independently that most insurers automatically decline LTC applications submitted by proposed insureds who exhibit these conditions or treatments. Figure 8-9 provides a partial listing of such conditions and treatments.

Figure 8-8. Typical questions asked during a face-to-face assessment.

To assess a proposed insured's mobility:

- Do you go outside your house at any time?
- Do you drive?
- Do you need support or help from another person when you go outside within walking distance of your home?
- Do you need to use any equipment such as a cane, walker, or wheelchair?

To assess the ability of a proposed insured to dress alone:

- Do you need help to dress or undress yourself?
- Are you able to get your clothes from the closet?
- Can you manage dressing with someone to stand by in case you need help, or do you need frequent assistance?

Figure 8-9. Partial listing of conditions and treatments preventing LTC coverage.

- Alzheimer's disease
- Cancer with evidence of distant metastasis within past ten years
- Cystic fibrosis
- Dementia, irreversible
- Emphysema, on oxygen
- Hospital or nursing home, current confinement, or current use of home or adult day care
- Kidney dialysis within past six months
- Memory loss within 12 months, including confusion, delirium, or disorientation, and any current use of medication for same
- Multiple sclerosis
- Muscular dystrophy
- Organ transplants (excluding kidney transplant five or more years ago)
- Oxygen use, current
- Paraplegia or quadriplegia
- Senility, all forms

Key Terms and Concepts

impairment guide
comprehensive general health questionnaire
rated policy
rating schedule
preexisting condition
flat rating
waiting period (*elimination period*)
impairment rider (*impairment waiver, exclusion rider*)
preexisting conditions clause
occupational rating classes
income replacement table
geriatrics
physiological age
cognitive impairment
dementia
Alzheimer's disease (*primary degenerative dementia*)
activities of daily living (ADLs)
instrumental activities of daily living (IADLs)
LTC field underwriting manual
personal history interview
face-to-face assessment
cognitive screen
delayed word recall (DWR) test

CHAPTER NINE

Group Underwriting Principles

Learning Objectives

After studying this chapter, you should be able to

- Discuss the principles involved in underwriting multiple-employer groups
- Name at least six types of groups with characteristics that may increase their insurance risk
- Explain the effects of geographic location on insurance risk
- Discuss the level of participation requirements for group insurance
- Explain the influence of age and gender on group underwriting
- Explain the requirements for including dependents in group coverage
- Discuss the impact on group underwriting of a group's expected persistency and prior coverage and claims experience
- Distinguish among three basic types of benefit schedules generally established for group coverage
- Explain the importance to group underwriting of plan administration and mode of commission payment

Chapter Outline

Scope of Group Underwriting

Risk Assessment Factors for Group Coverage

Risk Assessment Factors: The Proposed Group

Reason for Existence
Type of Group
Stability
Size
Nature of Business
Geographic Location
Employee Classes
Level of Participation
Age
Gender
Dependents
Expected Persistency
Prior Coverage and Claims Experience

Risk Assessment Factors: The Proposed Coverage

Plan of Insurance
Plan Administration
Mode of Commission Payment

A group insurance policy provides for a number of persons to be insured under the same policy. The insurance contract is formed between the insurer and the group policyholder, which may be an organization, such as an employer or an association. The persons who are insured under a group policy are not parties to the insurance contract and are usually underwritten as a group, rather than as individuals, although the members of some small groups are usually underwritten individually.

Group policies are generally marketed by (1) agents, (2) brokers, or (3) representatives who are employees of an insurance company and who work cooperatively with agents or brokers to complete sales of group products. Some insurers use all three types of marketers. Group insurance marketing usually follows certain steps. First, a marketer gathers information about the insurance coverage requested for a proposed group. The organization that will become the policyholder for a proposed group is generally called a ***prospect.*** After the marketer sends the information to the insurer, the risk is assessed by the group underwriter. If the proposed group represents an acceptable risk, the rates necessary to provide the requested coverage are calculated. Then the insurer develops a proposal, which the marketer presents to the prospect. If the prospect accepts the coverage at the stated rates, the group case is then installed as a new group policyholder.

The underwriting principles and procedures for all types of group insurance are essentially the same. Instead of approaching the discussion of group underwriting by product, therefore, we'll examine the overall principles and procedures of assessing group risks; we'll mention underwriting guidelines for specific products as necessary.

In this chapter, we'll begin our discussion of the principles of group underwriting. We will also examine the risk assessment factors considered in evaluating applicants for group insurance. In the next chapter, we'll discuss the procedures used for underwriting group coverage.

Scope of Group Underwriting

The overarching principle on which successful group underwriting is based is the same as that for individual underwriting: the purpose of underwriting is to assign proposed insureds to appropriate risk classes and to calculate an appropriate premium to pay for the coverage. In performing this duty, underwriters assess and accept proposed groups whose members, plan designs, and administrative processes fall within the parameters established by the insurance company for the group product. In general, a group underwriter

- Reviews the characteristics of the group of proposed insureds
- Evaluates the coverage and services requested
- Assesses the proposed group's premium and claims experience for renewal and transfer cases

If the requested coverage is within the insurer's parameters, the underwriter calculates the cost of the coverage and of the services to be provided to the insured group. The cost includes the expenses of administering the plan, establishing reserves, funding claims, and providing for commissions and profits. The premium rate charged for group coverage may be increased or decreased when the policy is renewed at the policy anniversary.

Fast Fact

Underwriting is one of the fastest growing jobs in the insurance field. In 1990 there were 11,405 life insurance underwriters working in the United States; by 1995 that number had grown to 15,172. Another 3,199 underwriters worked in the medical service and health underwriting fields.

Source: U.S. Department of Labor. Cited in Laurie J. Smith, "Help Wanted: Only the Nimble Need Apply," *Best's Review (Life/Health)*, November 1996: 29–34.

If the coverage requested is *not* within the insurer's parameters, the underwriter modifies the coverage offered and the premium so that the plan more nearly falls within the insurer's parameters. If the underwriter cannot develop an appropriate modification, then coverage for that group is declined.

In assessing the risk represented by a group, the underwriter ensures that all legal requirements are fulfilled. In addition, if group members are allowed to elect the type of coverage they will receive, the underwriter assesses the characteristics of the portion of the group that will be covered by each kind of coverage.

For example, suppose that a proposed group requests two basic types of health coverage—a standard plan and a managed care plan—and that the persons in the proposed group may choose one or the other type of coverage. In such a situation, the underwriter does not evaluate the risk of the whole group, but does evaluate the risk represented by each of the "subgroups"—that is, the persons covered by each plan. If most of the younger persons or most of the medically impaired persons have selected one of the coverage types, that choice can affect the projected cost of claims and, therefore, can influence the underwriting decision.

Underwriting for group products has considerable impact on subsequent administration of group products. Insight 9-1 reflects the importance of group underwriting.

Risk Assessment Factors for Group Coverage

What kinds of groups are acceptable for group insurance? Every group that is accepted for coverage by an insurance company must

Insight 9-1 My Thoughts On . . . The Importance of Group Underwriting

As a former manager of a contract issue department, I was able to observe the essential ties between underwriting and other company functions—in particular, how the application of underwriting principles had an impact not only on the issue department, but on other areas such as billing and collection, and contract administration. Now as the manager of a customer service center and a benefit payment area, I realize that the diligence of underwriting has an impact on the kinds and numbers of claims submitted to us. I have learned firsthand that the application of underwriting principles has a profound and far-reaching effect on many aspects of group insurance administration.

Group underwriting has important ramifications for most, if not all, aspects of a group insurance company's operations. An insurer's group insurance contracts, plan documents, contract issue system, and administration and claim payment processes are usually based on a standard structure to make administration and benefit payment efficient, timely, and cost-effective for the insurer, the group policyholder, and the plan member.

The group underwriter must be extremely circumspect in assessing a group for coverage, making sure to consider how the structure of a group contract may impact other areas of the insurance operation. Prudent underwriting requires that the underwriter communicate with other areas of the insurance company that may be affected by a deviation from the standard parameters for group insurance that have been established for the insurance product. These parameters are often the basis on which procedures and systems are established, and deviation from the parameters may lead to specific problems, such as

- Delays in issuing group insurance contracts and other documents
- Difficulty in administering group record changes
- Delays in payment of claims

Any of these problems can result in dissatisfied customers and marketers, and in additional expenses for the insurance company.

For example, a prospective policyholder may request some special conditions or wording in a contract. While those conditions or the wording may have little or no impact from a risk assessment perspective, and while they may not adversely affect the premium required to pay for the coverage, they may require manual intervention in writing the contract and the plan documents, and in the ongoing administration of the group plan. Because such manual intervention takes more time than fulfilling the standard procedures, the result is expense and delay.

Further, some deviations from the standard structure of a group plan may not be within the capacity of an insurer's computer system to handle. Therefore, although a group may present an acceptable level of risk, the insurer may not be able to issue the coverage because the administrative costs for the group will be unacceptably high. If an underwriter approves and accepts such a group only to find that its coverage cannot be administered within the structure of their computer system, the consequences may be negative.

The underwriting process may be considered to be the hub of a wheel, the spokes of which are connected to the marketing processes and the processes that support the effective administration of a group plan. An underwriting process should consider these other processes in forming a decision about the acceptability of a group for coverage and of the coverage requested.

Jerry J. Ross, FLMI
Manager, Customer Service and
Central Benefit Payment Office
Manulife Financial

meet that insurer's underwriting philosophy and guidelines, which include certain risk assessment factors.

Except for certain limited circumstances, group insurance generally does not require the same degree of evidence of insurability that individual insurance requires. Therefore, in order to ascertain whether a proposed group conforms to an insurer's underwriting philosophy and guidelines, the underwriter assesses the group according to specific risk assessment factors.

Figure 9-1. Risk assessment factors for group insurance.

Characteristics of the Proposed Group	Characteristics of the Coverage
■ Reason for existence	■ Plan of insurance
■ Type	■ Plan administration
■ Stability	■ Mode of commission payment
■ Size	
■ Nature of business	
■ Geographic location	
■ Employee classes	
■ Level of participation	
■ Age	
■ Gender	
■ Dependents	
■ Expected persistency	
■ Prior coverage and claims experience	

Most insurance companies consider two types of risk assessment factors in evaluating applications for group coverage. These types involve (1) characteristics of the proposed group and (2) characteristics of the coverage. Figure 9-1 summarizes these two types of risk assessment factors, each of which we will discuss in detail.

Risk Assessment Factors: The Proposed Group

In considering the nature of a proposed group, an underwriter typically assesses the following factors: the reason for the group's existence; the type of group and its stability; its size and the nature of its business; its geographic location and employee classes; the level of participation in the proposed plan of insurance; the age, gender, and dependents of the proposed insureds; and the group's expected persistency, prior coverage, and claim experience.

Reason for Existence

Most insurance companies in the United States and Canada generally adhere to the principle that an eligible group must have been formed for a purpose other than to purchase insurance coverage. This requirement helps protect insurance companies from antiselection that would result if a number of people, all of whom were poor insurance risks, were to join together for the purpose of obtaining insurance. Some insurers do underwrite groups that have been formed solely for the purpose of obtaining insurance. However, such groups that are accepted for coverage typically exhibit many of the characteristics of a standard, employer-employee group. That is, the group generally is formed of persons who are actively at work for approximately 40 hours per week on a regular basis, have reasonably steady income, and work in an industry considered average for risk. For example, several small businesses may form a group so as to buy insurance. If all members of the group work steadily in an industry or occupation that presents an acceptable level of risk, and have a regular income, some insurance companies would accept the group for coverage even though the group's intention in forming was to buy insurance.

Professional associations that apply for coverage are assessed to ensure that the reason for their existence is not solely to purchase group insurance. If a majority of the members of a profession belong to the association, most insurers assume that the group has a valid purpose aside from obtaining insurance.

Type of Group

The types of groups that generally are considered for group insurance include employer-employee groups (including private employers and public employers such as municipalities, county governments, and state governments), multiple-employer groups (including trade associations, trusts, and labor unions), professional associations, and debtor-creditor groups. For each of these types of groups, specific underwriting considerations influence risk assessment. In discussing these types of groups, for the sake of simplicity we will usually refer to all proposed or current group members as "employees."

Employer-employee group. Employer-employee groups are the most common type of group insured under group coverage. An ***employer-employee group*** consists of an employer, who is the policyholder, and its employees, who are the insureds. Such a group usually has certain inherent favorable underwriting characteristics, including

- Representation of a good balance of ages and a desirable cross-section of risk

- A generally healthy population that may have undergone a medical examination as part of employee selection

- Central control of employee records, helping to reduce administrative costs of insurance coverage and allowing for payroll deductions if the plan is contributory

- Reduction of the possibility of antiselection because the employer-employee group is formed for a purpose other than obtaining insurance

Although private employer-employee groups are the most common type of group seeking group coverage, employer-employee policies are often issued to such public employers as municipalities and county and state governments.

Some public employer-employee groups may present somewhat different underwriting challenges than private employer-employee groups present. For example, public employer-employee groups exhibit poor persistency; the public employers' budgets are often so tightly controlled that these employers tend to change insurance companies frequently in order to obtain coverage at the lowest annual cost. Moreover, because elected officials may hold office only briefly, many public employers experience frequent changes in insurers as new decision makers come into office.

To issue coverage to the employees of a municipality, an underwriter ascertains that a state statute enables such a group to form a contract for group coverage. Moreover, the underwriter validates the eligibility of each person to be insured because some politically appointed positions do not require full-time participation from their incumbents.

Multiple-employer group. A ***multiple-employer group*** is composed of two or more employers in the same industry who are allowed by law to establish a trust.* In assessing the risk for multiple-employer groups, including trade associations, trusts, and labor unions, the underwriter determines whether the group size is adequate to avoid antiselection and whether the coverage adheres to all the provisions of the trust agreement. In addition, the underwriter determines that all persons proposed for coverage are certified as eligible and demonstrate stable employment within the group. Moreover, the underwriter sees that the rates charged do not exceed the funds available for purchasing benefits. If an insurer is asked to guarantee that premium rates will not increase during the term of the insurance agreement, usually the underwriter establishes a rate that includes a percentage added in anticipation of cost increases resulting from inflation or from unexpectedly high claims.

Many insurers avoid antiselection in assessing multiple-employer groups by adhering to clearly defined underwriting guidelines and by checking prior coverage and claims experience, especially for small groups or for individuals who may have had unfavorable experience

* A trust is an arrangement whereby property is transferred to a trustee who has legal title to the property and administers it for the benefit of persons other than the trustee.

and who are seeking group membership in order to obtain coverage. If a small trade association wishes to obtain group coverage, an insurer may require individual evidence of insurability in the form of APSs and medical examinations.

Professional association. A ***professional association*** is composed of persons who have the same type of occupation or who share a common interest. Educator, health care professional, real estate agent, and police officer are some of the professions that typically form professional associations. Each member of a professional association normally pays the entire premium for coverage.

In assessing the risk represented by members of a professional association, the underwriter considers the industry experience of the marketer; if the marketer has previously submitted sound business of this type, the underwriter looks more favorably upon the risk. An underwriter who is uncertain about approving insurance for the members of a professional association may require each applicant to submit evidence of insurability, usually in the form of a health questionnaire and an APS. Members of a professional association are not usually required to undergo medical examinations because the members may be so widely scattered geographically that arranging and reporting the results of medical examinations would be too time-consuming and expensive.

Debtor-creditor group. A ***debtor-creditor group*** consists of a credit-granting institution, such as a bank, and its debtors. The underwriter usually verifies the financial strength of the credit-granting institution. Some jurisdictions have limited the amount of credit insurance that an insurer may issue and the duration of covered loans. In addition, in most jurisdictions, insurers are limited as to the premium rate they may charge for coverage to debtor-creditor groups.

Stability

From an insurer's perspective, an ideal group is relatively stable in composition, with a steady flow of new members to replace those who leave the group. Most insurers question the stability of (1) a group whose composition changes greatly and frequently, and (2) a group whose composition experiences very little change over a considerable period of time, for example, five years. An unusually high turnover rate produces unexpectedly high administrative costs and may indicate that persons are joining the group for the purpose of obtaining insurance coverage for a short time period. This type of antiselection generally produces an undesirably high claims cost. Similarly, an unusually low turnover rate produces an increase in the average age of group members. Because mortality and morbidity tend to increase as people grow older, a group with low turnover is likely to experience higher-than-average claims costs.

The fact that the size and membership of a group remain the same over a period of time does not necessarily mean that the group is stable from an underwriting perspective. Underwriters look for a balance between new, often younger, members entering the group and current, often older, members leaving it. If the numbers of members entering and leaving the group are not relatively well balanced—that is, if too many new members are entering and too few current members are leaving—the premium may be adjusted to account for possible antiselection and probably higher claims costs.

Insurers try to encourage stability within a group by setting eligibility requirements that define which employees can be covered under a group policy. If a group has experienced a high degree of turnover, for example, an insurer may establish a service requirement for the group. According to a ***service requirement,*** a person must be employed for a certain length of time—usually three to six months—before being covered under the group insurance plan. If a proposed plan includes a service requirement, the underwriter determines which employees are eligible under the plan.

Size

In the early days of group insurance, most insurers believed that a group with fewer than 100 insureds was too small for reliable estimation of likely mortality or morbidity. Today, because of increasing information about mortality and morbidity experience, the minimum group size has been reduced considerably. Some insurers, in fact, underwrite groups with as few as two members.

Fluctuations in a group's claims experience tend to decrease as the size of the group increases. Moreover, the larger a group, the lower the level of its administrative expenses as a percentage of the total premium amount the group pays.

Moreover, the smaller a group, the less predictable or credible the estimate of future claims costs. Therefore, the underwriter may have difficulty in determining an appropriate premium for a small group. To assist the underwriter in estimating a small group's probable claims costs and in calculating an equitable premium, most insurers use pooling and manual rating for small groups. ***Pooling*** is the practice of considering several small groups as one large group for risk assessment purposes. The larger the number of proposed insureds in the pooled group, the more likely that the underwriter can arrive at a fair estimate of the whole group's claims costs. ***Manual rating*** involves establishing premium rates for broad classes of groups, especially for those with no credible claims experience. We'll discuss manual rating in

Fast Fact

Although underwriting small groups is difficult, 65 percent of small businesses, most of which have fewer than 5 employees, do have some form of group insurance coverage. Forty-five percent of these businesses offer group health coverage to their employees, and 31 percent offer group life insurance.

Source: Nilufer R. Ahmed and Cheryl D. Retzloff, "The Changing Marketplace of U.S. Small Businesses," *LIMRA's MarketFacts,* July/August 1995: 4–6.

more detail in Chapter 10. Figure 9-2 summarizes the effects of group size on underwriting.

Nature of Business

The type of industry in which a group works influences the underwriting decision. Information on occupational hazards and experience information concerning the likelihood of persons in certain jobs to make excessive claims assist insurers in setting appropriate underwriting guidelines. The occupations of a majority of the participants in the group can be a significant underwriting factor, especially for accident or sickness hazards.

Some insurers establish pricing factors that modify the amount of premium charged to group members who work in specified industries. A ***pricing factor*** is a number that illustrates the risk represented by persons working in a specified industry. The pricing factor is multiplied by the standard premium to arrive at an equitable premium for a group's coverage. Insurers establish pricing factors by using experience-based statistics for various industries. A group whose members work in an industry with standard risk is assigned a pricing factor of 1.00—that is, the group is charged the standard premium for coverage. By contrast, a group whose job-related risk is considered greater than average is assigned a pricing factor that is greater than 1.00, and a group with job-related risk that is less than average is assigned a pricing factor less than 1.00. Figure 9-3 illustrates typical pricing factors assigned to various occupations.

Suppose that a proposed group has requested health coverage whose standard premium per person is $600 annually. According to Figure 9-3, if the members of the proposed group are employed in radio and television broadcasting, the annual premium for this coverage would be

Figure 9-2. Effects of group size on underwriting.

Smaller Groups	Larger Groups
■ Relatively larger fluctuations in claims experience increase the difficulty of assessing that experience	■ Relatively stable claims experience decreases the difficulty of assessing that experience
■ Relatively larger fluctuations in claims experience often require manual rating	■ Relatively stable claims experience often permits rating on the basis of the group's claims experience
■ Relatively higher expense level as percentage of total premium can increase the premium amount	■ Relatively lower expense level as percentage of total premium can decrease the premium amount

Figure 9-3. Typical pricing factors assigned to various occupations.

Occupation	Pricing Factor
Engineering surveying, geological work	0.90
Telephone communications	0.95
Gas production and distribution	0.95
Electric services	0.95
Radio and television broadcasting	1.00
Freight transportation arrangement	1.00
Sanitary services	1.14
Motor vehicle manufacturing	1.20

\$600 (\$600 × 1.00). If, instead, the group members are employed in motor vehicle manufacturing, the annual premium per person for the coverage would be \$720 (\$600 × 1.20). Finally, if the group members are employed in telephone communications, the annual per-person premium for the requested coverage would be \$570 (\$600 × .95).

The economic prospects of the industry in which a business operates can affect the underwriting decision. For instance, if an industry has recently suffered reductions in the numbers of employees or in the amount of available work because of a slowing in product demand, most insurers proceed cautiously in determining whether the business is likely to be able to pay the premiums.

The strength and financial condition of a business are also important in underwriting. Usually, a business or an organization must have been operating on a sound financial basis for at least one year in order for an insurance company to approve a group plan. General economic conditions and their relationship to the profitability of that business or organization may be another factor in determining the desirability of a specific group risk.

Some insurers do not issue certain types of coverage at standard rates to groups that have certain characteristics. For such groups, the coverage may be issued, but with an extra premium. The extra premium is charged because a particular characteristic of the group increases the risk of death or disability. For instance, a group that contains a large number of retired persons is subject to higher mortality than a younger group. The cost of life insurance for such a group usually includes an extra premium. Moreover, disability coverage on employees who work in hazardous occupations such as mining, logging, and quarrying generally incurs an extra premium because the employees are at increased risk for suffering a disabling injury.

Other types of groups considered to represent higher risk include the following:

- Groups having the appearance of employer-employee groups, but that involve other arrangements such as contracting or subcontracting
- Groups presenting an excessive risk for catastrophic loss, such as (1) groups in dangerous industries or professional sports, (2) those requesting coverage for aircraft pilots or other flight personnel, and (3) those engaged in water transportation, exploration, or research conducted at sea, in the air, or in space
- Groups requesting coverage for directors, partners, owners, or consultants who are not full-time employees of the proposed policyholder or of a covered subsidiary of the proposed policyholder
- Groups of fewer than 100 persons that request self-administration or administration by a third-party organization
- Groups engaged in seasonal industries (generally considered as working less than nine months per year) or subject to unusually high employee turnover, such as contractors, resorts, canneries, restaurants and hotels, laundries, and taxi services
- Groups requesting enhanced coverage for certain members such as officers and directors
- Groups requesting coverage for a high percentage of part-time employees

Geographic Location

Morbidity and mortality rates differ in various areas of the world and tend to be higher in areas that are susceptible to natural disasters. The underwriter takes these factors into consideration and also looks at the living conditions and the economic level of the proposed insureds, as well as the availability and cost of adequate health care in the area. Deficiencies in these factors can produce higher rates of mortality or morbidity and can affect the premium required for the coverage.

In some proposed groups, all members of the group are not located in the same place—for example, an organization may have multiple offices in a number of states, provinces, or countries. In assessing such groups, an underwriter considers all applicable laws and regulations concerning each of the locations involved. Some localities have established specific requirements for group coverage. For example, in Canada, maternity leave legislation varies among provinces. Several provinces require that an employee on maternity leave be entitled to collect disability benefits for the portion of her maternity leave that she is unable to work for health reasons, provided she is totally disabled according to the terms of the policy. In other provinces, women on maternity leave are not eligible to receive disability benefits until their expected return-to-work date.

Employee Classes

The persons to be insured by group coverage may be classified in various ways—for instance, by job title, salary amount, or length of service to an employer—and the amount of insurance available to each employee class may vary. We will discuss the relationship between classes and benefit levels later in this chapter.

Most insurers allow proposed groups that have 10 to 50 members to be covered to establish up to four classes; proposed policyholders that have more than 50 members may usually establish up to six classes. Classifications are typically broad enough to include a reasonable number of persons in each class. A class that includes only one or two persons would create the opportunity for antiselection.

In order for a group to be approved for coverage, assignment to a class must be established on a nondiscriminatory basis according to conditions pertaining to employment, and the policyholder may not select specific persons to be in any particular class. Moreover, laws in some jurisdictions prohibit classes based on marital status, gender, or age. Figure 9-4 illustrates some typical nondiscriminatory classes established for group insurance.

Figure 9-4. Typical nondiscriminatory classes for group insurance.

All salaried employees, OR
All salaried employees earning [specified dollar amount] per year and over, OR
All employees earning [specified dollar amount] per year and over

All salaried employees working [specified number of hours] per year, OR
All employees working [specified number of hours] per year

All salaried employees with [specified number of years] of service, OR
All employees with [specified number of years] of service

All officers, managers, and supervisors, OR
All officers and managers, OR
All officers

In groups other than employer-employee groups, persons proposed for coverage may be assigned to classes according to their membership in the group, their debtor relationship to a bank or other lending institution, or some other nondiscriminatory basis. Generally, certain classes of persons doing business with a prospect may not be included under group coverage unless they are certified employees of the group. For instance, attorneys, accountants, consultants, and contractors may do business with a prospect but are not employees of the prospect and are not eligible for group coverage. Similarly, stockholders of a company are not eligible for coverage under group insurance provided for the company unless they are also employees of the company.

Within a group, the mix of higher- and lower-income employee classes is important in setting the premium rate for a plan. For example, employees who earn high incomes are likely to produce higher-than-average claims for medical and dental care. One reason for this increased claims level is that persons with higher incomes are statistically more likely to seek expensive medical care or to seek it more often than are persons of more limited financial means. On the other hand, employees who earn low incomes may choose not to enroll in a contributory plan, so that the desired participation level is difficult to reach. As a result, the group plan may have a higher-than-desired rate of turnover.

Level of Participation

A ***noncontributory plan*** of group insurance provides that the insureds pay no part of the premium for their coverage. The group policyholder pays the entire premium, and coverage is automatic for all eligible members of the group. In a noncontributory plan, the level of participation is usually required to be 100 percent of all eligible group members. By contrast, a ***contributory plan*** of group insurance provides that the insureds pay some part of the premium for their insurance coverage and may choose whether to participate in the group insurance plan. In a contributory plan, the more closely participation in the plan approaches 100 percent, the more the standard risks in the group tend to compensate for the impaired lives and potential morbidity and mortality in the group, thereby reducing the effects of antiselection.

Consequently, for all but the largest groups enrolled in contributory plans, insurers normally require a minimum participation level of between 75 and 100 percent of eligible group members, depending on the size of the group. The larger the group, the more the participation requirement can be reduced because of the increased spread of risk. The following table illustrates minimum participation requirements established by one insurer for groups of various sizes enrolled in contributory insurance plans:

Number of Employees	Minimum Participation Requirement
Less than 250	75 percent
250–499	65 percent
500–749	60 percent
750–999	55 percent
More than 1,000	Case-by-case evaluation

The importance of a satisfactory level of participation can be illustrated by an example. Suppose a certain group of 100 people applying for group life insurance coverage is assumed to have an average inherent mortality that is 100 percent of standard. The group is composed of subgroups that have actual mortality ranging from 40 to 500 percent of standard, as follows:

Subgroup	Number of Employees	Size of Subgroup as a Percentage of Total Group	Mortality as a Percentage of Standard
1	40	40%	40%
2	40	40%	80%
3	10	10%	200%
4	10	10%	500%
	100	100%	

If the 100 group members were ranked in order of desirability as insureds, the employees in subgroup 1 would be considered most desirable because of their low relative mortality of 40 percent of standard. The employees in subgroup 4 would be considered least desirable because of their high relative mortality of 500 percent of standard. If we assume further that antiselection operates in the whole group, the persons in subgroup 4—those with the highest expected mortality—would be the most likely to participate in the group insurance plan, and the persons in subgroup 1—those with the lowest expected mortality—would be the least likely to purchase the group coverage. If only the persons in subgroup 4 enrolled in the plan, however, the insured group would have an overall mortality far in excess of standard. The expected cost of claims submitted under this coverage would be almost certain to exceed the assumptions made for the coverage when rates were established for it. Therefore, the insurance company could lose a great deal of money and could place its financial strength and the security of its other policyholders and insureds in jeopardy.

Ideally, a group applying for life coverage exhibits a wide range of expected mortality (or, for health and disability coverages, a wide range of expected morbidity), so that the overall mortality or morbidity of the group approaches 100 percent of standard, which is the assumed mortality or morbidity for the product at the premium rates established for it. The higher the level of participation in a plan—that is, the larger the number of eligible group members enrolled in it—the more likely the group's mortality or morbidity will approach standard, and the more acceptable the group becomes as an insurance risk.

Age

The age spread of a group should be sufficiently broad to produce a wide range of risks. Insurers are concerned about a group with a predominance of older persons because groups with a large proportion of older members tend to experience high rates of morbidity and mortality.

The largest controlling factor regarding age is the turnover rate of the group. A group with low turnover tends to increase in average age because fewer new, usually younger persons join the group. Ensuring a steady flow of new entrants can help to maintain the desired age spread in a group, particularly if the new entrants are young.

Gender

The ratio of males to females in a group is also an important underwriting factor. Women tend to experience lower mortality, but higher morbidity, than men tend to experience. All other factors being equal, a group with a large proportion of females represents a statistically lower risk for life coverage than does a group with a large proportion of males. Conversely, a group of males represents a statistically lower risk for health and disability insurance than does a group of females.

Dependents

Most insurance companies define a ***dependent*** as (1) a spouse or (2) an unmarried child, including an adopted child, stepchild, or foster child, who is under age 19 or to age 25 if disabled or a full-time student, and who relies on the insured person for support and maintenance. Most insurers consider a common-law spouse to be included within the definition of *spouse* for the purposes of group insurance coverage. Some insurers also treat the same-gender partner of an employee as that employee's spouse.

Generally, a dependent cannot be insured unless the eligible group member is also insured. If only a few eligible group members wish to insure their spouses, antiselection may become a factor, because the insured spouses may have existing health impairments. In addition, many insurers require that an eligible dependent not be confined to a hospital on the date that coverage begins for the eligible group member. If a dependent person is hospital-confined on that date, the effective date of coverage is usually delayed until the person has been discharged from the hospital.

Expected Persistency

A decision to change insurers is often made on the basis of quality of service and cost of the coverage. In order to help control the financial loss resulting when business is canceled during the first year, most insurers evaluate the degree to which a prospect will probably continue coverage over a period of years past the first few years, when commissions and the cost of adding the group business to the insurer's books reduce or eliminate the insurer's profit on the case.

Persistency is also important because, even if a group has unusually high claims costs in a given year, the group's experience may improve during the following years; a policy in force for a sustained period is more likely to overcome the effects of a single bad year of claims. A group that has frequently changed insurers is likely to be charged a higher-than-average premium to compensate the insurer for the additional risk of losing the business early.

Prior Coverage and Claims Experience

An application on a group that previously has been insured by another carrier and that is being transferred to a new insurer is given a thorough assessment. The underwriter looks at the reason for the transfer, the amount of premium the group paid to the other carrier, the claims experience of the group, the underwriting philosophy and guidelines of the previous carrier, and the amount of any increase in rates.

When coverage is transferred from one insurer to another, some insured individuals may have filed claims with the carrier who is losing the business. These persons must be protected from loss of benefits on already-filed claims when their group decides to change insurance carriers. The underwriter pays special attention to group members who are not actively at work and not disabled on the proposed effective date of the new coverage. In order to evaluate the risk for such persons, an underwriter determines which group members are absent because of vacation or leave of absence, and which are absent because of injury, sickness, or other conditions. Most insurers defer coverage on persons who are not actively at work on the date the new coverage becomes effective. Moreover, most insurers do not collect premiums on absent group members until those employees have returned to work on a full-time basis at their regular place of business.

Underwriting transferred business requires evaluation of the group's claims experience under the previous group policy. Most insurers require three years' documented experience of benefit changes and their effective dates, and of rates billed, premiums paid, claims incurred, and claims paid. Underwriters also examine all data on large claims, including the amount claimed, the current status of the claim (ongoing or terminated), and, for health insurance, the prognosis if the claim is ongoing. Other information that underwriters may request on transferred groups includes current billing statements, employee booklets that describe the current plan of benefits, and information about disabled employees and dependents.

Risk Assessment Factors: The Proposed Coverage

In assessing the degree of risk represented by a prospect, insurers generally consider the following factors related to coverage: the plan of insurance, including its eligibility requirements and benefits; plan administration arrangements; and the mode of commission payment.

Plan of Insurance

Important elements of plan design include eligibility requirements, benefit levels, and contract provisions. Details of these elements vary from one plan to another.

Eligibility requirements. Most insurers stipulate that only full-time, permanent employees and their dependents may enroll in a group plan of insurance. The underwriter is responsible for checking the eligibility of each person to be insured under a plan.

Under a contributory plan, not every employee must take part in the insurance coverage, although the required percentage of employees must be enrolled; the employees who do choose to use the coverage usually have 31 days to enroll in the plan after their date of eligibility. Employees who do not enroll during the 31-day period must usually provide evidence of insurability before being allowed to join the plan. This requirement is designed to prevent the antiselection that might occur if an employee who originally declined coverage subsequently learned that he had a serious impairment. However, some plans provide that an employee who has chosen not to participate in group coverage is allowed to enter the group plan without evidence of insurability within 31 days after acquiring a dependent.

Benefit levels. Benefit levels determine in large part whether a plan will be financially successful for both the insured and the insurer. A plan with excessive benefits may be overutilized so that claims experience will be too high, whereas a plan with too few benefits or with inequitable benefits for one or more employee classes may not appeal to employees and will, therefore, not achieve the desired percentage of employee enrollment.

Some plans provide the same benefit for all employees regardless of an employee's occupation, annual income, length of service, or any other criterion. A prospect may request, for example, that each employee be insured for $50,000 of basic life coverage, or for a specified level of medical and dental coverage. A plan that provides the same benefit for all employees does not divide employees into classes.

Other plans provide varying benefits according to specified criteria. In these plans, all employees to be covered by a plan are divided into classes, as previously discussed, and the schedule of benefits is identical for all employees in the same class. Setting benefit levels by class rather than by each individual's choice lessens the likelihood and impact of antiselection. Three basic types of benefit schedules are those that provide (1) benefits related to salary classification, (2) benefits related to occupational classification, or (3) benefits related to length of service. The underwriter's responsibility is to verify that each employee has been accurately classified and that antiselection does not appear to be a factor in the classification.

Fast Fact

At the end of 1995, there was $828 billion of group life insurance in force in Canada.

Source: Canadian Life and Health Insurance Association, "Key Statistics," *Canadian Life and Health Insurance Facts,* 1996: 4.

Benefits related to salary classification provide amounts of coverage for employees in each class established according to salary range. For example, the employees of a company might be divided into four classes according to annual income; each class is to receive the following flat amounts of basic life insurance:

Class	Annual Earnings	Insurance Coverage
A	Less than $15,000	$18,000
B	$15,000 but less than $20,000	$26,000
C	$20,000 but less than $25,000	$34,000
D	$25,000 or more	$42,000

This method of determining benefit amounts appears to be equitable in that each class above Class A in the benefit schedule shown is eligible for an increase of $8,000 in coverage more than the coverage available to the next lower class. However, this method does not provide a uniform ratio of coverage for each employee in a class. For example, within Class B of the benefit schedule shown, an employee earning $15,000 is eligible for basic life coverage of approximately 1.7 times the employee's earnings, whereas an employee earning $19,999 is eligible for basic life coverage of approximately 1.3 times the employee's earnings. Moreover, an employee earning $30,000 and an employee earning $60,000 are both eligible for $42,000 of basic life insurance coverage. Some employers assist employees in purchasing supplemental life insurance to help compensate for this lack of uniform benefits from one class to another.

Benefits related to occupational classification provide insurance coverage that is related to the occupation of each employee. For example, the employees of one company are divided into two classes according to occupational classification; the employees in each class are to receive basic life insurance according to the following formulas:

Class	Insurance Coverage
Company officers	3 times annual earnings, rounded to the next $1,000, to a maximum of $250,000
All other employees	1.5 times annual earnings, rounded to the next $1,000, to a maximum of $200,000

Some plans provide a flat amount of basic life coverage based on occupational classes, as the following table illustrates:

Class	Insurance Coverage
General employees	$ 50,000
Supervisors and department heads	$100,000
Company officers	$200,000

Benefits related to length of service provide increases in coverage according to the length of time an employee has worked for a policyholder. A typical basic life insurance benefit schedule of this type is as follows:

Class	Insurance Coverage
10 years or more of service	$100,000
More than 5 years but less than 10 years of service	$ 75,000
5 years or less of service	$ 50,000

Classes established according to length of service require the plan administrator to keep track of each employee's time in service.

In addition to these three types of classifications, some plans that offer retirement benefits reduce benefit schedules for older employees and for retired employees. Because the need for life insurance may diminish with age, many policyholders choose to include a provision for reducing or terminating coverage at or about the age when retirement normally takes place. Such a provision tends to keep the premium for the plan from increasing excessively. The following schedule of reductions in basic life insurance coverage is provided as an example:

Age at Which Reduction Occurs	Amount of Insurance Coverage
66	Original benefit reduced by 35%
70	Original benefit reduced by 50%
75	Original benefit reduced by 70%
80	Original benefit reduced by 80%

The amount of coverage, if any, provided for employees' dependents need not be consistent for all classes of employees. That is, the basic life and health benefits for the spouses and other dependents of all employees, regardless of employee class or annual earnings or any other criterion, does not have to be the same.

Contract provisions. The contract for a group health or long-term disability plan can include certain provisions, subject to legislated limitations, that affect the underwriting of the proposed plan. A preexisting conditions provision, for example, can protect the insurance company against antiselection by persons who have preexisting health conditions. The contract can also include a ***coordination of benefits (COB) provision*** to prevent duplication of benefits, that is, payment of the same medical expenses or disability benefits by more than one insurer or by a government program.

Many group plans include an ***actively-at-work provision*** that requires an employee to be actively at work on the date on which coverage becomes effective under the plan. Moreover, some insurers, because of the possibility of antiselection, require evidence of insurability when an employee wishes to purchase additional coverage. For example, suppose a group contract provides $30,000 of life insurance without evidence of insurability to each member of a class of employees. The contract may also allow those employees to buy additional amounts of insurance, but may require evidence of insurability for an employee wishing to buy more coverage. Some contracts provide that coverage will cease for a member of the covered group if that member goes on strike, takes a leave of absence, or is laid off from work.

Plan Administration

Keeping plan costs low and helping ensure the long-term satisfaction of the policyholder—and, thus, the persistency of the coverage—depends in large measure on the effectiveness of plan administration. The willingness and ability of the group policyholder to cooperate in administering the plan are essential. If the group plan is self-administered, the policyholder needs the ability to administer the plan effectively and to help control plan costs. In particular, the policyholder should be able to

- Promote the plan and encourage all eligible employees to enroll in order to reduce the probability of antiselection and high claims costs
- Certify the eligibility of each enrolled employee
- Collect and keep accurate records of each employee's contributions to the plan
- Maintain accurate and complete records of costs and claims
- Record additions, terminations, and status changes accurately and promptly (for example, changes in marital status, employee class, and earnings)
- Assist with claims submissions

The underwriter assesses the degree to which the policyholder is likely to administer the plan effectively or cooperate in plan administration.

Mode of Commission Payment

If the persistency of a proposed group is in question, the underwriter may determine that the marketer's commission should be spread over several years instead of being paid as a single first-year commission. An extended mode of commission payment enables the insurer to lower the first-year cost associated with a plan and to experience less loss if the plan lapses at the end of the first year.

Key Terms and Concepts

prospect
employer-employee group
multiple employer group
professional association
debtor-creditor group
service requirement
pooling
manual rating
pricing factor
noncontributory plan
contributory plan
dependent
coordination of benefits (COB) provision
actively-at-work provision

CHAPTER TEN

Group Underwriting Procedures

Learning Objectives

After studying this chapter, you should be able to

- Explain the purpose, contents, and attachments that are normally submitted with a Request for Proposal
- Identify the information that an underwriter derives from a proposed group's ERISA documents
- Explain the purpose and general contents of a master application
- Calculate the annual premium for a group using a specified unit price, a specified amount of coverage, and a specified number of employees
- Distinguish among manual rating, experience rating, and blended rating
- Explain how an underwriter calculates a claim experience figure that accurately represents a group's true experience for a period
- Describe the use of step rates to determine appropriate premiums for small groups
- Define and explain three types of post-issue underwriting used in group insurance

Chapter Outline

Information Sources for Group Underwriting

Request for Proposal

Proposal Attachments

Agent's Statement

ERISA Documents

The Proposal for Insurance

The Master Application

Rating Methods for Group Cases

Manual Rating

Experience Rating

Blended Rating

Rating Approaches for Small Groups

Post-Issue Underwriting for Group Insurance

Approval of Late Entrants

Approval of Benefit Changes

Renewal Underwriting

Having reviewed the principles of group underwriting, you are now ready to learn the procedures that group underwriters follow in assessing risks. These procedures generally include the same kinds of activities performed in underwriting individual coverages—that is, gathering information, assessing the risk, and making a decision on whether to approve the policy. If the group underwriter decides that the insurer can accept a risk, the underwriter also calculates the rate to be charged for the requested coverage.

You have learned that group insurance is marketed differently from individual insurance in that an insurer submits a bid for providing requested coverage. The document requesting that bid is one of the information sources used for underwriting. In this chapter, we'll examine this and other information sources for group underwriting, and we will study the contents of a proposal for insurance and a master application. Next, we'll discuss the methods used for rating group cases. Finally, we'll consider post-issue underwriting for group insurance.

Information Sources for Group Underwriting

The underwriter uses various resources to assess the risk represented by a group proposed for coverage. These resources may include a Request for Proposal, attachments submitted with the proposal, an agent's statement, and documents filed according to ERISA requirements. We'll discuss each of these resources in the following sections.

For small groups that require underwriting for each person proposed for coverage, the underwriter may also use APSs, inspection reports, financial reports, and other types of information typically used for individual underwriting. Because we have already discussed these documents in the chapters on individual underwriting, we will not repeat the information here.

Request for Proposal

After talking with a proposed policyholder and obtaining a Request for Proposal form, a marketer completes the ***Request for Proposal (RFP),*** a document that provides detailed information about the requested coverage and requests a bid from an insurer for providing that coverage. The information in the RFP enables the underwriter to assess the risk represented by the group and to make an accurate estimate of the premium required to pay for the requested coverage. If for some reason the requested coverage cannot be offered to the group, the underwriter can propose alternate coverage. If the insurer cannot offer coverage to the group, the underwriter declines the RFP.

An RFP includes the name and address of the group and its nature (employee-employer, debtor-creditor, and so on), the classes to be covered, and the amount of policyholder contribution toward the cost of the coverage. The RFP also outlines the types of coverage requested. If the proposed group has been covered by another carrier or has been self-insured in the past, the RFP also includes information about the previous insurance history of the proposed group: the premium amounts paid, the group's claim experience, and the length of time that coverage was in effect. The RFP may include a copy of the proposed group's previous insurance contract and other documents explaining the type and extent of coverages provided, as well as the cost of the previous coverage.

According to the information in the RFP, an underwriter attempts to determine the group's persistency and claim experience. The underwriter also determines whether the group contains enough participants to conform to the insurer's parameters for the requested coverage. If the RFP indicates that any classification of employees or members has been excluded from coverage, the underwriter determines whether the proposed group represents potentially adverse selection.

Usually, the RFP includes a list of ***current open claimants,*** who are group members receiving short-term or long-term disability income benefits. The list of current open claimants contains the following information about each claimant:

- Name
- Date of birth
- Date and nature of disability
- Expected date of return to work, if any
- Net monthly benefit amount

Some lists also contain the prognosis for each disability. The underwriter uses this information to assess the group's future claim liability, which may exclude benefits for current open claimants. Coverage on current open claimants does not transfer to the new insurance carrier when coverage is transferred. Instead, liability for current open claimants remains with the original insurance carrier.

A group that has an unusually high percentage of either young or old proposed participants typically receives different, usually more detailed, underwriting consideration compared to a group that has a more widely distributed range of ages. Underwriting for some types of coverages also requires more detailed consideration for groups with an unusually high number of dependents. Figure 10-1 illustrates an RFP submitted to a carrier of long-term disability income insurance coverage.

Proposal Attachments

An RFP is normally submitted with a number of attachments, including a benefit transmittal, a rate transmittal, and an employee census. Some of the information in an RFP typically refers to the

Figure 10-1. Request for Proposal for long-term disability income coverage.

NEUMEYER CORPORATION

Group Long-Term Disability Income

Corporate Headquarters:	Binghamton, NY
Industry:	Clothing manufacture
Current Carrier:	ABC Life & Health Insurance Co. since 1992
General Quotation Requirements:	Quotation deadline 1/4/97. Effective date 3/1/97 Quote a two-year rate guarantee
Employee Classes:	All full-time employees
Employer Contribution:	80%
LTD Benefit Percentage:	60%
Maximum Monthly Benefit:	$7,000
Minimum Monthly Benefit:	$100.00 or 10% of monthly pre-tax income
Elimination Period:	180 days
Preexisting Conditions:	Benefits payable after 12 months
Mental & Nervous Limitations:	Benefits payable for 24 months
Survivor Benefit:	None
Rehabilitation:	Mandatory

LTD Claim Experience

Year	Avg. # Lives	Paid Premium	Paid Claims
2/92–1/93	1,610	$110,330	$13,545
2/93–1/94	1,789	$122,589	$15,051
2/94–1/95	2,016	$138,416	$51,422
2/95–1/96	2,125	$174,873	$49,489
2/96–12/96 (11 mos.)	3,422	$258,163	$73,208

groups of employees, or employee classes, to be insured. An ***employee class*** is a group of employees categorized by earnings, rank, or position.

A ***benefit transmittal*** provides details concerning the insurance benefits being requested for each employee class, the effective date of coverage, how premium billing and claims will be administered, and other information concerning the type of plan being requested for the group. A benefit transmittal adds detail to the general description of benefits presented in the Request for Proposal.

A ***rate transmittal*** specifies the marketer's proposed rates for each type of insurance coverage for each class of employees. For instance, a rate transmittal developed for a proposed group may specify proposed rates for medical expense and dental coverage for each class of employees and their dependents, and for supplemental life coverage and accidental death and dismemberment coverage for the employees only. The final rates that the underwriter determines to be necessary for a group may differ from those proposed by the marketer.

An ***employee census*** lists demographic information about the proposed group as a unit and about individual persons within the proposed group. General information about the group includes a count of the total number of employees and the number for whom each type of coverage is to be provided. Information about individuals within the proposed group includes each employee's date of birth, gender, salary, job title or division of the organization in which the employee works, whether the employee has dependents for whom coverage is requested, and types and amounts of coverage requested. Figure 10-2 shows a portion of a typical employee census.

Figure 10-2. Portion of a typical employee census.

DOB	M/F	Salary	Division	Dependents	Life	*LTD	**WI
05/57	F	$33,904	0001	Y	$68,000	$1,800	$435
01/67	M	$27,050	0001	N	$55,000	$1,503	$347
10/49	M	$26,520	0002	Y	$54,000	$1,474	$341
09/47	F	$41,600	0001	Y	$84,000	$1,800	$534
03/52	M	$30,680	0003	Y	$62,000	$1,705	$394
11/65	M	$33,280	0001	Y	$67,000	$1,800	$427
10/45	F	$30,680	0003	Y	$62,000	$1,705	$394
07/39	M	$70,000	0001	N	$70,000	$1,800	$600

* The numbers in this column represent the amount of monthly long-term disability income benefits for which the employee is eligible under the contract.

** The numbers in this column represent the amount of weekly income coverage (for short-term disability) for which the employee is eligible under the contract.

Agent's Statement

The group marketer usually attaches to the Request for Proposal an agent's statement, which is a recommendation concerning the appropriateness of the requested coverage and the feasibility of providing that coverage to the specified group. The agent's statement is considerably important to the group underwriter in deciding whether to submit a bid for providing the coverage. As she does for individual applications, the underwriter evaluates the value of the marketer's recommendation by considering the insurer's experience with business submitted by that marketer. A marketer who has consistently submitted sound business to an insurance company is likely to have his recommendation considered favorably during underwriting. Conversely, a recommendation from a marketer who has submitted business of lesser quality or appropriateness in the past is likely to be less credible for underwriting purposes.

Moreover, insurers generally place a great deal of confidence in the comments of a marketer who specializes in the group market and who makes a considerable number of group sales of the type offered by the insurer. On the other hand, most insurers are cautious in evaluating proposed business from a marketer who

- Is unknown to the insurer or has not placed business with the insurer in the past;
- Is a marketer of a carrier that (1) is currently providing insurance for the group or (2) is known to provide the coverage requested; in either situation, the marketer may be attempting to transfer a less desirable group to the new insurer; or
- Has requested that coverage already in force be substantially increased, either for the entire group or for selected segments of it; such a request may indicate the presence of antiselection.

Figure 10-3 shows a sample agent's statement for group coverage.

Figure 10-3. Agent's statement for group coverage.

This company has been in business for over 47 years manufacturing and assembling movable windows. Its annual net profit has increased during the past 5 years from $1.3 million to $4.4 million. The current carrier has been underwriting the coverage for 7 years; the anniversary date is June 1, 1997. Major claims over $10,000 in the past 24 months have been nonexistent. I feel that the strength of the business and the stability of the group, coupled with its moderate claim experience, make it a prime candidate for benefit coverage under our policy.

ERISA Documents

In Chapter 3, we noted that documents filed according to requirements of the Employee Retirement Income Security Act (ERISA) may be helpful to the underwriter in evaluating the risk represented by a proposed group. Generally, underwriters use documents filed under ERISA reporting requirements only to assess the risk for self-funded groups. For groups that have previously been insured by another carrier, underwriters typically use information contained in the previous carrier's insurance contract and reports that the carrier has provided concerning claim experience of the group. ERISA documents that are helpful to underwriters are the summary plan description and the summary of material modification.

- The ***summary plan description*** defines details of the coverage. This document tells the underwriter the type of employee welfare benefit plan, the eligibility requirements, and the employer's claim administration procedure. For example, when a self-funded group wishes to change to a fully insured plan, the underwriter uses the summary plan description to determine the previous plan of benefits and the appropriate premium for the new plan.
- The ***summary of material modification*** outlines any benefit changes occurring within 210 days after the end of the plan's fiscal year. The underwriter determines whether any changes have been made. In some situations, changes in a plan alert the underwriter to seek the reasons for the changes.

Occasionally, to ensure that benefits match those agreed to under a trust, an insurer examines a trust agreement or collective bargaining agreement filed under ERISA requirements. The information gained from such an examination helps the underwriter determine (1) the insurer's potential liability in a situation in which the insurance benefits are required to match the benefits specified in the agreement, (2) the trustees' authority to contract for insurance, and (3) the disposition of monies in the event of a claim under the coverage.

The Proposal for Insurance

After underwriting on a Request for Proposal is complete, and if coverage has not been denied, the underwriter develops a proposal for insurance for the marketer to present to the proposed policyholder for consideration. A ***proposal for insurance*** provides a number of specifications for the insurance coverage approved by an insurer for a proposed group. A proposal for insurance enables a proposed policyholder to examine the coverage that the underwriter has approved for the group and to compare the cost and benefits of plans offered by several insurers.

Although each insurer develops its own format for a proposal for insurance, such a document usually includes the following information:

- The name of the proposed group, the eligible employee groups and dependents (if applicable), and the number of eligible employees and dependents (if applicable).
- A schedule of benefits that will be included in the group policy. Under a group insurance plan, a ***schedule of benefits*** is a table that specifies the amount of coverage provided for each class of insureds. If an insurer has been able to approve exactly the type of coverage listed in the group's Request for Proposal, the proposal for insurance specifies that type of coverage. If the insurer has not been able to approve the requested coverage, but has been able to offer another type, the proposal for insurance notes the differences between the requested coverage and the offered coverage.
- A list of rates used and the premium amounts quoted for each type of coverage. This information usually includes an ***illustration of net cost,*** typically covering two or more years, to show possible future rating and premiums, provided the group's claim experience remains within the parameters assumed for the insurance product.
- Underwriting principles and assumptions for the proposed coverage.
- Details concerning plan administration, including the responsibilities of the policyholder and the insurer.

Figure 10-4 shows a typical proposal for a self-administered billing plan of insurance.

For small groups, the proposal for coverage does not usually include an illustration of net cost, but does include all the other elements. The illustration of net cost is generally omitted from a small-group proposal because the claim experience of most small groups is not credible enough to entitle them to receive an experience refund (we will explain the experience refund later in this chapter). The proposal for coverage for a small group does include a description of all eligible employees and their dependents who will be insured under the proposed coverage.

A proposal for insurance provides an overview of the coverage offered to the proposed policyholder. If the policyholder accepts the proposal, the policy to be issued will contain complete details of benefits,

Figure 10-4. Typical proposal for a self-administered billing plan of insurance.

PROPOSAL FOR INSURANCE

Prepared for:	Olympic Gardening Services, Inc.
Eligibility:	All active full-time salaried employees who work a minimum of 30 hours per week with 90 days of service.
Number of eligible employees:	85

Schedule of Benefits

Elimination period: 180 days

Basic Life Coverage:

Class	Life Amount	AD&D Amount
Executives	$50,000	$50,000
Supervisors	$30,000	$30,000
Non-exempt employees	$20,000	$20,000

Supplemental Life Coverage:

Class	Life Amount
Executives	Three times basic annual salary less $40,000
Supervisors	Three times basic annual salary less $20,000
Non-exempt less than 1 year of service	One times basic annual salary less $10,000
Non-exempt 1 to 3 years of service	Two times basic annual salary less $10,000
Non-exempt 3+ years of service	Three times basic annual salary less $10,000

Weekly Income (Short-Term Disability) Coverage:

Class	60% of Basic Weekly Salary to a Maximum of:
Executives	$800
Supervisors	$600
Non-exempt less than 1 year of service	$300
Non-exempt 1 to 3 years of service	$350
Non-exempt 3+ years of service	$400

Rate Guarantee: 1 year

Rate Summary:

Coverage	# Employees	Volume	Rate/$1,000	Monthly Premium
Life	83	$2,770,000	$0.56	$1,551.20
Supplemental life	22	$2,095,020	$0.69	$1,445.56
Basic AD&D	83	$4,865,020	$0.05	$ 243.25
Supplemental AD&D	22	$2,095,020	$0.05	$ 104.75

Figure 10-4. Typical proposal for a self-administered billing plan of insurance. (continued)

Underwriting Principles and Assumptions

1. If the policyholder pays the entire cost of the insurance, all eligible employees must participate in the plan.
2. Employees must be actively at work on a full-time basis to become insured. Employees not actively at work on their effective date will become eligible upon return to active full-time employment.
3. If more than one coverage is quoted, coverages are not available separately unless otherwise so stated in this proposal.
4. Full-time employee: An employee must be working a minimum of 30 hours per week to be considered a full-time employee, unless otherwise specified in the schedule of benefits.
5. New employee: An employee hired after the effective date of the plan will become eligible for insurance after completing the probationary period specified in the policy.
6. Supplemental life maximum is $150,000 for each employee.
7. Evidence of insurability will be required for individual amounts of insurance, supplemental coverage only, which exceed $50,000 for employees under age 70 and $25,000 for employees age 70 and older.
8. Insurer will waive evidence of insurability for existing individual amounts of supplemental coverage shown on the proposal census. All increases and/or additional enrollees must submit evidence of insurability as stated above.

Plan Administration

Under this coverage, the policyholder will be responsible for:

- Delivering certificates to each insured
- Maintaining enrollment cards for all insureds
- Maintaining enrollment and benefit data on all insureds
- Providing a complete census of all insureds to the insurer no less frequently than once a year
- Computing the monthly premium due, by coverage when applicable, and remitting the same to the insurer within 30 days of the due date with the following details:
  - + Number of insureds
  - + Total volume
  - + Premium
- Certifying eligibility prior to submitting claims
- Submitting claim forms to the insurer for processing and adjudication. A copy of the enrollment card should be submitted with each claim to assure that the appropriate party is paid.
- Delivering claim checks to the appropriate parties
- Submitting to the insurer the medical questionnaires for individuals whose benefit amounts exceed the guaranteed issue maximum

Under this coverage, the insurer will provide:

- Master Contract to the policyholder
- Certificates for all insureds
- Enrollment cards to be completed by each enrolled member of the group
- Claim forms
- Claim processing and adjudication in the home office
- Conversion policies
- Medical questionnaires and individual underwriting for benefit amounts that exceed the guaranteed issue maximum

policy provisions, and limitations. A policyholder may request a specimen copy of a typical policy to examine prior to accepting or not accepting the proposal.

The Master Application

By means of a master application, a group prospect submits information required for underwriting. The ***master application*** contains the specific provisions of the plan of insurance being applied for and is signed by an authorized officer of the proposed policyholder. After underwriting, if the case is accepted, information from the master application is used to develop the ***master contract*** (also called a *master application*), which is the legal document certifying the relationship between the insurer and the group policyholder.

In some situations, the master application is not submitted until after (1) initial underwriting on the basis of general information provided to the insurer by the marketer and (2) tentative approval of the insurer's offer of insurance by the prospect. The master application contains detailed information about the policyholder, including the name of the ***correspondent,*** a person in the policyholder's organization who serves as liaison with the insurer. The master application also includes all relevant information about the proposed coverage, employee classes, premium, and plan administration. Finally, the master application certifies that all employees are actively at work at their usual place of business on the date the contract becomes effective. The names of all employees who are *not* actively at work are listed, along with the date last worked, the expected date of return to work, and the reason for absence.

Along with the master application, the prospect submits an enrollment card completed by each eligible employee. An ***enrollment card,*** also called an *employee application,* provides the following information about each employee:

- Name and address
- Date of birth
- Gender
- Social Security number in the United States or social insurance number in Canada (Canadian insurers require each employee's signed authorization to use the number for the purposes of identification and recordkeeping under a group plan)

- Name and relationship of beneficiary or beneficiaries

- Types of supplemental coverage selected by the employee (such as the amount of supplemental life insurance for the employee, a spouse, or children, or supplemental accidental death and dismemberment coverage)

The enrollment card also presents a statement that the employee signs to indicate his understanding of the coverage offered and his willingness to have his portion of the premium deducted from his salary. The statement includes a section that the employee may sign if he does not wish to enroll in the group plan. Figure 10-5 illustrates a typical employee statement.

The underwriter examines the master application and the enrollment cards to ensure that all information is complete and is consistent with the applied-for plan of insurance. If a group has been given tentative approval pending receipt of these information sources, the underwriter uses the information either to give final approval to the case or, if the information contains discrepancies or presents other underwriting problems, continues evaluating the case to arrive at a sound decision.

Figure 10-5. Employee statement on enrollment card.

I apply for coverage as indicated above, for which I am or may become eligible under the agreement with ABC Insurance Company, which is herein called the Company. I have read the above statements and represent that they are true and complete to the best of my knowledge. I authorize my employer/group to deduct from my pay and remit any required contribution for the cost of said coverage. This authorization is to remain in effect until the Company is notified by me in writing to the contrary.

I understand that the benefit(s) listed in the certificate(s) will be available subject to the Terms and Conditions thereof effective as listed in the certificate(s) of Coverage.

Signature of Applicant: ______________________

Date: ______________________

I do not wish to enroll at this time and understand that the opportunity to enroll at any future time will be subject to such arrangements as may be made with the Company.

Signature of Applicant: ______________________

Date: ______________________

Rating Methods for Group Cases

An underwriter is usually responsible for arriving at an adequate, equitable rate that the insurer will charge proposed and renewal policyholders. The rate needs to be adequate so that the insurer's costs of doing business and of settling claims are covered. The rate needs to be equitable so that each insured group pays a premium amount that fairly reflects the group's risk. At the same time, the rate must be competitive enough to attract prospects.

The premium for group insurance is calculated by taking into account several factors, generally including the following:

- Expenses associated with the insurance product
- Anticipated cost of claims
- Profit or contribution to insurer's surplus

Fast Fact

The rates for on-the-job injuries and illnesses vary significantly from profession to profession. For instance, in 1992 there were 13.1 occupational injuries or illnesses per 100 construction workers in the United States. Workers in finance and insurance, on the other hand, experienced just 2.9 work-related injuries or illnesses per 100 workers.

Source: U.S. Department of Labor. Cited in Health Insurance Association of America *Source Book of Health Insurance Data,* 1995: 152.

Of these factors, the most important is the anticipated cost of claims. Some jurisdictions have established minimum rates that insurers must charge to help protect the safety and solvency of insurance companies.

Determining the premium that a specific group will be charged for requested coverage involves two steps: (1) determining a unit price, called a ***premium rate,*** that will be charged for a specified amount of coverage; and (2) determining the premium that the group policyholder will be charged for the total amount of coverage requested. For instance, an underwriter may determine the annual premium rate for one type of life insurance coverage for a specific proposed policyholder to be $.17 per month per $1,000 of coverage. Seventeen cents is what the insurer charges each month to provide $1,000 of life benefits to an employee. Therefore, if the proposed policyholder wishes to insure each employee for $10,000, the policyholder would pay $20.40 per employee each year for that type of coverage, calculated as follows:

$.17 [the rate per thousand for the specified coverage]
× 10 [thousands of dollars of coverage]
× 12 [months]

If the policyholder has 500 employees, the annual premium for that coverage for all employees would be $10,200 ($20.40 × 500).

The benefit unit for term life insurance coverage is usually $1,000. For short-term disability income coverage, the benefit unit is typically $10 of weekly income; for long-term disability income coverage, the benefit unit is typically $100 of monthly income. The benefit unit for medical expense and dental coverage is not expressed as a dollar amount, but is expressed in terms of coverage for each covered person and that person's dependents. Because most medical plans provide the same coverage for each insured person, a U.S. insurer typically establishes one rate for each employee class, as follows:

Class 1: Employee

Class 2: Employee and spouse

Class 3: Employee and dependent(s)

Class 4: Employee, spouse, and dependent(s)

These classes are not as common in Canada as they are in the United States, but some Canadian companies establish such classes as employee and dependent(s) and single family (one employee and dependent[s]).

In calculating the premium rate to charge for group coverage, insurance companies generally use manual rating, experience rating, or a combination of the two. We will discuss these approaches and will then comment on the rating approaches used for small groups.

Manual Rating

Manual rating, as we mentioned in Chapter 9, involves establishing premium rates for broad classes of groups, especially for those with no credible claim experience. Sometimes the underwriter performs manual rating by considering the aggregate claim experience of a class of insureds, but does not consider the claim experience of a specific group.

Groups of any size are subject to manual rating if they have no specific claim experience on which the underwriter can base a calculation of premium rates. However, insurers that issue a large amount of certain types of coverage typically develop enough experience information to be able to determine future claims for many proposed groups, even those without claim experience. Additional sources of experience information include the Society of Actuaries' data reports and other governmental and trade organization publications.

In making a manual rate calculation, an underwriter first determines the ***net premium rate,*** which is the premium amount required to pay the cost of a group's anticipated claims. In determining the net premium rate, the underwriter relies on experience information from either the insurer's records or other sources. Depending on the type of coverage, the insurer may also consider such factors as age, gender, income, geographic location, and industry in which the proposed group is employed. Moreover, the underwriter may consider such elements of the plan as deductible amounts, coinsurance provisions, length of the probationary period, and length of the benefit period. In group insurance, the ***probationary period*** is the length of time that must pass before a new member is eligible to join the group plan.

Once calculated, the net premium rate is adjusted for expenses and profit or contribution to surplus. Many insurers also add a ***risk charge,*** an amount that represents a contribution to the insurer's reserves to pay for extremely large claims.

Manual rates usually stay in effect for a group for a specified period of time, usually 6 months for medical expense and disability income coverage and 12 months for life insurance coverage, until the insurer develops enough experience information for that group to be able to calculate rates based on the group's experience.

Experience Rating

Experience rating is the process of using a group's claim experience to calculate premium rates. This type of rating is generally used for large groups that have previously been insured and have a history of claims. An important assumption underlying experience rating is that a group's claim experience is likely to remain relatively constant from one year to another. In some years, a group may have higher or lower numbers of claims and dollar amounts of claims. Nevertheless, the likelihood is high that a group whose composition remains relatively constant is likely to experience about the same level of claims from one year to another.

Experience rating is used to establish initial premiums for groups requesting coverage for the first time from the insurer, as well as to calculate renewal premiums for groups that the insurer already covers. The underwriter examines health and short-term disability claim figures from as many as three years, if that many years of experience are available. For long-term disability income and life insurance coverage, underwriters examine claim figures for the past five years. However, if a group has had unusual claim fluctuations, the underwriter may consider claim information for a longer period. For instance, suppose a group had good claim experience for a period of 10 years, followed by 2 years of extremely poor claim experience. In such a situation, the underwriter examines the 12-year trend of claims and seeks to understand the cause of the recently poor experience. If the underwriter discovers sufficient reason for the downturn and is convinced that the poor experience is likely to end, the application may be approved.

When an insured group's claim experience for the previous year was favorable, an underwriter may calculate a lower-than-average premium rate for the next year. For a group that is renewing coverage, the insurer may decide, on the basis of its experience, to reduce the premium rates for the coming year. In some cases, a group with favorable claim experience becomes eligible for an experience refund.

An ***experience refund,*** also called a *dividend* or a *premium refund,* is the portion of a group insurance premium that is returned to a group policyholder whose claim experience is better than had been expected when the premium was calculated.

If a group's claim experience was unfavorable—that is, if claims were greater than anticipated when the premium rates were calculated—an insurer attempts to discover the reason for the excessive claims and may propose a higher-than-average premium rate for that group for the coming year.

We will first discuss the benefits of experience rating and then will examine the use of experience rating for calculating initial premiums and renewal premiums.

Advantages of experience rating. Experience rating has specific advantages concerning equity, effective competition, and avoidance of antiselection.

First, experience rating helps an insurer charge equitable premiums to each insured group. The amount of premium an insurer charges is established according to actuarial calculations whose intent is to ensure, as much as possible, that the premiums a group pays are adequate to cover claims, administrative expenses, and other business costs. Using a group's own experience to assess the premium due from that group is a fair way to charge each group for the amount of benefits it is likely to claim.

Fast Fact

One-quarter of all reported on-the-job injuries occur while a worker is attempting to lift an object.

Source: Health Insurance Association of America *Source Book of Health Insurance Data,* 1994: 145.

Second, experience rating enables an insurer to compete successfully with other insurance companies. In a free marketplace with adequate competition, a seller who most closely matches the cost of a product to the benefits of that product is more likely to succeed than are sellers who overprice their products. Similarly, an insurer that offers a group a premium rate based on that group's claim experience is able to match the cost of the product to the benefit the product has provided in the past and is likely to provide in the future. If an insurance company pooled all its group risks and charged the same premium to every group, the groups representing lower risk and potentially better-than-average claim experience would, in effect, subsidize the groups representing higher risk and potentially poorer-than-average claim experience. As a result, lower-risk groups would pay more for a product than the benefits they derived from it, and they would be likely to seek coverage from another insurance company with more competitive pricing.

Third, experience rating helps insurers to avoid the effects of antiselection. An insurer that offered all groups the same premium rate, regardless of each group's degree of risk, would probably find that lower-risk groups would resist paying more for the coverage and would tend to seek coverage from other insurance companies that could provide the same coverage at a lower premium. Meanwhile, higher-risk groups would tend to seek coverage from the insurer offering one premium rate because those groups could not obtain the same coverage at the same cost from other insurers that used experience rating. The resulting antiselection would probably harm the insurer's business, both present and future.

Calculating initial and renewal premiums. To figure a group's initial premiums, an underwriter calculates probable future claims. By assessing a group's claim experience, the underwriter develops a figure that represents the ***contractual claim liability,*** which is the amount of money necessary to pay the claims incurred by the group during a specified period. In developing the contractual claim liability figure, the underwriter uses reports indicating the total amount of claims paid during a specified period, which is usually one year. In our discussion, we will present a simplified view of the underwriter's calculations, which may, in reality, be much more complex and may include consideration of each group's claim reserves, a topic outside the scope of this textbook.

The total figure of claims paid during a period does not usually represent exactly the degree of contractual claim liability incurred by the insurer, because not all claims were incurred during the period, and not all incurred claims were paid or even reported during the period. To calculate a claim experience figure that more accurately represents the group's true experience for the period, the underwriter adjusts the figure representing the total claims paid during the period by separating the claims into three categories, as follows:

1. Total claims paid during the period
2. Claims incurred prior to the period and paid during the period
3. Claims incurred during the period but not yet paid

The claims for category 2 were incurred during a previous period and do not, therefore, represent claims incurred during the period being examined. By contrast, the claims in category 3 have not been paid and may not even have been reported. The claims in category 3 represent a liability that the insurer will likely have to pay in a future period. To represent fairly the claims in category 3 that have been incurred but not reported, the underwriter adds an amount that is estimated from the group's experience in previous periods or from the insurer's overall experience with the type of coverage for which the group's claim experience is being assessed.

Using these numbers, the underwriter then calculates the contractual claim liability as follows:

- From the total of claims in category 1, the underwriter subtracts the total of claims in category 2.
- The underwriter then adds the adjusted total of claims in category 3.

For example, from a report of a group's claim experience from May 1995 through April 1996, an underwriter develops the following information (figures have been rounded for ease of calculation):

1. Total claims paid = $296,000
2. Claims incurred prior to the period and paid during that period = $47,000
3. Claims incurred during the period but not yet paid = $57,000

The underwriter increases the figure for category 3 by $26,000 to indicate an estimate of claims incurred during the period but not yet reported, so that the total for category 3 = $83,000. The final calculation representing the contractual claim liability for the period is as follows:

$$\$296,000 - \$47,000 + \$57,000 + \$26,000 = \$332,000$$

The figures developed for an insurer's contractual claim liability for a group may be adjusted according to changes in the future coverage, if any. Changes that would usually result in adjustments involve benefit schedule changes, such as reducing the maximum long-term disability monthly benefit from $8,000 to $6,000; raising deductibles or coinsurance amounts; increasing life insurance amounts; or changing medical practitioners or covered medical procedures. Other changes that would normally produce adjustments include an increase or a reduction in the number of insured employees, a significant change in the employee mix (for instance, a large shift from white-collar to blue-collar employees), and assignment of employees to new job duties that pose considerable additional hazards.

The approach explained here for calculating initial premiums is also used to calculate renewal premiums, which we will discuss later in this chapter.

Blended Rating

Insurers sometimes use both manual and experience rating to calculate premiums. Sometimes adequate experience information is unavailable to permit an underwriter to base premiums solely on a group's history. However, including a measure of a group's prior experience helps to ensure that the premium is equitable and accurate. Therefore, ***blended rating*** is performed by assigning a credibility factor to the group's experience and including that factor in the premium calculations. A ***credibility factor*** is a percentage that represents the degree to which the underwriter has estimated that the available underwriting information accurately shows the risk represented by a group.

Suppose an underwriter assigns a 15 percent credibility factor to a group's experience. As a result, the underwriter assumes that 15 percent of the group's future claim cost will be based on the group's experience. The remaining 85 percent of the group's future claim cost will be based on the insurer's manual rating. The blended rate is determined by multiplying the premium calculated by manual rating and experience rating by the factor assigned to each, and adding the two products.

For instance, suppose that a group's premium is calculated as $300 by manual rating and as $250 by experience rating. The underwriter assigns a credibility factor of 85 percent to the manual rating and a credibility factor of 15 percent to the experience rating. The calculation of a premium by blended rating is as follows:

$$(\$300 \times .85) + (\$250 \times .15) = \$255 + \$37.50 = \$292.50$$

As in this example, the premium calculated by blended rating is typically lower than the premium calculated by manual rating alone, but higher than the premium calculated by experience rating alone.

Rating Approaches for Small Groups

Because small-group underwriting for life insurance and short- and long-term disability income coverage is similar to individual underwriting for these products, many companies send such small-group cases to an individual underwriter. After assessing the risk, if the case is acceptable, the individual underwriter forwards the case to a group underwriter, who performs the rate calculations.

Developing equitable rates for small groups requires the underwriter to exercise particular caution. Individual variations in age, health, and other risk factors increase in importance as group size decreases. In a group of eight people, for example, one person who represents a high level of risk can have a strong effect on the risk represented by the group. However, that same person, as part of a group of 500 persons, would have much less effect on the group's level of risk.

To calculate the rates to be charged to a small group, particularly for insurance that has limited numbers of benefits and limited amounts of coverage, underwriters at most insurance companies first assess the risk represented by each person in the group and assign each person a

Fast Fact

There are an estimated 5 to 6 million businesses in the United States with fewer than 100 employees—and over 80 percent of those businesses have fewer than 10 employees.

Source: Nilufer R. Ahmed and Cheryl D. Retzloff, "The Changing Marketplace of U.S. Small Businesses," *LIMRA's MarketFacts,* July/August 1995: 4–6.

rate according to ***step rates,*** which are rates based on the insurer's experience and expressed in age-graded, sometimes gender-specific tables. Then the underwriter can average the individual rates to determine the group rate. Employees with spouses usually pay an additional amount for spousal coverage. Figure 10-6 provides a sample calculation of the cost of insurance coverage using step rates for a small group of four employees.

Each insurer establishes its own numerical limits for a small group. When a proposed group falls within those limits, the insurer may require that each person in the group show evidence of insurability. The evidence required ranges from a simple health questionnaire completed by each group member to APSs and other medical evidence. An underwriter may require APSs and additional evidence on only those group members whose health questionnaires indicate the presence of possibly greater risk.

Especially for coverage proposed for new small groups, an insurer may guarantee the initial premium rate for only a short period, which most commonly is 6 months but may be as brief as 60 days. If the group's claim experience proves unfavorable, the insurer may increase the premium; alternatively, the insurer may decrease the premium for a group that has favorable claim experience. The insurer usually is permitted by law to change the premium with as little as 30 to 60 days' notice.

Risk factors that underwriters typically examine for each individual in a small group are age, gender, dependents, and the type of benefits for which the group requests coverage. Some insurers also consider the geographic location and the type of industry in which a group's employees are involved.

Figure 10-6. Calculation of small-group premiums using step rates.

Type of Coverage: Comprehensive major medical, $250 deductible

Name	Age	Spouse Covered?	Step Rate (monthly)
Sarah	29	Yes	$228.17
Mattie	52	No	$260.05
Kevin	38	No	$191.52
Dom	42	Yes	$242.38

Adding the step rates, the underwriter determines that the total monthly cost of coverage for the four employees is $922.12, and that the monthly premium for each employee is $230.53 ($922.12 ÷ 4). Some insurers modify the premium by charging a separate amount for an employee and for a spouse. In this case, the insurer might charge each of the four employees $161.37 and each of the two spouses $138.32, amounts that would produce the same amount of monthly premium ($922.12).

Post-Issue Underwriting for Group Insurance

Group underwriters are involved not only in approval of new risks, but in several kinds of post-issue underwriting. These kinds include approval of late entrants, approval of benefit changes, and renewal underwriting.

Approval of Late Entrants

Employees who choose not to enroll in a group plan when it is first offered may decide to enroll later. Sometimes these employees defer enrollment until they develop a health condition that would be covered by the plan. To avoid this kind of antiselection, insurers usually require late entrants to provide evidence of insurability. Such evidence is also submitted for a dependent whom the employee wishes later to enroll. Employees who are enrolled in a group plan and who then withdraw while still employed are usually required to submit evidence of insurability when they apply to re-enroll in the plan.

Evidence of insurability for late entrants varies from one insurer to another and from one plan to another. Generally, the more extensive the benefits, the more detailed the information required. Most insurers require late entrants to complete a questionnaire certifying their health status. Some insurers also require a medical examination and documentation concerning medical treatments received by the employee or dependents.

Approval of Benefit Changes

When an insured group wishes to increase the type or extent of benefits offered under a plan of insurance, the underwriter examines the group's claim experience. If that experience indicates that the group's rate should be increased to cover the additional benefits, the underwriter calculates the increase. On the other hand, the underwriter may find that a group that has had lower-than-expected claim experience (a concept defined in the next section) is eligible to increase benefits without an increase in premium. Similarly, a group that wishes to reduce its benefits can be eligible for a reduction in premium unless the group's experience has been unfavorable.

The underwriter is also involved when a policyholder wishes to offer insurance to employee classes that were previously excluded from certain types or amounts of coverage. If the employee classes to be added constitute only a minor addition to the whole group, the underwriter is usually able to approve the additional coverage without extensive information. If, however, the added classes constitute a considerable proportion of the whole group, the underwriter generally considers information about the age, gender, and salary of each person in the added classes. Moreover, the underwriter may need information about the geographic location of the new employees (for example, when a covered group purchases another company or establishes a branch office in another location), any previous coverage of the new employees, and the type of industry in which the new employees will be working, particularly if that industry involves hazards to which employees in the original insured group are not exposed.

Renewal Underwriting

Unlike individual life policies, group policies are subject to an annual renewal, during which underwriting takes place. In ***renewal underwriting,*** the underwriter reviews all the risk assessment factors considered when the group was originally underwritten and all changes in the group and its coverage between the previous underwriting and the current time. In addition, the underwriter assesses how efficiently the policyholder has administered the plan during the year. Problems identified are usually brought to the attention of the employer or group policyholder along with suggestions for corrective action.

Each year when the policy is renewed, the insurer uses experience rating to calculate a new premium rate that reflects the group's expected claim experience for the coming year. The ***expected claim experience*** is the dollar amount of claims that the insurer estimates the group will submit. The expected claim experience is calculated according to (1) the group's prior year's claim experience and (2) changes in the group's age, gender, and benefit payments that occurred during the previous year. The underwriter also takes into account any changes in the business segment occupied by an insured group or economic conditions affecting the financial strength of the insured group.

Generally, the information an underwriter receives from a marketer for a renewal of coverage includes a census of employees to be covered. This census is the same type of document as the census submitted for new policy underwriting.

For example, the Gartrell Corporation provides life insurance and medical expense insurance coverage for all its employees. The corporation's life insurance coverage provides for basic insurance as well as additional insurance that employees may choose to purchase. In addition, the corporation's medical expense insurance plan provides two levels of coverage—major medical and health maintenance organization (HMO). The underwriter who assesses the Gartrell Corporation's application for renewed coverage receives information on the number of employees enrolled in each line of coverage: those covered only by basic life insurance, those who purchased additional life insurance, those covered by major medical coverage, and those enrolled in the HMO. In addition, the underwriter receives information about the age, gender, occupation, and salary of each employee, and details about the number and type of claims submitted during the previous period of coverage. Claim experience is usually provided for the group as a whole and for individuals within the group.

If a group's claim experience and administrative expenses have fallen within the parameters established for the policy when it was written, the underwriter may renew coverage at the same premium rate as for the previous period. If, on the other hand, a group's claim experience or administrative expenses have exceeded the established parameters, the underwriter is likely to (1) increase the premium rate or (2) suggest a revision in benefits. Typical proposed revisions in benefits include increasing the amount of premium that each employee pays and adding programs to monitor the type of care delivered. Other approaches insurers may take to help underwrite a group with questionable claim experience are to pool the group's risk with the risk from other groups, to require premiums to be paid earlier in the year, and to institute some degree of self-insurance.

A group whose claim experience has been considerably less than the established parameters is likely to receive approval of future coverage and may receive a reduction in its premium rate or an experience refund. Calculation of renewal premiums follows the same approach as that used to calculate initial premiums.

Key Terms and Concepts

Request for Proposal (RFP)
current open claimants
employee class
benefit transmittal
rate transmittal
employee census
summary plan description
summary of material modification
proposal for insurance
schedule of benefits
illustration of net cost
master application
master contract
correspondent
enrollment card (*employee application*)
premium rate
net premium rate
probationary period
risk charge
experience rating
experience refund (*dividend, premium refund*)
contractual claim liability
blended rating
credibility factor
step rates
renewal underwriting
expected claim experience

CHAPTER ELEVEN

Scope and Organization of Reinsurance

Learning Objectives

After studying this chapter, you should be able to

- Name and define the entity that transfers risk and the entity that accepts risk in insurance and reinsurance transactions
- List and explain five reasons that an insurance company uses traditional reinsurance
- Identify two advantages of using reinsurance for coverage exceeding an insurer's retention limit
- Specify two limitations of using traditional reinsurance
- Explain the primary differences between primary-company underwriting and reinsurance underwriting
- Explain how regulation of reinsurance differs from regulation of insurance

Chapter Outline

Now that you're familiar with the principal activities and responsibilities of underwriting, we'll consider the subject of reinsurance. We have defined *reinsurance* as a form of insurance that allows an insurer to purchase protection that indemnifies or reimburses the insurer in the event of covered losses claimed under insurance policies it has issued. Briefly, reinsurance is insurance for an insurer. Reinsurance enables one insurer to transfer part of a risk to another insurer by paying the second insurer part of the premiums.

As you have learned, underwriting involves assessing the risk represented by a proposed insured or proposed policyowner or policyholder. (In discussing reinsurance, for simplicity's sake we will refer to both policyowners and policyholders as "policyowners.") In accepting these risks, each insurance company protects its financial strength by deciding how much financial responsibility it is willing to assume or retain on an individual or a group. The amount of insurance coverage that the insurer will carry at its own risk is generally known as the insurer's ***retention limit.*** The retention limit may be related to losses per insured person, losses per accident or event, or total losses per class of business (we will further discuss the retention limit later in this chapter). An insurer writes a policy that exceeds its retention limit by sharing the risk with a reinsurance company. Insurance companies and reinsurance companies establish relationships to facilitate such sharing of risk.

You may be wondering why an insurance company would choose to pay for reinsurance. After all, the insurer has marketed the case, has underwritten the coverage, and will receive the premium for it. Why doesn't an insurance company retain all its risks and keep all its premiums?

Part of the answer is that an insurance company gains specific advantages from *not* retaining all the risk associated with its cases. We'll discuss these advantages later in this chapter. The rest of the answer is that purchasing reinsurance for certain risks provides a win-win financial situation for both an insurance company and a reinsurer. From the perspective of an insurer, buying reinsurance allows the insurer to sell policies for amounts that exceed the retention limit. Reinsurance can be a cost-effective means of reducing an insurer's exposure to fluctuations in claims, lapses, and investment risk associated with insurance policies. Typically, an insurer pays a percentage of the premium to pass part or all of a risk to a reinsurance company and to compensate the reinsurer for the expenses, claims or mortality costs, and profit associated with reinsuring the coverage. The premium paid by the insurance company to the reinsurer may range between 2 and 10 percent (although high-risk or very high-amount cases may require 50 percent or more of the premium). Insurance companies do not cede more risk than necessary, however, because paying premiums to reinsurance companies reduces an insurer's profits.

From the perspective of a reinsurer, offering reinsurance is cost-effective because the reinsurer does not incur most of the costs of obtaining a case. The insurance company that is purchasing reinsurance has already borne those costs, including the expenses of product development, marketing, underwriting, billing and collections, and filing documents with regulatory agencies. Insight 11-1 discusses further the special relationship which is established between an insurer and a reinsurer, and which we will discuss in much more detail in Chapter 13.

An insurance company may use reinsurance in several ways, which are divided roughly into traditional and nontraditional uses. The traditional use of reinsurance is to transfer risk from the insurer to the reinsurer. This use is the one we will examine in detail in this textbook. (Reinsurers use the term "traditional reinsurance" to refer to reinsurance of new business and the term "surplus relief" to refer to reinsurance of in-force business. We will not focus on the distinction between reinsurance of new business and in-force business, but will discuss reinsured business in general.) The nontraditional uses of reinsurance involve many aspects of insurance financial planning and

Insight 11-1 The Good Old Days: Reinsurance Revisited

Why does reinsurance exist?

Look at it this way. Seller—in this case, a marketer—has a customer who wants $2 million in coverage. Seller's supplier of coverage has a retention limit of $1 million. Does Supplier tell Friend Seller, "Sorry, can't help you"? He does not. He doesn't want Friend Seller to go down the street, so he says, "Hey, man, you betcha, let's go."

Great, but now Supplier has to find a way to handle that $2 million. What does he do? He utilizes a reinsurer to get the monkey off his back.

What does this tell us? Almost all insurance companies need a reinsurer. All reinsurers *need* insurance companies—without insurance companies, there would be no reinsurers. In two words, there is a mutual need. My premise is that such a need calls for a relationship akin to what might be termed a partnership.

Accepting the concept of partnership, move on to the rules of the game. Usually, there is a basic document that outlines those rules. This document is usually described as an agreement, a contract, or a treaty. And it is an agreement that traditionally carries and should carry with it the adjective "gentlemen's." Why? Because, to put it simply, since every "t" can't be crossed and the myriad of transactions that take place between the partners cannot be reduced to writing, the character of the partners is of concern. They should be gentlemen.

Underlying the gentlemen's agreement is a principle that partners act at all times in the utmost good faith. It cannot be otherwise, if the gentlemen's agreement is to work; what is implied is fidelity, loyalty, honesty of intention. Each partner acts in accordance with standards of honesty and sincerity.

From Charles A. Will, "The Good Old Days: Reinsurance Revisited," *On the Risk,* 8(4), 1992: 16–22. Adapted by permission.

strategic planning, topics we will not discuss in detail because they are not primary activities of insurance administration.

In this chapter, we'll examine the scope of the relationship that an insurance company establishes with a reinsurance company. We'll discuss the reasons that insurers use reinsurance and the limitations of using reinsurance. Finally, we'll present some of the legal issues that affect the reinsurance relationship.

The Reinsurance Relationship

The reinsurance relationship between an insurer and a reinsurer is formed to enable the insurer to spread risk. Under reinsurance, the policyowners have a contractual relationship only with the insurer; they have no contractual relationship with the reinsurer. When risk is transferred to a reinsurer, or from one reinsurer to another, the insured person or group is not usually aware of the risk transfer (except in the case of assumption reinsurance, which we'll discuss later in this chapter).

A reinsurance agreement between an insurance company and a reinsurer typically provides that the insurer will send part of the premium to the reinsurer as payment for the reinsured coverage. The policyowners send their premiums to the insurer, not to the reinsurer. If a reinsurance company experiences financial difficulties and cannot pay claims submitted under the reinsurance agreement, the insurer is still obligated to pay all legitimate claims that policyowners submit under the coverage. Moreover, if an insurer cannot meet its financial obligations, the policyowner has no recourse to the reinsurer for indemnity at claim time.

Fast Fact

Life reinsurance is often placed by ceding life companies with affiliated life insurance companies. A.M. Best Co. reports that this reinsurance among affiliates totaled $580 billion in 1994.

Source: Kevin G. Maher, "Number of Life Reinsurers Dwindles as Market Grows," *Best's Review (Life/Health)*, March 1996: 40–46, 100.

When an insurer transfers all or part of a risk that it does not wish to retain, the insurer becomes a ***ceding company*** (also called the *reinsured*). A company that assumes the risk from the ceding company becomes a ***reinsurer*** (also called the *assuming company*). To transfer some or all of a very large risk to another reinsurance company, the reinsurance company may purchase reinsurance from a second reinsurer. The reinsurer that accepts a retrocedent's risk is known as a ***retrocessionaire.*** Figure 11-1 illustrates the transfer of risk by means of insurance and reinsurance.

The record of the transfer of risk from a ceding company to a reinsurer is an act known as a ***cession.*** The act of transferring risk from an insurer to a reinsurer is known as ***ceding.*** Transferring the risk from a reinsurer to a retrocessionaire is an act known as ***retrocession.*** In exchange for assuming all or part of a risk, the ceding company pays the reinsurer or the retrocessionaire part of the premium paid by insureds for the coverage. The reinsurer pays its share of any insured

Figure 11-1. Transfer of risk by means of insurance and reinsurance.

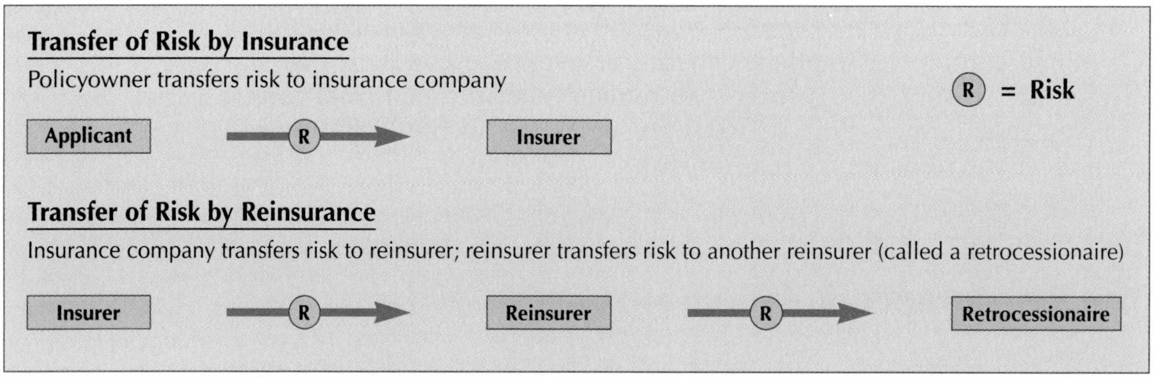

claims for which it has received a premium. Figure 11-2 illustrates a typical retrocession arrangement among an insurer, a reinsurer, and a retrocessionaire.

Reinsurance thus enables insurance companies to substitute certain known, fixed costs—paying premiums for reinsurance—for certain unknown, variable costs—the costs of claims covered by reinsurance. The transfer of risk tends to smooth the profits of the ceding company or the retrocedent. The amount of coverage provided by the reinsurer is defined in a ***reinsurance treaty,*** which is a statement of the agreement between a reinsurer and a ceding company. In Chapter 14, we'll examine the reinsurance treaty in detail. Until that point, however, we'll refer only to the "agreement" between an insurer and a reinsurer.

The reinsurance relationship includes the exchange of considerable information as the insurer and the reinsurer administer the reinsured coverage. Insight 11-2 discusses the importance of information systems in reinsurance administration today. In later chapters we'll discuss the importance of information exchanges by underwriting and claims in reinsurance administration.

Figure 11-2. Typical retrocession arrangement.

1. The insurer underwrites a life insurance policy for $5 million.
2. The insurer's retention limit is $1 million for such a risk.
3. The insurer cedes $4 million of the risk to a reinsurer
4. The reinsurer's retention limit is $2 million for such a risk.
5. The reinsurer cedes $2 million of the risk to a retrocessionaire.

After these cessions, the risk represented by the $5 million policy is spread in this manner:

Insurer:	Reinsurer:	Retrocessionaire:
Insures $1 million	Insures $2 million	Insures $2 million

Insight 11-2 My Thoughts On . . . Reinsurance Administration: Yesterday, Today, and Tomorrow

Twenty years ago, almost all reinsurance administration followed the format of having the ceding company prepare a cession form. This form would then be sent to a reinsurer to identify the transfer of risk above the ceding company's retention. The reinsurer would use this form to bill the ceding company for the premiums involved in the risk transfer. Each reinsurer had its own specialized mainframe administration and billing systems. Reinsurers dealt with only a few different kinds of policy plans.

Today, ceding companies transfer a high percentage of their risk by preparing their own billing and sending it to the reinsurer. Most of these administration systems are home grown programs developed by each ceding company. However, many mid-size and larger insurers have purchased reinsurance administrative systems developed by third parties or by reinsurers. Insurers also offer a much greater variety of plans of coverage. In addition, many insurers today cede blocks of policies to a number of reinsurers at one time, splitting each risk into percentages for each reinsurance pool member.

Third party vendors are selling personal computer-based administrations systems that have the capability of handling a great variety of traditional plans, interest sensitive plans, and universal life and variable plans. Moreover, context sensitive help features and menus allow for administrative staff to be trained more rapidly on using these programs.

The key element in today's reinsurance administrative system is the interface between the ceding company's own policy administration systems and information sources concerning new policy issues, as well as policy changes and terminations. A number of ceding companies with large amount of reinsurance records provide their reinsurers with electronic disks or cartridges containing reinsurance billing details.

Further insurance industry consolidation may result in ceding companies' providing direct electronic links with their reinsurers. Reinsurance billing information may be sent to reinsurers in this way. Reinsurers may use these links to verify death claims or to verify other types of reinsurance information.

Some third party vendors are considering doing reinsurance administration as a billable service to ceding insurers. The ceding company would arrange for the vendor to be able to extract policy information from the insurer's own system. The vendor would do the reinsurance billing and data transfers and would have the technical expertise needed to handle atypical transactions.

Richard P. Allen, FLMI
Director, Sales & Service,
Individual Reinsurance
CNA Insurance Companies

Reasons to Use Reinsurance

A ceding company transfers part or all of certain risks for several reasons, which include the following:

- Increasing underwriting capacity
- Obtaining underwriting expertise
- Minimizing mortality and morbidity risk
- Minimizing the persistency risk
- Fronting

Increasing Underwriting Capacity

In an increasingly competitive marketplace, an insurance company attempts to maintain a balance between accepting new business and exposing itself to excessive risk. For each new case that an insurer underwrites, legislation requires that the insurer establish sufficient reserves to pay anticipated claims. An insurer that accepts a great deal of new business must find a way to provide adequate reserves for the new cases. Rather than turn away well-qualified new business, most insurers turn to reinsurance as a way of strengthening their financial position.

Fast Fact

The trend in reinsurance is toward fewer but larger companies. The total U.S. reinsurance market in 1995 was $2.5 trillion. Some 43 percent of that market was held by 22 reinsurers. In 1994, the top 25 reinsurers held 42 percent of the market.

Source: Kevin G. Maher, "Number of Life Reinsurers Dwindles as Market Grows," *Best's Review (Life/Health)*, March 1996: 40–46, 100.

Reinsurance expands an insurer's ***capacity,*** which, in the simplest terms, is the largest amount of insurance the insurer is allowed to underwrite. An insurer's capacity is determined primarily by an insurer's financial worth, but it is also affected by the amount and nature of the insurer's in-force coverage. Capacity includes (1) the amount of risk an insurer transfers to reinsurers and (2) the insurer's retention limit, which we have defined as the maximum amount of coverage the insurer will carry at its own risk.

Using reinsurance enables an insurer to underwrite a greater amount of business than the insurer could underwrite independently because the insurer is able to transfer part or all of the risk to the reinsuring company. Because the insurer does not bear all of the risk, it does not have to establish the same level of reserves in anticipation of paying claims. When a ceding company purchases reinsurance, the company, in effect, adds to its own capacity the capacity of the reinsurer and, therefore, is able to accept a greater amount of financial risk than it could accept alone. In this way, reinsurance enhances an insurer's ability to expand the marketing for its products and to satisfy the needs of marketers and applicants for large policy amounts.

Both insurers and reinsurers establish retention limits (in this discussion, we'll refer to both insurers and reinsurers as the "insurer.") The retention limit defines the maximum amount of financial exposure an insurer is willing to keep as its own risk. An insurer's retention limit may be expressed as a percentage amount, as a dollar amount, or as a combination of these amounts. You can remember this term by thinking of it as the amount of coverage an insurer keeps, or "retains," as its own unshared risk and does not transfer to a reinsurer. Figure 11-3 illustrates a sample table of retention limits established by one insurance company.

The amount of risk above an insurer's retention limit is handled in one of two ways. The insurer may decide to accept the excess risk and reinsure it, or the insurer may decline the excess risk, an action that is rare.

Establishing a retention limit requires that a balance be found between the insurer's underlying business purpose—to earn profits—and

Figure 11-3. Table of retention limits.

	Standard Rating	Substandard Rating			
Issue Ages		**Tables 1 through 2**	**Tables 3 through 4**	**Tables 5 through 8**	**Tables 10 through 16**
0	$100,000	$100,000	$ 50,000	$—	$—
1–5	150,000	150,000	75,000	—	—
6–9	200,000	200,000	100,000	—	—
10–15	300,000	300,000	150,000	—	—
16–60	500,000	500,000	375,000	300,000	250,000
61–65	300,000	300,000	225,000	200,000	150,000
66–70	200,000	200,000	150,000	100,000	75,000
71 & above	100,000	100,000	75,000	60,000	40,000

Minimum Cession: $5,000

the insurer's obligation to its insureds not to undertake excessive exposure to risk and thus to jeopardize its financial strength. An insurer's retention limit for each type of insurance product is typically established by its board of directors according to a number of factors, including the following:

- Amount of the insurer's capital and surplus
- Volume of coverage currently in force
- Type of coverage
- Average age of expected policyowners for individual coverage
- Type of expected group for group coverage
- Expected level of claims and/or mortality experience
- Skill of the insurer's underwriting staff
- Cost of reinsurance
- Geographical distribution of risks
- Insurer's preference to be risk-taking or risk-averse

For life insurance coverage, the amount of insurance to be retained on each individual life can be a flat amount for all plans of insurance, all ages, and all mortality ratings, or it can be graded, with several internal retention limits in specific areas. Although an insurer usually sets a retention limit for each insurance product, that limit can be adjusted, according to the rating or risk class of each block of insureds and, for individual coverages, the age of the proposed insured at the time of policy issue. In practice, an insurer's maximum retention limit is usually applied to standard risks between the ages of 21 and 60. Most insurers also set lower retention limits for lower and higher ages, as well as for their substandard risk classes.

Generally, an insurance company establishes lower retention limits for greater risks—for instance, for coverage issued to persons of advanced age or to private pilots. Retention limits are graded downward as the extra mortality rating of the substandard classes increases. Some insurers set a lower retention limit for their term insurance plans in which, because of small reserves, the net amount at risk remains throughout the term at approximately the full face amount of insurance. Moreover, as an insurer's in-force coverage and capital and surplus grow, the insurer usually raises its retention limits because it can afford to retain more risk on its own.

Setting retention limits assists an insurer in reducing fluctuations in the claim level predicted for each line of business. The flat amount and the flat percentage schedules are the simplest to administer and permit the ceding company to retain more at higher ages and ratings than it could under a graded retention schedule. Figure 11-4 lists various types of retention schedules that insurers use.

Regardless of the retention schedule established for a product, the ceding company may set a ***reinsurance corridor,*** also called a *minimum cession,* which is an amount above the scheduled retention

Figure 11-4. Types of retention schedules.

Flat amount for all ages and mortality ratings
Example: $250,000 retention limit for any coverage, regardless of age and rating

Graded amounts based on mortality ratings and/or age, plan, or other basis
Example:

Age/Rating	Standard to 150%	175% to 300%	325% +
0–24	$100,000	$ 50,000	$ 0
25–65	$250,000	$175,000	$50,000
66–75	$175,000	$ 50,000	$ 0
76 +	$ 50,000	$ 0	$ 0

Flat percentage of each case
Example: 50% of each case will be retained, regardless of age and rating

Graded percentage of each case
Example: 25% of the risk up to $250,000

Combination amount and percentage
Example: $100,000 plus 25% of remainder up to retention limit.

limit. The insurer retains the amount specified as the reinsurance corridor as its risk in order to avoid purchasing a small amount of reinsurance. The reinsurance corridor typically takes effect only when the amount of coverage applied for is equal to or less than the insurer's retention limit *plus* the amount of the reinsurance corridor.

For instance, suppose that an insurer has established a flat retention limit of $50,000 for whole life coverage and a reinsurance corridor of $10,000. If the insurer underwrites and decides to issue a policy in the amount of $60,000, the insurer will retain the risk for the entire amount ($50,000 retention limit + $10,000 reinsurance corridor). On the other hand, if the insurer underwrites and decides to issue a policy in the amount of $65,000, the insurer will retain $50,000 as its own risk and will reinsure $15,000 of the risk. Establishing a reinsurance corridor enables a ceding company to avoid the expense of purchasing reinsurance on a case for which no significant risk transfer exists. Insurers with retention limits below $100,000 may have either no minimum cession or a very small amount of cession, say, $1,000.

The reinsurer's liability for each case or block of reinsured business is the total amount of coverage minus the amount of the insurer's retention limit and any applicable reinsurance corridor. For example, suppose an insurer's retention limit is $2 million for a certain type of policy, and the reinsurance corridor is $50,000. The insurer issues a policy of that type in the amount of $6 million. Note that in this case the reinsurance corridor does not apply because the total amount of the coverage exceeds the total of the retention limit *plus* the reinsurance corridor. If the $4 million above the retention limit is reinsured, that amount constitutes the reinsurer's liability. The $4 million in coverage may be spread among several reinsurers, particularly if the retention limit set by each reinsurer is less than the $4 million liability. Alternatively, one reinsurer may accept the whole $4 million of liability, but then, using retrocession, may reinsure all or part of the $4 million liability with another insurance company.

Sometimes an insurer decides to increase the amount of its retention limit on a certain line of business that has already been reinsured and to reduce the amount of reinsurance on the business. In such a situation, the insurer undertakes a procedure known as ***recapture*** in which the insurer takes back from the reinsurer a portion of the reinsured business. For example, suppose that a reinsurer's retention limit for a specific type of coverage is $100,000. The insurer issues a policy for $250,000 and reinsures $150,000 of the coverage. Later, the insurer's favorable claim experience for that type of coverage enables the insurer to raise the retention limit for the coverage to $150,000. In this situation, the insurer would recapture $50,000 of the coverage, leaving $100,000 reinsured.

Generally, reinsurance enables an insurer to increase its capacity to underwrite large-amount business, substandard business, and new product business.

Large-amount business. An insurer may wish to issue a policy for an amount that exceeds the insurer's usual retention limit for mortality or morbidity risks. For such large-amount individual cases, nearly all insurers transfer a part of the risk to a reinsurer in order to limit the amount of coverage that the insurer retains on the case so that the insurer does not exceed its retention limit.

For instance, an insurer may set its retention limit for term life coverage at $500,000 for a male between the ages of 25 and 65. If a male age 42 wishes to purchase $750,000 of term life coverage and presents an otherwise acceptable risk, the insurer may decide to issue the policy under the condition that the excess risk of $250,000 be transferred to a reinsurer. According to law, the ceding company accepts and is liable for the entire amount of coverage and, if a claim were submitted under that policy, the ceding company would have to pay the entire amount if the reinsurer did not pay it. The insurance contract and the reinsurance treaty are separate documents. The beneficiary of an insurance policy, therefore, has no legal claim against a reinsurer.

An advantage of using reinsurance for coverage that exceeds a ceding company's retention limit is that the ceding company can accept business that agents might otherwise have to place with another insurer. Enabling agents to submit cases of almost any size enhances an insurer's market position and ability to compete with other insurance carriers. Moreover, the sales force may be more loyal because it does not have to seek other insurers with which to place large-amount cases.

A further advantage of using reinsurance for excess coverage is that the ceding company's underwriters can gain experience in underwriting the large-amount cases. If the ceding company later increases its retention limit, the company will then be able to underwrite larger cases for which its underwriters have gained experience.

Substandard business. Some insurance companies do not wish to assume the risk for some medically substandard risks. To be of full service to their agents and proposed insureds, however, these insurers wish to offer such coverage. A solution to this problem is for an insurer to transfer all or part of the risk for substandard coverage to a reinsurer that is experienced in underwriting these risks. Coverage is issued by the insurer, but may be underwritten by the reinsurer. Typically the coverage reinsured is considered very high risk and is classified at 200 percent or more of anticipated mortality. That is, the risk has been evaluated as representing 100 debits or more in addition to the 100 percent of standard mortality.

New product business. An insurer may cede risks to reduce the amount of risk involved in offering a new insurance product. The insurer may wish to begin offering a new type of coverage in which it has little experience. To reduce the amount of risk it must assume for the new product, the insurer transfers some of the risk to a reinsurer.

In some cases, the reinsurer not only takes on some of the risk for the new product, but also helps the ceding company in product development because the reinsurer may have experience in that type of product. This type of arrangement usually lasts only until the ceding company has developed enough experience to offer the coverage independently. In the following section, we'll comment further on the connection between reinsurance and new product development.

Obtaining Underwriting Expertise

Reinsurers have access to the claim experience information of some of their client insurance companies, and also develop experience statistics based on the reinsurers' own cases. In addition, some reinsurers develop considerable expertise through many years of underwriting risks, some of them quite complicated. Some reinsurers, for example, specialize in issuing coverage on insureds who have experienced cardiovascular bypass surgery or who have specific, severe forms of diabetes. A reinsurer can, therefore, guide an insurer in establishing sound underwriting principles and procedures for the impairments about which the reinsurer has superior knowledge.

A new insurance company usually establishes a relationship with a reinsurer in order to benefit from the reinsurer's underwriting expertise and to receive advice on such matters as premium rates, policy wording, and claims. Moreover, an insurer that is developing a new product usually considers reinsurance during the product design process, particularly if the product has unusual features or must be priced very competitively. Most insurers prefer to establish a reinsurance relationship before they bring a new product to the market. If the insurer decides to offer the product and to obtain reinsurance for it, a reinsurer can assist the insurer in assessing the strength of the product by evaluating the product's underwriting standards, administration plan, premium structure and pricing assumptions, commission plan, and marketing approach.

The insurer also benefits from knowing whether its persistency and mortality forecasts for the new product are consistent with the levels at which a reinsurer prefers to establish a reinsurance relationship. If these levels are not consistent, the insurer may use the reinsurer's recommendations to modify the product, or may instead choose to apply for reinsurance from another reinsurer.

Many reinsurers develop expertise in assessing complicated or large-amount applications. An underwriter in a ceding company may need help in underwriting a new product or a challenging case, particularly one with which the insurer has little or no experience. In such a situation, the underwriter can benefit from the expertise of a reinsurer. For instance, suppose a man, age 42, applies for $3,000,000 of life insurance and names his business partner as the beneficiary. The applicant furnishes a complex financial statement showing that he has considerable property and a large investment in the business which he shares with his business partner. However, the applicant spends less than half his time working in the business. His medical history indicates that he has several impairments with residual effects. Underwriting this case requires considerable expertise in assessing both the financial and medical factors of the case. An underwriter in a ceding company might well seek assistance from a reinsurance underwriter in evaluating the risk represented by the applicant.

Other cases for which an underwriter at a ceding company might seek a reinsurer's expertise include various types of cancer therapy, organ transplants, and areas about which medical knowledge is evolving, such as sleep apnea or liver function test results. Ceding companies may also need other types of nonmedical expertise for financial underwriting or disability underwriting.

A ceding company can benefit from a reinsurer's knowledge and experience by consulting on difficult cases and, in the process, obtaining support for a more liberal and competitive underwriting decision than the ceding company might have reached without such consultation. Some reinsurers underwrite difficult cases more aggressively than ceding companies because (1) the reinsurers are reacting to competition from other reinsurance companies, (2) the reinsurers have gathered considerable experience in such cases, and (3) the reinsurers have developed advanced underwriting techniques and knowledge. Reinsurers also provide assistance to ceding companies in other ways, including

- Training staff in underwriting and claims
- Obtaining coverage for difficult cases
- Evaluating unusual claims
- Calculating retention levels

Minimizing Mortality and Morbidity Risk

To establish premiums that will enable an insurer to attract new business and yet remain financially sound, the insurer estimates the level of claims that will be submitted over a period of time. The insurer then establishes retention limits and premiums sufficient to fund that level of claims and sets aside reserves to pay the claims. However, if the estimated claim level significantly increases or occurs earlier than expected, the insurer may experience financial difficulty.

Variations in the level of claims can result from random occurrences as well as from catastrophic events or unexpected trends. As explained below, stop-loss coverage can provide protection for the insurer against such unexpected trends.

The principal reason for a ceding company to transfer all or part of certain risks to a reinsurer is to minimize the risk from large individual claims or unexpectedly large numbers of small claims. Reinsurance helps to smooth fluctuations in the ceding company's claims if a large-amount case is submitted or a large number of claims are submitted during a specific period of time.

Suppose that a ceding company has underwritten 1,000 policies for $250,000 apiece. The actuarial assumptions underlying these policies provide that claims under the policies will be submitted over a period of time, enabling the insurer to establish sufficient funds from premiums and investment income to pay all valid claims as they are submitted. For the purpose of this illustration, suppose that the insurer assumes that an average of 20 claims each year will be submitted, and that the insurer will pay an average of $5,000,000 annually in claims.

But suppose that, in a given year, an unusually large number of claims are submitted under those 1,000 policies. If the insurance company must pay far more than its estimated $5,000,000 in annual claims, the insurer may become financially unstable, and its ability to provide coverage for the remaining insureds may become doubtful. If, however, the insurer were able to share the risk for claim payments with a reinsurer, then the original insurance company would not have to deplete its funds in paying every claim. Rather, both the ceding company and the reinsurer would pay a portion of the submitted claims. In this fashion, reinsurance enables an insurance company to smooth fluctuations in claims.

Minimizing Persistency Risk

Ceding companies often transfer part or all of the risk in an effort to reduce the risk of loss from policy lapses and surrenders. A ***policy surrender*** is a type of policy cancellation that occurs when a policyowner sends a policy to an insurer and requests that (1) the insurance coverage be terminated and (2) the cash value of the policy be sent to the policyowner. In both a policy surrender and a policy lapse, coverage ends; surrendering a policy is a voluntary act on the part of the policyowner, whereas allowing a policy to lapse may or may not be voluntary.

Most insurance products produce a large risk for an insurer in the early years of a policy. First, the cost of putting most new business on an insurer's books exceeds the premiums paid during the first year. Additionally, an insurer must set aside sufficient funds to establish the reserve required to pay claims that may be submitted under the coverage. If too large a portion of an insurer's available funds is set aside for reserves, the insurer cannot legally continue to write new business that will require additional reserve funding. Transferring to a reinsurer all or part of the accountability for paying first-year expenses and establishing reserves enables an insurer to continue underwriting new business because a great portion of the insurer's funds is not allocated to such expenses.

Moreover, certain products typically have a large first-year commission or a considerable first-year cash value that encourages policy loans, either of which may exceed the product's first-year premium. Coverages with premiums that increase annually may also produce a large lapse risk for an insurance company. If such policies lapse or are surrendered within the first few years, the insurer (1) usually suffers a loss resulting from the heavy costs associated with putting the business on the books and (2) may have additional loss from the negative cash flow produced by the difference between the premium paid and the loans taken against the cash value.

Some insurers purchase reinsurance to help defray the first-year costs of issuing coverage and to spread the risk of earlier-than-expected lapses. Reinsurance agreements covering new products with unknown risk elements commonly provide for low retention limits for the ceding company in order that insurer and reinsurer may share these risks more equally.

Fronting

Sometimes an insurer wishes to issue policies in a jurisdiction in which the insurer is not licensed to do business. ***Fronting*** is a procedure by which an insurer that is licensed in a state or province issues a policy on a risk for and at the request of one or more other insurers with the intent of ceding the entire risk to the other insurer or reinsurers. Fronting provides a way for an unlicensed insurer to sell coverage in markets from which it would otherwise be prohibited. Some jurisdictions have adopted regulations designed to limit fronting by (1) limiting the volume of fronting business permitted, (2) limiting the percentage of business that an insurance marketer may cede by fronting, and (3) establishing audits and other monitoring procedures designed to detect fronting.

The principal benefits of fronting include the following:

- *For a policyowner.* Obtaining coverage from an unlicensed reinsurer that offers attractive premiums, terms, or customer service
- *For a ceding company.* Enabling an insurer to do business with an unlicensed reinsurer with highly specialized underwriting capabilities or other expertise

- *For a ceding company and a reinsurer.* Establishing and maintaining international relationships, often in an effort to expand business by offering coverage internationally

Limitations of Reinsurance

Despite the many advantages of using reinsurance, this approach to sharing risk has certain limitations. First, reinsurance cannot transform an uninsurable risk into an insurable risk by using reinsurance to cover the potential loss. Similarly, an insurer cannot change by using reinsurance an inadequately investigated and underwritten risk into a well-underwritten risk. Although reinsurance can help to control the severity of an insurer's losses, it cannot help to control the frequency of those losses.

In addition, an insurance company that overuses reinsurance to reduce its amount of risk can be harmed financially. Paying claims is a cost of doing business in the insurance industry. Attempting to avoid or excessively reduce claim-settlement cost by setting low retention limits will also reduce the amount of an insurer's working capital and, ultimately, can reduce the insurer's capacity to accept new business.

Using reinsurance does not eliminate the need for the ceding company to develop excellent products or to market them effectively. An insurer that fails to match products, distribution system, and prospective insureds may suffer low placements and a high lapse rate.

Reinsurance also does not transfer or eliminate the contractual legal liability that the ceding company has under a policy it issued to an insured. The reinsurance arrangements are separate and are not attached to a policy. For example, if for some reason, such as a dispute or insolvency, a reinsurer did not pay on a claim, the ceding company is liable to pay the claim in full. Therefore, reinsurance allows a ceding company to transfer risk, but not to transfer the legal liability under the policy.

Reinsurance Underwriting

Underwriting reinsurance risks is essentially the same as underwriting any risks, although reinsurance underwriters tend to see more unusual or problematic situations than do other underwriters. Ceding-company underwriting—that is primary underwriting—and reinsurance underwriting differ in two important ways.

First, in primary underwriting, the underwriter's judgment of the agent's integrity plays a role in the underwriting decision. In reinsurance underwriting, the underwriter is concerned primarily with the quality of the ceding company's underwriting department rather than with the agent's integrity. Under certain types of reinsurance agreements, the reinsurer has agreed in advance to accept the ceding company's underwriting judgment as its own. Particularly under these types of agreements, the reinsurance underwriter relies on the primary underwriter to develop adequate case files to support the underwriting decision.

Second, reinsurance underwriters consistently try to avoid asking for additional requirements on the cases submitted to them, but instead try to accept their ceding colleagues' judgment. Occasionally, if a file has not been sufficiently developed to satisfy a reinsurance underwriter, the reinsurer's underwriter may request additional information or may ask the ceding company's underwriter to consult on the case. However, such requests not only delay policy issue, but appear to question the thoroughness of the ceding company's underwriter.

The Application for Reinsurance

The application for reinsurance is the basic tool of reinsurance underwriting. The application identifies the ceding company, the plan of reinsurance, and the risk to be reinsured. It also specifies the type and amount of coverage applied for, including any special features or riders involved.

In some cases, the application also asks for the ceding underwriter's assessment of the risk. The application also shows any other reinsurers to which a file has been submitted for a quote. If retrocession is necessary, the application names the reinsurers that are already involved with the case so that the reinsurer may seek a retrocessionaire elsewhere. Insight 11-3 explains how the retrocession business has changed and what its future may be.

Reinsurers and the Medical Information Bureau

Like primary insurers, reinsurers use coded information supplied by the Medical Information Bureau (MIB) as an alert to the possibility that a proposed insured has undisclosed impairments that could materially affect the mortality or morbidity assessment of the case. All reinsurers are members of the MIB, although some of their clients are not.

Reinsurance companies may not make MIB information available to client companies, member or nonmember. However, a reinsurer can use MIB information in connection with a nonmember client's business if there is a reasonable expectation of reinsurance that is

Insight 11-3 If Risk Is Like an Iceberg, Then Retrocession Is . . .

Insurance risk is sometimes likened to an iceberg. The policyowner knows only the 10 percent above the water—the insurance company—while reinsurance is the unseen 90 percent. But reinsurers often need reinsurance themselves, and rely on the ocean floor of retrocession. Until 20 years ago, reinsurers' retrocessional needs were met primarily by other reinsurers and ceding companies looking for reciprocity. Direct writers with large capacity might also be used on occasion.

What is the state of the life retrocession business today, and where does it seem to be heading? In many ways, the conditions of the life retro market mirror those of first-line reinsurance.

■ **Pressure on prices:** The reinsurance market is intensely competitive on price, and the retrocession market is no different. If anything, reinsurers are trying to view retrocessions as sources of profit. They do so by seeking competitive rate quotes, pushing prices as low as possible, and asking for marketing allowances and / or experience refunds.

■ **Skyrocketing jumbos:** For many years, $10 million was the usual jumbo limit for automatic retrocession cover. A jumbo is the maximum amount of insurance in force and applied for in all insurance companies for which automatic reinsurance is allowed. In the 1990s, this limit shot past $15 million, paused briefly at $20 million, and then at $25 million. Today, many reinsurers want at least $30 million, and requests for $50 million and even higher are becoming more frequent.

■ **Shrinking world:** North American reinsurers, confronting a mature and less-than-ideally profitable market at home, are turning to foreign shores as new sources of volume and earnings. Retrocessionaires with international expertise can be valuable partners in these ventures. In turn, reinsurers either domesticated in or currently serving these markets are looking at North America to further their own interests.

■ **Annuities advance:** As the baby boomer generation ages, living too long is replacing dying too soon as a primary source of concern. Annuities are increasingly important as a source of insurance premiums, and bring with them new reinsurance and retrocession needs. Reinsurers of the guaranteed minimum death benefit risk also look to retrocessionaires for both technical analysis and the lessening of any potentially devastating risk.

■ **Service, service, service:** Reinsurers are asking retrocessionaires to provide a wide range of services as well as pure capacity. Assistance with product development, actuarial studies of ceded business, investment analysis, market perspectives—anything a ceding company might ask of a reinsurer is fair game.

None of these trends should be surprising, because they are all direct extensions of the evolving relationships between direct writers and reinsurers. A retrocessionaire, as the reinsurer's reinsurer, should expect all the new development and competitive pressures of the reinsurance marketplace to be passed along. Conversely, just as a ceding company should understand that a reinsurer is entitled to a reasonable profit in return for its services, a reinsurer should be willing to treat its retrocessionaire in the same way.

substantial in amount and duration. If such reasonable expectation is not present, the reinsurer can still use MIB information if it is used solely to protect the reinsurer's own business.

Legal Issues Affecting Reinsurance

Because a reinsurance agreement is formed between two businesses that are assumed to be able to protect themselves, the laws and regulations governing reinsurance are fewer and less detailed than those governing insurance. Rather than being heavily regulated by jurisdictional requirements, reinsurance is largely self-regulated. General reinsurance practice, based on a long-established reliance on the utmost good faith of the parties to a reinsurance agreement, tends to guide the performance of insurers and reinsurers in their reinsurance relationships. As you saw in Insight 11-1, the relationship between an insurer and a reinsurer has traditionally been compared to a "gentleman's agreement"—that is, an arrangement or understanding that is secured only by the honor of the persons or entities taking part in it. This aspect of reinsurance further assumes that, if an insurer and a reinsurer were to disagree about an issue relating to their mutual undertaking, they would rely on insurance and reinsurance experts to resolve the issue through arbitration, an approach we'll examine in Chapters 14 and 15.

Fast Fact

Foreign reinsurers play a significant role in the U.S. reinsurance market. In 1995, out of the 22 largest life insurance reinsurers in the United States, 6 of the companies were German-controlled, one was Swiss-controlled, and one was Canadian-controlled.

Source: Kevin G. Maher, "Number of Life Reinsurers Dwindles as Market Grows," *Best's Review (Life/Health)*, March 1996: 40–46, 100.

Not all treaties of reinsurance are managed by a gentlemen's agreement, however. Because of concern about potential reinsurer insolvency and about the legitimacy of claims submitted by insurers under reinsured contracts, both insurers and reinsurers are increasingly careful about the relationships they form. Furthermore, state and provincial regulators, auditors, acquiring organizations, and other parties consider reinsurance agreements as binding contracts that ought to be regulated. Regulators are especially concerned about ensuring that both insurers and reinsurers are financially strong and that sufficient information is available to evaluate their fiscal strength.

For reporting purposes, an insurance company is allowed to reduce its amount at risk by receiving accounting credit for amounts of risk passed along to reinsurers through reinsurance agreements. According to the NAIC Model Law on Credit for Reinsurance, an insurer may receive credit for reinsured risks if the reinsurance company (1) is licensed to operate in the jurisdiction or (2) is accredited as a reinsurer in the jurisdiction or (3) has been approved as a reinsurer in a state with requirements similar to those proposed in the Model Law or (4) has established a trust in a financial institution that can pay valid claims submitted under reinsurance agreements. This credit is used in financial statements to reduce policyowner liabilities to the extent that policies are reinsured under valid reinsurance agreements.

Some jurisdictions do not allow an insurer to reinsure the entire amount at risk unless the insurer obtains prior approval from a department of insurance or other regulatory authority. Moreover, many jurisdictions require insurers to pay a tax on the full amount of collected premiums, even if part of the business has been reinsured. Reinsurers sometimes reimburse the ceding company for the percentage of the tax that applies to the reinsured business. The percentage of the tax reimbursed may be equal to the percentage of reinsured risk, or may be based on a specified proportion—usually about 2 percent—of the policy premiums and the reinsurance premiums.

Four areas in which reinsurance is specifically regulated are licensing, financial condition, reinsurance intermediaries and marketers, and specific transactions.

Licensing

Laws of various jurisdictions govern the licensing requirements for reinsurance intermediaries and marketers, including agents and brokers. Such persons may be required to post a bond that will protect a reinsurer from financial loss, as well as to establish a procedure for compensating a reinsurer for negligent acts or mistakes of the agent.

Moreover, laws have attempted to govern the registration of unlicensed reinsurers, which are generally those that are organized or incorporated under the laws of other nations. Efforts are being made to require certain financial and other standards to which these unlicensed reinsurers must adhere.

Financial Condition

The amount of financial statement credit that a ceding company may take for reinsured coverages is regulated by law. In addition, most jurisdictions provide that a ceding company may not claim indemnity under reinsurance unless the ceding company has first paid a claim under the insurance coverage.

Another type of law affecting financial condition requires that a ceding company may claim financial statement credit only if (1) reinsurance is provided by an authorized or accredited insurer or (2) adequate funds have been reserved to pay potential claims under ceded coverage. Moreover, in the United States, a ceding company is required to list on its Annual Statement all the reinsurers or retrocessionaires owing reinsurance funds to the ceding company.

Reinsurance Intermediaries and Marketers

A reinsurer is generally prohibited from delegating excessive responsibility to reinsurance intermediaries and marketers, including brokers and agents. Legislation usually requires that a reinsurer and any agent have a written contract containing specified provisions and that the reinsurer must provide to regulatory authorities annual financial audits and other records concerning its marketers.

Specific Transactions

Certain specific transactions regulated by law include setoffs. A ***setoff*** occurs when a reinsurer that owes money to an insolvent insurer reduces, or "sets off," the amount of debt by an equal amount owed to the reinsurer by the insurer. For instance, if an insolvent insurer owes a reinsurer $100,000 in reinsurance premiums, and if the reinsurer owes at least $100,000 in claims to the insurer, the reinsurer may then reduce the total amount it owes the insurer by $100,000 in a setoff. Although the general practice of using setoffs is not prohibited by law, the NAIC has established several categories of setoffs that are not permitted.

Key Terms and Concepts

retention limit
ceding company (*reinsured*)
reinsurer (*assuming company*)
retrocessionaire
cession
ceding
retrocession
reinsurance treaty
capacity
reinsurance corridor (*minimum cession*)
recapture
policy surrender
fronting
setoff

CHAPTER TWELVE

Bases and Plans of Reinsurance

Learning Objectives

After studying this chapter, you should be able to

- Define automatic reinsurance, and list three benefits to an insurer of purchasing reinsurance on an automatic basis
- Name and define two types of limits used for automatic reinsurance
- Explain three ways an insurer may divide automatic reinsurance coverage among several reinsurance companies
- Explain the process of shopping for facultative reinsurance, including four possible actions an insurer may take on a facultative bid
- Distinguish between proportional and nonproportional reinsurance
- Explain two methods an insurer may use to determine the amount of coverage to cede through proportional reinsurance
- List and define three plans of proportional reinsurance and four plans of nonproportional reinsurance

Chapter Outline

Bases of Reinsurance

Automatic Reinsurance
Facultative Reinsurance
Facultative Automatic Reinsurance

Plans of Reinsurance

Proportional Reinsurance
Nonproportional Reinsurance

In the last chapter, you learned about the uses of reinsurance. Unlike many other insurance products, reinsurance is not offered as a predesigned coverage through standard policy forms. Rather, reinsurance is a customized product that is designed to fit the requirements of each case.

In purchasing reinsurance, insurers can choose from a wide variety of options that provide coverage tailored to their needs. A reinsurance agreement is flexible not only because it offers these options, but also because it may be modified later if the requirements of the parties change.

To help you understand the possible choices available when insurers and reinsurers negotiate reinsurance agreements, we'll explain the bases (types) and plans of reinsurance. In examining the bases of reinsurance, we'll discuss automatic, facultative, and facultative automatic reinsurance. Then we'll discuss proportional and nonproportional plans of reinsurance. Figure 12-1 outlines the reinsurance bases and plans that we'll examine in this chapter.

Bases of Reinsurance

An agreement for reinsurance generally establishes the basis on which each party to the agreement may participate or must participate in the reinsurance relationship. Reinsurance is established on either an automatic or a facultative basis. A variation of the facultative basis is coverage written on a facultative automatic basis.

Automatic Reinsurance

Automatic reinsurance is based on an agreement in which an insurer must cede specified types of cases or a block of business to a reinsurer, and the reinsurer must accept the risk for those cases up to a predetermined maximum. The agreement for automatic reinsurance generally specifies that the ceding company must retain as its own risk all coverage up to the retention limit, and then may pass excess risk to the reinsurer. When a reinsurer agrees to issue automatic reinsurance, it relies on the underwriting expertise and judgment of the ceding company and must accept all risks ceded under the automatic agreement even if the reinsurer's own underwriting judgment on a case differs from that of the ceding company.

Figure 12-1. Bases and plans of reinsurance.

Bases of Reinsurance	Plans of Reinsurance
Automatic	Proportional
	Yearly renewable term (YRT)
Facultative	Coinsurance
	Modified coinsurance
Facultative automatic	Nonproportional
	Excess-of-loss
	Stop-loss
	Spread-loss
	Extended-time
	Riders and policy provisions

Coverage amounts that exceed the reinsurer's maximum are usually ceded facultatively (we'll discuss facultative reinsurance in the next section). Some automatic reinsurance agreements, however, provide that a ceding company may make certain exceptions and may submit selected policies for underwriting by the reinsurer or by another reinsurer.

Within a specified time after a policy has been written, the ceding company sends the reinsurer notification that automatic reinsurance coverage has been issued on the case. The premium for policies ceded automatically is established in advance.

Automatic reinsurance is useful for increasing an insurer's capacity to underwrite new business. Moreover, automatic reinsurance removes the necessity for an insurer to seek reinsurance coverage for each case or block of cases that exceed the insurer's retention limit. In this way, the insurer is able not only to save administrative expenses and time, but also to issue policies much more rapidly than if the insurer took the time to negotiate placement of the policies with a reinsurer.

Automatic reinsurance generally assumes a long-term relationship and a high level of trust between the parties. Relying on the ceding company's underwriting criteria, the reinsurer must accept all cases submitted under the terms of the automatic reinsurance agreement. The ceding company may not withhold any of the specified types of cases even if the ceding company would prefer not to reinsure them. In addition, the ceding company may not send any case to another reinsurer if the case qualifies for coverage under the automatic reinsurance agreement. Finally, the ceding company may bind the reinsurer to a risk without giving the reinsurer underwriting evidence for the risk or asking the reinsurer's approval in advance.

Placing reinsured cases with several reinsurers. An insurer sometimes wishes to reinsure a single product or several products on an automatic basis with two or more reinsurers. Under such an arrangement, each reinsurer accepts a specified percentage of the cases or the coverage amount. As a result, each reinsurer is able to offer the insurer lower rates because competition encourages lower pricing. An advantage to the reinsurers dividing such coverage is that they do not have to compete with each other in underwriting and bidding to cover the cases.

To divide automatic reinsurance coverage among several reinsurance companies, an insurer typically uses an alphabetic split, pooling, or layering, although other approaches are also possible. An ***alphabetic split*** is a method of dividing insureds for reinsurance purposes by assigning part of the alphabet to each reinsurer and then sending that reinsurer all cases whose insured's surnames begin with one of the assigned alphabet letters. For joint life and joint and last survivor life insurance policies for which insureds have differing surnames, an insurer either (1) sends all policies to one reinsurer or (2) uses an alphabetic split and sends policies to each designated reinsurer according to the surname of the older insured person.

An insurer that uses ***pooling*** (also known as *quota share*) as a method of dividing automatic reinsured cases among a group of reinsurers arranges for each reinsurer to receive a specified percentage of the insured cases. Although the terms of agreement for each of the pool reinsurers are usually the same, the percentage of cases assigned to each reinsurer is not necessarily the same. One reinsurer, for instance, may receive half of the cases, whereas two other reinsurers may each receive 30 percent and 20 percent of the cases, respectively. Pooling of reinsured cases is usually done when the ceding company performs its own reinsurance administration. Insight 12-1 illustrates a proposed use of pooling for disability income coverage.

Layering is a method of dividing automatic reinsurance coverage among several reinsurers by allowing one reinsurer to cover all cases in excess of an insurer's retention limit up to a specified amount. Cases higher than the specified amount are ceded to a second reinsurer. For example, suppose ABC Insurance has established a retention limit of $100,000 on certain life policies. ABC Insurance cedes all amounts in excess of $100,000 and up to $500,000 to EFG Reinsurance. ABC Insurance cedes all amounts over $500,000 to XYZ Reinsurance.

A layering arrangement usually begins when a reinsurer, often a new company, wishes to establish a reinsurance relationship with an insurer. In order to obtain some of the insurer's business, the reinsurer agrees to accept coverage for cases that exceed a specified limit. Each reinsurer typically knows about and approves the inclusion of other reinsurers in a layering.

Insight 12-1 Reinsurance Should Be Playing a Larger Role in DI

With some creativity and cooperation, a totally new, pool-based reinsurance program could be designed to help stabilize the DI industry.

To understand how such a program could work, first consider the traditional DI reinsurance scenario.

For years, DI reinsurers have based their rates on the overall claim performance of the direct DI carriers. Carriers with good experience paid for the poor experience of others. Stung by several years of significant claim losses, a number of DI reinsurers—along with direct carriers—withdrew from the market.

Not surprisingly, those reinsurers remaining in the market were forced to raise their rates where possible. What's more, to prevent further losses, these reinsurers started paying more attention to the underwriting and claim practices of the direct writers, often dictating changes in policy provisions and internal procedures.

Examples include restricting lifetime benefits, replacing the traditional "own occupation" definition of disability with a more restrictive "own occupation and not working in any other occupation" definition, and requiring blood tests at lower income levels.

In contrast, the new pool-based reinsurance program could be designed to smooth out disability insurance claims during difficult times for participating companies; to provide a cap on the aggregate level of claims; and to provide underwriting, claim, actuarial, and financial support to those companies without being intrusive or mandating changes in their internal practices.

Over time, this should limit the cost of reinsurance to actual experience, capped by a stop-loss coverage, plus an administrative fee that includes the cost of the stop-loss protection.

It could work like this: Each company would decide what risk to cede to the pool. The company could use the pool to replace its traditional reinsurance, or it could cede business within its current retention and further reduce the volatility of its financial results.

For each participating insurer, an estimate could be made of expected incurred claims for the coming year. This would reflect the company's claim history and information from periodic audits of underwriting, claim, and marketing practices.

Each company would be assigned a share of the pool, equal to the ratio of its expected morbidity to the expected morbidity of the pool. (All other things being equal, the company with the most restrictive policy provisions, underwriting procedures, and claim practices would wind up with the smallest share.)

After the close of each year, the actual pool experience would be compared against expected pool claims, and if the actual claims exceed the expected by some "attachment point," say 125 percent, a stop-loss carrier would be responsible for the pool claims in excess of that point, and each participating company would be charged with its share of actual pool experience below that point.

A company's claims after reinsurance could be better or worse than the expected claim level, depending on overall pool experience. But in no event would claims after reinsurance exceed the attachment point (i.e., 125 percent of the companies' expected claims).

Consequently, the companies would, over time, have experience much closer to the expected claim level than their actual claims before reinsurance. The result: More predictable annual results!

In our opinion, this type of program would have multiple advantages. As indicated, it would allow each participating company to achieve more predictable financial results. Also, each company would benefit from aggregate stop-loss protection that would probably be unattainable on its own. And, each would make its own business decisions regarding policy design and underwriting, claim, and marketing practices.

Given the struggle in today's disability market, such a program could solve many DI dilemmas.

From Inger S. Harrington, James R. Grant, and Charles M. Waldron, "Reinsurance Should Be Playing a Larger Role in DI," *National Underwriter,* Life & Health/Financial Services Edition, February 19, 1996: 16, 23. Adapted by permission.

Other approaches that insurers may use to spread the risk among several reinsurers under automatic reinsurance agreements are to divide cases by (1) the insured's age at issue, (2) the state or province of residence of the insured, (3) the agent who sold the coverage, (4) the insured's use or nonuse of tobacco, and (5) the year of birth of the insured, giving one reinsurer the odd years and another reinsurer the even years, or assigning one reinsurer all policies issued to persons up to a certain age, and assigning those older to another reinsurer.

Limits for automatic reinsurance. Reinsurers establish not only a retention limit for the amount of risk they will carry on a specified case or product type, but also a binding limit. The ***binding limit*** is the dollar amount of risk that the reinsurer obligates itself to accept under an automatic agreement without making its own underwriting assessment of the risk. The binding limit, then, is the amount of coverage that the reinsurer must accept on a ceded case.

For instance, suppose a reinsurer has established a binding limit of $3 million. This limit indicates that the reinsurer must accept $3 million of coverage under a specified product. If an insurer with which the reinsurer has an automatic reinsurance agreement submits a case representing $4 million of risk, the reinsurer must accept $3 million of the risk. If, after underwriting the case, the reinsurer decides to accept the remainder of that risk, the reinsurer will then have reinsured a total of $4 million of that risk. If that amount exceeds the reinsurer's retention limit, the reinsurer may cede the excess amount to another reinsurer.

A reinsurer establishes a binding limit for each insurer and for each of that insurer's products according to the reinsurer's confidence in the insurer's underwriting expertise and both the underwriter's and the reinsurer's retention limits for the specified coverage. For example, an insurer whose underwriting staff lacks expertise in evaluating the risk for a certain type of coverage is likely to have a low binding limit for that coverage. The binding limit is usually expressed as either a dollar amount or as a multiple of the insurer's retention limit. The binding limit may be reduced for policies (1) that are issued to persons of specified ages or (2) that are given substandard ratings.

The binding limit is generally set at a level that permits most policies to be reinsured automatically. A high binding limit benefits both the insurer and the reinsurer by reducing their administrative costs. Moreover, a high binding limit benefits the reinsurer because it facilitates the reinsurer's acceptance of large-amount policies that otherwise have to be individually underwritten if they cannot be automatically reinsured.

In determining whether the binding limit on coverage for a specific individual has been met, the ceding company must include not only the amount of coverage represented by the new case, but also all other amounts of coverage that were previously issued to that individual by the insurer and that were reinsured by the reinsurer. Suppose, for instance, that an insurer has issued $2 million of key-person coverage on an individual life and has reinsured $1 million of that amount. If an additional $4 million of coverage on the same person is later applied for from the same insurer, and if the insurer hopes to reinsure all of that amount with the same reinsurer, the reinsurer must determine that the total reinsured amount of $5 million does not exceed the reinsurer's binding limit.

Most automatic reinsurance agreements establish a ***jumbo limit,*** which is an amount that the total insurance already in force and/or applied for with all insurers on any individual must not exceed for a ceded risk to be accepted automatically by the reinsurer. The jumbo limit is usually set quite high, in the range of $20 million or above. A reinsurer establishes a jumbo limit because it helps ensure that the reinsurer can participate in underwriting a large-amount case that the reinsurer may accept if it chooses, but may reject if the case represents a high level of risk and also exceeds the established jumbo limit.

If the insurer's total amount of coverage in force and applied for exceeds the reinsurer's binding limit, or if that total amount exceeds the jumbo limit, the case cannot be covered by the automatic reinsurance agreement. Instead, the case is usually evaluated separately and is submitted for facultative consideration, an approach we'll discuss in the next section.

Facultative Reinsurance

In contrast to automatic reinsurance, ***facultative reinsurance*** is based on an agreement in which the ceding company may choose whether to submit a case or a block of cases to a reinsurer, and the reinsurer may choose whether to accept each case or block of business. Facultative reinsurance agreements usually involve substandard risks or single policies that represent a considerable level of financial risk for the insurer. Facultative reinsurance also involves separate underwriting of each case and separate determination of a reinsurance rate for each case. Many insurers prefer to place cases facultatively because such placement enables an insurer to receive the benefit of the reinsurer's underwriting assessment before the policy is issued.

An agreement for facultative reinsurance usually provides that (1) the ceding company must give the reinsurer underwriting evidence on a case before any reinsurance becomes effective and (2) the ceding company may not bind the reinsurer on an automatic basis after the ceding company has submitted a case to any other reinsurer on a facultative basis. Facultative reinsurance is sometimes used as a way for an insurer and a reinsurer to establish a business relationship and to become comfortable with each other's business practices in the expectation that later the two companies will develop automatic reinsurance agreements.

In facultative reinsurance, the parties do not operate according to an ongoing agreement, as they do in automatic reinsurance, but instead establish a new reinsurance relationship with each case that is accepted for reinsurance. The insurer has no obligation to offer any case to a reinsurer, and the reinsurer has no obligation to accept any offer made by the insurer. Premiums and administrative expenses for facultative reinsurance are usually higher than those for automatic reinsurance, so that the cost of facultative coverage is relatively higher for the insurer to purchase.

Shopping for facultative reinsurance. To place cases it wishes to reinsure, an insurer generally requests bids from reinsurers. The insurer may already have a facultative reinsurance agreement established with such reinsurers, but may also request bids from other reinsurers with which the insurer has no current agreement.

In a practice known as ***shopping,*** insurers offer a case to several reinsurers and invite them to bid for the reinsurance coverage. An insurer sometimes tells each bidding reinsurer the names of the other reinsurers that have been invited to submit bids. A reinsurer is under no obligation to submit a bid in response to an insurer's request.

Shopping reinsurance has specific advantages, as follows:

- For cases that are unusual or difficult to evaluate, an insurer may gain the benefit of the reinsurer's underwriting expertise when the reinsurer's underwriters evaluate the case.

- Shopping enables an insurer to obtain competitive prices for reinsurance and, in many cases, to recover money on the cost of underwriting the coverage by placing a case or by assigning to the coverage a rating that is more likely to be acceptable to the applicant.

- Because some reinsurers specialize in providing coverage for certain serious impairments and can offer the coverage at standard or low substandard rates, insurers may be able to find coverage for difficult cases that otherwise would be impossible for them to accept as standard or low substandard. Shopping thus provides a marketing service for agents because it enables an insurer to place coverage that the insurer might otherwise not be able to accept or might have to charge a high premium to accept.

Whereas shopping may offer several advantages, it also has certain drawbacks, including the following:

- A few marketers may view reinsurance shopping negatively because they conclude that the ceding company's underwriting function may not be able to handle difficult cases or may be rendering excessively conservative decisions.

- Agents may bring pressure on the insurer and its underwriters to shop for reinsurance coverage because the agents want cases placed, even at additional cost.

- Duplicating and transmitting to reinsurers all the data associated with a case may be expensive and may, therefore, reduce an insurer's potential profit. Because such a case is often difficult and may involve multiple impairments and other challenging factors, the case file may be several hundred pages long.

- Reinsurance shopping is time consuming. In a competitive situation in which several insurers are being asked to cover a case and are, in turn, requesting reinsurance bids, the elapsed time may be considerable and may result in lost business for any insurer whose response is not delivered in a timely manner.

After receiving all bids, the insurer may award the coverage to one reinsurer or may split the case among several reinsurers. Specifically, the insurer takes one of the following actions on each bid and on the application for coverage:

1. The insurer may accept the bid and, therefore, share the risk with the reinsurer, and issue the coverage.

2. The insurer may reject the bid and issue the coverage without reinsuring it, provided that the coverage does not exceed the insurer's retention limit for that type of coverage. However, the insurer cannot bind its reinsurers on an automatic basis if the reinsurer has sent out the case facultatively.

3. The insurer may inform the insurance marketer that the risk may be covered on a modified basis—that is, the insurer will offer to issue a lower amount of coverage than was initially requested.

4. The insurer may reject the bid and deny the application for coverage.

5. The insurer may postpone the decision for a specified period—typically six months to one year—to see whether conditions affecting the risk improve. Such conditions might be the management of a business or the financial status of a business or an individual.

Facultative Automatic Reinsurance

A variation of facultative reinsurance is ***facultative automatic reinsurance,*** formerly called *facultative obligatory reinsurance,* which is based on an agreement by which the ceding company may choose to submit cases to a reinsurer, and the reinsurer must accept the cases as long as the reinsurer has sufficient capacity to do so. The ceding company does not have to submit cases to the reinsurer. In connection with the term "facultative automatic," the "facultative" portion of the term pertains to the ceding company, and the "automatic" portion of the term pertains to the reinsurer.

Generally, information about the risk is sent as rapidly as possible to the reinsurer, which must quickly determine if sufficient capacity is available. For individual coverages, the information consists of the proposed insured's name and date of birth, but not any other type of underwriting information. The reinsurer checks its information system to determine whether the coverage on the proposed insured exceeds capacity. If the reinsurer cannot accept the risk, the insurer must be so notified within a short time. If the reinsurer fails to notify the insurer, the reinsurer is bound to the risk and must reinsure the excess risk with its own reinsurers. Risks that are ceded under facultative automatic reinsurance may be subject to later review by the reinsurer.

Plans of Reinsurance

Many plans of reinsurance are available to insurers. In deciding what plan of reinsurance to use in reaching an agreement, the parties first decide whether the amount or percentage of the benefit to be paid by the reinsurer is to be specified or unspecified. That decision determines, by definition, whether the reinsurance will be issued on a proportional or a nonproportional basis. Following that decision, the parties decide what plan of proportional or nonproportional coverage will be used. Proportional and nonproportional reinsurance may be issued on either an automatic or a facultative basis, although automatic reinsurance is usually proportional reinsurance.

Proportional Reinsurance

If the reinsurance coverage is to be issued as ***proportional reinsurance,*** the parties agree to share premiums and claims according to a specified amount or a specified percentage. The reinsured amount may be fixed for each policy, or it may be established according to a scale that usually is reduced as the size of the policy increases. For instance, an insurer and a reinsurer may agree that the reinsurer will accept 50 percent of the face amount of life policies providing up to $500,000 of coverage. The parties may agree further that the reinsurer will cover 40 percent of the face amount for life policies between $500,001 and $1,000,000 of coverage and 30 percent of such policies exceeding $1,000,001 of coverage.

In determining the amount of coverage to cede through proportional reinsurance, insurers use either a quota share approach or an excess share approach. The ***quota share approach,*** also called a *pro rata approach,* provides that the reinsurer will accept the risk for a specified percentage of every risk of a certain type. The ceding company will retain the remainder of each such risk up to the ceding company's retention limit. Reinsurance premiums for the coverage are established at a fixed percentage of the insurance premiums, and the reinsurer pays a fixed percentage of all valid claims.

Suppose an insurer establishes a retention limit of $30,000 for a certain type of coverage. The insurer makes a reinsurance agreement providing that the insurer will retain 30 percent of each risk up to its retention limit, and that a reinsurer will accept the remaining 70 percent of each risk. According to this agreement, the insurer would accept cases up to $100,000, retaining 30 percent of each such case without exceeding its retention limit. On a $60,000 case, the insurer would retain $18,000 as its own risk and would reinsure $42,000 of the risk.

Fast Fact

Total net reinsurance premiums from all types of reinsurance grew 10.1 percent in 1995, the fourth year in a row that net premiums increased. A major factor in this increase was the growing tendency to seek international markets for reinsurance.

Source: Lynne Pease, "Group, Special Risk Premium up 10.1 percent in 1995," *National Underwriter,* September 23, 1996: 3.

If a ceding company uses a quota share approach to split reinsured coverage among more than one reinsurer, each reinsurer accepts a specified percentage of the coverage. Suppose an insurer had established agreements with two reinsurers, one of which would accept 30 percent of a risk and the other of which would accept 40 percent of the risk. On a $60,000 case, the insurer would retain $18,000 as its own risk, the first reinsurer would accept another $18,000 of the risk, and the second reinsurer would accept the remaining $24,000 of the risk.

Reinsurance purchased according to the quota share approach may be used to cover all of a ceding company's business or only certain types of coverage. Quota share coverage may cover one case or a block of business. Moreover, such reinsurance may expire when a policy or group of policies expires, or may continue on an ongoing basis and may be renewed automatically until the parties agree to cancel the reinsurance arrangement. Although most quota share coverage is issued on the basis of automatic agreements, some is issued on the basis of facultative agreements.

The ***excess share approach,*** also called the *surplus share approach* or *level retention,* provides that an insurer will cede specified amounts of coverage which exceed its retention limit. The reinsurer, therefore, accepts the risk for amounts in excess of the retention limit and pays claims that exceed the retention limit. Suppose that an insurer has established a retention limit of $60,000 for a certain type of coverage, but wishes to accept a case representing risk of $85,000. Under an excess share approach, the insurer accepts $60,000 of the risk and cedes $25,000 to a reinsurer.

Three plans of proportional reinsurance include yearly renewable term, coinsurance, and modified coinsurance. Figure 12-2 presents a comparison of proportional reinsurance plans.

Figure 12-2. Comparison of proportional reinsurance plans.

	Reinsured Risks	Accumulates Reserves on Reinsured Portion	Reinsurer's Responsibility
Yearly Renewable Term (YRT)	Morbidity/mortality	Reinsurer	Reimbursement to ceding company for death benefit paid on reinsured portion
Coinsurance	Morbidity/mortality; investment; early termination	Reinsurer	Proportionate share of death benefit
Modified Coinsurance	Morbidity/mortality	Ceding company	Death benefit of reinsured portion

Yearly renewable term (YRT). ***Yearly renewable term (YRT)*** reinsurance is a type of proportional reinsurance plan in which a ceding company buys an amount of yearly renewable term coverage that is equal to the net amount at risk on the portion of the policy being reinsured. The ***net amount at risk*** for a life insurance policy is the policy's face value, or death benefit, minus the policy's cash value, or reserve, and any policy loans at the end of a policy year. When a plan and its riders are reinsured under the same reinsurance agreement, the net amount at risk is calculated by including the amounts of both the plan and the riders. YRT reinsurance is often used to reinsure whole life coverage, disability coverage, and such interest-sensitive coverages as universal life.

The premium for YRT reinsurance is typically based on the age of the insured. The coverage is usually renewed annually when the ceding company pays the next year's premiums. Most reinsurance agreements provide that if the premium for YRT coverage is unpaid 90 days after the due date, the reinsurer has the option of notifying the ceding company that coverage will terminate if the overdue premiums, plus interest, have not been paid within 60 days from the date of notice. Therefore, if the reinsurer provides the ceding company with such notice, the reinsurance coverage will terminate 150 days after the premiums are still due and unpaid. Even if the coverage is terminated under these circumstances, the ceding company is obligated to pay the overdue premiums, plus interest to the date that the premiums are paid.

In purchasing YRT coverage, an insurer pays an annual premium to a reinsurer, but does not share premiums and expenses for the coverage. The reinsurer, in turn, agrees to reimburse the ceding company for any payment made on a reinsured claim. This reimbursement is limited to the net amount at risk for each policy. The insurer maintains adequate reserves to cover each policy, but reduces the amount of its reserves according to the amount of reinsurance purchased on the coverage.

Coinsurance. A type of proportional reinsurance plan in which an insurer and a reinsurer share the risk at a predetermined level is known as ***coinsurance.*** For instance, the insurer agrees to cover 40 percent of a risk, and the reinsurer agrees to cover the remaining 60 percent. As another example, the insurer may agree to cover $45,000 of a $60,000 risk, and the reinsurer agrees to cover the remaining $15,000. The principal difference between YRT reinsurance and coinsurance is that, under YRT, the reinsurer covers only the net amount at risk, whereas, under coinsurance, the reinsurer covers the face amount, policy reserve, policy expenses, and other elements of coverage.

Under coinsurance, the ceding company pays the reinsurer part of the premium paid by the insured, minus a proportionate share of the commission and premium taxes associated with the policy that is being reinsured and a portion of the ceding company's general overhead expenses. This share of the commission, taxes, and expenses is known as the ***reinsurance expense allowance.*** In return, the reinsurer agrees to pay the ceding company a proportionate part of benefits when a claim is filed and to contribute to all other policy benefits, including dividends. The ceding company also agrees to contribute to all other policy benefits, if any, including dividends. Finally, under coinsurance the reinsurer agrees to accumulate the required reserves for the reinsured portion of the policy. Whereas under YRT the reinsurer assumes only the mortality or morbidity risk, coinsurance provides that the reinsurer assumes the mortality or morbidity risk *and* the investment risk and risk of early termination of the policy.

Sometimes an insurer and a reinsurer use experience rating to provide appropriate dividends if the insurer's claims experience is more favorable than anticipated. Typically, however, coinsurance is not experience rated. Instead, a reinsurer usually offers a bonus to a ceding company for superior persistency or consistently high production levels that result in a considerable number of policies being placed with the reinsurer.

Modified coinsurance. Another proportional plan of reinsurance is ***modified coinsurance,*** under which the basic provisions of coinsurance are modified by having the ceding company maintain the entire policy reserve. At the end of each year, the reinsurer transfers to the ceding company an amount equal to the increase in the reserve for the reinsured portion of the policy, minus the interest that the ceding company has earned on the reserve for the reinsured portion of the policy. In the event of a claim, the reinsurer is responsible for the death benefit of the reinsured portion of the policy minus the reserve credited for that amount.

A central difference between coinsurance and modified coinsurance is that under modified coinsurance, the reinsurer does not share in the investment risk associated with an insurance product, whereas the reinsurer under coinsurance does share in that investment risk.

Nonproportional Reinsurance

In contrast to proportional reinsurance, ***nonproportional reinsurance*** provides that the amount or proportion of the risk carried by an insurer and by a reinsurer is not known when the reinsurance agreement is made. Usually, the risk level depends on the dollar amount or the number of claims submitted under the reinsured coverage. In establishing an agreement for nonproportional reinsurance, the parties do not specify the amount of premiums and claims that they will share.

Under a nonproportional agreement, the ceding company's losses usually must be greater than a specified loss limit before the reinsurer pays benefits on a valid claim. Generally, the amount or percentage that the reinsurer pays in a claim submitted under coverage issued on a nonproportional basis depends on the size of the claim.

The principal purpose of nonproportional reinsurance is to limit an insurer's total risk of loss on a policy or a block of business. By reducing claims fluctuations, nonproportional reinsurance helps an insurer achieve a greater measure of financial stability. Using nonproportional reinsurance enables an insurer to reduce or eliminate the financial impact of enormous losses that could result from claims submitted under large-amount coverage or in a catastrophic situation—that is, one in which a number of persons suffer considerable loss at one time.

Most insurers use nonproportional reinsurance to cover health and disability income policies rather than life policies. The potential claim amount for life coverage is typically specified in the policy, so that an insurer knows with reasonable certainty the level of potential claims. By contrast, if an insured person is gravely injured or suffers a lengthy or permanent disability, the potential claim amount for certain types of health and disability coverage may exceed the amount projected when the coverage was designed and priced. To cover such potentially large and unpredictable losses, insurers purchase nonproportional reinsurance.

Four plans of nonproportional reinsurance include excess-of-loss, stop-loss, spread-loss, and extended-time. Figure 12-3 presents a comparison of nonproportional reinsurance plans. In addition to using these types of plans, some insurers purchase nonproportional coverage for potential losses resulting from certain riders and policy provisions.

Excess-of-loss reinsurance. ***Excess-of-loss reinsurance*** is a type of nonproportional reinsurance providing that a reinsurer will pay the amount of a claim above a predetermined limit. The reinsurer's liability under excess-of-loss reinsurance is usually limited to a maximum amount

Figure 12-3. Comparison of nonproportional reinsurance plans.

	Reinsurer Will Pay	Type of Claim Covered	Top Limit of Reinsurance Specified?
Excess-of-Loss	Amount of claim above predetermined limit	Individual	Yes
Stop-Loss	Claims that exceed (1) a specified percentage of loss during specified period or (2) maximum dollar amount	Total percent or amount of claims incurred by ceding company	Yes
Spread-Loss	Specified percentage of specified kind of claims incurred by ceding company during specified period	Specified in reinsurance agreement; usually a certain type of policy coverage	No
Extended-Time	Disability income benefits for disabilities continuing beyond a specified period	Disability income	No

per event or per health claim. For example, suppose that an insurer issues a disability insurance policy that provides coverage up to $200,000 annually. The insurer sets a limit of $50,000 that it wishes to retain as its own risk and reinsures the policy under an excess-of-loss agreement for $150,000. If a claim is submitted under the policy, the insurer will pay the first $50,000 of the claim, and the reinsurance will cover the remainder up to $150,000, for a total potential disbursement of $200,000. Coverage under excess-of-loss reinsurance is typically guaranteed for one year, after which the reinsurance agreement is either renewed or discontinued at the reinsurer's option.

Stop-loss reinsurance. ***Stop-loss reinsurance*** is a type of nonproportional reinsurance providing that a reinsurer will pay claims that exceed (1) a specified percentage of the loss incurred during a specified period and/or (2) a maximum dollar amount. Stop-loss reinsurance does not cover individual claims, but covers total percentages or amounts of claims incurred by a ceding company. Unlike excess-of-loss reinsurance, stop-loss reinsurance does not specify a top limit of reinsured coverage for any single case. A stop-loss agreement, however, may specify a maximum amount of reinsurance that will be paid to satisfy claims submitted as a result of any single event.

For instance, suppose that an insurer has issued large amounts of life coverage on eight persons and has reinsured this coverage. The reinsurance agreement specifies that, during any calendar year, the reinsurer will pay all of the claims submitted under the coverage, providing that more than five claims are submitted during the year. The reinsurance agreement further specifies that the reinsurer will pay claims submitted as the result of a single event up to a maximum of $25 million. Suppose further that all eight of the insureds are killed in a typhoon, and claims submitted under their policies total $35 million.

Because more than five deaths occur as a result of the typhoon, the reinsurer will pay all of the claims on all eight reinsured lives up to the $25 million limit, but not for the $10 million in claims that exceed that limit. Note that if only four persons had died in the typhoon, and if no other claims had been submitted during the year under the reinsured coverage prior to this catastrophic event, the reinsurer would pay nothing for deaths resulting from the typhoon.

Spread-loss reinsurance. Another type of nonproportional reinsurance is ***spread-loss reinsurance,*** which provides for benefits covering a specified percentage of a specified kind of claim incurred by the ceding company during a specified period—for instance, 70 percent of whole life death benefits during a one-year period. The point at which the reinsurance benefits begin is usually set above 100 percent of the ceding company's actuarially predicted annual claims experience for the coverage.

For example, suppose a life insurer markets a term life product and expects to receive approximately 1,500 claims under that product annually. The insurer may purchase spread-loss reinsurance to cover a specified percentage of death benefits—say, 75 percent—above the expected 1,500 annual claims under the product. If the insurer receives only 1,389 such claims in a one-year period, no reinsurance benefits are payable. If, however, the insurer receives 1,680 claims during the period, the reinsurance coverage will pay 75 percent of the death benefits for the last 180 claims submitted during the period.

Some spread-loss reinsurance agreements are established for a multiple-year period, usually three to five years. Agreements for this type of spread-loss reinsurance typically provide that if, at the end of any year, the reinsurer has paid such a high level of claims that the premium reserve established for the coverage is exceeded, the reinsurance agreement between the insurer and the reinsurer may not be discontinued until the reinsurer has received sufficient premiums from the next period to compensate for the deficit. This provision remains in effect even if the deficit occurs in the final year covered by the agreement.

Extended-time reinsurance. A fourth type of nonproportional reinsurance is ***extended-time reinsurance,*** which typically covers disability income claims. Extended-time reinsurance generally provides that benefits are paid at the end of a specified period during which a covered disability has continued. For example, suppose that a person with disability income coverage loses a limb in an accident and is unable to work for an extended period of time. The reinsurance coverage on the policy specifies that reinsurance benefits will be paid for insurance benefits disbursed to the insured after a three-month period during which the insurer has paid disability benefits. From the date disability payments begin until the end of the three-month period, the ceding company alone is responsible for benefits. If the insured continues to receive disability benefits for more than three months, extended-time reinsurance benefits will begin.

Riders and policy provisions. Some insurers purchase reinsurance for certain features of coverage. Many reinsurers offer proportional and nonproportional specialized plans of reinsurance for such coverage features as waiver of premium and guaranteed purchase option or accidental death benefit.

A ***waiver of premium*** is a rider or policy provision by which an insurer agrees to give up its right to receive premiums if a policyowner fulfills a specified condition—for example, if the policyowner becomes disabled because of accident or injury, or if the policyowner who is paying premiums on coverage for a child should die and, therefore, not be able to pay the premium. Reinsurance for policies offering a waiver of premium pays the cost of the waived premiums and helps an insurer absorb the potential additional cost of providing insurance for a policyowner who is unable to pay premiums for the coverage.

A ***guaranteed purchase option,*** also called a *guaranteed insurability option,* is a rider or policy provision giving a policyowner the right to buy additional insurance of the same type as that provided in the original policy. The additional insurance can equal no more than an amount specified in the policy contract and can be purchased at specified premium rates and at specified times without new evidence of insurability. Reinsurance for policies having a guaranteed purchase option pays for claims submitted under the additional coverage. This type of reinsurance helps the insurer (1) spread the risk resulting from the increased coverage delivered without insurability evidence and (2) reduce the potential financial risk resulting from possible antiselection if an insured who develops impairments decides to exercise the option.

Both proportional and nonproportional reinsurance can help an insurance company manage its risks. Insight 12-2 illustrates some of the ways that reinsurance can help self-insured organizations to manage their risk as well.

Insight 12-2 Reinsurance Helps Cut Risk for Self-Insureds

Self insurance is an appealing alternative to many large- and smaller-size employers seeking to provide health care benefits to their employees and, at the same time, cut expenses.

Despite its charm, self insurance also carries risks—both old and new—about which every employer contemplating or using this option should know. Judicious reinsurance, however, can help manage those risks.

First, let's consider the risk traditionally confronting most self-insureds—a catastrophic claim year.

As every risk manager knows, a year of just a few very premature babies can be terribly costly for the self-insured employer. Purchasing a specific and aggregate stop-loss policy, thereby shifting risk to a reinsurer, can help an employer manage those costs.

In fact, for smaller employers, which have fewer employees to help absorb these expenses, obtaining such reinsurance is critical.

With the advent of managed care, another risk is appearing on the self-insured horizon: Cost-shifting by providers to patients covered by a plan without negotiated rates. The result is that self-insured employers which do not participate in a good managed-care network are likely to pay higher prices for medical services.

To prevent this cost shift, reinsurers provide incentives in the form of discounted rates to self-insured employers who contract with top-quality, managed-care networks. Discounts range from 10 to 50 percent, depending on the employer's stop-loss policy deductible and the caliber of their network.

Network quality is key. The issue, however, for many self-insured companies, particularly smaller ones with fewer resources, is how to ascertain that quality.

Quality networks generally meet these criteria: well-respected, accessible providers; good tertiary care facilities; quality utilization management; and competitive contracted rates that set fixed fees for specific procedures and treatments.

Self-insureds also face another new risk, related to finding a good medical network. To eliminate middleman costs, some employers are considering contracting directly with provider-sponsored networks.

But this route is risky.

The biggest risk is provider insolvency. Because these new provider-sponsored networks are not typically regulated as insurance companies and HMOs are, they are not subject to strict reporting and reserve requirements.

If the network sponsor goes belly-up, a self-insured might have to pay twice for the same services or, even worse, be sued. (The latter could happen when the network providers try to recover their expected fees.)

Finally, such an arrangement also may elicit state sanctions. Some states consider an employer prepaying directly for medical services—capitation fees to an unregulated provider-sponsored network—a murky form of insurance, subject to premium tax.

Clearly, employers contemplating such arrangements should make sure that prospective networks are stable, competent, well-capitalized, conforming to appropriate state regulations, and reinsured for catastrophic excess.

The self-insurance route may carry a variety of risks; however, it can be a cost-effective alternative for the employer using reinsurance and managed care to control the risks.

From Tracy Labonte, "Reinsurance Helps Cut Risk for Self-Insureds," *National Underwriter,* © The National Underwriter Company, Life & Health/Financial Services Edition, April 29, 1996: 20. Adapted by permission.

Key Terms and Concepts

automatic reinsurance
alphabetic split
pooling (*quota share*)
layering
binding limit
jumbo limit
facultative reinsurance
shopping
facultative automatic reinsurance (*facultative obligatory reinsurance*)
proportional reinsurance
quota share approach (*pro rata approach*)
excess share approach (*surplus share approach, level retention*)
yearly renewable term (YRT)
net amount at risk
coinsurance
reinsurance expense allowance
modified coinsurance
nonproportional reinsurance
excess-of-loss reinsurance
stop-loss reinsurance
spread-loss reinsurance
extended-time reinsurance
waiver of premium
guaranteed purchase option (*guaranteed insurability option*)

CHAPTER THIRTEEN

Establishing the Insurer-Reinsurer Relationship

Learning Objectives

After studying this chapter, you should be able to

- Explain how reinsurance is distributed by reinsurance companies, reinsurance pools, captive reinsurers, reinsurance intermediaries and consultants, and Lloyd's of London
- Contrast the reinsurance marketing functions of reinsurance intermediaries and consultants
- Discuss the principal ethical considerations involved in marketing reinsurance
- List and explain the factors a ceding company may consider in selecting a reinsurer
- List and explain the factors a reinsurer may consider in deciding whether to accept an insurer's business
- Describe the process an insurer follows in obtaining reinsurance quotations
- Discuss how reciprocity enables insurers to spread risk, and explain the advantages and disadvantages of a reciprocity relationship

Chapter Outline

When a relationship is formed between an insurer and a reinsurer, mutual trust and good faith are the basis of all transactions. From initial reinsurance marketing to treaty formation, the reinsurance relationship continues through numerous activities, usually including underwriting and claims.

This chapter and the two chapters that follow will discuss the course of the reinsurance relationship. In this chapter, we'll first examine the ways that the reinsurance relationship is initiated through marketing. We'll show how an insurer establishes a reinsurance relationship by searching for and selecting a reinsurer, and then by obtaining quotations for the desired coverage. After discussing the ethics of reinsurance, we'll examine a special type of reinsurance relationship known as reciprocity. In the next two chapters, we'll examine the characteristics of reinsurance treaties that are used to formalize reinsurance relationships, and we will discuss the activities involved in reinsurance administration.

Marketing of Reinsurance

The relationship between an insurer and a reinsurer begins when reinsurance is being marketed. Reinsurance for life and health coverages is marketed by reinsurance companies, by insurers that form a reinsurance pool, by captive reinsurers, and by insurance intermediaries and consultants. In addition, Lloyd's of London provides reinsurance for certain kinds of risks.

Reinsurance Companies

Reinsurers do not distribute coverage through exclusive agents. Instead, reinsurers market their products through account executives who are employed directly by each reinsurer. Most reinsurance companies employ account executives to market reinsurance coverage directly to ceding companies and, sometimes, to underwrite the coverage as well. As legal agents of their employers, account executives are usually paid a salary, but not commissions. Reinsurers that market insurance coverage through account executives are called ***direct-writing reinsurers*** and do not normally accept cases submitted by reinsurance intermediaries.

One advantage to an insurer of purchasing reinsurance directly from a reinsurance company is that the insurer and the reinsurer can develop a closer, more personal relationship than they might if they were represented by an intermediary. A disadvantage that can result from direct insurer-reinsurer negotiations is that each party to the transaction has a different goal: one is a buyer and the other is a seller, and, as a result, they may develop an adversarial relationship instead of a cooperative one. If a misunderstanding develops, the insured must find a way to represent its best interest without the intervention and expertise that an intermediary could provide. Another disadvantage to an insurer of negotiating directly with a reinsurer is that the reinsurer may seek to cover only the lower-risk portions of the insured's business. By using an intermediary, the insurer not only might receive offers to cover both lower-risk and higher-risk business, but also might receive competitive bids for each type of business and, therefore, obtain reinsurance at a relatively lower price. Generally, however, the direct market for reinsurance produces sound results for both insurers and reinsurers.

Reinsurance marketers are categorized as authorized or unauthorized. An ***authorized reinsurer,*** also known as an *admitted reinsurer,* is licensed or otherwise recognized by the insurance department in a jurisdiction. An ***unauthorized reinsurer,*** also known as a *nonadmitted reinsurer,* does not have the licensing or recognition of the insurance department in a jurisdiction. Only a reinsurer that is authorized to distribute its products may market those products within a specified jurisdiction. The practice of fronting, which we have previously mentioned, typically occurs when a reinsurer wishes to do business in a jurisdiction in which the company is considered an unauthorized reinsurer.

Reinsurance Pools

A ***reinsurance pool*** is a group of insurers that join together to offer reinsurance coverage and to smooth the claim fluctuations in the experience of each pool member. Pools are typically used for health coverages, especially for major medical insurance and for certain riders like waiver of premium (WP), but are rarely used for life coverages. Because a pool spreads the risk among several companies, the insurers in the pool have greater capacity as a group than each would alone to underwrite large risks and to offer coverage for difficult or nonstandard risks. The members of a reinsurance pool may choose to restrict reinsurance coverage only to the companies in the pool or only to companies *not* in the pool, or may offer coverage to companies both in and outside the pool.

Pools established to provide reinsurance for health coverages usually hire an outside organization to provide underwriting and claim administration services for pool members. Claim payment is usually handled in one of two ways, depending on the agreement made by the pool members. Each company may pay its own claims up to a specified limit, and claims above that limit are paid in equal shares by other pool members. Alternatively, each member of the pool may agree to pay a specified percentage of the total claims submitted to all members of the pool. In some pools, one company serves as a ***lead reinsurer*** that assumes responsibility for underwriting, communicating with, and handling claims for all insurers in the pool.

The term "pool" for reinsurance is also used by some insurers that establish a standard means of dividing reinsurance among a group of reinsurance providers selected by the ceding company. Although these selected providers do not function as a reinsurance pool as defined above, the providers are sometimes called a "pool" by the ceding company. Such a pool provides extended coverages for amounts above the ceding company's retention limit by sharing risks among the reinsurers. Figure 13-1 illustrates a sample division of reinsurance coverages among a group of reinsurance companies selected by a ceding company, which cedes some types of coverage to one group of reinsurers, and another type of coverage to a second group of reinsurers.

For example, if the insurer in Figure 13-1 wished to reinsure $2 million of a $3 million annual renewable term life insurance policy, the following amount of risk would be transferred to each company in the pool:

Reinsurer A—40% or $800,000
Reinsurer B—30% or $600,000
Reinsurer C—20% or $400,000
Reinsurer D—10% or $200,000

Captive Reinsurers

A ***captive reinsurer*** is a company established for the purpose of offering reinsurance for the risks submitted from a certain source, such as an insurance company. A captive reinsurer may be formed by a group of agents or other marketers in order to offer reinsurance for cases that the

Figure 13-1. Division of one insurer's reinsurance coverages among a group of reinsurers.

Type of Coverage Reinsured	Reinsuring Companies
Annual renewable term, 7-year term, and whole life	Reinsurer A—40% Reinsurer B—30% Reinsurer C—20% Reinsurer D—10%
Universal life and level term life	Reinsurer V—30% Reinsurer W—25% Reinsurer X—25% Reinsurer Y—10% Reinsurer Z—10%

agents themselves submit to an insurer. The reasons for forming a captive reinsurer include (1) taking advantage of the deductibility of premiums paid to a captive insurer as a business expense, (2) enabling the parent company to earn money by investing premiums paid to the captive reinsurer, (3) providing coverage tailored to the needs of the owners, and (4) encouraging marketers to produce a higher quality of business that can then be reinsured and that can return a portion of the profit directly to the marketers.

Three categories of captive reinsurers include ***pure captive,*** which is the most common kind of captive reinsurer and is a captive offering reinsurance to a parent company and its subsidiaries or affiliates; ***association captive,*** which is a captive offering reinsurance to a group of insurers that are usually in the same line of business; and ***broad captive,*** which is a captive offering reinsurance to not only its parent company, subsidiaries, and affiliates, but also other insurers. Captive reinsurers are regulated by the laws of the jurisdiction in which each reinsurer does business, as well as by the rules of the Securities and Exchange Commission (SEC) in the United States. Typically, a captive reinsurer holds a license in only one state or province.

Reinsurance Intermediaries and Consultants

A ***reinsurance intermediary,*** also called a *reinsurance broker,* markets reinsurance from several reinsurers directly to ceding companies. A reinsurance intermediary does not usually represent a certain reinsurer, but is generally considered to be an independent contractor. Intermediaries are often used to arrange reinsurance coverage for health coverages, but are rarely used to arrange reinsurance for life insurance.

One of the most important functions of a reinsurance intermediary is to assemble adequate reinsurance coverage for large cases, for which the intermediary may have to contact a number of reinsurers. For life reinsurance, a reinsurance intermediary is typically used only to place complex portfolios of risk or, very rarely, large-amount cases requiring a high level of expertise or strong industry contacts. For health, disability, and accident reinsurance, however, reinsurance intermediaries are routinely used.

Beyond the action of serving as liaison between insurer and reinsurer, a reinsurance intermediary also performs an educational function by informing the insurer about available reinsurance coverage options and about changes in the reinsurance market. The reinsurance intermediary may also counsel an insurer concerning establishing and maintaining a sound reinsurance program. Ideally, the reinsurance intermediary has ample access to international reinsurance markets and can provide an insurer with a large choice of reinsurance programs and choices.

The procedure followed by a reinsurance intermediary in obtaining reinsurance coverage for an insurer usually involves searching for the best coverage for a specific case or block of business. After determining an insurer's reinsurance needs, a reinsurance intermediary contacts reinsurers to obtain quotes for the coverage. If acceptable coverage is offered, the reinsurance intermediary prepares a reinsurance treaty between the ceding company and the reinsurer. During negotiations concerning the reinsurance treaty, the reinsurance intermediary represents the ceding company. Payment for the services provided by the reinsurance intermediary is usually made by the ceding company or the reinsurer on a contingent fee basis—that is, the intermediary is paid only for cases or blocks of business that are successfully placed with a reinsurer. Sometimes the ceding company or the reinsurer compensates the intermediary by paying a commission.

A reinsurance intermediary may perform several additional functions for life and health insurers. The reinsurance intermediary may present claim reports and information to the reinsurer, and may settle claims on behalf of the reinsurer. If the reinsurer and the ceding company disagree concerning a claim, the reinsurance intermediary represents the ceding company in resolving the disagreement. Finally, when the reinsurance treaty is renewed, the intermediary again represents the ceding company during negotiations and preparation of a renewal treaty. Some reinsurance intermediaries are given authority to serve as underwriters for reinsurers. As compensation for these services, a reinsurance intermediary is paid a commission by the reinsurer.

Reinsurance intermediaries often syndicate a ceding company's reinsurance, especially for large-amount cases, by splitting the coverage among several reinsurers. Syndicating reinsurance in this way enables an intermediary to place a large amount of business among several reinsurers, each of which might be less likely to accept the entire risk. Moreover, syndicating a ceding company's reinsured risks permits an insurer to obtain reinsurance for difficult-to-place risks without paying an increased premium to any one insurer for accepting the increased risk represented by the block of business.

According to recommendations made in the NAIC Reinsurance Intermediary Model Act, a reinsurance intermediary must be licensed and must give the ceding company full information concerning all transactions with reinsurers, including commissions and fees. According to the act, the ceding company must be allowed to audit all financial transactions and to review and obtain copies of all records associated with the reinsured business.

Some reinsurance companies accept reinsurance cases from consultants, although this method of marketing reinsurance represents only a small portion of the total reinsurance market. A ceding company pays a consultant a fee, but not a salary or a commission, for the service of marketing the ceding company's reinsurance coverage to a reinsurer and, usually, of supervising the administration and renewal of such coverage. Some consultants also help insurers design the required reinsurance coverage. A consultant is usually considered to be an agent of the ceding company. Independent reinsurance intermediaries also negotiate directly with insurers or pools on a commission basis.

Comparison of reinsurance intermediaries and consultants. Both the reinsurance intermediary and the consultant represent ceding companies and perform many of the same services for their clients. One difference between these two types of marketers is that a reinsurance intermediary is paid a fee by the ceding company or the reinsurer, whereas a consultant is paid a fee by the ceding company. Another difference is that, whereas a consultant is an agent of the ceding company, a reinsurance intermediary, at various times in the reinsurance relationship, may be an agent of the ceding company, of the reinsurer, or of both of them. Both parties rely on the insurance intermediary to arrange and administer sound business. Unless specific provisions are included in the reinsurance treaty specifying the agent relationship of the reinsurance intermediary, the agent relationship is determined by laws relating to agency relationships and by the usual practices followed in the type of reinsurance being marketed.

Figure 13-2 illustrates the similarities and differences in a reinsurance intermediary and a consultant in reinsurance marketing.

Many ceding companies choose to use reinsurance intermediaries because of the advantages of having such representation in the re-

Figure 13-2. Comparison of a reinsurance intermediary and a consultant.

	Reinsurance Intermediary	Consultant
Generally represents a ceding company, not a reinsurer	Yes	Yes
Helps determine a ceding company's need for reinsurance	Yes	Yes
Contacts reinsurers to obtain quotes for the coverage	Yes	Yes
Assists with treaty negotiations at initial placement and at renewal	Yes	Yes
Represents the ceding company during treaty and claim negotiations	Yes	Yes
Receives premiums from the ceding company and transmits them to the reinsurer	Yes	Sometimes
Presents claim information and reports to the reinsurer	Yes	Yes
Transmits claim payment funds from the reinsurer to the ceding company	Yes	Sometimes
Receives a commission from the reinsurer or the ceding company	Sometimes	No
Receives a fee from the ceding company	Yes	Yes
Serves as an agent of the ceding company	Varies	Yes

insurance marketplace. Specifically, the advantages to a ceding company of employing a reinsurance intermediary include

- Benefiting from the reinsurance intermediary's familiarity with a large number of reinsurance companies and types of available coverage
- Ensuring that the ceding company's best interests are considered in designing and negotiating the treaty of reinsurance
- Encouraging frank discussion of the ceding company's needs and the abilities of various reinsurers to meet those needs
- Enabling a ceding company that does not underwrite substandard or catastrophic risks on any basis to offer a full range of coverage to policyholders by having the intermediary send these kinds of risks to a reinsurer for risk classification and underwriting
- Benefiting from the intermediary's negotiation of favorable terms at time of treaty renewal

Lloyd's of London

Lloyd's of London functions as a clearinghouse for insurance coverage and is not itself an insurer or a reinsurer. Lloyd's is composed of a number of syndicates, each formed by a group of between 30 and 700 persons who qualify to market insurance coverage by virtue of their considerable financial strength. Unlike professional reinsurers, primary insurers, and reinsurance pools, the syndicate members of Lloyd's assume risks individually, not through a corporate entity. Each syndicate is managed by a managing underwriter and a staff whose principal responsibilities are to (1) provide underwriting, claim administration, and accounting services for syndicate members; (2) report claims and financial results; and (3) distribute profits to the members of the syndicate. The syndicates offer insurance and reinsurance for property and casualty risks and for medical, disability, and accidental death risks, and for life risks of a short-term nature.

Fast Fact

In the late 1980's, provider groups in the managed health care field had to go to Lloyd's of London or other foreign reinsurers with their business. By the mid 1990's, however, almost all domestic reinsurers offered managed-care coverage as both the market and the number of reinsurers expanded.

Source: Laura Mazzuca Toops, "Reinsurers Can Get Burned in Rush to Managed Care," *Best's Review (Life/Health)*, February 1996: 43–47.

Reinsurance Marketing Ethics

When a reinsurer markets its products directly to an insurer, the reinsurer adheres to the highest ethical standards by protecting information and data received from the insurer. During the course of negotiations aimed at establishing a reinsurance relationship, an insurer reveals to a reinsurer a considerable amount of sensitive information about the insurer's products, premiums, and insureds or proposed insureds. Even if the negotiations do not result in the establishment of a reinsurance relationship that is formalized by a treaty, the reinsurer preserves as confidential all information it has received in the course of the negotiations.

Fast Fact

"There is definitely an element of trust between the reinsurer and the direct insurer. It boils down to making sure everything is clear at the start of the contract. Reinsurers have to be extremely careful about confidentiality—if they abused that trust, they'd be out of business very quickly."

Graham Bancroft, Vice President of Life & Financial Reinsurance for Sun Life Assurance Company of Canada (personal communication, January 17, 1997).

If an insurer has used a reinsurance intermediary to negotiate for reinsurance, the intermediary is involved during all visits and in all other significant transactions between the insurer and the reinsurer. In order to avoid misunderstandings and to facilitate communication between the insurer and the reinsurer, the intermediary is included during every step of the negotiation process.

Another ethical consideration is that the reinsurer does not reveal information about the ongoing negotiations, nor about the reinsurance relationship (if one is developed), with any intermediary other than the one that represents the insurer. The intermediary usually has received permission from the insurer, in the form of a letter or other documentation, to discuss the insurer's needs for reinsurance. Although a reinsurer does not discuss the business with any intermediary except one authorized to represent the insurer, the reinsurer may deal with more than one intermediary that the insurer has appointed to discuss reinsurance on different types of products. For example, an insurer may appoint one intermediary to negotiate reinsurance for one product line, and another intermediary to handle reinsurance for a separate product line. In such a situation, the reinsurer may ethically enter into discussions with both intermediaries separately.

If an intermediary has successfully placed some reinsurance business with a reinsurer that later cancels the coverage, the reinsurer is prohibited ethically from resoliciting that same business directly from the insurer. Instead, if the reinsurer decides to make another offer to reinsure the same business, the reinsurer should contact the insurer only through the intermediary who handled the original negotiations. In addition, if an intermediary has brought business from an insurer to a reinsurer, ethical considerations dictate that the reinsurer contact the intermediary if the reinsurer wishes to offer another type of reinsurance to the same insurance company.

Selecting a Reinsurer

When an insurer decides to seek reinsurance, the insurer searches for a reinsuring partner. Insurers that search for a reinsurer typically talk with reinsurers whose representatives have called on them or use the services of a reinsurance intermediary or other marketer. The reinsurance relationship depends on good faith between the ceding company and a reinsurer and depends on their integrity. Although no perfect way exists to determine the integrity of a reinsurer, a good indication can be obtained by assessing a reinsurer's existing reinsurance relationships. To investigate and gather information about a prospective reinsurance company, a ceding company usually talks with some of the reinsurer's past and current clients. Speaking to people in insurance companies that have transacted business with a reinsurance company can provide valuable information.

In selecting a reinsurer, a ceding company considers a number of factors about the reinsurer, including

- Cost of coverage relative to the cost of similar coverage from other reinsurers
- Flexibility of product design, including the reinsurer's ability and willingness to tailor reinsurance packages to a ceding company's requirements
- Adequacy of customer service, including the reinsurer's ability to help the ceding company resolve problems of cash flow and accounting and to provide expert advice concerning the defense of difficult claims
- Underwriting ability and degree of reinsurance expertise
- Industry reputation of the reinsurer, especially its record of long-lasting, appropriately confidential relationships with ceding companies
- Location of the reinsurer (although most international reinsurers have local offices and expertise)
- Size and financial stability of the reinsurer, including its ability to accept the type and size of cases the ceding company wishes to reinsure and to make claim payments promptly

The location of a reinsurer may be helpful to a ceding company in facilitating a rapid flow of underwriting and claims settlement. Suppose, for instance, a ceding company located in Germany forms a reinsurance relationship with a reinsurer in Canada. Because of the time differences in the two locales, the ceding company can complete work on reinsured cases during its workday in Germany and relay the cases to the reinsurer in Canada for continued consideration during the Canadian workday. Underwriting and claim settlement can proceed in this manner on a virtually continuous basis, with resulting efficiencies for both parties to the reinsurance relationship.

Choosing a reinsurer that is financially stable is essential so that a ceding company may be confident that its risks are appropriately covered according to the terms of the reinsurance treaty. To evaluate a reinsurer's financial stability, a ceding company usually analyzes recent financial information from the reinsurer, including the following:

- Financial statements.
- An independent auditor's report that includes a letter concerning the reinsurer's internal controls.
- The 10-K report filed annually with the Securities and Exchange Commission (SEC) in the United States. A company's 10-K report provides excellent financial information because the 10-K must include certain items that a company could exclude from an annual report. For instance, a company might pay $100 million to acquire a subsidiary. Half the price of the acquisition might be for goodwill, so that the tangible net worth of the subsidiary is only $50 million. The company's annual report can show legitimately that the company paid $100 million for $100 million worth of assets. The company's 10-K report, however, would reveal the true tangible net worth of the subsidiary as only $50 million.
- Examination reports from the jurisdiction's department of insurance in the United States.
- Reports from the NAIC Insurance Regulatory Information System (IRIS), which enables state departments of insurance in the United States to review and assess the statutory annual statements that every insurer must file in each state in which the insurer is licensed to do business.

The perils of not checking the financial stability of a prospective reinsurer can be severe. Insight 13-1 presents an explanation of why such stability is important.

The reinsurance relationship is two-way. Therefore, the reinsurer also investigates insurers that apply for reinsurance coverage. In evaluating a proposed insurer-client, a reinsurer typically analyzes recent financial information about the insurer from the same sources as those listed previously for the reinsurer. In addition, the reinsurer investigates the insurer's business practices and its reasons for wishing to enter into a relationship of reinsurance. Among the factors a reinsurer considers in deciding whether to accept an insurer's business are the following:

Insight 13-1 Insolvent Reinsurers Pose Even Greater Risk

A ceding insurer needs to be able to recover amounts owed by an insolvent reinsurer. Recent court judgments in some states have generally ranked the claims of ceding companies against the assets of insolvent reinsurers as follows:

- Expenses incurred in the administration of the reinsurer's liquidation
- Wage claims by employees of the insolvent reinsurer
- Policyowner claims
- Claims of the federal government
- Claims of general creditors, which can include ceding insurers

The court decisions have resulted in ceding insurers' claims being given a lower priority than both policyholders and the federal government in the distribution of the assets of an insolvent reinsurer.

In view of these decisions, ceding insurers would be wise to determine the extent of a reinsurer's indebtedness to the federal government before doing business with the reinsurer. Ceding insurers should also monitor the solvency of their reinsurers.

Ceding companies may also want to negotiate the establishment of trust funds with authorized reinsurers. Such trust funds could include assets including cash, cash equivalents, or real estate or bond holdings. State insurance laws already require unauthorized reinsurers to place specified assets in trust for a ceding company that wants to obtain credit for reinsurance. However, state laws do not impose a similar requirement on authorized reinsurers.

From Cecelia Kemplar and William Duffy, "Insolvent Reinsurers Pose Even Greater Risk," *Best's Review,* Life/Health Edition, April 1994: 54–57. Adapted by permission.

- Actuarial studies of the business to be assumed
- The ceding company's anticipated profitability and termination rates
- The reinsurer's prior business experience with the ceding company, if any
- The reinsurer's prior experience with similar business and treaties
- Pricing information and ceding commissions, if coinsurance is to be involved
- Indication of the frequency and content of reports from the ceding company
- The ceding company's internal accounting controls relating to ceded reinsurance
- Provisions for the reinsurer to monitor the actual results reported by the ceding company, including means to investigate the reasons for and effects of significant deviations from anticipated results
- Reports of the ceding company's sales, underwriting practices, claims handling procedures, and actuarial policies

Reinsurance Quotations

An insurance company wishes to obtain competitive quotations for the business to be reinsured. Insurers either seek quotes or bids directly from reinsurers or use intermediaries to solicit quotes. If a ceding company has established a solid relationship with several reinsurers, the ceding company calls those reinsurers and solicits bids for the coverage. Alternatively, an insurer may use an intermediary to place the reinsurance. If an insurer wishes to use more than one intermediary to solicit quotations for reinsurance, the insurer takes one of two approaches. The insurer may restrict each intermediary to a specified segment of the reinsurance market so that multiple intermediaries will not seek a quotation for the coverage from the same reinsurer. In taking this approach, an insurer avoids sending intermediaries to the reinsurance market in such a way that reinsurers are forced to compete unfairly against themselves by providing quotations on the same business to more than one intermediary. Alternatively, the insurer may allow each intermediary to seek placement in any segment of the market, but require that if more than one intermediary approaches a reinsurer, the affected intermediaries coordinate their efforts and make a joint inquiry to the reinsurer.

To illustrate the second approach, suppose that an insurer is using three intermediaries to obtain reinsurance on a large block of business. Ten reinsurance companies, which we will call Companies 1–10, offer coverage appropriate for the business. Intermediary A plans to seek quotations from only Companies 1–4. Intermediary B plans to seek quotations from only Companies 5–10. Intermediary C plans to seek quotations from only Companies 9 and 10. Intermediaries B and C coordinate their requests in asking Companies 9 and 10 for quotations. Companies 9 and 10 typically develop only one bid apiece for the business. If Intermediaries B and C are successful in placing the business with either Company 9 or Company 10, the two intermediaries will divide the commission.

To provide each bidding reinsurer with information necessary to develop a quotation, the insurer gathers information about the business. Generally, the insurer provides information for the previous five-year period concerning the following elements of its business to date:

- Any large losses by product line, with reinsurance payments indicated

- Other losses by product line

- Gross and net premiums by product line

- Gross and net underwriting results by product line
- Total amount of risk exposure for current business

In addition, the insurer gathers information on the following elements concerning its underwriting approaches and corporate strategy:

- Underwriting procedures and practices, including a statement of risks that are prohibited or underwritten only on a limited basis
- Current and planned corrective measures for any problem areas of underwriting
- Statement of the insurer's strategic plans for the coming period, usually five years

After the quotations have been received from all reinsurers and/or intermediaries, the insurer selects a source or sources from which to purchase reinsurance. If a treaty proposal has been submitted with the quotation, the insurer also reviews the treaty terms to ensure that all requested terms have been included and that the treaty wording reflects the insurer's desired coverage.

Reciprocity

An additional type of insurer-reinsurer relationship involves reciprocity. ***Reciprocity*** is an arrangement by which two insurers or reinsurers exchange business in return for cessions or retrocessions. In return for business ceded to another insurer or reinsurer, an insurance company receives a share of business reinsured by the other insurer or reinsurer. When two parties agree to an arrangement of reciprocity, they usually draft and sign an ***exchange contract*** that specifies the details of the arrangement. Rather than use reciprocity, the majority of insurers and reinsurers retrocede or reinsure their risks through formal agreements.

Usually, the insurers involved in a reciprocity arrangement cede and reinsure the same type of business. If the exchanged business is not substantially the same, one insurer is likely to benefit from the arrangement more than the other insurer does. In addition, the two insurers generally do not compete in the same geographical or demographic area. Because the members of the reciprocity arrangement necessarily share extensive data about their products and insureds, the members cannot be in a competitive situation and still expect to benefit from exchanging business.

The purpose of reciprocity is to increase the spread of risk. The desired outcome of a reciprocity arrangement is to establish an acceptable quantitative and qualitative balance between the business ceded and the business received by each party to the arrangement. Reciprocity is an essential component of the international reinsurance market.

A reciprocity arrangement usually involves only two insurance companies—two direct insurers, a direct insurer and a reinsurer, or two reinsurers. An important difference between a reciprocity arrangement and a reinsurance pool is that, in a reciprocity, only two insurers are involved, whereas a reinsurance pool may, and usually does, involve more than two insurers. Moreover, reciprocity is normally not specified in a reinsurance treaty. Instead, the reciprocity is arranged through an exchange of correspondence between the insurers involved.

A reciprocity arrangement is usually based on either premiums or results. Premium-based reciprocity involves exchanging business purchased for the same or nearly the same amount of premium. Such an exchange may be adversely affected by such uncontrollable factors as tariff rates, inflation, and fluctuations in exchange rates. If the balance becomes inequitable, usually the two involved insurers make an adjustment in the amount of future business to be exchanged so that both insurers obtain approximately the same financial benefit. Results-based reciprocity involves exchanging business for which the projected claims experience is the same or nearly the same. Because projected and actual claims experience may vary widely, results-based reciprocity may not provide the desired balance. Adjusting variations in claims experience is a more difficult process than adjusting for variations in premium-based reciprocity.

Advantages of a Reciprocity Arrangement

Two insurers can gain potential advantages from a reciprocity arrangement. First, each insurer's claims experience may improve or become more stable because of the increased spread of risk. As a result, each insurer may enjoy increased capacity and may be able to expand or enhance existing product lines or to offer new types of coverage.

Second, the costs of administering coverage may decrease because each insurer may spread those costs over a larger premium volume. Ideally, the risks exchanged are covered by the same type or a very similar type of coverage. When a larger number of cases of the same or a similar type are administered, the cost per case typically decreases.

Third, the cost of purchasing reinsurance through treaties may decrease because each insurer is able to obtain reinsurance without establishing a formal treaty and paying another insurer for the reinsurance coverage. In international markets, this reason can become especially important because an insurer may not have to send currency out of the country and may, therefore, avoid potential financial disadvantages associated with currency exchanges. On an international scale, reciprocity arrangements may serve to reduce a country's balance of payments.

Disadvantages of a Reciprocity Arrangement

A reciprocity arrangement also has potential disadvantages. First, an insurer may suffer an unexpected increase in claims resulting from the business accepted through a reciprocal arrangement. If the claims increase results in a drain on the insurer's funds, the insurer's financial stability could be jeopardized.

Moreover, if an insurer establishes a reciprocity arrangement to accept business that differs from the insurer's own business, the insurer may experience an increase in the cost of administering the less familiar business. For instance, training the insurer's staff and designing appropriate computer applications to handle a new type of business can consume considerable resources.

Finally, the amount of business exchanged through a reciprocity arrangement typically varies according to the claims experience of previously exchanged business. When claims are lower than expected, reciprocal business usually flourishes. When claims are higher than expected, reciprocal business generally falters. Such fluctuations in business may result in administrative and financial problems for both the insurers involved in a reciprocal arrangement. Insurers involved in reciprocity arrangements must realize that absolute equality in the financial effects of the reinsurance ceded and assumed is impossible.

Key Terms and Concepts

direct-writing reinsurers
authorized reinsurer (*admitted reinsurer*)
unauthorized reinsurer (*nonadmitted reinsurer*)
reinsurance pool
lead reinsurer
captive reinsurer
pure captive
association captive
broad captive
reinsurance intermediary (*reinsurance broker*)
Lloyd's of London
reciprocity
exchange contract

CHAPTER FOURTEEN

Reinsurance Treaties

Learning Objectives

After studying this chapter, you should be able to

- List and explain seven conditions typically established by an automatic reinsurance treaty
- Name four types of materials that a facultative reinsurance treaty typically requires a ceding company to submit to a reinsurer
- Explain the contents of 12 common reinsurance treaty provisions
- Name three issues on which a ceding company and a reinsurer must agree at the time of termination of a reinsurance treaty
- Explain how a retrocession agreement is similar to and different from a reinsurance treaty

Chapter Outline

Establishing the reinsurance relationship requires a high degree of mutual trust. According to reinsurance tradition, the bond between an insurer and a reinsurer has been as much a "gentlemen's agreement" as a formal business arrangement. Insight 14-1 comments on the concept of the gentlemen's agreement in reinsurance. Notwithstanding this tradition, reinsurance arrangements today are also established by a formal written agreement, negotiated and signed by the parties involved.

As we mentioned in Chapter 11, a reinsurance treaty is a statement of the agreement between a reinsurer and a ceding company. Many reinsurance treaties are stated in very broad terms that provide the parties a great deal of discretion in conducting their business. Other reinsurance treaties place considerable constraints on the parties to the agreement.

Although the gentlemen's agreement approach to reinsurance still strongly influences business practices in the industry, the trend is to define the accountabilities of each party more specifically than had been done in the past. The reasons for the emphasis on formation of such stronger reinsurance treaties include (1) innovative product designs with which insurers and reinsurers may have little experience, (2) large-amount policies that create huge capacity needs for reinsurance, and (3) insurers' tendency, at the time each new product is marketed, to reconsider their needs and sources for reinsurance rather than to send all their business to only one or a few reinsurers.

In this chapter, we'll first discuss the contents of a reinsurance treaty, including the conditions specific to an automatic treaty and a facultative treaty. Then we'll examine the procedures used to prepare and later to terminate a treaty. Finally, we'll comment on a retrocession agreement and compare it to a reinsurance treaty.

Contents of a Reinsurance Treaty

A reinsurance treaty is designed to transfer risk from a ceding company to a reinsurer. An automatic reinsurance treaty and a facultative reinsurance treaty contain somewhat different provisions because the two treaties have different basic purposes. The basic purpose of an automatic reinsurance treaty is to specify the conditions under which a case qualifies for reinsurance under the treaty. By contrast, the basic purpose of a facultative reinsurance treaty is to specify the conditions under which the reinsurer may evaluate cases submitted for consideration.

Insight 14-1 My Thoughts On . . . The Gentlemen's Agreement in Reinsurance

In addition to the reasons for the more legalistic approach now common in the reinsurance industry—as discussed in this chapter—a generally more litigious business climate in recent years has contributed to an increasingly formal approach in reinsurance matters. Also, in past years the primary ceding company contact for the reinsurance representative was often the underwriting department, whereas now the actuarial department, among others, is frequently the primary contact, with complex actuarial matters often overriding purely underwriting considerations.

The above comments are not to be looked on as a judgment that the current reinsurance climate is good or bad, but as a statement of reality. There is frequently nostalgia in the ranks of ceding company and reinsurance company people with many years of experience in the industry. Nostalgia will not bring back the old days, however—nor, probably, should it. But even with the current climate of ceding company/reinsurer relationships, integrity and the old adage "my word is my bond" have not gone out of style. These elements are even more vital in maintaining a stable, profitable, mutually satisfying relationship between the ceding company and the reinsurer.

John C. Broshar, FLMI, ALHC (retired)
Vice President, Claims
Munich American Reassurance Company

In discussing the contents of reinsurance treaties, we'll first discuss the general requirements for automatic and facultative treaties. Then we'll examine the clauses that are usually found in every reinsurance treaty, regardless of its type. We'll conclude by explaining how treaties may be changed by amendments and addenda.

Conditions in an Automatic Reinsurance Treaty

Generally, the ceding company uses its normal underwriting standards in accepting cases later submitted for reinsurance. An automatic reinsurance treaty specifies the conditions under which a case is qualified to be reinsured. The conditions stated in most automatic reinsurance treaties include the following:

- The treaty might specify that underwriting risk classification will be determined by using the insurer's or the reinsurer's underwriting manual or an alternative method upon which the parties mutually agree. The reinsurer usually reserves the right to review risk classification information used by the insurer, either at the insurer's office or by written request. The reinsurer also reserves the right to review actual underwriting files to verify whether the insurer is properly classifying risks. If risks are not being classified properly, the reinsurer may terminate the treaty with respect to further new business. If the insurer subsequently changes any of its underwriting criteria or requirements, the changes may need to be discussed with and approved by the reinsurer prior to implementation.

- The ceding company may not submit any business of the type covered by the treaty to any other reinsurer. The ceding company may, however, send any case to the reinsurer to obtain its underwriting opinion before the ceding company accepts the case and submits it for automatic reinsurance. Some automatic reinsurance treaties further provide that a ceding company may submit cases that are ineligible for automatic coverage to the reinsurer for consideration on a facultative basis. Submission of such cases for facultative consideration requires the ceding company to send all necessary documents, as explained in the following section.

- The ceding company may not submit business that has previously been submitted to any reinsurer on a facultative basis. Sometimes this condition is restricted to periods within two years of the current request for reinsurance coverage.

- The ceding company will submit only cases that exceed its full retention. Some reinsurance treaties provide that if a ceding company retains less than its full retention, automatic reinsurance will still be in effect, but only up to the dollar amount retained by the ceding company—that is, the reinsurer will match the amount covered by the ceding company, but will not necessarily accept the full risk if the reinsurance would exceed the retained amount.

Fast Fact

As of 1996, there were approximately 50 reinsurance companies in the United States.

Source: "Reinsurance Roundtable," *Canadian Insurance*, July 1996: 24–26.

- The ceding company will submit only cases that meet the stated minimum cession—that is, the amount submitted for reinsurance must be equal to or must exceed the minimum that the reinsurer will accept.

- The ceding company will not submit cases that exceed the binding limit established for all in-force policies.

- The ceding company will not submit a total amount of coverage applied for and in force that exceeds the reinsurer's established jumbo limit.

An automatic treaty may also establish the conditions by which cases to be reinsured will be divided among several reinsurers—for instance, dividing the cases alphabetically, sending a percentage of the total risk to each reinsurer, or using any of the other approaches that we discussed.

Conditions in a Facultative Reinsurance Treaty

A facultative reinsurance treaty establishes the conditions by which (1) the ceding company submits cases to the reinsurer for risk evaluation and (2) the reinsurer determines whether each case represents a risk that the reinsurer wishes to cover. A facultative treaty may also state that the reinsurer's liability does not begin until the ceding company has notified the reinsurer of its acceptance of the reinsurer's offer.

A facultative treaty specifies the underwriting materials that the ceding company must submit to the reinsurer for each case. The required materials usually include the complete underwriting file, including

- The original application for insurance
- All medical examinations and reports
- Inspection reports and other information pertaining to the insurability of the risk
- Financial information necessary to justify the amount of insurance applied for
- The application for reinsurance
- Any other information necessary to assess the risk

A facultative treaty also specifies the date by which a reinsurer must respond to an insurer that has submitted a case to be considered for reinsurance on a facultative basis.

Common Provisions in Reinsurance Treaties

In general, a reinsurance treaty for either automatic or facultative coverage contains provisions relating to the following elements, each of which we'll discuss briefly:

- Parties to the agreement
- Type of reinsurance
- Covered classes
- Excluded classes
- Payment of reinsurance premiums
- Payment of claims
- Accounting and recordkeeping procedures

- Information exchanges
- Errors and omissions
- Execution, duration, and termination of the treaty
- Type of arbitration
- Provision for insolvency

Parties to the agreement. A reinsurance treaty includes a provision that names the insurer and the reinsurer as the sole parties to the agreement. Further, the provision states that the written treaty constitutes the sole agreement between the parties, and that the reinsurance agreement does not create a legal relationship between the reinsurer and the insured or the beneficiary under any reinsured coverage. Any change to the treaty is null and void unless it is made by amendment or addendum to the agreement and is signed by both parties.

Type of reinsurance. A reinsurance treaty also includes a provision that establishes the type of reinsurance upon which the parties agree. In a facultative treaty, for instance, the provision may state that "when the ceding company wishes to obtain reinsurance on individual life coverage, it may submit cases, and the reinsurer will consider such reinsurance on a facultative basis."

This provision also specifies the types of coverage that the parties agree upon. For example, such a provision may cover "life insurance policies and waiver of premium disability benefits and accidental death benefits in excess of the ceding company's regular retention for such benefits."

The provision also specifies how the net amount at risk in a yearly renewable term (YRT) treaty shall be defined for each type of coverage—for example, "The net amount at risk on insurance issued under a permanent plan shall be the difference between the total amount insured under the original policy and the terminal reserve on the original policy at the end of the policy year."

This provision in most reinsurance treaties also specifies that, if a change is made in the coverage amount of the original policy, the ceding company must inform the reinsurer of the change so that the reinsurer may adjust the reinsurance premium. Further, the provision may state that if a lapsed or canceled policy is reinstated, the reinsurance coverage is also reinstated. For facultative business, certain changes may require the reinsurer's approval.

Finally, if the ceding company changes its retention limit for a specified type of coverage, the ceding company may opt to increase or decrease the amount of reinsurance on that coverage, and to make appropriate changes in premium if the treaty has a recapture provision. The ceding company is usually not allowed to increase or decrease its retention limit on only selected policies, but must do so for a whole class of policies. Also, the treaty may state that a reduction will be made only if the ceding company retained its maximum limit on the risk at the time the policy was issued. The ceding company must give the reinsurer written notice of its retention increase and its intent to apply the increase to existing business.

Covered classes. The typical covered classes provision lists the risk classes included in the reinsured coverage—for example, "standard and substandard individual issues" and "all individual life plans requiring normal underwriting evidence."

Excluded classes. If any classes are excluded from coverage—for instance, substandard or tobacco user—they are listed. Other excluded classes may include residents of foreign countries and professional sports team members.

Payment of reinsurance premiums. All treaties specify the terms of reinsurance premium payment and the terms under which premiums for reduced or terminated coverage shall be refunded to the ceding company. The premiums for each covered class of risk are listed. This provision might state that "premiums for standard or substandard life insurance risks shall be calculated according to the appropriate rate per thousand applied to the net amount at risk." The provision may also provide a table of premiums, with entries for each type of coverage and class of risk covered under the treaty. This provision in most reinsurance treaties contains a statement indicating that the reinsurance rates provided for some coverages are guaranteed for only a specified period, usually one year.

The provision may specify that if the reinsurer is not required to pay state or provincial premium taxes on reinsurance premiums, the reinsurer must reimburse the ceding company for any such taxes that the ceding company paid on the portion of the original premium paid to the reinsurer as the reinsurance premium.

Most reinsurance treaties contain a provision specifying that the ceding company may terminate all or a portion of the reinsurance after a certain period if the ceding company's retention limit increases. Further, most treaties include a provision for calculating a reduced reinsurance premium if the amount of coverage under a policy is reduced or if a policy lapses or is surrendered.

Payment of claims. The portion of the treaty relating to payment of claims usually states that the reinsurer will pay benefits to the ceding company provided that the ceding company (1) pays due benefits in full and (2) notifies the reinsurer promptly of the claim. The treaty also states that in a case in which more or less than the full benefit is paid (for instance, when the benefit is increased or reduced because of misstatement of age or gender), or if unexpected claim settlement costs are involved (such as court or arbitration expenses, but not punitive awards), the parties will share in the amount of such expense increase or reduction according to their respective net amounts at risk under the coverage.

The reinsurance treaty further notes that proofs of loss that are acceptable to the ceding company will also be considered acceptable to the reinsurer. The ceding company is responsible for providing the reinsurer with copies of proofs of loss and must advise the reinsurer of all contestable claims submitted. The treaty usually permits the reinsurer to request a review of all claim documents and to deliver an opinion before the ceding company makes a final decision on the claim. This type of requirement is typically made when the reinsurer has a larger amount at risk than does the ceding company.

For contested claims, the treaty usually provides that the ceding company must inform the reinsurer of its intention to contest a claim or to proceed with arbitration or litigation. If contesting a claim reduces the ceding company's financial liability under the coverage, the liability of the reinsurer is similarly reduced.

Finally, the reinsurer typically agrees to pay a share of reasonable expenses for investigation and litigation of a claim, whether contested or not. The reinsurer does not, however, typically share in routine claim settlement expenses, unless it declines to participate in the denial of a claim and pays its share of the benefits.

Accounting and recordkeeping procedures. A reinsurance treaty usually contains a provision specifying that each party will keep accurate records of reinsurance transactions. Further, the provision states the means by which, each month, the ceding company must notify the reinsurer of insurance premiums due and claims paid. Many treaties include a provision specifying that any debts or credits in favor of or against either party to the agreement may be set off, so that only the balance is paid.

Most accounting and recordkeeping provisions specify that the ceding company bears all costs of medical examinations, inspection fees, and other expenses connected with underwriting and issue of the original policy.

If the parties agree to a dividend from the reinsurer to the ceding company, the provision usually states that the reinsurer will use its discretion in establishing a standard on which to base such a refund.

Information exchanges. Most reinsurance treaties include a provision that specifies the procedure for the parties to use in notifying each other of reinsurance transactions. Typically, the ceding company periodically sends the reinsurer a listing of cases automatically insured. Moreover, the reinsurer usually sends the ceding company a certificate of reinsurance on each facultative case.

The reinsurer generally reserves the right to inspect the insurer's books, records, files, and other documents pertaining to the coverages reinsured. Such an inspection typically takes place at the office of the insurer.

This provision in some reinsurance treaties also requires the ceding company to furnish to the reinsurer copies of its applications, policies, and rider forms. The ceding company may also be required to provide tables of rates and any other information necessary for the reinsurer to administer the business under the treaty terms. Moreover, the treaty may state that if new material is published, or if changes are made in the material already exchanged, the ceding company should send these to the reinsurer.

Errors and omissions. Transactions occurring during administration of a reinsurance treaty may involve a great deal of detail and may take place over a lengthy period of time. During this protracted time of many transactions, human errors may occur. The errors and omissions clause is intended to protect both the insurer and the reinsurer against the consequences of unintentional mistakes in administration of a reinsurance treaty.

All reinsurance policies contain a provision stating that neither party shall be held liable for errors in entries or omissions from records on any monthly statement or reinsurance record. Such an error may result from an oversight, from misunderstanding, or from an incorrect judgment or decision. The errors and omissions provision applies to handling and processing of individual cases, whether they are submitted to several reinsurers for bids or are submitted automatically or facultatively. The provision also applies to claims and reinstatement transactions. ***Reinstatement*** is the process by which an insurer puts back in force a policy that lapsed because of nonpayment of renewal premiums. If an error that affects reinsurance premiums or claim disbursements is found, the mistake is corrected in the month following the discovery of error, or as soon as possible thereafter.

Further, if either the insurer or the reinsurer unintentionally fails to comply with a provision of the treaty, and if such a failure is the result of misunderstanding, oversight, or faulty judgment, both parties are to be restored to the positions they would have occupied if the error or oversight had not occurred. For instance, suppose an insurer mails notices of 30 new cases to a reinsurer. In error, the notices are lost in the mail and are not delivered to the reinsurer for several months. After the error is discovered, the financial accounts of both the insurer and the reinsurer are mutually and equitably adjusted so that both companies hold the same financial position each would have held if the notices had been delivered to the reinsurer on time. However, any negligent or deliberate acts or omissions by the ceding company regarding the reinsurance provided are the responsibility of the ceding company and its liability insurer, if any, but not of the reinsurer.

Insurers and reinsurers use extreme caution when applying this provision because it covers only oversights. If the ceding company discovers a pattern of errors, it usually acts in good faith to locate other possible errors and to correct them if possible before claims occur.

Execution, duration, and termination of the treaty. A reinsurance treaty typically specifies the date of execution, or the effective date, of the treaty. Although many reinsurance treaties are created to be of unlimited duration, any treaty may be terminated at any time when either party provides notice of termination in writing to the other party. Usually, this notice must be provided 30 days before the date of termination, although some reinsurance treaties provide for longer notice periods. During the time between notification and termination, the reinsurer usually continues to accept (or, for facultative coverage, to consider) newly submitted cases.

If either party to the treaty fails to pay monies due under the agreement, the other party has the right to cancel all in-force reinsurance by giving written notice. Usually, the notice period is 30 days. If the failure to pay due monies is the result of a condition treated under the errors and omissions provision, the treaty cannot be terminated for failure to pay.

Type of arbitration. A provision in all reinsurance treaties provides that, if the insurer and reinsurer encounter a dispute or difference of opinion concerning the validity of the treaty, the matter must be submitted to arbitration. The arbitration proceeding will be held before a panel of arbitration consisting of three members (unless the parties can agree to nonbinding mediation by one independent person, a conflict resolution approach that is less expensive than an arbitration proceeding). Each of these arbitrators is typically a knowledgeable, active or retired executive from the insurance industry. The arbitration provision states the means by which arbitrators shall be chosen, the procedure to be used in settling the dispute, the means of paying reasonable expenses of arbitration, and the time allowed for settlement.

Provision for insolvency. Generally, reinsurance treaties contain a provision specifying that if the ceding company becomes insolvent, all reinsurance is paid directly to a legally established successor of the ceding company. In turn, the receiver or successor must inform the reinsurer promptly of a claim submitted under any reinsured policy. When a claim is submitted, the reinsurer may investigate the claim and, if necessary, defend the claim at the reinsurer's own expense. Some treaties provide that such expense for claim defense may be charged, with court approval, against the ceding company as part of the expense of liquidating its assets following the insolvency. The reinsurer generally reserves the right to offset past due reinsurance premiums against any claims payable under the treaty. In addition, some treaties contain clauses relating to the insolvency of the reinsurer—for example, such a clause may provide that the ceding company may cancel the treaty for new business if the reinsurer is deemed insolvent. Reinsurance treaties also include definitions of insolvency.

Although a reinsurance treaty may be drafted in general terms, the treaty must be carefully written. Figure 14-1 lists the characteristics of an effective reinsurance treaty.

Amendments and Addenda

After a treaty for reinsurance has been established, the parties' agreement may be modified by one or more separate agreements, termed *amendments* and *addenda,* that are established outside the reinsurance treaty. An amendment modifies or deletes an existing provision, whereas an addendum adds wording to a provision or adds a new provision. Because amendments and addenda identify specific changes to a treaty without negating or nullifying the original treaty, the parties do not have to renegotiate the entire treaty in order to make a minor addition, deletion, or correction. If a change is made to the original plan of insurance that is reinsured, the treaty covering the plan must be amended to reflect the change. An amendment or addendum is signed by both parties and becomes a legal part of the treaty.

Figure 14-1. Characteristics of an effective reinsurance treaty.

- **Clear language.** Precise wording helps ensure that all parties to a reinsurance treaty will be able to fulfill their obligations without disagreement or confusion. Because the persons who drafted the treaty may not be available to interpret the treaty language for persons who later must fulfill the terms of the treaty, clear language is especially important.
- **Standard, uniform wording.** Following the terminology currently in use in the reinsurance industry helps eliminate misunderstanding between the parties. Moreover, using the same term consistently helps clarify the treaty's meaning. For instance, a treaty using the term "ceding company" throughout is clearer than a treaty alternating synonymous terms such as "ceding company," "cedent," and "reinsured."
- **Self-contained treaty provisions.** Each provision should be self-explanatory. Provisions that overlap one another or that must be cross-referenced can cause confusion as to the intent and meaning of the treaty.
- **Adherence to reinsurance laws.** Adhering to the regulations ensures that all parties are protected by those laws.
- **Appropriate length.** An effective treaty should be concise and is typically much shorter than most other types of insurance contracts.

For example, suppose that an automatic reinsurance treaty provides that the reinsurer will accept 55 percent of the risk on a certain type of disability policy under a quota share arrangement. Later, the insurer decides to reduce the premium for such policies in order to expand the company's market share into a new geographic area. Resulting sales exceed the insurer's capacity to accept the additional risks, so the insurer wishes to increase the percentage of risk borne by the reinsurer from 55 percent to 60 percent. If the reinsurer agrees to accept the additional risk, the change to the two parties' reinsurance treaty may be accomplished by either amending the treaty provisions or adding a provision that establishes the increase in percentage reinsured. Figure 14-2 illustrates a typical addendum to a reinsurance treaty.

Preparation of a Reinsurance Treaty

Preparing a reinsurance treaty requires that the insurer provide the reinsurer with adequate information about the business to be reinsured. In general, reinsurance is negotiated much like group insurance: both these products are usually tailored to the needs of the purchaser, and all terms and rates may be negotiated until both parties to the contract are satisfied.

To submit information about the desired coverage, the insurer normally sends the reinsurer—or, if the business is to be submitted for bids, several reinsurers—a letter describing the product to be reinsured and outlining the most important conditions concerning the desired reinsurance. If the product to be covered is not new, the insurer includes whatever marketing and claims experience statistics are available concerning the business covered under the product. In the letter, the insurer indicates what rates it proposes to pay for the reinsurance and requests a quote for reinsuring the business. The insurer may also ask the reinsurer for advice about details of the product, such as policy

Figure 14-2. Typical addendum to a reinsurance treaty.

Addendum 2
to
Reinsurance Contract 6851

Between the Xavier Life Assurance Company and the Exceptional Reinsurance Company, originally effective January 1, 1993.

It is hereby mutually understood and agreed that, effective 12:01 A.M. Eastern Standard Time on January 1, 1997, the following paragraph is added to Article II, Exclusions:

B. Waiver of premium.

All other terms and conditions remain unchanged.

Figure 14-3. Letter from an insurer to a reinsurer requesting a reinsurance quote.

Mr. Byron Adams
ABF Insurance Company
Des Moines, IA 50309

Dear Byron:

We are in the process of developing a Joint Mortgage insurance plan, for introduction in mid March. The plan specifications are attached.

At this point, we do not have premium rates finalized. We are, however, looking for a reinsurer to follow our pricing philosophy on this product, which is different from a standard approach.

We will have two premium scales. One will assume two nonsmokers, a male and a female with extra mortality for AIDS. The other premium scale will assume two smokers, one male, one female and will assume extra AIDS mortality. The "good" rates will be competitive with rates offered for similar coverage by the banks.

I am not sure what volumes we may get, but the simplified issue process should appeal to most agents. Please let me know if you would be interested in reinsuring this plan, and if so, what your rates would be.

Yours truly,

Ellen Montford

provisions, pricing, and intended market. Figure 14-3 illustrates such a letter from an insurer to a reinsurer. If the insurer and a reinsurer have a facultative treaty in place, the insurer may use a letter to request a quote for including the new product under that treaty by using an amendment or an addendum to the treaty. Figure 14-4 illustrates such a letter.

In response to the insurer's letter, each reinsurer evaluates the request. If the reinsurer wishes to accept the risk, then the reinsurer quotes the rates, or reinsurance premiums, required for the reinsurance coverage. If the reinsurer cannot offer the requested level of reinsurance at the suggested rate, the reinsurer may offer to provide a lower level of coverage for the same or even a lower rate. Or, suppose an insurer has asked a reinsurer to accept 80 percent of the risk on a new product at a specified rate or schedule of rates. The reinsurer may counter the request by noting that it wishes to accept only 50 percent of the risk, but will do so according to a rate schedule that is lower than that quoted by the insurer. The reinsurer may also give advice to the insurer concerning the product. For instance, the reinsurer may

Figure 14-4. Letter requesting that a new product be added to an existing reinsurance treaty.

Ms. Lydia Bennett
ABC Insurance Company
Toronto, Ontario
CANADA M5J 2T6

Dear Lydia:

Enclosed is a draft of our proposed variable life policy, which has been submitted to our Superintendent of Insurance for approval. We ask that you add this product to our existing reinsurance agreement, and advise us of any relevant changes.

We look forward to hearing from you.

Sincerely,

Thomas Lee

Thomas Lee

note that, according to the reinsurer's experience with similar products, the insurer's proposed premiums for a certain class of proposed insureds are too high or too low.

The two parties may negotiate for a considerable period to reach an agreement on rates and coverage. The negotiations are usually handled by pricing actuaries at each company.

When the insurer has concluded negotiations with all reinsurers that have responded to the initial letter, the insurer makes a final decision on allocating the risk. The insurer then notifies each reinsurer of what award will be made of the business. The insurer may decide to split the business in various ways—for instance, to award 70 percent of the business to one reinsurer and 10 percent to each of three other reinsurers.

After the insurer and the reinsurer have agreed on the terms and rates for the coverage, the insurer usually develops the written treaty for review by and negotiation with the reinsurer. However, when a reinsurer is awarded 100 percent of the coverage on a case or a product, the reinsurer usually drafts the treaty for approval by the insurer.

If the insurer plans to split the coverage among several reinsurers, the insurer attempts to develop the same treaty for all reinsurers. Ideally, the insurer is able to reduce administrative problems by establishing the same procedures for every reinsurer—for instance, setting up the same claims handling procedures and limits for large-amount cases.

Although the treaty provisions are usually the same for every reinsurer, the specific rates for each reinsurer do not have to be the same. If one reinsurer, for example, offered to provide a portion of the coverage at a rate lower than the rate quoted by another reinsurer, the insurer is free to accept the lower rate from one and the higher rate from another. Similarly, one reinsurer may offer an insurer a 50 percent experience refund on a portion of the business, and another reinsurer may offer the insurer a 90 percent experience refund on another portion of the business. In such a situation, the insurer may accept both offers.

The drafted treaty is usually routed through a number of areas of the insurer's company, including the legal, actuarial, underwriting, claims, and accounting areas. The treaty may also be reviewed by certain persons among the insurer's upper management. If a treaty generally takes a standard approach to traditional types of reinsurance coverage, the review is less thorough than if the treaty takes an approach or covers a product that is new or unfamiliar to the insurer.

Reinsurance treaties do not usually have to be approved by state or provincial departments of insurance in most jurisdictions. Some jurisdictions do require that reinsurance treaties be filed before the treaties are executed. Normally, state and provincial departments of insurance review all reinsurance treaties at the time reinsurers are examined, usually once every three years.

Termination of a Reinsurance Treaty

A reinsurance treaty, whether automatic or facultative, usually remains in effect for years, even decades, as the parties continue a long-standing business relationship. Necessary changes are made to such a treaty by means of amendment and addenda as business requirements demand. However, any type of treaty for reinsurance may be terminated according to the termination provisions within the treaty.

As we have mentioned, reinsurance treaties provide that termination may be effected by one of the party's (1) informing the other of the intent to terminate and (2) allowing a specified notice period, usually 30 days, before the date of termination. If any of the parties to a reinsurance agreement undergoes an extraordinary business circumstance such as liquidation, merger, bankruptcy, or catastrophic loss of more than half of its capital, the party is usually allowed by a treaty provision to withdraw from the reinsurance agreement by invoking the ***extraordinary right of termination.***

When the parties to a reinsurance agreement enter the process of termination of the agreement, they must decide mutually how to handle certain issues, which include

- The date on which the reinsurance treaty and each party's obligations under it expire

- The disposition of premiums and other monies involved in the reinsurance transaction
- The specific losses, if any, for which the reinsurer is still liable and the time period for which such liability continues

Most often, the parties agree that the reinsurer is not liable for claims submitted past the date on which the treaty is terminated—that is, 30 days after notice to terminate has been given. Further, the parties usually agree that the reinsurer is to return all unearned premiums (that is, the amount of premium which has already been paid for coverage that would be in effect *after* the date on which the coverage is canceled) to the insurer, and that the insurer is to return appropriate amounts of commissions and other such funds to the reinsurer.

If a claim reserve has been established by the reinsurer, those monies must also be distributed equitably according to the termination provision. In some types of insurance, the claim reserve must remain available to pay claims for an extended time period. In such a situation, the claim reserve must be debited to the reinsurer—that is, paid to the insurer—over a lengthy period.

A reinsurance treaty that covers life insurance is considered to be of unlimited duration. Most reinsurance treaties for life coverage provide that in-force reinsurance cessions may not be terminated if the insurer continues to pay reinsurance premiums. In practice, however, either the insurer or the reinsurer may terminate the reinsurance agreement for new business written after a specified date that has been announced in writing by one party to the other party.

Retrocession Agreement

You recall from past discussion that a retrocession is a transfer of some or all of a very large risk from one reinsurer to another reinsurer. A ***retrocession agreement*** is a reinsurance treaty between two reinsurers involved in transferring risk from one to the other. In return for receiving coverage of some or all of the reinsured risk, the first reinsurer pays an appropriate reinsurance premium to the second reinsurer. Moreover, the second reinsurer may pay a certain percentage, usually 1 percent to 3 percent, of the first reinsurer's expenses. A reinsurer typically keeps its maximum retention on a risk before seeking retrocession coverage.

The provisions of a retrocession agreement are typically less precise than the provisions in a reinsurance treaty because the retrocessionaire is assuming risks over which it is at least twice removed and, thus, over which it has very little control. However, many of the provisions usually included in a reinsurance treaty can be incorporated into a retrocession agreement with few alterations.

Certain provisions of a retrocession agreement are quite different from those in a reinsurance treaty—for instance, the provisions specifying the currency and the geographic area in which business will be transacted. Because a retrocessionaire may accept risks underwritten over a wide geographic territory, the provision relating to the currency may include various foreign currencies and a broad geographic area. Moreover, the retrocession agreement usually specifies the type of business that is to be covered. The agreement states, for instance, whether the covered risks are assumed business or direct-written business.

Key Terms and Concepts

reinsurance treaty
reinstatement
extraordinary right of termination
retrocession agreement

CHAPTER FIFTEEN

Reinsurance Administration

Learning Objectives

After studying this chapter, you should be able to

- Distinguish between individual cession administration and self-administration of reinsurance
- Explain the uses of bordereaux, a grossup file, and a policy exhibit
- Describe the process used to conduct a reinsurance audit
- Name and explain seven administrative activities associated with reinsurance administration
- Explain the procedures typically followed during reinsurance arbitration, and name three reasons for using arbitration
- Discuss the requirements for handling insolvency of the ceding company and insolvency of the reinsurer

Chapter Outline

Methods of Administering Reinsurance

Individual Cession Administration
Self-Administration

Exchanging Information

Reinsurance Audit

Administrative Activities

Negotiating and Drafting Treaties
Underwriting Cases
Paying Premiums
Modifying Policies
Paying Claims
Recapturing Coverages
Evaluating In-Force Reinsurance

Resolving Disagreements

Handling Insolvency

Insolvency of the Ceding Company
Insolvency of the Reinsurer

When an insurer and a reinsurer have developed a business relationship, the two parties have numerous mutual obligations and expectations concerning administration of the reinsured coverages. Principal among these obligations and expectations is that each party will conduct business in an ethical manner and will establish and maintain a clear, accurate exchange of information and provision of contractually arranged services. In addition, the insurer typically seeks assistance from the reinsurer in developing new lines of business, in underwriting cases, in assessing and handling claims, and in providing guidance and advice concerning industry trends. In return, the reinsurer assumes that the insurer will provide timely, significant information concerning premiums, policy data, and claims.

In previous chapters, we have mentioned some of these interactions, and we'll examine others in this chapter. We are approaching reinsurance administration primarily from the perspective of the ceding company, but we will also mention some of the administrative activities that are the responsibility of the reinsurer.

We'll begin our discussion of reinsurance administration by explaining two methods of administering reinsurance—individual cession administration and self-administration. Because one of the most fundamental aspects of reinsurance involves the ongoing and timely exchange of information between insurer and reinsurer, we'll discuss this important activity and explain the procedures used for periodic reinsurance audits.

Next we'll consider the administrative activities of reinsurance administration, which generally include

- Negotiating and drafting treaties
- Underwriting cases
- Paying premiums
- Modifying policies
- Paying claims
- Recapturing coverages
- Evaluating in-force reinsurance

Besides these administrative tasks, reinsurance administration includes resolving disagreements between the parties and, if necessary, handling insolvency.

Methods of Administering Reinsurance

Two primary methods used to administer reinsurance are individual cession administration and self-administration.

Individual Cession Administration

Individual cession administration, also called *traditional cession administration,* is a system of reinsurance administration under which the ceding company sends a separate notification to the reinsurer for each cession, and the reinsurer prepares its own records of cession. Under individual cession administration, both the ceding company and the reinsurer maintain records of all ceded cases. As we mentioned in Chapter 11, the record of the transfer of risk from a ceding company to a reinsurer is sent by means of a document (or an electronic message) called a cession. A typical cession contains information about the coverage, including the policy number and cession number, plan of insurance and riders, amount of coverage and amount reinsured, and reinsurance premium amount for each year of coverage. Figure 15-1 illustrates a typical reinsurance cession.

Fast Fact

In Canada, there was $1.46 billion in reinsurance net premiums written in 1995—an increase of about $130 million over the previous year.

Source: "Reinsurer's Rank and Growth in Canada," *Canadian Insurance,* Annual Review of Statistics, 1996: 20.

Each month, the reinsurer sends the ceding company a series of reports that list all changes made to policies since the last report and the reinsurance premium due for each policy. After matching the reinsurer's information against the information in the ceding company's database, the ceding company then pays the reinsurance premium to the reinsurer. A ceding company with only a moderate amount of reinsured business usually finds individual cession administration to be more cost-effective than self-administration because checking the reinsurer's monthly reports requires less time than developing reports for the reinsurer. Some reinsurers request that facultative cases be handled by individual cessions, not by self-administration, because facultative cessions require that the reinsurer evaluate each case submitted.

Self-Administration

Self-administration, also called *bulk administration,* is a system of reinsurance administration under which the ceding company prepares most of the records for cessions and uses written or electronic lists, called *bordereaux,* to notify the reinsurer of cessions. A ***bordereau*** (the plural is *bordereaux*) is a report provided regularly by the ceding

Figure 15-1. Typical reinsurance cession.

The ______________________________ (the Reinsuring Company) hereby reinsures ABC Insurance (the Principal Company) under the terms and conditions of Y.R.T. Provisions 1965 which, together with this Guarantee and the Application for Reinsurance, constitute the whole contract.

On the life of ______________________________

Plan of Principal Policy ______________________________

____

Policy No. ____________ Policy Year Date ____________ Age at Issue ____________

Date of Birth ____________

Particulars of Reinsurance under this Guarantee

Residence for Premium Tax ____________ Currency ____________

Disability Benefit

Waiver of Premium to Age 60 Monthly Income to Age 65 ____________

Premium to be Waived ____________

Maturity Benefit at Age 65 on ____________

	PRINCIPAL POLICY	REINSURANCE GUARANTEE	
	FACE AMOUNT	FACE AMOUNT	RATINGS
Basic Policy			
Additional Life Risk			
Total Disability Waiver on			
Total Disability Income on			
Double Indemnity to Age 70 on			

				REINSURANCE PREMIUMS			
			PREMIUMS				
YEAR	AGE	LIFE RISK	Y.R.T.				TOTAL
		Extra and benefit premiums payable to					

The Schedule for later years applies just as though set out in full herein.

IN WITNESS WHEREOF the Reinsuring Company has by the hand of its proper officer signed this Reinsurance Guarantee at its office in the City of ______________________________

this ____________ day of ______________________, 19 ______ .

Checked ________ ______________________

________ ______________________

company to the reinsurer to transmit information about the premiums and claims associated with ceded risks. A bordereau is intended primarily to give a reinsurer current information about the risks that reinsurer covers. Information supplied by bordereaux includes monthly listings of premiums due, transactions occurring, and claims received, as well as quarterly and annual compilations of various statistics.

Two types of bordereaux are a ***premium bordereau,*** or *premium advice,* which includes detailed information, including the premium, of each case, and a ***claims bordereau,*** or *claims advice,* which also includes information about the claims status of each case. The action of providing a reinsurer with a list of total reinsurance premiums and other information is known as ***premium bordereau service.*** The action of providing a reinsurer with a report of claims submitted under reinsurance is known as ***claims bordereau service.*** These reports are issued on a regular basis, usually monthly or quarterly.

A reinsurer may choose to receive complete bordereau service, which includes reports on every case covered by that reinsurer, or selective bordereau service, which includes only exceptional cases—large-amount cases, those with frequent or large-amount claims, new business, and other specific categories. Most reinsurers choose selective bordereau service (1) to reduce the volume of information flowing between the partners and (2) to enable the reinsurer to make faster, more accurate analyses of exceptional cases.

In self-administration of reinsurance, the ceding company keeps records of each policy; the reinsurer may or may not maintain such records. For example, the reinsurer may require, for valuation purposes, a record of each policy for cases submitted to the reinsurer by electronic transfer. Selected information may be required for cases submitted to the reinsurer by written lists. The reinsurer may depend on the ceding company's bordereaux to provide the information needed to administer the reinsured coverage. The reinsurance treaty covering the self-administered coverage provides that the reinsurer may perform an audit of the insurer's policy records at any time.

If the bordereaux is submitted on paper rather than by electronic means, most reinsurers do not input the bordereaux information manually into their information systems because such an approach requires considerable time and employee expense. Instead, a reinsurer usually takes a sample of the entries on the bordereaux, typically 5 percent to 20 percent. The size of the sample depends on how satisfied the reinsurer feels with the insurer's expertise, accuracy of information, and trustworthiness.

In taking a 10 percent sample, the reinsurer enters every 10th name into its information system, including the reinsured's name, policy issue date, age, amount of coverage, rating, premium amount, plan of insurance, and total submitted claims. After the information is loaded into the information system, the system develops mathematical totals for the group—i.e., the total amount of coverage, the total premium amount, and the total amount of submitted claims. Then the system develops a ***grossup file,*** in which each of the figures is multiplied by a factor that produces a probable total figure for the whole group, not just for the sample. For example, if a sample of 10 percent was entered into the information system, the resulting sample totals would be multiplied by 10 to project a probable total of 100 percent for the whole group (10 percent × 10 = 100). If a 25 percent sample was entered, the sample totals would be multiplied by 4 (25 percent × 4 = 100); if a 50 percent sample was entered, the sample totals would be multiplied by 2 (50 percent × 2 = 100). The projected figures in the grossup file are used for actuarial studies on premium and claim volume, and for other assessments of the coverage.

Most insurers submit the bordereaux accompanied by a ***policy exhibit,*** which is an overall description of a block of reinsured business during a specified period of time, usually a month or a quarter. The policy exhibit contains a count of the number of cases in the block and information on the block at the beginning and end of the time period. The information typically includes the number of new cases added during the time period, as well as the beginning and ending totals of coverage, reinsurance premiums, policy changes, terminations, lapses, and claims. For cases submitted by electronic transfer, the reinsurer can summarize the transactions to develop its own policy exhibit.

Why would a ceding company choose to use self-administration? One reason is that an insurer that cedes a large volume of reinsurance usually finds self-administration more cost-effective than sending electronic records to its reinsurers. Because the insurer is handling most of the recordkeeping and reporting, the reinsurer may be able to offer lower reinsurance rates for self-administration. Another reason is that for certain products, such as interest-sensitive coverages and flexible-premium or variable-benefit coverages, calculating the net amount at risk and the reinsurance premium to cover the ceded portion of that net amount is complex and can be performed most efficiently by the ceding company, not the reinsurer.

One form of reinsurance administration pertains to pooling arrangements in which a number of reinsurers share the risk on coverages that have been retroceded by another reinsurer. Instead of receiving monthly reports on the premiums and claims associated with the pooled risks, the reinsurers receive quarterly reports and an annual report that provides year-end totals of the number of risks, the volume of insurance in force, reserves, premiums paid and due, and claims submitted and paid. The annual report is used to reduce the cost of compiling and delivering the report to the pool of reinsurers. The strength of such a pool depends on the highest levels of good faith and trust among its members. Any pool member may audit the information in such a report.

Fast Fact

Of the $25 billion total in life, health and accident reinsurance premiums in the United States, $7.5 billion comes from reinsurance on group accident and health policies, which is the fastest growing segment of the market.

Source: Laura Mazzuca Toops, "Reinsurers Can Get Burned in Rush to Managed Care," *Best's Review (Life/Health)*, February 1996: 43–47.

Exchanging Information

A reinsurer needs to know the amount of risk that it is assuming for each case or for each block of business. More specifically, the reinsurer needs to know the amount of reinsurance premium due from the insurer and the amount of claims submitted under the reinsured coverage. Typically, an insurer and a reinsurer specify that the insurer will provide the necessary premium and claim information to the reinsurer by means of bordereaux. Insight 15-1 describes an effective communication system between the underwriting functions of a reinsurer and a ceding company.

Reinsurance Audit

A ***reinsurance audit*** is a formal examination of an insurer's reinsurance records in order to evaluate whether those records contain accurate details. A reinsurance audit helps ensure that both parties to a reinsurance agreement understand and have complied with the terms of the treaty as agreed upon by both parties. A reinsurance audit may

Insight 15-1 Communication Between the Reinsurer and the Ceding Company

The relationship between the reinsurance and the ceding company's underwriters is in some ways similar to that between the direct underwriter and the marketer. In both cases, two-way trust must be the cornerstone for a mutually profitable endeavor.

The reinsurer must have trust in the underwriting skills and the integrity of the ceding company. The underwriter at the ceding company must also be able to trust that the reinsurer will attend to apparent discrepancies.

For example, suppose a case was submitted by facsimile transmission (fax) to three reinsurers simultaneously. Reinsurer A and Reinsurer B rated the case severely, whereas Reinsurer C offered to reinsure the case at standard rates. However, unknown to the ceding underwriter, Reinsurer C did not receive one of the supporting documents—a single-page APS—which stuck to another page during facsimile transmission.

Given the wide difference in underwriting ratings, should the ceding company accept the reinsurance offer from Reinsurer C and issue the policy as standard? Trust between the ceding company and the reinsurer requires that the ceding company's underwriter contact Reinsurer C to discuss the case. When one reinsurance quote is significantly different from all others, reinsurers hope that the ceding company will notify them of the disparity and ensure that the reinsurer has received all underwriting materials necessary to make a sound assessment of the case.

When a solid relationship exists between the reinsurer and the ceding company, not only will the reinsurer feel comfortable with the business assumed from that client, but less information may well be required to reach this comfort level. Just as a ceding company's underwriter sometimes waives requirements for a trusted marketer, the reinsurer may also occasionally waive requirements for an insurer in whom the reinsurer has developed a bond of trust.

Such a trusting relationship speeds the issue process, contributes to higher case placement ratios, and reduces the cost of putting business on the books. The benefits of trust are especially evident in competitive situations in which applications are written with multiple companies, but only one policy is to be placed.

From Andrew Kramer, "The Reinsurance/Direct Underwriter Relationship: A Reinsurer's Perspective," *On the Risk*, 7(3), 1991: 65–66. Adapted by permission.

focus primarily on underwriting or administration. Performing a reinsurance audit benefits both parties by

- Verifying that all policy details and reinsurance information are transferred correctly from the ceding company's file to the reinsurance file

- Ensuring that the insurer and reinsurer have established adequate internal controls of reinsurance information and procedures for paper and electronic administration

- Enabling both parties to discuss and resolve inconsistencies and work flow discrepancies related to insurance administration

- Providing evidence for external auditors and regulatory agencies that reinsurance is being properly ceded and administered

The ceding company is expected to perform self audits. However, self audits do not replace the need for an on-site audit to be performed by the reinsurer. Most reinsurance audits are performed by the staff of the reinsurer, who conduct the audit at the site of the ceding company. Prior to the audit, the reinsurer reviews at its offices certain information such as formats, treaties, premium calculations, and face amounts.

The date and duration of a reinsurance audit are sometimes selected several months in advance and are arranged at the convenience of the ceding company. The reinsurer generally sends the insurer a list of objectives for the audit and the types of materials and procedures the audit team will review. In return, the insurer provides the reinsurer with a procedures manual or other documentation covering steps in handling coverages to be reinsured. Having written procedures enables the audit team to become familiar with the ceding company's administrative approaches and, therefore, saves time during the audit.

The reinsurer requests that the insurer gather samples of the policy files (or microfiche or electronic files on the policies) that the reinsurer has selected. The reinsurer selects the sample to represent (1) the plans of insurance that are currently reinsured and (2) selected in-force policies and a few claims. The sample is selected on a random basis. An additional sample is chosen by the audit team during their visit to test the accuracy of the retention and reinsurance calculations.

During the visit, the audit team is given reasonable access to the insurer's records, although the insurer usually protects the confidentiality of files by prohibiting the audit team from making hard copies of certain documents and reports. Moreover, the audit team is typically permitted to speak with staff in areas that affect reinsurance administration. Generally, a reinsurer's team of auditors does not negotiate treaty provisions, but recommends enhancements to the ceding

Figure 15-2. Responsibilities of an audit team leader.

The leader of an audit team is responsible for ensuring that the audit team fulfills the following activities:

- Making sure that ceding company files agree with the reinsurer's files in all material aspects
- Checking the timing of notifying the reinsurer of claims and checking especially for delays
- Comparing ceding company reinsurance treaties with the reinsurer's treaties to make sure they are identical
- Reviewing the security surrounding policy forms and policy number sequence
- Determining whether written procedures exist for all or part of reinsurance administration
- Completing the audit of policy samples, including automatic requirements, facultative acceptances, reports of policy changes, monitoring of retentions, and all other requirements
- Determining that appropriate controls exist in all areas of reinsurance administration
- Reviewing a sampling of new business for proper reinsurance identification and placement

In addition, the leader of the audit team is responsible for making sure that all problems are discussed as they are identified and that sufficient information is gathered to ensure that problems can be discussed, evaluated, and resolved. The leader of the audit team also periodically reviews the status of the audit with team members, monitors the activities of new team members, provides the reinsurer's audit committee with oral and written reports of audit findings and details of specific items to be discussed in the closing meeting with representatives of the ceding company.

company's workflow or systems. The audit team also meets with representatives from the ceding company to present and discuss the results. Figure 15-2 lists the responsibilities of an audit team leader.

When the audit has been completed, the audit team presents its findings to the reinsurer's management. The reinsurer also sends a copy of the audit report to the management of the insurer. The report contains the audit results as well as recommendations. If required, the audit team or members of the reinsurer's management meet with the management and the reinsurance administration staff of the ceding company to review the results of the audit and to resolve discrepancies. Insight 15-2 discusses some of the reasons reinsurance auditors should be welcomed by insurers. Figure 15-3 presents portions of a sample checklist for a reinsurance audit.

Administrative Activities

Numerous administrative activities are associated with reinsurance administration. In the following section, we will discuss (1) negotiating and drafting treaties, (2) underwriting cases, (3) paying premiums,

Insight 15-2 Debunking the Myths of Reinsurance Audits

The Auditors Called. They're Coming In.
Few words in the business world are more capable of eliciting a predictable, collective groan. The general perception of an audit is that it's something to be endured, not enjoyed. It's dreaded, not welcomed, more wearying than exhilarating.

We believe that audits are getting a bad rap. It's time to separate fact from fiction, real from imagined, myth from truth. We want to spotlight the myths of reinsurance audits as well as the facts, in hopes that more people will change their minds about this very misunderstood process.

Myth 1: An Audit is Performed Solely for the Benefit of the Reinsurer.
An audit actually can be a value-added service that truly benefits the insurer. In fact, the very word "audit" now seems too limiting. We prefer to view such visits as consulting engagements, risk assessments, or due-diligence reviews that are for the benefit of both parties. In fact, we've had instances where clients have requested a visit because they've discovered problems in their processes and want a timely, satisfactory resolution.

Myth 2: An Audit is Fairly Narrow in Scope.
The traditional image of an audit is the ticking and tying of numbers, with a focus on account books and prescribed steps taken only in response to pressures applied by a third party. That image doesn't do justice to reinsurance audits today. Audits are now tailored to the business, the company, and the objective. It is not uncommon for recommendations to focus more on what an insurer can do to enhance operational efficiencies than be in compliance with established guidelines.

Considerable time now goes into understanding the entire company and its operations before auditors go on-site. The audit team can send a pre-visit questionnaire in an effort to better understand the organizational structure, systems interfaces, flow of data and communication between departments, management reporting, and issues related to the visit.

Myth 3: Auditors Spend Their Time in Back Rooms Reviewing Data.
A reinsurer seeking only to get comfortable with the accuracy and completeness of data doesn't necessarily need to visit the client company at all. Auditors can simply conduct appropriately designed "desk audits" of billing statements, claims, and other data. What cannot be verified through this process, however, is full inclusion, which is confirmation that all policies intended to be reinsured under an agreement—and only those policies—are reflected in the statements. This is where on-site reviews generally are focused. And if the job is done right, the auditors won't be found poring over data in a back room.

To test for full inclusion, auditors talk with everyone in the company who performs functions or makes decisions that impact reinsurance. This means not only those in reinsurance administration, but also the appropriate people in underwriting and new business, customer service, change processing, claims, systems, and even internal audit.

Myth 4: Auditors Look Only at the Past, Not to the Future.
Even when things are being done right, they can usually be done better. The audit team often is in a good position to provide suggestions and recommendations, if only because their exposure to so many insurers allows them to see patterns in problems facing the industry and solutions that have been attempted sometimes successfully, other times not. They also are aware of technologies that can be applied to further enhance administrative and operational efficiencies.

From Nick Stanger and Cheryl Burns, "Debunking the Myths of Reinsurance Audits," *Reinsurance Reporter,* Second Quarter 1996: 12–16. Adapted by permission.

(4) modifying policies, (5) paying claims, (6) recapturing coverages, and (7) evaluating in-force reinsurance.

Negotiating and Drafting Treaties

In a previous chapter, we discussed the contents of a reinsurance treaty. Negotiating and drafting an automatic or a facultative treaty

Figure 15-3. Portions of a sample checklist for a reinsurance audit.

Reinsurance Audit Questionnaire

Insurance Company: ______________________________

Part A: New Business

1. Is reinsurance file run independently from the direct policy master file?

   How is reinsurance file created and maintained for
   - automatic business?
   - facultative business?
2. Is allocation of automatic reinsurance correct?
3. Is allocation of facultative reinsurance appropriate?

   How is reinsurer notified of facultative policies?
4. Are special quotes, e.g., rates for coverages in excess of the rate guarantee, communicated by underwriters to reinsurance administration?
5. How are reinsurance requirements evaluated? Who determines amount and reinsurer?

   Are there appropriate checks to protect against over-retention or over-reinsurance?
6. Are there sufficient procedures to cancel not-taken policies off the
   - policy master file?
   - reinsurance file?
7. Is the method used to cancel reinsured not-taken policies appropriate and timely?
8. Is all the new business reinsured on a bulk basis?

   If not, how does the insurer distinguish policies reinsured on a bulk basis from policies reinsured on an individual basis?

Part B: Changes & Terminations

1. Are there appropriate indexing procedures and re-evaluation of reinsurance requirements upon
   - lapse?
   - changes in amounts at risk?
   - reinstatement?
2. How is the reinsurer notified of lapses?
3. Are there appropriate procedures to ensure a lapse due to nonpayment of premiums?
4. Are there proper procedures to ensure adherence to minimum cession limits of all reinsured policies—both initial and final limits?
5. What are the procedures for recapture?
6. Are unscheduled changes to amounts at risk reviewed appropriately and adequately maintained on the policy master file?

Figure 15-3. Portions of a sample checklist for a reinsurance audit (continued).

7. Is the notification to the reinsurer of scheduled and unscheduled changes of the amount at risk appropriate and timely?
8. Are the limits on increases to the amount at risk properly established and maintained?

   Are the scheduled increases proportionately reinsured for the lifetime of the policy?
9. Are the increases in the amount at risk for facultative policies referred to the reinsurer?

Part C: Accounting Procedures

1. Are the reinsurance premiums and commissions calculated and billed correctly by the system?
2. Are future renewal premiums set up correctly?
3. Is there more than one reinsurer involved in reinsuring this arrangement?

   Does the system pick up the right rates and terms for each reinsurer?
4. Does the system appropriately maintain the right set of rates and terms for riders?
5. Are the reinsurance renewal premium payments internally consistent with policyholder billing?
6. Is premium to be waived calculated correctly?

   How is reinsurer notified of waiver of premium claims?

   Is the premium accounting handled correctly under waiver of premium claims?

Part D: Other Questions

1. Can the client provide the following information:
   - lapse ratio
   - mortality levels
   - percent of smoker/nonsmoker business
2. Are juvenile rates available?
   Is a new nonsmoker declaration required once applicant exceeds age for juvenile rates?
   What percentage of the in-force business is issued on juveniles?
3. How is treaty information, especially changes to treaty terms, disseminated?
4. Are reinsurance administration procedures documented?
   Is there trained back-up personnel?
5. Is there anything that we could do to improve our service?
   Any particular items we can follow up upon return to our offices?

requires that the parties (1) discuss the provisions that each wishes to include and (2) resolve any differences.

When an insurer plans to develop a new product, one of the primary considerations is whether reinsurance is available at an attractive cost that the product's underlying actuarial assumptions can support. Most insurers planning to cede coverage under new products arrange for reinsurance in advance of offering the product on the market. After the insurer's marketing staff and actuaries have determined the new product's premiums, cash values, and reserves, the insurer typically requests bids for reinsurance from several reinsurers. The insurer also specifies the type of administration that will be used for the new product and any other special considerations required for it. Using this information, the reinsurer's actuarial staff calculates an appropriate reinsurance premium.

Underwriting Cases

Before the underwriting function of an insurance company decides to seek facultative reinsurance on a case, the insurer's underwriters may already have performed some underwriting on the case. After the case is submitted to one or more reinsurers for bids and after bids have been received, reinsurance underwriters assess the risk, decide whether to offer reinsurance, and, if so, may send the case information to the reinsurer's actuarial staff to develop an appropriate premium for the reinsurance coverage. After the insurer has received the risk assessment and premium information, its underwriters decide whether to accept the bid for reinsurance.

You'll recall that reinsurance underwriters have typically developed extensive knowledge on risk assessment for a variety of coverages and cases. Especially for nonroutine, challenging cases, the ceding company often relies on the reinsurer's expertise in evaluating the feasibility of accepting a case and calculating a reasonable premium.

You have also learned that an automatic reinsurance agreement allows a ceding company to bind a reinsurer on a risk without submitting underwriting evidence to the reinsurer or obtaining the reinsurer's approval in advance for the risk. You learned that a facultative reinsurance agreement requires a ceding company to submit underwriting evidence on a case to the reinsurer for assessment and acceptance before any reinsurance becomes effective. The ceding company may not bind the reinsurer on a risk without submitting such underwriting evidence.

Because the ceding company is not required to submit underwriting evidence to the reinsurer under automatic agreements, the ceding company performs all underwriting for such cases. The ceding company may consult with the reinsurance underwriter on cases covered by an automatic agreement.

The ceding company's underwriter must be aware of the provisions of the reinsurance agreement in force between the ceding company and the reinsurer, and must be careful not to cede to the reinsurer a case on an automatic basis if the face amount of the case exceeds the automatic binding limits outlined in the automatic agreement. If, for instance, an automatic reinsurance agreement provides that a reinsurer will accept all term life cases with face amounts up to $2 million, a ceding company should not cede to the reinsurer on an automatic basis any case that exceeds the automatic binding limit. Instead, the ceding company may submit such a case to the reinsurer for assessment on a facultative basis.

In addition to submitting cases that exceed the coverage limits established for automatic reinsurance, a ceding company may submit to a reinsurer cases that involve complicated risk factors, including substandard cases and experimental cases. For cases submitted on a facultative basis, the reinsurer may establish specific underwriting requirements that the ceding company must fulfill. The reinsurer usually follows the ceding company's underwriting requirement guidelines. The underwriter in the ceding company is responsible for obtaining the required underwriting information and submitting it to the reinsurer in a timely fashion. If a ceding company sends a case to several reinsurers in order to seek the most advantageous coverage and rate, the ceding company's underwriter must fulfill the underwriting requirements of each reinsurer.

In submitting underwriting evidence to a reinsurer, the ceding company's underwriter is obliged to provide all relevant evidence, especially if the evidence shows an increased or complex risk. Unlike the reinsurer's underwriter, the ceding company's underwriter typically has access to information from a marketer, such as an agent or a broker, and has more knowledge about the case than the reinsurer's underwriter has. The trusting relationship between insurer and reinsurer is based on honest and full disclosure of all evidence needed to provide a fair assessment of the risk. Even after a case is accepted for reinsurance, if the ceding company's underwriter receives information that would affect the risk assessment, that underwriter is obliged to send the information to the reinsurer. In such a situation, the reinsurer may revise the original underwriting decision according to the new information.

Paying Premiums

The insurer calculates the amount of reinsurance premium due, figuring it as the product of the sum reinsured and the reinsurance premium rate. For instance, if a reinsurer is to cover 80 percent of a $100,000 term life policy, or $80,000, at a rate of $1.30 per thousand, the annual reinsurance premium is $104 (80 × $1.30).

After calculating the reinsurance premium on each covered policy, the insurer submits the required premium along with the premium bordereau, which lists the reinsurer's share in each risk and other information about commission payments and allowances. Some conditions require alterations in the premium submitted. For example, if a policy is dated back more than three months before the date of the application, no reinsurance premium is usually payable for the period ending three months before the date of the application. Moreover, even if the premiums on the policy are payable on a date other than the anniversary of the policy's issue date because of payment of a special premium for a fraction of a year, the reinsurance premiums are nevertheless due on the policy's anniversary date.

Modifying Policies

Such modifications to policies as changing benefits, changing plans, and changing ratings require the insurer and the reinsurer to cooperate. For all policy changes, the assumption is that both the insurer and the reinsurer have a mutual obligation to maintain reinsurance in force on terms fair to both parties.

Some changes do not require the reinsurer's approval, but most insurers inform the reinsurer of the change anyway. For other types of changes, the insurer notifies the reinsurer of the change, and the reinsurer either approves the change or requires that the reinsurer's liability remain the same as though the change had not occurred. Rarely is the reinsurer in a position to disapprove a change in benefits, plans, or ratings, because the reinsurer is not a legal party to the contract existing between the insurer and its insureds.

Generally, if the ceding company increases the amount at risk, the reinsurer treats the increase as a new reinsurance cession. In such a situation, the reinsurer is not obligated to reinsure the increase unless bound to do so by an existing treaty. In contrast, if the ceding company decreases the amount at risk, the reinsurer decreases the amount of reinsurance in the same proportion. For example, if the amount at risk on a ceded policy decreases 20 percent, the amount of reinsurance coverage also decreases 20 percent.

Sometimes a ceding company places a policy for reinsurance and later discovers new underwriting evidence that reduces the mortality rating on the policy. In such a situation, the ceding company usually has the right to request the reinsurer to recalculate the reinsurance premium. If the reinsurer does not wish to quote a new rating, the ceding company has the right to terminate the reinsurance on that policy and to place the policy with another reinsurer.

If a ceding company alters the rate basis from smoker to nonsmoker rates, the evidence obtained is usually submitted to the reinsurer for approval unless the reinsurer has previously agreed to such potential changes. If the change in smoker rates is in accordance with the ceding company's normal underwriting practices, but the reinsurer does not concur with the change, then the ceding company typically recaptures the reinsurance.

When a ceding company has to reform a policy, the policy is restructured on a new premium rate basis from the date of issue of the initial policy. Then the reinsurer usually makes an adjustment for the difference in reinsurance premium without interest.

If a policy is terminated by death of the insured, by lapse, by surrender, or otherwise, the reinsurance terminates on the same date. If premiums have been paid on the reinsurance for a period beyond the date of termination, the reinsurer in most cases provides a premium refund. For some treaties, however, no refund is made on termination in the event of death. If the policy continues in force because of the operation of an automatic premium loan provision (or any other such provision by which the ceding company is compensated for its risk), then the reinsurance also continues. An ***automatic premium loan (APL) provision*** is a life insurance nonforfeiture option that allows an insurer to pay overdue premiums on a policy by establishing a loan against the policy's cash value. Moreover, the ceding company is obligated to pay the reinsurer the reinsurance premium for the period until the date of cancellation.

If a lapsed or cancelled policy is to be reinstated, the ceding company is obligated to give the reinsurer complete details concerning the basis on which the policy will be re-entered on the books. This information includes copies of any application for reinstatement, any personal declaration or medical examination, and any other underwriting documents. The reinsurer has the right to amend the reinsurance terms on the policy if it feels that the risk has changed significantly. If the reinsurer is not provided such information about a reinstated policy, the reinsurer calculates reinsurance premiums on the assumption that all underwriting requirements for the reinstated policy are the same as those required for any new policy for the same face amount issued at the same age. For certain limited coverages, however, the reinsurance treaty specifies that a reinstated policy is automatically reinsured on the date of reinstatement, with notice of reinstatement being mailed to the reinsurer within a reasonable time.

If any policy change increases or decreases the reinsurance premium, the reinsurer makes an appropriate modification to the premium amount due. In some circumstances—for example, when a reinsurer offers a reduction in premium to all insurers on a certain type of nonstandard coverage—the reinsurer notifies the insurer of the pending modification and makes the required financial adjustment. If a ceding company makes a change in premiums for a class of policies, and if that class is coinsured with a reinsurer, then the reinsurance premiums must be renegotiated.

Paying Claims

Cooperation between the claim staff of the insurer and the reinsurer usually produces advantages on both sides. The insurer gains the advantage of the reinsurer's expertise in handling claims, especially large-amount cases and those involving potentially expensive long-term care and rehabilitation. The insurer also benefits from access to the reinsurer's long-standing contacts with on-site professionals who may assist in claim investigation. The reinsurer gains the advantage of financial stability because close cooperation helps ensure that claim payments are equitable and prompt. In addition, the public reputations of both parties are enhanced by such ethical, professional business management.

The insurer initiates a claim for reinsurance by advising the reinsurer of claim payments made under the reinsured coverage. The proofs of claim that are acceptable to the ceding company are taken in good faith as sufficient by the reinsurer. The ceding company calculates the reinsurer's share in the claim payment according to the type of reinsurance that applies. For example, suppose an insurer and a reinsurer have established an automatic treaty covering health insurance. The treaty specifies that the reinsurer will cover 75 percent of all legitimate claims. If the insurer has paid a claim for $24,000 under the treaty, the reinsurer's share is $18,000 (so that the insurer actually disburses $6,000). The insurer submits regular reports on claims to the reinsurer through claims bordereau service. Small insurance companies typically request payment by electronic transfer of a reinsurer's share of benefit payments at the time of claim, especially for large claims.

The ceding company is responsible for paying all costs associated with settling routine claims. These costs typically include doctor and hospital reports, autopsy and coroner reports, and police investigation reports. Costs of settling unusual claims or contested claims, however, may be shared by the reinsurer, depending on the terms of the treaty. Although a ceding company may offer various settlement options to beneficiaries, reinsurers rarely participate in such settlement options, but instead pay proceeds in a lump sum to the ceding company. For disability coverages, however, a reinsurer does not pay proceeds in a lump sum, but disburses them to the ceding company at appropriate intervals according to the amount of disability benefits paid by the ceding company.

Most reinsurers allow the ceding company to settle claims (1) if the contestable period of a reinsured coverage has been completed and (2) if the ceding company retained more than 50 percent of the risk. If the contestable period has not been completed and/or if the ceding company did not retain at least 50 percent of the risk, then most reinsurers require the ceding company to submit all claim documents and to delay claim payment until the reinsurer has made a recommendation on the case. Most treaties require the reinsurer to render such a recommendation within a specified, usually brief period. The time allowed for investigation of a contestable claim may be considerably longer than the limit placed on claims in which the ceding company has retained less than half the risk.

What happens if, after investigating a reinsured claim, a ceding company determines that the benefit should be reduced? In such a case, the reinsurer shares proportionately in the reduction. Suppose that a claim for $100,000, submitted under coverage that is reinsured for 50 percent, is reduced after investigation to $80,000. The reinsurer's share of the benefit would be 50 percent of $80,000, not 50 percent of $100,000.

If a ceding company delays payment of policy proceeds and pays interest on the undisbursed proceeds, the reinsurer also pays interest on the undisbursed reinsured portion at the same rate that the ceding company pays. If payment on the reinsurance is delayed more than 30 days beyond the date of policy settlement, the reinsurer usually pays interest to the ceding company at the rate that the ceding company currently pays on delayed claims.

When an increase or a reduction occurs in the benefit amount because of an overstatement or misstatement of age established after the death of an insured, the ceding company and the reinsurer share in such increase or reduction in proportion to their initial liabilities under the policy. This principle also applies to a change in classification—for instance, from nonsmoker to smoker status. Any advanced payment of death benefit by the ceding company is the full responsibility of the ceding company unless the reinsurance treaty makes a provision to the contrary. If such payment is requested or offered within the contestable period, however, the ceding company usually must notify the reinsurer and submit all papers in connection with the claim to the reinsurer for consideration. In such a situation, both parties make a reasonable effort to agree before making settlement of a claim on that life.

Recapturing Coverages

When a ceding company decides to increase its retention limit on certain coverage, the ceding company may also decide to recapture reinsured business whose retention limit is lower than the new, higher limit. The ceding company is not required to recapture in-force business, but may choose to do so in order to reduce the cost of reinsurance. Most reinsurance treaties for yearly renewable term (YRT) coverage provide that amounts at risk of less than a specified amount, usually $10,000, are assumed to be recaptured automatically. However, all recapture requirements for coinsurance agreements, including recapture of small amounts, are usually negotiated separately. Many reinsurers require that coverage be maintained in force for a specified period, usually 10 years, although the length of the period varies from one plan of insurance to another.

Under the laws of most jurisdictions, at the time a ceding company raises its retention limit, the insurer must inform a reinsurer of its intention to recapture ceded business if in fact the ceding company so intends. If the ceding company fails to notify the reinsurer of its intention to recapture, most jurisdictions provide that the ceding company has thereby forfeited its right to recapture the reinsured coverage. No recapture is provided for facultative reinsurance *unless* the ceding company kept the full amount of its retention.

Evaluating In-Force Reinsurance

An insurer periodically reviews the amount and type of reinsurance in force and assesses whether the established form of reinsurance administration is being implemented correctly and cost-effectively. In addition to certifying that the insurer is keeping its full retention limits according to treaty provisions, such a review also enables the insurer to learn whether

- Cases are being ceded appropriately
- Claims are being handled properly and accurately
- Changes in policies are being reported in a timely fashion
- Certain coverages should be recaptured
- Operations should be reconfigured in order to reduce the costs of administration
- All reinsurers are provided the desired level and quality of service

Resolving Disagreements

You have learned that a reinsurance treaty usually provides that, if the insurer and reinsurer encounter a dispute or difference of opinion concerning the validity of the treaty, the matter is usually submitted to a panel of arbitration. For three reasons, using arbitration to resolve reinsurance disputes is considered preferable to litigation in a civil court. First, most disputes concerning reinsurance involve very technical and specific problems that a civil court might have difficulty resolving because of the lack of experts to evaluate the facts. Second, arbitration panels usually work more rapidly and inexpensively than civil courts. Third, arbitration panels generally reach equitable decisions without disclosing confidential business concerns of the parties involved. Nevertheless, most reinsurance treaties provide that either the insurer or the reinsurer may notify the other party in writing that it wishes to have the merits of a case determined by litigation in a court of law rather than by arbitration.

Most insurance treaties establish the procedure that must be followed in settling a dispute between the parties. Typically, a treaty provides that either party may request arbitration by notifying the other party, usually by registered letter. Within one month, each party selects an arbitrator, and those arbitrators usually are allowed 10 to 15 days to select the third arbitrator. If the arbitrators cannot agree on a third arbitrator, the treaty normally provides that each arbitrator shall choose one name from a list of three names submitted by the other arbitrator. Then the third arbitrator shall be chosen by lot from the two selected names. Some insurers require that if a third arbitrator cannot be selected, the two original arbitrators will be dismissed, and two new arbitrators chosen. Alternatively, some arbitration clauses provide that if arbitrators cannot choose a third member within a specified time, each arbitrator submits three names to a federal judge, who then chooses the third arbitrator.

A panel of arbitrators is allowed to establish its own procedures for handling a dispute and is normally relieved from all legal formalities. Members of the panel are subject to only four major restrictions, as follows:

1. Panel members must maintain absolute neutrality in all actions and decisions.

2. No arbitrator may unduly delay the performance of the panel's arbitration duties.

3. The panel may examine witnesses and experts who volunteer to testify, but may not require such persons (a) to testify, (b) to take an oath prior to testifying, nor (c) to submit written statements.

4. The panel must deliver its decision in writing to all parties, state the reasons for the decision it has reached, include the signatures of all arbitrators, and file the decision with a civil court. If any one of these requirements is not fulfilled, the decision will be considered incomplete and legally unenforceable.

The arbitration panel gives both sides a fair hearing by receiving oral or written arguments and typically renders its decision within a reasonable period, usually two to four months, from the time it begins work. Usually, reinsurance treaties provide that the arbitrators' decision shall be reached by majority vote, shall be binding on all parties involved, and shall not be subject to appeal. Most treaties also provide that the parties shall pay equally for reasonable expenses incurred during arbitration, including fees charged by arbitrators, and specify a time period during which arbitration must be completed.

Because of the community of interests that an insurer and a reinsurer share, the reinsurance relationship is based upon the good faith of both parties and continues for a lengthy period. Therefore, rapid resolution of disputes is highly desirable so that the business relationship between the two parties may continue without further disturbance. During arbitration, each party has an ethical obligation to disclose fully all relevant information and to provide access to all relevant documentation so that the arbitrator or arbitrators may reach a sound conclusion. Insight 15-3 presents some additional opinions about arbitration and litigation.

Handling Insolvency

When an insurer or a reinsurer becomes insolvent, the consequences can be very serious. If one of the parties is insolvent, the primary concern of both parties is to see that claims are paid under the contract. Any amounts owed by the parties involved should be offset, and only the balance should be paid.

Insolvency of the Ceding Company

Most reinsurance treaties provide that if the ceding company becomes insolvent, all reinsurance is paid directly to a receiver or other legally established successor of the ceding company, which pays all claims. The receiver or successor must inform the reinsurer promptly of a claim submitted under any reinsured policy. When a claim is submitted, the reinsurer may investigate the claim and defend the claim at the reinsurer's own expense. Some treaties provide that expenses for defending claims may be charged, with court approval, against the ceding company as part of the expense of liquidating its assets following the insolvency.

Most jurisdictions provide that in proportional reinsurance, a reinsurer has to pay only the share of the claim that is actually paid in an insolvency. For example, suppose that a reinsurer has entered into a 40 percent quota share treaty and that the ceding company becomes bankrupt. Suppose further that the liquidator allows payment of a $100,000 claim, but can pay only 25 percent of the claim ($25,000)

Insight 15-3 Working It Out

The increase in reinsurance disputes has spurred a corresponding rise in the use of arbitration and litigation as methods to resolve the disagreements. Both forms have come under attack recently.

Arbitration, once heralded as a quicker and less-costly remedy than litigation, has degraded into a sort of "mini-trial," critics contend. And litigation, preferred by some reinsurers that view this form of resolution as benefiting them in a dispute, has resulted in decisions that often are confusing and violate insurance industry custom and practice, claim its detractors.

The types of disputes that have arisen between ceding companies and their reinsurers fall into several categories. For the most part, however, the disputes relate to contracts between cedents and reinsurers—contracts, most observers agree, that historically tended to be loosely written.

A frequent contractual dispute involves material misrepresentation of fact on the part of the ceding company. The goal of a reinsurer here is to have the reinsurance contract rescinded, i.e., an adjudication that there never was a valid contract in the first place.

Other disputes center on the interpretation of contract wording and whether various coverage issues are encompassed within this language. For example, one area of disagreement concerns whether a reinsurer was notified "promptly" that the cedent had received a claim. In addition, the contract may provide the reinsurer with the right to associate with the cedent in the defense of a claim. In some cases, a reinsurer has stated that it did not receive notice of a claim in time to prepare an adequate defense, and thus the contract should be voided.

Other frequent disputes involve

- Offsetting claim payments against premium payments by cedents
- Defining "loss occurrence"
- Handling insolvent retrocessionaires
- Resolving coverage gaps due to underwriting errors and omissions

While congenial face-to-face meetings between reinsurers and cedents continue to resolve some disputes, most are resolved through a variety of resolution mechanisms. These include arbitration and litigation.

Arbitration

On the pro side for arbitration is that fact that an arbitration panel is generally composed of insurance or reinsurance professionals. According to one expert, "Arbitration saves time and money compared to litigation. The expertise of the arbitration panel ensures an intelligent decision process based on the custom and practice of the reinsurance industry, rather than strict rules of law." In addition, "the private, non-adversarial nature" of arbitration allows for a continued business relationship between the disputants "without the ill will that litigation may cause."

Other experts feel that arbitration is "as hard-hitting and confrontational" as litigation and can take as long as litigation as well. Further, the cost of arbitration can be as expensive as litigation when "the parties allow their attorneys to go into irrelevant side issues, do extensive discovery procedures, and litigate procedural disputes."

Further, the limited number of available arbitrators results in a personnel shortage. The pool of available arbitrators "is proving inadequate to meet the demands of the ever-increasing number of arbitrations," says one expert.

Litigation

The problem with court resolutions is that courts often have great difficulty in understanding the specialized practice of reinsurance. One expert notes the extreme difficulty of simplifying reinsurance principles and practices for a judge and jury. In brief, court interpretations "often lack the custom, practice, experience, and conscience of the industry," says another specialist, who adds that some court decisions have produced confusion.

From Russ Banham, "Working It Out," *Insurance Review,* November 1990: 34–40. Adapted by permission.

because the ceding company lacks funds to pay the full amount. Normally, the reinsurer would pay $40,000 on the $100,000 claim. However, because only $25,000 ($100,000 × .25) is being paid on the claim, the reinsurer is liable to pay only 40 percent of $25,000, which is $10,000.

Insight 15-4 Are Your Reinsurance Affairs in Order?

In keeping a reinsurance house in order, effective internal procedures must be installed and monitored to facilitate the effective administration of a company's program. Such procedures should involve the executive, underwriting, accounting, and claim units within the organization.

Executive

In addition to responsibility for the design and security of the overall program, the executive branch should receive a contractual summary of each agreement from intermediaries or reinsurers early to minimize any misunderstandings, particularly if the contract begins soon after or prior to the negotiations. It is important to carefully analyze the formal documents to ascertain that even the incidental or secondary provisions are well understood and do not adversely affect the company's operations, especially from a reporting or cash-flow perspective.

A key executive should also be charged with the communication and coordination of reinsurance activities affecting other units and with the ultimate responsibility to measure the bottom-line performance and effectiveness of the program.

Underwriting

From the outset, the underwriting unit must clearly understand cession guidelines and procedures necessary to effect reinsurance placement on the company's behalf. Such communications are particularly necessary if a company's program includes surplus treaties or facultative arrangements, which require decisions as to the amount of reinsurance necessary for a given risk.

Furthermore, the underwriting departments should be made aware of contract restrictions and representations pertaining to the reinsurance agreement. Nonadherence to such requirements may ultimately result in disputes with reinsurers or a denial of coverage by the reinsurer.

Accounting

From an accounting perspective, procedures must be in place to make sure that reinsurance premiums are properly allocated, not only among treaties, but also the individual underwriting years covered under the various contracts. Although contracts placed through intermediaries often include provisions which require that transactions be transmitted through such intermediaries, the ceding company should maintain records that reflect premium and loss transactions on a reinsurer-by-reinsurer basis.

The accounting unit must also maintain updated information on funding arrangements to avoid statutory penalties that would otherwise result from cessions to nonadmitted reinsurers.

Claims

The claim unit is generally responsible for handling losses for the ceding company's own account and must be cautious in handling claims that may impact the reinsurance agreements. In view of the potential for severe loss, reinsurers expect close adherence to agreed upon and professional claim procedures. Such procedures include proper communication to keep reinsurers apprised of developments and to afford an opportunity for reinsurers' cooperation in the decision-making process, especially in cases for which a reinsurer has the bulk of the exposure. Failure to adhere to those procedures and communication requirements may result in frequent inspections by the reinsurance company and ultimate denial of liability in certain cases.

Of greatest significance are the ceding company's ongoing procedures to monitor the recovery of reinsurance claims from the reinsurer and to implement the procedures necessary to effect such recoveries on a timely basis. In addition to an aggressive collection effort, the ceding company may need to engage in negotiations to collect due monies from difficult or troubled reinsurers.

In view of the importance of reinsurance coverages to a ceding company's bottom line, the administration of the reinsurance program must receive as much attention as does any other area that is critical to the company's profitability and survival.

From Paul Walther, "Are Your Reinsurance Affairs in Order?" *Best's Review,* Property/Casualty Edition, August 1994: 54, 56–57. Adapted by permission.

Insolvency of the Reinsurer

If a reinsurer becomes insolvent, the ceding company is still responsible for paying all claims submitted under reinsured coverages. Even if a policy is completely reinsured, the ceding company must pay the claim if the reinsurer is insolvent. Although the ceding company must still pay the reinsurer any premiums and other monies due, the ceding company usually may set off these payments by the amount of money owed by the reinsurer. That is, if a reinsurer owes a ceding company $100,000 in claims, and the ceding company owes the reinsurer $15,000 in premiums, the ceding company may set off the $15,000 due. In effect, the reinsurer owes the ceding company $85,000 in claims.

Many functions of an insurance company play a part in administering reinsurance. Insight 15-4 presents an overview of insurance functions involved in reinsurance administration.

Key Terms and Concepts

individual cession administration (*traditional cession administration*)
self-administration (*bulk administration*)
bordereau
premium bordereau (*premium advice*)
claims bordereau (*claims advice*)
premium bordereau service
claims bordereau service
grossup file
policy exhibit
reinsurance audit
automatic premium loan (APL) provision

CHAPTER SIXTEEN

Scope and Organization of Claims

Learning Objectives

After studying this chapter, you should be able to

- Describe the commitments included in the claim practices of most insurers
- Explain the principal accountabilities of a claim supervisor, a claim analyst, and support staff in claims
- Compare the organization of the workflow in claims to the organization of the workflow in underwriting
- Compare the basis on which claim analysts and underwriters receive increasing amounts of decision-making authority
- State six general procedures involved in claim administration
- Explain the principal claim considerations in deciding when insurance coverage began and ended
- Discuss the legal issues affecting claim administration

Chapter Outline

Claim Philosophy and Claim Practices

Cost Containment and Managed Care

Organization of Claims

Claim Supervisor

Claim Analyst

Claim Support Staff

Organizing the Workflow in Claims

Authority Levels for Claims

Activities in Claim Administration

Determining the Date When Coverage Began

Determining the Date When Coverage Ended

Legal Issues Affecting Claim Administration

Claim Settlements

Disputed Claims

Undisputed Claims

You have learned that one of the most important results of sound underwriting is protection of both an insurer and its insureds from excessive risk. Similarly, sound claim practices help ensure that an insurance company and its policyowners or policyholders are not exposed to the risk that will result if the insurer pays inappropriate claims. Effective claim administration fulfills the insurer's responsibilities to its insureds to (1) pay all valid claims promptly and accurately and (2) deny any claim that is not covered or that is fraudulent.

The claim analyst receives information on a claim and examines it for accuracy and completeness. After considering the facts of the claim, the claim analyst makes a decision to pay or deny the claim.

Persons handling claims are frequently in contact with the insurer's underwriters to check information submitted with an application or used to make an underwriting decision. The relationship between claims and underwriting is so important that many insurers have focused on establishing close ties between these two company functions. Figure 16-1 outlines some of the approaches insurers have used to foster cooperation between claims and underwriting.

Claim handling also involves consultation with the insurer's medical and legal staff and with marketers or specialized vendors who may help in gathering or verifying information related to a claim. Statistical information generated by the claim function is used by the insurer's actuaries in setting premium rates for existing and new products, as well as by the insurer's auditors in checking the overall accuracy of underwriting decisions by examining the type, size, and frequency of claims submitted under various products. Claims information is also used by the insurer's product development staff in developing new insurance products.

In this chapter, we'll give you an introduction to claims. We'll first explain the importance of an insurer's claim philosophy in guiding its claim practices. Then we'll introduce the concepts of cost containment and managed care and explain their importance in claim handling. Next, we'll define the job accountabilities of a claims supervisor, a claim analyst, and support staff in claims, and we'll mention the workflow methods that are normally used. After discussing the authority levels used in claims, we'll examine the basic activities involved in claim administration and review the most important legal issues affecting claim administration. In the following chapters, you'll learn more about claim administration for specific individual and group coverages and for annuities, as well as the procedures insurers follow during claim investigation.

Figure 16-1. Fostering cooperation between claims and underwriting.

Having a close relationship between claims and underwriting helps an insurer manage risk effectively, enhance the accuracy and quality of both underwriting and claim decisions, and therefore to compete successfully in a highly competitive environment. Recognizing the importance of this relationship, insurers have taken steps to foster cooperation between claims and underwriting by

- Involving staff from underwriting and claims during the development of new insurance products, and using data from both functions to evaluate the probable success of the new product
- Using staff from both functions to review policy documents, including applications and claim forms, to check for potential underwriting and claim problems
- Using staff from both functions to establish and revise procedures to ensure that a change in one function will not adversely affect the activities in the other function
- Physically establishing claims and underwriting near each other to facilitate personal communication and data exchanges
- If physical proximity is not possible, enabling both functions to communicate frequently and to consult on problems relating to the cases each is handling
- Providing cross training so that staff gain a deeper knowledge and better understanding of the work requirements and challenges of both functions

Claim Philosophy and Claim Practices

An insurer's ***claim philosophy*** is a precise statement of the insurance company's principles for conducting claim administration. The claim philosophy, which is usually developed for each company by its senior management, guides the decisions made by claim analysts. The claim philosophies of all insurers are focused on rapid, equitable, and courteous administration of claims.

Using the insurer's claim philosophy as a basis, the senior management of claims develops ***claim practices,*** which are expressed as statements that guide the day-to-day handling of claims. The claim practices of most insurers include the following commitments:

- To handle claims on a timely basis and to notify a claimant if an extended time period is necessary to gather information for a claim decision
- To apply the provisions of policies consistently
- To train claim staff so that they can perform their duties professionally and accurately, and can document claim handling appropriately

- To investigate questionable claims
- To obtain high-quality medical and legal advice when needed to make a decision on a claim
- To provide claimants with courteous, prompt, and complete explanations of claims for which benefits are not payable or are limited
- To permit claimants to submit additional supportive information on a denied or limited claim
- To provide satisfactory means for appeal of denied claims

The International Claim Association (ICA) has developed and distributed a written claim philosophy called the Statement of Principles that any insurance company may adapt for use in handling claims. The Statement of Principles is presented in Figure 16-2.

Figure 16-2. Statement of Principles of the International Claim Association.

International Claim Association
Statement of Principles

The International Claim Association, in recognition of the need to continue public trust and confidence in the insurance industry, reaffirms the following principles:

1. Any individual who has, or believes he has, a claim is entitled to courteous, fair, and just treatment; and shall receive with reasonable promptness an acknowledgment of any communications with respect to his claim.
2. Every claimant is entitled to prompt investigation of all facts, an objective evaluation, and the fair and equitable settlement of his claim as soon as liability has become reasonably clear.
3. Claimants are to be treated equally and without considerations other than those dictated by the provisions of their contracts.
4. Claimants shall not be compelled to institute unnecessary litigation in order to recover amounts due, nor shall the failure to settle a claim under one policy or one portion of a policy be used to influence settlement under another policy or portion of a policy.
5. Recognizing the obligation to pay promptly all just claims, there is an equal obligation to protect the insurance-buying public from increased costs due to fraudulent or nonmeritorious claims.
6. Procedures and practices shall be established to prevent misrepresentation of pertinent facts or policy provisions, to avoid unfair advantage by reason of superior knowledge, and to maintain accurate insurance claim records as privileged and confidential.
7. Reasonable standards shall be implemented to provide for adequate personnel, systems, and procedures to effectively service claims. These standards shall be such as to eliminate unnecessary delays or requirements, overinsistence on technicalities, and excessive appraisals or examinations. Claim personnel shall be encouraged and assisted in further developing their knowledge, expertise, and professionalism in the field of claim administration.

Reprinted by permission from the International Claim Association.

Cost Containment and Managed Care

One of an insurer's principal responsibilities is to conduct business in a responsible manner so that its financial resources remain adequate to pay claims. An insurer strengthens its financial position not only by using resources well, reducing waste, and encouraging efficiency in its business operations, but also by managing its expenses. An essential facet of expense management in insurance is making sure that every claim is assessed accurately and is paid appropriately. Particularly in handling health and disability claims, an insurer typically participates in decisions concerning the treatment given to insureds.

Many insurance companies are turning to managed care as a means of expense management. ***Managed care*** is the name given to a broad spectrum of techniques that integrate payment for and delivery of health care and that seek to manage the cost, accessibility, and quality of that care. Most forms of managed health care coverage include (1) a group of contracted health care providers; (2) limits on benefits to members who choose noncontracted providers for health care services; and (3) an authorization system that evaluates the level of care offered, the quality and cost of care, and accessibility to the care. Managed care enables insurers to practice ***cost containment***—that is, reduction of unnecessary expenses of reimbursement for health and disability income coverage—and to provide high-quality care without waste of money and resources.

Among the most common techniques involved in managed care is ***case management,*** which is a cost-containment process of handling the costs of illnesses and injuries by identifying alternate methods of treatment that can make the most efficient and cost-effective use of medical resources consistent with desirable results for each patient. Another common managed care technique is ***utilization review,*** a claim review approach by which an insurer analyzes a case to determine if the recommended treatment is both necessary and appropriate.

The primary aim of managed care is to reduce to a minimum the expenses of providing health and disability care without reducing the quality of that care. The role of an insurance company, and especially the role of its claim staff, is to ensure that claim assessment and payment are handled in a manner consistent with this goal of managed care. An insurer uses the expertise of medical practitioners in developing guidelines used to (1) govern reviews of medical treatment provided by medical caregivers and (2) assist insurers in determining what treatment is reasonable and necessary. Both an insurer and its claim staff are responsible for reviewing the actions of medical caregivers under managed care and for following the guidelines developed with the assistance of medical professionals. In handling claims under health and disability coverages, claim staff members do not second-guess medical caregivers nor assume that they know more about medical diagnosis and treatment than medical professionals know. Rather, claim staff members work closely with medical caregivers to ensure that reimbursement for delivered care is adequate, accurate, and equitable.

Organization of Claims

The claim function is organized so that tasks are distributed appropriately and so that the work may be accomplished efficiently and effectively. The work of claims is usually managed by a vice president of claims and, in large companies, by several managers, each handling a different type of claim. For instance, some insurers establish managers for life, medical and dental, and disability claims, whereas other insurers establish managers for individual and group claims. Insurers that have sold policies to large groups may assign a manager to oversee the claims for those groups, and some insurers establish teams to handle claims.

The day-to-day operations of claims are performed by persons filling the positions of claim supervisor, claim analyst, and support staff. We'll look first at the job accountabilities of the persons holding these positions, and then we'll discuss the ways that the workflow in claims can be organized.

Fast Fact

Every year from 1960 to the present, total death benefit payments made to beneficiaries of life insurance policies in the United States have increased. In 1960, $3.3 billion in payments was made to beneficiaries; in 1995, about $33.5 billion was paid.

Source: American Council of Life Insurance, *1996 Life Insurance Fact Book,* 1996: 45.

Claim Supervisor

A claim supervisor is usually promoted from the position of claim analyst to oversee the work of a number of claim analysts and support staff and to establish efficient claim handling procedures to ensure that all work is performed in an efficient, effective manner. The claim supervisor not only handles many difficult and large-amount claims, but also makes work assignments to claim analysts according to their experience and knowledge. To handle especially challenging claims, the claim supervisor may work with a group of experienced claim analysts to determine what additional information is needed, to find ways to obtain the information, and to evaluate it to reach an equitable decision.

The claim supervisor usually decides on the type and amount of training needed by each claim analyst and either delivers the training personally or arranges to have it delivered. If a state department of insurance has received complaints about claim handling, the claim supervisor usually responds to such complaints and provides documentation of the handling of those claims. The claim supervisor assists the actuarial function with claim audits, maintains records of products, and generates periodic production reports that show the type and quality of claim decisions made by claim analysts. Finally, the claim supervisor serves as liaison with the insurer's medical director and legal staff, and obtains information that claim analysts need to reach decisions.

Claim Analyst

At the heart of claim administration is the claim analyst, who works with paper and electronic materials to evaluate the merit of submitted claims and to make decisions on each of them. A claim analyst is responsible for

- Analyzing claims to determine the type of coverage held
- Assessing medical information
- Requesting additional information needed to determine benefits
- Determining the person or entity to pay
- Calculating payable benefits
- Explaining claim denials, payments, and contract provisions to marketers, clients, and health care providers through correspondence and telecommunication

Claim analysts generally receive extensive training in contract provisions and medical terminology and develop a solid knowledge of the legal considerations affecting claims. Insight 16-1 shows a letter from an industry executive to new disability income claim analysts, introducing them to the complexities of handling claims.

Many insurers establish groups of claim analysts who work together to resolve questions on difficult claims, much as the members of an underwriting team or committee cooperate to assess unusual cases. Some insurers also establish a group of two to four claim analysts who are authorized to approve routine or uncomplicated claims in much the same manner as the jet unit is used for underwriting. Claims that are handled in this manner usually are accompanied by complete information and present no problems in settlement.

Many insurers use electronic systems to evaluate and pay routine claims, particularly for health coverages. These systems can receive electronic information, make claim decisions, authorize payment of benefits, generate checks, and send proceeds to policyowners and beneficiaries. No human intervention is necessary for ordinary cases. Any claim that has unusual features that do not exactly match the param-

Insight 16-1 My Thoughts On . . . Welcoming New Analysts to Claim Administration

Welcome to the disability claim department! Today you start your training as disability claim analysts. It might seem that we are burying you with policy forms and other materials, but all this will be necessary as you progress in the department.

Let's review what we talked about when you interviewed for this position—what it takes to be a successful claim analyst, and what you must do to "get ahead" and acquire additional responsibility. First of all, it is important to become thoroughly familiar with all of our disability policy forms—to know and understand all the policy provisions and how each provision interacts with others. Also you will need to become well versed in medical terminology so that you will be able to recognize the conditions that disable a person.

You will learn about the average length of a disabling condition and about proper claim handling techniques. To help with all of this, you will be given resource materials, and you will have access to the materials from our claim library.

In addition to being technically correct, you will need to be able to speak effectively and to write letters that are coherent, grammatically correct, and free of insurance jargon so that clients can understand what you are trying to tell them. And you'll learn to say "no" to claimants and have them accept that answer on claims that are not payable.

After your introductory classes, you will be working closely with one of our experienced claim analysts. In the beginning, each of your claims will be audited before any final decision is made. When you have gained experience, your claims will be audited on a random basis. There will be periodic reviews with your immediate supervisor to determine where there might be some areas in which you need to gain additional expertise. During the review sessions, we will work together to set goals and standards for accomplishing those goals and monitoring your progress as a claim analyst.

The copy of your job description outlines the various steps that you will follow through the claim training process. You will see that advancement depends not only on the progress you make in handling claims, but also on your passing examinations on insurance industry courses.

R. J. "Sam" Schwarztrauber, ALHC
(retired)
Consultant and Team Leader
General American Life Insurance
Company

eters established for the electronic system is routed to a claim supervisor, who distributes such cases to claim analysts for handling.

Claim Support Staff

When claims arrive, in either paper or electronic form, support staff order information needed for a claim decision, establish files and assign case or file numbers to claims, exchange information with other functional areas of the insurance company, and perform other routine actions designed to facilitate the decision-making process. When a claim is approved, support staff ensure that a check is prepared and sent to the person or entity who is to receive benefits. In some insurance companies, support staff also handle telephone calls and electronic mail from clients and marketers, and send letters and claim forms to them.

Organizing the Workflow in Claims

The workflow in claims is organized according to the type and amount of claims to be administered. Every insurer establishes its own approaches to moving claims through the decision-making process. Systems similar to those used for underwriting may be used to handle claims. Thus, an insurer may choose to allocate claims according to a case assignment system, a work division system, or a combination of the two systems.

Fast Fact

In 1950, private health insurers in the United States paid $1.3 billion in claims. By 1993, insurance companies paid more than $254 billion.

Source: "Private Health Insurance Claims Payments by Type of Insurer," Health Insurance Association of America *Source Book of Health Insurance Data,* 1995: 41.

When claims are handled by a case assignment system, they are divided according to the type of claim (for example, dental, medical reimbursement, or disability income), the dollar amount of the claim, the geographic area from which a claim is received, or the group under whose coverage a claim is submitted. The claims received from persons insured under large group policies can be assigned to one or several claim analysts who specialize in handling only those claims. As with underwriting, each claim analyst is given sufficient authority to approve claims of a certain type and amount. Generally, the more experience a claim analyst gains, the higher the amount of claim that person can approve without having the claim reviewed by a more experienced analyst.

Under a work division system, claim staff may work independently to investigate and make decisions on claims, or they may be organized into work units similar to those used for underwriting, including teams and committees. Challenging claims are usually handled by highly experienced claim analysts and claim supervisors, and may be referred to the insurer's medical staff and legal staff if necessary. Insurers also use outside investigative agencies for claims that are still within the contestable period.

Some insurers establish branch offices whose primary purpose is to administer claims. One of an insurer's branch offices may be assigned to handle only claims submitted under one type of coverage, and other branch offices may handle claims submitted under other types of coverage. Alternatively, an insurer may send simple claims for small amounts of coverage to one branch office, where the claims can be handled electronically and benefits payments can be sent quickly to insureds or service providers.

Some insurance companies hire third-party administrators to handle claims, particularly routine claims. Information systems and electronic data transfer (EDT), which we discussed in Chapter 1, can speed the claim administration process by sending information rapidly among an insurer and its reinsurers, its marketers, its clients, and various sources of claim handling information.

The types of files necessary to support the claim handling work are similar to those used for underwriting. Whether an insurer uses paper or electronic files, or a combination of both, the claim analyst is responsible for maintaining a complete record of the progress and disposition of every claim. Particularly when a claim analyst reaches a decision to deny a claim, full written documentation to support the denial must be made a part of the claim file. Although some claims are completed within a short time, other claims—for example, those for long-term disability—can continue for months or years. The claim analyst updates such files and ensures that their contents are current.

Authority Levels for Claims

Like underwriters, claim analysts are given increasing amounts of decision-making authority as they gain experience and as they demonstrate enhanced ability and quality of judgment. A person who is new to claim handling is usually given small-amount, routine claims that present few difficulties or unusual circumstances. The new claim analyst's work is normally reviewed by a more senior claim analyst or by a claim supervisor. As the claim analyst gains more experience, he is given more decision-making authority and is assigned less routine, more challenging cases that may involve much higher coverage amounts, and his work is not as often subject to review by a more experienced person. Claims that require extensive investigation or compromise are usually handled only by experienced claim analysts and claim supervisors.

Because information systems can handle many types of claims quickly, accurately, and cost effectively, many insurers use them, especially for health claims that require small payments for routine treatments. The amount of decision-making authority given to an information system varies from one insurer to another. An insurer that has been able to develop an effective automated claim processing system that is based on extensive experience with the insurer's specific products can give that system considerable decision-making authority. Insurers are careful, however, not to allow a computer system to decide the merits of a claim unless the system has adequate information to make a decision equitably and correctly. Claims that do not fit the parameters specified for electronic handling are assigned to claim analysts for assessment and decisions.

Activities in Claim Administration

The claim administration process involves a number of activities that are essentially the same for most types of coverage. Generally, a person or system handling a claim determines whether the information submitted on a claim matches the coverage provided by a valid, in-force policy and, on that basis, makes a decision to approve or deny coverage. The general procedures involved in claim administration include the following:

- Establishing proof of loss, which may vary from one type of coverage to another
- Checking the status of the policy to determine that the contract was in force at the time the insured-against event occurred
- Verifying that the insurance contract coverage applies to the insured-against event
- If the claim is valid and payable, calculating the amount of the policy proceeds and the way they are to be paid (for instance, in a lump sum or in a series of payments)
- Identifying the person or party that should receive the policy benefits
- Authorizing payment of the policy benefits

Typical proofs of loss can include showing that the event insured against did take place, that the claimant has the contractual right to receive the policy benefits, or that the name and age of the beneficiary have been verified. In verifying that an insurance contract was in force when an insured-against event occurred, a claim analyst determines the date when coverage began. If coverage is no longer in force, the claim analyst determines the date when coverage ended. Because these dates are critical for all types of coverage, we'll discuss the determination procedures here in more detail.

Determining the Date When Coverage Began

To determine the date when coverage began, the claim analyst may have to take into consideration the effects of premium receipts, premium payments, modifications of coverage, and policy provisions. For group insurance, the claim analyst has additional considerations in determining the beginning date of coverage.

Premium receipts. In Chapter 3, we discussed conditional and binding premium receipts. If a proposed insured is covered by a conditional premium receipt and suffers a loss before the application is completely underwritten, the proposed insured may or may not receive policy proceeds, depending on whether the underwriting decision would have been to approve the application, offer modified coverage, or deny the application.

- If the underwriting decision would have been to approve the application, the policy proceeds may be payable.

- If the underwriting decision would have been to modify coverage, the policy proceeds are payable within the limits of the modified coverage.

- If the underwriting decision would have been to deny coverage, no policy proceeds are payable.

If a proposed insured is covered by a binding premium receipt (also called a *temporary insurance agreement* or *TIA*), a loss that occurs even before underwriting has been completed is treated as though the loss had occurred after policy issue. That is, even if a proposed insured would not have been approved for coverage or would have been approved for modified coverage, that proposed insured is due certain policy benefits as long as the terms and conditions of the TIA have been met. Most binding premium receipts do not provide full policy benefits, but instead limit the amount of coverage in some way. For example, under a binding premium receipt issued for an individual life insurance application, the maximum amount of coverage might be limited to $100,000 or $250,000, which would be an amount established by the insurer for all insureds proposed for coverage under that product. Moreover, most interim coverages do not provide benefits for preexisting conditions.

Premium payments. Occasionally a claim analyst has problems with a claim submitted under coverage whose renewal premium was paid by a check that did not clear a bank—usually because of insufficient funds (in other words, the check is written on an account that does not contain sufficient funds to cover the amount of the check). In such a situation, the insured has not paid for the coverage, so the policy contract is not in effect, and no benefits are payable. Most insurance contracts, however, allow proposed insureds a ***grace period,*** which is a specified period of time after a renewal premium is due and unpaid during which a policy, including all riders, remains in force. The length of the grace period varies from one type of insurance to another, but usually ranges between 10 days and 31 days. A premium that is paid during the grace period is considered to have been paid on time. Some insurers specify in their binding premium receipts that, if a check or other means of payment is not honored by a bank, no insurance will be in effect.

Sometimes problems arise at claim time when a proposed insured has failed to pay a full premium. If a proposed insured pays an insurance premium by payroll deduction, as is often done for group coverages, a claim problem can arise if the amount deducted at each pay period is less than a full premium payment. In such a situation, at the time of a claim the proposed insured may not have paid the full premium as provided by the insurance contract. Most insurers, however, honor these submitted claims unless the contract specifically states that insurance will be issued contingent upon payment of a full premium. Similarly, most insurers that permit proposed insureds to pay premiums by bank loan accept liability for coverage, even though a proposed insured could withdraw the loan application or fail to gain approval from the bank for the loan. If a proposed insured authorizes an insurer in writing to use dividend accumulations on an in-force policy to pay the premium for new coverage, and if those accumulations are insufficient to pay the premium, most insurers consider the premium to have been paid in full.

Modifications of coverage. What happens if an underwriter determines that coverage can be issued only with modification—for instance, a higher premium, a lesser amount of insurance, or a waiver of coverage? Normally the insurer is considered to be making a counteroffer to the applicant's original offer for a policy. Therefore, until the applicant either pays the higher premium or accepts the lesser amount of insurance or the waiver of coverage, no insurance is in force, and claims submitted under the insurance policy will be neither considered nor paid. If, however, a policy modification is minor and does not affect the risk represented by a proposed insured, most insurers choose to accept liability for losses incurred under the coverage even when the applicant has not yet accepted the insurer's counteroffer. For example, the insurer might modify a policy to correct a marketer's error in noting a proposed insured's place of residence or in submitting an outdated application form. If a claim is submitted under a policy that contains one or more waivers, the claim analyst undertakes an investigation to ensure that the claim is not excluded by a waiver.

Policy provisions. Most insurers specify in the application that, if the initial premium is not paid at the time of application, a proposed insured must remain in good health until the policy can be delivered. This requirement of good health can be stated in a ***change of condition provision,*** which specifies that, in order for a policy to become effective, all facts contained in the application must be true when the policy is delivered. Alternatively, some insurers include an ***insurability provision,*** specifying that, in order for a policy to become effective, the proposed insured must still be insurable by that insurer when the policy is delivered.

Group coverages. To determine the date when group insurance becomes effective, a claim analyst usually checks first to see that the coverage for the whole group has begun. The effective date of coverage is usually specified in the group insurance application and may be set to begin on the date that coverage from a previous insurer ceases. Having determined that group insurance coverage is in force, the claim analyst must then determine that the group member who has submitted a claim is covered by the group insurance. If a group policy contains an actively-at-work provision—defined in Chapter 9 as a provision under which an employee is required to be at work on the date insurance coverage begins—the claim analyst verifies that the claimant was at work on that date. To gather information about an employee's actively-at-work status, a claim analyst uses such documents as the employee's job description, a history of the employee's work attendance and absences, and work-related documents such as letters and memos that the employee may have sent on or after the date when insurance coverage became effective. If an employee was absent by reason of sickness, injury, or other cause on the day coverage began, the group coverage begins on the day the employee returns to work.

If the claimant is a new employee, coverage typically begins on the new employee's first day on the job or after a specified number of days on the job, usually 30, 60, or 90 days. If the insured group's actively-at-work provision states that an employee must be at work *in the usual place of business,* then the claim analyst must verify that the employee performed work in the location in which the employee normally works. This location is not necessarily the employer's location, because many persons are employed to work outside an office or in their own homes.

If a group policy requires new members to complete a waiting period before coverage becomes effective, the claim analyst checks to be sure that anyone hired recently has satisfied the waiting period. Similarly, a group policy may require that any potential member who did not enroll when coverage was first made available must show evidence of insurability if that person later decides to request coverage under the group plan. The claim analyst verifies that such a person who submits a claim has provided the required insurability evidence.

Determining the Date When Coverage Ended

Coverage comes to an end when an employee leaves an organization, and also as the result of a policy lapse, a policy surrender, or failure to reinstate a policy.

Policy lapse. As we have mentioned, a policy lapse occurs when an insurance policy terminates through nonpayment of premium before the policy has accumulated cash values. If a policyowner has not paid a premium by its due date, however, an insurer usually allows a grace period before terminating coverage. When a claim is submitted under coverage on which the premium has not been paid to date, the claim analyst checks to see whether an insurer's grace period might have extended the time of coverage and, if so, pays any appropriate claim submitted within that period. When a claim is paid during the grace period, the amount of overdue premium may be deducted from the benefit amount.

Payment of premium within the grace period is not considered to be a late payment. In contrast, payment of premium beyond the end of the grace period is considered to be a late payment. If the actions of an insurer or its marketer lead a policyowner to expect that delayed premium payments will not affect payment of claims, the insurer is generally held liable to pay claims submitted under the coverage. For example, if the policyowner was in the habit of giving premiums to the marketer to submit to the insurer, and then the marketer failed either to collect or to remit the premium, the insurer may be required by law to honor claims submitted under the coverage, even though the premium has not been paid.

Moreover, if an insurer has regularly accepted premium payments beyond the expiration of the grace period, the legal effect may be to extend the grace period. The insurer may be held liable to pay any claim submitted under coverage on which premium has not been paid because of the insurer's custom of accepting late payments. Similarly, if a marketer has regularly accepted premiums after the expiration of the grace period without requiring a policyowner to submit a reinstatement request, the insurer may be held liable for paying any claim submitted under coverage on which the premium has not been paid.

Policy surrender. As we have mentioned, a policy surrender occurs when a policyowner turns a policy in to an insurer in return for the policy's cash value. If a policyowner notifies an insurer that she wishes to surrender a policy for its cash value and then suffers a loss, the insurer must decide whether the policyowner is eligible to receive the policy's cash value only or full payment of benefits under the policy. The insurer's decision is usually based on its claim philosophy and claim practices, as well as on the laws and statutes of the jurisdiction in which the insurer does business.

Failure to reinstate a policy. After a policy lapses, a policyowner may wish to renew the coverage by reinstatement, which we have previously defined as the process by which an insurer put back in force a policy that lapsed because of nonpayment of renewal premiums. In handling a claim submitted under a policy for which reinstatement has been requested, a claim analyst determines whether the coverage has been placed back in force prior to the time the event resulting in the claim occurred. In particular, the claim analyst determines whether the reinstated policy has the same provisions, such as the incontestable provision and the suicide provision, as the original policy.

In most jurisdictions, the contestable period begins anew from the date the coverage is reinstated. In other jurisdictions, the contestable period does not start anew, but is calculated using the effective date of the policy that is being replaced—provided that the face amount of the policy has not been increased. The new contestable period applies only to statements made in the application for reinstatement. The length of the new contestable period is the same length as the original contestable period. If the face amount has been increased, an insurer cannot contest the original amount of the policy, but may contest the increased amount of coverage. The responsibility of the claim analyst is to check the applicable jurisdictional statutes and to apply the correct law to the reinstated coverage.

If an insured misrepresented information in the reinstatement application, the insurer can void the reinstated policy within the contestable period, if one applies. Moreover, if any misrepresentation is found, any claim that is subject to the incontestable provision and that is submitted within the contestable period is not eligible for benefits.

For reinstatement purposes, the suicide provision is treated differently in the United States and in Canada. Laws in the United States provide that a policy's suicide provision runs from the original date of the policy, not from the date when the policy was reinstated. In handling a death claim submitted under a reinstated policy, a claim analyst cannot deny coverage on the basis of the suicide exclusion. Therefore, in handling a death claim submitted under a reinstated policy for which the suicide exclusion provision has expired—regardless of the date when the contestable period begins—a claim analyst in the United States cannot deny coverage on the basis of the suicide exclusion even if the death is a suicide. Canadian laws, in contrast, provide that a policy's suicide provision runs from the date that the policy is reinstated.

But what about a claim that is submitted during the time between application for reinstatement and actual reinstatement? Such a claim may pose serious problems for a claim analyst because determination of the policy's in-force status may be difficult.

Legal Issues Affecting Claim Administration

Claim practices in the United States are covered by the provisions of the Fair Credit Reporting Act (FCRA), which we have already discussed in some detail. In gathering information to make claim decisions, claim analysts often use reports generated by consumer reporting agencies. According to the FCRA, credit reporting agencies must act fairly, impartially, and with respect for the consumer's right to privacy when preparing reports on individuals. Like underwriters, claim analysts are required to provide claimants with appropriate notice—pre-notice, supplementary notice, and post-notice—when using reports generated by credit reporting agencies. In addition, claim analysts must protect the confidentiality of information gathered during claim administration.

When an insurer denies a life, health, or disability insurance claim, the result can be a lawsuit brought on behalf of a policyowner or a beneficiary. If an insurer is found to have denied coverage properly, the cost of a lawsuit to the insurer is limited to expenses associated with defending the suit. Those expenses, however, can be considerable, as they include not only attorneys' fees and other legal expenses, but also the time required for the insurer's employees to gather information, consult with attorneys, give depositions, and testify in trials. Although insurers generally hire outside legal counsel to present the defense of a suit in court, the insurers often call on their employees, and sometimes on marketers, to help the outside legal counsel.

If an insurer is found to have improperly denied a claim, the insurer bears these same expenses and, sometimes, additional costs. A court can require an insurer that has been found to have improperly denied a claim to pay ***extra-contract damages,*** which are money awards that exceed the amount of policy benefits and which may be compensatory or punitive. ***Compensatory damages*** are money awards to pay a plaintiff for the damage he has suffered from the insurer's wrongdoing. ***Punitive damages*** are money awards intended to make an example of a defendant, to punish a defendant who has acted in a malicious, fraudulent, or oppressive manner toward a plaintiff, and thus to dissuade others from similar behavior. Insight 16-2 comments on punitive damages awarded as a result of claim error.

To protect itself against improper claim denial, an insurer usually provides in-depth, ongoing training for all claim supervisors, analysts, and support staff so that they will be informed about changes in laws and statutes affecting claim administration and will realize the importance of adhering to the insurance company's claim philosophy and practices completely, consistently, promptly, and professionally. Insurers further protect themselves from improper claim denial by ensuring that claim decisions are communicated in a timely fashion and in clear language to the policyowners and beneficiaries.

Most jurisdictions have enacted fraud acts that affect the operations of claims and which may involve an insured, a provider, or the employees of an insurer. Fraud acts generally require education on fraud issues for claim staff members, as well as for other employees of insurance companies. Moreover, fraud acts typically require that each insurer (1) establish investigatory units to handle questionable claim activities and (2) report instances of suspected claim fraud to insurance regulatory authorities.

The NAIC's Unfair Claims Settlement Practices Act specifies standards for the investigation and handling of claims. The Act defines unfair claim practices and notes that such practices are improper if they are (1) committed flagrantly and in conscious disregard of the Act or (2) committed with such frequency as to indicate a general business practice to engage in that type of conduct. Figure 16-3 lists the unfair

Insight 16-2 My Thoughts On . . . Punitive Damages

Since 1973, life and health insurers have been at risk of judgments requiring them to pay punitive damages. No clear standards yet exist for punitive damages awards, and jurisdictions have enacted punitive damages laws that vary considerably.

A court awards punitive damages against an insurer in order to punish the insurer when the court finds that the insurer breached the covenant of good faith and fair dealing implied in insurance contracts—that is, the insurer acted in bad faith. Although not all punitive damages awards against insurers result from the actions of claim analysts, claim mishandling has resulted in many such awards. An insurer's bulwark against punitive damages is claim analysts who handle claims *reasonably, promptly, thoroughly,* and *courteously.*

Reasonableness

Under the law in most jurisdictions, bad faith in the claim context means that the insurer denied a claim without a reasonable basis for the denial and that the insurer either knew that it did not have a reasonable basis for the denial or recklessly regarded the lack of a reasonable basis. A claim analyst must, therefore, give the interests of the claimant at least as much consideration as he gives to the interests of the insurer. When a claim is denied, the claim analyst should afford the claimant an opportunity to provide additional information or evidence in support of the claim. Moreover, a claim analyst who acts in good faith does not conceal significant information about the claim from the claimant. Such concealment would likely be discovered if the claimant filed a lawsuit. The court almost certainly would find such conduct unreasonable or even outrageous.

Promptness

Because delay in acting on a claim can result in harm to the claimant, a claim analyst must act promptly in investigating and settling a claim. Evidence of foot-dragging annoys juries, making punitive damages awards more likely. If part of a claim is payable, that part should be paid promptly, even if more investigation is necessary to determine whether the remainder of the claim is payable. If the claim analyst finds that a claim has been improperly denied, prompt payment of the claim is essential and might prevent a lawsuit or, if the claimant does file a lawsuit, might prevent a punitive damages award.

Thoroughness

The claim investigation must be done thoroughly, and the claim file must be well-organized and complete. If the claim analyst has legal or medical questions, those questions should be brought to the attention of the insurer's lawyers or its medical staff.

When a claim is denied, all the insurer's reasons for the denial should be explained clearly to the claimant. If a claimant successfully refutes claim denial reasons and the insurer continues to produce new reasons for denying the claim, a jury could conclude that the insurer was acting in bad faith.

Courtesy

A pleasant tone of voice and a professional demeanor are essential when speaking with a claimant. Letters to claimant and the entire claim file must reflect this courtesy and professionalism.

Muriel L. Crawford, J.D., FLMI, CLU, ChFC, CEBS (retired)
Associate General Counsel
Washington National Insurance Company
Author, *Life and Health Insurance Law*

claim practices defined under the Act that pertain to life and health insurance.

Claim Settlements

Sometimes a claim is resolved by settlement. Such a claim may be either disputed or undisputed.

Figure 16-3. Unfair claim practices defined under the NAIC Unfair Claims Settlement Practices Act.

- Knowingly misrepresenting to claimants and insureds relevant facts of policy provisions relating to coverages at issue
- Failing to acknowledge with reasonable promptness pertinent communications with respect to claims arising under policies
- Failing to adopt reasonable standards for the prompt investigation and settlement of claims arising under policies
- Not attempting in good faith to arrive at prompt, fair, and equitable settlement of submitted claims in which liability has become reasonably clear
- Compelling insureds or beneficiaries to institute suits to recover amounts due under policies by offering substantially less than the amounts ultimately recovered in suits brought by insureds or beneficiaries
- Refusing to pay claims without conducting a reasonable investigation
- Failing to affirm or deny coverage of claims within a reasonable time after having completed investigation related to such claims
- Attempting to settle or settling claims for less than the amount to which a reasonable person would believe the insured or beneficiary was entitled by reference to written or printed advertising material accompanying or made part of an application
- Attempting to settle or settling claims on the basis of an application that was materially altered without notice to, or knowledge or consent of, the insured
- Making claim payments to an insured or a beneficiary without indicating the coverage under which each payment is being made
- Unreasonably delaying the investigation or payment of claims by requiring both a formal proof of loss form and subsequent verification that would result in duplication of information and verification appearing in the formal proof of loss form
- Failing in the case of claim denials or offers of compromise settlement to promptly provide a reasonable, accurate explanation of the basis for such actions
- Failing to provide forms necessary to present claims within fifteen (15) calendar days of a request with reasonable explanation regarding their use

Disputed Claims

Some claim settlements result from a disputed claim in which the insurer and the claimant cannot agree on all the terms of the claim. For instance, a claimant may report that a disability is the result of an injury or illness, but information developed during the course of claim investigation may indicate strongly that the disability resulted from a preexisting condition excluded by a policy provision. If the insurer cannot gather sufficient proof to support its contention that the disability is not covered under the policy, the insurer may offer to settle the claim by paying the insured a lump sum instead of paying a series of disability benefits. The advantages to an insurer of settling a disputed claim are that the insurer saves the costs of committing its staff resources to the conflict over a lengthy period, as well as the costs of litigating the claim.

When a claim is disputed, the claimant and the insurer's legal staff may use the services of a mediator to help resolve the dispute. During such a mediation session, the claim analyst may be asked to provide specific information gathered during the investigation of a claim. In general, a mediation session considers information relating to

- The reason for the dispute
- The provisions of the policy
- Medical information, including the results of independent medical examinations
- Other information gathered by investigators

Undisputed Claims

Other claim settlements result from the insurer's attempt to provide a greater amount of benefits to a claimant early in the claim, rather than paying benefits over a period of time. Such an approach is appropriate when a claimant for disability income insurance needs a considerable sum of money to pay for unusual rehabilitation, to obtain education or training appropriate to another vocation, to purchase a business that can be handled even with the disability, or to invest the lump sum so as to realize a steady stream of income well into the future, beyond the time period during which disability benefits would be paid. Particularly when a disability income insurance policy covers only the insured's "own occupation," the insured may wish to receive benefits in a lump sum in order to have funds to begin another career.

Offering a lump-sum settlement is to the insurer's advantage because the costs of administering the claim over a period of time are eliminated. The lump-sum settlement is advantageous to the claimant, as well, because the lump sum can be used to arrange a suitable lifestyle that accommodates the disability. Providing a settlement for a claimant may result in a unique, innovative solution to the claimant's special needs. While disabled, few persons could expect to obtain such an amount of capital with which to restructure their lives.

In offering a lump-sum settlement, an insurer typically advises the claimant to seek professional advice on the legal, tax, accounting, and investment issues related to the settlement. In no case does the insurer provide such advice to a claimant because to do so would risk a possible charge of conflict of interest. Further, the insurer should consider what approach—lump-sum payment or series of benefit payments—is in the best interest of the claimant. The degree to which the claimant is financially dependent on a monthly benefit and the ability of the claimant to use a lump-sum payout to provide for his own well-being are issues that the insurer weighs in coming to a decision as to whether a settlement or benefit payments are more appropriate.

Key Terms and Concepts

claim philosophy
claim practices
managed care
cost containment
case management
utilization review
grace period
change of condition provision
insurability provision
extra-contract damages
compensatory damages
punitive damages

CHAPTER SEVENTEEN

Administering Life Insurance Claims

Learning Objectives

After studying this chapter, you should be able to

- Explain the importance of a claimant's statement, an authorization to release information, and a death certificate in handling a claim for life insurance
- Discuss the claim considerations for handling a death claim involving an insured's disappearance
- Describe the claim considerations for handling a death claim involving suicide
- Discuss the claim handling considerations for coverage that is supplemented by a waiver of premium for disability or an accidental death benefit rider
- Calculate the total amount of policy benefits by incorporating appropriate amounts for additions, deductions, and adjustments
- Explain how a claim analyst ensures that benefits are appropriately paid in various complicating circumstances
- Summarize the role of the claim analyst in handling policy settlement options

Chapter Outline

Handling Claims under Life Policies
Determining Whether a Loss Has Occurred
Determining Whether a Loss Is Covered

Developing Additional Information

Handling Supplemental Life Insurance Coverage
Waiver of Premium for Disability
Accidental Death Benefit
Family Benefit

Calculating the Amount of Policy Benefits
Amount of Death Benefits
Amount of Additions
Amount of Deductions
Adjustments for Misstatements of Age

Ensuring That Benefits Are Appropriately Paid
No Named Beneficiary
Death of the Beneficiary
Disqualification of the Beneficiary
Disappearance of the Beneficiary
Change in Beneficiary
Assigned Policy Proceeds
Payment to Attorneys or Tax Collectors
Unusual Claims
Administration of Settlement Options

A claimant for life insurance benefits may be a beneficiary of a policy, a person handling the estate of a deceased person, or a representative of a bank or other institution representing the interests of minor children or other persons needing special assistance. Administering individual and group life insurance claims requires a claim analyst to focus on a number of important elements because the analyst is responsible for ensuring that every claim is paid appropriately. Failure to pay claims accurately may subject the insurer to financial or legal complications and may hinder the insurer's ability to compete effectively.

The steps involved in handling life insurance claims include verifying whether a covered loss has occurred, determining whether supplemental benefits are payable, calculating the amount of policy benefits, and ensuring that the benefits are paid to an appropriate person and in an appropriate manner. In this chapter, we'll explain the general procedures involved in handling these aspects of individual and group life insurance claim administration. We'll also discuss some of the special considerations involved in handling life insurance claims accurately and equitably.

Handling Claims under Life Policies

After receiving notice of a claim, a claim analyst determines whether a loss has in fact occurred and whether that loss is covered under a policy.

Determining Whether a Loss Has Occurred

Notification of a death is usually sent to an insurer from a beneficiary or a marketer. To determine whether the insured-against loss occurred, the claim analyst collects certain items of proof including a claimant's statement, along with a death certificate or other acceptable proof of death. If the age of a deceased is in question—for example, if the age on the death certificate is different from the age in the policy records or on the application—the claim analyst usually asks for a birth certificate or other acceptable proof of age. If an insured has died outside North America, or if an insured has disappeared and death can only be presumed, the claim analyst follows different courses of action.

Claimant's statement. A ***claimant's statement,*** also called a *claim form,* is a document in which a claimant provides information concerning the deceased insured, including the date, place, and cause and circumstances of death. The claimant's statement also typically provides

- The names of all physicians or other practitioners who were consulted for any condition related to the cause of death or who were consulted within the past five years
- Information about all hospital confinement within the past five years
- The signature of the claimant, an authorized representative, or next of kin on an ***authorization to release information,*** a section of the claimant's statement that permits an insurer to obtain claim-specific information from medical caregivers and institutions, government agencies, other insurers, consumer reporting agencies, and numerous other sources

Figure 17-1 shows a typical claimant's statement for life insurance.

A claim analyst occasionally has difficulty obtaining a claimant's statement. A beneficiary or the next of kin of a deceased insured may be unwilling to sign the statement and to authorize collection of information about the insured. Usually the claim analyst tries to persuade the people closest to the insured to cooperate. In extreme situations in which no one cooperates with the investigation, the claim analyst may resort to obtaining a court order specifying what information may be obtained and the sources that may be used in gathering it.

Even when a claim analyst obtains a completed claimant's statement, the analyst may have difficulty obtaining detailed information from some sources. Concerns about patient privacy and confidentiality cause some medical caregivers to refuse to give insurers copies of a patient's entire medical file or to edit the medical records before releasing the information to the insurer. In some situations, attorneys or claimants try to control the information by requesting that all information be sent to them before it is sent to the insurer. The claim analyst then challenges the request to maintain the objectivity of information sources.

Death certificate. A ***death certificate*** is a document that attests to the death of a person and that bears the signature—and sometimes the seal—of an official authorized to issue such a certificate. Because of concerns about protecting the privacy of individuals and of ensuring the confidentiality of sensitive information, death certificates in some jurisdictions list only "natural causes" of death rather than specifying the

Figure 17-1. Claimant's statement for life insurance.

Full Name of Deceased	Number	Contract Number(s)
Home Address (Street, City, State, Zip)		Home Telephone Number ( )
Name of Last Employer	Last Occupation	Date Last Worked
Business Street Address	City/State/Zip	Business Telephone Number ( )
Please indicate desired method of settlement.	Was Policy Assigned?	Are any bankruptcy proceedings now pending against Deceased or any claimants?

CHILDREN OF DECEASED WHO ARE NOW LIVING:		CHILDREN OF DECEASED WHO HAVE DIED:		
Name and Address	Date of Birth	Name	Date of Birth	Date of Death

Date of Death	Cause and Circumstances of Death
Place of Death	

LIST ALL PHYSICIANS OR OTHER PRACTITIONERS CONSULTED FOR ANY CONDITION RELATED TO THE CAUSE OF DEATH.

Name	City/State	Dates Consulted

LIST OTHER PHYSICIANS OR PRACTITIONERS CONSULTED IN THE PAST FIVE (5) YEARS.

Name	City/State	Dates Consulted	Reason for Consultation

LIST ALL HOSPITAL CONFINEMENTS IN THE PAST FIVE (5) YEARS.

Name	City/State	From	To	Reason Confined

CONTINUED ON REVERSE SIDE – SIGNATURE REQUIRED

Figure 17-1. Claimant's statement for life insurance (continued).

CONTINUED FROM REVERSE SIDE

NAME OF DECEASED: ______________________________

AUTHORIZATION TO RELEASE INFORMATION

Upon presentation of the original or a reproduction of this authorization, I authorize any medical professional, hospital or other medical-care institution, insurance support organization, pharmacy, governmental agency, insurance company, employer, benefit plan administrator, accountant, or financial advisor to provide ABC LIFE INSURANCE COMPANY or any investigative service or other agent acting on its behalf, or an agent, attorney, consumer reporting agency or independent administrator acting on its behalf, information concerning employment, finances or insurance, advice, care or treatment provided the deceased person named above, including information relating to mental illness, use of drugs, use of alcohol, HIV (AIDS virus) and/or sexually transmitted diseases.

NOTICE Under applicable state law, any person who knowingly files a claim containing false or misleading information, or who conceals information with intent to defraud or mislead an insurance company or other person, may be guilty of a felony or subject to other criminal and/or civil penalties.

NEW YORK RESIDENTS ONLY Any person who knowingly and with intent to defraud any insurance company or other person files A Statement of Claim containing any materially false information, or conceals for the purpose of misleading, information concerning any fact material thereto, commits a fraudulent insurance act, which is a crime and shall also be subject to a civil penalty not to exceed five thousand dollars and the stated value of the claim for each such violation.

SIGNATURE OF CLAIMANT I represent the information on the front of this form is true and complete and I understand that such information will be used by ABC LIFE INSURANCE COMPANY for the purpose of evaluating a claim for insurance benefits.

____

Signature of Claimant, Authorized Representative, or Next of Kin | Date | Age | Social Security Number

____

Claimant's address | Street | City | State | Zip Code | Phone Number

____

Signature of Estate Representative (if not Claimant) | Date

(Please enclose a certified copy of Letters of Administration)

For claims assistance, please call ABC Life Insurance Company.

MAIL TO: ATTN: LIFE CO. BENEFITS

cause of death as being from a particular disease. Most insurers in the United States accept an official death certificate, either an original or a certified copy, as proof of loss. Most Canadian insurers accept an official death certificate, an APS, a coroner's certificate of death, or a hospital's certificate of death as proof of the death of an insured.

In some circumstances, an insurer requires additional evidence such as newspaper clippings or an autopsy report. Certain jurisdictions have held that an insurer may be required to accept as proof of death a document that attests to the death of an insured and that is signed by a person with knowledge of the insured's death. In such circumstances, the insurer generally obtains copies of official death records, if any are available, to corroborate information in the unofficial document.

Death outside North America. Claim analysts sometimes have difficulty establishing that a loss has occurred when the death of an insured takes place outside North America. Because many cases of fraud are connected to these types of claims, the claim analyst pays particular attention to establishing accurate information concerning such a death. If documents offered as proof of death are in a language other than English, the claim analyst must have the documents translated by a qualified person. Because investigating deaths occurring outside North America can be difficult, we'll discuss claim handling related to foreign death claims in Chapter 20.

Disappearance of the insured. Occasionally a claim analyst finds that the death of an insured person must be presumed because the person has disappeared. If a claim involves a death resulting from a specific peril that can account for an insured's disappearance, and if there are no other suspicious circumstances, the claim analyst generally approves the claim. For example, suppose a Boy Scout leader takes a group of Scouts on a hike in the mountains. A sudden thunderstorm causes flooding, and the Scouts see their leader swept away in a torrent. His body is not recovered. In such a situation, if the body were not found after a reasonable period and if no evidence of foul play were found, the claim analyst would more than likely approve the claim.

If an insured has disappeared and there is no specific peril and no definite proof of death, the claimant cannot provide proof of death in support of the life insurance claim, and without such proof the insurer is unable to pay the policy benefits without further investigation. If an insured has been continually absent from his home for a specified period, generally seven years in most jurisdictions, an application to a court may be made by an insurer or a claimant for an order presuming death. It is not always necessary to wait seven years provided evidence of death, such as an accident, is present. When reviewing the application, the court considers four elements:

1. Whether the insured has been missing from his home or usual residence for seven years

2. Whether the insured's absence has been continuous and whether any factors such as large debts, marital problems, or criminal indictments exist that would give cause for the disappearance

3. Whether the insured can be located by diligent search and inquiry

4. Whether the persons most likely to hear from the insured have not heard from him

If the court evaluates the evidence and is satisfied that the insured is more than likely deceased, the court issues a ***presumptive death certificate,*** which is a court-issued document stating that a person is presumed to be dead. However, if opposing evidence is submitted showing that the insured may still be alive, the case is usually referred to a jury for a decision. When a claim analyst receives a presumptive death certificate, any proceeds due on a death claim are processed according to the date of death shown on the court order.

If the claim analyst concludes that an insured person is determined to disappear and does not wish to have her location revealed, the claim analyst respects the insured's wishes. The claim analyst can, however, justify nonpayment of insurance benefits only by obtaining a signed, dated, and notarized statement from the insured attesting to identifying information such as date of birth, place of birth, and the names of such persons as the insured's parents, spouse, and children. Insight 17-1 presents additional information about disappearance claims.

Reappearance of the insured. Suppose an insured has been declared dead by a court and the policy proceeds have been paid in full. If the insured person later reappears, the insurer usually has the right to recover the money because it was paid under a mistake of fact. If the insurer paid less than the full amount of benefits in a compromise settlement, however, the insurer generally cannot recover the benefits because courts will not disturb a compromise settlement.

Determining Whether a Loss Is Covered

In deciding whether the insurer is liable to pay benefits for the loss, the claim analyst first determines the status of the policy and verifies the identity of the insured. Then the analyst examines all policy exclusions, including those concerning aviation, avocations, and suicide. If death of a proposed insured has occurred during underwriting and before the policy has been delivered, the analyst determines whether the insurer is liable for paying benefits.

Insight 17-1 Disappearance Claims

When some people think of a disappearance claim, they often develop the classic mental image of a person who, for no apparent reason, vanishes from the face of the earth. While such situations can and do occur, the claim professional will more likely than not be confronted with conditions that are not quite so obvious. In this discussion, I would like to define a disappearance claim as a death claim resulting from an incident in which the insured's body cannot be located. Perhaps the scope is a bit too broad, but I am intentionally making it that way to emphasize a point. Situations occur, and with a fair amount of regularity, in which what appears to be a legitimate and logical claim turns out to be anything but legitimate.

Disappearance claims come in many forms, but are frequently associated with sports-related accidents (scuba diving, snorkeling, mountaineering); travel-related accidents (airplane, train, ship and automobile mishaps); natural disasters (floods, earthquakes, avalanches, storms); and violent acts, including homicide. In broad terms, I consider disappearance claims as either legitimate or staged, good or bad, real or artificial, but it is frequently impossible to tell which is which on the surface. The vast majority of claims are legitimate, and the goal of the claim analyst, as always, is to develop the facts of the case and to make an accurate decision.

With no body available, suspicions arise, and justifiably so. In addition to the many problems commonly associated with a claim, perhaps the single most important question is whether the insured is really dead, particularly if the case offers no hospital records, no autopsy report, and no medical doctor present to certify the death. Common questions in the mind of the claim analyst are "When do I start the investigation?" and "Where and how do I start?"

I cannot emphasize the importance of initiating an investigation of a possible disappearance claim as soon as possible. As time passes, information is often harder to obtain, leads disappear, stories may change, and reconstruction of the facts becomes increasingly difficult. Equally important is to employ the services of a highly trained investigator. Disappearance claims are generally extremely complex, demand excellent interviewing and investigative skills, may require extensive travel, and can be dangerous as well. Further, contacting a reinsurance company may be helpful in developing the facts of a disappearance case, particularly if the reinsurer has begun to receive notices of death or disappearance of the same insured from multiple insurers.

It is a mistake to limit a disappearance investigation to the circumstances surrounding the insured's apparent death. Information concerning the insured's business, finances, health, interests, habits, associates, and activities can all help develop a better understanding of the case and may expose a motive for the disappearance or rule out a motive for it.

Finally, a few additional suggestions for the claim examiner faced with a disappearance claim:

- Do not accept stories at face value. Confirm accounts of what apparently happened by consulting multiple sources. Collaborative evidence may be gathered not only from persons, but from newspaper accounts, travel itineraries, and police, fire department, accident, Coast Guard, weather bureau, and oceanographic agencies.
- Conduct and record interviews in such a way that they will be usable later in the event of litigation.
- Consider monitoring the activities of interested parties such as a beneficiary or business partner.
- Be patient, persistent, and thorough.

From John B. Hitzeman, FLMI, ALHC, "Disappearance Claims," *Life Insurance Workshop Reports,* 1996: 53–59. Adapted by permission from the International Claim Association.

Aviation exclusion. You may recall from Chapter 5 that aviation exclusion riders are typically used in cases in which the aviation hazard (1) is too great for any coverage or (2) cannot be measured. If a policy contains an aviation exclusion and the insured dies while engaged in the excluded activity, no benefits are payable under the policy.

Avocation exclusion. An exclusion for avocation typically covers activities, such as skydiving, auto racing, and rock climbing, that are considered dangerous. An avocation exclusion usually provides that, if an insured dies from participation in a specified avocation, no death benefits—or, if the policy so states, only limited death benefits—will be payable.

Suicide exclusion. If an insured person dies as a result of verified suicide, the claim analyst checks the policy to determine the period during which death by suicide must be excluded from benefits—that is, the period during which a death by suicide is ineligible for coverage under the policy. Most jurisdictions provide for a one-year suicide exclusion period. Generally, this period begins in the United States on the date of original policy issue. If the original policy lapses and is reinstated, in most jurisdictions the period still is considered to have begun on the date when the original policy was issued. In Canada, the suicide exclusion period begins on the date of policy issue, so that if a policy has been reinstated, this period begins again on the date the policy is reinstated. The length of the new suicide exclusion period is the same as the length of the original period.

> **Fast Fact**
>
> Since 1980, approximately 1.3 percent of all deaths in the United States have been caused by suicide.
>
> **Source:** American Council of Life Insurance, "Causes of Death in the United States," *Life Insurance Fact Book*, 1996: 116.

If the claim analyst determines that an insured died by suicide within the exclusion period, the insurer returns only the premiums paid and does not pay policy benefits. Returning the premiums paid is considered to be payment of the limited benefit agreed upon when the application for insurance was submitted and when the insurer accepted the risk. Returning the premiums is not considered to be a refund, and the insurer is not considered to have rescinded the coverage. By invoking the suicide exclusion, the insurer is not contesting the policy nor attempting to rescind it, but instead is affirming the validity of the contract by applying the limited-benefit-for-death-by-suicide provision in the contract. During the investigation of a death by suicide, the claim analyst is governed by the statutes of the jurisdiction in which the coverage was issued.

In establishing that a person committed suicide, an investigator must establish the existence of and show a direct relationship among (1) the deceased's intention to commit suicide, (2) the deceased's self-destructive action, and (3) the death resulting from that action. If doubt exists about any of these factors, the claim analyst investigates further to determine, if possible, the cause of death. A death resulting from natural causes, accident, or homicide is not, of course, a death by suicide. However, some deaths, such as those from poisoning, vehicle collisions, drug overdoses, and weapons may be the result of accident, homicide, or suicide. The claim analyst must distinguish carefully among the facts relating to a death to be as certain as possible of the cause.

Concerning basic death benefits, most jurisdictions require that an insurer assume the burden of proof to show that a person committed suicide. In a case in which the facts indicate that an insured committed suicide, but no definite proof of suicide is discovered, courts generally have held that the death is not a result of suicide. Concerning benefits for accidental death, however, most jurisdictions require that the claimant or beneficiary assume the burden of proof that the cause of death was not suicide, but was the result of an accident.

An investigation of a possible suicide can be complicated by the reluctance of a deceased person's family and friends to admit that the deceased may have committed suicide. In order to deny or conceal that a suicide occurred, some persons may refuse to relate important information, such as recent conversations with the deceased, and may destroy evidence, such as a suicide note or an empty container of barbiturates. The claim analyst is called upon to be tactful, but persistent, in discovering the facts surrounding an insured's death and in reaching an accurate, equitable determination of the cause of death.

Death of the proposed insured during underwriting. When a proposed insured dies after the application has been submitted but before underwriting has been completed and the policy issued, claims and underwriting must work together closely to ensure that an equitable decision is made concerning payment of policy benefits. Information in the application and the circumstances of the death help determine whether the insurer is liable to pay policy proceeds.

Most individual life and health insurance applications and premium receipts contain a ***change in health statement*** that requires a proposed insured to notify the insurer in writing if her health or any material information in the application changes before the policy is delivered. Some insurers require the agent and the policyowner to sign a change in health statement at the time the policy is delivered. The change in health statement helps protect an insurer against antiselection that might result if an insured's health changes significantly during underwriting, and particularly if the insured dies during that period from such a health change. A typical change in health statement is shown in Figure 17-2. The change in health statement is similar to the change of condition provision discussed in Chapter 16. The change of condition provision states that, for a policy to become effective, all conditions described in the application must still be true at the time of delivery.

If an insurer wishes not to be liable for paying policy benefits because of a change in the proposed insured's health during the time of underwriting, the insurer is required in most jurisdictions to show that (1) the change in health directly affected the degree of risk for the case, (2) the proposed insured knew of the change in health, and (3) no

Figure 17-2. Typical change in health statement.

"I understand that no policy based on this application will be effective unless all of my statements and answers in this application continue to be true as of the date I receive the policy. I understand that if my health or any of my answers or statements change prior to delivery of the policy, I must so inform the insurer in writing."

ambiguity exists in its change in health statement. If a proposed insured dies as the result of a sudden event such as an accident or an acute condition about which the proposed insured had no prior knowledge, benefits are payable under the policy if a binding premium receipt was issued, and may be payable if a conditional premium receipt was issued.

What action does an insurer take if a proposed insured commits suicide during underwriting? Suicide is usually excluded during the contestable period by a statement in the life insurance contract. However, during underwriting, no contract has yet been issued. Most insurers rely on the language of the premium receipt, which should state clearly that coverage will be effective subject to the limitations contained in the policy applied for—and such a policy would contain the suicide provision.

We have mentioned the need for claim analysts to maintain a close working relationship with underwriters. Insight 17-2 discusses the need for mutual cooperation between claims and underwriting.

Developing Additional Information

After determining that a loss has occurred and that the loss is covered, the claim analyst next orders whatever additional information is needed to make a decision on the claim for life insurance benefits. Particularly if the policy is still contestable, the claim analyst gathers such information as medical records, motor vehicle reports, and criminal court records, and may also order an investigative consumer report.

By ordering medical records from available sources—medical caregivers, clinics, hospitals, and nursing homes, among others—the claim analyst can determine valuable information about the death. In ordering medical records, the analyst includes a copy of the claimant's authorization to obtain such records and makes each request very specific, spelling out such requirements as "all records within the last five years" and "all information relating to treatment for diabetes." Many medical caregivers are reluctant to provide medical information con-

Insight 17-2 The Reciprocity of Underwriting and Claims

Underwriting and claims have many similarities. Both are part of the same process of risk assessment. The critical difference is the timing. One process begins at the pre-issue stage, and the other at the pre-payment stage. Each area has accountability for ensuring that the insurance company participates in the right risks.

One of the ways to address the need to maintain and increase skills in both areas is to provide that seminars and lectures sponsored for underwriters are also open to claim staff, and vice versa. New developments in cancer research, genetic engineering, and laboratory technology have already resulted in many additions to the abbreviations and terms frequently seen in APSs. Familiarity with this information will greatly enhance claim analysts' ability to recognize situations in which claim files should be referred to underwriting colleagues so that the claim adjudication process will be conducted appropriately.

Having a good working relationship between claims and underwriting means that when a referral on a contestable case occurs, both claim and underwriting staff will understand what is expected and why. The relationship can be further enhanced by forming a committee consisting of claim and underwriting members, plus representatives from policyowner service. The role of this group is to review claims, to detect trends or areas of vulnerability, and to make recommendations to address the issues.

Claim staff are responsible for making sure that underwriters are aware of the impact of not clarifying ambiguous or contradictory statements on applications, of questions left blank, and of statements changed without obtaining the required signatures. Claim analysts and underwriters also need to be informed about the impact of possible misjudgments during underwriting. As an example, an applicant may state that he is a nonsmoker, although the urinalysis test results show some level of cotinine, a metabolite of nicotine. If the policy is nevertheless issued on a nonsmoker basis, problems may arise at claim time.

Communication is a critical element in any successful relationship. The proactive approach tends to be well received and helps to minimize those situations in which we sigh and think, "If only I had. . . ." The claim database is a veritable goldmine for underwriting, containing vast stores of information on varied causes of death, durations of illness, and many other topics of value to underwriters. Sharing this information and discussing any problematic issues will help ensure that risk assessment proceeds as it should: equitably, rapidly, and accurately.

From Miriam Bester, ALHC, ACS, "Reciprocity: Underwriting and Claims," *Life Insurance Workshop Reports,* 1994: 10–14. Adapted by permission of the International Claim Association.

cerning such sensitive conditions as AIDS and drug abuse without a detailed request asking for exactly that information.

Motor vehicle records can give the claim analyst historical information about the insured's driving habits, including convictions for reckless driving and driving under the influence of drugs or alcohol. Generally, the claim analyst must submit the insured's driver's license number in order to obtain the information. Records of criminal court proceedings reveal information about an insured's possible criminal activities.

During the course of investigating the claim, the claim analyst keeps the claimant informed of progress by sending status letters. Such letters are important to deliver top-quality customer service. If the claim analyst discovers information that indicates misrepresentation or fraud, that information must be conveyed tactfully to the claimant. In such a situation, the analyst explains the effect of misrepresentation or fraud on the claim decision and cites the sources of information on which the decision was based. If the claim is denied and the analyst sends the claimant a denial letter, that letter should include a statement indicating that if the claimant can provide additional information that might refute the information on which the denial was based, the insurer will consider such information in re-examining the claim.

Handling Supplemental Life Insurance Coverage

As we explained in a previous chapter, the insurance protection provided by most life insurance policies may be expanded by supplemental benefit riders, including those for waiver of premium for disability and accidental death benefit. If a claimant is covered by such supplemental riders, the claim analyst determines whether additional benefits are due under the policy.

Waiver of Premium for Disability

If a person becomes totally disabled and is insured under a life insurance policy that includes a waiver of premium for disability (WP) rider, the insurer waives payment of all premiums that become due during the period of disability. The duty of the claim analyst is first to verify that the claimant has satisfied the waiting period, if any is required, and then to verify that the claimant is in fact disabled according to the definition in the rider. To make this determination, the claim analyst typically uses such tools as the claim form, the disability information form, the claimant's medical records, including the Attending Physician's Statement, the claimant's financial records, and the claimant's job description and statements from the claimant's employer. If a claimant in the United States has been awarded Social Security disability benefits, the claim analyst obtains a copy of the Social Security Award letter from the insured.

The disability information form submitted by the claimant contains such information as

- The initial date of disability
- The claimant's occupation
- Additional sources, if any, of disability income, including names and addresses of providers of such benefits

As soon as possible after the disability claim is submitted, the claim analyst usually tries to develop a complete job description, containing a list of all the claimant's duties. The job description may be obtained from the insured or the employer although some employers limit the information they will provide to verification of the date of hire, the date last worked, and the reason the claimant is not currently working. The claim analyst also verifies that the claimant has a job to which he can return—in other words, that the claimant's original job has not been discontinued.

Initial review of a disability claim is especially important if the disability appears to be one that will continue for a year or longer. The experience of most insurers indicates that disabilities lasting one year or more are likely to continue past two years. Therefore, gathering information on such a possibly long-term claim is essential to ensure that the claim is valid. Typically, the claim analyst gathers not only the usual information from the claim form, medical and financial records, and job-related data, but also determines the claimant's education and work background, often by interviewing the claimant and, if necessary, by using a specialist trained in such investigations. Income tax forms can also reveal whether a claimant has multiple income sources and whether the claimant is able to perform the duties of an occupation other than his primary employment. Even if an insured has personal wealth that is adequate to pay premiums, the waiver of premium for disability would be approved if the insured became disabled under the terms of the insurance contract. If a claimant is able to perform the duties of another occupation, he may be considered partially rather than totally disabled.

If the claim analyst finds that the claimant has also filed a claim for disability income coverage or a waiver of premium request with another insurer, the claim analyst usually sends a letter of inquiry to the other insurer to verify the claim-related information. Sometimes the other insurer will have developed information that will enable the claim analyst to make a rapid judgment on the claim. In addition, the claim analyst verifies that if the life insurance policy contained waivers of coverage for participation in certain activities, such as specified dangerous avocations, the disability did not result from such participation.

Most insurers review each active waiver of premium case at least annually to determine whether the claimant is still disabled and eligible to receive the benefits of the waiver of premium rider, and to certify that the total of claims paid has not exceeded the maximum benefit payable, if the coverage has such a limit. Claims for disabilities that the insurer's experience has shown are usually short-term may be reviewed more frequently, usually every three to six months. Generally, a claim analyst telephones the claimant at home or at work to ask about the claimant's medical condition and to check the type of work, if any, that the claimant is able to perform. The claim analyst may also request copies of the most recent tax returns from the claimant and may contact the claimant's medical caregivers by telephone or mail to update the insurer's files and to verify the claimant's current status. For some cases, the claim analyst instigates a more detailed investigation to ensure that the waiver of premium benefit is justified. If a claimant does not supply proof of continued disability, most insurers notify the claimant that she is being removed from waiver status and that she will be responsible for paying future life insurance premiums if she wishes the coverage to remain in force.

Waiver of premium claimants who have received benefits for two years are generally classified in one of two ways:

1. Claimants who show little possibility of eventual rehabilitation

2. Claimants who may be expected to improve or for whom new medical treatments may promise partial or complete recovery

The claim analyst usually verifies the continuing status of a claimant in the first group by obtaining a statement annually from the claimant's medical caregiver. For a claimant in the second group, the claim analyst typically continues to update the case annually, gathering information to demonstrate the claimant's current condition and ability to work and pay life insurance premiums.

When a claim analyst handles a waiver of premium claim submitted under group coverage, the claim analyst checks two additional items. Specifically, the claim analyst determines whether the claimant has satisfied the group policy's actively-at-work provision and the employee class definition, if any. For example, if the group policy provides waiver of premium benefits only for salaried employees, and not for exempt employees or those who are union members, the claim analyst verifies that the employee who has submitted a waiver of premium claim is a salaried employee. If the claim analyst finds that the employee's disability began before the original effective date of the group coverage, the analyst usually does not approve waiver of premium benefits. The claim analyst also determines that the claimant satisfies the policy's definition of full-time employee, if the coverage is only for such employees. To make such a determination, the claim analyst may examine payroll records and the employee's enrollment card.

Occasionally the information gathered in administering a disability claim shows serious inconsistencies and factual contradictions. The claim analyst investigates such a case in great detail. We'll consider some of the approaches used in handling questionable claims when we discuss misrepresentation and claims fraud in a later chapter.

Accidental Death Benefit

The purpose of the accidental death benefit (ADB) rider is to provide an additional death benefit above the face amount of the policy if the insured's death occurs as the result of an accident. An insurer may charge an extra premium for ADB coverage issued to persons who have hazardous occupations or may decline to issue the ADB rider.

Some policies contain accidental death benefit provisions with certain limitations related to the insured's age, the time span during which death occurred, and the proximate cause of death. An age limitation specifies an age range during which benefits will be paid and cites ages below or above which benefits will not be paid. For instance, an accidental death benefit provision may specify that benefits will be paid only until age 70. A beneficiary of an insured who dies at age 71 cannot, therefore, expect accidental death benefits to be paid under the policy. Some provisions specify that an insured must reach a certain age—for instance, five years—before benefits will be payable.

Another type of provision limits the span of time between the date that an injury occurred and the date that death occurs if the death is to be considered accidental. Most insurers specify 90 days as the maximum time span allowed between an injury and a death, although some policies allow longer periods. For instance, if a policy provides a 90-day limit on this span, and an insured is injured on February 10 and dies the next June 10, no accidental death benefits would probably be paid under the policy.

Some cases can present conflicting information concerning the ***proximate cause*** of a death—that is, the event that directly caused a death, or the event that led to an unbroken chain of events resulting in death. Provisions of most insurance policies limit accidental death benefit coverage only to accidents that directly caused a person to die. For instance, an insured might suffer a heart attack or a stroke—a natural event—that resulted in a fatal vehicle accident or other mishap. In such a case, the claim analyst examines the autopsy report and medical records to ascertain the immediate cause of death. If the death resulted from the natural event, no accidental death benefits would be payable. If the death resulted from the mishap, accidental death benefits would probably be payable.

Another type of situation in which the limit of proximate cause of death may apply involves an injury that causes an illness or a disease, which then causes death. In such a situation, the injury is considered to be the proximate cause of death, and accidental death benefits are payable. As an example, suppose a swimmer is struck by a motorboat and inhales a quantity of water. Although the swimmer does not immediately drown, he develops pneumonia, from which he dies within several weeks. In this situation, the proximate cause of the swimmer's death was the motorboat accident, and accidental death benefits would probably be payable.

If an insured person dies during an altercation, the claim analyst seeks to determine whether the death was foreseeable by the insured. The claim analyst usually interviews all witnesses and other concerned persons so as to determine as nearly as possible the circumstances of the death and whether the death was accidental. In addition, the claim analyst investigates the relationship between the deceased insured and any persons involved in the altercation, particularly if any

Fast Fact

Through the mid-1990's in the United States, between 2.1 and 2.3 percent of all deaths were caused by accidents other than motor vehicle accidents, which accounted for about 1.9 percent of all deaths.

Source: American Council of Life Insurance, "Causes of Death in the United States," *Life Insurance Fact Book*, 1996: 116.

of those persons is a beneficiary of the policy. For some cases, the claim analyst obtains information from law enforcement officials.

Family Benefit

An insured with individual life insurance coverage may add a family benefit rider to insure the lives of a spouse and children. Such a rider usually provides coverage in a lesser amount on the spouse and each child than on the primary insured. After a policy with such a rider is issued, children who are born or adopted into the family, or who become part of the family by marriage, are usually covered when they reach the age of at least 15 days (or whatever minimum age the rider specifies). A child born in or out of wedlock is usually covered by a family benefit rider, but foster children are generally not covered by this type of rider.

The claim analyst verifies that any person whose death occasions a claim under a family benefit rider is either a spouse or a natural child, adopted child, or stepchild of the primary insured. The documents that the claim analyst uses for such verification include a marriage certificate, a birth certificate, and an adoption certificate.

Some family benefit riders provide that, on the death of the primary insured, the spouse and children receive paid-up life insurance. When a claim is submitted under such a rider, the claim analyst verifies that the deceased person was a family member covered by the paid-up policy. Although most insurers require that life insurance policies on a single life be returned to the insurer when a death claim is submitted, insurers do not generally require that a policy with a family benefit rider be returned because the rider continues to provide coverage on other family members. The claim analyst may request a copy of the original policy, however, to verify its provisions, and may ask that the original policy be returned at the death of the last person insured under the policy. In addition, the insurer may require that the policy be returned if misrepresentation is ever found or if the insurer is returning premiums because the primary insured commits suicide during the suicide exclusion period.

Calculating the Amount of Policy Benefits

In figuring the amount of life insurance benefits to be paid to a claimant, the claim analyst determines three amounts: (1) the amount of death benefits, (2) the amount of any additions to that figure, and (3) the amount of any deductions from that figure. In making the total calculation, the claim analyst checks many details of the coverage, including information about policy dividends, policy loans, policy premiums, additional coverage and accidental death benefits, and various kinds of interest. The analyst may also adjust the amount of policy benefits for misstatements of age.

Amount of Death Benefits

Because a life insurance contract is not a contract of indemnity, the claimant is not reimbursed for an actual amount of loss. Instead, the amount of death benefits due upon the death of the insured is based on the face amount of the policy. The claim analyst begins, therefore, by determining the amount of the basic death benefit payable. Usually the basic death benefit is the face amount of the policy. However, if the policy was in force under a reduced paid-up insurance nonforfeiture option, for instance, then the basic benefit payable is less than the face amount. Or if the policy application contained a misstatement of age, the policy's face amount will be adjusted to account for the misstatement.

Amount of Additions

The claim analyst next determines any amounts that should be added to the amount of basic death benefits. Amounts that can be added include the following:

- Paid-up additional insurance
- Accidental death benefits
- Excess premiums paid in advance
- Policy dividends not yet paid
- Policy dividends left with the insurer to earn interest
- Interest on delayed claims payment
- Loan interest paid in advance

Amount of Deductions

The claim analyst is also obligated to deduct certain amounts from the basic death benefits. These amounts include the following:

- Premiums due but unpaid during the grace period
- Loans against the policy
- Interest on any policy loans

If the insured had died during the grace period and had neglected to pay the premium due by the end of that period, the amount of premiums due would be subtracted from the death benefits. Further, if the policyowner had taken out a loan against the policy, the amount of the loan and any interest on that loan would be deducted from the amount of death benefits.

To illustrate additions and deductions, we'll use an example. Suppose a policyowner purchased a life insurance policy in the amount of $200,000 plus $150,000 of accidental death benefits. The policy bore no dividends. Later, the policyowner chose to buy $60,000 of additional coverage. At the time of his death, which resulted from an accident, he (1) had paid $500 in advance premiums and (2) had an outstanding policy loan of $22,000 plus $1,500 of interest on that loan. The claim analyst calculated the total amount of benefits payable under this policy as follows:

Face value of policy	$200,000
+ ADB	150,000
+ Additional coverage	60,000
+ Premium paid in advance	500
– Unpaid policy loan	22,000
– Unpaid interest on policy loan	1,500
Total death benefit payable	$387,000

Adjustments for Misstatements of Age

As you have learned, the premium for most individual life insurance policies is affected by the age of the insured. Similarly, life insurance premiums for small-group coverage may require individual premiums that are affected by the age of each insured person. In either situation, the claim analyst verifies the age of the deceased insured to be certain that the premiums paid have accurately reflected the amount of risk borne by the insurer. If the claim analyst determines that the age of the insured was misstated on the application for insurance, and if a different age on the application would have resulted in a different premium being charged, then the analyst adjusts the amount of death benefits appropriately. Such an adjustment is permitted throughout the life of the policy and is not affected by the incontestability clause.

Generally, an adjustment for misstatement of age results in a death benefit amount equal to the death benefits that the premium paid would have purchased at the correct age, according to the insurer's published premium rates at the time of policy issue. Suppose, for example, that an insured stated her age as 38 when she purchased $150,000 of whole life insurance. She was charged an annual premium of $1.42 per thousand, or $213 (150 × $1.42). At the time of her death, the claim analyst discovered a discrepancy between the insured's age as stated on the application and her age at time of death—in fact, the insured was 45 years old when she applied for coverage. According to the insurer's published premium rates at the time of policy issue, the paid premium of $213 a year would have purchased approximately $136,000 of whole life insurance. Therefore, the amount of death benefits due is approximately $136,000, plus and minus any amounts as we have discussed in the previous sections. If the insured's age had been lower than 38 at the time of application, the amount of coverage that the premium would purchase would probably have been more; in that situation, the claim analyst would adjust the amount of death benefits upward accordingly.

The burden of proof for showing that an insured is *older* than the age stated on the application rests with the insurer. The burden of proof for showing that an insured is *younger* than the age stated on the application or than the age calculated by the insurer rests with the claimant. Proof of an insured's age may be established by various documents, including

- A copy of the insured's birth certificate or birth record
- A certificate of baptism, bar or bat mitzvah, or other religious ceremony that establishes the insured's age at the time of the ceremony
- A record of birth written in a family Bible

If none of these proofs of age is available, the claim analyst may accept other proofs of age, such as banking or medical records, school records, marriage records, census records, police or motor vehicle records, passport information, and similar official or semi-official documents that contain references to the insured's age. The number and type of acceptable records vary from one case to another and from one insurer to another, but generally depend on the quality and apparent accuracy of the records and on the amount of death benefits.

Besides checking age information on the claim form and using the sources we have mentioned, the claim analyst also attempts to verify an insured's correct age by noting such elements as

- The ages of the insured's children
- The date when the insured retired
- Records of government- or employer-paid retirement benefits
- The cause of death, which should be consistent with the age of the insured

Besides increasing the death benefits payable, an adjustment for age may cause an insured to be ineligible to receive certain benefits. If the accidental death benefit, for instance, is payable only until an insured reaches a specified age, usually 65 or 70, then an insured whose age at death exceeds the limit will probably not be eligible for accidental death benefits.

Ensuring That Benefits Are Appropriately Paid

To ensure that death benefits are appropriately paid, the claim analyst must determine the right person or entity to receive the benefits and the correct manner in which the benefits are to be paid. Usually the beneficiary—a spouse, a child or children, an estate, a trust, a charity, or almost any other entity—is clearly named on the insurance application. However, a number of circumstances can complicate the claim analyst's responsibility to ensure that the benefits are paid to the correct person. These circumstances include situations in which no named beneficiary exists; the named beneficiary has died, been disqualified, or disappeared; a change in beneficiary has occurred; policy proceeds have been assigned; or unusual circumstances exist that require special handling of policy proceeds. After we examine these complicating circumstances involving determination of the right payee, we'll briefly discuss the administration of settlement options used for paying policy benefits.

No Named Beneficiary

If a policy does not name a beneficiary, the claim analyst usually designates the benefits as payable to the estate of the deceased insured. According to the laws of some jurisdictions, however, in such a situation the policy proceeds are payable to a designated class of beneficiaries who become eligible when no beneficiary has been named or when no named beneficiary survives the insured.

Death of the Beneficiary

If the beneficiary named in an application for insurance has predeceased the insured, the claim analyst checks the application and other information in the case file to determine whether an alternate beneficiary was named. Such a beneficiary, called a ***contingent beneficiary*** or *secondary beneficiary,* is the person or entity named to receive life insurance benefits if the primary beneficiary has died before the insured. If no contingent beneficiary was named, the proceeds are paid to the estate of the insured.

Disqualification of the Beneficiary

In some unusual cases, a beneficiary is deliberately responsible for the death of an insured and is legally disqualified from receiving policy proceeds. If an insurer can show that the beneficiary applied for insurance on the life of the insured with the intent of profiting from the insured's death, then the insurer is required to return only the amount of premiums paid with interest. If, however, the policy was applied for in good faith, but the designated beneficiary is judged to have been deliberately responsible for the insured's death, then the insurer must pay the policy proceeds, but not to that designated beneficiary.

The insurer usually delays payment of the proceeds until the investigation into the death of the insured is complete. If the investigation continues for a long period, the insurer generally deposits the amount of policy proceeds with a court for disbursement after a legal decision has been reached concerning the beneficiary's guilt or innocence. In some situations, the insurer is allowed to pay the proceeds to a contingent beneficiary or to the insured's estate instead of paying the proceeds to a beneficiary if the beneficiary has been convicted of the death of the insured. A verdict of "not guilty" in a criminal action is separate from the verdict in a civil suit, so that a beneficiary found not guilty in a criminal case can be denied policy proceeds if he is held in a civil trial to have wrongfully caused the insured's death.

Disappearance of the Beneficiary

If a named beneficiary has disappeared and cannot be located within a reasonable period, the insurer generally follows the laws and statutes prevailing in the state or province in which the beneficiary's last address is located. Most states have adopted variations of the NAIC Uniform Disposition of Unclaimed Property Act and, therefore, an insurer usually holds the proceeds for a specified period—typically five to seven years—and then deposits with the state all proceeds that cannot be paid to a missing beneficiary. The state holds the money in trust for such a beneficiary, who may petition the state for the property. In all the Canadian provinces except Quebec, an insurer deposits unpayable proceeds with a court, which then determines the proper payee. In Quebec, three years after proceeds become payable, insurance companies are required by law to deposit proceeds payable to untraceable beneficiaries with the ***public curator,*** a person authorized to handle the affairs of missing persons, among others.

Fast Fact

Tracking a beneficiary can sometimes be difficult because of the long-term nature of most life insurance policies. For instance, according to a Canadian Life and Health Insurance Association survey, 58.2 percent of life insurance policies had been in effect for 30 or more years when they became claims; 72 percent of the policies had been in effect for 20 or more years.

Source: Canadian Life and Health Insurance Association, "Analysis of Death Benefit Payments," *Canadian Life and Health Insurance Facts,* 1996: 16.

Change in Beneficiary

When an insured has changed the beneficiary of a policy, the claim analyst verifies that the change was accurately made and that the new beneficiary is eligible to receive the policy proceeds. Almost every beneficiary is a ***revocable beneficiary***—that is, a beneficiary whose right to policy proceeds can be cancelled or reduced by the policyowner at any time before the insured's death. At the time the insured dies, the insurer will pay the policy proceeds to the beneficiary named in the policy. If a policyowner has named an ***irrevocable beneficiary***—that is, a beneficiary whose right to policy proceeds cannot be cancelled by a policyowner unless that beneficiary consents to the cancellation—then the insurer must pay the benefits to that irrevocable beneficiary. Only when an irrevocable beneficiary dies or signs a release may the policyowner name another beneficiary.

In Canada, the law provides that a spouse, child, parent, or grandchild named in any life insurance policy issued before July 1, 1962, was a ***preferred beneficiary,*** and the policyowner thereafter could not change the beneficiary to anyone outside this group of family members and could not obtain a policy loan or surrender nor assign the policy benefits without the written consent of the preferred beneficiary. The rights of a preferred beneficiary continue until that beneficiary dies, is divorced from the spouse-insured, or signs a release. Policies issued in Canada after July 1, 1962, do not have to follow the legal concept of preferred beneficiaries. However, a claim analyst must follow the earlier law for claims arising from any policies issued before the designated date.

In addition, if the claim analyst determines that the person who made the beneficiary change was mentally incompetent, then the change is legally ineffective, and the original beneficiary receives the policy proceeds. The claim analyst is not legally bound, however, to question the competence of every policyowner who changes a beneficiary. If an insurer pays the policy proceeds to a new beneficiary and then discovers later that the beneficiary change was made by an incompetent policyowner, the insurer is usually not bound by law to pay the proceeds a second time to the original beneficiary. If a former beneficiary wishes to challenge a change of beneficiary, the burden of proof is upon the former beneficiary to prove the incompetence of the policyowner to make the change.

Assigned Policy Proceeds

Some or all of the rights to receive the proceeds of a life insurance policy can be transferred to another person or entity by means of an ***assignment.*** A policyowner may transfer these rights to another person or persons or to an entity such as a business or a trust. An ***absolute assignment*** is an irrevocable transfer of all the rights of a life insurance policy from one party to another. A ***collateral assignment*** is a transfer of some ownership rights from one party to another, usually for a temporary period. Insurance policies are often assigned as collateral for the balance due on a loan, for example, and after the loan is paid, all rights under the policy return to the policyowner. The claim analyst is not responsible for checking into every possible assignment of an insurance policy. Insofar as possible, the claim analyst pays the proceeds to the correct person or entity, but the claim analyst does not have the responsibility to check for any possible assignment or to take responsibility for ensuring that no outstanding absolute or collateral assignment exists.

Payment to Attorneys or Tax Collectors

If an attorney notifies a claim analyst that he represents a claimant, the analyst usually sends the proceeds to the attorney for subsequent payment to the claimant. Some insurers prefer to make checks for such payments payable to the claimant, and others make the checks payable jointly to the claimant and the attorney.

If an insured owes taxes, a tax collector cannot legally collect policy proceeds to satisfy the tax debt. A tax collector can, however, lay claim to the cash value of a life insurance policy as payment for unpaid federal income taxes. A claim analyst may need to consult with the insurer's lawyers to determine appropriate treatment for complex tax collection issues.

Unusual Claims

A claim analyst occasionally encounters a claim that has unusual characteristics or that requires special handling. Such unusual claims may involve adverse claimants, community-property laws, divorce, simultaneous deaths, or accelerated death benefits.

Adverse claimants. When a claim analyst receives conflicting claims from two or more claimants, the analyst is responsible for (1) consulting with the insurer's legal function and (2) conducting a thorough claim investigation according to the insurer's established procedures for handling adverse claimants. During the investigation, the analyst notifies the adverse claimants of the conflicting claims and provides each claimant with complete information concerning the facts of the case, including details about the beneficiary designations, policy provisions, assignments, and any other relevant information.

If the claimants can reach a resolution between themselves, the claim analyst receives written notice of their decision and pays the policy proceeds in accordance with that decision. If the claimants cannot reach such a resolution, however, the claim analyst is responsible for initiating ***interpleader,*** a claim settlement method by which an insurer pays the proceeds to a court, advises the court that the insurer cannot determine the correct party to whom the proceeds should be distributed, and asks the court to decide the proper recipient or recipients. Particularly when a claimant sues the insurer for the proceeds, most insurers immediately respond with interpleader in order to have an appropriate decision made by the court.

Community-property laws. If a policyowner lives in a state governed by community-property laws, the claim analyst must consider those laws in determining the correct beneficiary. ***Community-property laws*** provide that a spouse is entitled to receive an equal share of earned income and an equal share of property acquired by the other spouse during a marriage. When a person dies in a state governed by community-property laws, the spouse is entitled to at least half of all community property. When a person applies for and is issued an insurance policy on her life during marriage and pays the premium with community funds, the policy is considered to be community property. The policy proceeds are also community property if the beneficiary is the estate of the insured or someone other than the spouse. If the beneficiary is the policyowner's spouse, the proceeds are usually considered the spouse's separate property.

If a policyowner-insured who is a resident of a community-property state dies and leaves all life insurance proceeds to the spouse, the claim analyst has no problem in determining the beneficiary. But suppose that a policyowner-deceased insured who has been living in a community-property state selects someone other than the spouse to receive life insurance benefits. Or suppose that a deceased policyowner-insured had once lived in a community-property state for a period of time, during which he had paid premiums on life insurance coverage for which his spouse was not the designated beneficiary.

In these circumstances and an endless variety of others, an insurer could be placed in the difficult position of determining to whom benefits should be paid, what proportion of benefits should be paid, and, indeed, whether any insured had ever lived in a community-property state. To require an insurer to make such time-consuming, detailed claim investigations would result in high expenses and lengthy delays in claim handling. To release insurers from such a burden, community-property states have passed ***exculpatory statutes,*** which are laws that permit an insurer to pay life insurance proceeds according to the terms of a policy without fear of double liability. If the insurer has received prior written notice of a conflicting claim, the insurer must respond to that notice. Otherwise, the insurer is legally liable to pay the policy proceeds to the named beneficiary, regardless of other conditions. To prevent possible conflict resulting from appearing to ignore or avoid a spouse's legal property right, however, insurers generally obtain a release from a surviving spouse before paying policy proceeds above a certain amount—usually $10,000—to anyone other than the spouse.

Divorce. When a claim analyst handles a life insurance claim on the life of a divorced spouse who did not change the beneficiary designation from her former spouse, under the laws of most jurisdictions the analyst pays the proceeds to the former spouse. If a divorce decree specifies that a person must continue to pay premiums on life insurance and name the divorced spouse as beneficiary, no problem exists if the person complies with the decree requirements.

However, sometimes the policyowner-insured continues to pay premiums, but names someone other than the former spouse as beneficiary. In such a situation, if the claim analyst has received no notice of a new beneficiary and pays the policy proceeds to the former spouse as beneficiary, the insurer is not liable to pay benefits a second time if the new beneficiary submits a claim.

Simultaneous deaths. In some situations, an insured and the primary beneficiary die simultaneously. If the claim analyst cannot determine with certainty the order of death, insurers generally apply laws designed to handle this problem. The applicable law in the United States is the Uniform Simultaneous Death Act; in all Canadian provinces except Quebec, it is the Uniform Life Insurance Act; and in Quebec it is the Quebec Insurance Act.

According to these laws, when both the insured and the primary beneficiary die at the same time and the order of their deaths cannot be determined, the insurer is to presume that the insured survived the beneficiary—that is, the beneficiary died first. Paying the policy proceeds under this law may require payment to the insured's estate or to another named beneficiary. Some policies specify how the proceeds shall be disbursed in the event of simultaneous death. If a policy contains such a specification, that specification determines how proceeds are paid. To cover situations in which a beneficiary survives an insured by a brief time, other policies use a ***survivorship clause,*** also called a *time clause,* which provides payment of proceeds to the beneficiary provided the beneficiary lives longer than the insured for at least a specified period such as 10 days or 30 days.

Accelerated death benefits. Some insurers offer life insurance policyowners the option of taking an ***accelerated death benefit,*** which is a portion of a policy's benefits paid during life to a terminally ill insured who has a remaining life expectancy of less than a specified period usually ranging between six months and two years. The amount of the death benefit payable under the policy to the named beneficiary is then reduced by the amount of the accelerated death benefit that was paid out to the insured. Each insurer that offers an accelerated death benefit option designs its own requirements and benefit payout percentages, but the usual range is between 60 and 80 percent of the basic life benefit.

In administering claims for the accelerated death benefit, most insurers are concerned with establishing eligibility, accurately handling irrevocable beneficiaries and absolute assignments, and avoiding fraud.

- Determining an insured's eligibility for the accelerated death benefit requires that the insured meet the insurer's definition of terminal illness and of life expectancy. For example, an insurer may specify that an insured who has been diagnosed HIV positive is not considered to have a terminal illness. However, if an insured develops the form of pneumonia (pneumocystis carinii) associated with full-blown AIDS, the insurer may consider that the insured then has a terminal illness and has a life expectancy within the insurer's defined parameters for accelerated death benefit eligibility.

- If an insured has named an irrevocable beneficiary or has made an absolute assignment of policy proceeds, the claim analyst must obtain a signed acknowledgment of such actions from the persons affected. Because only a portion of the death benefits are accelerated, the insurance protection provides some degree of protection for beneficiaries and assignees.

- To avoid fraud, most insurers reserve the right to obtain an independent medical evaluation of an insured who wishes to be considered eligible for accelerated death benefits. If an insured wishes to be considered eligible to receive accelerated death benefits during the contestable period, the claim analyst helps to avoid fraud by verifying every element of the claim and the insured's medical condition before approving the payment of benefits. For group coverages, the risk of fraud tends to be less because the employer generally has knowledge of the employee's medical condition.

Some organizations known as viatical settlement companies purchase life insurance policies at a discount from the face amount from terminally ill policyowners. In such a transaction, the viatical settlement company then becomes the owner of the policy and, when the insured person dies, receives the death benefit. Insight 17-3 describes the purposes of viatical settlements delivered by such companies.

Insight 17-3 Viatical Settlements: Exploitation or Genuine Need?

The doctors all agree. The life insurance policyowner has eight months to live, at most. He has practically exhausted all his financial resources. Then he sees an advertisement that says, "Cash for Life Insurance!" and starts thinking: "I have that policy on my life. I wonder how the family would feel about getting some of that money right now?"

The proliferation of viatical settlement companies has been rapid. In 1989 there were two, one in New Mexico and one in Florida. Now there are more than 30 operating in the United States.

Ads Can Be Misleading

"Coping with AIDS should not be a financial burden," reads one viatical settlement company's ad. "Financial concerns can hinder your ability to cope with a personal crisis on your own terms. . . . We can help."

One difficulty with these ads is the implication that the insurance industry is totally indifferent to the plight of dying policyholders. Nowhere is it suggested that policyholders should first check with the marketer who sold them the policy, the local agency, or the home office to discover what arrangements the carrier is willing to make. The life insurance business guards its public image carefully. Even if they have lost touch with their life insurance agent, terminally ill policyholders will usually find the local agency more than happy to go to bat for them.

A Call for Regulation

"That's why viatical settlement companies that are currently neither licensed nor regulated need to be handled in an aggressive manner, and it needs to be done now," says David Lyons, Iowa's insurance commissioner. "We're particularly concerned because these arrangements are marketed to an extremely vulnerable population. In the current unregulated marketplace, no disclosures are required about the possible alternatives and the consequences of entering into those agreements. Determining the possibility of getting an accelerated death benefit from the life insurance company should be the first question asked. The last thing a company wants to do is make the end of a policyholder's life anything other than as comfortable as possible, " he declares.

A Source of Controversy

From the very beginning, viatical settlement companies have been controversial within the insurance community. Reaction has ranged from skepticism to downright hostility. Some think of them as ambulance chasers of the worst sort and have suggested outlawing them altogether.

However, viatical settlement companies fill a genuine need when insurance companies decide against considering a pre-death settlement. And, after all, changing one's beneficiary is legal.

Several jurisdictions have set up some regulatory mechanism to monitor and regulate viatical settlement firms, requiring licensing of the companies and their brokers or agents as well as consumer disclosure requirements. Others may soon follow as concern over their expanding activity mounts.

The Need for Disclosure

The National Association of Insurance Commissioners (NAIC) has proposed a model law to bring these companies under the authority of state insurance departments. The model bill incorporates many of the stipulations contained in the laws enacted by the states that already have regulation. The model law would require companies to acquire a license from the insurance commissioner and submit a detailed plan of their operations. To protect the seller, companies would have to disclose alternatives to the viatical settlement; the fact that proceeds may be taxable; that the consumer could be ruled ineligible for Medicaid or other government benefits by accepting payment; the policyholder's right to negate the contract; and when the funds would be made available to the policyholder.

Adapted by permission from *LAN*, April 1994: 115–116.

Administration of Settlement Options

A life insurance policy provides certain options for the way the proceeds are paid to the beneficiary upon the death of the insured. The most common of these options include paying the benefits in a lump sum, paying the benefits in installments during a fixed or lifetime period, and paying the benefits in fixed amounts. Some policies allow a beneficiary to leave the proceeds with the insurance company to earn interest for a certain period before the principal is disbursed.

If payment of a lump sum is the option chosen by either the insured or the beneficiary, the claim analyst requests a check to be made payable to the beneficiary and sees that the payment is sent to the beneficiary or to a bank or other financial institution. If policy proceeds are to be paid in installments during a fixed or lifetime period or for fixed amounts, the claim analyst sends the beneficiary an ***installment certificate*** that specifies the amount of each benefit payment and/or the period during which benefit payments will be made. The installment certificate also specifies whether a beneficiary is permitted to withdraw all or part of the proceeds during the payment period.

If policy proceeds are being left with the insurance company to earn interest, the claim analyst usually sends the beneficiary a ***certificate of indebtedness,*** which specifies a guaranteed minimum interest rate that an insurer will pay on the proceeds and the frequency with which the insurer will make interest payments to a beneficiary. Like an installment certificate, the certificate of indebtedness also specifies whether the beneficiary may withdraw all or part of the proceeds. Insight 17-4 comments on a procedure used by some insurers to disburse policy proceeds which are being held in an insurer's account.

Key Terms and Concepts

claimant's statement (*claim form*)
authorization to release information
death certificate
presumptive death certificate
change in health statement
proximate cause (of a death)
contingent beneficiary (*secondary beneficiary*)
public curator
revocable beneficiary
irrevocable beneficiary
preferred beneficiary
assignment
absolute assignment
collateral assignment
interpleader
community-property laws
exculpatory statutes
survivorship clause (*time clause*)
accelerated death benefit
installment certificate
certificate of indebtedness

Insight 17-4 My Thoughts On . . . Retained Asset Accounts

It has been approximately a decade since the insurance industry took the step to introduce and promote the use of retained asset accounts (RAAs) for payment of death benefits. A *retained asset account* is an interest-bearing money market checking account that is established by an insurer for the beneficiary of a life insurance policy, and into which the insurer deposits the policy's death benefit. Initially, RAAs mainly benefited individual insurance policy beneficiaries, but later was expanded to beneficiaries on group life contracts as well.

The mechanics of RAAs are relatively simple. An insurer establishes an RAA with one of several banks that provide such a service. The RAA is usually, but not always, a closed-end checking account. The insurer and the bank develop marketing or promotional items, checkbooks, and other materials to be sent to a beneficiary in a special kit. The kit typically includes a certificate of the amount deposited, the checkbook, and a brochure explaining how the account works. The beneficiary can write a check immediately for the entire amount deposited by the insurer or may withdraw a portion of the total amount as funds are needed.

Amounts left on deposit continue to draw interest at a rate agreed on by the insurer and the bank. The rate usually changes weekly and is credited to each account monthly. A common misconception is that the funds are transferred by the insurer to the bank that performs administration of the RAAs. In fact, the proceeds remain with the insurer. The bank provides the beneficiary and the insurer with accounting data as if the funds actually resided in the bank's checking account. Checks written by the beneficiary are drawn against the bank, which then requests needed monies from the insurer.

The effects of this program have been favorable for beneficiaries, who no longer complain that a check was not delivered or that interest was lost on the proceeds during mail time or third-party handling of disbursements. RAAs also allow funds to remain with the insurer as the beneficiary uses the funds on an as-needed basis, while the unused proceeds continue to accrue interest.

At General American Life, the RAA program during the most recent 12-month period saw a double-digit growth in the number of accounts, average balances, and dollars in the account. Also noteworthy is that the number of our accountholders who have maintained RAAs for three years or more continues to grow. RAAs have developed into a positive force within the insurance industry to promote excellent customer service, to improve insurer earnings, and to permit the flexible use of insurance proceeds as an investment tool.

William G. Kasalko, ALHC
Executive Director, Policyholder Services
General American Life Insurance Company

CHAPTER EIGHTEEN

Administering Medical Expense Insurance Claims

Learning Objectives

After studying this chapter, you should be able to

- Explain the function and benefits of diagnostic and treatment codes for claims handling
- List the items of information on a typical medical or dental claim form concerning the insured, the medical caregiver, and drugs and medicines
- Define a coordination of benefits (COB) provision and explain its function
- Explain five types of medical exclusions and limitations, and give at least three examples of each type
- Explain the purpose of preadmission certification and the process used to obtain it
- Define and explain the purpose of a subrogation clause in a medical insurance policy
- Calculate the payable benefits according to a schedule of benefits
- Distinguish among benefits payable according to a maximum limit, reasonable and customary limits, and Diagnostic Related Groups (DRGs)
- Calculate the deductible amount for a comprehensive medical plan and for a major medical plan with a corridor deductible

Chapter Outline

Determining Whether a Loss Has Occurred

Diagnostic and Treatment Codes

Medical Expense Claim Form

Itemized Receipt

Determining Whether a Loss Is Covered

Exclusions and Limitations

Other Policy Provisions

Calculating the Amount of Policy Benefits

Diagnostic Related Groups

Schedule of Benefits

Maximum Limit

Reasonable and Customary Limits

Ensuring That Benefits Are Appropriately Paid

Deductibles

Coordination of Benefits

Payment of Benefits

Cooperating in Case Management

Although a life insurance policy generally produces only one claim for each insured, medical expense insurance policies can produce dozens of claims during the lifetime of an insured. Claims for medical services, including dental services, range in amount from a few dollars for prescription drugs to thousands of dollars for complex surgeries and long-term treatments. In a typical medical claim area, claim analysts might receive hundreds of claims in a single day. Each claim must be handled promptly, accurately, and completely, in accordance with the insurer's claim philosophy, its other business practices, and legal requirements.

To enable claim analysts to be more accurate and to handle medical expense claims more rapidly, some insurers that cover large groups assign one or more claim analysts to handle only the claims arising from a specific group. The claim analysts learn the details of the specific policy covering such a group and, therefore, do not have to reread the policy for every claim.

Claim analysts who handle medical expense and dental claims need much of the same kind of technical knowledge that underwriters need. That is, medical and dental claim handling involves assessing the validity and accuracy of technical information about diseases and physical and mental conditions. Claim analysts also need expertise in handling claims under managed care. Like life claims, medical expense and dental claims may be resolved quickly or may take weeks or months to complete if a considerable amount of additional information is necessary to reach a decision.

In the first chapter of this textbook, we explained the importance of information systems in enhancing the activities involved in insurance administration. Nowhere are information systems more useful than in handling medical expense and dental claims. The sheer volume of such claims makes it imperative that an insurer incorporate effective information systems and train claim analysts in their correct and efficient use. Most insurers have implemented sophisticated medical expense and dental claims handling systems that not only verify information about the coverage and the insured, but also calculate benefit amounts, produce checks or transfer funds electronically to pay benefits, and generate printed explanations of benefits so that each policyowner receives specific information about the amount of benefits paid for each claim. In most insurance companies, only claims requiring special examination are handled individually by a claim analyst. Whether a computer or a person evaluates a claim, the same steps are generally involved. In our discussion of medical and dental claim administration, we will review those steps in some detail and will refer always to a claim analyst, although for many coverages the administration process is often implemented by an information system.

Generally, medical and dental policies include a provision requiring that a claim be submitted within a specified period—usually 30 to 90 days—from the date the loss was incurred. Because claim analysts need to gather additional information for certain claims, insurers prefer to receive claims promptly so that such information-gathering may take place as soon as possible after the loss has occurred, while records are readily available and medical caregivers' memories are still fresh. Claims may be submitted by either the medical caregiver, the insured, or a marketer, according to the provisions of the policy. Whether a claim is submitted by paper or by electronic transmission, most insurers offering group health coverage use a uniform claim form or electronic format developed under the guidance of the Health Insurance Association of America (HIAA) in the United States or the Canadian Life and Health Insurance Association (CLHIA) in Canada. Submitting claim information in a uniform manner enables persons submitting claims to provide complete, accurate information and enables claim analysts to examine claims rapidly and precisely.

In certain respects, handling medical expense and dental claims is similar to handling any other kind of claim. The claim analyst is responsible for verifying that the reported loss occurred and that both the insured and the loss are covered by the policy. If benefits are due, the claim analyst is also responsible for seeing that they are paid appropriately. In this chapter, we'll discuss these and other details of administering medical and dental indemnity claims.

Fast Fact

One researcher has estimated that a typical large, computer-dependent company will pay $100 million to change its computer software so that its programs do not mistake the year 2000 for the year 1900. Programs that are not changed either will not run or will incorrectly compute dates and other figures.

Source: Suzanne E. Stipe, "Year 2000 Doomsayers Finally Get Insurers' Attention," *Best's Review (Life/Health)*, September 1996: 39–42.

Determining Whether a Loss Has Occurred

Medical expense and dental claims are usually submitted either (1) manually on paper claim forms completed by insured persons and their medical caregivers or (2) electronically by medical caregivers and their staffs who communicate directly with insurers. In determining whether a loss has occurred, the claim analyst typically interprets the diagnostic and treatment codes included in paper or electronic submissions. When paper is submitted, the claim analyst examines the claim form and any itemized receipts from medical caregivers.

Diagnostic and Treatment Codes

To facilitate communication among medical caregivers and insurers, including underwriters and claim analysts, special codes have been developed to describe specific medical and dental diagnoses and treatments. ***Diagnostic and treatment codes*** are special codes that describe specific medical and dental diagnoses and treatments. These codes include (1) a brief, specific description of each diagnosis or treatment and (2) a number that identifies each diagnosis or treatment. Diagnostic and treatment codes enable anyone familiar with the coding system to tell immediately what information is being reported.

One of the most commonly used codes for medical *diagnoses* is the ***International Classification of Diseases and Related Health Problems,*** which is generally referred to as the ICD and to which claim analysts refer by its most current edition—e.g., the 10th edition is called ICD-10. One of the most commonly used codes for medical *treatments* is the ***Physicians' Current Procedural Terminology,*** generally referred to as CPT. Dental treatments and procedures are usually coded according to the American Dental Association Code or the Canadian Dental Association Code.

The categories used in these codes enable medical and dental caregivers to classify diagnoses and treatments with considerable precision. As an example, the American Dental Association Code divides dental procedures into such categories as diagnostic, preventive, restorative, oral surgery, orthodontics, and so on. The procedures within each of these general categories are then subcategorized, and each procedure is given an identifying number. For instance, the procedures included in the restorative category include the subcategories of restorations of amalgam, silicate, filled or unfilled resin, gold foil, and inlay, as well as crowns. Among the code numbers assigned to various types of crowns are the following:

02720	Crown (resin with high noble metal)
02721	Crown (resin with predominantly base metal)
02722	Crown (resin with noble metal)
02740	Crown (porcelain/ceramic substrate)
02750	Crown (porcelain fused to high noble metal)

Like dental diagnoses and procedures, medical procedures are similarly organized into categories, with an identifying number assigned to each procedure. Figure 18-1 shows some of the codes commonly used to identify diagnoses and treatments associated with appendicitis.

In examining medical codes reported on claims, the claim analyst first determines whether the codes are accurate and complete. Suppose that a claim analyst received a claim for an appendectomy with the diagnosis coded 540 (acute appendicitis with peritonitis including rupture of the appendix) and the treatment coded 44960 (appendectomy for ruptured appendix with abscess or generalized peritonitis). Because the diagnosis code and the treatment code appear to be consistent, the claim analyst would note no problem with that portion of the claim.

But suppose instead that the diagnosis was coded 540.9 (acute appendicitis without mention of peritonitis) and the treatment was coded 44960 (appendectomy for ruptured appendix with abscess or

Figure 18-1. Codes commonly used for diagnoses and treatments of appendicitis.

Diagnosis Codes	Diagnosis
540	Acute appendicitis with peritonitis, including rupture of appendix
540.1	Acute appendicitis with peritoneal abscess
540.9	Acute appendicitis without mention of peritonitis
542	Other appendicitis, including chronic or recurrent attacks
Treatment Codes	**Treatment**
44900	Incision and drainage of appendiceal abscess
44955	Appendectomy performed at time of another major procedure
44960	Appendectomy for ruptured appendix with abscess or generalized peritonitis

generalized peritonitis). In such a situation, because the codes appear to be inconsistent, the claim analyst would check with the medical caregivers and the insured to verify the diagnosis and the treatment, and to clarify the apparently conflicting information. The claim analyst might, for instance, request a copy of the operative report that describes the medical procedures followed. Similarly, a claim analyst would verify the facts concerning a root canal reported on a tooth that the insurer's database shows was extracted at an earlier time, or a pediatric procedure reported for an adult.

The codes enable a medical caregiver to provide fairly complete information quickly and accurately. The codes also permit the claim analyst to understand what diagnosis or procedure has been reported. For instance, when a claim analyst receives a dental claim coded 02721, she knows that the reported procedure is a crown restoration involving resin with predominantly base metal. In addition, the medical and dental coding systems help eliminate errors resulting from illegible handwriting or inconsistent ways of explaining the same treatment or diagnosis. Further, the coding systems permit an insurer to program its information systems to handle routine claims quickly. Using the codes, the claim analyst can determine whether each treatment fits the requirements of ***medical necessity***—that is, a criterion requiring that the prescribed medical procedure is one that (1) is considered effective and that is normally used for the specified illness or injury and (2) does not exceed in scope, duration, or intensity the level of care needed to provide safe, adequate, and appropriate diagnosis or treatment.

Generally, an inconsistency in a diagnosis code indicates a simple human error that can be corrected by communicating directly with the medical caregiver. For example, most insurers do not pay benefits for both an office visit and an emergency room visit for the same injury or illness on the same day. Similarly, most insurers do not pay separate benefits for both a surgical procedure and preoperative and postoperative office visits related to that procedure. When a claim analyst notices that a medical caregiver has reported overlapping codes—say, for both a surgical procedure and a postoperative checkup—the analyst notifies the medical caregiver and, unless unusual circumstances apply, does not approve benefits for postoperative visits because they are generally included in the cost of the surgical procedure.

Occasionally a code indicates an apparently incorrect, unnecessary, or nontraditional treatment for a given condition. In such a situation, the claim analyst gathers information from the caregiver, medical facilities, and the insured to assess the condition or treatment and determines whether the medical caregiver correctly or incorrectly delivered medical care for the condition. The claim analyst may also consult with the insurer's medical director and other medical staff. Most insurers are willing to pay benefits for some new or nontraditional treatments, but the advantage to the patient of such a treatment must be clear before the claim analyst approves payment of benefits. In extreme situations, the claim analyst may detect fraud in medical care delivery. In a later chapter, we'll discuss the issue of claim fraud.

Medical Expense Claim Form

The medical or dental claim form provides basic information from both the insured and the medical caregiver. The information provided by the insured generally includes

- The name, address, gender, and date of birth of the patient—that is, the person incurring the loss
- The relationship of the patient to the insured (dependent or self)
- The nature of the illness or injury on which the claim is based
- The name, address, gender, and date of birth of the insured
- Authorization from the patient (or, if the patient is a minor, from the insured) for all physicians, hospitals, medical caregivers, pharmacists, or other agencies and organizations to release information concerning the patient's records

The claim form also asks whether the patient is covered by other insurance, whether the illness or injury resulted from the patient's occupation, and whether the claim is the result of an accident. If the claim is the result of an accident, the claim form asks whether the claimant expects to receive or has received payment for medical or dental expenses from another source as the result of a lawsuit or settlement. Space is provided for additional information concerning these responses.

Fast Fact

In 1990, Americans paid about $13.7 billion for nontraditional health care treatments. While most paid for the treatments themselves, 14 percent were completely reimbursed, and 31 percent were partially reimbursed.

Source: Daniel M. Stern, "Insuring Alternative Medicine," *Life Association News,* June 1996: 75–80.

The claim form information provided by the caregiver generally includes

- The name, address, and Tax Identification Number of the medical caregiver
- The name of the patient
- The nature of the illness or injury, including appropriate diagnostic codes
- The type of services rendered, including appropriate treatment codes
- The dates on which services were delivered
- The locations at which services were delivered
- The charges for those services

If the patient or the caregiver includes bills for drugs and medicines, each bill usually shows

- The name of the person for whom medication was prescribed
- The date(s) of purchase and the charge for each prescription
- Each prescription number, the nature of each medication, and the drug identification number (DIN)
- The name and address of the pharmacy

Itemized Receipt

A caregiver typically provides each patient with an itemized receipt that gives detailed information about diagnosis and treatment. The information on such a receipt usually includes the name of the caregiver, a specific diagnosis, the expenses involved in diagnosis and treatment, and the date on which those expenses were incurred. As proof of claim, most insurers require original itemized receipts, not photocopies. Itemized receipts may be given by any caregiver, ranging from a physician or paramedic to a laboratory, a hospital, or an outpatient clinic.

Most itemized receipts include diagnostic or treatment codes and therefore can be interpreted accurately and rapidly. If, however, such a receipt contains only a written description of diagnosis or treatment,

Figure 18-2. Portion of a typical medical receipt.

Date of Service ______________ Name ______________________________

Address ____

Social Security No. __________________________ DOB ____________________

Procedures	Laboratory	Diagnosis
57500 Cervical Biopsy	82465 Cholesterol	789 Abdominal Pain
58100 Endometrial Biopsy	82565 Creatinine	795.0 Abnormal Pap
57511 Cryotherapy	82728 Ferratine	285.8 Anemia
59000 Amniocentesis	82947 Glucose	250 Diabetes
59050 Fetal Monitoring	86317 Hepatitis C	617.9 Endometriosis
58990 Hysteroscopy	86996 OB Profile	620.2 Ovarian Cyst

Remarks ____

Provider Signature ______________________________________

the claim analyst usually communicates with the caregiver to clarify the information. Figure 18-2 illustrates a portion of a typical receipt from a physician specializing in obstetrics and gynecology.

Determining Whether a Loss Is Covered

To determine whether a loss is covered, a claim analyst verifies that both the insured and the loss are covered under the policy. If a claimant has been covered under a group policy that has been converted to individual coverage, the claim analyst verifies that the premiums have been paid and that the coverage is in force.

If the claimant is the primary insured, the claim analyst usually has little difficulty determining whether the person is covered for the stated loss. However, for family insurance or group insurance, the claim analyst determines whether the claimant is a qualified dependent of the primary insured. Most policies define a ***covered person,*** that is, one who is eligible for coverage consistent with the policy's definition of a dependent or spouse. Generally, dependents include not only the spouse, but also unmarried dependent children—natural, adopted, and stepchildren—who are under age 19 (or, if a full-time student, under age 23 to 25, depending on plan provisions) and who are chiefly dependent upon the insured for support and maintenance.

If the claimant is a qualified dependent or a primary insured eligible to be covered under a spouse's medical insurance, then the claim analyst checks whether the claimant is also covered under another plan of insurance that allows for coordination of benefits. As we mentioned in Chapter 9, a coordination of benefits (COB) provision prevents duplication of benefits, that is, payment of the same medical expenses or disability benefits by more than one insurer or by a government program. A COB provision specifies which of two health insurance plans will be considered as the "primary" provider of benefits—that is, which plan will pay benefits first on a claim. The second plan may provide additional benefits, but total reimbursement from both plans may not exceed the full amount of the claim. The purpose of a COB provision is to ensure that an insured's benefits from all sources do not exceed 100 percent of incurred medical or dental expenses. Like all insurance coverage, medical coverage is intended to provide reimbursement for some or all expenses, but not to provide a profit for the insured. Some individual health insurance policies also contain an ***overinsurance provision*** which specifies that, under certain circumstances, policy benefits will be reduced if the insured has more insurance than needed to cover medical or dental expenses.

The claim analyst also checks the policy to be sure that the loss reported on the claim is covered under the policy and has not been excluded by a rider. Some insurers have entered all policy provisions into a database so that claim analysts can quickly check details of coverage. Because many individual and group policies have been individualized and contain various kinds and levels of coverages and exclusions, the claim analyst may refer to a file copy of the policy contract to ensure that the claim assessment of the losses is accurate.

Exclusions and Limitations

Checking the exclusions and limitations in a policy may take considerable time because the claim analyst needs to verify that delivered medical or dental care for which benefits are requested meets the policy requirements. Policy exclusions and limitations specify as exactly as possible the conditions that a policy will and will not cover. They can cover a wide range, and they differ from one policy to another.

The most common types of medical and dental exclusions and limitations include the following:

- *Those defining the medical caregiver.* Some policies specify that covered medical care must be delivered by a licensed dentist or a resident physician or an intern, but not a nurse or nurse's aide, who is employed by or officially associated with a specific kind of medical facility. Generally, a physician is defined as a practitioner of the healing arts, licensed and legally qualified to treat sickness and injury. Most policies specify that a physician cannot be an immediate family member of an insured (that is, not a spouse, parent, child, or sibling) and may provide only services within the scope of her license.

- *Those defining the medical facility.* Most policies state that coverage extends only to certain types and levels of facilities. A policy may not cover treatments and procedures delivered in a patient's home, in a medical caregiver's office, or in an outpatient clinic. For example, a policy may define a "continued care facility" and establish specific requirements for it as (1) being equipped and staffed to provide care and treatment for patients who are sick and injured, (2) being supervised by a medical staff, and (3) having a nurse available at all times. Treatment delivered at a facility that is reported to be a continued care facility, but that does not meet the policy's definition, may not be covered under such a policy.

- *Those defining the type of medical procedure.* Many policies limit or exclude benefits for corrective treatments (such as orthopedic shoes, eyeglasses, hearing aids, and some dental restorations), preventive treatments (such as vaccinations, inoculations, and weight reduction programs), and some diagnostic treatments (such as sight and hearing examinations, certain X-rays, heart scans, coronary artery disease risk assessment programs, and any diagnostic treatment when no injury or illness exists). Most dental policies exclude certain dental procedures including installation of crowns for cosmetic purposes only.

- *Those defining the type of medical condition.* Most policies define the type of medical conditions for which treatment is covered. For example, a typical definition of "sickness" is any sickness or disease that first makes itself known after the policy is in force and while the policy is in force. Similarly, an "injury" may be defined as an accidental bodily injury that results in loss independently of sickness and other causes. For example, a policy may define the covered conditions associated with normal pregnancy and childbirth—for instance, false labor, occasional spotting, morning sickness, and other conditions. Some individual health policies do not provide benefits for a preexisting condition, which is an injury that occurred or a sickness that first appeared or manifested itself during a specified period before the policy became effective. In group insurance, a preexisting condition has generally been defined as a condition for which an insured received medical care during a specified period, usually three to six months, prior to the effective date of coverage. Generally, a medical condition has been considered to be no longer preexisting after the earlier of (1) a period of 3 consecutive months during which the insured receives no medical care for the condition and (2) a period of 12 months during which the insured has received coverage for the condition under the insurance contract. In the United States, legislation restricts group health plans, insurers, and some health care providers from denying coverage because of preexisting conditions. Only insureds with "creditable coverage" under a health plan are protected under the legislation. The period during which a group health plan may deny coverage for a preexisting condition is reduced by the period during which an insured has had creditable coverage under another previous group plan.

- *Those defining the fees charged by the medical caregiver and the medical facility.* Most policies set limits on the amount of coverage provided for certain medical procedures, for the maximum benefits allowed for one period of illness or for a single injury, and for the number of medical procedures allowed within a stated period of time. These limits may be established according to the usual and customary fees for such treatments within the applicable geographic area. In addition, all policies specify the charges that will be covered by the policy. Figure 18-3 illustrates a typical list of charges covered by a medical insurance policy.

Figure 18-3. Typical list of charges covered by a medical insurance policy.

- Hospital charges for the average semiprivate room and board during necessary hospital confinement
- Confinement in an intensive care unit or cardiac care unit of a hospital
- Hospital charges for services and supplies
- Treatment by a physician or surgeon
- Anesthesia and its administration
- X-ray and laboratory examinations
- Services of a radiologist for diagnosis or treatment
- Services of a professional physical or speech therapist acting under the direction of a physician
- Professional ambulance service for emergency transportation to the nearest hospital
- Services and supplies furnished by an ambulatory surgical facility
- Medical supplies such as blood and blood plasma, surgical dressings, casts, splints, crutches, oxygen, and approved drugs and medicines
- Specified expenses for care provided by a hospice or licensed home health care agency

Besides the limitations and exclusions noted above, some policies contain other prohibitions to coverage. All health insurance policies prohibit payment for unnecessary care or treatment. In addition, many health policies also exclude coverage for expenses of the following kinds:

- Routine health care and checkups
- Routine physical examinations
- Cosmetic surgery unless needed to repair damage suffered in an accident covered under the policy, for reconstructive surgery, or for restoration to normal bodily function
- Self-donated blood and blood replacement
- Custodial care
- Any work-related illness or injury that is covered by workers' compensation insurance
- Intentionally self-inflicted wounds or illness, or wounds suffered in an assault on another person or in an attempt to commit a crime

Some health insurance policies provide that an insured must obtain a ***preadmission certification,*** sometimes called *precertification,* which is a statement from the insurer approving nonemergency, inpatient hospital treatment. A typical preadmission certification requirement in a policy is worded as follows:

> *Certification is required when you or any covered person is to be hospital-confined as an inpatient.*

Preadmission certification is usually required for surgical, maternity, substance abuse, mental health, and other types of hospital admissions. Preadmission certification is generally not required for treatments delivered as emergency medical care.

In order to provide such certification, an insurer requires the claimant's attending physician to demonstrate a genuine medical need for prescribed care in advance of the time that care is to be delivered. Information required from the physician includes (1) the diagnosis or reason for hospital confinement, (2) signs and symptoms indicating a need for such care, (3) the proposed treatment or surgical procedure, and (4) the expected number of days of confinement. Most insurers require a physician to provide this information at least two days before the hospital admission; many insurers allow the information to be transmitted to the insurer by telephone or by electronic submission. If an insured must be confined to a hospital longer than the period approved through preadmission certification, the insurer usually obtains medical information from the physician to determine the medical necessity of the extended stay. If the continued admission is certified, the claim analyst approves payment for the extended period.

Some insurers assign staff to consult with medical caregivers in planning alternative ways of delivering care, such as using a hospice or home care instead of hospital care, when appropriate. A ***hospice*** is a facility that helps ease the physical and psychological suffering of a person who has a terminal illness. Generally, a hospice does not attempt to provide a cure for an apparently terminal condition. For some cases, the insurer obtains a second medical opinion before approving surgery or other kinds of care. The claim analyst checks to be sure that preadmission certification has been obtained and that, if an insurer has recommended alternative forms of care delivery, those recommendations have been heeded.

If a medical caregiver has delivered certain types of care without obtaining preadmission certification, an insurer usually reduces the amount of payment provided for the treatment even if the care would have been approved had it been submitted for preadmission certification. Further, if the claim analyst determines that an insured has been treated as an inpatient in a hospital and has not obtained preadmission certification, the analyst invokes whatever provision the policy makes for such an omission. In most situations the insured is responsible for paying (1) an additional deductible above the usual deductible that may apply to an overnight hospital stay and (2) an additional percentage of the room and board charges. If an insured applied for preadmission certification but was denied such permission, the claim analyst invokes the policy provision for such action, which usually requires the insured to pay a larger amount of the total cost of the hospital stay or, under some contracts, to be eligible for no plan benefits.

Other Policy Provisions

In addition to checking the exclusions and limitations contained in a policy, the claim analyst verifies whether the policy contains certain other provisions that permit the insurer to pay for services not generally covered by the basic policy. For example, a policy that offers extended care coverage might permit a claimant to receive benefits to pay for skilled nursing care—from a registered nurse or a licensed practical nurse—working in an outpatient clinic or in the patient's home. Another policy might enable a terminally ill patient to receive benefits for hospice care, drugs, and counseling. Although many medical policies do not pay for prescription drugs, hearing aids, vision correction, psychiatric treatment, and experimental medical treatments, some policies do provide some or all of these benefits. Rather than assume that a claim is covered, the claim analyst is responsible for checking a policy in detail, for paying full benefits for all covered treatments, and for denying benefits for all claims not covered by the policy provisions.

The claim analyst also verifies whether a policy contains a subrogation clause. ***Subrogation*** is a contractual right that permits an insurer to recover payments made to an insured for medical care if that insured receives payment for damages through a legal action. You will recall that a medical claim form contains a question concerning whether a claimant expects to receive or has received payment for medical expenses as the result of a lawsuit or settlement. If a claimant is reimbursed for medical expenses as the result of such a legal action, the insurer is eligible to recover whatever monies the insurer has paid in medical benefits.

For example, suppose an insured is involved in an automobile accident, and the insurer pays $15,000 for medical costs resulting from the accident. The insured later sues the person who caused the accident and is awarded $45,000 by the court. If the insured's policy contains a subrogation clause, the insurer can recover up to $15,000 to offset the medical expenses incurred. Figure 18-4 contains a typical subrogation clause.

Calculating the Amount of Policy Benefits

After a claim analyst assesses the information associated with a claim and has determined that the claim should be paid, the next step is to determine the amount of benefits to be paid under the policy. Insurers generally use one of several approaches to determine the amount of

Figure 18-4. Subrogation clause.

Upon payment of medical benefits, the insurer will be subrogated to all rights of recovery the insured may have against a third party. This right extends to the proceeds of any settlement or judgment, but is limited to the amount of benefits that the insurer has paid. In this regard, the insured must

- Do nothing to prejudice any right of the insured to recover
- Execute and deliver any required information
- Do whatever else is necessary to secure such rights

payable benefits. Diagnostic related groups (DRGs) is a prospective payment method, and a schedule of benefits, a maximum limit, and reasonable and customary limits are retrospective payment methods.

Diagnostic Related Groups

In an attempt to reduce some of the costs of unnecessary medical care, the Medicare system in the United States introduced diagnostic related groups as a method of paying claims, and some insurers have adopted this method. ***Diagnostic Related Groups (DRGs)*** is a prospective payment method providing that a payor will pay hospital charges not according to the number and types of services delivered, but according to the diagnosis for a patient. If a hospital can deliver care for a certain diagnosis at a lower cost, the hospital is entitled to keep the full amount allowed for treatment of a patient having that diagnosis. If a hospital spends more in treating such a patient than is reimbursed, however, the hospital loses money on the transaction.

Under a DRG system, a patient's diagnosis is translated to a DRG, and the payor reimburses hospitals, but not other medical caregivers, for that DRG according to a payment schedule. If a patient's diagnosis cannot be classified under a DRG, the patient's case is handled individually to determine how much to pay for each medical service. Certain kinds of hospitals—those specializing in care for cancer, psychiatric disorders, long-term care, and children's diseases, and those providing rehabilitation services—are exempt from the requirements established for DRGs.

In handling a claim based on DRGs, the claim analyst determines whether the DRG to which a patient is assigned is appropriate. Specifically, the claim analyst checks to be sure that the hospital has provided a DRG that accurately describes the patient's condition and that the treatment provided is consistent with that DRG. The claim analyst also verifies that the patient was not discharged too early from the hospital as part of a cost-containment effort. For some conditions, premature discharge may result in later medical complications for which the insurer may be liable.

Schedule of Benefits

For claim purposes, a ***schedule of benefits*** is a listing of medical treatments and the maximum benefit amounts an insurer will pay for each treatment. Using a schedule of benefits enables a claim analyst retrospectively to determine the amount of policy benefits due. This schedule is not to be confused with the schedule of benefits used in group insurance to specify the amount of coverage provided for each class of

Figure 18-5. Portion of a typical schedule of benefits.

Procedures	Benefit Amount
Hysterectomy	$1,650 per procedure
Cesarean section	$1,370 per procedure
Appendectomy	$1,025 per procedure
Tonsillectomy	$ 380 per procedure

insureds, a topic we discussed in Chapter 10. Figure 18-5 illustrates a portion of a typical schedule of benefits.

A typical schedule of benefits might state the percentage of charges that will be reimbursed or paid for certain medical costs. For instance, a schedule of benefits may specify that an insurer will pay for 80 percent of the first $5,000 of medical expenses and 100 percent of expenses above $5,000. As an example using these figures, suppose that an insured underwent a surgical procedure and was confined in a hospital for three days. The total medical expenses were $13,500. The insurer would pay 80 percent of the first $5,000 of medical expenses, or $4,000, and 100 percent of the remaining expenses of $8,500 ($13,500 – $5,000), for a total of $12,500 in benefits ($4,000 + $8,500).

A schedule of benefits under managed care might provide that the insurer will pay for 90 percent of medical care provided by a medical caregiver within a network and will pay 70 percent of medical care provided by a medical caregiver outside the network. Therefore, an insured who incurs expenses of $10,000 using an in-network caregiver will have $9,000 of those expenses paid by insurance, whereas an insured who incurs expenses of $10,000 using an out-of-network caregiver will have $7,000 of those expenses paid by insurance.

Maximum Limit

Another retrospective approach to calculating policy benefits is a ***maximum limit*** approach, which involves payment of a specified amount of total benefits for claims arising from a single injury or incident, or one period of sickness. A maximum limit approach may also establish the maximum number of days of coverage for specific services—for instance, the number of days of hospital admission or of treatment in a rehabilitation center. Many health insurance policies also contain a ***lifetime maximum benefit,*** which is the maximum amount that the policy will pay for all eligible medical expenses an individual incurs while insured under the policy. An example of maximum limits for certain procedures is shown in Figure 18-6.

Figure 18-6. Examples of maximum limits for health insurance.

Procedures	Maximum Limit
Treatment for mental and nervous condition	$15,000 lifetime
Inpatient treatment	45 days per person per calendar year
Outpatient care	25 visits per person per calendar year
Substance abuse	$15,000 lifetime *and* 30 days inpatient care per person per calendar year *and* 30 outpatient visits per person per calendar year
Physical therapy	$1,000 per person per calendar year

Reasonable and Customary Limits

By establishing ***reasonable and customary limits,*** an insurer retrospectively specifies that the amount paid for a claim must conform to the amount most frequently charged for each medical procedure in a given geographical area. An insurer may obtain information about reasonable and customary amounts from such sources as the Health Insurance Association of America (HIAA). Alternatively, large insurers generally develop enough historical information to determine what rates are reasonable and customary in the areas in which their insureds receive medical treatment.

Reasonable and customary limits are usually confined to surgical benefits, but some insurers use them for other types of charges such as office visits, hospital room and board, anesthesia, radiology, and laboratory services. The amounts allowed under reasonable and customary limits can vary significantly from one geographical area to another and are generally higher in urban areas and lower in rural areas.

Under a policy that uses reasonable and customary limits, an insured might submit a claim for $500 for a specific treatment. If the reasonable and customary charge for that treatment in the insured's geographical area is $450, the insurer will most likely limit the benefit to $450. On the other hand, if the reasonable and customary charge for that treatment in the insured's geographical area is $600, the insurer will consider the charge of $500 as acceptable for the treatment. If the insurer typically pays for the specified procedure at 80 percent of the total charge, in the first case the insurer would pay a benefit of $360 ($450 × .80) and in the second case would pay a benefit of $400 ($500 × .80).

Ensuring That Benefits Are Appropriately Paid

After examining a claim and determining the extent of the insurer's liability for it, the claim analyst decides whether the amount of benefits should be reduced as a result of deductibles, applicable exclusions or limitations, or coordination of benefits with other insurers or with other providers. After making such determinations, the claim analyst finally submits the claim to be paid.

Deductibles

The claim analyst first reduces the amount of covered expenses by any applicable deductible. Some basic or hospital-surgical medical plans have no deductibles, so that the insurer pays the first dollar of medical costs up to any specified dollar or percentage limit. In such a situation, the claim analyst does not subtract any deductible amount from the benefits due.

Comprehensive medical plans, by contrast, usually require an ***initial deductible,*** which is an amount an insured must pay before any medical expenses are paid by an insurer. After the initial deductible is paid, the insurer pays the remaining amount, usually up to a specified dollar or percentage limit. If a policy contains a provision for ***coinsurance***—which is the percentage of all eligible medical expenses, in excess of the deductible, incurred as a result of sickness or injury and which the insured is required to pay—the claim analyst calculates the amount of coinsurance and deducts that amount from the benefit amount.

Suppose that a policy has a $500 deductible and pays 80 percent of covered medical expenses above the initial deductible. The remaining 20 percent of the amount in excess of the deductible is the amount that is to be paid as coinsurance. If an insured has incurred $5,000 of covered medical expenses, payments are made as follows:

The insured pays
$500 initial deductible
$900 coinsurance ($5,000 – $500 = $4,500; $4,500 × .20 = $900)

The insurer pays
$3,600 in benefits ($5,000 – $500 = $4,500; $4,500 × .80 = $3,600)

Major medical plans often include an all-causes deductible, and a few plans have a per-cause deductible. An ***all-causes deductible*** is a deductible that must be satisfied only once during a specified period of time, usually one year, no matter how many illnesses or injuries result in medical expenses. A person covered under a major medical policy with an annual all-causes deductible of $500 would pay only $500 in deductibles regardless of the number of different illnesses or injuries that resulted in medical expenses during the year. By contrast, a ***per-cause deductible*** is a deductible that must be satisfied for each separate illness or injury that results in medical expenses. A person covered under a major medical policy with an annual per-cause deductible of $500 would pay $500 for each illness or injury that resulted in medical expenses.

Most major medical plans require a ***corridor deductible,*** which is an amount that an insured must pay above the amount paid by his basic policy before any benefits are payable under the major medical policy. You might think of the corridor deductible as a "bridge" between the basic policy and the major medical policy. After the basic policy has paid all possible benefits, the insured must pay a bridge amount before the major medical policy begins to pay benefits.

Suppose that an insured has exhausted the $30,000 in benefits offered by her basic medical policy and submits a claim under major medical coverage, which has a $2,000 corridor deductible. The insured is responsible for paying that corridor deductible, and the major medical policy then begins to cover claims in excess of $32,000 ($30,000 covered by the basic policy plus the $2,000 deductible).

Coordination of Benefits

The claim analyst is responsible for ascertaining as accurately as possible whether an insured is covered under any other insurance that is paying benefits for the expenses claimed. We have already defined coordination of benefits and have explained how an insurer evaluates the amount to be paid under a policy when a claimant is also covered under another policy. For example, when an insured is covered not only by a medical insurance policy but by a health maintenance organization (HMO) or by a government-sponsored program such as Medicare, Medicaid, or social insurance, the claim analyst determines how much of the cost has been covered by the HMO or the government-sponsored program and how much should be covered by the policy. These determinations can be complex and are beyond the scope of this textbook.

Payment of Benefits

After calculating the amount of benefits due to a claimant, the claim analyst requests that payment be sent to the appropriate recipient. In many situations, the claimant has signed an ***assignment of benefits,*** which is a statement on the claim form that directs an insurer to pay benefits directly to a medical provider rather than to an insured. A typical authorization of benefits statement says simply, "I authorize payment of medical benefits to the undersigned physician or supplier for service(s) described." If an insured has not signed an authorization of benefits statement, the claim analyst usually sends the benefit payment directly to the insured. After making a decision on each claim, the claim analyst sends the claimant an ***explanation of benefits (EOB),*** which is a detailed statement showing each treatment or medication submitted as part of a claim, the insurer's decision concerning payment of each charge, any amount that is considered as a deductible or a copayment, an explanation of any charge for which part or all of the charge will not be paid, and the total amount sent to the medical provider.

What happens if an insured dies before a medical claim is settled? If the insured signed an assignment of benefits statement, the claim analyst directs that payment be made to the medical caregiver. Otherwise, payment is usually made to the estate of the deceased insured. Some jurisdictions require an insurer to give notice to the tax department of life insurance benefits paid to an estate, and some jurisdictions require an insurer to withhold a proportion of such benefits to be used for paying taxes on the proceeds.

Cooperating in Case Management

As medical care becomes more sophisticated—and, usually, more expensive—insurers continue to try to keep the costs of providing care as low as possible without compromising the quality of that care. A claim analyst may be involved not only in handling claims, but in cooperating with medical caregivers, patients' families, and cost-containment specialists employed by the insurer in helping to ensure that expenses involved in providing care in high-cost cases do not reach undue levels.

As we discussed in Chapter 16, case management is a cost-containment process of handling the costs of illnesses and injuries by identifying alternate methods of treatment that can make the most efficient and cost-effective use of medical resources consistent with desirable results for each patient. The goal of case management is not just to save money for the insurer, but to ensure that each patient receives appropriate care without taking unnecessary measures. Case management may involve such alternatives to hospitalization as hospice care, home care, rehabilitation, and counseling. A claim analyst involved in case management is usually given sufficient authority to approve certain expenses associated with the medical care of an insured. Because management of a case may continue for months or years, a claim analyst is trained in keeping accurate records of the case so that, if responsibility for handling the case is transferred to another claim analyst, the case file will provide accurate, detailed information.

Key Words and Concepts

diagnostic and treatment codes
International Classification of Diseases and Related Health Problems (ICD)
Physicians' Current Procedural Terminology (CPT)
medical necessity
covered person
overinsurance provision
preadmission certification (*precertification*)
hospice
subrogation
Diagnostic Related Groups (DRGs)
schedule of benefits
maximum limit
lifetime maximum benefit
reasonable and customary limits
initial deductible
coinsurance
all-causes deductible
per-cause deductible
corridor deductible
assignment of benefits
explanation of benefits (EOB)

CHAPTER NINETEEN

Administering Disability Income Insurance Claims

Learning Objectives

After studying this chapter, you should be able to

- Define and explain *contestability, elimination period,* and *benefit period* in connection with disability coverage
- Distinguish among five forms of disability
- Distinguish among four types of renewability for individual disability coverage
- Explain the several exceptions and limitations of disability coverage
- Name and define supplementary benefits under disability income coverage
- Name and explain the kinds of claim information available from five information sources
- Explain how offsets function in the calculation of benefits under disability income coverage
- Discuss the special disability income claim considerations for continuing claims and claims for mental illness and substance abuse
- List and define types of questionable claims
- Describe and explain three circumstances in which disability income benefits may be terminated
- Explain the differences in settling disputed and undisputed claims

Chapter Outline

General Provisions of Disability Income Contracts
Injury and Sickness; Contestability; Elimination Period; Benefit Period; Definition of Disability; Benefit Amount; Renewability; Exceptions and Limitations

Supplementary Benefits under Disability Income Coverage
Waiver of Premium for Disability; Cost of Living Increase; Rehabilitation Benefit; Transplant Donor Benefit; Future Increase Option

Information Sources for Disability Income Claims
Disability Income Claim Form; APS and Medical Information; Financial Information; Personal Information; Employer Information

Administering Disability Income Claims
Coordinating Other Disability Income Benefits
Managing Benefits for Mental Illness and Substance Abuse
Managing Benefits for Continuing Claims
Administering Contestable Claims
Administering Questionable Claims

Administering Rehabilitation

Terminating Disability Income Benefits
End of Maximum Benefit Period
End of Disability
End of Employee or Group Eligibility

Settling Disability Income Claims
Disputed Claims
Undisputed Claims

When a person insured under disability income insurance is unable to work because of a disabling injury or illness, the insurer generally compensates that person for a portion of the income she lost because of the disability. This form of coverage may be long-term or short-term and may provide a variety of benefits depending on the specific policy provisions. Disability income insurance usually does not provide medical expense coverage.

Disability income benefits may be provided under life insurance and health insurance, as well as under specialized types of business insurance such as disability buy-out coverage, business overhead expense policies, and key person disability coverage. Health insurance can provide several different kinds of disability income benefits, depending on which benefits an insured individual or group elects to include in the policy.

We have already discussed the underwriting principles used in assessing applicants for disability income coverage. You'll recall that the underwriter checks both primary and secondary income sources in determining the amount of disability income coverage for which an applicant is eligible. Because disability income benefits are not intended to replace all of an insured's regular earnings when he is disabled, the benefit amount is less than the amount of those earnings. The benefit amount is usually figured as a percentage (normally between 60 and 75 percent) of regular income; some policies specify that the insurer will pay a flat income benefit if the insured becomes disabled. The percentage method is most often used for group disability coverage, whereas the flat benefit amount is most often used for individual disability coverage. Generally, the benefits under disability income insurance are provided in a series of monthly payments. Like medical insurance, disability insurance is subject to the abuses of overinsurance and fraud, two issues we will discuss in the next chapter.

Administering disability claims requires a great deal of judgment and insight. The facts of every case are slightly different, and the claim analyst usually has to consider a number of factors before making a decision on a claim. Because consistency in claim decisions is critical, and because decisions on disability income claims are often difficult to reach, most insurers arrange periodic meetings of disability claim staff to discuss claim issues. In some insurance companies, claim analysts meet with underwriting, legal, marketing, and actuarial staff to review underwriting practices, policy provisions, and claim practices. Insight 19-1 comments on the need for

Insight 19-1 My Thoughts On . . . A Reality Check for Disability Management

Everyone knows that common sense is an inherent trait and that we all have it (or we assume we do) to some degree. We also know that from time to time something mysterious seems to happen to our common sense. We vacillate, we waver, we drift in some poetic way away from the ground rules of our daily lives and our work. When we arrive back on earth from the cosmos we have traveled to, we are shocked and amazed to realize that there is something awry, something amiss, and we lament, "What *was* I thinking?" and "How *could* I have missed that?"

As capable as we may be, it seems this happens even to the best of disability income case workers and managers. I know because I work in disability case management, and over the years I have reviewed hundreds, if not thousands, of claim files and cases from a multitude of case workers.

The collective result of disability claim administration is that huge numbers of workers have been helped to return to gainful, productive lives in work that is suitable to their physical and mental abilities. These people otherwise might have remained by the wayside, labeled only as disabled. In disability case management, we know that the disability period is transitional, relating to the time between the onset of the medical condition which forces a worker out of the workplace and the management of that condition so that the worker's abilities can be assessed. The case worker or manager makes these determinations and then develops a plan aimed at maximizing the worker's abilities for suitable work or creating new abilities through retraining or other vocational options. It is during this process that I recommend a *reality check.* It is meant to ensure that our common sense is not on a cosmic vacation and that our disability management plans make good sense and focus on the circumstances of each disabled worker.

Consider the case of a disabled truck driver who insisted that with financial assistance he could become self-sufficient again if he could buy his own tractor-trailer and hire someone to make the necessary runs across the country. He anticipated that he would garner the contracts needed to get his business up and going, and in no time would be able to buy more trucks and add more drivers. There was no question that this man had the knowledge about the operation of the right kinds of trucks and that he was committed to his dream of owning a business. We urged him to solicit advice from his banker and to submit a business plan that would demonstrate how his dream could be made a reality. No business plan ever arrived, yet the truck driver confirmed regularly that he was looking into the venture. Time went by, and no substantial progress was made. Everyone concerned was becoming a little frustrated, but no one really knew why.

Eventually, we undertook a complete review of the truck driver's disability claim file—a large file, as this man had been disabled off and on for many years. We found deep in the file a neuropsychological profile which revealed that the man was below average on several of the ranges of testing so that, ultimately, he would have had little chance of success in running a business. He had not prepared a business case because he could not appreciate the complexity of running a business.

The point? If the file had been reviewed thoroughly when the insured initiated a discussion about developing his own business, this man would not have been encouraged to proceed in this way. As an employee in a different industry, he would have had a far better chance of success with challenges that he could meet.

Use this as your example to take a reality check from time to time in handling disability income claims. If a case seems perplexing, there is usually a good reason. Check all the facts, and be thorough. Verify that you have followed your usually successful protocol for case management. Call on your common sense, and if it's on an unapproved leave, send it a reality check!

Kerry Turner, FLMI, ALHC, HIA
Manager, Life and Disability Claims
Blue Cross Life Insurance Company

disability claim administrators to maintain a clear perspective in handling claims.

In this chapter, we'll begin by explaining the basic and supplementary provisions of disability income contracts with which claim analysts must be familiar. Next we'll examine the information sources that claim analysts use for examining disability claims. Then we'll discuss administration of disability income claims, contestable claims, questionable claims, rehabilitation, termination of claims, and claim settlements.

General Provisions of Disability Income Contracts

Handling disability income claims requires the claim analyst to be completely familiar with the definitions and provisions of the insurance product. The general provisions of disability income insurance contracts cover the definitions of injury and sickness, contestability, elimination period, benefit period, disability, waiver of premium, benefit amount, and renewability. Moreover, both individual and group disability income policies include certain exceptions and limitations. Such exceptions and limitations usually include preexisting conditions, disability exclusions, and coverage while on military duty. In discussing these policy provisions, exceptions, and limitations, we'll explain the actions that the claim analyst typically takes for each.

Fast Fact

Of all disability income policies, group insurance is growing the fastest: between 1994 and 1995 the insurance industry saw an increase of 42.26 percent in the net premiums written on this type of policy.

Source: Roger L. Blease, "Group Disability Income Net Premiums Written," *Best's Review (Life/Health)*, August 1996: 54.

Injury and Sickness

Every disability income policy defines injury and sickness as each will be covered under the contract. Generally, an ***injury*** is defined as an accidental harm resulting from an unforeseen external force (1) causing trauma to a person's body and (2) occurring while the disability income policy is in force. Moreover, an injury is normally defined as a condition resulting independently of sickness. Usually a ***sickness*** is an illness or a disease that (1) includes pregnancy unless it is specifically excluded under the contract and (2) begins while a person is insured under the policy.

Contestability

Most short- and long-term disability income policies provide for a specified contestable period. Any material misstatement or material misrepresentation that an insured may have made in the application for insurance is grounds for rescission of the policy. For any claim in which a material misstatement or a material misrepresentation appears to be evident, the claim analyst is responsible for determining whether the contestable period is still in effect.

Elimination Period

Some disability income policies specify an elimination period that must pass following the beginning of a covered disability before an insured is eligible to receive benefits. The purpose of an elimination period in disability income insurance is to eliminate the expense of administering small amounts of benefits for injuries or illnesses that last only a brief time. The claim analyst verifies that any required elimination period has been satisfied before approving disability income benefits.

Short-term disability income insurance provided under group insurance typically provides no elimination period for disability caused by an accident or a scheduled surgery, and an elimination period of one week for disability resulting from illness. The elimination period for long-term disability coverage provided under a group contract is usually 30 days to 6 months. The elimination period for individual coverage varies widely, but most policies provide that the longer the elimination period, the lower the cost of the coverage.

Benefit Period

The ***benefit period*** of a disability income policy is the length of time during which disability income benefits will be paid. The benefit period may last from less than a year to age 65 or 70. Some long-term contracts specify that disability income coverage will be offered until the insured's normal retirement age, and some contracts provide for lifetime disability income benefits.

Definition of Disability

In order to be eligible to receive benefits under a disability income contract, an insured must meet the contract's definition of disability. The claim analyst ascertains whether an insured has met the policy's definition of a particular level of disability, which may vary from one policy to another. The levels of disability covered under disability contracts typically include total disability, presumptive total disability, residual disability, partial disability, and recurring disability.

Total disability. The most commonly used definition of ***total disability*** in both short-term and long-term DI contracts includes the complete and continuous inability of an insured at the beginning of his disability to perform the essential duties of his regular occupation. The majority of long-term DI contracts add a second definition relating to disability that continues beyond a specified period. A typical definition of both the first and second definitions is as follows:

"Total disability" means your inability, as a result of injury or sickness, to perform the substantial and material duties of your principal occupation for the first 24 months of continuous disability. After the first 24 months of continuous disability, "total disability" means the inability to engage in any occupation for which you are qualified by reason of education, training, or experience. You must be under a physician's care and receive regular medical attention during a period of total disability.

As the example indicates, the total disability definition for long-term disability usually specifies that after an insured has been disabled for a specified period, usually two to five years, the person is considered totally disabled only if the disability prevents him from fulfilling the requirements of *any occupation* for which he is reasonably fitted by education, training, or experience. Insurers typically distinguish between an "own occupation" disability—one that prevents an insured from performing the essential duties of his regular occupation—and an "any occupation" disability—one that prevents an insured from performing the essential duties of any occupation for which he is reasonably fitted.

Some policies specify that if an insured cannot perform the duties of his own previous occupation, but can perform the duties of another occupation, he is still eligible for total disability income benefits, but at a reduced rate—usually 50 percent of full disability income benefits. The wording of the policy determines whether benefits are paid to an insured who is able to work at a job for which he is reasonably fitted, but which is not his previous occupation. From one jurisdiction to another, the applications of the "own occupation" and "any occupation" distinctions vary widely.

Insurers generally establish specific criteria for determining whether a disabled person can engage in an occupation—for which she is reasonably fitted—other than her primary one. These criteria usually include

- The insured's previous work experience in the primary occupation and in any other occupation
- The insured's previous education and training
- The insured's earnings history and overall standard of living
- The insured's age
- Impairments of the insured's physical and mental activities
- Current opportunities for the insured to work
- Applicable laws and statutes

Most insurers provide that if a disabled insured returns to work in an occupation different from her principal occupation, that occupation does not have to be one that is degrading, that does not provide sufficient income, or that endangers the insured's health or well-being. If an insured is able to return to work in another suitable occupation for which she is reasonably fitted, but does not choose to do so, the insurer is usually legally entitled to stop payment of full benefits and to pay only the level of benefits to which the insured would be entitled if she were to return to work at another occupation for which she is reasonably fitted.

Presumptive total disability. A disability income policy may specify that if an insured suffers a presumptive total disability, that insured is eligible to receive disability income benefits. A ***presumptive total disability*** is a condition that automatically causes an insured to be considered totally disabled. Such a loss is usually severe, such as total and permanent blindness, loss of speech or hearing in both ears, or loss of two limbs.

If a disability income contract contains this type of provision, the claim analyst verifies through medical documents and consultation with medical caregivers that a specified loss has occurred and that the insured is eligible for benefits under the policy. After appropriate verification of the presumptive total loss, the claim analyst approves payment of benefits from the date of loss. For a presumptive total disability, the elimination period is usually waived. If an insured with a presumptive total disability is able to return to work, even in his own occupation, most insurers do not reduce the amount of disability income benefits nor cease payment of benefits for as long as the disability lasts. The benefit period for presumptive total disability usually lasts until the end of the policy's maximum benefit period.

Residual disability. Under most disability contracts an insured is considered to have suffered a ***residual disability*** if he is not totally disabled, but is still unable to function as before the sickness or injury, and therefore suffers a reduction in income of at least the percentage—typically 20 percent to 25 percent—specified in the DI plan. Some insurers, in addition to the reduced income requirement, also specify that meeting the definition of residual disability requires that an insured need ongoing medical care and/or be unable to work for the length of time needed to perform his usual occupational duties.

Many insurers require that, in addition to the elimination period, an insured also satisfy a qualification period before becoming eligible for benefits for a residual disability. A ***qualification period*** is the length of time—usually between 30 and 90 days—that an insured must be totally disabled before she becomes eligible for residual disability income benefits.

In determining the amount of income that has been lost as the result of a residual disability, the claim analyst first establishes the amount of income the insured earned before the onset of the disability. Most insurers calculate the amount of pre-disability income as the average of income for the 12-month period immediately preceding the onset of the disability. If an insured who suffers a residual disability is able to earn income from a source other than the former occupation, that amount of income is considered in computing the amount of disability benefit.

To calculate the amount of residual disability benefit due to an insured, most insurers multiply (1) the monthly benefit that would be due if an insured had suffered a total disability by (2) the percentage of earnings lost. For example, suppose an insured earned an average of $4,000 per month prior to becoming residually disabled. He was covered by a disability income policy that would reimburse him for 70 percent of his pre-disability earnings if he were totally disabled. He would, therefore, receive a benefit of $2,800 per month if he were completely disabled ($4,000 × .70). During his disability, he is able to earn $3,000 per month. His percentage of earnings lost is 25 percent ($4,000 – $3,000 = $1,000 ÷ $4,000). To calculate the amount of residual disability benefit due this insured, the claim analyst multiplies (1) the benefit that would be due if the insured had suffered a total disability ($2,800) by (2) the percentage of earnings lost (25 percent) to arrive at a residual disability benefit of $700.

Partial disability. Although many disability income policies sold recently provide only for residual disability and not for partial disability, claim analysts need to know how to handle claims under partial disability provisions included in many older disability policies. A ***partial disability*** involves inability, resulting from sickness or injury, to perform one or more of the main duties of an insured's former occupation or to perform the duties on a full-time basis.

A person who qualifies for partial disability may be able to perform some or all of the less important duties of his former occupation, or may be able to perform his main duties on a part-time basis. To qualify for benefits under most disability policies, an insured must be under the care of a physician during the period of disability. After an insured has experienced a period of total disability, he may be able to return to work at his own or another occupation and may then be considered partially disabled.

In making a decision on partial disability, the claim analyst determines the job duties that are included in an insured's full-time occupation and the type and extent of the insured's disability that prevents her from fulfilling those duties. Claims for partial disability require careful monitoring by the claim analyst to ensure that the insurable loss is continuing and that the insured is unable to do her regular work. The claim analyst maintains a record of the medical treatments provided for the insured and verifies the extent of the partial disability throughout the period during which the loss is claimed. A case involving an insured who is self-employed and who claims partial disability requires special care, usually including a claim representative's visit to the insured's place of work to verify the facts of the claim.

In determining the benefit amount under a partial disability provision, a claim analyst does not consider the percentage of income lost. Instead, the benefit that is usually payable under partial disability is equal to half of the benefit that would be paid for total disability. Most insurers limit to six months the length of time during which partial disability income benefits will be paid. Therefore, benefits for partial disability can be considered short-term, whereas benefits for residual disability can be considered long-term.

Recurring disability. Sometimes an insured experiences a period of total or residual disability, recovers from the disability, and is able to return to work. The condition that originally caused the disability may recur, with the result that the insured is once again totally or residually disabled. A ***recurring disability*** is one that is the result of the same cause as for an original disability and that reappears after (1) the original period of disability and (2) an intervening period of recovery.

Most disability income policies provide that if such a disability (1) recurs within six months from the date the previous disability ended and (2) results from the original sickness or injury, then the insurer will consider the new disability period as a continuation of the original disability period. If more than six months has elapsed since the end of the previous disability and if the new disability results from the original sickness or injury, most insurers consider the new disability *not* to be a continuation of the previous disability and establish new elimination and benefit periods. Benefits for recurring disability help the insured because the elimination period is waived. However, the length of the benefit period remains unchanged.

Benefit Amount

If a disabled insured were to receive an amount of disability income benefits equal to or greater than his income prior to the disability, he would have little incentive to return to work. As we have noted, disability income coverage is intended to replace some, but not all, of an insured's earnings. The amount of benefits is usually set during underwriting. If an insured's salary has increased significantly since the time of underwriting the coverage, or if an insured has developed significant other sources of income—for instance, from investments or a second job—the benefit amount remains as agreed in the contract for total disability. Residual benefits, if any, may be lower because of the additional income.

Renewability

In handling claims under individual disability policies, a claim analyst reviews a policy's specifications for renewability to determine whether the insured is, in fact, still covered by the policy. Generally, renewability is an essential feature of a disability income policy because it determines whether an insurer continues to be responsible for the risk over a period of time. Four types of renewability provisions are those for noncancelable, guaranteed renewable, conditionally renewable, and optionally renewable coverage.

Noncancelable. The most liberal form of renewability for disability income coverage is ***noncancelable,*** which means that, until the insured reaches a specified age (usually age 65), the insurer will not cancel the coverage, increase the premiums, or change the policy provisions as long as the premiums are paid. An insured who reaches age 65 and is still employed for at least a specified minimum number of hours per week (usually between 20 to 30 hours) may, under some disability income contracts, continue the disability income coverage by paying a higher premium for as long as employment continues. A claim analyst evaluating a noncancelable disability income policy has only to verify that the premiums are paid to date on the coverage.

Guaranteed renewable. ***Guaranteed renewable*** disability income coverage offers the same continued coverage as noncancelable coverage *except* that the insurer may increase the premiums, not for an individual insured, but for all the policyowners within a defined class of insureds. Classes may be defined by age group, gender, policy type, occupation, or other specific criteria. In verifying that a guaranteed renewable policy is still in force, the claim analyst checks whether the premiums are paid to date and whether any increase in premium that has been communicated to the insured has been reflected in recent premium payments.

Some disability income policies state that coverage is "noncancelable and guaranteed renewable" to a specified age. Such policies are noncancelable—even though the term "guaranteed renewable" appears—and the insurer cannot raise premiums until the insured reaches the specified age.

Conditionally renewable. A disability income policy that is ***conditionally renewable*** sets criteria that the insured must meet in order to renew the coverage. The most frequently established criterion is continued employment or ongoing membership in a professional or other organization. Verifying coverage under a conditionally renewable disability income policy requires the claim analyst to check that the insured continues to meet the criteria established for that coverage. A refusal to renew a conditionally renewable DI policy cannot be based on the health of the insured.

Optionally renewable. ***Optionally renewable*** disability income coverage enables an insurer to change premium rates at any time and to cancel the coverage with sufficient notice to an insured.

Exceptions and Limitations

The exceptions and limitations of disability income policies generally relate to preexisting conditions, certain specified disabilities for which benefits will not be paid, and coverage while on military duty.

Preexisting conditions. Except for conditions covered under legislation discussed in Chapter 18, most insurers do not pay disability income benefits for total disability caused by preexisting conditions during the first two years (or whatever period is legally established for a jurisdiction) that the policy is in force. The two-year period is measured from the date when the policy first becomes effective. Under a disability income policy, a preexisting condition is generally defined the same as it is for any other individual policy—that is, as a condition for which an individual received medical care during a specified period of time prior to the effective date of the proposed coverage. An injury or a sickness is considered to have "made itself known" when the symptoms are sufficiently evident to cause a prudent person to seek medical attention, care, or advice. Generally, any conditions that are fully disclosed on the application for insurance but are not excluded or limited by the policy are not considered to be preexisting conditions.

Specified disabilities. If a disability is named in a policy as one for which no coverage is offered, then claims for such a disability will not be paid. Most disability income policies include as specified disabilities such conditions as injuries or sickness that result from an act of declared or undeclared war, as well as suicide or attempted suicide, whether an insured is sane or insane.

Coverage while on military duty. Some disability income policies provide that on the first day that an insured enters full-time active duty in any branch of the armed forces of any country, disability income coverage is suspended until full-time active duty is completed. Generally, full-time active duty does not include active duty training that lasts for two months or less.

Some insurers allow a person who was previously insured under a disability income policy and who leaves full-time active military duty within a specified period of time—usually five years—to reinstate the disability income coverage without evidence of insurability by giving the insurer 60 days' notice of intent to reinstate the insurance. Premiums for the reinstated coverage are usually calculated at the insured's previous age—that is, the age at which the disability coverage was discontinued because of the insured's entry into full-time active military duty. A disability income policy that is reinstated under these conditions covers only losses caused by an injury or a sickness that begins within a specified period—usually 10 days—after the policy is reinstated.

Supplementary Benefits under Disability Income Coverage

The supplementary benefits included under many disability income policies are waiver of premium for disability, a cost of living increase benefit, a rehabilitation benefit, a transplant donor benefit, and future increase options.

Waiver of Premium for Disability

Unlike a waiver of premium for disability provision in a life insurance policy, a waiver of premium provision in a disability income policy automatically becomes effective as soon as monthly disability income benefits become payable. Generally, a ***waiver of premium for disability*** provision in a disability policy provides that after an insured has been disabled for a specified period—usually 60 to 90 days—premiums will be waived for as long as the insured is disabled. If the insured has paid any premiums during the specified period, those premiums are refunded. In this situation, the "specified period" generally refers to the elimination period or another period cited in the policy. The claim analyst is responsible for ensuring that such premium refunds are correctly and promptly made.

Cost of Living Increase

After an insured has received total disability income benefits for a specified, uninterrupted period, usually 12 consecutive months, a ***cost of living increase benefit*** feature provides an increase in the monthly disability benefit. This increase is typically a percentage of the monthly benefit amount. The assumption underlying a cost of living increase benefit is that an employed person would probably continue to receive periodic salary increases. If a policy contains a cost of living increase provision and the insured continues to be disabled, the claim analyst authorizes an increase in the benefit amount according to the terms of the provision.

Rehabilitation Benefit

During any period when an insured is receiving total or partial disability income benefits, the ***rehabilitation benefit*** provides that an insurer may reimburse the insured for the expenses associated with participation in a rehabilitation program. The definition of a rehabilitation program is specified in the policy contract and typically requires that any such program must be operated by a federal, state, or provincial government or must be offered by a licensed hospital, vocational school, business school, or accredited college. Rehabilitation may include physical, educational, or vocational assistance. Some insurers offer rehabilitation reimbursements to some insureds even if the policy contract does not contain this type of provision, particularly if the insured seems to be motivated to work and if rehabilitation will cost less than projected disability income benefits.

Fast Fact

According to a Health Insurance Association of America study, insurers that offered group disability insurance lines and that used case management programs saw a return of $30 in savings for every dollar they spent on the programs.

Source: Bill Gradison, "Management Programs Serve Customers and Insurers," *Best's Review (Life/Health)*, February 1996: 64.

Most insurers require an insured who wishes to receive such rehabilitation benefits to consult with the insurer and reach agreement on the type and extent of rehabilitation services that will be reimbursed. In addition, most policies set a dollar limit on the total amount of rehabilitation benefits or on the type of rehabilitation services that will be reimbursed. The dollar limit is usually a multiple, such as 10 or 12, of the policy's maximum monthly disability benefit. For example, if a DI policy paid a maximum monthly disability benefit of $1,000 and the rehabilitation limit was 12 times the maximum monthly disability benefit, the total amount that the policy would pay for rehabilitation services would not exceed $12,000.

Transplant Donor Benefit

A ***transplant donor benefit*** specifies that if an insured undergoes surgery to donate a part of his body to another person, the insurer will treat that surgery as a sickness and will pay benefits for it. If the surgery results in total disability, benefits will be paid under the policy. Most insurers limit the transplant donor benefit by requiring that a transplant surgery occur at least 12 months after the policy's effective date. Among other facts, the claim analyst verifies that the required time period has passed since the policy date.

Future Increase Option

Some insurers allow insureds to exercise a ***future increase option*** to buy additional disability income protection without providing evidence of insurability. The waiting period and the maximum benefit period for each increase are usually the same as for the original policy. The premium for each increase is figured at the rates in effect at the insured's attained age at the time the increase is purchased. If any extra premiums or riders are attached to the original policy because of an impairment stated on the policy application, they also apply to future increases. Once an insured exercises a future increase option, the insurer generally requires proof that the insured's earnings meet the insurer's financial underwriting requirements so that the insured does not attempt to purchase coverage which she cannot afford and which might provide an incentive to avoid work.

Information Sources for Disability Income Claims

Evaluation of a disability income claim involves not only establishing the presence of a disability, but also attempting to determine the future ability of the insured to perform the duties of her current job or of another job. Moreover, the evaluation may focus on planned rehabilitation for the insured so that she will be able to return as soon as possible to work at her own occupation or at another occupation.

Evaluating a disability claim is complex because many factors can contribute to an insured's experience during and upon recovery from an illness or injury. Among these factors are the insured's attitudes toward illness, work, and the current employer; the insured's current and future financial status; economic conditions and prospects for financial stability in the insured's occupation and current job; the motivation and ethics of the medical caregivers who treat the insured; and the insured's alternatives for medical treatment, rehabilitation, and future employment. Any of these factors can play a significant role in the outcome of an illness or injury suffered by an insured.

In handling claims under disability income coverage, the claim analyst typically uses two basic sources of information: the claim form and the attending physician's statement (APS). More medical, financial, personal, and employment information may be requested if necessary. If the claim analyst needs financial information for a claim, financial documents including income tax documents are usually used. The claim analyst may also consult with an employee counselor to evaluate the insured's capacity for alternative employment.

Disability Income Claim Form

When a disability claim analyst receives notice of a claim, the analyst immediately sends the insured a claim form for filing proof of loss. Most insurers require that the claim form be submitted within a specified time, usually 30 to 90 days, after the onset of disability, but most insurers also permit an insured to submit a claim form after this time, particularly if the nature of the disability prevented the insured from submitting the claim in a more timely manner. Normally, an insurer will not deny or reduce any claim if the insured could not reasonably have been expected to provide proof of loss within the time required.

Claim forms for both short-term (also called *weekly income*) claims and long-term claims ask for essentially the same kinds of information, but a claim for long-term disability income benefits typically requires considerably more information than does a claim for short-term disability income benefits. Both short-term and long-term disability claim forms contain a section that the insured completes and a section that the attending physician completes. If either type of claim is submitted under group coverage, the claim form also contains a section that the employer completes. Each insurer determines what information it wishes to gather in order to make a claim decision as accurately and efficiently as possible. Figures 19-1 and 19-2 illustrate claim forms for short-term and long-term disability income claims.

Using information on the claim form, the claim analyst assesses the type of illness or injury and the cause of the disability. The cause of disability is especially important, for two reasons. First, the insurer's liability for coverage depends on whether the cause fits the policy's definitions. Some policies, as we have noted, provide different elimination periods depending on whether a disability results from an illness or an accident. If an insured has submitted a disability claim under coverage that specifies a one-week elimination period for disability resulting from an illness, but no elimination period for disability resulting from an accident, the date on which payments may begin depends on the nature of the cause. The claim analyst verifies the cause in order to ensure that benefits are appropriately paid, neither sooner nor later than provided in the policy.

Second, coverage depends on whether the cause of disability is a risk excluded from the policy. Most disability policies exclude such causes of disability as attempted suicide, self-inflicted injuries, and occupationally related disabilities or sicknesses that are covered under a government program such as Workers' Compensation. Some disability policies exclude or provide only limited coverage for disabilities resulting from mental or nervous conditions or from participation in specified dangerous avocations.

APS and Medical Information

The APS is critical for disability income claim analysis because it provides detailed information about the nature and cause of the disability, along with supporting evidence that includes the physician's diagnosis, the results of laboratory and other tests, the types of treatment and

Figure 19-1. Short-term (weekly income) disability claim form under group coverage.

PART I - Employee:

Your Employer's Name			Group Number	
Your Name	Ctf No./Social Security No.		Birth Date Mo. Day Yr.	Sex ☐ M ☐ F
Your Home Address (Street Address - City - State - Zip)				
This Claim Is For ☐ Illness ☐ Accident		Illness/Injury Is Work Related ☐ Yes ☐ No		
Nature of Illness or Injury				

IF ACCIDENT	Date Accident Occurred	Time ☐ A.M. ☐ P.M.	Place
	Details of Accident		

I hereby authorize ______________________ and/or ______________________
(insert your primary doctor's name) (insert the name of your hospital)

to release to ABC Life Insurance Company or its representative any and all information with respect to myself which may have bearing on the benefits payable under this plan. I certify that the above information in support of this claim is true and correct. A copy of this authorization shall be considered as effective and valid as the original. This authorization shall be valid for sixty days.

Date ______________________ Signature of Insured ______________________

PART II - Employer's Certification: Please include a copy of the job description with this form.

Name of Employee				
Group Number	Certificate No.	Employment Date	Insurance Eff. Date	Insurance Class

I certify that the Employee is ☐ a full-time active employee working a minimum of 30 hours per week or ☐ on disability leave.

If employment has been terminated, give date: ______________

Is illness due to occupational causes? ______________

Date absence began: ______________ Date returned to work: ______________

Amount of earnings: Weekly $______________ Monthly $______________

If premium for Weekly Income is contributory, give percent of employee's contribution: ________%

Name of Employer	Mailing Address

Date ______________________ Signed by ______________________
Representative of Employer

(continued)

Figure 19-1. Short-term (weekly income) disability claim form under group coverage (continued).

PART III - Attending Physician's Statement:

Patient's Name	Date of Birth

Diagnosis and concurrent conditions: ______________________________

PHYSICAL IMPAIRMENT (*as defined in Federal Dictionary of Occupational Titles)

☐ Class 1 — No limitation of functional capacity; capable of heavy work* No restrictions. (0-10%)
☐ Class 2 — Medium manual activity* (15-50%)
☐ Class 3 — Slight limitation of functional capacity; capable of light work* (35-55%)
☐ Class 4 — Moderate limitation of functional capacity; capable of clerical/administrative (sedentary*) activity. (60-70%)
☐ Class 5 — Severe limitation of functional capacity; incapable of minimal (sedentary*) activity. (75-100%)
☐ Remarks:

MENTAL/NERVOUS IMPAIRMENT (if applicable)

(a) Please define "stress" as it applies to this claimant.

(b) What stress and problems in interpersonal relations has claimant had on job?

☐ Class 1 — Patient is able to function under stress and engage in interpersonal relations (no limitations)
☐ Class 2 — Patient is able to function in most stress situations and engage in most interpersonal relations (slight limitations)
☐ Class 3 — Patient is able to engage in only limited stress situations or engage in only limited interpersonal relations (moderate limitations)
☐ Class 4 — Patient is unable to engage in stress situations or engage in interpersonal relations (marked limitations)
☐ Class 5 — Patient has significant loss of psychological, physiological, personal and social adjustment (severe limitations)
☐ Remarks:

Do you believe the patient is competent to endorse checks and direct the use of the proceeds thereof? ☐ Yes ☐ No

Is condition due to injury or sickness arising out of patient's employment? ☐ Yes ☐ No

Date symptoms first appeared or accident happened: ______________________________

If patient was referred by other physician, give name: ______________________________

Address of other physician: ______________________________

Date patient first consulted you for this condition: ______________________________

Is patient still under your care for this condition? ☐ Yes ☐ No

Patient was continuously totally disabled (unable to work) from ______________ through ______________

Patient was partially disabled from ______________ through ______________

If still disabled, date patient should be able to return to work: ______________________________

Physician's Name (Type or Print)	Degree	SS# or ID#	Telephone ( ) -
Mailing Address			

Date	Signature of Attending Physician

Figure 19-2. Long-term disability claim form under group coverage.

EMPLOYEE'S LONG-TERM DISABILITY BENEFITS APPLICATION

TO BE COMPLETED BY EMPLOYEE

CLAIMANT

1. Full Name (Last, First, Middle Init.) | 2. Social Security Number | 3. Phone Number

4. Address | City | State | Zip Code

5. Date of birth (Mo. Day Year) | 6. Height | 7. Weight | 8. Sex ☐ M ☐ F | 9. Marital status ☐ Single ☐ Married ☐ Widowed ☐ Divorced | 10. Spouse's date of birth (Mo. Day Year) First Name | 11. Is spouse employed? ☐ Yes ☐ No

12. Number of children (Under age 19) | 13. List names and dates of birth of unmarried children who have not finished high school.

EMPLOYMENT

14. Employer's Name | 15. Group Policy No.

16. Occupation (List the duties of your occupation at the time of disability)

17. Date of accident or date first noticed symptoms of illness: (Mo. Day Year) | 18. I have been unable to work because of the disability since: (Mo. Day Year) | 19. I returned to work on a part time basis on: (Mo. Day Year) | 20. I returned to work on a full time basis on: (Mo. Day Year)

21. Is your accident or illness related to your occupation? ☐ Yes ☐ No | 22. If "yes," explain

Have you or do you intend to file a Workers' Comp. claim? ☐ Yes ☐ No

CLAIM HISTORY

23. Describe how and where accident occurred or describe the onset and nature of your illness.

24. Date you were first treated for your illness or injury. (Mo. Day Year)

25. Treated by:

Hospital: ______ (Name, Street Address, City, State, Zip Code)

Doctor: ______ (Name, Street Address, City, State, Zip Code)

26. Have you ever had the same or similar condition in the past? ☐ Yes ☐ No
If yes, complete No. 27.

27. Treated by:

Hospital: ______ (Name, Street Address, City, State, Zip Code)

Doctor: ______ (Name, Street Address, City, State, Zip Code)

INCOME

28. Describe other income you are receiving:

Yes	No	Type	Amount	Date Began	Date Term.
☐	☐	Social Security (disability or retirement)	$ ______	______	______
☐	☐	State disability	$ ______	______	______
☐	☐	Retirement (normal, early or disability)	$ ______	______	______
☐	☐	Workers' Compensation	$ ______	______	______
☐	☐	Group disability benefits	$ ______	______	______
☐	☐	Other (describe) ______	$ ______	______	______

BENEFIT

29. Have you, or do you plan to apply for benefit described above?

Type ______ Date application filed ______

Type ______ Date application filed ______

30. If your request for benefits is approved do you want us to withhold amounts from each benefit check for Federal Income Tax purposes? ☐ Yes ☐ No If "yes" Amt. $______
Indicate amount per week $20.00 min. ______ Signature

The above statements are true and complete to the best of my knowledge and belief.

______ Signature of Employee ______ Date

(continued)

Figure 19-2. Long-term disability claim form under group coverage (continued).

EMPLOYER'S REPORT OF CLAIM

TO BE COMPLETED BY EMPLOYER

CLAIMANT

1. Employee's Name	2. Social Security No.	3. Date of Birth

4. Address   City   State   Zip Code

EMPLOYMENT

5. Insurance Class	6. Employee Date of Hire	7. Date employee became insured for LTD	8. Date employee was actually last present at work

9. Occupation at time last worked (attach job description)

10. Work schedule at time last worked
No. of days per week ________ No. of hours per day ________

11. Reason for stopping:
☐ Sickness ☐ Granted LOA ☐ Laid Off
☐ Retired ☐ Dismissed ☐ Other
☐ Resigned ☐ Vacation

12. Has employee returned to work?
☐ Yes ☐ Part-time ☐ Full-time
☐ No Date ________ Date ________

INCOME

13. How is employee paid?
☐ Straight Salary ☐ Hourly
☐ Salary & Commissions
☐ Commissions Only ☐ Salary & Bonus

14. Employee's Basic Monthly Earnings
$ ________ LTD Benefit ________
(If salary is based on less than 12 mos. — No. of mos. ________)

15. Employee's % of LTD premium contribution: Employee pays ________ Employer pays ________

OTHER BENEFITS

16. Has insured received other disability payments since time last worked?

Salary Continuance: ☐ Yes Wkly. Amt. ________ Date benefits cease ________ ☐ No

Insured Short Term: ☐ Yes Wkly. Amt. ________ Date benefits cease ________ ☐ No

Other Type: ________ ☐ Yes Wkly. Amt. ________ Date benefits cease ________ ☐ No

17. Did claim result from job activity?
☐ Yes (Explain)
☐ No

18. Has Workers' compensation claim been filed? ☐ Yes ☐ Pending ☐ Denied (Enc. copy)

19. Workers' compensation Wkly. Amt.
$ ________
(Inc. copy of 1st report of accident)

RETIREMENT

20. Is employee covered by employer sponsored retirement plan? ☐ Yes ☐ No

21. Does retirement plan contain a disability provision? ☐ Yes ☐ No

22. Is employee or will this employee be eligible for a disability or retirement pension? ☐ Yes If "yes" type: ☐ No

Monthly Amount $ ________
☐ Disability
☐ Retirement
☐ Other ________
Commence Date of Benefits: ________
(enclose copy of summary plan description)

NOTE: If any portion of this pension benefit is attributable to the employee's contribution, please provide details including the percentage of his/her contribution to the total contribution.

CERTIFICATION

23. Employer's Name (state association and name of policyholder, if other)	24. Telephone No.	25. Group Policy No.

26. Address

27. Employer (Taxpayer) I.D. Number (EIN) ________ - ________
OR
28. Public Employer Social Security No. 69 ________ - ________

29. Name of person completing this form (please type or print)

30. Signature of Authorized Insurance Representative   Title   Date

Separate and send this form (with other enclosures) to address on reverse side. Give remaining portions to claimant for completion.

(continued)

Figure 19-2. Long-term disability claim form under group coverage (continued).

ATTENDING PHYSICIAN'S STATEMENT

Name of patient | Date of birth

HISTORY

(a) When did symptoms first appear or accident happen?

(b) Date patient ceased work because of disability?

(c) Has patient ever had same or similar condition? ☐ Yes ☐ No If "Yes" state when and describe

(d) Is condition due to injury or sickness arising out of patient's employment? ☐ Yes ☐ No ☐ Unknown

(e) Names and addresses of other treating physicians

DIAGNOSIS

(a) Diagnosis (Including complications)

(b) If pregnancy, est. date of delivery

(c) Subjective symptoms

(d) Objective findings (Including current x-rays, EKG's, laboratory data and any clinical findings)

TREATMENT

(a) Date of first visit

(b) Date of last visit

(c) Frequency ☐ Weekly ☐ Monthly ☐ Other (Specify)

(d) Nature of treatment (Including surgery and medications prescribed, if any)

PROGRESS

(a) Has patient ☐ Recovered? ☐ Improved? ☐ Unchanged? ☐ Retrogressed?

(b) Is patient ☐ Ambulatory? ☐ House confined? ☐ Bed confined? ☐ Hospital confined?

(c) Has patient been hospital confined? ☐ Yes ☐ No If yes, give Name and Address of Hospital

Confined from ______________ through ______________

CARDIAC

(a) Functional capacity (American Heart Ass'n.)
☐ Class 1 (No limitation) ☐ Class 2 (Slight limitation)
☐ Class 3 (Marked limitation) ☐ Class 4 (Complete limitation)

(b) Blood Pressure (last visit) ______________ systolic/diastolic

IMPAIRMENTS

(a) Physical Impairments (*As defined in Federal Dictionary of Occupational Titles)

☐ Class 1 – No limitation of functional capacity; capable of heavy work* No restrictions. (0-10%)
☐ Class 2 – Medium manual activity* (15-30%)
☐ Class 3 – Slight limitation of functional capacity; capable of light work* (35-55%)
☐ Class 4 – Moderate limitation of functional capacity; capable of clerical/administrative (sedentary*) activity. (60-70%)
☐ Class 5 – Severe limitation of functional capacity; incapable of minimum (sedentary*) activity. (75-100%)
Remarks:

(b) Mental Impairments (If applicable)

(a) Please define "stress" as it applies to this claimant.

(b) What stress and problems in interpersonal relations has claimant had on job?

☐ Class 1 – Patient is able to function under stress and engage in interpersonal relations (no limitations)
☐ Class 2 – Patient is able to function in most stress situations and engage in most interpersonal relations (slight limitations)
☐ Class 3 – Patient is able to engage in only limited stress situations and engage in only limited interpersonal relations (moderate limitations)
☐ Class 4 – Patient is unable to engage in stress situations or engage in interpersonal relations (marked limitations)
☐ Class 5 – Patient has significant loss of psychological, physiological, personal and social adjustment (severe limitations)
Remarks:

PROGNOSIS

(a) Is patient now totally disabled? PATIENT'S JOB ☐ Yes ☐ No ANY OTHER WORK ☐ Yes ☐ No

(b) Date patient became disabled due to present illness

(c) When do you expect a fundamental or marked change in the future? ☐ 1 Mo. ☐ 1-3 Mo. ☐ 3-6 Mos. ☐ Never Applies To: ☐ Patient's Job ☐ Other Work

REHAB

(a) Is patient a suitable candidate for occupational rehabilitation? PATIENT'S JOB ☐ Yes ☐ No ANY OTHER WORK ☐ Yes ☐ No

(b) Can present job be modified to allow for handling with impairment? ☐ Yes ☐ No

(c) When could trial employment commence?
Date: ______________ PATIENT'S JOB ☐ Full-time ☐ Part-time
Date: ______________ ANY OTHER WORK ☐ Full-time ☐ Part-time

REMARKS

(Limitations, Therapy, etc.)

Name (Attending Physician) Print | Degree | Telephone

Street Address | City or Town | State or Province | Zip Code

Signature | Date

medication recommended, and the places and dates of treatment. By reviewing the APS, the claim analyst can usually determine a great deal about the nature and extent of the disability and the probable prognosis.

Some physicians are reluctant to state that an insured is in fact disabled, usually because a physician may not know the details of an insured's occupation and is, therefore, not in a position to judge the presence of disability. Such physicians will, however, provide sufficient information for the claim analyst to determine whether the insured is disabled under the terms of the policy. Because a claim for disability is not as easily verified as a claim for death or a claim for medical reimbursement, the claim analyst who handles disability claims needs special training in evaluating the nature and extent of physical and mental impairments and in determining to what extent such impairments hamper the performance of specific job duties.

To encourage a physician to help determine the presence and extent of a disability, a claim analyst sometimes sends the physician information about the policy provisions relating to disability and a copy of the insured's job description from the employer. Using this information, the physician can help the claim analyst determine whether the insured is disabled under the terms of the policy and whether the insured is capable of performing some or all of the specified job duties. If a physician cannot or will not verify a claimed disability, the claim analyst usually requires the insured to undergo an examination by an independent medical caregiver named and paid by the insurance company. The independent medical caregiver is usually a specialist who is familiar with the type of injury or illness involved in the disability and who can provide an objective assessment of the insured's condition. An independent medical evaluation is also sought when an insured's own physician appears to be biased in giving an opinion of a disability or when the opinion may be beyond the scope of the physician's training—for example, when a general practitioner attempts to evaluate an insured's psychiatric condition.

Moreover, the claim analyst may consult the insurer's medical director, who can provide insight into medical diagnoses and treatments and can advise the claim analyst during the investigation of a disability income claim. Among other actions, the medical examiner may suggest sources of information on particular disabilities and methods of rehabilitation, guide the claim analyst in choosing medical tests for unusual injuries or illnesses, and consult with the independent medical caregiver prior to examination of the insured. None of these professionals—the attending physician, the independent medical caregiver, or the medical director—makes a final decision on a claim. After consultation with these professionals, the claim analyst is responsible for making that decision.

To obtain further medical information about a claimant, the claim analyst can consult the MIB and the Disability Insurance Records System (DIRS), which is managed by the MIB and which provides insurers with information designed to alert them to the presence of overinsurance—particularly other coverage applied for or in force. This information is especially important for individual disability policies during the contestable period.

Financial Information

One of the responsibilities of the claim analyst is to request the correct financial documents to verify the income loss to a disabled insured and to examine those documents closely so as to determine the appropriate amount of benefits. If an insured has suffered a disability, the claim analyst requires financial documents to verify the amount of financial loss suffered. Generally, a W-2 form in the United States or a T4 form in Canada, as well as a 1099 or other tax form to identify income from other sources, is sufficient to establish the level of the insured's previous income.

If a disabled insured is the sole proprietor of a business, the claim analyst may require federal income tax returns for the business, along with a profit and loss statement, to verify the level of income that the insured derived from the business. If a disabled insured is a partner in a business, a copy of the partnership tax return usually provides enough information for the claim analyst to establish the income level of the insured. Other forms of businesses such as regular corporations and "S" corporations—in which income and expenses are reported as though the corporation were a partnership—require that other financial documents be submitted in support of a disability claim.

Personal Information

For some disability income claims, the disability may continue for an unusually long time although the insured appears to be only moderately ill or injured. The claim analyst may need to develop personal information on an insured to determine whether the disability is responsible for the insured's slow recovery or whether other factors are playing a part. The claim analyst has access to the same kinds of investigatory techniques that the underwriter has, including personal interviews with the insured. Particularly if an insured's disability appears to be one that will continue over a period of time, the claim analyst may wish to telephone or visit with the claimant and establish a personal relationship that will enhance the ability of the insurer to pay the claim equitably.

Although inspection reports are not widely used for investigations of disability income claims, the analyst does have access to such resources. The usual information developed by an inspection report focuses on the degree of an insured's disability, the presence of overinsurance, and verification of information on income and employment. Moreover, claim analysts sometimes consult with the insurer's legal staff or with accountants inside or outside the insurance company to verify the details of financial records, particularly for large-amount claims under business disability coverages. Surveillance is sometimes used to discover whether an insured is working at an undisclosed occupation or is engaging in other activities that are inconsistent with the disability. Insight 19-2 discusses some of the considerations involved in using surveillance to gather claim information.

Employer Information

If a claim analyst determines that he needs further information concerning the insured's employment, he usually asks the employer for the necessary information. The type of information usually requested includes details about an insured's job duties, compensation, and place and hours of work. Figure 19-3 illustrates a sample job analysis form for a long-term disability claim. The claim analyst may also need to determine whether the employer anticipates continuing to employ the insured if the insured is able to return to work. If the insured can work only under certain conditions, such as reduced hours or revised responsibilities, the claim analyst attempts to learn whether the employer is willing to accommodate those needs.

Administering Disability Income Claims

After examining the information submitted with a disability claim, the claim analyst orders whatever additional information is needed. As soon as all necessary information has been collected, the claim analyst makes a decision on the claim and notifies the claimant of that decision.

If the decision is to deny the claim, the claim analyst sends a letter to the claimant, explaining the basis for the denial. If the decision is to pay the claim, in whole or in part, the claim analyst sends a letter to the claimant and specifies the benefits to which the claimant is entitled. A copy of the letter is usually sent to the marketer who originally sold the disability income policy.

Insight 19-2 Surveillance as an Investigative Tool

Advances in lenses and camera technology have made it possible to clearly document an insured's activities from great distances without the insured's knowledge. This technological revolution provides the disability claims professional with the means to verify the insured's version of the impact of disability on daily activities. With proper preparation, surveillance can be used to substantiate or refute disability.

Conventional wisdom in using surveillance is that it is wasted on highly subjective conditions such as mental and nervous disorders. However, given the technology available today, along with careful documentation of the insured's restrictions, limitations, and symptoms, surveillance of exaggerated mental or nervous conditions can be successfully used in some cases to control unfounded claims. A consulting psychiatrist or psychologist may be required to identify questionable mental or nervous disability claims and to comment upon the significance of activities documented through surveillance based upon the disabling condition.

One example of successful termination of a psychiatric claim based upon surveillance involved a 40-year-old executive with an undergraduate degree in psychology. The insured claimed total disability due to depression arising from business reversals. When disability became extended, medical documentation was requested. Care was found too infrequent and was provided by an elderly psychiatrist. Efforts to contact the insured on an unannounced basis at his mailing address or to reach him by telephone were unsuccessful. It was necessary to leave calls on an answering machine, and calls were not returned for days or weeks.

In a scheduled interview with an insurance company representative, the insured confirmed in writing that his daily activities consisted of "watching television." He allegedly had little interest in social life and rarely left his apartment. The insured maintained that he was chronically exhausted and had symptoms that were consistent with depression.

Surveillance of the insured revealed that he was out and about, driving extensively while dressed in expensive clothing and carefully groomed. He was in frequent social contact and was shown on surveillance tapes smiling, laughing, and conversing at length with those he came into contact with. On one occasion, he spent the evening traveling from one night spot to another with several other persons.

Review of the surveillance information with a psychiatric consultant confirmed that these findings were inconsistent with the claimed disability from depression. The claim was successfully terminated based upon these findings and an independent medical examination. The key in using surveillance to evaluate a mental/nervous claim is to establish whether the surveillance findings are consistent with the behaviors expected for the given diagnosis.

Another difficult area is partial disability. Surveillance can confirm or refute the insured's detailed description of his daily activities and restrictions or limitations. Careful documentation of the file can provide a benchmark against which the surveillance can be measured. For example, an insured whose partial disability is based upon an inability to work more than a certain number of hours per day may be documented through surveillance as working full time.

It may be desirable to meet with the insured to discuss discrepancies between the insured's claimed activities and his actual activities documented by surveillance. File statements made by the insured can be challenged and correction invited. An insured may provide a credible discussion of activities, restrictions, and limitations that will allow proper administration of the claim. A claimant who believes he has been "caught" may refuse to respond. Another approach is to send details of the surveillance to the insured's attending physician or an independent physician after the physician has provided an opinion based upon the insured's description of symptoms, activities, restrictions, and limitations.

From the *Individual Health Insurance Workshop Reports,* 1993: 1–9. Adapted by permission from the International Claim Association.

Figure 19-3. Job analysis form for long-term disability.

To Be Completed By The Employee's Supervisor

This claim is for (Employee's Name)

Employee's Social Security Number	Date of Disability (Month, Day, Year)

A. General information about the employee's job

Job Title	Minimum education or training required

Does the employee perform supervisory functions?

☐ Yes ☐ No If yes, how many people are supervised? ________________ Describe job duties.

Check the items below that relate to the employee's job. Use these definitions for the frequency of occurrence:

Occasionally means the person does the activity up to 33% of the time.
Frequently means the person does the activity 34% to 66% of the time.
Continuously means the person does the activity 67% to 100% of the time.

	Occasionally	Frequently	Continuously
Relate to others	☐	☐	☐
Written and verbal communication	☐	☐	☐
Reasoning, math and language	☐	☐	☐
Makes independent judgments	☐	☐	☐

Which of the following describe the employee's working environment? Check all that apply.

☐ Unprotected heights ☐ Changes in temperature or humidity ☐ Exposure to dust, fumes and gases
☐ Being near moving machinery ☐ Driving automotive equipment ☐ Other hazards

Is the employee required to travel?

☐ Yes ☐ No If yes, complete the following information:

How does the employee travel? (Automobile, plane, train, etc.)	Where does the employee travel?	What percent of the time does the employee travel?

B. Information about the physical aspects of the employee's job

Check the items below that relate to the employee's job and complete the information requested. Use these definitions for the frequency of occurrence:

Occasionally means the person does the activity up to 33% of the time.
Frequently means the person does the activity 34% to 66% of the time.
Continuously means the person does the activity 67% to 100% of the time.

Activity	Frequency of Occurrence				
	Occasionally	Frequently	Continuously		
☐ Standing	☐	☐	☐		
☐ Walking	☐	☐	☐		
☐ Sitting	☐	☐	☐		
☐ Balancing	☐	☐	☐		
☐ Stooping	☐	☐	☐		
☐ Kneeling	☐	☐	☐		
☐ Crouching	☐	☐	☐		
☐ Crawling	☐	☐	☐		
☐ Reaching/working overhead	☐	☐	☐		
☐ Climbing:	☐	☐	☐		
☐ Stairs	☐	☐	☐		
Number of stairs: ________					
☐ Ladders	☐	☐	☐	Describe Activity	Weight
Height of Ladder: ________					
☐ Pushing	☐	☐	☐	____________	______ lbs.
☐ Pulling	☐	☐	☐	____________	______ lbs.
☐ Lifting/Carrying	☐	☐	☐	____________	______ lbs.

(continued)

Figure 19-3. Job analysis form for long-term disability (continued).

Can the job be performed by alternating sitting and standing?
☐ Yes ☐ No

Does the job require using the feet to operate foot controls?
☐ Yes ☐ No If yes, on what type of equipment?

How important is good vision in the job?

What are the major tasks requiring use of one or both hands?	One Hand	Both Hands
	☐	☐
	☐	☐
	☐	☐
	☐	☐

C. Information about the job as it relates to the disability

Can the job be modified to accommodate the disability either temporarily or permanently?
☐ Yes ☐ No If yes, explain

Is it possible to offer the employee assistance in doing the job (through use of technology or personal assistance for example)?
☐ Yes ☐ No If yes, explain

D. Attachments and Signature (Attach a copy of the employee's job description)

Name of person completing this form

X

Signature Title Date

Telephone ( ) Fax ( )

As part of information gathering before making a claim decision, the claim analyst verifies whether the claimant is also covered by another form of disability coverage. An important goal of the claim analyst is to ensure that a claimant does not receive a disproportionate amount of compensation from various sources of disability insurance. Generally, all disability programs, whether public programs or private coverage, provide that a claimant may not receive a total of more than 60 to 80 percent of pre-disability earnings. The purpose of such a limitation is not to reduce the costs of claims, but rather to encourage disabled persons to return to work if recovery is possible.

In the United States, two pieces of legislation affect the handling of disability claims. One is the Family Medical Leave Act (FMLA), which provides that an employer must allow an employee to take unpaid leave if the employee's own serious health condition makes job performance impossible. Generally, a serious health condition in this context is one that (1) will require absence from the workplace for more than three calendar days and (2) requires continuing treatment from a health care provider. The FMLA also provides treatment for pregnancy and certain chronic conditions such as diabetes and asthma even though treatment at any time might last less than three calendar days.

Another piece of legislation that affects the handling of disability claims is the Americans with Disabilities Act (ADA), which provides that if an employee suffers a disability, the employer must make certain accommodations to enable the employee to continue employment. For example, if a disabled employee must work from a wheelchair, the employer is obligated to make certain changes in the employee's work station to accommodate the wheelchair. If an employee has developed an ongoing disease such as diabetes, the employer is obligated by the ADA to make allowances in the employee's schedule of work so that the employee can make periodic insulin level checks and eat if necessary. The claim analyst, aided by the insurer's legal staff, verifies that an employee who wishes to return to work is accommodated under the provisions of the ADA.

The ADA also requires that employers in the United States help eliminate employment discrimination with respect to job application procedures, job training and discharge, and other terms, conditions, and privileges of employment. When an employee suffers a disability that is likely to be long-term, but that is not so serious that the employee could not work at some occupation, the claim analyst oversees the case and sometimes helps the employer determine whether accommodations can be made that will permit the employee to return to work on a full- or part-time basis.

Coordinating Other Disability Income Benefits

In addition to disability income benefits under a contract of insurance, an insured may be eligible for disability income coverage provided by a number of other sources. In the United States, ***Workers' Compensation*** is government-mandated insurance that provides benefits to covered employees and their dependents if the employee suffers a job-related injury, disease, or death. Workers' Compensation is administered by each state, and its benefits vary considerably from one state to another. Social Security Disability Income (SSDI) in the United States and social insurance under the Canada Pension Plan (CPP) and the Quebec Pension Plan (QPP) in Canada (as well as through the Unemployment Insurance Programme) provide disability income benefits when a worker is so severely impaired physically or mentally that he cannot perform any substantial work and is not expected to recover within 12 months. A person must be disabled for at least 5 months before becoming eligible to submit a claim for disability benefits through such government-sponsored insurance programs. These programs also encourage workers to return to work by providing benefits for a 9-month trial work period (during which the worker tries to return to work) and an additional 3-month grace period. In addition, some states in the United States provide residents with disability income payments for disabilities that are not work-related. Moreover, some employers in the United States and Canada include disability income benefits under their group life insurance coverage.

The claim analyst notifies an insured who is covered by more than one type of disability coverage of any applicable ***offset,*** which is a federal tax law requirement that allows an insurer to use the benefits paid under one type of insurance coverage to reduce the benefits paid for another type of coverage. The purposes of an offset are (1) to ensure that a disabled person does not receive an excessive total amount of benefits and (2) to encourage the disabled person to return to work. The types of coverage usually resulting in offsets to disability income coverage include Social Security in the United States and social insurance in Canada, as well as Workers' Compensation, employer sick leave benefits, and other disability income coverage (for instance, an insured who becomes covered by a group disability policy at work may also be covered by an individual policy he purchased earlier). Some disability income policies further specify that the amount of disability or retirement benefits paid to an insured's spouse or children may also be considered in calculating the offset to disability income benefits.

When a claim analyst determines that a claimant is eligible for disability coverage under Social Security, the analyst sends the claimant a notice that the offset will be used in determining the amount of benefits that the insurer will pay. Some insurers provide a claimant with several options, usually (1) to reduce the amount of monthly disability income benefits from the insurer by the amount of disability benefit paid by Social Security or another source, or (2) to pay the monthly benefit with no reduction until the claimant has time to apply for Social Security disability benefits. When the Social Security benefits begin, the claimant is then obligated to notify the insurer that such payments have begun and to repay the excess amount he has received from the insurer. Figure 19-4 shows a typical statement of long-term disability payment options.

Managing Benefits for Mental Illness and Substance Abuse

Because disabilities resulting from mental illness and substance abuse are often more difficult to specify and define than are disabilities resulting from physical sickness and injury, insurers are challenged to manage such claims carefully. Particularly for difficult-to-define conditions such as depression or anxiety, the claim analyst has to make decisions based on information that is more subjective than the data that usually accompanies a claim for physical injury or illness.

Figure 19-4. Statement of long-term disability payment options.

LONG TERM DISABILITY PAYMENT OPTIONS

Insurer ____________________ (Herein referred to as "we" and "us")

Policy No. __________ Claim No. __________ Date Disability ____________________

Issued to ____________________ Address ____________________

Claimant ____________________ Address ____________________

The policy under which you are covered provides that Long Term Disability benefits will be reduced by the amount of Social Security benefits which **you and your spouse and family** are eligible to receive. The policy also provides that if you do not apply for Social Security benefits, the policy benefits will be reduced by the amount of Social Security benefits **you and your spouse and family** would be eligible to receive if application had been made.

We understand that the Social Security Administration has not yet made a decision concerning your benefits. Until the Social Security Administration makes a decision, your Long Term Disability benefits can be handled in one of two ways:

☐ 1. We can estimate the amount of Social Security benefits **you and your spouse and family** will receive and reduce your monthly policy benefit by this amount. If Social Security benefits are estimated, the monthly policy benefit will be adjusted when we receive proof of the amount awarded by Social Security or that Social Security benefits have been denied and the denial is not being appealed. If you Social Security application is denied and the denial is not being appealed, the amount estimated will be returned to you in a lump sum.

☐ 2. We can pay you a monthly benefit with no reduction for estimated Social Security benefits until Social Security makes a decision. This may result in an overpayment by us. You must supply us with a copy of the Social Security decision and repay any overpayment. In addition, if Social Security makes an award, we will reduce your monthly policy benefit by the amount of Social Security benefits **you and your spouse and family** receive according to the policy provisions. If you want to elect this option but have not yet applied for Social Security benefits you must agree to apply for them immediately. If you do not apply for Social Security benefits, we will use approach #1.

Please tell us which approach you want to use by checking box #1 or box #2 and signing this form. If you make no selection, we will use approach #1. If you have any questions, please contact us.

____________________	____________________
(Insured)	(Witness)
____________________	____________________
(Address)	(Address)
____________________	____________________
(Date)	(Date)

Generally the most effective way to manage benefits for mental illness and substance abuse is to define in the policy the conditions that are covered, the level of coverage for each, and any other requirements for payment of benefits. The responsibility of the claim analyst is to verify that an insured who has applied for such benefits has complied with the policy requirements and definitions.

In handling a claim for mental illness, the claim analyst often performs a work site assessment to determine the claimant's usual job duties. The assessment is the first step in deciding the extent to which the claimant is prevented by mental illness from performing his job functions. During a ***work site assessment,*** a claim analyst or an investigator interviews an employer and reviews the actual job duties and the claimant's level of success in performing those duties. The claim analyst or investigator also obtains a specific job description for the claimant, learns the criteria by which the claimant's performance is evaluated, and determines whether such factors as downsizing or legal difficulties have affected the claimant's job. If a claimant is self-employed, the analyst or investigator obtains as much detail as possible about the claimant's work by using client appointment records, contracts, financial documents, and interviews with clients.

Managing Benefits for Continuing Claims

An insured may be disabled for a considerable period of time, during which the claim analyst is responsible for remaining informed about the insured's condition and his ability to return to some form of employment. Most insurers require a disabled insured to submit proof of continuation of the claim, usually at monthly intervals. An exception is made for insureds who are clearly totally disabled and whose medical prognosis indicates little chance of recovery to near-normal functioning. For such insureds, most insurers require only semiannual or annual proof that an insured continues to be disabled and, therefore, eligible for benefits.

The length of time a person is disabled for a specified injury or illness can vary widely. Most insurers develop information based on their experience and on published medical information about the typical disability period for injuries and illnesses, and use that information in evaluating claims. Claim analysts use that information as a guide in assessing a claim. Such information might indicate, for example, that a fracture of the femur (thigh bone) near the hip can be expected to cause a disability ranging on average from 8 to 12 months, whereas a person who undergoes a hip replacement is typically considered disabled for 4 to 5 months.

Sometimes insurers base the expected length of disability on the type of work that an insured performs. For instance, if an insured who usually performs a job requiring sedentary activity undergoes surgical repair for hammertoe, the expected length of disability may range from three to four weeks. By contrast, a person whose work requires light to medium physical activity may be expected to be disabled during recovery from the surgery for a period ranging from four to six weeks.

The claim analyst does not consider this information to be absolute, however. Some insureds who suffer specified illnesses or injuries may be able to return to work within a shorter time than the periods specified, whereas other insureds may require extensive treatment or physical therapy and may not be able to return to work for periods longer than those stated.

Estimating the length of time an insured will be disabled is one of a claim analyst's most important duties, but this task is difficult because the duration of a disability can vary depending on several factors. An insured's previous medical condition can affect the length of disability: a person who was quite healthy prior to an illness or injury may recover more rapidly than a person who was not in good health before becoming disabled. Other factors that can affect the length of a disability include the insured's age, the severity of the disability, the presence of complications and other physical and mental conditions, the type of treatment available for the disability. In addition to these factors, an insured may or may not be motivated to return to work, may have a greater or lesser economic need to return to work, or may not be able to find work suitable for his present physical and mental condition.

Most proofs of continuing claim are brief, consisting of a statement of continuing disability that is completed by the insured or by someone familiar with the insured's condition. Few insurers require a new APS each month, although if a disability appears to be short-term, the claim analyst may need APS information in order to determine that the disability is in fact continuing.

Requiring proof of a continuing claim is not intended to harass disabled persons, but is intended to help an insurer disburse claim funds in a responsible manner. If an insured continues to be unable to perform job duties according to the terms of the disability contract, the insurer continues to pay benefits according to the contract's provisions. However, an insurer that paid unjustified benefits for disability or any other cause would place itself and other insureds in some financial jeopardy. As we have mentioned previously, one of an insurance company's principal accountabilities is to pay all legitimate claims and to deny all others. Obtaining proof that a claim continues to be legitimate exemplifies an insurer's responsible conduct of business.

If an insured recovers from a disability and is no longer eligible to receive disability income benefits, the insured or, for group coverages, sometimes the employer sends the insurer a notice of recovery from disability. After receiving such a notice, the claim analyst stops

Figure 19-5. Notice of recovery from disability.

NOTICE OF RECOVERY FROM DISABILITY

(This form to be sent to the Insurance Company by the Employer as soon as possible after the Employee recovers)

THIS IS TO INFORM YOU THAT ______________________________
(Name of Employee)

insured under Group Policy No. ______________________ Certificate No. ____________

returned to work on ______________________, 19____, having recovered from his recent disability

on ______________________, 19____.
(Last Day of Actual Total Disability)

____
Employer

Date ______________________, 19____

By ______________________

Form 1113 Rev. 1-90

payment of disability income benefits. Figure 19-5 shows a typical notice of recovery from disability.

Administering Contestable Claims

You recall that most disability income contracts provide for a two-year contestable period for material misstatements or material misrepresentations in the application for insurance. In addition, group disability income contracts generally provide that, to be covered under the contract, a group member must meet certain requirements. For example, a person who wishes to enroll in a group plan after the usual date for such enrollment or who wishes to obtain an amount of insurance higher than the usual amount offered must submit evidence of insurability. If that evidence includes deliberately false information, the coverage may be voided, and no benefits will be due if a claim was filed.

Further, a person who claims to be insured under a group contract is sometimes shown to be ineligible for the group coverage. For instance, if a group contract requires that all eligible insureds must work at least 36 hours per week, a claimant who works only 30 hours per week is not eligible in many jurisdictions for benefits under the group contract.

Administering Questionable Claims

Some disability claims raise questions that must be answered before the claim analyst can make a decision to pay or deny them. A claim analyst investigates most questionable claims, but may turn over complex or highly unusual claims to an outside investigative agency. For most questionable claims, additional information from the insured, the policyholder, medical caregivers, and independent medical examiners enables the claim analyst to reach a decision.

The most common circumstances in which claims may be considered questionable and may require additional investigation include late notice of claim, occupational injuries, termination of employment, problematic diagnosis, vague diagnosis, ambiguous prognosis, extended prognosis, and infrequent medical attention.

Late notice of claim. If notice of a claim is not submitted within a reasonable period of time after a disability is alleged to have begun, the notice is considered late. Because most genuinely disabled insureds need money to replace lost income and, therefore, tend to file disability income claims promptly, a late notice of claim may indicate a suspicious claim. The claim analyst determines whether an investigative report is needed of the claimant's activities during the period of alleged total disability. After a claimant has returned to work, a medical examination is of no value in determining the degree of disability during the period when the claimant was not at work.

Occupational injuries. If an injury that occurred in the work environment has produced disability, a government-sponsored insurance program such as Workers' Compensation may be liable for disability coverage. The claim analyst conducts a thorough investigation to see whether the claimant is eligible for other coverage.

Termination of employment. If a claimant's employment has been terminated for any reason—including voluntary resignation or retirement, discharge, and temporary layoff—the claim analyst typically investigates to determine the cause of termination. Because an employee who has been terminated from work usually seeks employment elsewhere or applies for unemployment compensation, the claim analyst checks whether the claimant is able to work or has filed a claim for disability income benefits from another source. Insight 19-3 addresses the issue of disability income claims filed in connection with corporate reductions in staff.

Problematic diagnosis. The diagnosis offered for a claimant's disability may be nonspecific or vague. In either case, the claim analyst undertakes an investigation to determine the exact diagnosis.

If an attending physician reports symptoms rather than a diagnosis, the claim analyst probes to determine the exact diagnosis. For instance, a diagnosis stating that a patient is experiencing only nausea,

Insight 19-3 Disability Claims Spiked after Job Cuts

Downsizing and corporate restructurings may have trimmed the payroll, but where disability claims are concerned, the reverse is true, according to a survey by CIGNA Group Insurance Managed Disability, Philadelphia, and American Management Association, New York City.

The two organizations collaborated on a survey of nearly 300 large and mid-sized AMA-member companies who underwent organizational staff changes between 1990 and 1995 as a result of downsizing or corporate restructuring.

The results show that job eliminations during the period contributed to a rise in claims for both occupational and nonoccupational disabilities—of blue collar workers *and* salaried employees—particularly in areas related to tension and stress.

What's more, they show that disability claims have risen not just among employees whose jobs were cut, as traditionally occurs during periods of job elimination, but also among a group which CIGNA terms the "survivors." These are the people who retained their jobs after the changes.

Some of the specific findings:

- Seventy percent of the surveyed companies reported an increase in disability claims during the period.
- Companies that cut jobs were more likely to report increases in seven of the eight listed disability categories than companies that didn't cut jobs. Example: 32 percent of those cutting jobs reported increases in disabilities related to mental/psychiatric/substance abuse, and 15 percent reported increases in cardiovascular/hypertension-related disabilities, as compared to companies that did not cut jobs.
- Of companies reporting job cuts, 33 percent saw an increase in occupational claims and 24 percent reported an increase in non-occupational claims among hourly blue-collar wage earners. Among salaried workers at these companies, there were increases as well; 24 percent and 16 percent, respectively.
- Companies cutting jobs were more likely to see claims from white-collar workers than did companies that did not cut jobs. Examples: At the job-cutting companies, 13 percent reported an increase in occupational disability claims at the supervisory level and 7 percent reported an increase in claims from managers, versus 12 percent and 5 percent, respectively, among companies that did not cut jobs. (In the non-occupational category, the same pattern held: Among job-cutting companies, 13 percent and 10 percent, respectively, reported claims increases, whereas among companies that did not cut jobs, only 10 percent and 5 percent, respectively, reported increases.)
- The average duration of short- and long-term disability claims (non-occupational) ran an average of 25 percent longer at companies that eliminated jobs than those at firms that did not.

The survey findings suggest that insurance marketers and benefits advisors need to help employers deal with disability issues related to restructurings.

Adapted by permission from *National Underwriter* © 1996, The National Underwriter Company Life & Health/Financial Services Edition, December 9, 1996: 11, 14.

dizziness, enlarged lymph nodes, tremor, seizures, or backache is not sufficient to present a clear picture of a claimant's physical condition. Any number of conditions could be the cause of such symptoms.

A diagnosis that is so vague that it reveals little about a claimant's true medical or psychological condition is incomplete for claim purposes. Such a diagnosis provides no details on which the claim analyst can base a reasonable assessment of the claim. For example, a diagnosis may state only that a claimant suffers from anemia, arthritis, anxiety, pneumonia, hepatitis, or stroke with no accompanying details or explanations. Any of these conditions could be of minor or major concern, depending on extent. Given such a vague diagnosis, the claim analyst typically interviews or requests further written information from the physician in order to discover precisely what condition has caused the claimant's disability.

Problematic prognosis. A prognosis that is ambiguous or unreasonably extended usually requires careful investigation to determine the extent of disability. Occasionally a physician indicates only that a claimant's prognosis is "unknown," "indefinite," or "uncertain" and refuses to state a date by which the claimant may be expected to return to work. Certain medical conditions do defy accurate estimates of continuing disability. However, for other conditions—particularly those for which the prognosis seems inconsistent with the cause of disability—the claim analyst persists in trying to learn from the physician a reasonable estimate of recovery time.

Sometimes an attending physician repeatedly extends the period of time during which a claimant will be disabled. If the physician offers only an indefinite prognosis or changes the previous estimate of the date of return to work, and if the nature of the disability does not appear to warrant such an extended prognosis, the claim analyst generally attempts to elicit from the physician specific information about the disability and the specific work activities in which the claimant may reasonably be expected to take part.

Infrequent medical attention. When a claimant appears to need medical attention only infrequently, the claim analyst is alerted to the possibility that the reported disability should be investigated. An independent medical examination and an activities check of the claimant are usually considered in order to determine whether the apparently infrequent medical attention is all that is warranted.

Administering Rehabilitation

In addition to examining and making decisions on disability claims and monitoring the progress of claimants, some claim analysts are responsible for administering rehabilitation programs for eligible insureds. ***Rehabilitation*** is the process of helping a disabled person return to work, either at her own occupation or at another occupation if she is unable to perform the duties of her own occupation. Rehabilitation may include medical treatment, vocational training, job placement, and any other activities that help a disabled insured return to gainful employment.

Rehabilitation can provide a valuable service to an insured by enabling him to reenter the work force. Further, rehabilitation can be beneficial to an insurer by saving a significant amount in claim costs. Because rehabilitation is so important to both insureds and insurers, many insurance companies have established specialized teams of highly trained rehabilitation specialists who assist claim analysts in handling all such cases.

An insurer's rehabilitation program typically handles cases of many kinds, including musculoskeletal injuries, blindness, hearing impairments, cardiovascular and respiratory problems, substance abuse, and depression and other mental or nervous conditions. So much progress has been made in the development of special equipment such as voice activated computers, specially designed work areas, and supplementary equipment that many persons who would have been unemployable in the past can now return to work, sometimes in their original occupations with appropriate modifications to accommodate their disabilities. The provisions of the ADA, as we have mentioned, require employers to make reasonable accommodations so that disabled persons may return to the workplace. Moreover, vendors specializing in rehabilitation can help an insurer manage many rehabilitation activities including evaluating the skills of disabled persons, delivering career counseling, performing job market surveys, and designing and building the devices needed to enable disabled persons to return to work.

Rather than allow a considerable length of time to pass before beginning rehabilitation efforts, most insurers approach disabled insureds early in the period of disability to assess the prospects of an insured's being able to return to work. The longer a claimant receives disability payments, the more difficult it is for that person to take the steps necessary to prepare herself for active participation in the workplace and the less likely the person is to be motivated to return to work. To gather information about an insured's training, education, and experience, the claim analyst typically asks the insured to complete a brief questionnaire, which the claim analyst can use to guide planning for the insured's rehabilitation. Figure 19-6 illustrates such a rehabilitation information questionnaire.

As we have mentioned, many disability income policies include a rehabilitation provision specifying that the insurer will pay for the costs of rehabilitation training. Further, many disability income policies provide that a disabled insured who wishes to return to work will be granted a trial period, usually of one year, during which benefits will continue to be paid, typically in an amount that is reduced by some percentage according to the amount the insured is able to earn during that period. For example, if an insured is able to earn $2,000 per month during the trial year, his monthly disability income benefits might be reduced by 50 percent of those earnings, or $1,000. If, during or following such a trial work period, the disabled employee decides

Figure 19-6. Rehabilitation information questionnaire.

Name ________________________________ Policy Number ____________________

We are currently interested in receiving your response to the following questions so that we may continue to evaluate your claim and to understand your circumstances and needs. Please complete these questions and return the questionnaire to us in the enclosed postage-paid envelope.

1. Educational Background

Circle highest grade completed 1 2 3 4 5 6 7 8 9 10 11 12

Did you attend college? ____ Yes ____ No

Major field of study____________________

Degree(s) received____________________

Were you in the armed forces?____ Yes ____ No

Branch of service____________________

Highest rank____________________

Specialty____________________

Please list any additional education or training you have had (carpentry, auto repair, sales, etc.).

2. Work Experience

Please list chronologically all the jobs you have had.

Dates	Type of Work	Physical Requirements	Supervisory Experience, if any

3. How do you spend your time during the day? ____________________

4. How do you feel about returning to work? ____________________

5. If work was available that met your abilities and limitations, would you be interested in exploring the possibility of doing it? Please explain. ____________________

6. Do you have a special interest in specific occupations or work activities? Please explain.

7. Have you made efforts to explore work-related possibilities? Please explain. ____________

Please feel free to make any additional comments on the reverse side of this questionnaire.
We appreciate your cooperation.

____________________________ ____________________
Signed Date

that he is not yet able to return to work, the full long-term disability income benefits will resume.

Terminating Disability Income Benefits

Disability income benefits terminate in several circumstances: when a policy's maximum benefit period is reached, when a claimant is no longer disabled under the terms of the policy, and, for group coverage, when an employee or a group is no longer eligible for coverage.

End of Maximum Benefit Period

When an insurer has paid benefits to the end of the maximum benefit period, the claimant is no longer eligible to receive disability income payments. An insured who has received benefits under the "own occupation" definition of disability may reach the time limit of benefits paid under this requirement and may then be eligible for benefits paid under the "any occupation" definition. If the policy provides for payment of benefits *only* if an insured cannot work at his own occupation, then all benefits terminate at the end of the maximum benefit period.

End of Disability

A claim analyst may terminate benefits to a claimant at any time that the analyst concludes that the claimant is no longer disabled according to the policy requirements. Making such a decision requires the analyst to gather sufficient information to be certain that the claimant is no longer eligible for benefits.

End of Employee or Group Eligibility

Termination of coverage under group insurance typically results when

- An employee is no longer a member of an eligible class covered under a group policy
- The employee's class is no longer eligible for coverage under the policy
- The employee is no longer employed by the organization that is the policyholder for the group coverage
- The group policy lapses because of nonpayment of premium
- The group policy is canceled or not renewed

Most group policies contain a provision that if the policyholder fails to pay any premium within the grace period, the policy terminates at midnight on the last day of the grace period. A policyholder that does not wish to renew a group policy or that wishes to cancel the policy may do so, usually by giving advance written notice to the insurer. Similarly, an insurer that does not wish to renew a policy may usually do so by giving written notice to the policyholder on any premium due date, at least 31 days in advance if (1) the number of employees insured is less than 10; or (2) fewer than 100 percent of the employees eligible for a noncontributory plan are insured under it; or (3) fewer than 75 percent of the employees eligible for a contributory plan are insured under it; or (4) the policyholder fails to furnish information that the insurer may reasonably require.

Settling Disability Income Claims

Instead of paying claims throughout a benefit period, sometimes insurers offer a claimant a ***claim settlement,*** which is a lump-sum payment of money from the insurer to the claimant in exchange for the claimant's agreement to release the insurer from further responsibility for coverage under the policy. In effect, a claim settlement cancels the coverage under the disability policy. When an insured accepts the terms of a settlement offer, the insured usually signs a full, final, and complete release of all liability.

Most insurers present the offer of claim settlement in writing to the insured. Such an approach has the advantages of (1) indicating that the offer is freely made and that the insured is free to accept or reject the offer and (2) verifying that the insurer has given full consideration to the financial needs, vocational opportunities, and other factors of the insured's case. Typically a settlement offer is made as negotiable, meaning that the claimant may make a counteroffer if the terms of the insurer's offer are not satisfactory. If the claimant rejects the settlement offer, the insurer has a continuing contractual obligation to pay disability income benefits according to the provisions of the policy. A claim settlement may be offered whether a claim is disputed or undisputed.

Disputed Claims

Some claim settlements result from a disputed claim in which the insurer and the claimant cannot agree on all the terms of the claim. For instance, a claimant may report that a disability is the result of an injury or illness, but information developed during the course of claim investigation may indicate strongly that the disability resulted from a preexisting condition excluded by a policy provision. If the insurer cannot gather sufficient proof to support its contention that the disability is not covered under the policy, the insurer may offer to settle the claim by paying the insured a lump sum instead of paying a series of disability income benefits. The advantages to an insurer of settling a disputed claim are that the insurer saves the costs of litigating the claim and of committing its staff resources to the conflict over a lengthy period.

Undisputed Claims

Other claim settlements result from the insurer's attempt to provide a greater amount of benefits to a claimant early in the claim, rather than paying benefits over a period of time. Such an approach is appropriate when a claimant needs a considerable sum of money to pay for unusual rehabilitation, to obtain education or training suitable to a new vocation, to purchase a business that can be handled with the disability, or to invest a sum so as to realize a steady stream of income well into the future, beyond the period during which disability income benefits would be paid. Particularly when a policy covers only the insured's "own occupation," the insured may wish to receive benefits in a lump sum in order to have funds to begin another career.

Offering a lump sum settlement is to the insurer's advantage because the costs of administering the claim over a period of time are eliminated. The lump sum settlement is advantageous to the claimant as well, because the lump sum can be used to arrange a suitable lifestyle that accommodates the disability. While disabled, few persons could expect to obtain such an amount of capital with which to restructure their lives.

In offering a lump sum settlement, an insurer typically advises the claimant to seek professional advice on the legal, tax, accounting, and investment issues related to the settlement. In no case does the insurer provide such advice to a claimant because to do so would risk a possible charge of conflict of interest. Further, the insurer typically considers what approach—lump sum payment or series of benefit payments—is in the best interest of the claimant. The degree to which the claimant is financially dependent on a monthly benefit and the ability of the claimant to use a lump sum payout to provide for his own well-being are issues that the insurer weighs in reaching a decision about a settlement.

Key Terms and Concepts

injury
sickness
benefit period
total disability
presumptive total disability
residual disability
qualification period
partial disability
recurring disability
noncancelable
guaranteed renewable
conditionally renewable
optionally renewable
waiver of premium for disability provision
cost of living increase benefit
rehabilitation benefit
transplant donor benefit
future increase option
Workers' Compensation
offset
work site assessment
rehabilitation
claim settlement

Most people who submit claims for benefits from insurance companies are honest. Claimants occasionally make mistakes in providing information on claims, but generally their intent is to submit legitimate claims and to receive only legitimate benefits. A small percentage of persons who submit claims, however, intend to manipulate the claim system in order to obtain benefits to which they are not entitled.

Particularly in health care, insurance fraud has increased rapidly. The volume of money generated by providing medical and dental care tempts some people to make health care a target for claim abuse. Further, the managed-care environment has produced lower median income for some physicians and other caregivers, a few of whom have sought to recover lost revenue by engaging in claim fraud.

Persons who submit fraudulent claims cost the insurance industry more than $100 billion in claims every year, according to NAIC estimates. Further, those who submit fraudulent claims drive up the costs of private health insurance and government health coverage programs; produce increases in employers' premiums for workers' compensation coverage; and seriously damage the strength and reputation of insurers. Moreover, insurers may have inadequate funding to pay claims, may lose present or future business because of customer dissatisfaction, and may have to reduce their staffs. Every insurer has an obligation to protect itself and its insureds from these negative outcomes, including the loss of public trust and support that can seriously damage the industry.

Abuse of claims is usually associated with misrepresentation or fraud. We have already defined misrepresentation, which, in insurance, is the act of making false or misleading statements. Fraud is the result of intentional misrepresentation. False information on an insurance application or a claim might be provided by an applicant, a marketer, a medical caregiver, or anyone else who is in a position to provide information that would bias an insurer toward issuing a policy. You will recall that if an application contains erroneous information, an insurer is allowed by law to deny coverage. If an insurer does not discover the misrepresentation until after the policy is issued, the law allows the insurer to rescind the policy on the basis of material misrepresentation. You will also recall that *rescission* is an equitable remedy under which an insurer seeks to void a policy or to have it declared void by a court. We will further discuss rescission and material misrepresentation later in this chapter.

Claim fraud is an action by which a person intentionally uses false information in an unfair or unlawful attempt to collect benefits under a policy. Claim fraud can be committed by an insured, a beneficiary, a medical caregiver or provider, a marketer, an attorney, an employee of an insurance company, or any other person who is in a position to influence a claim decision or to benefit from illicit claim payments. From false billings and bribes to unnecessary and overpriced prescriptions, the varieties of fraud are limited only by the ingenuity of those who intend to take advantage of insurance companies.

In this chapter, we'll begin by explaining some of the characteristics of fraudulent claims and the persons who commit claim fraud. After discussing specific types of claim fraud connected to life, health, and disability income coverages, we'll conclude the chapter by discussing insurers' responses to claim fraud and the ways insurers attempt to prevent such fraud.

Characteristics of Fraudulent Claims

Generalizing about fraudulent claims is difficult because the characteristics of such claims vary widely and depend on the creativity of persons who are determined to gain illegitimate benefits. However, when a claim analyst receives a claim that includes problems on the claim form or on the APS, or when characteristics of the claimant or the coverage are questionable, the analyst develops as complete information as possible about the claim to validate the claim decision.

We do not suggest that the following discussion of the characteristics of fraudulent claims covers every possibility. It does, however, show you some of the principal indications that a claim may not be legitimate. Claims that have these characteristics are checked in detail to be sure that they are valid.

Problems on the Claim Form

The claim analyst checks further and obtains additional information about a claim form exhibiting any of the following problems:

- All claimant and physician information appears to have been completed in the same handwriting.
- Erasures, white-outs, and typeovers indicate that information has been modified.
- Important information is omitted or differs from other information in the insurer's files, or questions are unanswered.
- The diagnosis and other medical information are the same, word for word, on a series of claim forms.

- Medical terms are misspelled or inconsistent with the total diagnosis and treatment.
- The claimant fails to sign the statement authorizing the insurer to obtain additional information from medical caregivers, the MIB, insurers, and others.
- Instead of providing a street address or an employer's address, the claimant lists a post office box.
- The claim form is a photocopy, not an original.

Problems on the APS

The claim analyst checks especially closely an APS or other medical document that shows any of the following characteristics:

- Instead of actual records, only a very general statement of diagnosis and treatment is provided.
- A subjective diagnosis such as stress or headache is provided.
- Symptoms and length of disability appear extreme for the claimed medical diagnosis.
- Non-emergency medical services are provided on a Sunday or a holiday.
- APSs from one physician change considerably in the manner of reporting medical information, signatures, or other significant aspects.
- APSs contain a rubber stamp of a physician's signature.
- The APS is a photocopy, not an original.

Problematic Characteristics of the Claimant

The claim analyst checks especially closely a claim exhibiting any of the following characteristics concerning the claimant:

- The claimant demands rapid settlement of the claim; threatens involvement of attorneys, insurance organizations, or the claim analyst's supervisor; or volunteers to come to the insurance company to collect the proceeds.

- The claimant exhibits unusual knowledge about medical procedures, insurance coverages, and claim handling.

- Without a significant reason, the claimant consults medical caregivers who do not practice in the claimant's geographic area.

- Even in an alleged emergency, the claimant insisted on seeing his own doctor instead of going to a hospital for treatment.

- Documentation from the claimant's employer is not written on business letterhead or contains inconsistent dates and statements.

- The claimant names the same employer, medical caregivers, and attorneys as other claimants who have submitted questionable claims.

Problematic Characteristics of the Coverage

The claim analyst checks especially closely a claim under coverage that has any of the following characteristics:

- The coverage was issued within the last six months.

- The coverage is still in the contestable period.

- The coverage appears to be excessive for the risk.

- The application for insurance was submitted by a marketer who has also submitted applications for other persons submitting questionable claims.

Those Who Commit Claim Fraud

Among those who commit claim fraud are insureds and beneficiaries, marketers, medical caregivers, and insurance insiders. Less than one-fourth of claim fraud is committed by insureds and beneficiaries; by far, medical caregivers commit the highest percentage of claim fraud.

In addition to being alert to possible fraud committed by any of these persons or entities, the claim analyst remains alert to possible collusion. ***Collusion*** is a secret agreement between two or more persons to perform an act in order to defraud a third person. In insurance claims, the parties to collusion may be an insured, a beneficiary, a medical caregiver, a marketer, or an insurance insider. Collusion is very difficult to prove because the persons in collusion usually verify each other's versions of the facts. When a claim analyst discovers evidence of collusion, the usual action is to notify the insurer's legal division and proceed according to the directions of the legal staff.

Insureds and Beneficiaries

An insured or a beneficiary may try to obtain benefits to which she is not entitled by submitting multiple claims, fabricated claims, or modified claims. An insured or a beneficiary may alter bills for services, submit claims for services that were not delivered or for providers that do not exist, or submit claims for dependents who are ineligible or do not exist.

Medical caregivers usually notify insurers that an insured is eligible for benefits under more than one plan. If an insured denies that other coverage exists and the claim analyst discovers that claims were filed with other insurers, the claim analyst may establish an intent to defraud and may turn the case over to the insurer's legal staff. The claim analyst is also alert to medical bills that have been altered in any way, particularly by changing the amount charged for a rendered service. Many insurers know the fees usually charged for medical services in a certain geographic area and can recognize unusual amounts reported on bills. Particularly if an insured or a beneficiary attempts to receive payment directly for charges that are usually assigned—such as payments for surgeries and hospitalizations—the claim analyst is justified in investigating very closely to determine if the claim is genuine.

If the claim analyst suspects that a provider does not exist, the analyst first calls the telephone number on the bill or claim form, checks the identification or tax identification number of the provider, or contacts the licensing authority to determine whether the alleged provider was licensed to practice at the time the service was allegedly rendered. The claim analyst may also contact the postal authorities to determine who receives mail at the alleged provider's address and whether mail is forwarded from that address.

To determine whether a claimed beneficiary is eligible for benefits, as well as whether an impostor is receiving medical treatment by assuming the identity of a real beneficiary, the claim analyst usually obtains a written statement from the insured or the beneficiary to verify the name, address, and physical description of the person receiving medical treatment and the patient's true relationship to the insured. The claim analyst also obtains complete medical and hospital records, which ordinarily contain information describing the patient and may contain the patient's signature.

Fast Fact

Claim fraud in Workers' Compensation alone costs the insurance industry in the United States $5 billion each year.

Source: National Insurance Crime Bureau, "NICB Reports Workers' Compensation Prosecutions Hit All-Time High in 1995," January 12, 1996.

Sometimes an insured is not attempting so much to collect monetary benefits as to gain access to certain medicines, especially controlled substances. If the insured submits an unusual number of receipts for renewed drug prescriptions, or if the same prescription numbers appear on several claim forms, the claim analyst checks further.

To avoid prosecution for mail fraud, some insureds and beneficiaries hand deliver claims to an insurer and insist on coming to the insurer's office to pick up benefit checks. Such behavior is suspicious, as is any person who wants a claim paid quickly. If an insured or a beneficiary repeatedly contacts a claim analyst or threatens legal action if the claim is not settled rapidly, the claim analyst documents such behavior on the insured's claim record and makes sure that a full claim investigation is completed.

An insured or a beneficiary who commits any one of these actions is not necessarily involved in claim fraud. The claim analyst looks for patterns of behavior and makes a comprehensive evaluation of each case to determine whether claim fraud is present.

Marketers

Although most marketers are honest in their dealings with clients and insurers, some marketers commit fraud by committing theft of premium, annuity, or investment payments, or by selling unauthorized or fictitious policies. Moreover, marketers sometimes conspire with proposed insureds to obtain coverage without reporting all relevant information on the application. For example, the marketer may not submit complete information about the medical history of an applicant for health insurance or may overstate the amount of income earned by an applicant for disability income coverage. When an insured later submits a claim for benefits, the insured pays the marketer a portion of the benefits. To guard against such activity, an insurer must know its marketers and the quality of business they submit. Insight 20-1 explains some of the problems resulting from collusion between marketers and proposed insureds.

Most insurers maintain records on the underwriting and claim experience of business submitted by marketers. If an insurer notices a pattern of excessive, suspicious, or fraudulent claims on business submitted by one marketer, the insurer attempts to determine whether the marketer is involved in fraudulent activity. The marketer may not be so involved—for example, persons who intend to defraud an insurer may approach the same marketer simply because the marketer services a particular insurance product in the geographic area in which those persons live.

Other actions that insurers take in attempting to reduce marketer fraud include the following:

Insight 20-1 Shady Agent, Viatical Mix Creates Recipe for Fraud

Disreputable agents and the popularity of viatical settlements have prompted an increase in adverse risk selection. The existence of viatical settlement companies, which buy the rights to death benefits from life insurance policies, has increased the probability of fraud and accompanying financial difficulty for life insurers. In particular, the combination of viatical settlement companies, AIDS, and disreputable agents has given insureds a way to access the money in a life insurance policy.

Life insurers generally do not want to insure people who are terminally ill. Until recently, the combination of agent, application, and the underwriting process dealt with the situation adequately. According to James E. Melville, president of Universal Guaranty Life Insurance Company, "Before AIDS there were very few terminal health conditions that lasted longer than the two-year contestable period. The insurer was protected if there was material misrepresentation on the application and the insured died within two years. However, a person who is HIV positive but does not have full-blown AIDS has a life expectancy that is severely limited, yet longer than two years."

In the past, insurers had few worries about fraudulent life insurance claims because, as Melville says, "The insured had to die to collect. Besides, the insured wasn't the one who got the money. However, an insured who lies on an application and lives two years can sell the policy to a viatical company. In such a situation, it is not the insured's brother, parent, or significant other who gets the proceeds—the insured gets the money."

Viaticals are predisposed to help HIV-positive persons, Melville says, quoting statistics that indicate 90 percent of the people viaticals deal with are HIV positive. Apparently the existence of viatical companies enables insureds to have benefits paid to themselves.

Melville's company discovered that it had approximately $23 million face amount of such insurance on the books. The coverage had been placed by agents who were actively soliciting applications for insurance in a manner designed to attract prospective insureds with health conditions the agent knew the insurer would not knowingly accept. In one case, according to Melville, an agent advertised, "If you are HIV positive, I can make you a millionaire." The advertisement went on to detail a program whereby the applicant would get a sanitized medical record from a doctor the agent would provide, and then the agent would submit dozens of applications to dozens of companies for amounts small enough to be below the insurers' blood testing limits.

No easy solutions to this problem exist. Melville says that industry coordination and cooperation will help resolve it, as will increased internal vigilance and close examination of new business. Encouraging lawmakers to repeal the 24-month limit and to enact criminal and civil penalties for fraudulent applications will also help.

From Charles E. Schmidt, Jr., "Shady Agent, Viatical Mix Creates Recipe for Fraud," *Best's Review*, Life/Health Edition, March 1996: 68–70.

- Performing background checks on prospective marketers
- Prohibiting marketers from using the insurer's name on a checking account
- Prohibiting marketers from writing personal checks for an insured's premium, annuity, or investment payments
- Stating prominently on every insurance application the instruction to make checks payable only to the insurer
- Mailing confirmation to policyowners when new policies are issued and when existing policy values are used to pay the premium for new policies

- Telephoning policyowners to confirm large policy loans or surrenders

- Issuing a Personal Identification Number (PIN) to policyowners for making telephone withdrawals, including loans and surrenders

- Reviewing all policyowner addresses to identify those that match a marketer's address

Medical Caregivers

Although most medical caregivers report claims fairly, a few are dishonest. From the doctor who claims to have treated many more patients than she could possibly have seen in a given time period to laboratories which churn out an impossibly high number of tests, medical caregiver fraud can take many forms. Medical caregivers who might commit fraud include physicians, dentists, pharmacists, chiropractors, hospitals, clinics, home health care agencies, laboratories and other diagnostic facilities, durable medical equipment suppliers, and others connected with delivery of medical care and equipment. Fraud committed by medical caregivers is especially serious because, in addition to producing higher insurance premiums and escalating costs of public insurance programs, provider fraud causes the public to look unfavorably on the health care profession and, even worse, can damage the quality of health care available to patients by rendering an incomplete or inaccurate diagnosis in the interest of reporting a higher-cost procedure or treatment. Insurers generally train claim analysts to be aware of the indicators of provider fraud not only to save money in ineligible claims, but also to protect insureds and beneficiaries from the effects of such fraud.

The types of fraud committed by medical providers vary widely. Besides submitting claims for cosmetic surgeries as medically necessary procedures, as discussed in Insight 20-2, medical caregivers also commit fraud by

- Providing a false or misleading diagnosis

- Ordering unnecessary treatments or tests

- Authorizing medical care that has not been approved or that is unusual for a specified condition

- Extending medical care beyond the period needed or providing treatments more frequently than necessary

Insight 20-2 Questionable Medical Necessity: Cosmetic Procedures

Physicians and patients may offer a variety of questionable explanations for the medical necessity of certain cosmetic procedures. For example, if a nasal reconstruction was done for cosmetic reasons, explanations may include nasal obstruction, difficulty in breathing, and chronic sinusitis. Subsequent investigation may show no history or treatment for these conditions, and the operative report may indicate an obvious cosmetic procedure.

Blepharoplasty, or excessive overhanging skin of the upper eyelids, presents similar opportunities for fraud. Although the claim report may state that surgery was done because the insured could not see or that vision was obstructed laterally and superiorly, a review of the visual fields and photographs may not indicate any functional loss of vision. The procedure, therefore, would be considered cosmetic. Likewise, "herniated fat pads" listed on the claim form and operative report may be used to justify cosmetic repair of the lower eyelids as a medical necessity.

In reduction mammoplasty, a surgeon may list symptoms of chronic neck and back pain and strap marks on the shoulders. Though this diagnosis may be valid in some cases, an investigation may disclose no history or workup for other causes of spinal problems. The procedure may, therefore, be cosmetic.

Adapted by permission of the publisher, from "'White Fraud' in Health Claims," *Lincoln National Reinsurance Medical Resource*, January/February 1991. Published by Lincoln National Life Insurance Company.

- Certifying a disability that does not exist, certifying a disability based on nonmedical factors such as lack of education or work experience, or certifying a disability in an area in which a medical caregiver is not qualified to render judgment

- Billing for services not rendered, or using a DRG that will allow payment of higher benefits

- Providing discounts for services to patients, but not noting such discounts on insurance claims

- Inflating the amount of claimed fees to cover the insured's copayment or deductibles so that, in effect, the insurer is paying 100 percent of the cost of medical care

- Colluding with insureds by refusing to provide medical records or by failing to respond promptly to insurers' requests for such records

- Upgrading procedures

Upgrading procedures, including upcoding, unbundling, and exploding, are particularly troublesome for insurers. Insurers detect these kinds of attempted fraud by training claim analysts about medical conditions and coding conventions.

Upcoding is a fraudulent claim procedure by which a medical caregiver reports a code for a more serious, and usually more expensive, diagnosis or treatment. For example, if a surgeon removes a small mole, he may report that the mole was larger so that the insurer will pay greater benefits. Further, Medicare typically does not pay for an X-ray as part of a routine checkup, but does pay for an X-ray if a medical caregiver indicates the presence of heart disease. Some unscrupulous caregivers, therefore, upcode X-ray patients' reports to indicate heart disease even if no medical basis exists for that diagnosis.

Unbundling is a fraudulent claim procedure by which a medical caregiver reports and charges separate fees for two or more procedure codes to describe a single medical treatment instead of reporting only one code to cover the entire procedure. For example, the caregiver may report separately a primary treatment and an incidental treatment that is usually included in the primary treatment, and charge a full fee for each procedure.

Exploding is a fraudulent claim procedure by which a medical caregiver increases the cost of a procedure by including a number of other procedures not deemed medically necessary. For example, a physician may require several medically unnecessary tests to be included in a routine blood test, so that the final charge totals far more than the cost of the routine test alone.

In examining claims submitted by medical caregivers, the claim analyst determines whether the diagnoses and treatments are consistent with the bills and with other information supplied by the insured. Comparing bills from various providers, undertaking an audit of hospital and other provider records, and verifying diagnoses and treatments with the insured are some of the many approaches used by insurers to ascertain whether a claim is valid.

Insurance Insiders

Claim analysts and other employees of an insurer can commit claim fraud by submitting false claims, intentionally miscalculating benefit payments and stealing the difference between the actual and false amounts, and delaying benefits processing to improve the reported results—i.e., not immediately reporting a number of approved claims so that the insurer's auditors will not become aware of the analyst's fraudulent activities. In rare instances, claim analysts have accepted bribes from medical caregivers or vendors in exchange for approving claims, have included fictitious or terminated employees on lists of persons employed under group coverage, and have sold confidential claim-related information to persons intent on committing fraud.

The signs of insider claim fraud are sometimes difficult to see, but alert management and well-trained staff can help discover fraud if it exists. Some of the most obvious signs include the following:

- Significant, unexplained fluctuations in operating costs and benefit payments
- Claims apparently approved without appropriate documentation
- Normal claim handling processes changed and system safeguards overridden without adequate explanation
- Evidence that a claimant's address was changed for a few days and then changed back to the original address
- Evidence that claim benefits have been mailed to a claim analyst's residence or mailbox
- A significant number of files containing copies rather than original documents, or documents with evident changes affecting the payout of benefits
- Lifestyle elements such as bankruptcy, addictions, and divorce that may result in financial pressure on employees
- Lifestyle changes involving unusual expenditures for such items as cars, clothing, or travel

As soon as an insurer suspects insider fraud, the person or persons who may be committing fraud are identified and investigated. During an investigation of insider fraud, others of the insurer's areas such as legal, personnel, and accounting are usually informed and are kept apprised of the investigation's results. Depending on the nature of the claims and the financial amount involved, an insurer may check some or all claim transactions in which fraud is suspected.

To demonstrate their high ethics and their intent to remove fraud from claim handling, most insurers are committed to prosecuting incidents of insider fraud as fully as they would prosecute fraud committed by persons outside the insurance company. Instead of only terminating an employee found to have committed claim fraud, most insurers file criminal charges and demand restitution. Insight 20-3 comments on ways some insurers have found to combat fraud committed by persons inside an insurance company.

Fraud under Various Coverages

No type of insurance is completely protected from fraud. In this section we will examine some of the most common types of fraud submitted under life, health, and disability income coverages.

Insight 20-3 Insurers versus Internal Fraud

Insurance fraud is a major concern and priority, but fraud involving employees of insurers has received relatively scant attention. Some argue that the industry should set its own house in order so that it can set an example for the public.

Preventing internal fraud is a complex but important issue for any organization. For insurers, however, fraud control is especially complex and doubly important. Insurance companies are in the business of receiving, investing, and paying out money. Trust will be placed in employees to handle this cash appropriately. Because insurer's deal with the public's money, the need to take control and establish a fraud prevention program is critical.

The following is a four-part fraud-risk assessment exercise. Its purpose is to identify possible opportunities within the insurance company to commit fraud, and then, depending on the assessment of each fraud risk, to redesign controls for each one.

1. *Brainstorming about fraud opportunities.* The first step is to set up discussions or brainstorming sessions with groups of employees from all levels of each department, to examine the opportunities that exist to commit fraud. Before the group meets, give the participants a survey asking about the chances for fraud in their area, the internal controls or procedures that affect their work, and how those controls are being, or could be, bypassed. The survey responses will identify which controls may be circumvented or overridden, and which controls are operating differently than believed or intended. The survey results are used as the basis for group discussion. During the brainstorming session, a record of the proceedings should be kept to make sure all issues are covered and all risks captured for future consideration.

2. *Preparing a fraud-opportunity matrix.* To develop such a matrix, down the left side of a page, list the various internal controls or procedural exposures or weaknesses discussed. Across the top of the page, write three headings: level of staff; functional area; and seriousness of risk (low, medium, high). The three columns should be completed for each exposure to help identify important data that will be required to address the identified risks. Emphasis should be placed first upon those risks that are likely to cause considerable economic risk to the insurance company.

3. *Scoring the matrix.* After the fraud-opportunity matrix has been developed, estimate the potential financial impact of each instance of internal fraud by combining the probable occurrence of fraud with the probable dollar loss. Scoring the matrix provides information about the specific activities that give rise to the most likely losses and provides the basis for establishing a fraud-prevention plan.

4. *Designing a fraud-prevention plan.* With the matrix scored, the focus shifts to redesigning existing controls, creating new controls, or improving the monitoring of controls already in place. It is necessary to consider how the identified risks relate to each other and to the overall system of internal controls. Because components of a complete internal control system are interrelated, a change to one component may have implications for the entire system. The fraud-prevention plan should usually be prepared by a team consisting of the controller, internal audit manager, manager of the Special Investigation Unit, a representative of each department being reviewed, and perhaps an outside consultant. The plan should be sufficiently detailed to allow for effective implementation of the recommendations, but not so detailed as to inhibit the staff from adapting the plan to workplace realities.

In implementing the fraud-prevention plan, changes to controls should be put into practice in an organized fashion and should be monitored appropriately to allow fine-tuning and to ensure that the recommended alterations will work. A beneficial side effect of the fraud-prevention exercise is the increased awareness by an insurer's staff of the seriousness of internal fraud.

From James McAuley, "Internal Affairs," *Canadian Insurance,* May 1995: 14–15. Adapted by permission.

Life Insurance Fraud

When a claim analyst receives a claim under a life insurance policy, the analyst determines whether the policy is still within the contestable period—that is, the date of the claim loss is within two years from the date the policy was issued. If the policy is contestable, the claim analyst assesses the case to determine whether extensive investigation is necessary. Among the factors important in such an assessment are

- Face amount of the policy—cases involving higher face amount policies are subject to more detailed assessment
- Circumstances of the death—unusual or mysterious incidents warrant greater investigation
- Age of the insured—unusual circumstances relating to age, such as a 35-year-old insured's death attributed to natural causes, warrant closer checking

If a death claim appears to require more than usual investigation, the claim analyst gathers information from a variety of sources. These sources may include the beneficiary, family members, employer and co-workers, medical caregivers, the marketer who sold the policy, neighbors and friends, and others who have knowledge of the insured and his death. The claim analyst also gathers information about the insured's medical history and about other insurance coverage. If the claim analyst determines the presence of possible material misrepresentation, the analyst consults with the insurer's underwriters to determine whether complete, accurate information was submitted with the application and, if not, whether the underwriting decision would have been different had the accurate information appeared on the application.

If the death was accidental, the claim analyst verifies all details surrounding the accident, including the time, place, circumstances, and other details of the accident and its contribution to the insured's death, and checks to see if homicide or suicide could have been a factor in the accident. The analyst also interviews witnesses to the accident and any law enforcement personnel associated with the event. If an autopsy was performed, the claim analyst obtains a copy of its results.

When a death occurs in the United States or Canada, the claim analyst usually has access to sufficient information to make a clear determination on most claims. However, if a death occurs outside these countries, the claim analyst may have some difficulty obtaining the information needed to reach a claim decision.

Initially the claim analyst must determine whether the insured in fact existed and whether the death of that person in fact occurred. Persons intent on committing life insurance fraud may purchase coverage on a nonexistent person and then make a claim on that person's alleged death. Because birth certificates, identification papers, death certificates, and other official records can be purchased or forged, and because in some countries a body can be purchased and used to represent the deceased insured, the claim analyst is responsible for verifying that documents submitted in support of a foreign death claim are legitimate. Even if documents are certified by a local United States or Canadian embassy, such certification indicates only that embassy officials have attested to the names of the persons listed in a document. Embassy certification does not guarantee that documents are authentic. However, embassy officials may be able to verify or disprove certain details of a claim, such as local medical, police, and burial practices.

One particular problem in developing sufficient documentation for a foreign death claim is that in some countries medical records are extremely difficult to obtain. Some countries, for example, consider a person's medical records to be her personal property and do not maintain records in a central location such as a physician's office, clinic, or hospital. As a result, the claim analyst must contact the deceased person's family to obtain medical records and must determine whether those records are complete or have been changed. To obtain medical records from some countries, an insurer must petition a court, hire local legal representation, and wait one to three months for the copies of records to arrive. The cost in money and time of obtaining such records and of conducting other types of investigations related to foreign death claims can be very high.

Fast Fact

As much as 10 percent of the health care expenditures each year in the United States are the result of some sort of fraud; since the nation spends over $1 trillion per year on health costs, the loss to fraud may exceed $100 billion per year.

Source: Health Insurance Association of America, *Fraud: the Hidden Cost of Health Care,* 1996: 1.

The claim analyst may also check with the underwriting staff to review the information submitted in support of the application for insurance. Inconsistencies in the underwriting and claim information—for example, the address, place or date of birth, medical history, or avocations—can help the claim analyst determine how to proceed in handling the claim.

Moreover, consulting with a reinsurer about a foreign death claim is useful because the reinsurer may have considerable experiences with death claims from all over the world and may have handled a variety of foreign death claims. The reinsurer may have branch offices in the country in which the death occurred and may, therefore, be able to assist the claim analyst in obtaining information directly from officials in the country.

The claim analyst must be alert to any inconsistencies in foreign death claims. Figure 20-1 lists some additional characteristics of questionable claims for death occurring in foreign countries.

Health Insurance Fraud

Detecting fraud in health insurance claims, including workers' compensation claims, requires the claim analyst to be aware of the characteristics of legitimate claims and to recognize details on a claim that may indicate the presence of fraud. Because a health claim analyst receives numerous claims each day, the analyst learns to develop a "sixth sense" about claims that do not fit the usual pattern. An un-

Figure 20-1. Some characteristics of questionable foreign death claims.

- Medical records are incomplete or were completed all at one time, rather than at the times medical treatments were delivered to the patient
- Medical records report medical treatments that are inconsistent with the cause of eventual death of the insured
- Several of the insured's dependents live in their native country and have not lived in the country in which life insurance was issued
- Documents submitted in support of the claim are photocopies or carbon copies, not originals

usual claim in itself does not indicate fraud, but may warrant additional investigation before it is approved.

Every insurer develops its own list of indicators of possible health insurance fraud. Some of the most common indicators include

- A policy that lapses soon after a claim is filed
- A claim for an injury occurring just prior to a strike, layoff, or job termination
- A claim for a complaint that was not mentioned or reported at the time of an injury or accident
- A claim for which multiple claimants provide conflicting information or statements
- Mysterious or vague information concerning a claimant's identification, work history, or income
- Medical records submitted directly by the claimant or the marketer instead of by the medical caregiver
- An unusual number of claims submitted by one claimant or one family within a short time period
- False documentation such as driver's license, Social Security number, and medical documents
- A claim submitted for injury resulting from an unwitnessed accident or from an accident viewed by unreliable or unbelievable witnesses

In addition, a claim analyst checks every claim that reports severe injuries which are inconsistent with the facts of an accident or illness.

If a claimant is not at home on several occasions when the claim analyst telephones to discuss the claim, or if a medical caregiver appears reluctant to submit complete medical records, the claim analyst does not approve the claim until adequate information on the case has been developed.

Claims filed under workers' compensation may indicate fraud if any of the following elements are present:

- A work-related injury that was not reported promptly, that is not usual in the claimant's line of work, that was not witnessed, or for which specific, consistent details are not available
- Claimant suffers repeated accidents or has been recently hired or terminated
- Claimant complains long after receiving medical permission to return to work, or frequently misses scheduled medical appointments
- Claimant's income from workers' compensation and other sources equals or exceeds wages

Disability Income Insurance Fraud

Fraud in disability income (DI) claims can take many forms. In general, DI fraud involves deliberate inclusion of false information or omission of information that would enable an insurer to make an accurate determination of benefits due under DI coverage. The misinformation can be provided by a claimant, an employer, a medical caregiver, or other information source.

Among the types of DI misinformation are the following:

- The level of work activity of which an insured is capable—for example, the reported information may state that the insured can work for only four hours per day or can fulfill only limited duties, when in reality the insured can work for longer periods and can perform more types of work;
- The occupation and duties at the beginning of disability;
- The type and amount of supplies and treatments necessary for the insured—a medical caregiver or other provider may exaggerate the level of assistance required;
- Level of income—an insured may report that she has less income than she really does in the hope that no offset will reduce the amount of insurance benefits;

- Failure to disclose a preexisting condition or other disability coverage—in either of these situations, the misinformation can cause an insurer to pay benefits to which the claimant is not entitled; and
- Failure to disclose other insurance coverage.

If a claim analyst is responsible for following up on a disability income claimant and receiving periodic reports on the claimant's continued disability, the analyst would become suspicious if the claimant was not at home on several occasions when the claim analyst telephoned for a progress report or other information. Investigative reports and surveillance can be used to determine whether a disability in fact exists and continues. Where appropriate, a medical examination at the insurer's expense can be used to substantiate a claimed disability.

Sometimes an insured who claims disability income benefits appears to be able to work, but refuses to do so. If a claim analyst has reason to believe that the insured could perform work under the provisions of the policy, the analyst may decide to ask that the insured undergo a medical examination at the insurer's expense. In addition, the claim analyst may ask a rehabilitation vendor to perform a rehabilitation analysis of the insured. Generally the claim analyst selects a vendor located in the insured's geographic area and sends the vendor the claim information necessary to conduct the rehabilitation analysis.

During the rehabilitation analysis, the vendor may interview the claimant, members of her family, medical caregivers, neighbors, and other persons who have knowledge of the claimant's ability to be rehabilitated and return to work, in either her own occupation or another occupation. During the interviews, the rehabilitation vendor gathers information concerning the claimant's

- Age, education, training, experience, and hobbies
- Occupational abilities and interests
- Financial status and needs
- Social and personal activities
- Current and future medical prognosis
- Physical limitations and restrictions
- Motivation to undertake rehabilitation

The rehabilitation vendor may also study the labor market in the claimant's geographic area, prescreen employers, and, if the claimant is actively seeking work, assist in the employment process.

After concluding the interviews, the vendor provides a narrative report of the findings and makes recommendations for handling the case. If a reinsurance company is providing coverage for the case, a copy of the vendor's report is forwarded to the reinsurer.

Insurers' Responses to Claim Fraud

An insurance company does not pay any fraudulent claim. If a claim analyst can demonstrate that any person or entity (such as a clinic or hospital) committed fraud during the claim process, the insurer refuses to pay the claim.

When an insurer has established the presence of fraud in connection with a submitted claim, generally the insurer undertakes criminal or civil litigation. The insurer may also undertake professional discipline, report perpetrators to authorities, or undertake rescission or reformation.

Undertake Litigation

When an insurer has established the presence of fraud in connection with a submitted claim, generally the insurer undertakes criminal prosecution or civil prosecution of those alleged to have committed the fraud. Criminal prosecution involves pursuit through the court system with the intent of proving criminal fraud. Civil prosecution, which is usually undertaken if criminal prosecution fails, involves an attempt to recover monetary damages through the court system.

Sometimes an insurance company pays a claim and later discovers that fraud was involved with the claim. In such a situation, the insurer may attempt to recover benefits paid by requesting reimbursement from the insured. If the insured cannot or will not repay the benefits, the insurer may take legal action to recover the amount of benefits paid, as well as all or a portion of the costs incurred in handling the fraudulent claim.

Undertake Professional Discipline

In addition to criminal or civil actions, an insurer may attempt to have a medical caregiver disciplined because of fraudulent actions. Professional discipline involves referral of a case to an appropriate licensing agency, which may reprimand the medical caregiver or, in extreme cases, temporarily suspend or permanently revoke the caregiver's license to practice.

Report to Authorities

Insurance companies that develop information relating to fraud typically report every instance to insurance departments and to fraud bureaus or fraud units, as well as to postal inspectors if the fraud is carried out by using mail services. In addition, in the United States, insurers report claim fraud to the U.S. Attorney General's Office, the Federal Bureau of Investigation, and the Internal Revenue Service.

Undertake Rescission or Reformation

When an insurer has gathered sufficient information to prove that material misrepresentation or fraud has occurred, an insurer may seek to rescind the policy. The basis for such a rescission is material misrepresentation, a misstatement on the application or its supporting documents that is relevant to the insurer's acceptance of a risk. A misrepresentation is material if, had the truth been known about the misstatement, the insurer would not have issued the policy or would have issued it on a different basis, perhaps as a rated policy or as a policy with fewer or lower benefits. An insurer may not, however, seek to rescind a life insurance policy on the basis of material misrepresentation after the expiration of the contestable period. In the United States, the one exception to this rule is fraudulent impersonation of a proposed insured. In Canada, insurers retain the right to contest the validity of an insurance contract *at any time* in the event of fraudulent misrepresentation of material fact.

Claim staff sometimes consult with the insurer's legal staff before undertaking rescission. In addition, the claim staff usually obtain a report of the underwriting action taken on the case and a statement from the marketer concerning the circumstances under which the insurance sale was made. This information helps the insurer to make an equitable, good-faith decision on the case.

Rescission is often the outcome when a proposed insured has not revealed material information on the application for insurance or when material information has not been revealed during the underwriting investigation. The claim analyst usually discovers that information has been withheld during investigation of a claim for benefits. For example, if an insured has withheld pertinent facts about a medical condition such as AIDS, alcohol or drug abuse, cancer, cardiovascular problems, and other serious or potentially serious medical conditions, the insurer generally rescinds the coverage on the basis that the application did not provide information which, if provided, would have caused the underwriting decision to be different.

Instead of rescinding the coverage, an insurer may offer to reform the policy. ***Reformation*** is an equitable remedy under which an insurer revises or reinterprets a contract to express the original intent of the parties to the contract. In reforming a policy, the insurer states precisely what is covered under the policy and usually includes an exclusion rider for a specific medical condition or other impairment. If the formerly unrevealed information indicates that the risk is greater than formerly thought, the insurer may also rate the policy and charge a premium higher than that originally charged for the coverage. Reformation generally produces a reduction in coverage, whereas rescission produces a termination of coverage. For a small group that might lose its coverage because of misinformation about one member of the group, reformation allows an insurer to continue to provide coverage for the group while modifying the coverage to account for the previously unrevealed impairment of the one member.

In some cases, the claim analyst discovers that an applicant or a group had no intent to make a material misrepresentation. For example, a proposed insured may not have understood the implications of medical information supplied by a medical caregiver and, therefore, did not advise the marketer or the insurer of the medical facts. In such a situation, an insurer does not always rescind or reform a policy even though information submitted on the application or during underwriting is incomplete or misleading.

If a policy being considered for rescission or reformation is reinsured, the insurer sends copies of the underwriting report and the agent's statement to the reinsurer, as well as a copy of the letter notifying the insured of the insurer's decision to rescind or reform the policy. Notifying the reinsurer about a rescission is important because, if the policyholder proceeds to litigation, the reinsurer typically either (1) chooses to assist the insurer during the litigation or (2) pays the amount reinsured to the insurer and then has no further liability in the case. Whatever the reinsurer's decision, the reinsurer is not a party to litigation; the full responsibility for proceeding through the litigation process rests with the insurer, although the reinsurer may assist with such matters as selecting attorneys who are experienced in insurance litigation and providing advice on certain types of legal proceedings. Moreover, the reinsurer may provide useful guidance and assistance to the insurer by suggesting investigative approaches and experienced vendors, and by advising the insurer if a pattern or trend of such fraudulent claims has become evident in the reinsurer's experience.

Preventing Claim Fraud

Generally the best defenses against claim fraud are well-informed consumers and alert, well-trained insurance company staff. Consumers who understand the primary function of insurance—to pay for covered losses that would cause financial difficulty for insureds—are not likely to consider insurance coverage as an entitlement or as a source of unmerited wealth. Similarly, the employees of an insurance company can discover fraud in many of its forms and can follow the insurer's procedures for investigating suspicious cases and, when necessary, turning over incidents of fraud to the insurer's legal staff. Insight 20-4 presents information concerning some of the ways that insurers can combat claim fraud.

Insurers combat claim fraud in many ways. Among the most important are effective product design, insurance applications, and underwriting, as well as claim analyst and consumer education, internal controls, vendor investigations, specialized claim software, field visits to marketers and branches, and cooperation with law enforcement agencies and state departments of insurance.

Product Design

During the process of designing an insurance product, an insurer can build in at least some protection against fraudulent use of the product. When any coverage is offered as guaranteed issue, insurers generally

Insight 20-4 Fighting Fraud

For insurers, the process of uncovering and battling fraud begins in the claim department because once a claim has been paid, it is almost impossible to recapture the money. For this reason, the insurer's best line of defense is a well-trained claim professional. Fraud today has reached a crisis level, and the potential for abuse will increase as benefit amounts and durations increase.

The Health Insurance Association of America (HIAA) recommends that insurers take the following steps to prevent, detect, and control fraud:

- *Adopt a clear and consistent policy on fraud. Do not overlook abusive billing statements.* It pays to examine and challenge every suspicious claim, no matter how seemingly insignificant. Insurers must prosecute fraud when it is uncovered, work closely with law enforcement agencies, report fraud to state licensing boards, and take civil action to gain restitution.
- *Centralize all fraud detection efforts in a special unit to achieve coordination, integration, and communication.* The staff in these units must be highly trained and must work closely with other departments, including the insurer's attorneys.
- *Share information as a key weapon in the fight against fraud.* Sharing information must take place within the boundaries of legal guidelines. The information may be used as a guide for conducting investigations. Claim decisions must be based on the results of an investigation, not on information obtained from other insurers.
- *Institute strong anti-fraud messages in sales and marketing presentations.* For example, an insurer can add fraud statements to marketing materials, benefit brochures, and claim forms, and can train claim analysts to identify suspicious claims.
- *Use the explanation of benefits (EOB) to educate and motivate consumers to spot and report suspicious claims and activities.* The EOB must be explicit and easy to read, but because providers make honest mistakes, the message should not be accusatory.
- *Become involved in fraud seminars, workshops, regional and local networks, and national associations.* Make every effort to create awareness among employees at every level of the harmful effects of fraud.

W. J. West, State Farm Insurance Companies, *Best's Review,* Life/Health Edition, January 1993. © A. M. Best Company. Adapted by permission.

offer only moderate sums of coverage. Moreover, insurers usually offer only moderate sums of daily benefits for accident coverages because large sums might encourage some insureds to depend on the daily benefits instead of returning to work. The amount of benefits offered and the conditions under which benefits are offered should be adequate to compensate an insured who is sick or injured, but should not be so great that they encourage fraud.

Insurance Applications

In designing an application for insurance, insurers generally include a question concerning whether a proposed insured is covered by any other insurance. The fact that a proposed insured is already covered under one or more existing policies does not in itself become a reason to deny an application for additional insurance. Asking the question, however, helps determine whether a proposed insured might become overinsured if the applied-for policy were issued.

Some persons, intent on obtaining multiple policies of the same type of coverage, submit applications to various insurers simultaneously. Therefore, their answer to the question concerning whether they already have "other insurance" can be negative because the other insurance has not yet been issued. Such a response is, of course, misleading to any insurer who is asked to accept the new risk. To forestall such a tactic, insurers usually include a question on the application about whether the applicant has applied for any other policies.

Nearly all applications also include one or more questions about preexisting injuries or other conditions that might increase the risk. A proposed insured who intends to misrepresent information may fail to provide accurate answers to such questions and later submit a claim for an injury that allegedly is the result of an accident, but in fact is a preexisting condition. To prevent such losses from such fraudulent claims, insurers need information about preexisting conditions, or at least evidence that the application contained false information denying such conditions.

Underwriting

In our previous discussion of underwriting, we emphasized the importance of detailed checking of any facts that seem inconsistent or questionable on an application for insurance and on any supporting documents. Underwriters and claim analysts need to work closely together to ensure that both underwriting and claim handling are accurate and that appropriate decisions are made in both instances. Underwriters typically share with claim staff certain information concerning the reasons for underwriting decisions; similarly, claim staff inform underwriters of claim decisions and any problems that have resulted from such a decision.

We have also discussed the issue of moral hazard—that is, a characteristic that may exist when the reputation, financial position, or mental state of an applicant or a proposed insured indicates that the person might cause a loss intentionally or might fail to limit a loss after it occurs. One of the most important aspects of accurate underwriting is checking for the presence of moral hazard and, if it is found, either denying the applied-for coverage or modifying the offered coverage so that the insurer is not placed at unreasonable risk. In helping to lessen the impact of moral hazard, the underwriter verifies that the amount of coverage requested (1) meets an evident need and (2) is appropriate for the potential loss. Further, the underwriter is especially cautious if a proposed insured's financial condition is perilous—for example, if he seems to have no means to repay debts or meet other financial obligations.

Internal Controls

To help prevent claim fraud committed by an insurer's employees, insurers generally institute the kinds of internal financial controls that prevent one person from performing every transaction involved in receiving and evaluating claims, and issuing and accounting for benefit payments. For instance, an insurer generally establishes procedures to prevent any one employee from processing claim transactions and also producing payment checks and making accounting entries for those checks. An insurer that issues manual checks keeps the check stock locked and requires that each check be accounted for by management. All large-amount claims are reviewed by senior claim staff, who also have responsibility for receiving and investigating returned checks and preventing those that are still negotiable from being given to other staff. Just as underwriters are allowed to approve applications within established limits, each claim analyst is given permission to approve claims only up to a dollar limit appropriate with that analyst's training and experience.

In addition, insurers establish internal information controls that not only establish a sequence of security passwords for claim records, but also separate the sources of information from the users of that information. As an example, many insurers pass records of group members' coverage directly to the claim system from a billing system or other source external to claims. Similarly, medical caregiver records are created and maintained by non-claim employees.

Moreover, insurers try to prevent insider fraud in claims by establishing information systems that track and check claim-related approvals, payments, and records. In hiring employees to handle claim responsibilities, insurers carefully check references, verify information with prior employers, and sometimes hire an investigative agency to provide criminal checks and credit histories of job applicants. Some insurers also make job offers contingent upon a job applicant's passing a drug test.

Another type of internal control is a claim audit, which permits an insurer to verify the types of decisions made by claim analysts and the disbursements of benefit payments. An internal audit may be performed by a special unit composed of the insurer's employees; occasionally an insurer employs an outside agency to conduct such an audit. Many insurers have established special investigative units (SIUs) to handle all suspicious activities involving claims. Insight 20-5 discusses the characteristics and uses of SIUs.

Insight 20-5 Special Investigative Units

Insurance fraud in the United States, whether committed by claimants, providers, employees, or insurers, is pervasive and expensive. It poses a serious problem for insurers and policyowners alike. Faked deaths and phony accidents are classic examples of insurance fraud. The geographically limited nature of these crimes is such that state law enforcement tools are not enough for deterring, arresting, and punishing those who would enrich themselves through filing fraudulent insurance claims. Historically, the investigation has been conducted by the regular claim staff with help from management.

To help combat insurance fraud, several states have enacted antifraud legislation. Included as part of the legislation in some of the states has been the requirement for the formation of Special Investigative Units (SIUs) to address suspected cases of fraud. Although all states do not yet require insurers to have SIUs, most insurers have established these units because the insurers conduct business in many states. Utilization of SIUs is, therefore, likely to apply on many suspected cases of fraud, no matter where the case may be located.

As an investigative unit, an SIU can be composed of persons inside or outside the claim area. The unit may include persons currently employed by the insurer, and the SIU may hire additional employees or contract with another entity to fulfill its duties. A SIU usually includes representatives of the legal, auditing, and claim functions. The number of members of the SIU is decided by the insurer or by state statute and can be based on the number of lives insured by the company. Training for SIU staff on all fraud-related issues and on Unfair Claims Practices statutes and regulations is important.

In conducting investigations, the SIU generally considers these rules:

- Distribute only information that they know or suspect to be false.
- Distribute fraud information only to those who can help with the investigation, those who have a common interest in the investigation, or others who have a need to know.
- Develop reasonable procedures so that the investigations can obtain accurate information.
- Do not use information obtained as part of a fraud investigation, or the threat of such an investigation, to pressure claim settlement.
- Make claim decisions independently, not in conjunction with other insurers.
- Consult with legal counsel before pursuing criminal charges.
- Conduct investigations *only* for the purpose of investigating fraud.
- Avoid investigative techniques that are abusive or not reasonably calculated to yield pertinent information.
- Conduct investigations in good faith and without malice.
- Be alert to evidence that disproves fraud as well as to evidence that proves it.

After a suspected case of fraud is detected and evaluated, the case is referred to the authorized person of the insurer who conducts or oversees claim investigation. If the case warrants further investigation, it is then referred to the SIU.

From Arthur E. Garner, FLMI, "Special Investigative Units," *Life Insurance Workshop Reports,* 1996: 8–10. Adapted by permission of the International Claim Association.

Generally, an internal claim audit examines claim financial records, operating procedures, and recordkeeping systems. For instance, an audit may verify the original claim, the supporting documentation, the payee, and the payment amount against the financial reports issued concerning the claim.

Generally, insurers tend to audit high-amount claims, but they also examine ordinary claims in a random, unpredictable manner. Because examining every transaction would require excessive time and expense, the audit is usually based on a statistical sample of transactions.

Specialized Claim Software

By using specialized claim software to monitor the claim examination and decision processes, individual insurers save millions of dollars annually and help preserve the integrity of the insurance industry. Claim software can identify simple human error and can prompt a claim analyst to seek ways to correct it. Suppose that the usual length of hospitalization following a specified minor surgery is two days. However, a claim analyst approves a claim for five days of hospitalization following this type of surgery. The insurer's claim software is programmed to provide a warning automatically when the length of hospitalization exceeds the usual length by more than one day. In such a situation, the claim analyst would be advised of the discrepancy and would probably check the documentation submitted with the claim to see whether an extended hospital stay was justified.

Equally important, claim software can help in detecting fraudulent activity, particularly in identifying suspicious patterns of claim submission, medical caregiver billing, and other unusual claim-related practices. Claim software can provide extensive analysis of client claim data and can pinpoint unusual patterns of activity. If claims submitted from a medical caregiver begin to show an abnormal pattern—for instance, when most of the claims are for high amounts instead of showing the usual balance among high, medium, and low amounts—the insurer is alerted to the possibility of fraud.

During internal audits, claim software can also provide reports on each claim analyst's patterns of approval of various types of claims and can reveal whether claim decisions appear to be appropriate. Moreover, specialized software can provide a profile of physicians and other caregivers, enabling an insurer to compare a physician's diagnoses and treatments against a normative pattern established for each specific medical condition.

Field Visits

Making frequent visits to marketers and field offices can help an insurer to check standard operating procedures and to ensure that marketers and claim analysts are performing their duties in an ethical manner. Some insurers also perform audits of marketers' insurance applications to verify that the level of each type of business submitted is consistent with the standards established by the insurer.

Insurers also help marketers understand the importance of avoiding clients who appear intent on committing insurance fraud. Some guidelines for marketers are included in Insight 20-6.

Vendor Investigations

A wide range of investigative services is available from vendors. Insurers typically authorize and pay for such investigation not only when a claim requires extensive investigation, but also when fraud is suspected. The services provided by investigative vendors include

- Accident investigation
- Surveillance
- Asset searches
- Subpoena service
- Polygraph testing

Insight 20-6 How Agents and Brokers Can Avoid Trouble

Insurance agents and brokers face a legal minefield every time they do business. Mistakes and misunderstandings can ruin a once-friendly business transaction. However, marketers can take several steps to avoid problems.

■ *Put it in writing.* Get into the habit of taking notes from all meetings or conversations with clients. Being able to produce documentation is critical.

■ *Don't assume.* Assuming that a client knows or understands something can lead to more than embarrassment. The complexities of insurance make it essential to explain all details, no matter how obvious, to the client.

■ *Listen to the client.* Pay special attention to what clients say. Answer questions promptly and completely, and take extra care to address complaints or criticisms.

■ *Stay informed.* Insurance is a complex business, and marketers require constant education to remain up to date. Associations, trade journals, and continuing education can keep marketers current about the latest products and regulations, as well as the policies and procedures of each insurer. Marketers must also keep licenses and registrations current.

■ *Be candid with insurers and clients.* The best way to avoid problems is to address them before they occur. Be proactive when contracting with new insurers. Disclose any adverse information immediately, keep existing insurers updated on what is happening with the marketing organization. Advise insurers of any changes or situations that may reflect on their relationship with the marketer.

From Stefan E. Keller and Tony D'Orazio, "Investigating Agents," *Best's Review,* Life/Health Edition, September 1993: 32. © A. M. Best Company. Adapted by permission.

- Assistance with jury panel selection
- Witness location
- Personnel background screening
- Loss prevention surveys
- Physician peer reviews

Law Enforcement Agencies and State Departments of Insurance

One of the insurance industry's strongest allies is law enforcement, whose concern is to protect the public from crime in all its forms. Working with law enforcement agencies to provide evidence and enabling claim analysts to guide law officers in investigating specialized types of fraud are two important approaches by which insurers help to combat insurance fraud.

In addition, insurers cooperate with state insurance departments and other appropriate authorities to report required information on an annual or a more frequent basis, as statutes dictate. In general, insurers report the following types of information to state departments of insurance:

- Number of policies in force and number of claims
- Number of suspected fraud cases and number of proven fraud cases
- Fraud cases according to product line and according to persons involved
- Cost of investigation, including legal expenses

Claim Analyst and Consumer Education

Knowing what to look for on a claim is one of the most important skills a claim analyst develops. Every insurer provides training to its claim analysts concerning appropriate procedures to follow in handling claims and methods of detecting claim fraud. Many insurers gather representatives from claims, underwriting, product development, and legal for periodic updates on preventing insurance fraud.

Among the important fraud-related information for employees to know is that they should report all questionable activity and not conceal or promise not to reveal suspected fraud even if a person suspected of fraud promises to withdraw a claim or return the benefits. Further, an employee needs to know that discussion of fraud investigations should be conducted only with persons who are authorized to investigate the matter. Discussion of a case of suspected fraud could expose both the insurer and the employee to liability for defamation of character.

In addition, most insurers provide other information to claim analysts, including claim handling procedural updates and reports on claim trends. Moreover, if an insurer receives a claim that turns out to be fraudulent, the claim can be circulated to all claim analysts for their review. Many insurers also provide periodic workshops and classes for claim analysts to inform them about new types of fraudulent claims, new laws and statutes affecting claim handling and claim fraud, and new methods the insurer is using to identify fraudulent claims.

Helping consumers understand the detrimental effects of fraud can guide consumers to make intelligent choices concerning the purchase and use of insurance. Many jurisdictions require claim forms to include a statement noting that supplying false information on a claim is a criminal offense. Insurers and insurance groups also try to improve media coverage concerning the costs of insurance fraud and the results of insurance fraud detection activities. Many insurers provide educational materials to schools and civic groups, and make company management available for informational presentations. Insurers also may take an active role in community affairs, sponsoring various educational and community improvement activities, and otherwise indicating their interest in contributing to the strength of the community.

Key Terms and Concepts

claim fraud
collusion
upcoding
unbundling
exploding
reformation

CHAPTER TWENTY-ONE

Scope and Organization of Policyowner Service

Learning Objectives

After studying this chapter, you should be able to

- Explain four benefits of providing effective customer service
- Discuss various ways to organize and deliver policyowner service
- Describe the ways that insurers deliver service to marketers and information to insurance regulatory organizations
- State the importance of conservation and the approaches insurers use to conserve the business of policyowners and marketers
- List and explain the qualities of effective policyowner service
- Explain five ways by which insurers try to deliver effective policyowner service
- Discuss ways that insurers evaluate the quantity and quality of policyowner service

Chapter Outline

Benefits of Providing Effective POS

Organization of POS
Other Providers of POS

POS to Customers
POS for Insureds and Beneficiaries
POS for Marketers
POS and Insurance Regulatory Organizations

POS and Conservation
Conservation and Policyowners
Conservation and Marketers

Qualities of Effective POS

Delivering Effective POS
Determining Strategies for Effective POS
Automating and Simplifying POS Delivery
Documenting POS Policies and Procedures
Ensuring Excellent Telephone Communication

Evaluating POS
Evaluating the Quantity of POS
Evaluating the Quality of POS

To this point in your study of the functions involved in insurance administration, you've seen the importance of underwriting, reinsurance handling, and claim administration. You've also seen the many ways in which these aspects of insurance administration cooperate with one another, with other functional areas of the insurer, and with marketers and insurance regulators to ensure that insured persons and groups are treated equitably. Now we'll turn our attention to a fourth aspect of insurance administration, policyowner service. Because effective service to clients is a cornerstone of successful organizations, policyowner service is an essential part of the insurance administration functions.

In this discussion, we will distinguish policyowner service from customer service. In general, as we mentioned in Chapter 1, customer service refers to the activities, consistent with contractual provisions, that help keep customers satisfied with the insurer. These activities are designed to satisfy the needs and wants of the insurance company's customers. In Chapter 1 we also told you that, as a part of customer service, policyowner service (POS) includes all the service activities performed for marketers and for the persons or parties who own or hold insurance policies and annuities. Although marketers have a different relationship to an insurer than do the other persons served by POS, most insurers do establish service to marketers as a part of POS.

In our discussion of policyowner service, we will refer to POS as both (1) the functional unit that performs specified activities and (2) the activities performed by POS staff. Further, in order to simplify the discussion, we will use the term *policyowner* to refer to policyowners (of individual coverage), policyholders (of group coverage), and insureds (both individual and group). Where necessary, we will explain how individual and group POS differs.

Unlike the sale of many other products, the sale of insurance products establishes a relationship between the seller and the buyer—the insurer and the policyowner. During the often lengthy period when an insurer and a policyowner are linked by the provisions of an insurance contract, various customers—purchasers, insureds, beneficiaries, and others—may have many questions that require prompt attention if the insured is to be satisfied with the insurer's service and products. In addition, the insured may require certain changes to be made in the contract—name, address, coverage type and amount, beneficiary, and others. In addition to making these changes, the insurer may continue to collect premiums, make loans, pay dividends, provide information, and undertake other kinds of business related to the insurance product.

POS is the part of insurance administration that responds to these questions and circumstances and that helps ensure that clients' needs and desires are met during the contract period. In short, POS helps maintain important contractual and business connections between the insurer and its insureds. Moreover, POS enhances the insurer's reputation for taking good care of its clients and thereby assists marketers of the insurer's products in making further sales. Finally, POS helps an insurer to preserve its existing business and to compile information for reports to insurance regulatory organizations.

In this chapter, we will begin by explaining the benefits of providing top-quality service to customers and the numerous ways of organizing such service. After outlining the types of service that insurers deliver to various types of customers and insurance regulatory organizations, we will examine the relationship between POS and policy conservation. In subsequent sections of the chapter, we'll discuss the qualities and ways of delivering and evaluating effective POS. In the next chapter, we'll look at some of the details of delivering POS in connection with various kinds of insurance coverage and annuities.

Benefits of Providing Effective POS

An insurance company that establishes and maintains superior POS enhances business in a number of ways:

- *Building long-term customer loyalty.* Customers who are satisfied with the service an insurer provides are more likely to continue productive relationships with the insurer. For example, satisfied insureds are likely to renew and increase their current coverage and to buy new products. They may also recommend the insurer to friends and family members. Moreover, marketers who receive high-quality service are likely to feel that selling the insurer's products will result in satisfied insureds and continuing commissions. Further, an insurer with a reputation for effective customer service increases its ability to attract new customers and to recruit and retain its sales force.

- *Improving profitability.* Retaining business and marketers can greatly increase the profit margin of an insurance company. Avoiding the wasted time and resources required to rebuild lost business and to locate and train a sales force allows the insurer to direct those resources into building its business.

- *Differentiating an insurer from its competitors.* Coverage from various insurance companies may seem about the same to many potential purchasers. One way in which an insurer can distinguish itself from others is to offer POS that fulfills customers' needs as rapidly, completely, and courteously as possible.

- *Enhancing the insurer's work environment.* Working for an organization that prides itself on delivering top-quality service to its customers makes employees feel proud and helps motivate them to excel at their jobs. In contrast, poor POS can cause employees' morale to drop as they cope with the stressful effects of dealing with unhappy or angry customers.

Organization of POS

Like underwriting and claims, POS may be organized in a variety of ways according to the types of business an insurer does, and according to the preferences and operating approaches of each insurer's management. Some insurers establish one department or area to deal with every kind of service to its customers. Other insurers divide the activities of POS in other ways, such as by product, by client, by type of service requested, by marketer, and by function. Many insurers establish teams to handle various aspects of POS.

In organizing POS by product, an insurer usually trains specific employees to respond to the questions concerning one or two products—for example, an individual disability income product or a group life insurance product. An employee who understands all the details of a product, especially a complex one, is able to provide top quality service to customers.

An insurer may decide instead to organize POS employees according to clients served. Some employees may handle inquiries only from marketers, while other employees may respond to requests from large group clients. Particularly when an insurer provides coverage for a very large group, assigning certain employees to handle the service for that group may prove efficient. The employees learn the needs and typical requests of the group and can develop response systems that provide rapid, accurate POS.

Yet another way of organizing POS is to assign employees to different types of requests for service. Using this organizational mode, an insurer would assign certain employees to make address or beneficiary changes, others to work with policy loans, and so on. In dividing POS according to function, insurers typically establish such divisions as policy administration, premium billing, coverage transfers incoming from other insurers, conservation, loans, cancellations and surrenders, annuities, and marketer service.

Other Providers of POS

Besides the employees who directly provide POS, other employees also provide service to policyowners. In discussing underwriting, reinsurance, and claims, we have mentioned a number of ways in which employees of these functions interact with various customers. In reviewing policy applications and renewals, underwriters consult with marketers and vendors; employees working with reinsurance may consult with a reinsurer's staff and inform marketers of ongoing negotiations; and claim employees communicate regularly with insureds and marketers.

Moreover, other employees outside the specific POS area deliver policyowner service in a variety of ways as part of their daily activities. For instance, employees in accounting handle premium billing and collection; information systems employees handle data input and information processing; and employees on the legal staff are involved in legal problems related to policyowner service. Employees in POS interact frequently with employees in these and other functional areas to obtain information and guidance in handling various requests for information and in resolving problems associated with coverage.

The insurer's top management also enhances POS by performing strategic planning and employee training that provide for high-quality POS delivery. An insurer's top management knows that effective POS strengthens the insurer's competitive position and helps the organization to grow and remain strong. Moreover, potential clients generally prefer to purchase insurance products from insurers with a reputation for attending promptly and successfully to the needs of their customers. Therefore, an insurer can increase its sales effectiveness by establishing a solid reputation for good policyowner service.

POS to Customers

POS provides essential contacts with insureds and beneficiaries, annuitants and annuity owners, and marketers. Keep in mind that a policyowner is not always an insured—for example, a wife may purchase a life or disability income policy insuring her spouse, or a business may buy coverage on the life of key employees. In this discussion, we'll focus on the general principles of POS, not on all the details that an employee in POS has to master.

In this section, we'll outline the general types of POS delivered to insureds, beneficiaries, annuitants, and annuity owners, and we will discuss these services in more detail in the next chapter. After explaining the types of services that POS delivers to marketers, we'll explain the interactions of POS and insurance regulatory organizations.

POS for Insureds and Beneficiaries

Most of the interactions between POS and insureds and beneficiaries involve dispensing information and processing changes to policies. The interactions of POS and beneficiaries usually involve claim handling. Specifically, POS transactions for insureds generally include

- Providing information and answering queries from insureds
- Changing the owner and/or the beneficiary of a policy
- Changing addresses
- Changing coverage or adding riders
- Determining cash values, loans, and dividends
- Sending premium due notices and handling premium payments
- Handling annuity payments and distributions

POS for Marketers

POS helps attract and retain effective marketers to sell an insurer's products. Marketers are very much interested in whether an insurer provides high-quality service to policyowners because selling an insurer's products is easier if the insurer has a reputation for providing effective policyowner service.

To help marketers in soliciting and selling business, POS provides information and education about insurance products. Such information and education are valuable especially if the insurance products or annuities are complex. In addition, POS helps marketers understand how to submit information about proposed insureds—for instance, to know which forms should be completed, which need to be completed in duplicate, and what additional kinds of information might need to be submitted with an application for specific types of coverage or for proposed insureds with certain kinds of medical conditions. In these ways, POS helps marketers submit complete application information and, therefore, increases the probability that underwriters can make a prompt evaluation of the application.

Marketers also need information to service their existing customers. Many insureds consider the marketer to be their link to the insurance company and, therefore, communicate directly with the marketer when they have questions or problems. Answering customer questions promptly is vital to the continuation of an insurance relationship; in

Fast Fact

The first accident insurance policy in the United States was issued in 1864 as an oral agreement for $1,000 in coverage on James Bolter of Hartford for the time each day he spent walking from his house to the post office. The annual premium was two cents.

Source: Joseph Nathan Kane, *Famous First Facts: A Record of First Happenings, Discoveries, and Inventions in the United States,* 3rd ed. New York: H. W. Wilson Company, 1964: 315.

fact, marketers' commissions often depend on the continuation of the insurance relationship. Moreover, the marketer typically bears the burden of a policyowner's irritation if the insurer makes errors in transactions, is unresponsive to requests for information, or otherwise fails to meet policyowner expectations. POS provides information and service to help the marketer provide top-quality service directly to insureds. Establishing and maintaining a productive relationship between POS and marketers is of great importance in enhancing the marketers' effectiveness and the insurer's competitive position.

POS may also handle calculation and payment of commissions to marketers. If an insurer enables marketers, at a policyowner's request, to make certain contractually permitted changes to policies and annuities and to submit the changes either electronically or on paper to the insurer, POS usually oversees and maintains records of the change processes. If an insurer provides information to customers by means of a telephone or other communication system, POS is generally responsible for updating that information.

POS and Insurance Regulatory Organizations

POS complies with requirements of supervisors of insurance and state and provincial departments of insurance by maintaining accurate, complete, and current records of complaints. POS also compiles and submits annual reports of complaints to insurance regulatory organizations. State and provincial departments of insurance generally reconcile insurers' annual reports of complaints with records of complaints submitted directly to those departments. In jurisdictions that have established standards of promptness in handling complaints, state and provincial departments of insurance determine how adequately each insurer has responded to filed complaints and what, if any, actions were taken to resolve problems in response times.

In explaining the nature of each complaint, an insurer generally establishes categories that describe typical complaints. Then POS employees assign each complaint to the category that most accurately describes it. For example, an insurance company might establish the following categories for complaints related to claims: claim procedures, delays, unsatisfactory settlements or settlement offers, and denial of claim. Any claim-related complaint that does not fit adequately into one of these categories would be placed in a "miscellaneous" category. In explaining the disposition of each complaint, the insurer usually specifies that for each complaint (1) a satisfactory explanation was given to the person who submitted the complaint, (2) corrective action was taken, or (3) no corrective action was deemed necessary.

Insurers gather information on complaints not only to satisfy regulatory requirements, but also as a management tool to help determine actual and potential weaknesses in the ways they are doing business. An increase in one type of complaint generally indicates a need to examine the causes and circumstances of the complaints and to take whatever remedial action is appropriate. Complaints that are deemed serious or that could negatively affect an insurer's image are usually referred to the legal staff. Such complaints may involve customer demands for reinstatement beyond the period allowed, allegations that instructions to the insurer or its marketers were not followed, or allegations that the insurer's employees or marketers behaved in an incompetent, negligent, or dishonest manner.

POS and Conservation

Another important function of POS is to preserve the insurer's existing business. ***Conservation*** is the process of ensuring that policies, once issued, are retained on an insurer's books for as long as possible. Many insurers consider conservation of existing business to be as important as selling new policies.

Conservation efforts are essential because a policyowner is free at any time to cancel the coverage provided under a policy. That is, the policyowner has no obligation to continue to pay premiums and receive coverage under the contract of insurance. Coverage under a policy may be ended by a lapse or a surrender. As we mentioned in Chapter 5, a policy lapse is a type of policy cancellation that occurs when an insurance policy terminates through nonpayment of premium (and, for life insurance, before the policy has accumulated cash values). As we discussed in Chapter 11, a policy surrender is a type of policy cancellation that occurs when a policyowner sends the policy to the insurer and requests that (1) the coverage be terminated and (2) the cash value of the policy be sent to the policyowner.

Fast Fact

In 1985, the overall lapse rate for life insurance policies was 12.3 percent; by 1995 the lapse rate had fallen to 7.2 percent.

Source: American Council of Life Insurance, *Life Insurance Fact Book,* 1996: 67.

Because an insurer has incurred numerous expenses in underwriting and issuing a policy, the insurer does not wish to experience a high cancellation rate from either lapses or surrenders, particularly within the first four or five years of coverage. Unless an insured continues a policy in force for at least several years, the insurer generally cannot offset its initial costs. Moreover, a policy begins to offer a return to an insurer only after those initial costs have been recovered. Therefore, the insurer makes every effort to provide top-quality customer service to every customer in order to retain business. Ideally, the insurer would like to conserve every policy sold. In reality, this goal is difficult, but POS is one of the most important ways by which an insurer tries to conserve business. In undertaking conservation efforts, POS works with policyowners and marketers.

Conservation and Policyowners

A strong relationship between an insurer and its policyowners is one of the best conservation methods. Answering policyowners' questions, making requested changes, and providing other types of services enable the insurer to demonstrate its interest in enhancing its relationship with its insureds. By monitoring all customer complaints, an insurer can often identify and seek to help insureds who may appear concerned about their coverage or who otherwise indicate any degree of dissatisfaction with their relationship to the insurance company. Insight 21-1 provides comments on the importance of including conservation in POS.

POS may also contact policyowners who have not paid premiums in a timely manner to indicate the insurer's interest in continuing the business relationship and to seek ways by which the policyowners' needs may be satisfied. Some insurers provide rewards to POS employees who "save" policies that have lapsed or been submitted for

Insight 21-1 My Thoughts On . . . POS and Conservation

Initiating a conservation call to a policyholder serves many functions in a life insurance company operation. The first, and probably most often thought of role, is to preserve the in-force business and ensure a continued flow of premium dollars. Keeping new business on the books is especially critical since many policies require a period of seven to eight years before they truly become profitable. It is during this time when the initial expenses of underwriting, issuing, and servicing the business are recovered.

But conservation is also just plain good customer service. For example, a policyowner with a cash value producing policy may see those funds as a vehicle to meet a temporary cash flow need. The policyowner often assumes that the only way to access those funds is through a full policy surrender. A telephone call or letter to the client explaining the alternatives of receiving cash through a loan or a partial surrender is sometimes all it takes to conserve a policy that otherwise would have been surrendered. And the policyholder has been well served. She can now meet her financial needs while maintaining valuable insurance protection—a true win-win situation!

There are times when the conservation call reveals that replacement of the business is taking place. But that doesn't always mean lost business. It is important to reach the policyowner to discuss his current coverage. A well-trained customer service representative can help a client to realize the value of preserving his current policy. Communicating with the client can reveal why he plans to leave the company and transfer the coverage to another insurer. Perhaps he wants new coverage because his needs have changed, and he simply wants less coverage or a lower premium. With the flexibility of many of today's policies, these needs can often be met by making a change to the policyowner's existing coverage.

A key to a successful conservation program is to provide employees with training on conservation techniques. Start by emphasizing the importance of conservation for your company. And make sure the staff is well versed in the various policy options available. The more the staff members understand how each policy operates and the options that are available to policyowners, the more versatile they will be in their conservation attempts. Sometimes all it takes to conserve a policy is a friendly customer service call.

Susan Calame, FLMI/M, ACS
Manager, Customer Service
Westfield Life Insurance Company

surrender. The POS employees usually save a policy by discussing the coverage with the policyowner, trying to determine the reason for the lapse or surrender, and taking appropriate steps to encourage the policyowner to keep the policy in force. However, insurance companies generally try to make conservation of a policy come as the result of a genuine, unforced customer decision so that the business will likely remain in force.

In most insurance companies, POS employees who handle lapses and surrender requests are trained to offer contractual options such as reduced paid-up insurance or policy loans that may persuade policyowners to leave the coverage on the insurer's books. If a policy has been in force for a specified period of time—usually at least six months—and has lapsed, most insurers offer an extended reinstatement period from the due date of the premium without requiring evidence of insurability. Some insurers also provide for reinstatement without requiring the payment of unpaid premiums in order to provide policyowners an opportunity to continue coverage that may have lapsed as a result of temporary financial hardship.

Insurers also help conserve business by informing insureds of upcoming changes in premiums or coverage. For policies that require higher premiums at certain ages, a POS employee may inform each insured of the change and may ask whether the insured is interested in discussing other coverage options with a marketer. If a certain type of coverage terminates on a specific birthday of the insured—for instance, the 60th or 70th—most insurers send policyowners a letter stating that the coverage will terminate on that date and asking whether the insured would like to have a marketer explain how to continue coverage with the insurer. Because customers may feel resentful if the only time they hear from an insurer is on the occasion of such a change, however, many insurers make efforts to maintain frequent contact with customers throughout the length of the business relationship. Some insurers mail an annual summary of benefits statement that explains all existing coverages and the benefits paid during the previous year. Another way that insurers stay in touch with customers is to ask about their satisfaction with the insurer's service, a topic we will discuss later in this chapter.

Simplifying the payment of premiums is another approach insurers use to conserve business. Because coverage whose premiums are paid on a monthly basis by check is the most likely to lapse and to experience problems with late payments, many insurers allow insureds to pay premiums through ***electronic funds transfer (EFT),*** an automatic premium payment approach whereby a policyowner authorizes his bank to withdraw funds from an account to pay each renewal premium. Some insurers also pay benefits—particularly small amounts, such as those paid for certain health claims—by EFT.

Figure 21-1. Additional approaches to conservation of insurance business.

- Giving marketers access to information about payments insureds make to flexible-premium policies so that marketers may take action if payments decline or fall below the required level
- Providing multiple reminders of premiums due, such as a premium statement 15 days before the premium is due, a past due notice 20 days after the due date, a late payment notice and a telephoned reminder to the policyowner 30 days after the due date, and a final reinstatement notice 55 days after the due date
- Sending notices of late premiums to both insureds and marketers, in the hope that marketers will encourage insureds to maintain the coverage
- Conferring with policyowners who make maximum loan requests, which are sometimes encouraged by competing marketers who plan to replace policies as soon as the loan has been processed
- Advising policyowners who request a policy surrender about the alternatives to making such a change, such as a policy loan or a decrease in the face amount, and providing a list of reasons not to relinquish the coverage
- Offering insureds who leave a group insurance plan various options for continuing their coverage on an individual basis
- Offering a toll-free telephone number and electronic communication to policyowners who wish to get in touch with the insurance company
- Maintaining records of policyowners' responses to such questions as "How satisfied are you with your marketer and with our products?" in order to identify specific problems and devise solutions to them
- Providing extensive, ongoing training for all staff and management in understanding policy provisions and features, and in providing effective policyowner service
- Monitoring and testing the effectiveness of various notices, letters, and scripted telephone reminders to determine the most cost-effective and efficient approaches that help conserve business
- Tracking the relationship between conservation and persistency, estimating the financial impact to the insurer of both lost and conserved business, and publicizing the results to all staff and management to demonstrate the importance of conservation efforts

Insurers have devised a number of other ways to conserve business. Figure 21-1 lists a number of those approaches.

Conservation of orphan policyowners. An ***orphan policyowner*** is one whose original marketer is no longer available to provide service. The marketer may have moved from the area, stopped marketing the insurer's products, retired, or died, or the policyowner may have moved to another geographic area that is not served by his original marketer. Without regular communication from the marketer, a policyowner may be likely to cancel or surrender the policy and purchase coverage from another insurer whose marketer can provide ongoing service.

To help conserve the business represented by orphan policyowners, most insurers attempt to contact such persons and recommend a marketer who is in the same geographic area. Alternatively, an insurer may contact a nearby marketer directly and ask that the orphan policyowner be contacted. Insurers generally offer some financial incentive to marketers to encourage them to "adopt" orphan policyowners and provide them with effective service. Some insurers have established a program to communicate regularly with every policyowner so that even if a policyowner becomes an orphan, she will still feel that she has strong ties to the insurance company and can obtain answers to questions and solutions to problems.

Some insurers have established electronic tracking of marketer activities in order to identify marketers who are no longer active and may have left orphan policyowners. The sooner an insurer can identify an orphan policyowner, the more likely the insurer can conserve that person's business. Insight 21-2 comments on the importance of developing an effective marketing program for orphan policyholders.

Fast Fact

Since at least the 1950's, the lapse rate for life insurance policies that have been in force for less than 2 years has been 2 to 5 times higher than for policies that have been in force for several years.

Source: American Council of Life Insurance, *Life Insurance Fact Book,* 1996: 67.

Conservation through superior claim service. Customers who purchase insurance generally interact with an insurer or its marketers at two times: when the coverage is sold and renewed, and when a customer submits a claim. For health insurance, a customer may interact with the insurance company numerous times. When customers are dissatisfied with claim service, they are likely to feel frustrated. Therefore, POS employees in insurance companies that provide top-quality service usually communicate regularly with employees in claims to encourage rapid, accessible, customer-focused, and simplified claim handling. Customers want their claims processed as rapidly as possible; they want easy ways to get in touch with the insurer to submit a claim; and they want personal treatment and clear explanations while their claims are being handled. Insurers whose claim handling satisfies these customer desires can expect to enhance their relationship with customers.

Conservation through customer feedback. Because conservation of business requires clear communication between the insurer and its customers, most insurers communicate regularly with customers to demonstrate the insurers' interest in meeting customer needs. In addition, most insurers evaluate customers' needs through telephone surveys and printed questionnaires. Some insurance companies have established electronic feedback systems to gather information about customers' needs, preferences, and knowledge of insurance products and services. In designing such an electronic feedback system, an insurer must take into consideration the need to preserve customers' privacy and confidentiality. Transmitting contract numbers, personal identification numbers, and other confidential information may inhibit

Insight 21-2 In Pursuit of Orphan Excellence

With a substantial portion of an insurer's in-force business falling into the orphan category, it is evident that, with proper cultivation, orphans represent an enormous potential in helping an insurer achieve its new business, conservation, and public image objectives.

The bulk of orphans consists of insureds whose marketers are no longer under contract with the insurer and whose records either have not been reassigned to other marketers for servicing, or who have been reassigned to marketers who failed to follow through. A smaller percentage of the orphan group consists of policyowners who are not receiving service, even though the original marketer is still under contract to the insurer.

The orphan market has the following significant advantages over other markets an insurer may be considering for development:

- The qualification of prospects is easier because the demographic and need information is already in the insurer's records.
- Fewer telephone and mail contacts are required to obtain a face-to-face interview.
- The closing ratio at point of sale is better because of predetermined needs, exercisable policy options, and cash availability.
- The average size sale tends to be larger and the premium per $1,000 higher because of age and product selection.
- The probability of referrals and cross-product sales is greater because of the customer's confidence in the insurer.
- The business written tends to stay in force longer.

In order to achieve dramatically increased results from its orphan market, an insurer must significantly restructure its support functions. Among the actions to take are these:

- Install computerized procedures that merge leads on policyowners and orphans with other available support functions such as direct mail and point-of-sale marketing materials, and that enable marketers and agency managers to carry out effective service and selling activities.
- Provide detailed training materials that explain simple, cost-effective service and selling approaches to policyowners and orphans.
- Establish procedures for the equitable redistribution of policy records among agencies to ensure that an orphan policyowner's records are kept on file in the agency best equipped to provide follow-up service.
- Set up financially acceptable programs to encourage marketers to release the records of policyowners whom they have no further desire to retain as clients, in order to reassign or transfer the records to another marketer.
- Establish compensation plans, recognition programs, and expense reimbursement procedures to reward employees and marketers who make significant contributions toward achieving the insurer's defined orphan objectives.
- Develop conservation control procedures for making ongoing comparisons, on an agency and marketer basis, of actual and expected persistency of blocks of business.

For many insurers, the orphan market is a large and valuable asset yielding current returns far below its true potential. Tapping its real worth will require an insurer to analyze all of its current marketing, administrative, and related support functions to determine specifically where changes are needed. Further, individual marketers, agencies, and home office executives will have to reconcile any divergent objectives regarding orphan policyowners. Finally, an insurer's top management need to commit the resources needed to optimize both new business and retention of orphan business.

Adapted by permission from "In Pursuit of Orphan Excellence," *LIMRA's MarketFacts*, November/December 1990: 8–9.

customers' willingness to use such a system, so most insurers do not require that kind of information.

Some insurers' electronic feedback systems permit customers to respond freely about any topic. Typically, such a system provides space for typing comments, prefaced by an invitation such as this one:

We welcome your questions and invite you to ask our experts questions about life and health insurance—24 hours a day, 7 days a week. We also welcome your thoughts about the way we have treated you as a customer and how we might serve you better. Please write your questions and comments in the space below, and then click on "SEND" to e-mail your response to us. We will immediately acknowledge receipt of your response, and we'll provide you with a prompt answer.

Other electronic feedback systems provide surveys to which customers may give responses. Figure 21-2 illustrates one such electronic feedback survey system maintained on the Internet.

Conservation and Marketers

Most insurers have found that the principal cause of lapse or transfer of business is lack of marketer involvement with policyowners. By educating marketers about the need to match coverage to the specific needs of proposed insureds and by providing prompt, accurate responses to marketers' questions, the insurer demonstrates its intent to support the marketers' sales and retention efforts and to encourage submission of high-quality business. Some insurers also structure their commissions to reward marketers whose business remains in force for an extended period. For instance, an insurer may pay a marketer a ***persistency bonus,*** a sum that represents an increase in the marketer's commission when a policy continues in force beyond an initial period, usually five years. Moreover, some insurers require that every surrender form be accompanied by a memo from the marketer explaining the reason for the request and requesting that the policyowner making the request be contacted by telephone by a POS employee.

Some marketers attempt to generate commission income by replacing policies they have originally sold with new policies underwritten by a different insurer. To help prevent such replacements, insurers who receive notice of surrenders and lapses not only get in touch with the marketer, but send a letter to the policyowner with information comparing the coverage and the premiums of the previous policy and the new policy. Insurance companies sometimes penalize marketers whose conservation percentage is low by excluding the marketer from various promotional competitions or by reducing the amount of commission paid to the marketer on other policies.

In attempting to conserve business, insurers also train marketers in providing top-quality policyowner service and check regularly with marketers to encourage them to provide continual service to policyowners. In addition, insurers try to recruit marketers who are concerned with selling only coverage that is appropriate for customers' needs; provide those marketers with information about the insurer's underwriting principles and requirements; and maintain records of the persistency of each marketer's business. Insight 21-3 comments further on the important relationship between POS and the marketer.

Figure 21-2. Excerpts from electronic feedback survey system of one insurer.

Thank you for taking the time to complete and return our user survey. The personal information you provide, such as your name, address, and e-mail address, won't be used as part of a TIAA-CREF direct marketing effort. It's solely to help us understand who is using our online evaluation service, TIAA-CREF At Your Service, and how we can improve it.

The following types of information are currently available online from *TIAA-CREF At Your Service*. Please rate how important it is to you to be able to get each type of information online through the Internet.

1a. Current unit values and interest rates of TIAA-CREF investment funds
( ) Very important ( ) Somewhat important ( ) Not very important ( ) Not at all important

1b. Information about the performance history of TIAA-CREF funds
( ) Very important ( ) Somewhat important ( ) Not very important ( ) Not at all important

1c. Excerpts from current publications
( ) Very important ( ) Somewhat important ( ) Not very important ( ) Not at all important

1d. Answers to frequently asked questions
( ) Very important ( ) Somewhat important ( ) Not very important ( ) Not at all important

1e. Texts of current prospectuses
( ) Very important ( ) Somewhat important ( ) Not very important ( ) Not at all important

The following services are not currently available through *TIAA-CREF At Your Service*. Please rate how interested you are in being able to do each of the following online through the Internet.

2a. Obtain information about the current value of your TIAA-CREF accounts
( ) Very interested ( ) Somewhat interested ( ) Not very interested ( ) Not at all interested

2b. Project the value of your TIAA-CREF investments given various assumptions
( ) Very interested ( ) Somewhat interested ( ) Not very interested ( ) Not at all interested

2c. Use e-mail to reach a TIAA-CREF representative
( ) Very interested ( ) Somewhat interested ( ) Not very interested ( ) Not at all interested

2d. Make allocation changes among your TIAA and CREF accounts
( ) Very interested ( ) Somewhat interested ( ) Not very interested ( ) Not at all interested

2e. Transfer funds among TIAA and CREF accounts
( ) Very interested ( ) Somewhat interested ( ) Not very interested ( ) Not at all interested

2f. Purchase TIAA-CREF financial products
( ) Very interested ( ) Somewhat interested ( ) Not very interested ( ) Not at all interested

2g. Get an online version of your annuity benefits report
( ) Very interested ( ) Somewhat interested ( ) Not very interested ( ) Not at all interested

2h. Get an online version of your quarterly confirmation of transactions
( ) Very interested ( ) Somewhat interested ( ) Not very interested ( ) Not at all interested

2i. Get updates on available TIAA-CREF services and products
( ) Very interested ( ) Somewhat interested ( ) Not very interested ( ) Not at all interested

What other information, services, or products not currently available online, if any, would you like to see included?

____

____

How important is it for you to be able to make financial transactions using the Internet?
( ) Very important ( ) Somewhat important ( ) Not very important ( ) Not at all important

Have you read advertisements or notices about financial products and services (such as insurance, mutual funds, and banking services) on the Internet in the past year? ( ) Yes ( ) No

If "Yes": What companies do you think have done a particularly good job in providing information about their financial products and services on the Internet?

Note: This survey also invites information about a customer's use of the Internet, interest in online financial planning software, employment status, occupation, gender, name and address, and knowledge about financial planning for retirement.

Adapted by permission from TIAA-CREF, New York, NY.

Insight 21-3 My Thoughts On . . . POS and the Marketer

Marketers—whether they be captive or independent—we all too often take their names in vain. If a POS staff member were asked to describe the field force, what would be the first words to come to mind? Demanding? Wants everything now? Only has commissions in mind? However, a POS staff member may wish to reconsider this opinion of some of the most hard-working core of people in the insurance business.

See if you can put yourself in the marketer's place. Your customer is busy and wants some answers immediately. In today's competitive environment, if you as a marketer can't provide that information quickly, chances are that your client will go elsewhere. Losing this customer can have a direct effect on your future contact base, not to mention your paycheck! Feel the pressure? The need for immediacy?

As a POS staff member, you can bet that if a marketer demands information on a case right away, it's because he or she is receiving pressure from a client. And in this age of technology, if you're not able to provide that information quickly, you and your company are going to be left behind. What makes the difference is being able to satisfy marketers' demands with a smile and a warm, human attitude. Keep in mind that the marketer is doing his or her best to provide service to the customer—who is also your policyholder!

In 1992 our POS department changed its name from Policyholder Services to Client Services in an effort to acknowledge the importance of our relationship with our field force. We also wished to acknowledge our renewed commitment to view and treat the marketer as one of our most important customers. Now, when a marketer calls about the tax ramifications of an annuity withdrawal or about any other information relating to a client's coverage, we view this interaction as an opportunity not only to provide service to the policyholder, but also to build a relationship with that policyholder's marketer. In providing information to the marketer, we are allowing the marketer to serve clients in ways beyond the norm. We are providing an opportunity for personal contact that can make or break the service relationship and that can greatly enhance our business. This three-way alliance, if properly nurtured, will further the interests of the client, the marketer, and the insurance company.

Providing top-quality policyowner service is not always easy. CSRs are often the bearers of bad news, such as the fact that a premium payment has not been received, or that a long-time client is considering a replacement. We always try to keep in mind that POS staff serve as a buffer between the marketer and the insurer. It's a delicate balancing act, but care and tact can go a long way toward ensuring that everyone involved is satisfied.

Kim Gibson, FLMI, ACS
Client Services Manager
United Heritage Mutual Life Insurance Company

Qualities of Effective POS

Effective POS is prompt, courteous, complete, accurate, and confidential. An insurer that can deliver POS with these qualities can enhance its strength and competitive position, and can keep its insureds and other customers satisfied.

Prompt POS helps turn customers into friends and strengthens the organization. By contrast, delays may result in frustrated customers, reductions in new business, lapses and surrenders of coverage, and even legal actions against the insurer. An insured who has to wait an unreasonable period of time to obtain a policy loan or to receive information about submitting a claim may well be irritated. To enhance the promptness of response to customers, many insurers have established increased hours of service.

Courteous POS representatives strengthen the bond between an insurer and its customers. Considering the feelings of customers and making every effort to handle transactions politely can have only positive results and can make transactions a pleasure for everyone involved.

Providing complete service is sometimes a challenge for POS, especially when requests for service cover a variety of transactions or when transactions are complicated or unusual. Attending to the small details of each transaction helps ensure that no errors will prevent completion of the transaction and that the customer will be fully satisfied. Providing complete service—that is, responding to all facets of a request—saves time for customers, marketers, and POS employees, and reduces the insurer's expense in unnecessary follow-up correspondence and customer contacts. Insight 21-4 explains the need to meet or exceed customer expectations by understanding what those expectations are.

Accurate information in POS is critical because giving a customer the wrong data can result in an inaccurate and potentially damaging decision. If, for instance, a POS representative advises a marketer that a certain insured has changed the beneficiary of a policy, the marketer may later offend the insured or the beneficiary by mentioning the wrong person as the beneficiary or otherwise proceeding as though another beneficiary had been named. Especially when money is involved in POS, accuracy is important in avoiding inconvenience to customers and embarrassment for the insurer. Most insurers enhance accuracy by creating checklists, worksheets, procedures manuals, and online reference materials that guide POS employees through the steps of transactions, particularly those that are complex or have various options. In addition, insurers provide either manual or online logs by which POS employees can record every customer transaction undertaken.

Confidentiality is essential in POS as in all other aspects of insurance administration. A contract of insurance between an insurer and a policyowner establishes a strong responsibility on the part of the insurer to ensure the privacy of customers. The POS representative must remember, for example, that usually only the policyowner and the insurer are parties to the insurance contract. No beneficiary or other person is a party to the contract. Therefore, no one except the policyowner has the right to request information from the insurer about the status of a policy—not even whether the policy is in force, whether its premiums have been paid to date, whether a policy loan has been requested, or who the beneficiary may be. Insurers generally establish specific guidelines concerning what information may be released to which persons so that POS employees will not make errors that may damage the confidential bond between insurer and policyowner.

Insight 21-4 My Thoughts On . . . Understanding Customer Expectations

Amid the rush to embrace new buzzwords such as "sustainable competitive advantage through customer satisfaction" or "delighting customers," we in the insurance industry face a fundamental challenge: Do we know what our customers expect, and can our systems and business processes support these lofty objectives? My blunt assessment will be "no" on both counts. This problem is one that many insurers should be, and are, working to change.

Market research and customer survey methods can provide a great deal of insight into what customers want or need. Most insurers also collect customer feedback on service perceptions. Our challenge is to turn this general information into specific processes to deliver on individual customer expectations. Otherwise, all this measurement risks being nothing more than an expensive applause meter.

The insurance industry has not simplified the customer interface as successfully as other industries. Let's consider three diverse product categories: cars, running shoes, and computers. Each of these product categories has experienced huge gains in product performance, complexity, and potential applications. However, one can argue that any of these products has never been easier to understand and to use. Life insurance should be no different. Our systems and processes need to make the complex simple at the user interface in order for customer expectations to be met. Ultimately, consumers and insurance industry regulators will expect no less.

Policy performance is a very important element of customer satisfaction, but not the only one. The same principles about setting the right expectations apply to other aspects of the customer relationship. Certainly it makes sense to under-promise and over-deliver where possible. However, customer expectations are escalating. Ten years ago, a ten-minute wait in a bank line may have been acceptable. Today, we have a major bank in Canada that credits customer accounts with $5 if the wait exceeds five minutes or if an automatic teller machine is out of service!

To be successful in the future, an insurance company will need to have established systems and processes in partnership with our marketers that align with meeting or exceeding customer expectations. Essential elements of these systems and processes are the following:

- Policy financial performance will be monitored and reported to the client at the frequency and level of detail desired by each individual client.
- Customer representatives and/or marketers will have a complete record of customer contacts and interactions.
- Administrative commitment regarding frequency of customer contact, types of communication, and service preferences will be delivered on a consistent basis.

Exactly how a successful insurance company chooses to execute these elements will depend on chosen distribution and marketing strategies. But I am convinced that these will be merely the price of admission to compete.

Erik H. Mathiesen, FLMI, ACS
Assistant Vice President,
Customer Service
Manulife Financial

Adapted by permission from *Resource*, August 1995: 18–19, 21.

Delivering Effective POS

Every insurer wants to deliver POS in such a way that all customers are satisfied. Determining specific strategies for POS delivery, automating and simplifying service delivery procedures, ensuring that POS policies and procedures are appropriately documented and accessible, and establishing excellent telephone communication are some of the approaches by which insurers deliver effective POS.

Determining Strategies for Effective POS

The POS implementation strategies used by insurance companies vary according to the types of coverage involved and the type, frequency, and complexity of the service transactions required. The strategies adopted by each insurer reflect that organization's attitude toward POS delivery and serve as a guide for employees in their interactions with the insurer's customers.

The POS strategies generally focus on all types of customer interactions, including written and spoken communications and face-to-face meetings. As an illustration of such strategies, Figure 21-3 shows the POS strategies formulated by one health insurer.

Automating and Simplifying POS Delivery

Replacing traditional paper documents with online and electronic documents enables many insurers to provide faster, more accurate POS. Moreover, streamlining routine changes into one or two steps or only one document helps POS employees deliver rapid service. Efficiency translates into productivity in POS as in other areas of the insurance business.

Documenting POS Policies and Procedures

To ensure consistency and accuracy among all POS employees in delivering service to customers, insurers document the policies and

Figure 21-3. POS strategies of one health insurer.

- We will treat all customers, internal and external, as individuals with value.
- We will approach every customer contact from the customer's point of view.
- We will treat each customer contact as an opportunity to build a relationship, not just to process a transaction.
- We will ensure that our customers receive accurate and timely responses.
- We will ensure that each POS employee has the technical and thought process skills to consider all possible implications before taking appropriate action.
- We will continually seek to improve our written communication by using personalized letters and by acknowledging important events in the lives of our customers.
- We will continually seek to improve our spoken communication by returning all telephone calls within 30 minutes of receipt and by asking permission before placing any customer on hold, informing the customer first of the anticipated hold time.
- We will continually seek ways and implement technologies to make it easier for customers to do business with us.

Adapted by permission from USAA Life Insurance Company.

procedures that employees are to use. Insurers use many means of documenting such policies and procedures, including manuals kept on each employee's desk and online systems that provide each POS employee with information on how to handle practically any situation that may arise during the course of delivering POS.

Some insurers also use online screens to help employees track individual files. With such screens, an employee can record every customer interaction and thereby develop a complete history of each transaction. Although such detailed information is not necessary and usually is not collected for routine transactions, it can be invaluable in handling lengthy or complex transactions on which more than one POS employee may work, or which may have to be transferred temporarily to a manager for consideration and advice.

One of the most important ways of ensuring consistency in POS is to inform every employee promptly about changes in policies and procedures. If an insurer uses an online documentation system, such changes can be highlighted or presented in a bright color to capture employees' attention. If an insurer uses a printed manual, employees are typically required to update their manuals regularly, substituting new pages for old ones and otherwise ensuring that each employee is proceeding according to the most recent procedures and policies. Most insurance companies assign one employee to be responsible for updating documentation and communicating the changes to all the staff.

Ensuring Excellent Telephone Communication

Although other technologies have become increasingly important in maintaining communication between an insurer and its customers, the telephone continues to provide an essential link. In remaining aware of customers' needs and in gathering information to fulfill them, POS employees use telephones extensively.

Because some of the persons who telephone POS employees wish to express strong feelings of anxiety or displeasure, the communication skills training for POS employees covers certain topics that can enhance the employees' ability to handle calls well. In particular, POS employees are taught (1) to empathize with callers, allowing them to vent their feelings, and (2) to understand that customers are not angry at POS in particular, but at the situations about which they are calling. By repeating and summarizing the caller's concerns, the POS employee can validate those concerns and help the caller understand that the employee is eager to help. Rather than indulge in blaming, denying fault, or making excuses, the POS employee asks questions to help control the dialogue and to obtain information needed to resolve problems.

In being trained to communicate effectively with customers, POS employees are taught not to use technical terms used by insurance industry employees, but instead to use everyday language and to keep their responses simple and specific. Rather than saying, "Your EOB just arrived, and co-payments and deductibles are being accounted for so that our comm center can cut a check," a POS employee might be trained to say, "We now have everything we need to handle your claim, and we'll mail your check this afternoon."

Providing POS by telephone over a long period can lead to employee frustration and burnout. Therefore, most insurers allow telephone service representatives to rotate off this service for certain hours each day or to work in other POS areas for weeks or months before returning to telephone duties. Insurers also involve telephone service representatives in new product design to help prevent some of the problems that might later arise when the product is serviced.

Evaluating POS

Because POS is important to the success of an insurance company, most insurers examine both the quantity and the quality of their POS services. Although evaluating the *quantity* of POS delivered is easier than evaluating its *quality,* both aspects of POS are essential in tracking customer satisfaction.

Evaluating the Quantity of POS

Insurers typically count various elements associated with POS, including the average speed of answering telephone communications, the rate at which callers abandon a call because it has not been promptly answered, and the length of time required to complete various transactions such as completing loan and dividend withdrawals or responding to a policyowner's or marketer's request for information. Establishing turnaround times for accomplishing specific POS activities is the most common method used by insurance companies to assess the quantity and speed of service delivered. An insurer may review the amount of time required to fulfill a typical customer request—for example, a policy loan—and may decide that three days or two days or one day is the standard by which all such requests should be fulfilled. Thereafter, the insurer maintains records of the length of time for POS employees to "turn around" or fulfill each policy loan request and calculates the average time required to fulfill a typical request. If an insurer discovers that its turnaround times vary significantly from the standards set, management investigates the cause of the variance and, if necessary, takes steps to help employees more closely adhere to the standard. These steps may involve hiring additional staff or temporarily assigning other staff to POS and enhancing certain systems, such as tracking systems and procedures information systems.

Usually, measures of turnaround time include (1) the day that a request is received and (2) the day the request is fulfilled. If mail is involved, a mailing date is used as a measure of turnaround time. Typical turnaround times vary from one insurer to another. Generally, however, fulfilling a policy loan request takes between one to three days; a beneficiary change, three to five days; a policy replacement, one to three days; and a cash surrender, three to five days. Some insurers specify that their stated standards do not reflect the best possible or even optimal service, but serve as a measure of the minimum acceptable average level of performance.

Counting the number of POS transactions and comparing that count to established standards is accomplished manually or electronically. Generally, the transactions count is completed weekly and is examined by management to assess trends, to identify problems, and to inform POS employees of how well they are fulfilling their accountabilities. The number and complexity of transactions accomplished are expected to increase as a POS employee gains experience. Because accuracy is critical in POS, the number of transactions is not as important as the quality of those transactions.

Evaluating the Quality of POS

Most insurers establish various systems to track the quality of POS. For example, randomly selected customers may receive mail surveys or telephone inquiries, asking the customers' views on the type of POS they have received and inquiring about their level of satisfaction with it. Customers may be asked to comment on such elements as the following concerning telephoned and written POS:

- Friendliness and professionalism of POS staff
- Understandable communication
- Timeliness of service
- Accuracy in completing a request
- Overall level of service

Insurers also establish focus groups, composed of customers, to discuss such elements as these and to suggest specific ways in which POS may be improved. In addition, many insurance companies carefully assess customers' complaints to determine their cause and possible methods of avoiding them or improving the insurer's ability to respond to them effectively.

Further, many insurers have established telephone or online feedback systems that enable a customer to provide POS assessment directly to the insurer. A customer who is uncomfortable using such technology is given the option to speak directly with a POS representative.

To track the quality of service delivered by individual POS employees, many companies require managers to monitor a percentage of the transactions undertaken by each employee. The manager may examine files of completed cases and those in progress and may listen to live or taped telephone calls between customers and the employees. Generally, a manager looks especially carefully at cases that are returned to a POS employee for additional work as the result of an error in the initial transaction. Sometimes the manager makes follow-up telephone calls to customers to ask how well their cases were handled and to solicit suggestions for improving the service. Insurers also use peer review, by which POS employees monitor and evaluate each other's service delivery. Peer review requires careful training so that the assessments will be consistent. Figure 21-4 illustrates a portion of a checklist used to evaluate the quality of telephone conversations between POS employees and customers.

Finally, insurers use questionnaires, focus groups, and other means of enabling POS employees to give feedback concerning their jobs and to recommend ways of improving the work accomplished in POS. On the basis of employee feedback, insurers typically revise procedures, organizational methods, and standards when such revisions seem to promise enhanced quantity and quality of POS.

Figure 21-4. Checklist used to evaluate the quality of POS telephone conversations.

- ☑ Identify self and offer assistance
- ☑ Determine the reason for the call
- ☑ Express help/regret/acknowledgement appropriately
- ☑ Request and verify caller information
- ☑ Accept appropriate responsibility for actions taken or not taken
- ☑ Provide accurate, complete information
- ☑ Summarize action to be taken and verify customer's understanding
- ☑ Offer additional assistance
- ☑ Avoid insurance jargon
- ☑ Use appropriate presentation: pace, inflection, enunciation, courtesy, personalization
- ☑ Use a proper approach to placing customer on hold or transferring customer to another department
- ☑ Accurately record the call

Key Terms and Concepts

conservation
electronic funds transfer (EFT)
orphan policyowner
persistency bonus

CHAPTER TWENTY-TWO

Practices in Policyowner Service

Learning Objectives

After studying this chapter, you should be able to

- Explain the general procedures used to change the owner or beneficiary of a policy and to assign ownership of a policy
- Discuss the POS activities involved in changing coverage, adding riders, determining cash value, administering loans and dividends, sending premium due notices, and handling premium payments
- Explain how POS handles variable insurance products
- Describe the ways POS fulfills such policyowner needs as obtaining a duplicate policy and surrendering, converting, reinstating, or terminating a policy
- Explain how POS handles returned mail
- Summarize the relationships between POS and underwriting

Chapter Outline

Providing Information and Answering Queries
Information for Individual Insurance
Information for Group Insurance

Changing the Owner's Name or the Beneficiary
Assigning Policy Ownership

Changing an Address

Changing Coverage or Adding Riders

Determining Cash Value and Administering Loans and Dividends

Handling Variable Insurance Products

Handling Premium Payments

Fulfilling Other Policyowner Needs
Obtaining a Duplicate Policy
Surrendering a Policy
Converting a Policy
Reinstating a Policy
Terminating a Policy

Handling Returned Mail

The Relationship of POS and Underwriting
Change in Type of Insurance
Rate Reduction
Additional Benefits

In the last chapter, you reviewed the general activities involved in policyowner service and the specific services rendered to marketers and insurance regulatory organizations. In this chapter, we'll discuss in more detail the ways that an insurer's POS staff handle transactions related to various types of insurance coverage.

Efficiency is very important in POS because of the need to handle each request accurately, courteously, and promptly. POS staff receive extensive and ongoing training in the many details of responding well to policyowner requests and in the provisions of various policy contracts. Further, insurers provide marketers and policyowners with forms to request various types of POS transactions. Although some insurers use a separate form for each type of transaction, most insurance companies have developed multipurpose forms that group similar types of transactions and thereby reduce the complexity of fulfilling policyowner needs. For example, an insurer may group together on one form the requests for change of ownership, beneficiary, name, address, and assignment. On another form may be grouped requests for cash surrender, policy loan, allotment of dividends, and reinstatement. Each insurer designs its own service request form and may include all available policyowner services or only selected ones. Some insurers develop separate forms for specific services; we will examine some of these types of forms later in this chapter. Besides requests submitted on such forms, POS also accepts requests submitted by telephone and by electronic means.

Providing Information and Answering Queries

POS staff are responsible for responding to numerous requests for information and complaints about various aspects of coverage and service. The training for POS is intensive and complex in order to provide the staff with the breadth and depth of information they need to fulfill policyowners' needs. A complete list of the types of questions fielded by POS staff would fill many pages, but the most frequently encountered policyowner questions relate to

- Changing the owner's name or the beneficiary
- Changing an address
- Changing coverage or adding riders

- Determining cash value and administering loans and dividends
- Handling premium payments
- Fulfilling other policyowner needs, including obtaining duplicate policies and surrendering, converting, reinstating, or terminating a policy
- Handling returned mail

In the following discussion, we will first distinguish between the types of information generally requested for individual and for group insurance. In discussing other types of POS activities, we will not distinguish between these types of coverage unless such a distinction is necessary, as many of the POS activities apply equally to individual and group insurance.

Information for Individual Insurance

Individual policyowners often have questions about coverage and need assistance in handling claims and other administrative details. An insurer's POS staff provide valuable information to policyowners, thereby not only providing customer satisfaction, but also helping to conserve coverage.

From the time a policy is sold until the relationship between the individual insured and the insurer comes to an end, a policyowner may wonder about almost anything related to the coverage. When a child is born, a marriage dissolves, a spouse dies, a medical caregiver moves or retires, an insured suffers a debilitating illness or injury, or other life changes occur, a policyowner may need information. Successful insurers train POS staff to know the answers to the most commonly asked questions and to be familiar with information sources necessary to locate the answers to uncommon queries. An experienced POS staff member can be invaluable in tracking down information requested by a policyowner.

Information for Group Insurance

In regard to group insurance, POS plays a part in ensuring that a group policy is installed correctly and completely. You have learned that *installation* is the term used to include the series of activities involved in issuing a master contract and its individual certificates to an insured group. The role of POS in group installation generally involves providing information and answering queries about the plan's eligibility requirements, benefits, and provisions, as well as the portion of the premium, if any, that each employee must pay.

Because group members tend to support a group insurance plan more completely if they feel that the plan is an employer's or organization's plan rather than an insurance company's plan, the announcement of the policy purchase is typically made by the employer or group that sponsors the group coverage. The role of the insurer when this announcement is being planned is to provide sample letters, brochures, enrollment forms, and other information to the persons who announce the purchase. POS may have a part in preparing these materials.

While a self-administered group policy is in force, a representative of the insurance company delivers POS by answering questions and assisting the group in administering the coverage effectively. This representative maintains close contact with the insurer's claim staff to identify and help resolve any problems that may become apparent. For instance, if a group member is having difficulty in providing adequate information relating to a claim, the insurer's representative may advise the employee or the group plan administrator about the required information and ways to obtain it. To provide adequate assistance to group members, the insurer's representative must be well informed about the coverage, the claim administration process, and the general administration of group products.

Besides providing information as requested, the insurer's representative also enhances communication by making periodic calls on each insured group. During these calls, the representative checks the activities of the group plan administrator in administering the plan, informs the administrator of changes in laws and insurance practices that affect the group plan, and provides guidance if the plan administration fails to meet the insurer's standards. The representative also helps conserve the business by discussing the group's evolving needs for coverage and suggesting changes to the coverage. By evaluating the group's claim history, the representative helps prepare the group for the next year's rates, which often depend on the level of claims made by the group during the preceding year. The representative also presents the administrator and other group officials with rating information based on employee census information, incurred claims, and other information relating to the group's experience. If necessary, the representative may recommend changes to the coverage, including increased or decreased deductibles, changes to coinsurance requirements, or changes to contractual provisions.

Fast Fact

At the peak of the Great Depression in 1935, 15.2 percent of all life insurance company assets were lent to policyowners against the cash value of the policies. At the end of 1995, only 4.5 percent of company assets were in policy loans.

Source: American Council of Life Insurance, *Life Insurance Fact Book*, 1996: 105.

Changing the Owner's Name or the Beneficiary

The name of the owner or beneficiary of a policy may need to be changed for several reasons. Sometimes a name has been misspelled, and correction is needed to satisfy an owner or a beneficiary. More

Figure 22-1. Name change form.

☐ Insured ☐ Owner ☐ Beneficiary

From ______________________ Former Signature ______________________
First, Middle, Last

To ______________________ Present Signature ______________________
First, Middle, Last

Reason for name change: ☐ Marriage ☐ Divorce ☐ Correction
☐ Other (attach certified copy of court order)

commonly, a name change results from marriage, divorce, adoption, or a court order. Most insurers require a policyowner to complete and sign a form requesting the name change, and many insurers also require a copy of a marriage license, divorce decree, or other documentation verifying the requested change. When a name change is requested because of naturalization of citizenship, many insurers require as proof a notarized sworn ***affidavit,*** which is a written statement made before an official who is authorized to administer oaths. After a name change has been made, POS sends the policyowner verification of the change. Figure 22-1 illustrates a name change form used by some insurance companies to indicate a name change in an insured, a policyowner, or a beneficiary. Note that this form would be used only when a beneficiary changes his or her name, not when the policyowner wishes to change the beneficiary of the policy.

POS staff must be familiar with the numerous and often complex ways in which beneficiaries may be designated. Many different persons and entities may be named as beneficiary. These include spouse and children of an insured person, other persons who may be unrelated to the insured, trustees under trust agreements or wills, the estate of the insured, and others. Moreover, a policyowner may specify contingent, concurrent, or irrevocable beneficiaries, and may further specify distribution of proceeds per stirpes or per capita. These beneficiary designation terms are defined in Figure 22-2.

Many insurers establish guidelines for submitting beneficiary changes. The guidelines are designed to prevent mistakes in recording a policyowner's beneficiary choice and to avoid delays in the event of a claim. Among the most common guidelines are the following:

- The full name—given name and surname—of the beneficiary is required; initials are not acceptable. For example, "John & Louise Jones" is acceptable, but "Mr. and Mrs. John Jones" is not acceptable.

- The relationship of the beneficiary to the policyowner must be specified.

Figure 22-2. Beneficiary designation terms.

- *Contingent beneficiary.* The person or entity designated to receive life insurance policy proceeds if the primary beneficiary should die before the person whose life is insured. Also called *secondary beneficiary* and *successor beneficiary.*
- *Concurrent beneficiaries.* The designation of more than one person or entity to share, if living, in payment of the proceeds on the death of the insured. The shares will be distributed equally unless otherwise provided.
- *Irrevocable beneficiary.* The designation of a beneficiary that cannot be revoked or changed without the written consent of such beneficiary.
- *Per stirpes.* A method of dividing policy benefits among the living members of a class of beneficiaries (such as children or grandchildren of an insured person) and the descendants of deceased members of that class. Children of a deceased member share their deceased parent's or other relative's portion of the benefit equally as representatives of the deceased person. For example, a policyowner-insured who has three children—Abraham, Benjamin, and Carol—might provide that each child would receive one-third of the policy proceeds, per stirpes. If Benjamin died before the insured died, then at the insured's death Abraham and Carol would each receive one-third of the proceeds, and the heirs of Benjamin would receive equal shares of the remaining one-third of the proceeds. If Benjamin died without heirs, however, Abraham and Carol would each inherit one-half of the policy proceeds. Many insurers prohibit the use of some classes in per stirpes beneficiary designations, such as "nieces and nephews of the insured" or "children of the insured's brother," because such classes are not specific in naming the persons who are to be included in the division of the proceeds.
- *Per capita.* A method of dividing policy benefits among beneficiaries without regard for different degrees of relationship. Each beneficiary receives an equal portion of the proceeds. For example, a policyowner-insured who has three children—Abraham, Benjamin, and Carol—might provide that each child would receive one-third of the policy proceeds, per capita. If Benjamin died before the insured died, then at the insured's death Abraham and Carol would each receive one-half of the proceeds, whether or not Benjamin had heirs.

- Dates of birth for minors must be provided.
- Use of the words "or," "either/or," "and/or" makes the designation unacceptable because the intent is not clear.
- Names that are scratched out or marked over, or that contain correction fluid marks, are not acceptable.
- The beneficiary's address, social identification or Social Security number, *and* date of birth must be provided.
- Dollar amounts may not be specified for any or all beneficiaries. Instead, fractions (such as one-half or two-thirds) should be used to specify unequal shares.
- The enrollment card or beneficiary form must be signed and dated by the policyowner.

- If a trust is designated, the exact date and legal name of the trust must be provided. Because some trust documents are difficult to interpret, some insurers attach a disclaimer noting that the insurer is not obligated to inquire into the terms of the trust agreement and will not be liable after the policy proceeds have been paid.

Changing the name of an owner or a beneficiary requires that numerous insurance records be modified. The master policy file, the billing file, the marketer's file, and other documents should all be in accord with one another. Generally, an insurer's information system automatically changes a name in all locations when it is changed in any location. Therefore, if an insured, for example, requests a change in her name, that change will be reflected throughout the insurer's records. If the insured later files a claim under the coverage, her name will already be changed in the insurer's claim files, so that the claim may be handled quickly and efficiently. A copy of the face page of the policy or an endorsement to the policy is usually sent to the policyowner to verify that the requested change has been made. Further, if a settlement option has been selected for a life insurance policy, POS may require the settlement option certificate to be submitted to the insurer and a new settlement option to be selected and certified.

POS staff are also aware that a beneficiary designation may be changed by a person who holds a power of attorney and who has been given specific power to make the change of beneficiary. A ***power of attorney*** is a written statement that authorizes one person to act on behalf of another person. A person who holds a power of attorney for a policyowner may designate and change beneficiaries if

- The power of attorney is properly executed—that is, it is notarized or executed or recorded by a proper public official

- One of the powers granted includes the power to make or enter into contracts on behalf of the person granting the power of attorney

If a policyowner grants such a power of attorney to someone, both the policyowner and the person holding the power of attorney may designate beneficiaries. If the policyowner changes the beneficiary *after* the person holding the power of attorney has changed the beneficiary, any subsequent change of beneficiary by the person holding the power of attorney should *not* be accepted until investigation shows that the power of attorney is still valid. POS may decide to notify the insurer's legal staff of such a situation so as to comply fully with all applicable laws and statutes. Notice of the change of beneficiary designation must always be sent to both the policyowner and the person holding the power of attorney.

Changes of beneficiary cannot be made by telephone, but the request can be submitted by phone. POS mails a change of beneficiary form which, when returned, is verified by the policyowner's signature on file. If the original beneficiary was designated irrevocably, that person is also required to sign the request for a change of beneficiary before the change can be made.

Assigning Policy Ownership

As we noted in Chapter 17, assignment of a life insurance policy is a transfer of some or all of the rights to receive the proceeds of a life insurance policy. The insurance company is not a party to the assignment, which involves only the ***assignor***—the person or entity that transfers ownership rights—and the ***assignee***—the person or entity that receives ownership rights. Ownership of some or all of the rights to a policy is most often transferred when an insured wishes to use the cash value in a life insurance policy as collateral for a loan or when a divorce results in one party's assumption of full ownership of an insurance policy. As you learned in Chapter 17, irrevocable transfer of all the rights of a life insurance policy is known as absolute assignment, whereas the transfer of some rights of policy ownership is known as collateral assignment. Figure 22-3 illustrates an absolute assignment form.

In an absolute assignment, the assignee, in effect, becomes the owner and the beneficiary of the policy, and the assignor may no longer change the beneficiary or exercise the conversion privilege. At death, only the assignee can choose a method of settlement because the assignee now has all these rights. In a collateral assignment, the rights assigned revert to the assignor when specified requirements—such as repayment of a loan—have been satisfied. When such requirements have been fulfilled, the assignee notifies the insurer that the assigned rights of ownership are being returned to the assignor.

Because the insurer is not a party to the assignment, the insurer rarely asks the reason for the assignment. The role of POS in an assignment is to record the change of ownership so that rights of ownership are granted to the proper party and so that, in the event of a claim, benefits may be disbursed to the appropriate party.

Before recording an assignment, POS checks whether the policy has an irrevocable beneficiary. If so, that beneficiary must sign the request for assignment. If the irrevocable beneficiary refuses to sign the request, no assignment can be made. The insurer also reviews the policy provisions to determine whether any problems exist.

Figure 22-3. Absolute assignment form.

Absolute Assignment

Policy # ______________________ Life of ______________________

The undersigned hereby assigns and transfers without any exception, limitation, or reservation whatsoever to

[Name and address of each assignee]

all (his, her, its, their) assignable benefits, interest, property, and rights in the policy described above.

The nature and effect of this assignment shall be as indicated in the following expressions of intent and purpose, namely

- This assignment is ☐ for a valuable consideration ☐ without a valuable consideration.
- If two or more assignees are named above, their interests under this assignment shall be as indicated in the line before which an "X" is inserted below.
  - ☐ Joint owners with right of survivorship between them
  - ☐ Common owners with no right of survivorship between them
  - ☐ Life interest, use, and enjoyment in ______________________ [Name of life owner]

with absolute control and power of disposition in such assignee during his or her lifetime; remainder interest in other assignee(s). If there are two or more assignees entitled to receive remainder interests, such interests shall be of the nature indicated in the line before which an "X" is inserted below:

- ☐ Joint owners with right of survivorship between them
- ☐ Common owners with no right of survivorship between them

- This assignment cancels and rescinds any reversionary provision in favor of the assignor or his estate, whether contained in the policy or in any writing or provision pertaining to the policy.
- This assignment does not affect or change the beneficiary designation or settlement presently contained in the policy assigned. Proceeds payable on death will be paid in accordance with such designation or settlement unless same be hereafter changed by the assignee(s), when the right to make such change exists under the policy.

Changing an Address

One of the most common changes requested is a change of address for an individual policyowner and, less often, a change of address for a group of insureds. Having correct addresses for all policyowners is very important for an insurer in order that notices, checks, and correspondence may be communicated promptly. The address involved is typically the address to which premium notices and other communications from the insurance company are sent.

When POS receives an address change request by telephone, the caller is usually required to provide the Social Security or social insurance number, current address, and other identifying information to verify authorization to make the change. Like changing a policyowner's or beneficiary's name, changing an address requires that all of an insurer's records reflect the change. After the changes are made, POS mails a verifying letter to the policyowner.

Sometimes changing an address indicates that another marketer or branch office will provide service to a policyowner or a group of insureds. An insured who moves from one state or province to another, for example, is likely to become orphaned from the original marketer and may also be required to send claims to a new claim handling center. In such a situation, the insurer may assign the orphaned policyowner to a new marketer and, if so, notify both the marketer and the policyowner of the change. If the policyowner is to send claims to a new location, the policyowner is so notified, and the policyowner's claim records are forwarded to the new claim center.

A policyowner who has paid premiums by electronic funds transfer (EFT) may wish to continue paying premiums in that way in a new location. If the same bank can continue to serve the account, POS usually helps the policyowner make arrangements to change to a bank branch in the new location. If the same bank cannot serve the policyowner, some insurers enable POS staff to provide the policyowner with a list of banks in the new area that can supply that service or, if such service is not available, POS notifies the policyowner that another premium payment method will be necessary. In the latter case, POS provides information to the policyowner concerning the new method of remitting premiums.

Changing Coverage or Adding Riders

Policyowners often wish to increase or decrease the amount of coverage provided by a policy, to add or delete persons from coverage, or to modify the coverage by adding riders to it. Perhaps a policyowner has been promoted and earns a higher income, so he wishes to increase the amount of disability income coverage. Or perhaps a family has added one or more children or other dependents, and needs to increase the amount of life insurance on the wage earners. Changes to group insurance coverage are typically frequent as employees join and leave an organization. When a business is purchased and several formerly key employees are laid off, the key person coverage on those employees needs to be removed. In response to these and other types of requests, POS handles the ongoing changes in insurance coverage.

Increasing the amount of coverage may be accomplished by

- Increasing the dollar amount of insurance or the period during which benefits will be paid
- Reducing the deductible amount or the elimination period
- Adding a new type of benefit not offered under the existing coverage

Because increasing the amount of coverage may increase the risk for the insurer, granting a policyowner an increase in coverage may require additional underwriting, depending on the type of coverage, the amount of coverage already in force and requested, the age and impairments of the persons to be covered under the policy, any indications of changes in the health of the insured, and the insurer's underwriting guidelines.

Decreasing the amount of coverage may be accomplished by

- Reducing the dollar amount of insurance or the period during which benefits will be paid
- Increasing the deductible amount or the elimination period
- Removing one or more benefits offered by the existing coverage

Decreasing the amount of coverage generally does not require additional underwriting, as such a reduction does not increase the insurer's risk. Therefore, POS can usually approve a decrease in coverage on receipt of a signed request from a policyowner.

Previously we discussed riders and their uses in revising the amount and type of coverage provided under various types of insurance. Among the many benefits that can be added by riders are guaranteed insurability, accidental death benefit, and waiver of premium for disability. We noted that in applications for new coverage, the decision whether to approve a rider is usually left to underwriting. When an insured makes a request for such a revision of coverage, however, POS first evaluates the degree of additional risk involved, if any, and sends the request to underwriting only if the additional risk may be considerable.

A policyowner requests changes of coverage by submitting a special form to the insurer. Figure 22-4 illustrates part of a typical form used to request a change of coverage.

In deciding whether to approve a requested rider, POS typically evaluates such factors as

- The type of rider requested
- The amount of coverage involved

Figure 22-4. Portion of a request for change of coverage.

For Contract/Policy Number ______________________

Add Optional Benefits:

☐ **Disability Waiver of Premium:** If you suffer an accident which results in a covered disability, this option guarantees that your premium will be paid for you while you are disabled.

☐ **Waiver of Monthly Deduction:** If you suffer an accident or illness which results in a covered disability, this option guarantees that your cost of insurance will be paid for you while you are disabled.

☐ **Accidental Death Benefit (ADB) of $** ______________________**.** If you die as the result of a covered accident, this option will pay your beneficiary an *additional* amount above the face amount you have selected for the policy.

Increase Coverage:

☐ Increase coverage to $ ______________
☐ Increase Accidental Death Benefit to $ __________________

Rate Review:

☐ Change from Tobacco User to Non-tobacco User
☐ Medical/avocation rate review

- The insured's risk classification, impairments, age, and occupation
- The length of time the original policy has been in effect
- The interval since the last evidence of insurability was submitted
- For health insurance, the insurer's experience with the current policy for all insureds and with the claim experience for the particular policyowner

Many insurers use tables that show acceptable ranges in each of these areas and that enable POS staff to make decisions concerning whether to approve a rider to a policy. If adding the rider results in no more than a minimal increase in the insurer's risk, usually POS can approve the rider very quickly. If, however, the risk to the insurer may be considerable or if POS does not have sufficient information to make a decision, then POS informs the policyowner that additional proof of insurability will be required. In such a situation, POS asks underwriting for assistance in assessing the risk.

Adding a rider to a policy usually results in an increase in premium, so POS advises the policyowner of the required increase and establishes a premium payment schedule. Then POS either prepares a rider and sends a copy to the policyowner to attach to the policy, or, in some cases, prints an entirely new policy with the rider included.

Removing or canceling a rider requires no underwriting action because the risk to the insurer is decreased when the coverage is changed. Instead, POS calculates the new premium, submits a new premium bill to the policyowner, and, if necessary, remits a premium refund.

Determining Cash Value and Administering Loans and Dividends

The ***cash value*** of an individual life insurance policy is the amount of money, before adjustment for factors such as policy loans or late premiums, that a policyowner will receive if the policyowner (1) wishes to obtain a policy loan, (2) allows the policy to lapse, or (3) cancels the coverage and surrenders the policy to the insurer. Cash value is a feature of most types of permanent life insurance such as whole life and universal life.

Policy loans made on individual life insurance coverage are actually cash advances issued to policyowners. The policyowner may repay the policy loan with interest. If the loan is not repaid, the amount of the policy loan, plus interest, is deducted from the amount of death benefits paid under the policy. Some insurers accept telephone requests for loans of amounts lower than a specified maximum amount. Figure 22-5 illustrates a sample request for a policy loan.

Figure 22-5. Request for policy loan.

Policy Loan Request

☐ Maximum Loan Value OR ☐ For loan of $ ____________

- The policy is hereby assigned to the insurer as security for the said loan and interest under the terms of this agreement.
- Interest will be due and payable on the loan in arrears or in advance as stated in the policy. The rate of interest will be stated in the policy.
- If the loan and interest thereon together with all other indebtedness under the policy at any time exceeds the policy's cash value, all liability of the insurer under the policy will terminate, subject to any right of reinstatement provided in the policy.
- Any provision of the policy requiring endorsement by the insurer for a loan is hereby waived.
- The undersigned hereby certify that they are of the age of majority.

When receiving a request for a policy loan, POS examines the policy record to ensure that the request has been made by an eligible person and that, if the policy has been assigned or has an irrevocable beneficiary, the necessary signatures of the assignee or beneficiary (or a spouse in a community property jurisdiction) are correctly provided. By comparing the signatures on the loan form to the signatures on the insurer's records, POS verifies that the person or persons requesting the loan are entitled to do so. If the signatures do not match, POS typically sends a letter with a loan form to the insured and instructs the insured to return the form with a notarized signature. POS may verify that the policyowner has specified a loan repayment method. Although the policy loan does not have to be repaid, most insurers offer policyowners a choice of one of the following loan repayment plans:

- *Dividend plan.* The insurer applies available dividends plus future dividends against the loan amount.
- *Coupon plan.* The insurer supplies the policyowner with coupons to return with periodic payments against the loan amount.
- *Automatic check plan.* The policyowner authorizes the insurer to write a check for a set amount on the policyowner's bank account each month until the loan is repaid.
- *Lump sum plan.* The policyowner is authorized to enclose a check or money order for the entire loan plus the loan interest due.
- *Partial loan repayment plan.* The policyowner is authorized to enclose a check or money order for a partial loan payment.

After computing the cash value of the policy and verifying that it is adequate to fulfill the requested loan, POS then issues a check in that amount. If the cash value is inadequate to fulfill the loan, most insurers issue a check for the greatest amount available and notify the policyowner of the reason for not granting the full amount requested.

Most insurers offer policyowners the option of obtaining an automatic premium loan to cover unpaid premiums. In most jurisdictions, such an option is available only if the policyowner requests it. As we mentioned in Chapter 15, an automatic premium loan (APL) provision in a policy allows an insurer to pay overdue premiums on a policy by establishing a loan against the policy's cash value. If a policyowner chooses an APL and fails to pay a premium on a timely basis, the insurer automatically grants a loan if the policy's loan value is sufficient to cover the amount of premiums plus interest. When an automatic premium loan is established, it may signal a potential lapse

Fast Fact

Policy loans made against the cash value of life insurance policies totaled $95.9 billion through the end of 1995. These outstanding loans to policyholders equaled 4.5 percent of insurance companies' total assets.

Source: American Council of Life Insurance, *Life Insurance Fact Book,* 1996: 105.

or surrender of the policy. POS therefore attempts to conserve the business by notifying the policyowner and the marketer that the loan has taken effect.

A ***policy dividend*** is a payment made by an insurer to a policyowner and can be paid on both individual and group insurance coverage. On individual coverage, a policy dividend is a refund of excess premium paid to the owner of an individual participating life insurance policy. Generally, a policy dividend on individual coverage reflects the insurer's decision to reduce the cost of the coverage by returning to the policyowner a portion of the premium already paid. A person who owns a participating life insurance policy elects a dividend option at the time of policy application. The policyowner is usually free to change the selected option at any time while the policy is in force. The available options usually include

- Receiving cash payment of dividends on a periodic basis, usually quarterly or annually
- Applying dividends to pay some or all of the premiums on the policy
- Applying dividends to pay some or all of the loan on the policy, if any
- Allowing dividends to accumulate at interest, adding to the policy's cash value
- Using dividends to buy additional insurance

On group coverage, a policy dividend is the portion of a group insurance premium that is returned to a group policyholder whose claim experience is better than had been expected when the premium was calculated.

POS is responsible for computing the amount of policy dividends available at any given time and for making appropriate changes to the insurer's records when a policyowner changes the dividend option. If the policyowner chooses to receive cash payment of dividends or to withdraw some or all of the dividends that have been left to accumulate with interest, POS calculates the amount of dividends and makes appropriate disbursements to the policyowner. Although dividend earnings are not taxable, any interest earned on accumulations is taxable. POS is responsible for calculating any amount of taxes due.

If a policyowner wishes to apply existing dividends to buy additional insurance, POS verifies that the additional coverage is allowable without further evidence of insurability. Elements generally considered include the amount of insurance already in force, the amount of coverage that dividends would purchase, and the applicant's risk classifi-

Fast Fact

About 34 percent of all Canadian life insurance policies qualify for policy dividends. In 1995, Canadians used 65 percent of those policy dividend dollars to buy either additional amounts of insurance or annuities.

Source: Canadian Life and Health Insurance Association, *Canadian Life and Health Insurance Facts,* 1996: 18.

cation. If such evidence is necessary, POS usually notifies both the policyowner and the insurer's underwriting staff of the required evidence.

Handling Variable Insurance Products

Variable life insurance is a form of whole life insurance under which the death benefit and the cash value of the policy change according to the investment performance of funds that are kept separate from an insurer's other investments. Most variable life insurance products permit a policyowner to choose from several separate funds and to change the selection at least annually and sometimes more often. In purchasing variable life insurance, the policyowner, not the insurer, assumes the risk concerning the amount of the death benefit and the policy's cash value.

Like other forms of life insurance, variable products require POS to handle loans, surrenders, and changes in name, address, beneficiaries, and premium mode. In addition, policyowners of variable life products need assistance from POS in (1) reallocating money from one investment fund to another and in (2) designating the allocation of future premium payments. In the first instance, a policyowner wishes to move currently invested money from one type of investment to another—for example, from a money market or bond account to a growth and income stock account. In the second instance, a policyowner wishes to specify the investments into which future premiums will be placed. Most insurers allow policyowners to make reallocation choices by telephone or in writing, although some insurers require written notification of the policyowner's desire to reallocate funds.

Handling Premium Payments

Some insurance companies assign to POS the responsibility for sending premium due notices and handling the payment of premiums. In order to continue a policy in force, a policyowner must send premium payments to the insurer according to an established schedule, which may be monthly, quarterly, semiannually, or annually. POS sends notices to insureds to remind them of premiums due and maintains records of premiums due and paid.

If a policyowner is late in paying a premium, most insurance companies send the policyowner a ***policy grace notice*** (also called a *lapse notice*), which is a written notification that the policy's grace period is about to expire. As we noted in Chapter 16, the grace period is a specified period after a renewal premium is due and unpaid during which a

Figure 22-6. Example of wording in a policy grace notice.

There is no longer sufficient surrender value in your policy to prevent termination or lapse of the policy. Accordingly, your policy has entered a grace period and will lapse if sufficient premium to continue your policy is not received before the end of the grace period.

In order to continue your coverage in force, you must pay the minimum premium, which is $____________. This premium must be received on or before the grace period expiration date, which is ________________.

We appreciate your business and hope that you will remit your premium promptly.

policy, including all riders, remains in force. If a premium is paid during the grace period, the premium is considered to have been paid on time. The policy grace notice is mailed to a policyowner as a reminder that the premium is due within the grace period. Figure 22-6 shows one version of wording used in a policy grace notice.

Some policyowners wish to increase or decrease the frequency of premium payments. For example, a policyowner who has previously paid monthly premiums for health insurance may wish to change to a semiannual or annual premium payment mode because the premium charged for less frequent payments is usually somewhat lower than for more frequent payments. Insurers sometimes do not permit changes in premium payment frequency because of complications resulting from due dates that are inconsistent with a policy's anniversary. If a policy has a waiver of premium provision and the premiums are currently being waived, an insurer generally does not allow a change to a more frequent premium payment mode. Generally, when a policyowner submits a request for a change of premium payment frequency, POS can approve it if the request meets the insurer's premium payment requirements.

If insurance coverage provides for a change of premium at the time an insured reaches a specified age, POS sends the policyowner a premium bill that reflects the new premium. In addition, POS notifies the staff responsible for paying marketers' commissions to modify the premium-based commission amount due, if any, to a marketer. POS also handles various other age-related changes to certain coverages. For example, a health insurance policy may provide that an insured may continue to be covered if the insured is still employed past a certain age. Similarly, some types of coverage terminate when an insured reaches a specified age, and other types of coverage provide that an insured becomes eligible for alternative coverage at a stated age. For these and other types of changes, POS is responsible for notifying policyowners of coverage changes and premium rates, and arranging premium payment according to policy provisions.

In order to conserve business, most insurers require POS to send marketers a list of insureds whose premium payments have fallen 20 to 90 days overdue. This list is usually updated weekly or biweekly. Marketers thus have an opportunity to contact policyowners who have not paid their premiums in a timely manner and to encourage them to retain the coverage or to modify it so that the coverage and the premium amount more nearly match their current needs.

Fulfilling Other Policyowner Needs

In addition to the POS services already discussed, certain other needs of policyowners are fulfilled by POS. These needs include obtaining a duplicate copy of a policy or surrendering, converting, reinstating, or terminating a policy.

Obtaining a Duplicate Policy

A policyowner or other person may need to obtain a duplicate copy of a policy when the original policy has been lost or destroyed, or is otherwise unavailable. A duplicate copy of a policy is stamped to indicate that it is a duplicate, and the insurer's file contains a record of the duplicate issuance. Some insurers require a policyowner to state in writing that if the original policy is found, the duplicate policy will be returned to the insurer. Figure 22-7 illustrates a typical lost policy request form.

Figure 22-7. Lost policy request form.

For Contract/Policy Number ____________________

I request a: ☐ Certification of my policy (no charge)
☐ Duplicate policy ($30 fee enclosed to cover expenses)

My policy was: ☐ Lost
☐ Destroyed
☐ Other ______________________________

Send the above to: ☐ Policyowner ☐ Marketer ____________________

The undersigned hereby represents that the above numbered policy was lost or destroyed. This policy is not now assigned, nor has it been otherwise transferred or encumbered in any manner. No person, firm, or corporation has or claims the right to possession of this policy.

I agree that should the original policy be found or in any way come into my possession, I will return the duplicate policy to the insurer.

Before issuing a duplicate copy of a policy, POS helps to avoid potential legal problems by obtaining verification that the duplicate copy is needed and that the original copy is gone. If a problem arises in attempting to verify the loss of the original policy, POS usually issues a certificate of insurance rather than a duplicate policy. The ***certificate of insurance,*** also known as a *certificate of coverage,* verifies that coverage exists, but does not contain all the details of provisions and riders that the original policy may have contained.

Surrendering a Policy

A policyowner may decide to surrender a policy by requesting that coverage cease and that the insurer send the policyowner the cash value of the policy. When POS receives such a request, it first makes certain that the person who submitted the request is legally entitled to surrender the policy. If a policyowner has assigned some or all of the rights to the policy, then the policyowner is not allowed to surrender it without the assignee's authorization. Figure 22-8 illustrates a typical cash surrender request form.

Before administering a request to surrender a policy, POS usually attempts to conserve the business by contacting the policyowner to ask whether an alternative action might fulfill the policyowner's needs. For instance, POS might suggest that the policyowner use accumulated dividends to pay premiums or request a policy loan for the same purpose, or reduce the amount of coverage if the original amount is no longer needed.

Processing the request for policy surrender requires POS to calculate the cash value and to deduct the amount of any outstanding loans. Some insurers also require the policyowner to submit the policy to the insurer before the surrender is completed and the cash value is disbursed to the policyowner.

Figure 22-8. Cash surrender request form.

Return your policy OR complete a Lost Policy Request Form.

I request payment of the cash surrender value in exchange for surrender of the attached policy.

Effective Date: ______________________

Apply proceeds to Policy # ______________________ (if applicable)

Reason for surrender (check all that apply):

☐ Changing insurance needs ☐ Affordability

☐ Replacing with new insurance from another insurer

☐ Other ______________________

Converting a Policy

A ***conversion privilege*** is a policy provision that permits a policyowner to convert group insurance coverage to coverage under an individual insurance policy or, in certain prescribed situations, to change coverage from one type of policy to another—for instance, to change from an individual term insurance policy to an individual whole life insurance policy. An employee who ceases employment through retirement or termination may be eligible to continue certain types of group coverage by exercising the conversion privilege if one is included in the group contract. Generally a policyowner who exercises the conversion privilege is not required to submit evidence of insurability, particularly if the increase in risk to the insurer is only slight.

POS does check several items, however, in handling a request for policy conversion. First, POS makes sure that the conversion occurs during the conversion period if one is specified in the policy contract. In addition, most insurers require that the first premium payment for the new, or converted, policy be remitted when the conversion request is made. After verifying that the correct premium has been submitted, POS prepares a new policy and updates the policyowner's records to reflect the converted coverage.

Reinstating a Policy

As we have mentioned, reinstatement is the process by which an insurer puts back in force a policy that lapsed because of nonpayment of renewal premiums. Reinstatement provides advantages for both the insurer and the insured. The insurer is able to keep business on its books without incurring the high first-year expenses. The insured is able to have insurance protection that may no longer be offered to new applicants or for which the insured may not be able to qualify otherwise because of advanced age or impairments developed since the original coverage was issued. Moreover, a reinstated policy usually maintains the original, usually lower premium and typically can be reinstated with more liberal underwriting standards than would apply to an application for new coverage. Figure 22-9 shows a typical application for reinstatement of coverage.

When a policyowner applies for reinstatement of a lapsed policy, POS determines whether the policy contains a ***reinstatement provision,*** which is a provision that describes the conditions a policyowner must meet in order for an insurer to reinstate a policy within a specified time after lapse. The right to reinstate a policy is generally not available if the policyowner has surrendered the policy for its cash value. The reinstatement provision does not obligate the insurer to reinstate the policy.

Most insurers require applicants for reinstatement to pay back premiums. Some insurers, however, allow policies that meet certain strict

Figure 22-9. Application for reinstatement.

Policy # ____________________

Insured ____

Name of Employer ______________________________

Application for Reinstatement of Policy Described Above

1. Your present occupation: ____

2. Have you for any reason received medical attention or advice since the date you became covered by the policy in question? If so, give the nature of the illness, date, and name of the physician:

   ____

   ____

   ____

3. Do you declare that you are of sound constitution and temperate habits, and that you are now in good health? ______________________

4. Are you now, have you in the past, or do you intend to engage in any form of aviation? ________________________

5. Name and address of family physician:

   ____

   ____

I hereby certify that the above declarations are complete and true, and I agree that no reinstatement shall take effect until this application is approved by the insurer at its home office.

Date _________________ Signature _____________________________________

criteria to be reinstated without payment of back premiums in order to encourage reinstatement of policies that may have lapsed because of temporary financial hardship, as explained in Figure 22-10. Approval of a reinstatement application is typically subject to evidence of current insurability, which is usually a statement of good health or a health certificate.

If these types of documentation reveal no significant changes in the applicant's health since the original policy was issued, POS reinstates the policy without further investigation. However, if evidence shows the possibility of significant change, POS usually directs the

Figure 22-10. Reinstatement by redating.

Some insurance companies attempt to conserve canceled business, especially that of smaller amount policies, by permitting lapsed policies to be reinstated without requiring the payment of back premiums. Policies which have lapsed but which meet certain criteria can be reinstated by advancing the policy date and the paid-to date (the date to which premiums were paid up) by the number of months that the policy has been lapsed. No back premiums are collected.

A policy reinstated in this manner generally must meet the following criteria:

- The policy must be less than two years old and have no cash value.
- It must have been lapsed for more than 60 days but not more than six months beyond the paid-to date.
- The face amount plus any supplementary term coverage cannot exceed a specified amount, usually $20,000 to $30,000.
- Redating can occur only once during the life of the policy.

underwriting staff to ask for additional evidence of insurability. After this evidence is reviewed, the underwriter can recommend one of three actions:

1. Grant reinstatement as requested.
2. Decline reinstatement if the risk has increased so much that the underwriter cannot justify allowing the person to remain in the original risk class.
3. Offer to reissue the policy at a higher premium charge.

Approval of routine reinstatements involving adequate documentation of unchanged health conditions may be done by POS staff. More complex applications for reinstatement involving deteriorated health or high amounts of coverage are usually referred to underwriting.

Terminating a Policy

If a policyowner does not renew a policy contract, or if premiums have not been paid on a policy and the policyowner does not respond to a series of premium due notices, then POS terminates the policy in accordance with the insurer's established procedures. A letter or notice is sent to the policyowner stating that the coverage has been terminated. Most insurers also instruct POS to notify marketers when coverage has been terminated so that the marketers may determine the cause for the termination.

Handling Returned Mail

Many areas of an insurance company designate staff to handle mail that has been returned. Claims and underwriting, to name two, are careful to investigate returned mail and to send it to its intended recipients, if possible. POS is also concerned with handling returned mail because of the need to conserve business, to operate in a cost-effective manner, and to ensure that requested changes, loans, and other transactions are completed promptly and accurately.

For most insurers, the first step in attempting to resend mail to its intended recipients involves checking whether a more current address has been received. An insurer's information system may contain such address information. If, after checking the system, POS discovers that no current address has been entered, a code is put into the system to show that mail was returned and that no further mail should be sent to that address.

Many insurance companies subscribe to a national database that allows POS to search for a more current address by entering a recipient's name, Social Security or social identification number, date of birth, and last known address. Insurers usually pay only for successful searches—that is, searches that result in identification of a usable address.

For mail related to variable insurance and other regulated products, POS usually intensifies the search by calling directory assistance in the city of the last known address and attempting to seek a new address. In many instances, POS calls a marketer to inquire about the location of the addressee.

At the completion of a search, if POS has been unable to find a viable address, another code is usually entered into the information system to indicate that the insurer not only received returned mail, but could not locate a mailing address. Having made a good faith attempt to find the addressee, POS files the undelivered mail and hopes that the client will later contact the insurer.

The Relationship of POS and Underwriting

We have already mentioned several circumstances, such as using dividends to buy additional insurance and reinstating a policy, in which POS staff consult with underwriting. In addition, several types of policy changes may involve underwriting.

An insured's financial situation, insurability status, or insurance needs can make it necessary or desirable for the insured to request a change in the terms of a policy contract after it has been in force for some time. The insured may wish to (1) change the policy to a different type of insurance, (2) obtain a rate reduction, or (3) add benefits to the original policy. An insured who wishes to make such changes in policy terms must complete a policy change application, specifying the requested changes.

The underwriter's primary concern, as you have learned, is to evaluate the risk represented by a proposed insured and an insured who wishes to make a change in coverage. In considering requested policy changes, the underwriter considers (1) whether a proposed change increases the net amount at risk and (2) whether the insured's original insurability status has changed. POS and underwriting work closely to ensure that each requested change is promptly evaluated and that those involved—principally the policyowner and, sometimes, the marketer—are kept informed of progress on the case.

Change in Type of Insurance

For an insured who wishes to make a change in the type of insurance, the underwriter considers several factors, among them the reason for the requested change. A policyowner may want to change the insurance program into a higher-premium plan with a greater investment in the policy. This type of change usually poses no problem for the underwriter, as the insurer's net amount at risk will decrease more rapidly under the higher-premium plan than under the original plan. An underwriting problem may result, however, if the waiver of premium benefit is included in the contract, because the higher premium for the new plan will increase the amount at risk for the waiver of premium benefit. Thus, a premium increase above a certain dollar amount may require additional evidence of insurability.

When an insured requests a change to a lower-premium plan, generally no significant increase or only a moderate increase in the insurer's amount at risk occurs. Underwriting for such a request can be more liberal than the original underwriting because the first-year acquisition costs, such as the agent's commission, have already been paid. In many insurance companies, therefore, policy changes and conversions involving only moderate increases in the amount at risk are approved by POS without referral to an underwriter *if* all of the following are true:

1. The insured has no history of impairment or rating.

2. The height and weight of the insured are within current standard limits.

3. All answers on the health declaration of the policy change form are negative.

Figure 22-11. Health declaration section of a policy change request form.

Amendment of Application
and
Certification of Health Status

The application for Contract/Policy Number __________________ is hereby amended as follows:

Except as explained in number 3 below, it is represented and certified that since the date of the original application and the date of the medical examination,

1. The answers to the questions on the original application and on the medical examination form remain true and complete as of today and that there has been no change in the health of the proposed insured that would call for or warrant a change in the answers provided.

2. The proposed insured has not consulted or been examined or treated by a physician or other physical or mental health advisor.

3. (State details for any exceptions to 1 and 2 above.)

____

____

____

It is agreed that the omission of any written exception in the space immediately above shall have the same force and effect as if the word "None" were written in that space.

It is further understood and agreed that if approved by the insurer, this Amendment of Application will become part of the policy and that the policy is issued in reliance upon the truthfulness of the representation contained hereon.

Signed this ____________ day of ________________________, __________.

______________________ Witness	______________________ Proposed Insured
______________________ Marketer	______________________ Signature of Applicant if other than Proposed Insured

Figure 22-11 shows a sample health declaration section of a policy change request form.

Rate Reduction

Another type of requested change is reduction or removal of a previously assigned rating or extra premium. Most rate reductions are made in situations in which an insured has received a substandard rating.

In general, a rate reduction is considered either (1) if the insured was originally rated incorrectly or (2) if the reason for the rating is no longer present—for instance, when a disease or condition is either cured or brought under an acceptable degree of improvement or control. An insured person who was rated for being overweight and who later loses the excess weight will more than likely receive a rate reduction if other medical factors remain the same. Such a decision is typically made by an underwriter, whose expertise is necessary to evaluate all pertinent medical indicators.

Many insurance companies advise new policyowners that they can request reconsideration for an extra premium rating at certain times, usually on the first or second policy anniversary date. When POS receives such a request, it is typically forwarded to underwriting for evaluation.

Unlike conversion, rate reduction is not a contractual right. A request for a rate reduction usually requires the insured to submit an application that is similar to the original application, but not as detailed. Such a request also requests evidence of insurability to demonstrate that the insured's case warrants a reduction in the current substandard rating. POS is generally responsible for providing the necessary forms to the insured and for answering questions concerning the procedure followed in considering such a request.

Additional Benefits

After a policy is issued, an insured may wish to add benefits, as we have already mentioned. Such requests are usually handled in a routine manner by POS, but, in some cases, underwriting may require evidence of insurability in order to reappraise the risk. Each insurer establishes its own procedures to define those benefits and levels of coverage that do and do not require the involvement of underwriting.

Key Terms and Concepts

affidavit
power of attorney
assignor
assignee
cash value
policy dividend
variable life insurance
policy grace notice (*lapse notice*)
certificate of insurance (*certificate of coverage*)
conversion privilege
reinstatement provision

CHAPTER TWENTY-THREE

Administering Annuities

Learning Objectives

After studying this chapter, you should be able to

- List and explain five ways in which annuities are classified
- Calculate the amount of annual annuity benefits that would be paid under an annuity contract of a specified face amount and a specified guaranteed rate
- Define 10 provisions of annuity contracts
- Use a chart of surrender charges to calculate the surrender charge for an annuity of a specified face amount in a given year of the contract
- Explain how insurers provide information and annual reports to annuitants
- Discuss the requirements for changing names and addresses, ownership, beneficiaries, and payment options for annuities
- Explain how an insurer collects premium payments and handles annuity charges
- Discuss the annuity administration activities involved in handling withdrawals, surrenders, and loans
- Explain how an insurer disburses annuity proceeds

Chapter Outline

Classification of Annuities
Number and Tax Status of Premium Payments
Frequency of Benefit Payments
Time When Benefits Begin and End
Number of Annuitants
Guaranteed and Variable Annuity Values

Provisions of Annuity Contracts
Withdrawal Provision
Surrender Provision
Bailout Provision
Waiver of Surrender Charge Provision
Ownership Provision
Beneficiary Provision
Change of Ownership or Beneficiary Provision
Entire Contract Provision
Incontestability Provision
Misstatement of Age Provision

Administering Annuities
Providing Information about Annuities
Establishing Accounts and Maintaining Records
Changing Names, Addresses, Beneficiaries, and Payment Options
Collecting Premium Payments
Transferring Funds between Accounts
Handling Annuity Charges
Handling Withdrawals, Surrenders, and Loans
Handling Annuitization
Disbursing Death Claim Payments

To this point in our discussion of insurance administration, we have discussed the administration of underwriting, reinsurance, claims, and policyowner service. In this chapter we'll conclude our study of insurance administration by reviewing the activities involved in administering annuities.

To provide a brief review of this specialized type of product and to explain the wide variety of information required to administer annuities, we'll begin by defining some terms. In insurance, an ***annuity*** is a contract that provides for an insurer to make a series of payments at specified intervals. A person who receives the benefit payments from an annuity is called the ***annuitant*** or the *payee.* Under a life annuity, the annuitant is the person whose lifetime is used as the measuring period to determine how long benefits are payable. Sometimes the annuity benefit payments continue until the death of the annuitant, and sometimes they continue for a specified period regardless of whether the annuitant is still living. The ***annuity owner,*** also called the *contract holder,* is the person, persons, or entity that applies for and purchases the annuity. Usually the owner of an annuity is also the annuitant, although it is possible for one person to own an annuity and another person to receive the payments from the annuity. In our discussion we will refer to the annuity owner as the annuitant.

Annuities are sold to individuals and to groups. Most annuities sold to groups are used as vehicles for investing the assets of a group retirement plan. The trustees of a retirement plan purchase a group annuity and provide a certificate for each participant in the group plan. When a participant in the group plan retires, benefit payments from the annuity provide periodic retirement benefits.

In this chapter we'll begin by explaining various ways in which annuities may be classified so that you'll see the large number of types of annuities. Next we'll explain several contract provisions commonly used in annuities and the principal activities involved in annuity administration.

Classification of Annuities

An employee who administers annuities needs to know a great deal about each type of annuity sold by the insurer and how to handle a variety of issues that arise during administration of the annuities. Many types of annuities exist. In general, annuities are classified according to (1) the number and tax status of premium payments, (2) the frequency of benefit payments, (3) the time when benefits are to begin and end, (4) the number of annuitants covered by the contract, and (5) whether the annuity values are guaranteed or variable.

Number and Tax Status of Premium Payments

An annuity may be purchased by (1) a single, usually large sum; (2) a series of equal-amount premiums; or (3) a series of flexible premiums that may vary between a set minimum amount and a set maximum amount. The annuity functions generally in the same way regardless of whether the premium is paid in a single sum or in a series of payments.

In addition, an annuity may be classified as nonqualified or qualified depending on whether the annuity is associated with a certain type of employee benefit plan that meets specified tax requirements. Plans that satisfy these requirements are known as *tax-qualified plans.* An annuity that is purchased to fund or distribute funds from a tax-qualified plan is purchased with pretax dollars. This type of annuity is known as a ***qualified annuity*** and is exempt from current income on both the purchase amount and the earnings on that amount during the accumulation period. Annuities may be used to fund a number of qualified plans, including pension plans, profit sharing plans, 401(k) accounts, tax sheltered annuities, Keogh plans, simplified employee pensions (SEPs), and individual retirement accounts (IRAs) and spousal-IRAs. When benefits are disbursed under the contract for a qualified annuity, taxes are due on the whole sum disbursed, because the money was not previously taxed.

By contrast, a ***nonqualified annuity*** is an annuity funded with money that has already been taxed by the federal government. By definition, any annuity that is not defined as a qualified annuity is considered to be a nonqualified annuity. The contributions to a nonqualified annuity are not tax deductible. Earnings on a nonqualified annuity accumulate tax deferred until the benefits are disbursed. When benefits are disbursed under the contract for a nonqualified annuity, no taxes are due on the amount paid for premiums, but taxes are due on any sums earned in interest and on any amount in excess of the premiums paid. Nonqualified annuities are generally used as supplemental retirement plans.

Frequency of Benefit Payments

The length of the annuity period determines the frequency of periodic annuity benefit payments. The ***annuity period*** is the length of time between each of the payments in a series of periodic annuity benefit payments. An annuity period of one month provides that annuity benefit payments will be paid each month. An annuity period of six months provides that annuity benefit payments will be paid twice each year. Although the annuity period can be 12 months, 6 months, or 3 months, the most common period is 1 month.

Time When Benefits Begin and End

The ***maturity date,*** also known as the *annuity commencement date,* of an annuity is the date on which an insurance company begins paying the annuity benefit payments. Generally, the maturity date can be immediate or deferred. An ***immediate annuity*** is one for which benefit payments begin between one annuity period and one year after the annuity is purchased. In other words, the annuitant begins to receive income from the contract immediately. For example, if the annuity period of an annuity is six months and the annuity is an immediate annuity, the first benefit payment will be disbursed six months after the purchase date of the annuity. The principal function of an immediate annuity is to convert a sum—the single premium—into a stream of income.

In contrast, a ***deferred annuity*** is one for which benefit payments begin more than one annuity period after the annuity is purchased. The funds in the contract are allowed to grow, tax deferred, until a distribution is made. For most deferred annuities, benefit payments begin one or more years after the annuity is purchased. The principal purpose of a deferred annuity is to provide a means for the annuitant to accumulate funds until a future time.

Every immediate annuity is purchased with a single premium. A deferred annuity may be purchased with a single premium or with a series of periodic payments, which can be equal or flexible in amount.

The time between the purchase of a deferred annuity and the beginning of benefit payments is known as the ***accumulation period,*** also called the *accumulation phase.* (Obviously, an immediate annuity has no accumulation period.) During the accumulation period, an insurer invests the premiums so that the annuity builds value. In administering an annuity, an insurer's staff calculates the annuity's ***accumulated value,*** which is equal to the amount of premiums paid for the annuity *plus* the interest credited to the contract *minus* the amount of (1) any withdrawals and withdrawal charges and (2) any applicable tax, fees, or other charges.

The time when annuity benefit payments end is also specified in the annuity contract. A ***life annuity*** provides periodic benefit payments that are payable as long as the annuitant is alive to receive them, even if the accumulated value of the annuity is completely paid out. When the annuitant dies, the benefit payments come to an end. A life annuity can be a *temporary life annuity,* which limits the number of annuity payments to a stated length of time, such as a 10-year life annuity. A life annuity can also be a *whole life annuity,* which provides for annuity payments to continue throughout an annuitant's entire life. An ***annuity certain*** provides periodic benefit payments for a stated

Fast Fact

In the United States, 2.9 million individual annuities were issued in 1995. About 95 percent of those were deferred annuities. About 21.4 million deferred annuities were in force at year's end.

Source: American Council of Life Insurance, *Life Insurance Fact Book,* 1996: 37.

length of time regardless of whether the annuitant lives or dies. The benefit payments continue to the named beneficiary during the specified period even if the annuitant dies. Some annuity certain contracts provide for payment of remaining benefits in one lump sum.

Number of Annuitants

Most annuities are sold to individual annuity owners, but some annuities provide an income to more than one person. A ***joint and survivor annuity*** provides benefit payments that continue until both or all of the individuals die. We'll discuss this type of annuity in more detail later in this chapter.

Guaranteed and Variable Annuity Values

The manner in which an annuity contract provides for investment earnings on the accumulated value depends on whether the deferred annuity is a fixed-benefit annuity or a variable annuity. Under a ***fixed benefit annuity,*** an insurer guarantees a minimum interest rate on the accumulated value of the annuity and, therefore, at least a specified amount of periodic benefits for each dollar applied toward the purchase of the annuity. The amount to be paid typically varies according to the age at which the annuity benefits begin and the payout option selected. Figure 23-1 illustrates a portion of the guaranteed annuity rates for a deferred life annuity. The chart shows the amount that will be paid per $1,000 of accumulated value for each of three options: a whole life annuity, a 10-year temporary annuity, and a 20-year temporary annuity.

According to the information in Figure 23-1, if the annuitant of a whole life annuity began receiving annuity benefits at age 60 from

Figure 23-1. Guaranteed annuity rates per $1,000 of accumulated value for a deferred life annuity.

Age	Whole Life	10-Year	20-Year
45	4.39	4.37	4.30
50	4.68	4.64	4.53
55	5.06	5.00	4.81
60	5.58	5.47	5.12
65	6.30	6.07	5.44
70	7.31	6.83	5.71
75	8.77	7.72	5.89
80	10.88	8.61	5.97

a \$150,000 deferred life annuity, she would receive \$837 per month (5.58 × 150). If she chose a 10-year temporary life annuity, payable at age 60, she would receive \$820.50 per month (5.47 × 150). If she waited until age 65 to receive benefits under a 10-year temporary life annuity, she would receive \$910.50 per month in benefits (6.07 × 150). These amounts are guaranteed under the annuity contract. The insurance company may elect to pay higher benefits under such a contract, but may not pay less than the guaranteed rates.

Under a ***variable annuity,*** an insurer agrees to pay periodic benefits that may vary according to the performance of a separate account (known in Canada as a *segregated account*). A ***separate account*** is an investment account that is totally separated from an insurance company's other, general investment accounts. The separate account is, therefore, entirely separate from the insurer's liabilities and is not subject to claims from creditors of the insurance company. Subaccounts within a separate account do not offer a guaranteed interest rate or other type of return on earnings, and the annuity purchaser, not the insurance company, bears the full investment risk.

Usually, variable annuity contracts permit each annuitant to choose from several subaccounts within the separate account—and, therefore, to select the amount of risk he is willing to take on various amounts of the total investment—and to move money from one subaccount to another. The subaccounts are invested in various types of stocks, bonds, mutual funds, and other investments. The value of a subaccount within a separate account fluctuates depending on the value of the investments in which the account's funds are invested.

The amount of money earned by the investments in the separate account helps determine the amount of periodic benefit payments made under the annuity contract. If the underlying investments prosper and the value of the annuity increases, the amount of benefit payments increases accordingly. By the same token, if the investments do not do well and the value of the annuity decreases, the amount of benefit payments decreases as well.

Because a variable annuity transfers the investment risk from the insurer to the annuitant, variable annuities are considered to be securities contracts and are subject to federal regulation. This federal regulation generally requires that in the United States and Canada, a marketer of variable annuities (1) must be licensed as an insurance agent in the jurisdiction in which the annuities are sold, and (2) in the United States, must be registered with the National Association of Securities Dealers (NASD) as a marketer. Moreover, an insurer that issues annuities within a given jurisdiction must be licensed as an insurance company by that jurisdiction and must ensure that its annuity policies comply with all applicable laws and regulations. Insight 23-1 explains how variable annuities may be considered investments.

Insight 23-1 My Thoughts On . . . Investing in a Variable Annuity

A variable annuity allows a contract holder to accumulate assets on a tax-deferred basis during the contract holder's working years to support a lifetime stream of income during the retirement years. An important aspect of a variable annuity is the minimum death benefit guarantee. This guarantee provides that if the contract holder dies during the accumulation period of the contract, the beneficiary will receive the greater of (1) the contract value at the time of death or (2) the total dollar amount that was invested (minus any withdrawals that have been taken).

Determining where to invest the assets of a variable annuity can be difficult. Contract holders generally have a choice of subaccounts in which to place their money and may choose among (1) fixed or guaranteed investments and (2) variable investments. Many contract holders want the safety of guaranteed investments. Yet, compared to fixed or guaranteed investments, variable investments can produce a better opportunity for growth.

Variable annuities allow a contract holder to decide how much of each periodic premium payment will be allocated to various subaccounts, each of which has a different objective and strategy for making money. Single premiums may be directed to a fixed account—an interest-bearing account—and then automatically transferred to various subaccounts on a systematic basis. This process is called automatic dollar cost averaging.

The theory of dollar cost averaging allows the contract holder to turn the characteristic fluctuation in the unit value of the variable subaccounts into an advantage. This benefit is achieved by investing equal dollar amounts at regular intervals. When prices are low, more units of a subaccount can be purchased. When prices are high, fewer units are purchased. Over time, more units are purchased at a lower price level, making the average cost at which the units were purchased generally lower than the average price. Dollar cost averaging does not ensure a profit and does not protect against a loss in a declining market; however, it has proven its value when used consistently over an extended period.

The key to dollar cost averaging is simply investing equal dollar amounts at regular intervals through periods of varying price levels. Automatic dollar cost averaging is designed to reduce the chance that a contract holder will invest a large amount under a contract when the unit value is high, resulting in a large reduction in the value of the investment if the value of the unit then declines.

Assume an investment in a variable annuity of $150 each month for 10 months, for a total of $1,500. Subaccount prices fluctuate during this period, but the investment amount does not. If the unit price varies as follows from month to month, the periodic investment of $150 will purchase these numbers of units:

Month	Unit Price	Number of Units $150 Will Purchase
1	$ 6	25.00
2	$ 8	18.75
3	$ 10	15.00
4	$ 10	15.00
5	$ 8	18.75
6	$ 6	25.00
7	$ 4	37.50
8	$ 2	75.00
9	$ 2	75.00
10	$ 4	37.50
Total	$1,500	342.50

At the end of 10 months, the $1,500 total investment has purchased 342.5 variable annuity units. If we divide $1,500 by 342.5 units, we find that the average *cost* per unit is $4.38. Yet the average *price* per unit, determined by adding the 10 monthly prices ($6 + $8 + $10 + $10 + $8 + $6 + $4 + $2 + $2 + $4 = $60) and dividing by the number of months is $6. A lump sum of $1,500 invested at the beginning of the period at the average price of $6 would have purchased only 250 units—yet, by using dollar cost averaging, the investor has accumulated 342.5 units during that same period.

Lisé White, FLMI, ACS, AIAA
Assistant Vice President
Security Benefit Life Insurance Company

Provisions of Annuity Contracts

The contract provisions included in each type of annuity vary according to the design of the annuity product. Common provisions of annuity contracts include the withdrawal provision, surrender provision, bailout provision, and waiver of surrender charge provision. Not all annuities contain all of these provisions. All annuities do, however, contain provisions concerning ownership, beneficiary, change of ownership or beneficiary, entire contract, incontestability, and misstatement of age. You may notice that many of the provisions commonly included in annuities are similar to provisions included in many life insurance contracts.

Withdrawal Provision

A ***withdrawal provision*** permits an annuitant to withdraw funds from an annuity's accumulated value during the accumulation period. The withdrawal provision specifies the dollar amount or percentage of the accumulated value that may be withdrawn during a specified period, which is usually a year. A typical withdrawal provision would allow an annuitant to make one withdrawal—during each contract year—of any amount up to 10 percent of the contract's accumulated value without incurring a withdrawal charge. Subsequent withdrawals in a contract year or withdrawal of amounts greater than 10 percent would be subject to a withdrawal charge. A ***withdrawal charge*** is a flat amount or a percentage of the amount withdrawn that is deducted from the annuity when a withdrawal is made from the annuity account during the accumulation period. Typical withdrawal charges are illustrated in Figure 23-2.

Figure 23-2. Typical withdrawal charges for an annuity.

Contract Year of Withdrawal	Percent Charge of Accumulated Contract Value
1	8
2	6
3	4
4	3
5	2
6	1
Thereafter	0

Under certain conditions, an insurer waives the withdrawal charge. For example, suppose an annuitant chooses to withdraw the annuity's accumulated interest on a periodic basis. If the amount of accumulated interest is less than a specified amount, the insurer generally reserves the right to pay that interest only on an annual basis in order to reduce the cost of administering the annuity. In such a situation, the insurer may waive the withdrawal charge.

The withdrawal provision may also establish a minimum amount that must be withdrawn during a specified period. To enhance cost efficiency and to avoid having to administer small-amount withdrawals, many insurers establish a minimal withdrawal amount, such as $100.

Surrender Provision

An annuity's ***surrender provision*** allows an annuitant to withdraw all available value from the annuity—that is, to take the annuity's ***surrender value,*** which is the net cash value of the annuity, minus fees and any other applicable charges. When an annuity is surrendered, the contract terminates. A ***surrender charge*** is an amount deducted from the accumulated value of annuity when it is surrendered early in the contract. Like withdrawal charges, surrender charges generally decrease gradually each year after the beginning of the contract and disappear in six to eight years. The percentages typically used for withdrawal charges, as shown in Figure 23-2, are applicable to surrender charges as well.

As an example, suppose an annuity contract that is in its second year has an accumulated value of $200,000, allows an annual withdrawal of any amount up to 10 percent of the accumulated value, and has a 6 percent withdrawal charge. To calculate the total surrender value of this annuity contract, an annuity administrator would proceed as follows:

Accumulated contract value		$200,000
10 percent surrender-free amount	–	20,000
Amount subject to surrender charges		$180,000
6 percent surrender charge	×	.94
Net amount after surrender charge		$169,200
10 percent surrender-free amount	+	20,000
Total surrender value		$189,200

Note that the 10 percent surrender-free amount is deducted *before* the surrender charge is calculated and is then added to the net amount *after* the surrender charge amount is deducted.

Bailout Provision

The ***bailout provision*** of an annuity enables an annuitant to surrender the annuity contract, usually without a surrender charge, if the interest rates paid on a fixed annuity decrease below a specified level. The bailout provision protects annuitants from having to pay a surrender charge in the event that the renewal interest rate is below the rate guaranteed in the annuity contract.

Waiver of Surrender Charge Provision

To allow the insurer to waive surrender charges in certain situations, some annuities contain a ***waiver of surrender charge provision.*** As an example, an insurer may waive the surrender charge when the annuitant or contract owner becomes disabled or confined in a nursing home or other long-term care facility. The waiver of surrender charge provision releases the annuitant or contract owner from paying surrender charges on withdrawals.

Ownership Provision

The ***ownership provision*** establishes the owner of the annuity as the person so named in the application. Generally, if the owner of an annuity is a trustee, the insurer reserves the right in the ownership provision to deal directly with the trustee without regard for the provisions of any trust agreement. As a result, provisions in a trust agreement typically do not allow waiving or altering any part of the annuity contract.

Beneficiary Provision

According to a typical annuity ***beneficiary provision,*** if the annuity owner dies before benefit payments begin under the annuity policy, the accumulated value of the annuity is paid to the named beneficiary. If during the accumulation period any beneficiary named in the annuity application dies before the owner dies, proceeds will be paid to any surviving beneficiaries upon the death of the owner. In other words, the death of a beneficiary does *not* automatically make that beneficiary's heirs eligible to receive benefits under the annuity contract. Some annuities provide in the beneficiary provision that if a beneficiary does not survive an owner for a specified period—usually, 24 hours—that beneficiary will be considered to have predeceased the annuitant, and the proceeds will be distributed to any surviving beneficiaries. Contract owners may change beneficiaries at any time prior to annuitization (which we will discuss later in this chapter).

Change of Ownership or Beneficiary Provision

An annuity policy is a piece of property. Like any other property, such as a house, car, or boat, the annuity may be sold or given by the annuity owner to someone else. Most annuities provide by the ***change of ownership or beneficiary provision*** that the contract owner (in many cases, the annuitant) may change the owner or the beneficiary at any time during the annuitant's lifetime. Any such change must generally be recorded at the home office of the insurer, whether or not the annuitant is living at the time of the recording (that is, the recording may take place after the death of the annuitant if the annuity owner made the request for the change before the annuitant's death). Because some changes of ownership may result in a taxable event, the owner is generally advised to seek tax counsel before requesting the change. Typically, federal tax authorities view the transfer of an annuity as a distribution because the original owner is assumed to have received something of value equal to the value of the annuity. Even if the transfer of ownership results from a gift by the original owner to the new owner, the transfer is still considered a distribution.

Entire Contract Provision

An ***entire contract provision*** establishes that the annuity contract and the application for the annuity contract form the entire contract. All statements made during the process of applying for the annuity will, in the absence of fraud, be considered representations and not warranties. A ***representation*** is a statement of facts upon which an insurer bases its decision to issue a product, such as an annuity. A ***warranty*** is a statement made by a party to a contract that will invalidate the contract if the statement is not literally true. Therefore, the entire contract provision typically states that any information provided by an applicant for an annuity is considered to be not a literal fact, but an acceptable fact unless proven false by the presence of material misrepresentation or fraud. The entire contract provision functions to exclude (1) any oral agreements that are not written into the contract and (2) other written documents.

Incontestability Provision

Annuity contracts include an ***incontestability provision*** stating that the annuity contract is not contestable after it has been in force during the lifetime of the annuitant for two years from the contract date.

Misstatement of Age Provision

According to the ***misstatement of age provision*** included in most annuities, if the age or gender of an annuitant has been misstated, the

Insight 23-2 My Thoughts On . . . Information for Annuity Administration

Annuity administration requires an understanding of the annuity contract provisions, Internal Revenue Code sections, state insurance laws, securities laws, and the markets in which these products are sold. Good business decisions regarding the administration of annuity contracts can be made only with an understanding of these concepts and how they interrelate.

It goes without saying that an annuity administrator should read each annuity contract very carefully to determine what its provisions are. Annuity contracts vary not only from one insurer to another, but also within each insurance company.

As an example, what you might think of as a "typical nonqualified annuity contract with joint owners" may have certain requirements which, if not followed carefully, may produce problems in administration. Handling requested exceptions in such a contract can result in costly mistakes and legal quagmires. Suppose that one of the joint owners of the contract wishes to make a partial withdrawal, or even to surrender the contract, using only his own signature and not including the signatures of the other owner or owners of the annuity. Is such an approach permissible? Only by reading the provisions of the contract can an administrator learn what is permitted by that contract. Depending on the contract provisions, the joint owner's request may or may not be allowed.

In nonqualified annuity contracts, many problems are not discovered until the death of one of the persons involved in the annuity contract (i.e., the owner, joint owner, or annuitant). Annuity administrators may then find misunderstandings regarding income tax consequences or who is to receive the death proceeds. This situation is particularly true if the owner and the annuitant are different individuals or entities.

For example, an annuity contract could provide that the beneficiary receives death proceeds when the annuitant dies, and the surviving joint owner receives proceeds if the owner dies. The income tax consequences may also be different, depending on which scenario occurred. The annuity administrator needs to understand these relationships and consequences.

Mary Jo Ardington, CLU, ChFC
Associate Counsel
Lincoln National Life Insurance Company

amount payable under the annuity contract will be the amount that the premiums would have purchased for the correct age. Usually, misstatement of age is not important until the contract is annuitized. At that time, the insurer typically requires proof of age in the form of a birth certificate, baptismal record, driver's license, or similar document.

In order to administer annuities accurately and promptly, annuity administration staff need a clear understanding of contract provisions and their implications, as well as numerous other types of information. Insight 23-2 comments on some of the many kinds of information with which annuity administration staff must become familiar.

Administering Annuities

Now that you have a general idea of the many kinds of annuities and their various features, you can understand the immense amount of information that staff who administer annuities must obtain and keep updated. Annuities are not more complicated than insurance products to administer, but annuity administration does require a considerable number of activities. These activities usually include the following:

- Providing information and annual statements about annuities
- Establishing accounts and maintaining records
- Changing names and addresses, ownership, beneficiaries, and payment options
- Collecting premium payments
- Handling annuity charges
- Handling withdrawals, surrenders, and loans
- Transferring funds between various annuity investment accounts
- Disbursing annuity proceeds according to the provisions of each annuity contract

In the United States, employees who handle investment-based products like variable annuities must be registered with the National Association of Securities Dealers (NASD). In addition, in order to ensure compliance with requirements of the Securities and Exchange Commission, all of an insurer's employees who discuss such products in person and on the telephone are licensed.

Providing Information about Annuities

Fast Fact

Canadian companies were paid $5.7 billion in premiums or contributions for annuities in 1995, with 88 percent of that amount being paid into deferred retirement products.

Source: Canadian Life and Health Insurance Association, *Canadian Life and Health Insurance Facts,* 1996: 11.

Keeping annuitants informed about the status of their annuities is an important activity of annuity administration. For each annuity, the insurer maintains an accurate record of deposits, withdrawals, loans, and other transactions, and makes that information available to the annuity owner and the annuitant upon request. The insurer also apprises the annuitant of any mandated tax changes or other legislated changes that might affect the annuitant.

In addition, an insurer produces and sends to each annuity owner an annual statement containing information about the account value, the surrender value, the renewal interest rate, and additions and deductions to the policy made during the contract year. Some insurers send such information to annuity owners on a more frequent basis. Most jurisdictions require that a statement be sent at least annually to all owners of qualified annuities.

Establishing Accounts and Maintaining Records

In establishing an account for an annuity, the annuity administration staff use information submitted with the annuity application. Generally, an application for an annuity requires information similar to that required in an application for life insurance. Typical information required by most annuity applications is shown in Figure 23-3.

If an applicant wishes to purchase a variable annuity, most applications require that the applicant sign a statement verifying that he has received a ***prospectus,*** which is a document that describes the main features, typical investment vehicles, and administration procedures of an investment product. Like any organization offering investment-based products, an insurer is required by federal securities laws and regulations to disclose all material facts about an investment so that a prospective investor—in this case, a person who purchases a variable annuity—may make an informed decision about the merit of the investment.

An application for an immediate annuity must be accompanied by proof of age because adjusting the amount of the benefits at the time of the annuitant's death would not be practical. At that time, the benefits have already been paid (periodically, during the annuitant's lifetime), and an overpayment of benefits cannot be recovered. By contrast, if underpayment of benefits has occurred, the annuitant is no longer alive to receive the additional benefits.

When a company purchases an annuity to provide funds for an employee's pension, that employee's current salary and date of hire are

Figure 23-3. Typical information required by annuity applications.

- Proposed annuitant's name, address, and Social Security or social identification number
- Annuitant's marital status, gender, and birthdate
- Proposed annuity owner's name and address
- Type of annuity requested
- Effective date of the contract
- Premium amount (fixed or variable) and frequency (single, monthly, quarterly, semiannual, annual)
- Beneficiary (primary and contingent), including date of birth, Social Security or social identification number, and the relationship of each beneficiary to the proposed annuitant
- Information concerning whether the requested annuity is intended to replace any existing insurance or annuity currently in force and, if so, the name of the insurer or annuity issuer, policy or annuity number, year of issue, and reason for replacement; some annuity applications also ask the marketer to verify whether a new annuity is intended as a replacement
- The premium amount, if any, submitted with the application
- Any special requests, such as a specific date of issue or payment of premiums by electronic funds transfer (EFT)

usually requested. In addition, some legislation requires that a marketer demonstrate the suitability of the annuity for the employee by providing information about (1) the number of dependents of that employee and (2) the amount of total family income.

Maintaining the records associated with annuities requires annuity administration staff to update each record in accordance with requested changes such as those discussed in the next sections. In addition, a record is kept of the value of each annuity to facilitate payment of proceeds, calculation of taxes due, and preparation of annual statements. Finally, the record of each annuity contains a copy of the tax code section that governs that type of account in order to determine taxable amounts and other requirements that the code may place on the annuity account.

Changing Names, Addresses, Beneficiaries, and Payment Options

Changes of names, addresses, and beneficiaries are fairly routine. An owner submits a request to the insurer, and the changes are made in the insurer's records. If an annuity contract provides for an irrevocable beneficiary or a collateral assignee, the signatures of these persons must accompany a request for a change of beneficiary. Most insurers also require that these types of requests include a daytime telephone number so that the change may be verified. In addition, insurers generally mail a notification of such changes to an owner's former address to help prevent mistaken or fraudulent change requests from being implemented.

When an immediate annuity is purchased, or when other types of annuities become annuitized, the owner chooses a payment option by which the benefits will be disbursed. Generally, the payment options for annuities include

- The value of the annuity in a lump sum or in installments for a fixed period
- The value of the annuity in a life annuity
- Investment of the value of the annuity to the insurer and periodic payment of the interest earned on that value

Some annuities provide that an owner may change the payment option at any time during the accumulation period while the annuity contract is in force. After the annuity is annuitized and a payment option chosen, no change is permitted in the payment option.

Collecting Premium Payments

Annuity administration includes collecting and maintaining accurate records of annuity or premium payments. Further, if an annuitant wishes to allocate certain amounts of each variable premium payment to various investment funds, or to change the allocation of such amounts, annuity administration staff ensures that the requested fund allocation is made in a timely manner and that the annuity's records are brought up to date.

Transferring Funds between Accounts

Transferring funds between variable annuity subaccounts may involve existing funds or future allocations, or both. To effect these kinds of changes, an owner submits a change request to the insurer's annuity administration staff.

If a variable annuity contract provides that funds may be transferred from one annuity subaccount to another, the owner usually has only to submit a request by telephone or on paper to effect the transfer. Suppose that an annuity has $50,000 invested in a capital appreciation subaccount and $60,000 invested in a growth and income subaccount. The owner may wish to transfer $20,000 from the first subaccount to a bond subaccount and to transfer $35,000 from the second subaccount to a money market subaccount. In such a situation, after the insurer receives the owner's transfer request, the funds are electronically transferred, and the record of that annuity is updated to reflect the new investments. Confirmation of the transaction is sent to the owner.

An owner may wish to change the way in which future premiums are allocated among subaccounts for a variable annuity. As an example, an owner may wish to increase the percentage of each monthly premium invested in one of an insurer's funds. Most insurers provide that the percentage of a premium payment allocated to an account must equal at least 10 percent—that is, an owner may not divide a premium payment into portions smaller than 10 percent. For instance, if an owner has divided her premium payments among five of an insurer's available investment accounts, the allocation of premium might look like this:

Capital Appreciation Subaccount	30 percent
Growth and Income Subaccount	25 percent
World Government Subaccount	25 percent
International Stock Subaccount	10 percent
Bond Subaccount	10 percent

Under the terms of most variable annuity contracts, this owner would be allowed to instruct the insurer to allocate different percentages to any or all of these accounts or to other subaccounts offered under the contract provided that if a portion of the premium is allocated to any fund, that portion must be at least 10 percent.

Handling Annuity Charges

Administering annuity contracts includes handling whatever annuity charges are included in each type of annuity contract. Considerable diversity exists in the amount and types of charges made for annuities. Some insurers establish a fixed charge made at the time an annuity is issued, whereas other insurers establish periodic charges. A typical annuity contract may contain one or more of the following types of charges:

- *Contract fee.* The ***contract fee*** is a flat amount charged either at the time the annuity is issued or annually. The contract fee is intended to help pay for the costs of administering the annuity.
- *Transaction fee.* The ***transaction fee*** is a flat charge per premium payment or other specified transaction.
- *Percentage of premium charge.* Instead of a transaction fee charged per premium payment, an annuity contract may specify a ***percentage of premium charge,*** also called a *load,* to be deducted by the insurer from each premium paid. The percentage of premium charge may be reduced after the contract has been in force for a certain number of years or after the total amount of premiums paid has reached a certain level.
- *Withdrawal charge.* As we have mentioned, the withdrawal charge is a flat amount or a percentage of the amount withdrawn that is deducted from the annuity when a withdrawal is made from the annuity account prior to the date of annuitization.
- *Surrender charge.* As we have mentioned, the surrender charge is an amount that is deducted from an annuity when it is surrendered. Generally, a surrender charge is not levied against earnings with the annuity.

Some insurers establish the surrender charge as a reduction in the interest rate credited to the fixed annuity account. That is, if an annuity provides for a guaranteed interest rate of 7 percent per year and the annuity is surrendered early in its life, the surrender charge may be half or more of that guaranteed amount of interest. The penalty, then, is that the owner receives a smaller amount of interest on the annuity for the period during which the annuity was held than the owner would have received if the annuity had been held for several additional years. During the first year of some annuities, owners are offered a guaranteed interest rate that is lower by one to two percentage points than the rate the annuity guarantees to pay in years subsequent to the first. Owners who keep their annuity contracts in force for an extended period, therefore, are rewarded by higher interest rates in years subsequent to the first year of the contract.

Under certain circumstances, an insurer waives the surrender charge. Two such circumstances are the following:

- The owner dies before the annuity's maturity date
- The surviving spouse of a deceased owner continues the annuity contract within a year of the death of the owner

Some insurers combat early withdrawal of funds or surrender by discouraging marketers from selling annuities to persons who are unable financially to pay the premiums and who may, therefore, be likely to withdraw funds or surrender the annuity in its early years. To discourage unsound marketing, insurance companies use a ***commission chargeback,*** which requires a marketer to return the first-year commission on an annuity product sold to an annuitant who dies or withdraws the funds from an annuity within the first year after issue.

Handling Withdrawals, Surrenders, and Loans

Annuity administration involves maintaining records of funds subtracted from annuity accounts and disbursing those funds accurately and promptly.

Withdrawals and surrenders. An owner may withdraw funds accumulated in an annuity or surrender the annuity at any time *prior* to (1) the maturity date of the annuity, (2) the death of any annuity owner, or (3) the death of any annuitant if the owner is not a natural person (but is, for example, a business). The amount of funds withdrawn is usually subject to a certain limit, typically 90 percent of the account value *or* a dollar amount that is specified in the annuity contract. Withdrawals made before an owner reaches a specified age, usually 59½, are typically subject to a 10 percent federal tax penalty in addition to standard income tax liability. Withdrawals from or surrenders of a nonqualified annuity are subject to tax only on the earnings, not on the principal amount, whereas withdrawals from or the surrender of a qualified annuity are subject to tax on the principal and the earnings. When an owner makes withdrawals from a variable annuity that may be invested in various subaccounts, the withdrawal request form specifies the amount of money to be withdrawn from each specific subaccount.

In the United States, some annuity surrenders are the result of 1035 exchanges, by which owners ask that funds held in an annuity be sent to another seller of annuities. When an insurer receives a 1035-exchange request, the annuity administration staff first checks whether the owner has signed the request. If the annuity contract requires submission of the contract form to the insurer, the staff asks the owner in writing to send the annuity contract to the insurer. After sending the amount of surrendered funds to the replacing company, the insurer mails a 1099 form, indicating to tax authorities that funds have been disbursed, to the owner, and codes the funds as 1035 funds, which are not taxable. If the surrendered funds are being rolled over directly into another qualified investment such as an Individual Retirement Account (IRA), the annuity administration staff checks for the owner's signature and for any requirement that the annuity contract be submitted to the insurer.

Owners of nonqualified plans may choose when to begin receiving payments, although many insurers begin payments by the time the annuitant reaches a specified age, usually 80. For qualified annuity contracts, federal legislation requires that annuitants must begin making withdrawals when they reach the age of 70½ (by April 1 of the year following attainment of age 70½) and if they no longer have earned income. ***Minimum distribution requirements*** are instituted by federal law and establish the least amount that must be withdrawn each year from a nonqualified or qualified account. In general, the minimum distribution is calculated by dividing the amount in an account as of December 31 (in this case, the accumulated value of the annuity) by the annuitant's life expectancy *or* by the annuitant and designated beneficiary's joint life expectancy. As an example, if the accumulated value of a single life annuity is $180,000 and the annuitant's life expectancy is 15 years, the annuitant must withdraw a minimum of $12,000 each year after the annuitant passes age 70½.

Insurers write to such annuitants prior to the time they reach the specified age, informing them of the need to begin making withdrawals, or, as some insurers phrase it, "taking distributions." If an annuitant does not respond to the insurer's letter, some insurers process an automatic withdrawal of the minimum distribution amount and mail a check each year to the annuitant. Other insurers inform an annuitant of the minimum required distribution requirement, but leave the annuitant responsible for requesting the distribution.

Loans. Some annuity policies include a loan feature that allows the owner to withdraw funds from the annuity by "borrowing" an amount equal to the distribution. The difference between a loan and a partial withdrawal is that a loan can be viewed as a temporary distribution. A

Figure 23-4. Annuity loan repayment statement.

> I hereby agree to make payments of principal and interest on this loan no less frequently than quarterly for the term of the loan, which shall not exceed (number of years, usually no more than 5) unless such loan is for the purchase of my principal residence. If any required loan payments have not been made within 61 days of the date payment is required, the insurer shall treat the loan as in default and will automatically repay the entire outstanding loan balance with a partial withdrawal of surrender value from the contract. The amount withdrawn will be treated as a taxable distribution to me.

partial withdrawal, on the other hand, is more like a surrender because it is a permanent withdrawal. If the annuity owner does not intend to repay the loan, a partial withdrawal is usually recommended.

When an owner makes a loan from an annuity, the annuitant is required to sign a statement verifying that the loan will be repaid according to specified terms. Figure 23-4 shows a typical annuity loan repayment statement.

Handling Annuitization

Annuitization is the conversion of an investment fund into a series of payments. At the time an annuity is purchased, the annuity owner selects a time when annuity benefits are to begin. As we have mentioned, payment of proceeds of an immediate annuity begins one annuity period after the annuity is purchased. Some annuities specify that proceeds may begin if the annuitant becomes disabled according to the definition of disability provided in the annuity contract. Benefits payable on the death or disability of an owner are not subject to a tax penalty, regardless of the age of the owner.

Every annuity contract contains the payout option selected by the owner at the time the annuity was purchased. An annuity's ***payout option*** is the method by which the annuity proceeds will be disbursed. The payout option is usually the same as the name of the annuity—that is, if an annuity owner chooses a straight life payout option, the annuity is called a straight life annuity. The choice of payout options varies from one annuity product to another. Among the most common types of payout options are the following:

- A ***straight life annuity*** provides periodic benefit payments for the lifetime of the annuitant. This type of annuity provides that if the annuitant is living on the starting date of the annuity (the date the payments begin), the insurer will make periodic payments to the annuity owner until the death of the annuitant. After the annuitant dies, the benefits cease, regardless of the value of the annuity fund at the time of death. Therefore, if the annuity owner received only one or a few payments before the annuitant died, the remaining value of the annuity fund becomes the property of the insurance company. Likewise, if the annuitant lived beyond the life expectancy used to calculate the annuity payment, the insurer would continue making annuity payments to the annuity owner. The annuity owner thus assumes the risks of the annuitant outliving the value of the annuity fund, while the insurance company assumes the risk of the fund outlasting the annuitant. As an example, if an annuitant selects a straight life annuity that begins paying benefits in January 2001 and if the annuitant dies in June 2006, benefits will be paid only between January 2001 and June 2006. Given an equal fund amount, the straight life annuity provides the largest payment of any other type of annuity payment method. All the other methods, however, protect the annuity owner from losing the total amount of the remaining fund value if the annuitant dies earlier than expected.

- A ***life income with period certain annuity*** provides periodic benefit payments throughout the annuitant's lifetime and during at least a specified period regardless of whether the annuitant is living. The annuitant selects the certain period, which typically ranges from 5 to 20 years. For example, if an annuitant chooses a life income with period certain annuity that begins paying benefits in January 2001 and has a 15-year period, the annuity will continue to pay benefits until December 2015, whether or not the annuitant is still living at the end of the period. If an annuitant dies before the specified period has elapsed, the insurer makes the remaining payments to a named beneficiary. If the annuitant lives longer than the specified period, benefits continue until the annuitant's death.

- A ***life income with refund annuity*** provides benefits during the lifetime of the annuitant *and* guarantees that benefits will continue until the insurer has disbursed at least an amount equal to the purchase price of the annuity. If an annuitant chooses this type of annuity and dies before the purchase price has been paid in benefits, the insurer pays to the beneficiary the difference between the amount of benefits paid and the purchase price.

- A joint and survivor annuity, as we mentioned earlier in this chapter, provides benefits to two or more people—typically, to two persons who receive benefits throughout both their lives. If one of the persons dies, the joint and survivor annuity continues paying benefits to the second person (the survivor of the pair) for as long as that person lives. A joint and survivor annuity may cover the lives of more than two persons. The terms of a joint and survivor contract may provide that the benefit amount will be reduced by a dollar amount or by a percentage after the first person dies. For instance, a contract may state that after the first annuitant dies, the benefit amount will be reduced by 50 percent.

- A ***fixed period annuity*** provides that periodic annuity benefits will be paid for a specified length of time.

- A ***fixed amount annuity*** provides that periodic annuity benefits will be paid in a specified amount for as long as the accumulated value of the annuity lasts.

Figure 23-5 illustrates how each of these options pays contractual benefits.

In disbursing annuity proceeds, an annuity administration staff member first reads the annuity contract to determine the annuity's maturity date and the payout option selected. The staff member next calculates the amount of proceeds payable. Some of the details involved in calculating the amount of proceeds payable under a typical immediate annuity and a typical deferred annuity are shown in Figure 23-6.

Sometimes an annuity owner wishes to delay the maturity date of an annuity and to begin receiving benefits at a later time. Insurers usually notify annuity owners of the maturity date of an annuity to remind them of the date on which annuity benefits become payable.

Disbursing Death Claim Payments

If an annuitant has died during a policy's accumulation period and a beneficiary submits a claim for survivor benefits, the annuity administration staff member handles the claim in the same manner in which a claim for individual life insurance benefits is handled—in other words, the staff member requests proof that the annuitant has died and then disburses the benefits in accord with the provisions of the annuity contract. The beneficiary may choose to receive the death benefit as a lump sum payment or may elect another settlement option offered by the insurance company. Some annuity contracts may be continued in the name of a surviving spouse. In such a case, the surviving spouse receives the same benefits the annuitant would have received and for the same time period as provided in the annuity contract.

In disbursing annuity benefits, the insurer must adhere to all provisions of applicable tax codes. In general, the death benefits under an annuity contract are not qualified for tax exclusion. If the amount of the annuity death benefit, plus dividends received by the beneficiary, is in excess of the sum of the premiums paid for the annuity, the

Fast Fact

In 1995, about $165.7 billion was paid to Americans from life insurance and annuity benefits, not including life insurance from fraternal organizations or benefits paid by the federal government.

Source: American Council of Life Insurance, *Life Insurance Fact Book*, 1996: 40.

Figure 23-5. Payment of annuity benefits.

Straight Life Annuity
Pays benefits for as long as the annuitant lives.

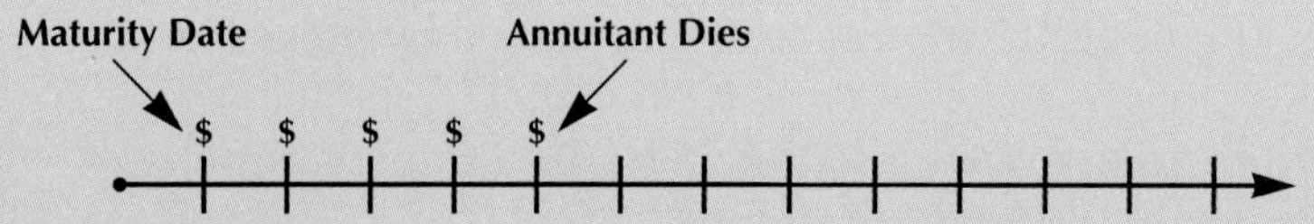

Example: An annuitant with a straight life annuity lives four years beyond the annuity's maturity date.

Life Income with Period Certain Annuity
Pays benefits for as long as the annuitant lives and guarantees that payments will be made for at least a certain period of time, even if the annuitant dies during that period.

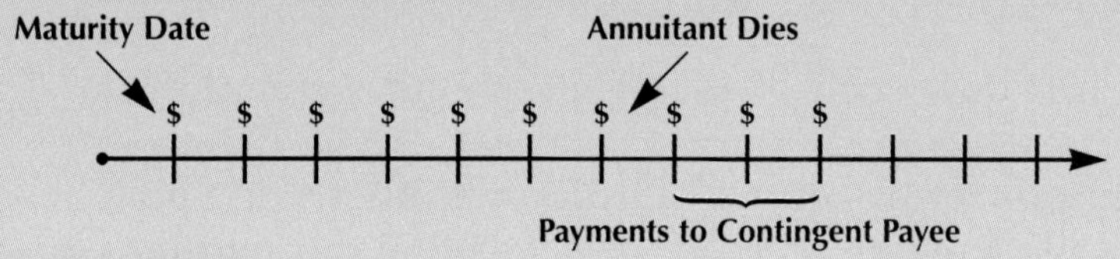

Example: An annuitant has a life income annuity with a 10-year period certain. She dies before the period certain expires.

Life Income with Refund Annuity
Pays benefits throughout the annuitant's lifetime and guarantees that at least the purchase price of the annuity will be paid in benefits.

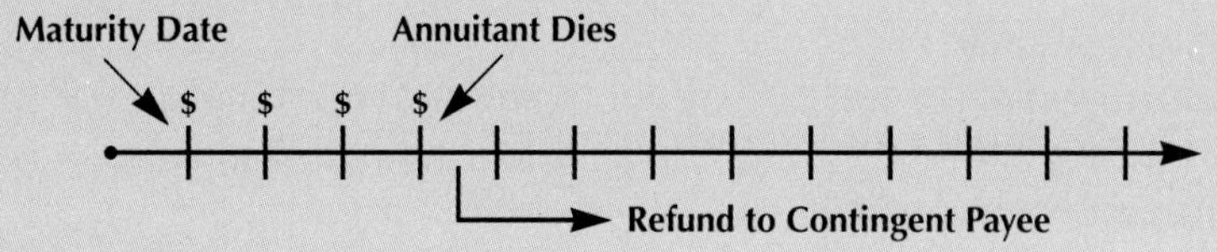

Example: An annuitant has a life income with refund annuity. He dies after the annuity's maturity date, but before recovering the purchase price of the annuity.

Joint and Survivor Annuity
Provides a series of periodic payments to two or more individuals, and those payments continue until both or all of the individuals die.

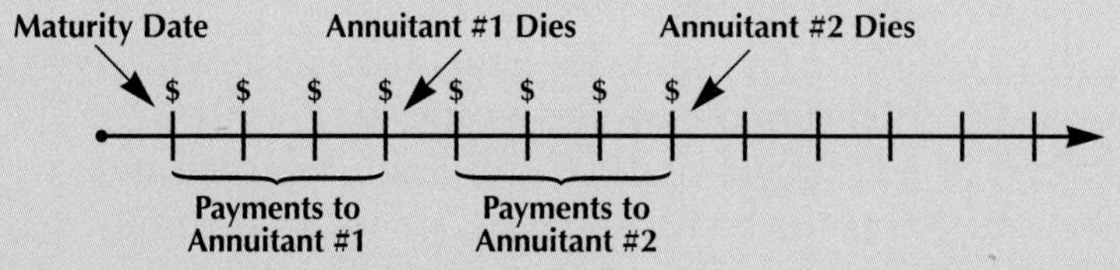

Example: Annuitant #1 and Annuitant #2 have a joint and survivor annuity. Annuity benefit payments continue until both annuitants die.

Fixed Period or Fixed Amount Annuity
Pays annuity income benefits for a specified period of time (fixed period option), or pays a preselected periodic benefit amount for as long as the annuity's accumulated value lasts (fixed amount option).

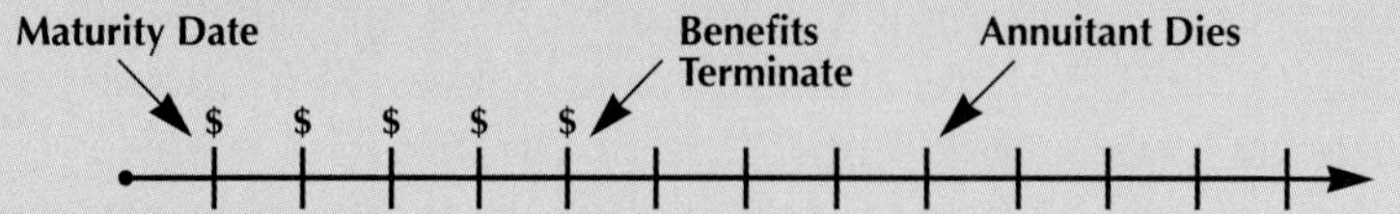

Example: An annuitant has an annuity with a fixed period option. The fixed period terminates before the annuitant dies.

Figure 23-6. Calculating the amount of proceeds payable under an immediate annuity and a deferred annuity.

For an immediate annuity, the amount of proceeds was calculated at the time the annuity was sold—that is, the insurer decided on the amount of annuity benefits it could provide for the amount of premium paid and the annuity period selected. If the annuity is a life annuity, the insurance company requires proof of the annuitant's age.

For a deferred annuity, the staff member determines the maturity date, calculates the amount of annuity benefits payable under the selected payment option, and authorizes the payment of those benefits. Calculating the amount of benefits involves consideration of the total amount of premiums paid, the interest or other earnings accumulated in the annuity account, and the number or amount of periodic payments due to the annuitant, the beneficiary, or the survivor.

excess amount must be included in the beneficiary's taxable income. An insurer usually withholds sufficient funds from the benefits to pay federal income taxes and files required tax forms with appropriate tax agencies. However, in some jurisdictions the annuity owner may choose not to have income tax withheld. If an annuity owner makes such a choice, the insurer is obligated by law to advise the annuity owner of her obligation to pay any applicable federal income taxes at the time they are due.

Key Terms and Concepts

annuity
annuitant (*payee*)
annuity owner (*contract holder*)
qualified annuity
nonqualified annuity
annuity period
maturity date (*annuity commencement date*)
immediate annuity
deferred annuity
accumulation period (*accumulation phase*)
accumulated value
life annuity
annuity certain
joint and survivor annuity
fixed benefit annuity
variable annuity
separate account
withdrawal provision
withdrawal charge
surrender provision
surrender value
surrender charge
bailout provision
waiver of surrender charge provision
ownership provision
beneficiary provision
change of ownership or beneficiary provision
entire contract provision
representation
warranty
incontestability provision
misstatement of age provision
prospectus

Key Terms and Concepts, continued

contract fee
transaction fee
percentage of premium charge (*load*)
commission chargeback
minimum distribution requirements
annuitization
payout option
straight life annuity
life income with period certain annuity
life income with refund annuity
fixed period annuity
fixed amount annuity

Glossary

1035 exchange. A transaction in which the cash surrender value of a replaced policy is used as the initial premium for a new policy; named for Section 1035a of the United States Internal Revenue Code. (7)

20 percent rule. A method of determining an allowable life insurance coverage amount; stipulates that a maximum of 20 percent of an applicant's gross earned income can be used to buy life insurance. (6)

absolute assignment. An irrevocable transfer of all the rights of a life insurance policy from one party to another. (17)

accelerated death benefit. For life insurance, a portion of a policy's benefits paid during life to a terminally ill insured who has a remaining life expectancy of less than a specified period, which usually ranges between six months and two years. (17)

accidental death benefit (ADB). A rider that provides an additional death benefit above the face amount of a policy if an insured's death occurs as the result of an accident. (7)

accounting. The process of collecting, analyzing, and reporting financial data. (1)

accumulated value. For an annuity, an amount equal to the amount of premiums paid for the annuity *plus* the interest credited to the contract *minus* the amount of (1) any withdrawals and withdrawal charges and (2) any applicable tax. (23)

accumulation period (also called the *accumulation phase*). The time between the purchase of a deferred annuity and the beginning of benefit payments. (23)

actively-at-work provision. In a group insurance plan, a provision that requires an employee to be actively at work on the date on which insurance coverage becomes effective under the plan. (9)

activities of daily living (ADLs). Actions that generally include eating, bathing, dressing, mobility (transferring from bed to chair or getting out of bed), and toileting. (8)

actuarial (function of an insurance company). The function of an insurance company that applies mathematical principles to insurance so as to predict the rates of illness, injury, disability, and death among insureds. Also calculates legal reserve liabilities and the premium rates for insurance products, and conducts research on trends in mortality and morbidity rates, policy lapses, policy loans, company expenses, and interest rates. (1)

affidavit. A written statement made before an official who is authorized to administer oaths. (22)

agent's statement. A section of an insurance application or a letter in which a marketer comments about the applicant or the proposed insured. For group insurance coverage, the agent's statement includes comments concerning the feasibility of providing the requested coverage to a proposed group. (2 and 10)

all-causes deductible. A deductible that must be satisfied only once during a specified period of time, usually one year, no matter how many illnesses or injuries result in medical expenses. (18)

alphabetic split. A method of dividing insureds for reinsurance purposes by assigning part of the alphabet to each reinsurer and then sending that reinsurer all cases whose insured's surnames begin with one of the assigned alphabet letters. (12)

Alzheimer's disease (also called *primary degenerative dementia*). A cognitive disorder that causes deterioration of a person's intellectual and cognitive functions, including memory, orientation, intellect, and judgment, and that can cause deterioration of a person's speech and motor functions. (8)

annual report. A financial document that an incorporated business issues to its stockholders and that usually includes independently audited financial statements, along with information from the organization's management team concerning the current and future business position and performance. (6)

annuitant (also called the *payee*). A person who receives the benefit payments from an annuity. (23)

annuitization. The conversion of an investment fund into a series of payments. (23)

annuity. A contract that provides for an insurer to make a series of payments at specified intervals. (23)

annuity certain. An annuity that provides periodic benefit payments for a stated length of time regardless of whether the annuitant lives or dies. (23)

annuity owner (also called the *contract holder*). The person or entity that applies for and purchases an annuity. (23)

annuity period. The length of time between each of the payments in a series of periodic annuity benefit payments. (23)

antiselection. The tendency of people who suspect or know they are more likely than average to experience loss to apply for or renew insurance to a greater extent than are people who lack such knowledge of probable loss. (2)

assignee. In an assignment, the person who receives ownership rights. (22)

assignment. The transfer of some or all of the rights to receive the proceeds of a life insurance policy from one person or entity to another person or entity. (17)

assignment of benefits. A statement on a claim form that directs an insurer to pay benefits directly to a medical provider rather than to an insured. (18)

assignor. In an assignment, the person or entity that transfers ownership rights. (22)

association captive. A captive reinsurer offering reinsurance to a group of insurers that are usually in the same line of business. (13)

attending physician's statement (APS). A report by a physician who has treated, or who is currently treating, the proposed insured. (4)

authorization to release information. A section of a claimant's statement that permits an insurer to obtain claim-specific information from medical caregivers and institutions, government agencies, other insurers, consumer reporting agencies, and numerous other sources. (17)

authorized reinsurer (also called an *admitted reinsurer*). A reinsurance marketer that is licensed or otherwise recognized by the insurance department in a jurisdiction. (13)

automatic premium loan (APL) provision. A life insurance nonforfeiture option that allows an insurer to pay overdue premiums on a policy by establishing a loan against the policy's cash value. (15)

automatic reinsurance. A reinsurance agreement in which an insurer must cede specified types of cases or a block of business to a reinsurer, and the reinsurer must accept the risk for those cases up to a predetermined maximum. (12)

bailout provision. In an annuity contract, a provision that enables an annuitant to surrender the annuity contract, usually without a surrender charge, if the interest rates paid on a fixed annuity decrease below a specified level. (23)

balance sheet. A financial document that provides a statement of a business' financial position on a certain date; includes information on the business's assets, liabilities, and net worth. (6)

beneficiary provision. In an annuity contract, a provision establishing that, if any beneficiary named in the annuity application dies before the annuitant dies, proceeds will be paid to any surviving beneficiaries upon the death of the annuitant. (23)

benefit period. In a disability income insurance policy, the length of time during which disability income benefits will be paid. (19)

benefit transmittal. In a Request for Proposal, an attachment that provides details concerning the insurance benefits being requested for each employee class, the effective date of coverage, how premium billing and claims will be administered, and other information concerning the type of plan being requested for the group. (10)

binding limit. The dollar amount of risk that a reinsurer obligates itself to accept under an automatic agreement without making its own underwriting assessment of the risk. (12)

binding premium receipt (also called a *temporary insurance agreement [TIA]*). Provides insurance coverage of a specified amount for a specified time, usually for the time required to underwrite the case. (3)

blended rating. In group insurance, an approach to setting a premium rate by assigning a credibility factor to the group's experience and including that factor in the premium calculations. (10)

block of policies (also called a *block of business*). A group of policies issued to insureds who are all the same age and the same gender, and in the same risk classification. (2)

bordereau. A report provided regularly by a ceding company to a reinsurer to transmit information about premiums and claims associated with ceded risks. (15)

broad captive. A captive reinsurer that offers reinsurance to not only its parent company, subsidiaries, and affiliates, but also other insurers. (13)

build chart. A chart used to evaluate build; based on established studies, it indicates average weights for various heights for each gender, along with the mortality debits associated with increases in weight. (4)

business financial supplement. A specialized questionnaire that requests information concerning the type of business, the current financial condition of the business, and the purpose for which insurance is being requested. (7)

business insurance. Insurance coverage intended to serve the insurance needs of a business organization rather than those of an individual. (7)

capacity. The largest amount of insurance that an insurer is allowed to underwrite. (11)

captive reinsurer. A company established for the purpose of offering reinsurance for the risks submitted from a certain source, such as an insurance company. (13)

case assignment system. In underwriting, a work-organization system that establishes a basis for giving a case to an appropriate person or group for underwriting. Most common case assignment systems distribute case files according to (1) the face amount requested, (2) the type of application or policy change, (3) the geographic origin of the application or the location of the marketer submitting the application, or (4) the last name of the applicant. (2)

case management. A cost-containment process of handling the costs of illnesses and injuries by identifying alternate methods of treatment that can make the most efficient and cost-effective use of medical resources consistent with desirable results for each patient. (16)

cash value. For an individual life insurance policy, an amount equal to the sum, before adjustment for factors such as policy loans or late premiums, that a policyowner will receive if the policyowner (1) wishes to obtain a policy loan, (2) allows the policy to lapse, or (3) cancels the coverage and surrenders the policy to the insurer. (22)

ceding. The act of transferring risk from an insurer to a reinsurer. (11)

ceding company (also called the *reinsured*). An insurance company that transfers all or part of a risk that it does not wish to retain. (11)

certificate of indebtedness. A document sent by a claim analyst to a beneficiary when policy proceeds are being left with an insurance company to earn interest; specifies a guaranteed minimum interest rate that the insurer will pay on the proceeds and the frequency with which the insurer will make interest payments to the beneficiary; also specifies whether a beneficiary is permitted to withdraw all or part of the proceeds during the payment period. (17)

certificate of insurance (also called a *certificate of coverage*). A document that an insurer issues instead of a duplicate policy when a problem arises in attempting to verify the loss of an insurance policy; verifies that insurance coverage exists, but does not contain all the details of provisions and riders that the original policy may have contained. (22)

cession. The record of the transfer of risk from a ceding company to a reinsurer. (11)

change in health statement. A statement in an individual life or health insurance application or a premium receipt requiring a proposed insured to notify the insurer in writing if the insured's health or any material information in the application changes before the policy is delivered. (17)

change of condition provision. A policy provision specifying that, in order for the policy to become effective, all facts contained in the application must be true when the policy is delivered. (16)

change of ownership or beneficiary provision. In an annuity contract, a provision stating that the contract owner may change the owner or the beneficiary of the annuity at any time during the annuitant's lifetime. (23)

churning. An unethical activity by which a marketer induces a policyowner to cash in a policy and buy another, even though replacing the policy is not in the policyowner's best interest. (7)

claim (function of an insurance company). The function of an insurance company that assesses each claim made under insurance coverage and decides whether each is justified. (1)

claim fraud. An action by which a person intentionally uses false information in an unfair or unlawful attempt to collect benefits under a policy. (20)

claim philosophy. A precise statement of an insurance company's principles for conducting claim administration. (16)

claim practices. Statements that guide the day-to-day handling of claims for an insurer. (16)

claim settlement. A lump-sum payment of money from an insurer to a claimant in exchange for the claimant's agreement to release the insurer from further responsibility for coverage under the policy. (19)

claimant's statement (also called a *claim form*). A document in which a claimant provides information concerning a deceased insured, including the date, place, and cause and circumstances of death. (17)

claims bordereau (also called *claims advice*). A type of bordereau that includes information about the claim status of each case. (15)

claims bordereau service. The action of providing a reinsurer with a report of claims submitted under reinsurance. (15)

cognitive impairment. A reduction in a person's ability to think, reason, or remember; can involve a number of mental conditions, including forgetfulness, memory loss, decreased ability to think clearly, reduced mental keenness, confusion or disorientation, and delirium or amnesia. (8)

cognitive screen. A test designed to determine a person's powers of recollection or short-term memory. (8)

coinsurance. In reinsurance, a type of proportional reinsurance plan in which an insurer and a reinsurer share the risk at a predetermined level. (12) In medical insurance coverage, the percentage of all eligible medical expenses, in excess of the deductible, which is incurred as a result of sickness or injury and which an insured is required to pay. (18)

collateral assignment. A transfer of some ownership rights from one party to another, usually for a temporary period. (17)

collusion. A secret agreement between two or more persons to perform an act in order to defraud a third person. (20)

commission chargeback. A requirement that a marketer return the first-year commission on an annuity product sold to an annuitant who dies or withdraws the funds from an annuity within the first year after issue. (23)

committee underwriting. A risk selection approach in which a committee of highly qualified persons from inside and outside the underwriting function are called together for case assessment. (2)

community-property laws. Laws providing that a spouse is entitled to receive an equal share of earned income and an equal share of property acquired by the other spouse during a marriage. (17)

compensatory damages. Money awards to pay a plaintiff for the damage he has suffered from an insurer's wrongdoing. (16)

compliance (function of an insurance company). The function of an insurance company that is responsible for ensuring that the insurer and its marketers follow all applicable state, provincial, and federal insurance requirements and regulations, as well as the requirements of organizations that regulate insurance. (1)

comprehensive general health questionnaire. A document that seeks information on an applicant's total health condition rather than focusing on a specific disorder or disease. (8)

conditional premium receipt. A type of premium receipt that makes the applied-for insurance coverage effective on the date of the application without necessitating the delivery of the policy. (3)

conditionally renewable. A type of disability income insurance policy that sets criteria which an insured must meet in order to renew the coverage. (19)

conservation. The process of ensuring that policies, once issued, are retained on an insurer's books for as long as possible. (21)

consumer report. A consumer reporting agency communication that contains information about a person's credit worthiness, credit standing, or credit capacity, as well as information about the person's general reputation or personal characteristics. (3)

consumer reporting agency. A person or an organization that regularly prepares consumer reports and furnishes them, either for profit or on a cooperative, non-profit basis, to other persons or organizations. (3)

contingent beneficiary (also called a *secondary beneficiary*). The person or entity named to receive life insurance benefits if the primary beneficiary has died before the insured. (17)

contract fee. For an annuity, a flat amount charged either at the time the annuity is issued or annually; intended to help pay for the costs of administering the annuity. (23)

contractual claim liability. In group insurance, the amount of money necessary to pay the claims incurred by a group during a specified period. (10)

contributory plan. A group insurance plan which provides that the insureds pay some part of the premium and that they may choose whether to participate in the group plan. (9)

conversion privilege. A policy provision that permits a policyowner to convert group insurance coverage to coverage under an individual insurance policy or, in certain prescribed situations, to change coverage from one type of policy to another—for instance, to change from an individual term life insurance policy to an individual whole life insurance policy. (22)

coordination of benefits (COB) provision. A provision in a group health or long-term disability insurance plan that prevents duplication of benefits—that is, payment of the same medical expenses or disability income insurance benefits by more than one insurer or by a government program. (9)

correspondent. In group insurance, a person in a policyholder's organization who serves as liaison with an insurer. (10)

corridor deductible. An amount that an insured must pay above the amount paid by his basic policy before any benefits are payable under the major medical policy. (18)

cost basis. For an insurance policy, an amount that is equal to the total net premiums paid, *plus* accumulated dividends and *minus* certain specified costs. (7)

cost containment. The reduction of unnecessary expenses of reimbursement for health and disability income insurance coverage. (16)

cost of living increase benefit. In a disability income insurance policy, a provision for an increase in the monthly disability income insurance benefit after an insured has received total disability income benefits for a specified, uninterrupted period, usually 12 consecutive months. (19)

covered person. For group insurance purposes, a person—not the primary insured—who is eligible for coverage consistent with a policy's definition of a dependent or spouse. (18)

CPT. See *Physicians' Current Procedural Terminology.*

credibility factor. In group insurance, a percentage that represents the degree to which an underwriter has estimated that the available underwriting information accurately shows the risk represented by a group. (10)

creditor insurance. Insurance designed to cover the economic loss suffered by a creditor if one of its borrowers dies before the debt is paid. (7)

credits. An applicant's medical, personal and lifestyle, and financial characteristics that have a favorable effect on mortality; these are assigned "minus" values such as –25. (4)

current open claimants. In group insurance, group members receiving short-term or long-term disability income benefits. (10)

current ratio. The result of a calculation made by dividing a company's current total assets by its current total liabilities to determine the company's liquidity. (7)

current assets. The items or entities a company presently owns or to which it has a legal claim, including buildings, inventory, investments, and other items and entities. (7)

current liabilities. For a company, usually all the debt that is due and payable within the next year. (7)

customer service. The activities, consistent with contractual provisions, that help keep customers satisfied with an insurer. (1)

death certificate. A document that attests to the death of a person and that bears the signature—and sometimes the seal—of an official authorized to issue such a certificate. (17)

debits. An applicant's medical, personal and lifestyle, and financial characteristics that have an unfavorable effect on mortality; these are assigned "plus" values such as +25. (4)

debt-to-equity ratio. The result of a calculation made by dividing a company's total debt by its net worth to determine the company's solvency. (7)

debtor-creditor group. One type of group insured under group coverage; consists of a credit-granting institution, such as a bank, and its debtors. (9)

declined class. A risk class used only for proposed insureds whose impairments and anticipated extra mortality are so great that the underwriter cannot justify issuing insurance coverage for them. (2)

deferred annuity. An annuity for which benefit payments begin more than one annuity period after the annuity is purchased. (23)

delayed word recall (DWR) test. A type of cognitive screen that examines the ability of a proposed insured to remember a number of common words. (8)

dementia. One of the most common types of cognitive impairment; a general term used for mental deterioration that is characterized by loss of certain intellectual abilities such as memory, judgment, and abstract thinking, of such a degree as to interfere with social functioning. (8)

dependent. For insurance companies, generally (1) a spouse or (2) an unmarried child, including an adopted child, stepchild, and foster child who is under age 19 or to age 25 if disabled or a full-time student, and who relies on the insured person for support and maintenance. (9)

diagnostic and treatment codes. Special codes that describe specific medical and dental diagnoses and treatments; include (1) a brief, specific description of each diagnosis or treatment and (2) a number that identifies each diagnosis or treatment. (18)

Diagnostic Related Groups (DRGs). A prospective payment method providing that a payor will pay hospital charges not according to the number and types of services delivered, but according to the diagnosis for a patient. (18)

direct response products. Insurance products sold to consumers by an insurer without the assistance of a marketer; usually sold through direct mail, advertising in print and other media, or telephone solicitation. (7)

direct-writing reinsurers. Reinsurers that market insurance through account executives. (13)

electronic data interchange (EDI). A computer-to-computer information exchange. (1)

electronic funds transfer (EFT). An automatic premium payment approach whereby a policyowner authorizes a bank to withdraw funds from an account to pay each renewal premium. (21)

employee census. In a Request for Proposal, a document that lists demographic information about both a proposed group and individual persons within the proposed group. (10)

employee class. A group of employees categorized by earnings, rank, or position. (10)

employer-employee group. For group insurance purposes, a type of group that consists of an employer that is the policyholder, and its employees who are the insureds. (9)

enrollment card (also called an *employee application*). In group insurance, a document that provides the following information about each employee: name and address; date of birth; gender; Social Security number in the United States or social insurance number in Canada; name and relationship of beneficiary or beneficiaries; and types of supplemental coverage selected by the employee. (10)

entire contract provision. In an annuity contract, a provision establishing that the contract and the application for the contract form the entire contract. (23)

estate settlement. The process of paying a person's debts after death. (6)

excess-of-loss reinsurance. A type of nonproportional reinsurance providing that a reinsurer will pay the amount of a claim above a predetermined limit. (12)

excess share approach (also called the *surplus share approach* or *level retention*). One way of determining the amount of insurance coverage to cede through proportional reinsurance; provides that an insurer will cede specified amounts of coverage which exceed the limits of its retention limit. (12)

exchange contract. In an arrangement of reciprocity, a contract that specifies the details of the arrangement and that is drafted and signed by the two parties. (13)

exclusion rider. A rider that limits a policy's benefits by excluding from coverage certain specified types of risk, such as death resulting from an aviation accident or disability income coverage payments for a specified, usually preexisting impairment. (2)

exculpatory statutes. Laws that are passed by community-property states and that permit an insurer, without fear of double liability, to pay life insurance proceeds according to the terms of a policy. (17)

expected claim experience. The dollar amount of claims that an insurer estimates a group will submit. (10)

experience (of an insurer). The inferences drawn from the cumulative events of a certain type (for example, claims) which, taken together, express historical trends with respect to an insurance product. (2)

experience rating. In group insurance, the process of using a group's claim experience to calculate premium rates. (10)

experience refund (also called a *dividend* or a *premium refund*). In group insurance, the portion of a group insurance premium that is returned to a group policyholder whose claim experience is better than had been expected when the premium was calculated. (10)

expert system. A computer application that manipulates information based on established facts and an insurer's experience data to suggest solutions to problems. (1)

explanation of benefits (EOB). A detailed statement showing each treatment or medication submitted as part of a claim, an insurer's decision concerning payment of each charge, any amount that is considered as a deductible or a copayment, an explanation of any charge for which part or all of the charge will not be paid, and the total amount sent to a medical provider. (18)

exploding. A fraudulent claim procedure by which a medical caregiver increases the cost of a procedure by including a number of other procedures not deemed medically necessary. (20)

extended-time reinsurance. A type of nonproportional reinsurance that typically covers disability income insurance claims; generally provides that benefits are paid at the end of a specified period during which a covered disability has continued. (12)

extra-contractual damages. Money awards that exceed the amount of policy benefits and that may be compensatory or punitive. (16)

extraordinary right of termination. In a reinsurance agreement, a treaty provision that allows one of the parties to withdraw from the agreement because the party has undergone an extraordinary business circumstance such as liquidation, merger, bankruptcy, or catastrophic loss of more than half of its capital. (14)

extra-percentage table. A table rating chart showing a group's extra mortality expressed as a percentage of standard mortality. (4)

face-to-face assessment. An evaluation that involves a meeting between a proposed insured and an interviewer who represents an insurance company and who is usually employed by a vendor. (8)

factor table. A table that shows the maximum amount of insurance, expressed in multiples of a person's salary or total income, that an insurer will typically approve without question in each of several age ranges. (6)

facultative automatic reinsurance (formerly called *facultative obligatory reinsurance*). A reinsurance agreement by which a ceding company may choose to submit cases to a reinsurer, and a reinsurer must accept the cases as long as the reinsurer has sufficient capacity to do so. (12)

facultative reinsurance. A reinsurance agreement in which a ceding company may choose whether to submit a case or a block of cases to a reinsurer, and the reinsurer may choose whether to accept each case or block of business. (12)

Fair Credit Reporting Act (FCRA). Enacted in 1970, legislation that helps ensure that credit reporting agencies, when preparing reports on individuals, act fairly, impartially, and with respect for the consumer's right to privacy. (3)

family benefit. A rider that insures the lives of an insured's spouse and children. (7)

family income. Funds needed to replace the ordinary living expenses formerly paid by the income of a deceased person whose wages or other income supplied the needs of a family. (6)

FCRA. See *Fair Credit Reporting Act.*

field underwriting. The process of gathering initial information about a proposed insured and screening persons for whom a specific type of insurance coverage may be appropriate. (2)

field underwriting manual. A document developed by an insurance company for marketers to use when making initial assessments of proposed insureds; presents (1) information on the insurer's underwriting philosophy, (2) specific guidance on completing applications and on submitting changes and reinstatements, (3) brief, simple definitions of common medical terms, (4) information on specific medical impairments, and (5) other company-specific considerations, such as risk factors and age and amount limitations for specific insurance products. (4)

financial status. A person's current income expressed in terms of amount, sources, and permanency, and by the person's net worth. (6)

first-to-die policy. A type of joint-and-last-survivor policy which provides that proceeds will be paid when the first of two or more insured persons dies. (7)

fixed amount annuity. An annuity which provides that periodic annuity benefits will be paid in a specified amount for as long as the accumulated value of the annuity lasts. (23)

fixed benefit annuity. A type of annuity under which an insurer guarantees at least a specified amount of periodic benefits for each dollar applied toward the purchase of the annuity. (23)

fixed period annuity. An annuity which provides that periodic annuity benefits will be paid for a specified length of time. (23)

flat extra premium method. A method of assessing the medical risk represented by a proposed insured; used mainly in cases involving extra mortality that is considered to be either constant or decreasing with age. (4)

flat rating. A rating method that is generally used for impairments which present an accident hazard but no additional health hazard and for which the extra risk does not increase with age. (8)

fronting. A procedure by which an insurer that is licensed in a state or province issues a policy on a risk for and at the request of one or more other insurers with the intent of ceding the entire risk to the other insurer or reinsurers. (11)

future increase option. In a disability income insurance policy, an option that allows an insured to buy additional disability income insurance without providing evidence of insurability. (19)

geriatrics. The branch of medicine dealing with the diseases and conditions of aging. (8)

grace period. A specified period after a renewal premium is due and unpaid during which a policy, including all riders, remains in force. (16)

grossup file. In bordereau sampling, an information file in which mathematical totals for a sample of cases are multiplied by a factor that produces a probable total figure for a whole group, not just for the sample. (15)

guaranteed insurability (GI). A rider that gives a policyowner the right to buy additional insurance up to a specified amount at a specified premium rate and at specified times without providing new evidence of insurability. (7)

guaranteed-issue products. Insurance products designed so that each applicant who meets certain conditions established by the insurer is automatically issued a policy. (7)

guaranteed purchase option (also called a *guaranteed insurability option*). A rider or policy provision giving a policyowner the right to buy additional insurance of the same type as that provided in the original policy. (12)

guaranteed renewable. One type of renewability for disability income insurance; offers the same continued coverage as noncancelable coverage *except* that the insurer may increase the premiums, not for an individual insured, but for all the policyowners within a defined class of insureds. (19)

history checkup. A medical checkup that was very likely prompted by a symptom or health problem. (4)

history statement. An APS concerning a specific health condition that has been admitted by a proposed insured. (4)

hospice. A facility that helps ease the physical and psychological suffering of a person with a terminal illness. (18)

human resources (function of an insurance company). The function of an insurance company that monitors the availability of qualified workers; recruits and screens applicants; helps select qualified employees; plans and presents appropriate orientation, training, and development for each employee; administers employee benefit programs; and performs other such activities.

ICD. See *International Classification of Diseases and Related Health Problems.*

illustration of net cost. For a proposal of insurance for group coverage, an explanation of rates that typically covers two or more years and shows possible future rating and premiums, provided the group's claim experience remains within the parameters assumed for the insurance product. (10)

immediate annuity. An annuity for which benefit payments begin between one annuity period and one year after the annuity is purchased. (23)

impairment. Any aspect of a person's health, family history, occupation, activities, or lifestyle that could increase that person's expected mortality or morbidity risk. (2)

impairment guide. A list of common impairments and the probable underwriting decision for each. (8)

impairment rider (also called an *impairment waiver* or an *exclusion rider*). An attachment to a policy to exclude from coverage (1) a loss arising from a specified disease or physical impairment or (2) a specific body part. (8)

income replacement table. A table that presents the limits on the amount of disability income insurance—usually expressed as an amount of monthly benefit—an insurer will issue based on an applicant's earned income. (8)

income statement (also called a *profit and loss statement*). A financial document that provides information on the net results of a business's operations during a certain interval such as three months or one year; the document attempts to match the revenues or income for the specified period with the expenses or costs of doing business during that period. (6)

incontestability provision. In an annuity contract, a provision stating that the contract is not contestable after it has been in force during the lifetime of the annuitant for two years from the contract date. (23)

individual cession administration (also called *traditional cession administration*). A system of reinsurance administration under which a ceding company sends a separate notification to a reinsurer for each cession, and the reinsurer prepares its own records of cession. (15)

industrial insurance. A form of insurance that is marketed under the home service system and that relies on marketers to sell specified products and to provide premium collection and other policyowner service functions within a defined geographic territory. (7)

information systems (function of an insurance company). The function of an insurance company that facilitates data processing and enables the resulting information to be made available to employees who need it. (1)

initial deductible. In comprehensive medical plans, the amount an insured must pay before any medical expenses are paid by an insurer. (18)

injury. In a disability income insurance policy, an accidental harm resulting from an unforeseen external force (1) causing trauma to a person's body and (2) occurring while the disability income insurance policy is in force; normally defined as a condition resulting independently of sickness. (19)

inspection report. A type of investigative consumer report developed by a consumer reporting agency concerning a proposed insured's personal life, activities, occupation, and economic standing. (5)

installment certificate. A document that is sent by a claim analyst to a beneficiary when policy proceeds are to be paid in installments during a fixed or lifetime period or for fixed amounts; specifies the amount of each benefit payment and/or the period during which benefit payments will be made; also specifies whether a beneficiary is permitted to withdraw all or part of the proceeds during the payment period. (17)

instrumental activities of daily living (IADLs). Actions that generally include doing one's own finances, taking care of cooking and laundry, and shopping for food and clothing. (8)

insurability provision. A policy provision specifying that, in order for the policy to become effective, the proposed insured must still be insurable by that insurer when the policy is delivered. (16)

insurable interest. The condition in which a person or an entity would suffer a genuine loss if an insured-against event occurs. (5)

insurance administration. The activities associated with assessing risk and issuing policies, obtaining reinsurance, handling claims, providing policyowner service, and administering annuities. (1)

integrated image processing. A computer-based approach to capture, index, store, retrieve, and distribute documents in electronic form. (1)

interim insurance law. Legislation which generally holds that, if a marketer has accepted payment of an insurance premium, the applicant is covered until the insurer notifies the applicant that insurance coverage has been terminated and returns the premium. (3)

International Classification of Diseases and Related Health Problems (ICD). One of the most commonly used codes for medical diagnoses. (18)

interpleader. A claim settlement method by which an insurer pays policy proceeds to a court, advises the court that the insurer cannot determine the correct party to whom the proceeds should be distributed, and asks the court to decide the proper recipient or recipients. (17)

investigative consumer report. A type of consumer report that includes information gathered during interviews with persons such as friends, neighbors, business associates, and others who are associated with or who have knowledge of a consumer. (3)

irrevocable beneficiary. A beneficiary whose right to policy proceeds cannot be cancelled by a policyowner unless that beneficiary consents to the cancellation. (17)

jet unit. A risk selection approach that establishes a group of two to four employees to screen applications which meet specific criteria and to approve certain types of applications for immediate policy issue. (2)

joint-and-last-survivor policy. A life insurance contract that is written on more than one life. (7)

joint and survivor annuity. A type of annuity which provides benefit payments that continue until both or all of the individuals die. (23)

jumbo limit. A maximum amount, established in most automatic reinsurance agreements, which the total insurance already in force and/or applied for with all insurers on any individual must not exceed in order for a ceded risk to be accepted automatically by a reinsurer. (12)

juvenile insurance policy. A life insurance policy purchased by an adult to cover the life of a child. (7)

key person. An owner or employee of a company whose absence would cause a serious loss to the business. (7)

key-person insurance. Insurance coverage that protects a business from losses that would occur when a key person dies. (7)

layering. A method of dividing automatic reinsurance coverage among several reinsurers by allowing one reinsurer to cover all cases in excess of an insurer's retention limit up to a specified amount. (12)

lead reinsurer. In a reinsurance pool, a company that assumes responsibility for underwriting, communicating with, and handling claims for all insurers in the pool. (13)

legal (function of an insurance company). The function of an insurance company that helps an insurer follow the laws and regulations affecting the insurer's relationships with customers, prospective customers, employees, marketers, other insurers, vendors, and government agencies. (1)

life annuity. A type of annuity that provides periodic benefit payments which last as long as the lifetime of the annuitant. (23)

life income with period certain annuity. A type of annuity that provides periodic benefit payments throughout the annuitant's lifetime *and* during at least a specified period regardless of whether the annuitant is living. (23)

life income with refund annuity. A type of annuity that provides benefits during the lifetime of the annuitant *and* guarantees that benefits will continue until the insurer has disbursed at least an amount equal to the purchase price of the annuity. (23)

lifetime maximum benefit. For a health insurance policy, the maximum amount that the policy will pay for all eligible medical expenses an individual incurs while insured under the policy. (18)

liquidity. The ease with which a company can convert its assets into cash for an approximation of their true value. (7)

Lloyd's of London. An organization that functions as a clearinghouse for insurance coverage and is not itself an insurer or a reinsurer; composed of a number of syndicates, each formed by a group of between 30 and 700 persons who qualify to market insurance coverage by virtue of their considerable financial strength. (13)

LTC field underwriting manual. A guidebook that provides general underwriting criteria for a number of medical conditions. (8)

managed care. The name given to a broad spectrum of techniques that integrate payment for and delivery of health care and that seek to manage the cost, accessibility, and quality of that care. (16)

manual rating. In group insurance, a process of establishing premium rates for broad classes of groups, especially for those with no credible claim experience. (9)

marketer. Any person or entity that sells insurance. (1)

marketing. The function of an insurance company that identifies its customers, defines and develops the products that customers want, conducts sales activities, and distributes products to customers. (1)

master application. In group insurance, a document that contains the specific provisions of the plan of insurance being applied for and that is signed by an authorized officer of the proposed policyholder. (10)

master contract. In group insurance, a legal document certifying the relationship between an insurer and a group policyholder. (10)

material misrepresentation. A misstatement that is relevant to an insurer's acceptance of a risk. (3)

maturity date (also called the *annuity commencement date*). For an annuity, the date on which an insurance company begins paying benefit payments. (23)

maximum limit. A retrospective approach to calculating policy benefits that involves payment of a specified amount of total benefits for claims arising from a single injury or incident, or one period of sickness. (18)

Medical Information Bureau (MIB). A non-profit organization established to provide coded information to insurers concerning impairments that applicants have admitted to or that other insurance companies have detected in connection with previous applications for insurance. (4)

medical necessity. A criterion that is determined by a claim analyst for medical treatments; provides that the prescribed medical procedure is one that (1) is considered effective and that is normally used for the specified illness or injury and (2) does not exceed in scope, duration, or intensity the level of care needed to provide safe, adequate, and appropriate diagnosis or treatment. (18)

medical report. A document designed to be completed by both the proposed insured and a physician; the most extensive of the three types of Part II applications. (4)

minimum distribution requirements. Federal requirements establishing the least amount that must be withdrawn each year from a qualified annuity account. (23)

misrepresentation. The presence of false or misleading statements on an application for insurance. (3)

misstatement of age provision. In an annuity contract, a provision stating that, if the age of an annuitant has been misstated, the amount payable under the annuity contract will be the amount that the premiums would have purchased for the correct age. (23)

modified coinsurance. A proportional plan of reinsurance under which the basic provisions of coinsurance are modified by having the ceding company maintain the entire policy reserve. (12)

moral hazard. A characteristic that may exist when the reputation, financial position, or mental state of an applicant or a proposed insured indicates that the person might cause a loss intentionally or might fail to limit a loss after it occurred. (5)

morbidity. The relative incidence of sickness and injury occurring among a given group of people. (2)

mortality. The relative incidence of death occurring among a given group of people. (2)

motor vehicle record (MVR). A document that typically contains information about a person's driving history, including information about traffic violations and arrests and convictions for driving-related incidents. (5)

multiple-employer group. For group coverage, a group composed of two or more employers in the same industry who are allowed by law to establish a trust. (9)

NAIC Model Privacy Act. Legislation patterned on the NAIC Model Privacy Act to establish standards for the collection, use, and disclosure of information gathered in connection with insurance transactions by insurance institutions, marketers, and insurance-support organizations. (3)

net amount at risk. For a life insurance policy, an amount equal to the policy's face value, or death benefit, minus the policy's cash value, or reserve, and any policy loans at the end of a policy year. (12)

net income. A financial total expressed very generally as the money remaining from a company's sales after deductions have been made for sales costs, operating expenses, and taxes. (7)

net premium rate. In manual rating, the premium amount required to pay the cost of a group's anticipated claims. (10)

net worth. The difference between a person's assets and liabilities. (6)

new business. The general term used to describe all the activities required to market insurance, submit applications for insurance, evaluate the risks associated with those applications, and issue and deliver insurance policies. (1)

noncancelable. For disability income coverage, one type of renewability providing that, until an insured reaches a specified age (usually age 65), an insurer will not cancel the coverage, increase the premiums, or change the policy provisions as long as the premiums are paid. (19)

noncontributory plan. In group insurance, a plan providing that the insureds pay no part of the premium for their coverage. (9)

nonmedical basis. A way of applying for insurance without being required to undergo a medical examination. (2)

nonmedical limits. The total amounts of insurance that will be issued to an applicant at one time without requiring a medical examination. (4)

nonmedical supplement. A type of Part II application which contains health history questions that a marketer asks of a proposed insured. (4)

nonproportional reinsurance. Reinsurance which provides that the amount or proportion of the risk carried by an insurer and by a reinsurer is not known when the reinsurance agreement is made. (12)

nonqualified annuity. An annuity funded with money that has already been taxed by the federal government. (23)

numerical rating system. A method of assigning numbers to individual proposed insureds according to the degree of risk they present to the insurer and then using the numbers to determine the appropriate risk class for each proposed insured. (4)

occupational rating classes. Groups of occupations established according to the relative degree of risk they present for disability income insurance. (8)

offset. A federal tax law requirement that allows an insurer to use the benefits paid under one type of insurance coverage to reduce the benefits paid under another type of coverage. (19)

optionally renewable. For disability income coverage, one type of renewability that enables an insurer to change premium rates at any time and to cancel the coverage with sufficient notice to an insured. (19)

orphan policyowner. A policyowner whose original marketer is no longer available to provide service. (21)

overinsurance. An amount of applied-for insurance that is excessive in relation to the loss that is insured against. (4)

overinsurance provision. In some individual health insurance policies, a provision that, under certain circumstances, policy benefits will be reduced if an insured has more insurance than needed to cover medical or dental expenses. (18)

ownership provision. In an annuity contract, a provision that establishes the owner of an annuity as the person so named in the application. (23)

paramedical report. One type of Part II application; contains (1) the proposed insured's answers to the same medical history questions that are included in the nonmedical supplement and the medical report and (2) the results of a physical examination of the proposed insured conducted by a paramedical examiner. (4)

Part I (of a life insurance application). A section that identifies the proposed insured (and the policyowner, if different from the proposed insured), specifies the amount and type of insurance coverage requested, and provides basic insurability information. (4)

Part II (of a life insurance application). A section that consists of medical information regarding the proposed insured; may take one of three forms: (1) a nonmedical supplement, (2) a medical report, or (3) a paramedical report. (4)

partial disability. A condition that involves inability, resulting from sickness or injury, to perform one or more of the main duties of an insured's former occupation or to perform the duties on a full-time basis. (19)

partnership insurance. A type of business insurance which provides cash that surviving partners can use to purchase the interest of a deceased partner from that partner's heirs. (7)

payout option. For an annuity, the method by which the annuity proceeds will be disbursed. (23)

per-cause deductible. A deductible that must be satisfied for each separate illness or injury that results in medical expenses. (18)

percentage of income rule. A guideline for the amount of money an applicant can afford to spend on insurance according to the applicant's income. (6)

percentage of premium charge (also called a *load*). An amount that is deducted by an insurer from each annuity premium paid. (23)

permanent flat extra premium. A premium amount that is usually charged for cases in which a nonmedical risk is expected to remain constant throughout the life of the policy. (4)

persistency. An underwriting factor that refers to how well a policy or group of policies remains, or persists, in force. (5)

persistency bonus. An amount paid by an insurer to a marketer to represent an increase in the marketer's commission when a policy continues in force beyond an initial period, usually five years. (21)

personal computer. A type of relatively small computer designed for use by an individual. (1)

personal history interview. A fact-finding interview that is usually conducted as a telephone conversation between an underwriter and a proposed insured or a medical caregiver of the proposed insured. (8)

personal information. Any information that can be connected to a specific person and that includes information about the person's habits, character, occupation or avocations, financial situation, credit history, health, and any other topic. (3)

personal insurance. Insurance purchased by individuals for the ultimate benefit of persons who have a direct financial interest in the life of the proposed insured. (6)

personal interview report. A document that contains the same type of information as an inspection report, but uses *only* the proposed insured as a source. (5)

Physicians' Current Procedural Terminology (CPT). One of the most commonly used codes for medical treatments. (18)

physiological age. The relative age or youthfulness of a person's vital organs and their functioning. (8)

policy dividend. A payment made by an insurer to a policyowner as a refund of excess premium paid to the owner of an individual participating life insurance policy or the portion of a group insurance premium that is returned to a group policyholder whose claim experience is better than had been expected when the premium was calculated. (22)

policy exhibit. An overall description of a block of reinsured business during a specified period of time, usually a month or a quarter. (15)

policy grace notice (also called a *lapse notice*). A written notification that a policy's grace period is about to expire. (22)

policy issue. The function of an insurance company that prepares the insurance contract, modifies the applied-for coverage according to instructions from the underwriter, and facilitates the delivery of the policy to the customer. (1)

policy lapse. A termination of insurance coverage that occurs as a result of nonpayment of premium. (5)

policy surrender. A type of policy cancellation that occurs when a policyowner sends a policy to an insurer and requests that (1) the insurance coverage be terminated and (2) the cash value of the policy be sent to the policyowner. (11)

policyowner service. A type of customer service that includes all the service activities performed for marketers and for the persons or parties who own or hold insurance policies and annuities. (1)

pooling (also known as *quota share*). In reinsurance, a method of dividing automatic reinsured cases among a group of reinsurers and arranging for each reinsurer to receive a specified percentage of the insured cases. (12) In group insurance, the practice of considering several small groups as one large group for risk assessment purposes. (9)

post-notice. One type of notice, required by the FCRA, that must be sent to an applicant if an insurer makes an adverse decision based wholly or partially on information contained in a report from a consumer reporting agency. (3)

power of attorney. A written statement that authorizes one person to act on behalf of another person. (22)

preadmission certification (also called *precertification*). A statement from an insurer approving non-emergency, inpatient hospital treatment. (18)

preexisting condition. A condition for which an individual received medical care during a specified period of time prior to the effective date of the proposed coverage. In group insurance, a condition for which an insured received medical care during a specified period, usually 3 to 6 months, prior to the effective date of coverage. (8, 18, 19)

preexisting conditions clause. For individual health insurance policies, a clause which states that, until coverage has been in force for a specified time—typically two years—no benefit is payable if the impairment producing the claim (1) existed prior to the issue date and (2) was not disclosed on the application. (8)

preferred beneficiary. According to Canadian law, a spouse, child, parent, or grandchild named in any life insurance policy issued before July 1, 1962; when a preferred beneficiary was named, the policyowner thereafter could not change the beneficiary to anyone outside this group of family members and could not obtain a policy loan or surrender nor assign the policy benefits without the written consent of the preferred beneficiary. (17)

preferred class. A risk class generally used to designate proposed insureds whose anticipated mortality is significantly lower than average and who represent the least degree of risk. (2)

premium bordereau (also called *premium advice*). A type of bordereau that includes detailed information, including the premium, of each case. (15)

premium bordereau service. The action of providing a reinsurer with a list of total reinsurance premiums and other information. (15)

premium-paying customers (of an insurance company). Persons and entities that include an insurance company's insureds, policyowners and policyholders, and annuitants and annuity owners. (1)

premium rate. In group insurance, a unit price that will be charged for a specified amount of coverage. (10)

premium receipt. A written acknowledgment that an insurer has received the initial premium submitted with an application for insurance. (3)

pre-notice. One type of notice, required by the FCRA, requires insurers to disclose clearly and adequately to an applicant that an investigative consumer report may be made. (3)

presumptive death certificate. A court-issued document stating that a person is presumed to be dead. (17)

presumptive total disability. A usually severe medical condition, such as total and permanent blindness, loss of speech or hearing in both ears, or loss of two limbs, that automatically causes an insured to be considered totally disabled. (19)

pricing factor. A number illustrating the risk represented by persons working in a specified industry. (9)

Privacy Act of 1974. One Congressional act that has encouraged insurers to treat personal information carefully; protects the employees of federal agencies by establishing requirements for the collection, retention, use, and distribution of personal data. (3)

probationary period. In group insurance, the length of time that must pass before a new member is eligible to join the group plan. (10)

professional association. For group coverage, a group composed of persons who have the same type of occupation or who share a common interest. (9)

profitability. A measure of the productivity of a company's assets and its return on investment. (7)

proportional reinsurance. Reinsurance in which the parties agree to share premiums and claims according to a specified amount or a specified percentage. (12)

proposal for insurance. A document that provides a number of specifications for the insurance coverage approved by an insurer for a proposed group. (10)

prospect. In group underwriting, the organization that will become the policyholder for a proposed group. (9)

prospectus. A document that describes the main features, typical investment vehicles, and administration procedures of an investment product. (23)

proximate cause (of a death). The event that directly caused a death, or the event that led to an unbroken chain of events resulting in death. (17)

public curator. A person authorized to handle the affairs of missing persons, among others. (17)

punitive damages. Money awards intended to make an example of a defendant and to punish a defendant who has acted in a malicious, fraudulent, or oppressive manner toward a plaintiff. (16)

pure captive. A captive reinsurer that offers reinsurance to a parent company and its subsidiaries or affiliates. (13)

qualification period. In a disability income insurance plan, the length of time—usually between 30 and 90 days—that an insured must be totally disabled before he or she becomes eligible for residual disability income insurance benefits. (19)

qualified annuity. An annuity that is purchased to fund or distribute funds from a tax-qualified plan and that is purchased with pretax dollars; this type of annuity is exempt from current income on both the purchase amount and the earnings on that amount during the accumulation period. (23)

quick ratio (also called an *acid-test ratio*). The result of a calculation made by dividing a company's current assets (cash, liquid and short-term investments, and accounts receivable, but not including inventories) by the company's current liabilities; used to determine a company's ability to liquidate debt immediately. (7)

quota share approach (also called a *pro rata approach*). One way of determining the amount of insurance coverage to cede through proportional reinsurance; provides that the reinsurer will accept the risk for a specified percentage of every risk of a certain type. (12)

rate transmittal. In a Request for Proposal, an attachment that specifies the marketer's proposed rates for each type of insurance coverage for each class of employees. (10)

rated policy. A policy issued to a person considered to have a greater-than-average risk of loss. (8)

rating (an application). Approval of a higher-than-average risk by charging a higher-than-usual premium rate for the insurance applied for, by reducing the amount of coverage to be provided, or by doing both. (2)

rating schedule. A table that enables an underwriter to convert the total of rating debits to a rating percentage. (8)

reasonable and customary limits. A specification that the amount paid for a claim must conform to the amount most frequently charged for each medical procedure in a given geographical area. (18)

recapture. A procedure in which an insurer takes back from a reinsurer a portion of the reinsured business. (11)

reciprocity. An arrangement by which two insurers or reinsurers exchange business in return for cessions or retrocessions. (13)

recurring disability. A disability that is the result of the same cause as for an original disability and that reappears after (1) the original period of disability and (2) an intervening period of recovery. (19)

reformation. An equitable remedy under which an insurer revises or reinterprets a contract to express the original intent of the parties to the contract. (20)

rehabilitation. The process of helping a disabled person to return to work, either at his own occupation or at another occupation if he is unable to perform the duties of his own occupation. (19)

rehabilitation benefit. During any period when an insured is receiving total or partial disability income benefits, a benefit by which an insurer reimburses an insured for the expenses associated with participation in a rehabilitation program. (19)

reinstatement. The process by which an insurer puts back in force a policy that lapsed because of nonpayment of renewal premiums. (14)

reinstatement provision. A provision that describes the conditions a policyowner must meet in order for an insurer to reinstate a policy within a specified time after lapse. (22)

reinsurance. A form of insurance that enables an insurer to be indemnified, or paid, for covered losses claimed under insurance policies it has issued. (1)

reinsurance audit. A formal examination of an insurer's reinsurance records in order to evaluate whether those records contain accurate details. (15)

reinsurance corridor (also called a *minimum cession*). In reinsurance, an amount retained by a ceding company above its scheduled retention limit. (11)

reinsurance expense allowance. Under coinsurance, a specified share of the commission, taxes, and expenses the ceding company pays the reinsurer. (12)

reinsurance intermediary (also called a *reinsurance broker*). A person or entity that markets reinsurance from several reinsurers directly to ceding companies. (13)

reinsurance pool. A group of insurers that join together to offer reinsurance coverage and to smooth the claim fluctuations in the experience of each pool member. (13)

reinsurance treaty. A statement of the agreement between a reinsurer and a ceding company. (11)

reinsurer (also called the *assuming company*). An insurance company that assumes the risk from a ceding company. (11)

renewal underwriting. In group insurance, an underwriting review of all the selection factors considered when a group was originally underwritten and all changes in the group and its coverage between the previous time of underwriting and the current time. (10)

replacement. The act of surrendering an insurance policy or part of the coverage of an insurance policy in order to buy another policy. (3)

representation. A statement of facts upon which an insurer bases its decision to issue a product, such as an annuity. (23)

Request for Proposal (RFP). A document that provides detailed information about requested insurance coverage and that requests a bid from an insurer for providing the coverage. (10)

rescission. A legal action by which an insurer seeks to void a policy or have it declared void. (3)

residual disability. A disability that occurs when an insured is not totally disabled, but is still unable to function as before a sickness or an injury, and therefore suffers a reduction in income equal to a percentage—typically 20% to 25%—specified in the disability income insurance plan. (19)

retention limit. The amount of insurance that an insurer will carry at its own risk. (11)

retrocession. The act of transferring the risk from a reinsurer to a retrocessionaire. (11)

retrocession agreement. A reinsurance treaty between two insurers involved in transferring risk from one to the other. (14)

retrocessionaire. A reinsurer that accepts a retrocedent's risk. (11)

return on equity. A measure of the profitability of a company that has issued stock; determined by dividing the company's net income by the stockholders' equity in the company. (7)

revocable beneficiary. A beneficiary whose right to policy proceeds can be cancelled or reduced by the policyowner at any time before the insured's death. (17)

risk assessment. The process of ascertaining the degree of risk represented by each proposed insured person or group according to a range of criteria established when the insurance product was designed and priced. (2)

risk charge. An amount that represents a contribution to an insurer's reserves to pay for extremely large claims. (10)

risk class. A group of insureds who represent a similar level of risk to an insurance company. (2)

routine checkup. A medical checkup that was not motivated by a symptom or health problem. (4)

schedule of benefits. Under a group insurance plan, a table that specifies the amount of coverage provided for each class of insureds. (10) For claim purposes, a listing of medical treatments and the maximum benefit amounts an insurer will pay for each treatment. (18)

second-to-die policy (also called a *survivorship policy*). A type of joint-and-last-survivor policy which provides that payment of proceeds will occur when the second of two or more insured persons dies. (7)

self-administration (also called *bulk administration*). A system of reinsurance administration under which the ceding company prepares most of the records for cessions and uses written or electronic lists, called *bordereaux,* to notify the reinsurer of cessions. (15)

separate account. An investment account that is totally separated from an insurance company's other, general investment accounts. (23)

service requirement. In group insurance, a stipulation that a person must be employed for a certain length of time—usually 3 to 6 months—before being covered under a group insurance plan. (9)

setoff. A reduction of the amount of debt a reinsurer owes to an insolvent insurer by an equal amount owed to the reinsurer by the insurer. (11)

shopping. The process of offering a case to several reinsurers and inviting them to bid in order to provide the reinsurance coverage. (12)

sickness. In a disability income insurance policy, an illness or a disease that (1) includes pregnancy unless it is specifically excluded under the contract and (2) begins while a person is insured under the policy. (19)

sole proprietorship insurance. A type of business insurance which provides coverage so that when the owner of a sole proprietorship dies, the insurance pays for the buyout of the business from the owner's heirs by the person or persons designated to become the new owner or owners. (7)

solvency. A company's ability to pay its debts on time. (7)

specialized medical questionnaire. A questionnaire designed to gather information on certain potentially serious impairments. (4)

split-dollar plan. A type of business insurance that covers the life of an employee and that is paid for jointly by the employee and the employer. (7)

spread-loss reinsurance. A type of nonproportional reinsurance that provides for benefits covering a specified percentage of a specified kind of claim incurred by the ceding company during a specified period. (12)

standard class. A risk class that includes persons whose anticipated mortality is regarded as higher than the mortality predicted for persons in the preferred class, but lower than the mortality predicted for persons in the substandard class. (2)

statement of cash flows. A financial document that indicates the amounts of actual cash received or paid in the day-to-day operations of a business. (6)

statement of changes in financial position (also called a *sources and uses of funds statement*). A financial document that provides information on the resources that a business used during a certain period and the ways in which those resources were used. (6)

step rates. Rates based on an insurer's experience and expressed in age-graded, sometimes gender-specific tables. (10)

stock repurchase insurance (also called *stock redemption insurance*). A variation of partnership insurance that provides the remaining stockholders of a company with money to purchase the stock of a deceased partner. (7)

stockholders' equity. The net worth of a firm determined by subtracting its total liabilities from its total assets. (7)

stop-loss reinsurance. A type of nonproportional reinsurance providing that a reinsurer will pay claims that exceed (1) a specified percentage of the loss incurred during a specified period and/or (2) a maximum dollar amount. (12)

straight life annuity. A type of annuity that provides periodic benefit payments for the lifetime of the annuitant. (23)

subrogation. A contractual right that permits an insurer to recover payments made to an insured for medical care if that insured receives payment for damages through a legal action. (18)

substandard class (also called *special risk*). A risk class that usually includes persons whose anticipated mortality is significantly worse than average. (2)

summary of material modification. An ERISA document that outlines any benefit changes occurring within 210 days after the end of the plan's fiscal year. (10)

summary plan description. An ERISA document that defines details of group insurance coverage, including the type of employee welfare benefit plan, the eligibility requirements, and the employer's claim administration procedure. (10)

supplementary notice. An FCRA-required notice to a consumer concerning a report by a consumer reporting agency; specifies the nature and scope of the investigation. (3)

surrender charge. An amount deducted from the annuity when it is surrendered early in the contract. (23)

surrender provision. A provision in an annuity contract that allows an annuitant to withdraw all available value from the annuity. (23)

surrender value. The net cash value of an annuity, minus fees and any other applicable charges. (23)

survivorship clause (also called a *time clause*). A policy provision that covers situations in which a beneficiary survives an insured by a brief time; provides payment of proceeds to the beneficiary provided the beneficiary lives longer than the insured for at least a specified period, such as 10 days or 30 days. (17)

table of underwriting requirements. A document that specifies the kinds of information the underwriter considers in assessing the insurability of a proposed insured. (2)

table rating method. A method by which insurers adjust premium rates to compensate for extra mortality; in this method, substandard risks are divided into broad groups according to their numerical ratings, and the extra mortality for each group is expressed as a percentage of standard mortality as has been shown by the insurer's actual mortality experience and as presented in an extra-percentage table. (4)

team underwriting. A risk selection approach in which underwriters work in small groups. (2)

temporary flat extra premium. A method of assessing the medical risk represented by a proposed insured; used for an impairment for which the extra mortality risk is expected to decrease and eventually disappear over a limited time period. (4)

temporary life annuity. An annuity that limits the number of annuity payments to a stated length of time, such as a 10-year life annuity. The payments are made only if a designated person is then alive. (23)

third-party applicant. A person who applies for insurance coverage on the life of another person. (5)

total disability. In both short-term and long-term disability income insurance contracts, a condition that includes the complete and continuous inability of an insured at the beginning of a disability to perform the essential duties of her regular occupation. (19)

transaction fee. For an annuity, a charge per premium payment or other specified transaction. (23)

transplant donor benefit. In a disability income insurance policy, a provision specifying that if an insured undergoes surgery to donate a body part to another person, the insurer will treat that surgery as a sickness and will pay benefits for it. (19)

twisting. An illegal practice in which a marketer misleads a policyowner concerning replacement or provides an incomplete comparison of the two policies to the disadvantage of the policyowner. (7)

unauthorized reinsurer (also known as a *non-admitted reinsurer*). A reinsurance marketer that does not have the licensing or recognition of the insurance department in a jurisdiction. (13)

unbundling. A fraudulent claim procedure by which a medical caregiver reports and charges separate fees for two or more procedure codes to describe a single medical treatment instead of reporting only one code to cover the entire procedure. (20)

undeliverable (also called *not taken*). Descriptive term for a policy that is refused by a buyer when a marketer attempts to deliver it. (2)

underwriting (function of an insurance company). The process of (1) assessing and classifying the degree of risk represented by a proposed insured or a group of insureds with respect to a specific insurance product and (2) making a decision to accept or decline the risk. (1)

underwriting guidelines. General standards that specify the parameters within which an applicant may be assigned to one of the risk classes established for each insurance product. (2)

underwriting manual. A document that typically provides descriptive information on impairments and serves as a guide to underwriting action. (4)

underwriting philosophy (also called an *insurer's underwriting objectives*). A set of ideas that guide an insurer's risk selection and classification procedures and generally reflect the insurer's strategic business goals and product pricing assumptions. (2)

underwriting worksheet. A document that contains records of telephone calls, letters and other communications, documentation of requests for reinsurance, lists of reports and other information requested, and other notations that will explain clearly the manner in which a case has been handled from the time it was submitted to an insurance company. (3)

upcoding. A fraudulent claim procedure by which a medical caregiver reports a code for a more serious, and usually more expensive, diagnosis or treatment. (20)

utilization review. A claim review approach by which an insurer analyzes a case to determine if the recommended treatment is both necessary and appropriate. (16)

variable annuity. A type of annuity under which an insurer agrees to pay periodic benefits that may vary according to the performance of a separate account (known in Canada as a *segregated account*). (23)

variable life insurance. A form of whole life insurance under which the death benefit and the cash value of the policy change according to the investment performance of funds that are kept separate from an insurer's other investments. (22)

waiting period. For medical expense coverage, a specified length of time, counted from the date of policy issue, during which an insured's medical expenses are not covered. For disability income insurance, a specified length of time, beginning with the onset of disability, during which benefits are not payable (also called the *elimination period*). (8)

waiver of premium. A rider or policy provision by which an insurer agrees to give up its right to receive premiums if a policyowner fulfills a specified condition. (12)

waiver of premium for disability. In a life insurance policy, a rider which provides that, in the event an insured is totally disabled as defined in the rider, the insurance company will waive the payment of all premiums that become due during the period of disability. (7) In a disability income insurance policy, a rider which automatically becomes effective as soon as monthly disability income insurance benefits become payable and which provides that after an insured has been disabled for a specified period, premiums will be waived for as long as the insured is disabled. (19)

waiver of premium for payor benefit. A provision stating that an insurer will waive payment of the policy's premiums if an adult policyowner becomes disabled or dies prior to an insured child's attainment of a specified age, usually 21. (7)

waiver of surrender charge provision. In an annuity contract, a provision that allows an insurer to waive the surrender charge when the annuitant or contract owner becomes disabled or confined in a nursing home or other long-term care facility; releases the annuitant or contract owner from paying surrender charges on withdrawals. (23)

warranty. A statement made by a party to a contract that will invalidate the contract if the statement is not literally true. (23)

whole life annuity. An annuity that provides for annuity payments to be made only if a designated person is alive, with the payments continuing for that person's entire life. (23)

withdrawal charge. For an annuity, a flat amount or a percentage of the amount withdrawn that is deducted from the annuity when a withdrawal is made from the annuity account early in the contract. (23)

withdrawal provision. In an annuity contract, a provision that permits an annuitant to withdraw funds from an annuity's accumulated value during the accumulation period. (23)

work division system. A system for organizing underwriting which divides cases according to the person or group that underwrites them; types of work division include independent underwriting, team underwriting, jet unit underwriting, and committee underwriting. (2)

work site assessment. In disability income insurance, an evaluation conducted when a claim analyst or an investigator interviews an employer and reviews the actual job duties and the claimant's level of success in performing those duties. (19)

Workers' Compensation. In the United States, government-mandated insurance that provides benefits to covered employees and their dependents if the employee suffers a job-related injury, disease, or death. (19)

yearly renewable term (YRT). A type of proportional reinsurance plan in which a ceding company buys an amount of yearly renewable term coverage that is equal to the net amount at risk on the portion of the policy being reinsured. (12)

Index

A

B

C

D

E

G

H

I

J

K

L

P

Q

R

U

V

W

XYZ